SOCIOLOGY
The Study of Society

SOCIOLOGY
The Study of Society

James B. McKee
Michigan State University

HOLT, RINEHART AND WINSTON

New York · Chicago · San Francisco · Philadelphia
Montreal · Toronto · London · Sydney · Tokyo · Mexico City
Rio de Janeiro · Madrid

Publisher **Ray Ashton**
Acquisitions Editor **Patrick V. Powers**
Senior Developmental Editor **Rosalind Sackoff**
Administrative Editor **Jeanette Ninas Johnson**
Senior Project Editor **Herman Makler**
Production Manager **Patrick Sarcuni**
Art Director **Robert Kopelman**
Text Design **Beverly G. Haw, A Good Thing, Inc.**
Cover photograph **Reginald Wickham**

Library of Congress Catalog Card Number: 81-506
ISBN 0-03-041851-8

Address correspondence to:

383 Madison Avenue
New York, N.Y. 10017

CBS COLLEGE PUBLISHING
Holt, Rinehart and Winston
The Dryden Press
Saunders College Publishing

ACKNOWLEDGMENTS

Part Opening: p. 1, Owen Franken/Stock, Boston

Chapter 1

p. 5 (top), Robert Eckert/EKM–Nepenthe (bottom), Chris Maynard/Stock, Boston; **p. 10** (top), Camera Press/Photo Trends (bottom), Robert Eckert/ERM–Nepenthe; **p. 12,** Beryl Goldberg; **p. 14** (top), Alex Webb/Magnum Photos (bottom), Roger Mallock/Magnum Photos; **p. 19,** V. Lawrence/Stock, Boston

Part Opening: p. 31, Owen Franken/Stock, Boston

Chapter 2

p. 36, Richard Kalvar/Magnum Photos; **p. 37** (left and right), Robert Eckert/EKM–Nepenthe; **p. 39,** Photo Trends; **p. 44** (top), Photo Trends (bottom), Culver Pictures; **p. 48,** Syndication International/Photo Trends

Chapter 3

p. 53, Henri Cartier-Bresson/Magnum Photos; **p. 63** (top), J. R. Holland/Stock, Boston (bottom), Erika Stone; **p. 64,** Kenneth Murray/Nancy Palmer Photo Agency; **p. 68** (top), Dennis Stock/Magnum Photos (bottom), John Maher/EKM–Nepenthe; **p. 71,** Cary Wolinsky/Stock, Boston

Chapter 4

p. 80, Owen Franken/Stock, Boston; **p. 81,** Jean-Claude Lejune/Stock, Boston; **p. 87,** Beryl Goldberg; **p. 90,** Ellis Herwig/Stock, Boston; **p. 92,** Owen Franken/Stock, Boston

Chapter 5

p. 103, Cary Wolinsky/Stock, Boston; **p. 111,** Christopher Manon/Stock, Boston; **p. 113** (left), John Maher/EKM–Nepenthe, (right), Barbara Alpen/Stock, Boston; **p. 116,** Ellis Herwig/Stock, Boston; **p. 118,** Joel Barry/Nancy Palmer Photo Agency

Part Opening: p. 121, Hartmann/Magnum Photos

Chapter 6

p. 125, Stuart Cohen/Stock, Boston; **p. 126,** © Beryl Goldberg 1975; **p. 127,** Cary Wolinsky/Stock, Boston; **p. 134,** Owen Franken/Stock, Boston; **p. 141,** Dennis Stock/© 1970 Magnum Photos

Chapter 7

p. 152, Jean-Picase Roget/Stock, Boston; **p. 156,** Ken Heyman/Magnum Photos; **p. 159,** Owen Franken/Stock, Boston; **p. 161,** Cornell Capa/Magnum Photos

Chapter 8

p. 167, The Bettmann Archive; **p. 177,** W. B. Finch/Stock, Boston; **p. 179,** Tim Carlson/Stock, Boston; **p. 184,** Donald Dietz/Stock, Boston; **p. 185,** John R. Maher/EKM–Nepenthe

Part Opening: p. 189, Stock, Boston

Chapter 9

p. 193, Michael Dobo/Stock, Boston; **p. 195,** Syndication International/Photo Trends; **p. 201** (left), Charles Harbutt/Magnum Photos (right), Elizabeth Hamlin/Stock, Boston; **p. 207,** Burt Glinn/Magnum Photos

Chapter 10

p. 217 (left), Robert V. Eckert/EKM–Nepenthe (right), Bruce Davidson/Magnum Photos; **p. 223** (top left), Nick Sapieha/Stock, Boston (top right), Arthur Grace/Stock, Boston (bottom right), Erika Stone (bottom left), Tim Anderson/Photo Trends; **p. 228,** © Beryl Goldberg 1980; **p. 232,** © 1974 Norman Hurst, Stock, Boston

Chapter 11

p. 237, Daniel S. Brody/Stock, Boston; **p. 241,** Robert Eckert/EKM–Nepenthe; **p. 248,** Bruce Davidson/© 1968 Magnum Photos; **p. 249** (left), Cary Wolinsky/Stock, Boston (right), © Donald Dietz, 1980/Stock, Boston; **p. 255,** Constantine Manos/Magnum Photos

Chapter 12

p. 264, © Stephanie Diskins, 1973/Photo Researchers, Inc.; **p. 266,** Wayne Miller/Magnum Photos; **p. 273,** Bruce Roberts/Photo Researchers, Inc.; **p. 276,** Charles Harbutt/Magnum Photos; **p. 278,** Peter Southwick/Stock, Boston

Part Opening: p. 287, Jean-Claude Lejune/Stock, Boston

Chapter 13

p. 293, Lupe/Stock, Boston; **p. 294,** Ken Heyman/Magnum Photos; **p. 298,** Leonard Freed/Magnum Photos; **p. 300,** © Erika Stone, 1978; **p. 305,** © Michael Malyszko/Stock, Boston

PREFACE

The introductory textbook is one of the tools available to the teacher who undertakes the never easy task of teaching an introductory-level course in any discipline. A good textbook can contribute considerably to what the teacher can accomplish. Its usefulness to the student is not only in its clear presentation of the basic material of the discipline, but also in that it can be read and reread, studied and underlined. *Sociology: The Study of Society* aspires to be useful in just that way.

The writing of this book grew out of the second edition of my *Introduction to Sociology*. Instead of simply preparing a third edition, however, I have written a new text. It is based upon the earlier text and some material from it has been incorporated into the new work. However, I have not abandoned what many users and readers felt was most useful about my prior text. In particular I have tried to retain a humanistic tone, a sense that sociology is relevant because it has something to say about the human condition in a world grown larger, more complex, and more interdependent. At the same time I have sought to maintain an appreciation of the effort to make that voice a rational and scientific one.

One of the reasons for regarding this as a new book is the alteration in the basic organization of the text, including the addition of some wholly new chapters. In Part 1 the usual first two chapters have been combined into a single one but without sacrificing the introduction to theory and research which many instructors wish to include. In fact, materials on doing research have been strengthened in order to provide a more detailed description of the process. Part 2 opens

with Chapter Two, where the concepts of conflict and change are introduced, after roles, relations, and social structure, as basic ideas which need to be brought in early and utilized in the ensuing discussion. In developing the concept of culture in Chapter Three, I have tried to make students understand what the counter-culture was and what of it remains significant; and I have also discussed popular culture and consumer culture as dimensions relevant to their immediate lives.

Part 3 is organized to emphasize the basic world trend to large-scale organization. A new chapter on the trend from small to large organization (Chapter Five) has replaced a former chapter on small groups. Chapters on society, bureaucracy, and urban structures then flesh out this trend.

Part 4 offers a more extended section on social inequality. A chapter on wealth, poverty, and the welfare state, following a chapter on social class, is a new and innovative one, which offers a more comprehensive coverage than would be done by just a chapter on poverty. That is followed by a separate chapter on racial and ethnic minorities, which ends with an updated discussion of the issues involved in affirmative action. Then comes a new chapter on sexual inequality; it seemed more sound sociologically to place the issue of sex and gender in the section on social inequality than under the more innocuous heading of sex roles.

The section on institutions, Part 5, retains the same chapters but they are considerably updated. In particular the chapter on the economy provides a basic discussion of such concepts as capitalism, socialism, industrialism, technology, as well as development and dependency. Part 6 provides a new chapter on social deviancy and social problems, while collective behavior has been treated in a single chapter.

I have tried to reflect contemporary issues and developments for which sociology has something to say, and to bring in some of the newer literature of the 1970s which gives to sociology a current relevance. In doing so, I have sought out the most recent empirical data, including the most recent census data available at the time of writing.

In response to a constant problem, I have tried to make the text more readable for undergraduates by providing concrete examples and by avoiding where possible too much abstract discussion. A summary of each chapter and special boxed inserts have been provided. A glossary of terms has been appended.

A comprehensive Instructor's Manual has been prepared by Virginia McKeefery-Reynolds of Southern Illinois University. Each chapter in the manual includes a summary, key objectives, extended lecture assistance, and test questions. These chapters also contain additional materials we think will be useful to the instructor.

A number of sociologists read earlier drafts of the manuscript, and I appreciate their careful reading and critical comments. They are Eugene Fappiano, Southern Connecticut State College; Glenn Stevick, Mt. Aloysious Junior College; Huron Polnac, Ranger Junior College; Donald Gilbart, Hillsboro Community College; Virginia McKeefery-Reynolds, Southern Illinois University; Chad Richardson, Pan American University; Hugh Lena, Providence College; Larry Reynolds, Central Michigan University; and Thomas Yacovone, Los Angeles Valley College.

Among these reviewers, I again owe a special thanks to Larry Reynolds, who always understood what I was trying to do and knew how to be helpful. I would be seriously remiss, furthermore, if I did not gratefully acknowledge the critical readings and detailed suggestions of Tom Yacovone, who caught many errors, omissions, and awkward or misleading phrasings, and who kept insisting that I remember what a text was supposed to do for its readers. I also wish to express my appreciation to my colleague and friend, Barrie Thorne, for her invaluable assistance in preparing the chapter on sexual inequality. None of these persons, of course, is in any way responsible for the final work; that responsibility can only be mine.

Rosalind Sackoff of Holt, Rinehart and Winston assumed editorial responsibility from the outset; her hard work, diligence, and editorial acumen is reflected in the total product. Others of the staff have made their professional contributions to the book and I am appreciative. As is always the case, I am indebted to my wife, Alice, for her patience and unstinting support and for her readiness to assist in meeting deadlines.

J. B. McK.

CONTENTS

Part One: **Sociology and Society**   **1**

   Chapter 1:   **The Study of Society**   **3**

     The Meaning of Society   4
     Sociology: The Study of Society   8
     The Theoretical Task   11
     The Uses of Sociology   15
     Studying Society   18
     Summary   28

Part Two: **The Study of Social Life**   **31**

   Chapter 2:   **Interaction: The Bases of Society**   **33**

     Interaction: Social and Symbolic   33
     Roles and Relations   35
     Social Structure   40
     Social Change and Social Conflict   41
     Summary   50

   Chapter 3:   **Culture**   **52**

     The Idea of Culture   52
     The Elements of Culture   56
     Some Aspects of Culture   60
     Subculture and Life-Style   61
     Counterculture and Alternate Life-Style   64
     Popular Culture and Mass Culture   69
     Summary   74

   Chapter 4:   **Socialization: The Person in Society**   **77**

     Human Nature and Human Being   77
     Socialization   78

Social Control	91
Individualism, Identity, and Alienation	93
Summary	98

Chapter 5:   The Basic Trend: From Small to Large Groups   101

The Social Group	102
The Primary Group	105
Peer Groups	105
Small Groups within Large Groups	110
The Consequences of the Basic Trend	112
Summary	119

Part Three: Society and Groups   121

Chapter 6:   Society and Groups   123

The Concept of Society	123
The Development of Complex Society	124
Social Institutions	128
Modern Society	129
Beyond Modern Society	133
The Good Society	140
Measuring Society	142
Summary	143

Chapter 7:   Bureaucracy in Modern Society   146

The Nature of Large Organizations	146
The Origins of Bureaucracy	147
Formal Structure	149
Informal Structure	152
Bureaucrats and Professionals	153
The Bureaucratic Personality	155
Bureaucracy and Social Power	158
Bureaucracy in a Postmodern Society	160
Summary	163

Chapter 8:   Urban Structures   166

Urbanization	166
The Metropolitan Area	168
The Decline of Local Autonomy	171
Urban Ecology	172
Urbanism	175
The Suburban Community	177
The Metropolis	180
The Crisis of the Cities	182
The Future of Community	185
Summary	186

Part Four: **Stratification**   **189**

Chapter 9:   **Social Class**   **191**

Interpreting Inequality   191
Class and Status   193
Social Class in Industrial Society   199
Social Class in Communist and Capitalist Societies   204
Blue-Collar/White Collar: Class and Occupation   205
Social Mobility   208
The Persistence of Inequality   211
Summary   212

Chapter 10:   **Wealth, Poverty, and the Welfare State**   **215**

Wealth and the Wealthy   216
The System of Poverty   218
The Welfare State   230
The Future of Inequality   233
Summary   233

Chapter 11:   **Racial and Ethnic Inequality**   **236**

Racial and Ethnic Minorities   236
Explaining Minority Status   244
Race and Racism   250
Affirmative Action   253
The Future of Race Relations   257
Summary   259

Chapter 12:   **Sexual Inequality**   **262**

Sex and Gender   262
Sexual Domination   268
Women in American Society   271
The Feminist Movement: Toward Sexual Equality   280
Summary   283

Part Five: **Institutions and Social Structure**   **287**

Chapter 13:   **The Family**   **289**

The Universality of the Family   289
Capitalism, Industrialism, and the Family   292
Class, Ethnicity, and Family Life   295
The Changing American Family   298
The Future of the Family   302
Summary   307

Chapter 14:   **Education**   **311**

The Functions of Education   311
Social Class and Education   314

Race and Education   320
Higher Education   324
The Control of Education   328
Reforming Education   331
Summary   333

Chapter 15:   **Religion and Science**   **336**

Religion and Science as Worldview   336
Religion and Society   337
Science in Society   351
The Future of Science and Religion   357
Summary   358

Chapter 16:   **Economy and Society**   **362**

The Organization of Economy   362
Capitalism as an Economic System   364
Industrialism and Technology   369
Conflict and Control in the Economy   371
The World as an Economic System   375
Summary   379

Chapter 17:   **Politics and Society**   **383**

Power and Authority   383
Nation and State   385
The Political Party   388
Elites and Power   394
Centralizing and Decentralizing Power   398
Political Participation   402
On Political Economy: A Final Note   404
Summary   405

Part Six: **The Study of Society**   **409**

Chapter 18:   **Social Deviance and Social Problems**   **411**

Deviant Behavior   413
Problems of Social Organization   422
Solving Social Problems   428
Summary   431

Chapter 19:   **Collective Behavior: Crowds, Publics,
               and Social Movements**   **434**

The Crowd   434
Publics and Public Opinion   440
Social Movements   446
Collective Behavior: A Concluding Note   453
Summary   454

Chapter 20:   **Environment and Social Change**   **457**

The Ecological Perspective   458
The Ecological Crisis   459
Population   465
The Crisis of Growth   473
Reshaping Society: Finding an Ecological Balance   476
Summary   479

Glossary   483

Name Index   489

Subject Index   493

Part 1

SOCIOLOGY AND SOCIETY

Man is the measure of all things.
Protagoras

One

THE STUDY OF SOCIETY

A gifted poet once wrote about a man who cursed and wept because he did not live in days of old when armored knights roamed the land:*

Miniver Cheevy, child of scorn
   Grew lean while he assailed the seasons;
He wept that he was ever born,
   And he had reasons.

Miniver loved the days of old
   When swords were bright and steeds were prancing;
The vision of a warrior bold
   Would set him dancing.

Like so many other people, Miniver Cheevy wanted to be somewhere else, in another time and place. So do a lot of other people. And most people, even you and I, wish at least sometimes to be someone else or to be someplace else, or both.

Most of us cannot do that in reality, so we do it in fantasy. We imagine and we daydream. That makes it possible for us to see ourselves as some other kind of person, in some other social world, living a more interesting kind of life. Like Miniver Cheevy, we cannot really exchange our present life for another, but we

* Edward Arlington Robinson, "Miniver Cheevy."

can temporarily escape it by daydreaming and by immersing ourselves in forms of popular culture.

Some people read science fiction, where imaginative writers construct whole new societies of the future. Many suburban housewives today read historical romances, where innocent heroines are threatened by dark forces but are always rescued by strong, masculine heroes. Many people apparently are absorbed in the reading and viewing of explicit sexual adventures, where they imagine that sexual prowess and conquest will offer the supreme achievement of life. Still other people are absorbed in the tangled web of life in the soap operas, where intrigue and juicy scandal occur daily.

In whatever way each of us does this, we are letting ourselves, at least in fantasy, recognize that social life could offer possibilities other than the ones we know and live within. Yet in every one of these possibilities, real or imagined, we would take for granted that there would be a society, this one or another. Why? Because we all know that to be human is to live in society, not outside of it. Only in a fearful nightmare are we likely to imagine ourselves all alone, isolated from others, devoid of human contact. Any better possibility we dream about is still a *social* life.

All of this seems fairly obvious; surely we know it so well we need hardly be reminded. In growing up we discover for ourselves how much being human involves us in a life shared with others. We learn this, not all at once, but gradually, so gradually in fact that we may go through life taking it for granted but never consciously thinking about it. It is the intention of this book to make you think consciously about what it means to live in a society, about what a society is, about how it is organized and how it changes. That, somewhat simply, is what sociology is all about.

THE MEANING OF SOCIETY

While we can easily enough recognize that we live our lives inside a society, not outside or independent of it, we often do not fully grasp what this means. For one thing, we become the unique person each of us is only within a particular society that encourages, or at least allows, certain forms of personal development—and discourages, even forbids, others. In some cases, forms of personal development fall beyond what is humanly possible within that society. Miniver Cheevy could not be a warrior bold with bright sword on a prancing steed, because nobody can in the twentieth century. That is beyond the limits of what his society can offer him for personal development.

No one society, then, offers us the entire range of the humanly possible. History provides us with a long record of ways to be human long since lost in practice, though sometimes still alive in books and movies, and so still available to us in fantasy. From anthropology we learn of very different peoples and what may seem to us their strange though sometimes quite attractive ways to be human. In each case different kinds of societies provide different ways to be human.

In living our own lives, we do so necessarily within the roles and routines of our own society, which constrain us to be and do some things and not to be and do some other things. We never escape society, which was there before us and will be there after us, though it may change during our lifetime, a little or a lot.

To live within a society means to be involved in a small and personal world of everyday life, of the familiar and manageable, of people we know and love (or even hate). We experience in face-to-face relations family, friends, neighbors, co-workers, fellow students,

teachers, employers, traffic cops, local merchants, and the like. Our daily activities interlock with theirs.

There once was a time when this small world of daily life could be the limits of a society, for there were tribes and little villages for which no larger world existed. But that is long since past; now society extends into a larger world which we do not directly experience but relate to only impersonally and indirectly. Large and remote systems penetrate our small worlds. In Washington, laws may be made which affect our daily lives—laws about equal rights for women, about student loans, about job discrimination, and the like. If the United States goes to war, a local draft board will act as the agent of a vast and impersonal system to decide who shall go to fight (and possibly die) in some distant place on the globe.

Our own small daily world of town, neighborhood, or campus then, is not a world unto itself. It is, instead, part and parcel of a large society, which always extends well beyond the range of our daily experience. In the past, when people's lives were entirely bound within the small world of daily life, the common sense developed from living within this small world seemed sufficient to understand what was happening and what to expect. But for few of us is that any longer the case; modern society includes so much more than our own small worlds that the experience of everyday life is not an adequate guide to understanding society. Sociology came into being for just that reason. Something else besides common sense was needed to understand what society was all about.

Why Is There Society?

Perhaps it is foolish to ask this question. After all, nobody is advocating that society be abolished; indeed we all take its existence for granted. Nonetheless, it is still useful to ask the question, since understanding why society exists helps us to understand what it is.

To answer this question we must start with two basic observations about the nature of individuals:

1. At birth the human organism is helpless to meet its own needs. Others must protect and care for it or it will die. Also, it needs others from whom it can learn how to do the things necessary to live. Human life can be sustained only if the slowly growing human organism (slowly growing compared to most

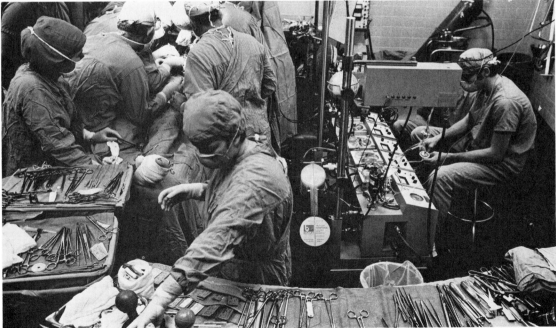

From the simplest to the most complex activities, it is cooperatively that human beings accomplish the many tasks that ensure survival.

other animals) is cared for while it learns how to do the things necessary to take care of itself.

2. The above, in turn, tells us that the human organism is not genetically programmed, that is, its specific behavior is not provided by some set of inherited instincts. Instead, all human beings must go through a prolonged, complex *learning* process. We become human by this learning process, and this, in turn, requires persistent association with other human beings.

Human beings, then, do not come into the world ready-made by nature, already fitted out with the necessary instincts to adapt to the natural environment. The consequences which flow from this basic point are fundamental to an understanding of why there *is* society.

In the first place it means that human beings have had to work out for themselves ways to survive. Possessing no instinctive knowledge and skills, human beings have learned from experience, have developed useful skills, and have made tools and constructed shelter from whatever materials the environment made available.

Secondly, human survival can only be accomplished if human beings act *collectively*. Cooperation can accomplish things no one person could manage alone. From the earliest period of human existence, providing food and shelter, while also bringing into being a new generation, taking care of it and teaching it what it must know, required that individuals cooperate with one another. They had to develop some organized way to see that what needed to be done got done. Some tasks need to be shared, some to be divided among different persons. African Bushmen, for example, hunted down game, while their women collected roots, fruits, nuts, and other vegetable foods, a task that could be carried out while taking care of infants. And both sources of food were necessary, since hunting did not provide a regular and predictable source of food.

From this perspective human society is the outcome of collective *adaptation* to a natural environment, a process of finding how to live cooperatively in such a way as to make nature yield enough to sustain life. By cooperative activity among humans learning from one another, skills are acquired; knowledge is ac-

cumulated; techniques and tools are developed; and all are transmitted to the next generation. It seems that human life must have been carried on in social groups, however small and primitive, from the very beginning of human existence.

There is a basic lesson to be learned from this: out of their struggle with nature, human beings provided for their biological survival *and* they produced a social life. The answer to our question—why is there society?—is surely not startling or even surprising, but is nonetheless basic: society is produced by the cooperative activity of human beings, and the human organism becomes human only in a society. Neither the fully human organism—the person—nor society comes from nature ready made; neither, that is, is genetically produced.

Society and Nature   To stress the issue of survival may seem quaint today when modern people possess science and a powerful technology and are thus able to harness and control the forces of nature in many ways. We mine the earth for coal and minerals, extract gas and oil from deep within the ground, change the course of rivers and dam them to create great bodies of water, change arid land into fertile soil by irrigation, drain swamps, tunnel through mountains, domesticate wildlife, and in so many ways turn the natural environment to our own use.

Until recently we exploited and changed the environment without concern for the future, but extensive pollution and the destruction and depletion of natural resources rudely remind us that we are still dependent on a thriving and healthy physical environment. There is, then, a necessity for us to live in some kind of sensible relation with nature, and for society to strike a balance with nature. Otherwise, the destruction of nature will be the destruction of society. Modern people still need to adapt to the environment, even though science and technology have radically altered the terms of that adaptation. (We shall return to this issue in some detail in Chapter 18.)

Society and the Individual   But the more technology makes possible a society that places us comfortably back from the edge of survival, the more we are individually dependent upon the complex social organization needed to sustain life at new levels of material living. As individuals we may worry less about collective survival, more about our own individual fate. Even

IS SOCIETY REAL?

If the human organism becomes fully human only in a society, and if society in turn is the product of the cooperative activity of human beings, then, is society as "real" as the person?

One of the great names in the founding of sociology, Émile Durkheim (1858–1917), argued that society is a reality *sui generis* (of its own kind), a "thing" apart from and different from individuals. While society was created by the association of individuals, it was nevertheless, he asserted, more than the attributes of these individuals; the whole is greater than the sum of its parts. "We can see . . . that society does not depend upon the nature of the individual personality."

The existence of society, Durkheim thought, could not be explained by referring to the psychological characteristics of individuals. Society had its own characteristics, which, after all, is what is meant by saying that it is a reality *sui generis.* That also meant that society, as a different reality than the person, was not to be explained by psychology. As a reality external to the individual, it needed its own separate mode of study. That, for Durkheim, was sociology. "It is not realized that there can be no sociology unless societies exist, and that societies cannot exist if there are only individuals."

While not all sociologists would agree with Durkheim's definition of society as a reality *sui generis,* they would all probably agree that a person *experiences* society as an objective reality that constrains and coerces him or her. As Durkheim noted, society is an arena of *social facts*, things external to individuals which constrain them. Individuals experience the social fact as an independent reality which they did not create and cannot wish away. Laws, customs, moral rules, and official (bureaucratic) practices are, among others, examples of social facts. They are, Durkheim insisted, "obligatory" in that they require some behavior from the individual quite independent of his or her personal preferences. It is in this obligatory character of social facts that Durkheim finds proof of the reality of society.

then we are forced to recognize that our personal destiny, for good or bad, is thoroughly tied into the social organization of our society. We depend on teachers and schools (including colleges), for example, to learn an occupation and get a "better" job. We may even be vaguely aware that what chance we have to learn a particular occupation, particularly one that ranks high, may depend less on our individual talents and energies than on where our family is located in the class structure.

Furthermore, complex changes in society that we only dimly recognize, let alone understand, may alter the pattern of our own lives and force on us new decisions and choices. Every day, for example, many Americans migrate from the northeastern states to the southwestern ones—from Frostbelt to Sunbelt—because corporations close up old plants in the one re-

gion and build new ones in the other. By looking for a job or for a better economic opportunity, the individual is lured to a new place where, indeed, economic growth requires more labor. When viewed on the individual level, such migration looks like a matter of personal choice. But when viewed on the societal level, it is seen as the movement of the working population following the relocation of industry.

The Reality of Society It seems obvious that we often experience society as a separate and independent reality which creates us and then persistently controls and constrains us (see "Is Society Real?"). While it is useful to view society this way, as one of sociology's founders, Émile Durkheim, so effectively taught us, we must be careful not to let this conception of society as a separate reality be carried to the point of detaching it from human activity and its social nature. Society does not exist without individuals through whose actions it is carried on. Society and person, then, are *interdependent;* neither exist without the other.

Because modern society is a vast and complex process, we can easily lose our recognition of this fact that society does not exist without individuals through whose activity it is carried on. Because the origins of society are far back in time, we can miss the point that society was humanly created. Because, as individuals, we feel helpless before daily demands on our time and energy, and powerless to effect any change, we may give little recognition to the fact that it is also by human effort, collective and organized, that society changes.

SOCIOLOGY: THE STUDY OF SOCIETY

Studying society can hardly be claimed to be anything new; as far back as we have records, scholars and scribes have described and analyzed the social life shared by a people. Yet sociology as a discipline goes back in name and identity only to the early decades of the nineteenth century, barely a century and a half.

Sociology grew at a time of new and creative social thought that transformed and modernized all of the social sciences. New specialized disciplines broke away from the long-established fields of history and philosophy. Political economy, for example, separated into *political science* and *economics* when, under a growing capitalism, the economic system was thought of as separate and apart from the political process, especially the state.

Anthropology originated in the interest that Europeans developed in non-Western peoples after three centuries of exploration, colonization, and trade. After the explorers, colonizers, and traders, and the missionaries seeking converts to Christianity, came the anthropologist, the Western specialist on non-Western peoples.

The Origin of Sociology

The new discipline of sociology emerged in response to the vast social upheaval which so radically changed the shape of society in Europe: the French Revolution, for one, which marked the rise to political power of new middle classes, instead of aristocrats and kings; the Industrial Revolution, for another, which, together with capitalism, brought about industrial society. The origins of these changes were at least two centuries further back, but it was in the early nineteenth century, just after the French Revolution, that thoughtful people began to realize just how revolutionary they were.

Once under way the revolutionary transformation of society relentlessly altered the way everyone was to live. Rural people moved into urban centers, peasants changed into workers, and cities grew where villages had once stood.

Two significant consequences followed from this: (1) people's daily range of personal experiences became too limited in scope to provide them with sufficient familiarity with their own social world, for that world was growing to be vast and complex; (2) their world changed before their eyes even as they learned about it. People soon learned that they could not assume that their world would be the same as the world of their parents, or that the world of their children would be like their own.

For many social thinkers the radical transformation of society produced both hope and anxiety. Political democracy and rising standards of living were sources of hope. Yet there also emerged a deep anxiety over the future. Did all this change threaten the continuity of society itself? Did the breaking up of old ways of life and the decline of once sacred and unquestioned values bode ill for the future of family and community?

Scholars recognized that an old order—the Christian unity of medieval society—was gone, replaced by a new order of unfamiliar and uncertain features. Among a varied group of intellectuals in nineteenth-century Europe—some radical, some conservative—there developed a new consciousness about society, a recognition of how revolutionary had been the change in human society, how uncertain had the future become. From such concerns as those, sociology was born.

Human Society as Problematic

Any time social change so alters the familiar social world that it is no longer adequately understandable or explainable by the usual ways of thinking common to a society, people examine it with a new level of social awareness. Such a sustained and intense level of social awareness has existed now for over a century and a half. Sociology, created out of this modern social awareness, has attempted to provide answers to questions generated about the old and new forms of society.

There were questions such as these: How are people able to sustain social order and avoid chaos and disorder? What are the basic elements necessary to the existence of society? Is common religious belief necessary to sustain society? What are the sources of social change? How does society control individual conduct? What is the necessary relationship of the individual to the group? What is the importance of the small and traditional group in society—family and community, for example—both for the individual's relation to society, and for the organization of society? How do the social classes relate to one another? Is social inequality necessary in human society? Does class conflict necessarily lead to social revolution?

Throughout the nineteenth century sociology took shape and substance from the effort to grapple with these many questions. The founders of sociology tended to ask global, all-encompassing questions posed at the highest level of generality. And for good reason; they were trying to get a basic grasp of fundamental change from a feudal, authoritarian, preindustrial society to an industrial, democratic, urban society, something that had never before existed in human experience.

If many early sociologists were inquiring into the larger meaning of societal transformation, there were still many others asking more specific questions and answering them by going out and observing social life. Some explored the vast unmapped dimensions of the social worlds of the working poor, who were then a majority of the population. Perhaps the most influential of these was a detailed, factual study of the living conditions of the poor in London in the 1880s and 1890s, undertaken by a wealthy British industrialist, Charles Booth, and published in several volumes from 1891 to 1903 as *Life and Labour of the People of London.*

The origin of sociology, then, is rooted equally in two different though related tasks: The formulation of a theory of industrial society, and observation and description of the lives of people in new, urbanized environments.

If sociology emerged as a distinct social science

from this process, many others besides sociologists engaged in the task. Looking at the world sociologically is not a monopoly of sociologists. Instead, sociologists share with others, particularly journalists, the task of describing changing and contradictory patterns in personalities, cultures, and groups found within the boundaries of modern society. The best of journalists and novelists have often been good descriptive sociologists. But the sociologist intends to be both describer and theorist, moving carefully back and forth from the level of observable facts to the more abstract level of theory based upon the analysis of those facts.

The Sociological Perspective

How human beings organize and carry on a stable social life interests sociologists. They are interested in the *collective* (the shared, the common, the organized) aspects of social life, rather than the individual.

Some sociologists study the small social groups that abound in social life, getting a close-up focus on some small social world, whether that be a neighborhood, or a boys' gang, or a family, or a kinship unit. This enables the sociologist to get closer to the individual, to see how each person develops social relations with other persons in these small settings. Here we can see how human beings experience social life in all its joys and triumphs, its pain and suffering, how they learn to adjust to changes and social forces beyond their reach, how they struggle to control some immediate but significant dimension of their own life.

These small worlds exist within larger groups and organizations, and we need to understand how they are shaped and constrained and changed by the larger world into which they fit. It is for that reason that other sociologists focus on the larger structures of social life —its institutions, social classes, bureaucracies, and even total society—in an effort to get a grasp on "the big picture."

Most sociological studies tell us about these immediate worlds of everyday life that individuals actually experience, or about the larger structures which so forcefully shape and limit our immediate environments. While our everyday life often makes the smaller context more "real" to us, social reality is both the small world of everyday life and the larger, constraining structures. Consequently, sociological study must encompass both.

One source for the origin of sociology was the effort to understand the new urban environment that industrialism created, particularly that of the working class; housing conditions of the urban poor are here illustrated by an engraving from the *Illustrated London News* of 1875. Society today includes so much more than our immediate world that our everyday experiences are frequently not enough for us to understand society. The need for sociologists and society are even more important.

Private Troubles and Public Issues One useful way to get at the connection between the small, immediate environment of our personal world, and the larger social structure which constrains and shapes it, is to use the distinction that C. Wright Mills made between personal troubles and public issues.[1] A personal trouble is a private matter: difficulty in finding a job or getting into a professional school, easing marital or family tensions, and the like. An issue, in turn, is a public matter, having to do with such things as the rate of unemployment and what government can or should do about it; or about seeing to it that women and minorities are given an equal chance at jobs and education.

Consider, as one case in point, a black youth in the ghetto, a school dropout, angry and resentful, unable to find a job. That is his personal problem. But when economists point out that the unemployment rate of black youth is the highest of any group in the nation (as high as 40 percent in some large cities), it is no longer a matter of the faults and limitations of a black teenager but an issue about the structure of the job market and its limited capacity to offer employment.

Consider, again, the college graduate who drives a taxi or tends bar (most generally a male). His personal trouble overwhelms his entire life: he has the degree and qualifications to be, say, a teacher, but he can't find a teaching job. His years of struggle and sacrifice now seem in vain; perhaps, after all, he has failed. But a declining birthrate has reduced the need for schools, and many are closed and teachers laid off. The chance to be a teacher is now less than it once was, and many who might have been teachers may have to settle for something else.

Or consider the woman who no longer has a husband and who is struggling to support herself and her children on an inadequate income. Life is a series of never-resolved troubles. Although in the 1970s the woman-headed family was no longer so unusual and, furthermore, was on the increase, the overall earning power of women nevertheless is still far less than that of men. As a consequence, families headed by women as a rule have a much lower income than families headed by men. And, in turn, both are exceeded by the two-income family in which both parents are employed.

The troubles that beset these people, that frustrate and anger them, that give them sleepless nights and bad dreams, are not primarily of their own making. Their individual fates are rooted in structural changes and developments such as high unemployment for black youth, a declining birthrate, unequal economic opportunity for women—and to deal with these are beyond their individual capacities. Their singular, personal fates in life are not simply to be accounted for in terms of what kind of individuals they were, but in terms of larger structural changes that shaped in impersonal but powerful ways what they were to get out of life. Personal troubles are the individual forms which public issues take; the small milieu of everyday life must be seen as located within the changing pattern of large institutions.

To be able to see that personal troubles can be explained only by linking them to the larger scope of institutions and organizations is what C. Wright Mills meant by the *sociological imagination:*

> The sociological imagination enables its possessor to understand the larger historical scene in terms of its meaning for the inner life and the external career of a variety of individuals . . .
>
> It is the capacity to range from the most impersonal and remote transformations to the most intimate features of the human self—and to see the relations between the two.[2]

It is never easy to move from the large, impersonal level of economic systems, such as capitalism, to the level of everyday life and the individual, whose very individuality is shaped and formed within the limited possibilities provided by these systems. But that is what the study of society, possessed of the sociological imagination, tries to do.

Defining sociology as the study of society, then, means studying all the social relations, from the small-scale ones of everyday life and face-to-face social relations, to those large and remote systems whose very remoteness must not blind us to the fact that it is within the limits of their forms that our own life-chances are cast.

start with family, to school to church, the neighborhood then city, state, country

THE THEORETICAL TASK

When sociologists study social relations both small and immediate, large and remote, they are concerned with both the *empirical* and *theoretical* aspects of their study. The empirical is concerned with observing social behavior carefully and systematically, enabling the sociologist to gather a reliable body of facts: the *data* of the study.

When Émile Durkheim undertook his pioneering study of suicide, for example, he was guided by a set of assumptions about social order and integration which was to give a particular meaning to the fact of suicide: to interpret it as evidence of strong or weak social integration. To do that, he first demonstrated that known facts about suicide did not support then common theories that suicide was genetically caused and so was inherited, or was due to mental disorder, or to climate.

Durkheim's assumptions led him to believe that social integration would affect social behavior in predictable ways. This, in turn, led him to collect a *very* different set of facts about suicide from others who had studied the matter. He collected facts about religious affiliation, marital status, military participation, and economic and political stability to support his thesis that suicide occurred *inversely* with social integration; that is, those *most* integrated into a stable group life, Durkheim believed, were *less* likely to commit suicide. Thus, his facts demonstrated a higher rate of suicide among unmarried than among married people; a higher rate among the more individualistic Protestants than among Catholics, and among Catholics than among the most communal of all, Jews; and a higher rate among civilians than among career soldiers.

From this analysis, Durkheim was able to demonstrate that suicide is more than an individual act of a distraught person. It is a social phenomenon that occurs with greater or lesser frequency depending upon the integration of group life. People with few or weaker ties to some community are more likely to commit suicide in response to personal crises; those with a strong attachment to a network of close social relations are much less likely to do so.

Durkheim's classic study of suicide has long been a model of how the empirical and the theoretical are joined. One has no meaning without the other. Without theory the empirical is a jumble of unrelated facts that make no sense. Without facts, theory is a set of suppositions and conjectures that can make no claim to being true.

Sociologists today strive to develop limited theories of specific aspects of social reality, such as a theory of poverty, of power, of the family, of community organization, or of political parties. But when they do that

they are always guided by a more general *theoretical orientation,* a perspective on social life which begins with some basic assumptions, raises certain questions, poses particular problems, and which thus examines social life from a particular angle. The most significant of these perspectives are the *functional,* the *conflict,* and the *interactionist.*

The Functional Perspective

From the perspective of functionalism, society is viewed as a stable social system made up of interrelated parts. Each part "fits" with the others to make a well-ordered system, and each part contributes something to maintaining that system. That is its *function.*

The family, for example, contributes to the organization of society by ensuring legitimate biological reproduction of society's members, by caring for the young until they become adults, and by socializing the young into the existing culture. In modern societies, schools are developed to extend and develop further some of these functions, such as making the young literate and training them in skills required in modern occupational systems.

Teaching the young to handle language competently is a function of the school.

To determine what are the functions of a part for the system as a whole requires that the sociologist not confuse *purpose* with *consequence*. What people intend when they act is not always the same as the consequences of their actions. Sociologists, therefore, define *function* as an *objective consequence* for the maintenance of the system. Some functions are clearly recognized and intended—*manifest* functions—while many others are unrecognized and unintended, but are no less objectively real; these are *latent* functions.

When schools provide mass training in literacy and a set of basic skills for all children, they are doing something both intended and recognized. But when schools "track" children into different academic programs, preparing some for college and others for lesser opportunities, they may be doing something largely unrecognized and unintended. If tracking provides a better education for the children of the middle and upper classes than is provided for other children, as often happens, then the latent function of the schools is to maintain existing forms of social inequality. (We shall explore this matter in some detail in Chapter 14.)

Whatever is functional, however, is not necessarily "good" nor is whatever is *dysfunctional*—that is, that which disrupts or interferes with the ongoing system—necessarily "bad." The sharp increase today in working wives, for example, is a development which, whatever its other consequences and meanings, is dysfunctional for the family *in its traditional form.* The employment of wives outside the home disrupts the sexual division of labor around which the family has long been organized (husband works and provides family income, while wife cares for children and home). Such employment, therefore, makes it difficult if not impossible to maintain the traditional, male-dominated family. Such a consequence is "bad" only if one believes the family should remain unchanged in its basic structure.

The Conflict Perspective

Though functional analysis emphasizes how all parts of a society fit together to maintain a well-ordered social structure, it often neglects to examine the conflict that is always present in society. From the conflict perspective, conflict is not an occasionally disruptive force; rather, it is a constant feature of all human societies, as is social change.

It was Karl Marx who made clear to modern sociologists how persistent and pervasive conflict is in society, and who saw conflict between social classes as the basic force for change. Marx understood fully what the functionalists say, namely, that any society is a functioning system. But he also understood that it is also an ever-changing system.

As a constant feature of society, conflict appears in many forms. Some of these are *legitimate* ones, deliberately constructed to allow conflicting groups to act in their own interests, but also to keep them from seriously disrupting the established order. Elections, collective bargaining and even strikes, as well as peaceful picketing and demonstrations, are prime examples.

But sometimes conflict does take violent form and disrupts the established order, as, for example, when demonstrations end in rioting and perhaps looting. It also happens through terrorist acts, in guerrilla struggles, in spontaneous rebellions such as race riots, and in revolution and war. When conflict takes this form, only rarely can peace be achieved without social change.

Focusing on conflict and change leads sociologists to examine society in terms of power, domination, and inequality. The scarcity of valued objects—money, goods, privilege, status, and prestige—leads to an unequal distribution of these among individuals, groups, and societies. Such inequality does not always or necessarily lead to conflict, however. If there is a consensus which establishes the legitimacy of unequal distribution—and dominant groups always create a legitimizing ideology—there is no conflict.

Conflict, however, is always widespread in and among societies, testifying to how difficult it is to achieve such a consensus between the privileged and the deprived. What the dominant groups or classes in society, or the dominant societies in the world system, claim to be consensus is more often simply compliance of the dominated in the face of power.

The Interactionist Perspective

Still another perspective on social life is the *interactionist,* which looks primarily at how people *interact,* that is, act toward and respond to one another at the same time. Interactionists, then, are more likely to focus on more immediate, face-to-face encounters,

As long as these protesting construction workers stay behind the barricades, their demonstration is socially defined as legitimate. If the conflict becomes violent, as below, some social change will usually occur in order to establish peace.

rather than on such large abstractions as "society" or "economy."

One source of the interactionist perspective is Max Weber's conception of the individual as an actor who attaches a subjective meaning to his or her behavior. Any person's action has always to be understood from the point of view of the actors involved in the situation. For the sociologist, then, the task is not only to observe what people *do,* it is also to understand what they *mean* and *intend* by what they do.

These meanings are conveyed through symbols— words, gestures, signs, and the like—which are learned and shared within any interacting group. In American sociology this symbolic interaction has derived many of its insights from the work of George Herbert Mead in the 1920s.

One basic sociological assumption underlies the interactionist perspective: that it is through their social interaction that human beings construct a social life for themselves, maintain it, and change it. Society and its social groups come into being in no other way. The reality of our existence, in short, is socially constructed.

Interaction, then, is the basic process from which all forms of group life emerge. For that reason, we will begin our study of society in Chapter 2 with the concept of interaction as our starting point. We will also examine conflict in society in that chapter. A concern for function will appear throughout our analysis, but particularly in the analysis of social institutions (Chapters 13 to 17).

THE USES OF SOCIOLOGY

Sociologists have always claimed that their discipline could be useful to society in some way. Being useful, however, has never been the issue, for all sciences are useful. But how and in what way—that has been argued about.

Being a Science

To make sociology into a science has been a major goal for many sociologists. For them the usefulness of sociology comes about only by its growth as a science. If there could be a science of society, they feel, then society could be more rational than at any time in history.

For this to occur, such sociologists argue, sociology should stick to its task of developing as a science and remain free of any kind of entanglements with practical affairs. Not only should sociologists carry out their research objectively, they should remain free of commitment to any of the institutional values of society; in short, they should practice *value-neutrality* and as *scientists* not make value-judgments or advocate moral or political positions. At some time in the future—perhaps a quite distant future—a science of society could tell us *how* to change society, though it could not tell us *what* that change should be.

For other sociologists, this is all an illusion: they say it is not possible to be value-neutral. A sociologist, they point out, is also a parent, a teacher, a citizen, and a neighbor; he or she belongs to a family, a community, a professional organization, or a political party. In these groups the sociologist shares with others values that cannot help but be carried over into sociological work. Values cannot be shed like a coat on a warm day.

Still other sociologists argue that sociology should not try to be value-neutral, and that to do so becomes an excuse for being morally irresponsible or morally indifferent. Often, they argue, it becomes a reason for not doing what often takes courage anyway—to criticize society.

However, sociologists have never in practice been as neutral as they claimed to be. Along with anthropologists, psychologists, and even biologists, they have, for example, taken sides on the race issue and challenged the myths that claim that whites are genetically superior to nonwhites. Furthermore, they rely on research grants from government agencies, private foundations, and even corporations as a way of funding their research, and these organizations make no claim to being neutral. Indeed, the relation with these funding organizations involves sociologists in a lot of practical research.

Practical Uses

Sociology has grown rapidly in the last two decades, in part because of its practical use to government agencies making policy, to politicians seeking to persuade publics, to administrators trying to control and direct people's actions, to corporations wanting to "handle" employees or market their products better. Most large organizations in modern society use sociological research to advance their specific goals and interests.

A recent influential book, which sought to describe the many ways in which sociology was useful, viewed it as a process of collaboration between a client—most likely an organization rather than an individual—and a research sociologist.[3] The client was engaged in action, setting general policies, making day-to-day decisions. Implementing the client's goals, the editors asserted, reflects "the prevailing uses of sociology."[4] Here is a partial list of some of the practical uses explored: the law and medicine, social work and social welfare, management, the military establishment, law enforcement, the management of educational establishments, consumer behavior, foreign policy, social planning, manpower development, public health, and desegregation.

Such practical usefulness to established institutions and organizations as these brings clients to sociology and assures a source of research funds. But other sociologists deplore and criticize this practicality. To them, these practical sociologists too often help the powerful and those with special interests to have their way with ordinary people who, as citizens, employees, or consumers, are manipulated, controlled, or administered. Practical for whom, then, becomes a critical question.

Ideological Uses

Among the practical uses of sociology are those that are primarily *ideological,* dealing with ideas about and images of social life, and with values that are basic to judgments people make about aspects of social life. In every society there is a set of prevailing images that serves to justify how social life is organized and how power and wealth are distributed. C. Wright Mills notes that:

The images and ideas produced by social scientists may or may not be consistent with these prevailing images, but they always carry implications for them.[5]

He suggests that sociological ideas have an ideological impact, intended or not, when:

By justifying the arrangement of power and the ascendancy of the powerful, images and ideas transform power into authority.

By criticizing or debunking prevailing arrangements and rulers, they strip them of authority.

By distracting attention from issues of power and authority, they distract attention from the structural realities of the society itself.[6]

Obviously, the implications of sociological ideas can be both helpful and harmful to those organizations and elites whose interests are served by sustaining prevailing images. They are not, therefore, likely to leave the matter to chance. Instead, they seek out sociologists to provide what Mills called "ideological ammunition."[7]

Every interest and power, every passion and bias, every hatred and hope tends to acquire an ideological apparatus with which to compete with the slogans and symbols, the doctrines and appeals of other interests. As public communications are expanded and speeded up, their effectiveness is worn out by repetition; so there is a continuous demand for new slogans and beliefs and ideologies. In this situation of mass communication and intensive public relations, it would indeed be strange were the social studies immune from the demand of ideological ammunition, and stranger still were social researchers to fail to provide it.[8]

Both practical and ideological use of sociology are most likely to meet the needs and help to solve the problems of the established organizations of society. Sociology can be useful for management and administration, for social control and cultural manipulation. And even if it not be conscious intent, such a sociology is basically supportive of society's institutions and organizations, its power structure and its class structure. In a basic sense, that makes it *conservative,* because it seeks *to conserve* the prevailing forms of social life against the pressures and demands for change.

Social Reform   To claim that a practical use for sociology is conservative will probably be vigorously disputed by many sociologists—and, indeed, needs further qualification in order not to be unfair and misleading. Most sociologists do not see their activities as conservative, and they often describe and analyze the problems and deficiencies of American society. They do not hesitate, furthermore, to criticize the practices and social interests which perpetuate these problems.

There is a long list of social problems on which sociologists have done research: crime and delinquency, racial discrimination, alcoholism and drug addiction, poverty, urban slums and ghettoes, aging, and public health, among many others. They have sympathized with and tried to understand the perspectives of the underdogs and the disadvantaged, such as the poor and racial minorities, and have tried to get the majority to see these people as victims, not villains. They have tried to encourage a social tolerance of them and to promote a willingness to bring them into the mainstream of social life.

In pointing to the need for social reform—and its possibilities—such reform-minded sociologists have been advocates of social change. They want those in positions of power and policy-making to respond rationally to the pressures and demands for social change, not to ignore them or, worse yet, suppress them.

But if using sociology for social reform is not conservative, neither is it radical. The reforms commonly supported by sociological work—racial desegregation, equal educational opportunity for all races and both sexes, the reduction of poverty, for example—do not require any radical transformation of the social structure. What they do require is a new set of practices and policies accepted by the dominant groups and organizations of society, the development of new ways to include those formerly left out, which will equalize opportunity and remove the barriers that too often held back so many.

Such reforms do not seek to change these dominant groups and institutions in any basic way, however. The reform-minded sociologists accept as given the basic institutional structure of society, particularly its economic and political organization. They also accept the existence of class structure and its pattern of inequality. Furthermore—and perhaps most importantly—their reform practices proceed from a basic assumption, namely, that without any radical change the present society can carry out these reforms and by doing so remedy or eliminate the social problems that plague us. It is that assumption that some other sociologists hold in doubt.

Critical Uses Some sociologists conceive of sociology as having a usefulness of another kind. They ask for a sociology which confronts the issues crucial for the lives and life-chances of everybody. They want a sociology not committed to existing institutions, but not automatically opposed to them, either. They want a sociology free from partisan commitment, whether that be to the General Motors Corporation, the CIA, the Democratic Party, or the Department of Housing and Urban Development (HUD). They want a sociology, then, which is not a servant of power—any power.

Like the reform-minded sociologists, they want to change those practices and policies which unfairly, even oppressively, exclude some from having a fair chance in life. Unlike them, they do not necessarily assume that such changes can be accomplished without more radically altering and transforming the basic set of social structures around which society is organized. Just how radical social reform has to be is just what sociological work must determine; it cannot be presumed in advance.

Sociologists committed to such a critical use of sociology want to ask questions of social and political significance while also asking questions that are theoretically important. About forty years ago Robert Lynd called for just such a sociology in his renowned book, *Knowledge for What?*:

> No protestations of scientific objectivity and ethical neutrality can excuse the social scientist from coming down into the arena and accepting as his guiding values, *in selecting and defining his problems,* those deep, more widely based cravings which living personalities seek to realize.[9]

A generation later C. Wright Mills again argued for such a sociology, one in which the *sociological imagination* enabled students of society—and that includes more than sociologists; the best novelists and journalists, for example—to understand how the small troubles of individuals are in fact but dimensions of larger public issues.

In the work of Lynd and Mills, and in a long line of sociologically imaginative thinkers going back to Karl Marx, a new generation of sociologists renewed and refreshed the old conviction that the purpose of knowledge was to solve our problems and to change the world. To do that, a critical sociology had to be not only scientific, but it also had to be *humanistic* and *liberating:*

Humanistic, because it gives priority to the needs, hopes, and aspirations of the mass of human beings, rather than to privileged groups and dominant institutions. In doing so it critically measures any society and its institutions and practices against such values as human freedom, social equality, and justice;[10]

Liberating, because its fundamental commitment is to participate in the task of understanding the world in order to change it and so to liberate people from false and demeaning self-images, from confining and growth-denying roles and institutions.

To be humanistic and liberating does not contradict the scientific commitment to be rigorously logical or to be objective and dispassionate in observing social life. It is not an excuse to distort reality by bias. A critical sociologist fails to be either scientific or liberating as sentiment and compassion are allowed to distort any description of social reality.

Critical sociologists are not engaged in making propaganda or in producing partisan argument. Nor do they spin out romantic idealizations of ordinary people. After all, the actors in the human dramas we observe are not giants or pygmies, gods or robots; they are not Superman or Dracula. They come in quite human size, with human strengths and weaknesses, capacities and limitations.

Clearly, then, critical sociologists share with all other sociologists a recognition of the importance of objective social analysis. Furthermore, probably most sociologists want sociology to be useful in ways which promote human betterment. What they disagree about is how that should be done. Most of them probably would agree with Alvin W. Gouldner:

> Social science can never be fully accepted in a society, or by a part of it, without paying its way; this means it must manifest both its relevance and its concern for the contemporary human predicament. Unless the value-relevances of sociological inquiry are made plainly evident, unless there are at least some bridges between it and larger human hopes and purposes, it must inevitably be scorned by laymen as pretentious word-mongering.[11]

We hope to make it plain that sociology at its best is much more than "pretentious word-mongering."

STUDYING SOCIETY

Before we turn fully to *what* sociologists study, there is value in knowing something about *how* sociologists study society.

We live in an age of science, and consequently the dominant model for discovering "truth" is the model set forth by the scientific method. The scientific method provides a reliable and objective means for acquiring systematic and accurate knowledge. It does so by asking questions and then formulating possible answers (hypotheses) so carefully stated that they can be rigorously tested by reliable and objective observation of events and processes in the "real" world.

Doing Social Research

When sociologists use the scientific method to study human situations, there is a basic logic to how they do their research. Though there are different techniques and different ways to design a research project, six basic steps in doing research are (1) defining the problem, (2) reviewing the literature, (3) formulating hypotheses, (4) choosing a research design, (5) collecting data, and (6) analyzing and interpreting the results.

What to Study: Defining a Problem   There is an old saying: Ask a stupid question and you'll get a stupid answer. An updated version of that old saying refers to the limitations of those wonderfully ingenious computers: Put garbage in and you'll get garbage out. Sociological research is never any better than the questions sociologists ask. Poor questions produce nothing, or garbage. Good questions formulate a problem worth pursuing.

The beginning of sociological research, then, is to ask the right question and to determine what needs to be known to answer it. This has never been a simple or obvious matter in any science. One can ask *why* about anything, but scientists have to decide *what* questions are worth asking.

Asking the wrong question is a frequent error in science. A case in point is the old nature-nurture controversy: Does heredity or environment determine behavior? In that form the question is unanswerable, for it is not an either/or matter; both heredity *and* environment affect behavior, and they seem not to be clearly separable from one another. Only when social scientists stopped asking the wrong question could any progress be made.[12]

While some questions are wrong, others are merely trivial; not every question matters for science. What makes a question worth asking and qualifies it as a scientific problem is that answering the question will in some way—by confirming or revising—affect what we now take to be knowledge.

What we already know is also the basis for deciding what more we want to know, for there are always

Computers can count, correlate, and organize vast quantities of social data for research, as this scene from the M.I.T. Laboratories demonstrates. But what comes out of the computer can be no better than what went in.

inconsistencies, uncertainties, contradictions, and missing pieces in all established knowledge. A great deal of social research is generated from this. This was the reason, for example, why two sociologists decided to study employed black workers; as they noted, most research has been about the poorest blacks, uneducated, and either unemployed or underemployed:

> Little attempt has been made to study those who have steady jobs, live with stable families in respectable neighborhoods, and stay out of trouble. What about working-class and middle-class blacks who have made it?[13]

But that is not the only source of questions for research, at least for the social sciences. Society continually changes, and when it does it often opens up whole new areas of concern, raises previously unanticipated questions, and, more importantly, calls into question some of our already-established knowledge. The turbulent decade of the 1960s, for example, forced sociologists to study violence, riots, and social movements more closely and in more detail than ever before, and also to reexamine the place of youth in American society. In turn, the change into the 1970s has raised new issues about feminism and the rapidly changing status of women; about forms of religious commitment, particularly among the young; about the emergence of multinational corporations in a world-system of capitalism; and about such concrete issues as busing for solving the racial problem in education.

Reviewing the Literature Anyone who undertakes to do research looks to see what others have done before, how they have done it, and what they have found. There is an already existing record of how sociologists have carried on research on any particular sociological problem and there is a body of knowledge about that problem to be learned and used.

Very often there is a rich research literature, as, for example, in the study of crime and delinquency, minorities, or the family. Any new research must then build upon what is already known, fill in gaps, or test the established knowledge against changing circumstances.

Sometimes, in contrast, there may be little in the research literature to draw upon. In the 1960s and 1970s, for example, when sociologists began to study new social movements among minorities, youth, and women, they found that there was not much sociological literature on social movements in general and even less on these particular ones. In such cases, sociologists turn to the historical literature, for historians have studied social movements in American history, such as the populist movement of the late nineteenth century, and to anthropology, which possesses studies of nativistic religious movements.

Formulating Hypotheses A research problem has to be stated in a form that enables the researcher to test a specific proposition. A testable proposition is a *hypothesis;* it predicts a specific relationship expected to be found in the data. Thus, a sociologist studying the increase of married women in the labor force could hypothesize that women no longer remained at home because they had children, or that more women now than in the past, even with children, had no or little male support and had to work.

The research process either confirms that the hypothesized relationship does in fact exist, or it disconfirms it. Even disconfirming an hypothesis, however, provides new knowledge, for then sociologists know that certain relationships do not exist, even if many people believe they do. Such knowledge may be as important as that provided by the confirming of an hypothesis. Many people, for example, believe that the death penalty will significantly deter serious crime, but many tests of such an hypothesis, made by comparing over time homicide rates in states with and without capital punishment, failed to confirm the hypothesis.[14]

Variables Testing hypotheses requires the researcher to measure *variables*. Variables are often measured quantitatively, as *age, number* of children, *income* of

households, *years* of schooling, and others that vary in amount and degree. Other concepts do not vary in degree but take on two or more values. Some of these are dichotomous, as *male* and *female*. Others include several values: for example, *married, single, divorced,* or *widowed*.

The needs of a research project may lead researchers to combine quantities and values, as, for example, the *rate* of suicide among married and unmarried; the *percentage* of black and white people who are poor; the *proportion* of married women with children who are employed; or the *percentage* of Republicans, Democrats, and Independents among the college-educated.

Depending on how a variable is used in research, it is either a *dependent* or an *independent* variable. The dependent variable is the one the researcher is seeking to explain. This is done by showing how the dependent variable is affected by other variables, the independent ones.

If one wanted to explain partisan (Republican or Democratic) voting, for example, then these two partisan choices would be the dependent variables. Every factor that differentiated between voting Republican or Democratic would be an independent variable.

Such variables could be *age* (more younger than older people vote Democratic); *race* (blacks very largely vote Democratic); *income* (the wealthier people are, the more likely they are to vote Republican); *religion* (most Protestants vote Republican, most Catholics vote Democratic); and so on until enough independent variables have been measured to account adequately for the dependent variables.

Choosing a Research Design Specifying the hypotheses to be tested and the variables to be measured is but a first step in designing the research. How to gather the kind of data which will adequately test the hypotheses requires that the researcher decide on the population to be studied, the variables to be examined, and the mode of research appropriate to the problem, such as a survey, an experiment, fieldwork, documentary, or historical. (These several modes for designing a research project will be discussed further below.)

Collecting Data Whether questions come from the incompleteness of what is already known, or from changes in the social world that demand explanation, sociologists try in the most logical and rigorous way they can to find answers. And, consistent with the scientific method, answers require evidence. Facts must be obtained; in the language of research, *data* must be gathered. In asking and answering questions, the sociologist is *empirical,* that is, he/she gathers data by careful observation of social reality.

Observing the social world always meets up with a particular difficulty. Many things are *invisible.* Did you ever "see" a group's *morale,* a community's *values,* an organization's *goal?* The answer, of course, is no. What you do see, when you try to observe, are people's actions, and from these you *infer* that a group's morale is low, or that a community has certain values, or that a particular role exists.

Making inferences from observations can be a tricky matter, and two competent people may infer quite different things from the same observed facts. Social researchers try to meet this problem by constructing *indicators.* They do this by specifying the particular observations from which their inferences are made. Then others can check them out.

Low morale in an army, for example, might be inferred from such indicators as reenlistment rates, proportions of AWOLS, and maintenance of military discipline. In a factory, in contrast, the useful indicators of morale could be the daily rate of absenteeism, job turnover, quality of work, unauthorized work stoppages, and complaints filed with the grievance procedure.

To Sample or Not   Guided by what they want to know, sociologists have to decide whether it is practical to observe all of the population of people or events under study. Such considerations as time and money may lead them to use a *sample,* a small proportion of the total population.

A scientific sample will be so drawn that all the variation in the population important to the study will be present in the sample in the same proportion. If the sample were of the voters in a municipal election, for example, it would need to have the same proportion of voters by race, sex, age, income, occupation, and education, as these categories appear in the total population. The larger the sample, the more representative it can be, but usually large samples collect only a limited amount of data about each unit (each person interviewed, for example) through the use of a carefully worded questionnaire.

Analyzing and Interpreting the Results   The gathering of data may give us a rich description of some particular slice of social life and provide us with a lot of facts about some segment of the population. But the sociologist wants to do more than compile data. Facts must be related to the hypotheses first posed to see if an answer has emerged. To do that, there must be a *generalization* from the facts. Only then can a sociological explanation be developed.

The findings of any study will be compared to past research, to see to what extent, if any, they support past findings, or break new ground. Since a research project is never the last word, a researcher always concludes the study by pointing out what new hypotheses could be tested or new variables measured.

To generalize from the data is to move from the *empirical* realm of hypothesis-testing and data-gathering to the realm of *theory.* (We shall return to look again at theory.)

It should not be thought that all social research proceeds exactly according to these six steps. Sometimes, for example, when little is known, there may be no basis for stating a hypothesis; in that case, the research may be limited to gathering data from which hypotheses for future research can be developed. But these steps provide a model of what, ideally, is good social research.

The Major Methods of Research

In choosing a research design, as we saw above, a sociologist selects from among several different modes of research. The most common of these are survey research, the case study, experimental, fieldwork, documentary, and historical. While most studies are carried on through only one of these, it is possible to combine them, as, for example, to use both fieldwork observation and a survey, which means to collect data both by direct observation and by interviewing.

Survey Research   Surveys provide sociologists with a convenient and economical way to gather a great deal of standard data about some social group or category of people—the "population" under study. The *respondents* may fill out a self-administered questionnaire, or they may be questioned by interviewers. Whichever is done, the intent is to get exactly the same information from *everyone.*

Asking questions in such a way as to get valid information from respondents is not an easy matter. Long experience in devising questionnaires and conducting interviews has provided a substantial stock of knowledge about sources of bias. *Loaded* (emotionally tinged) words, for example, bring distorted responses. Similarly, complex and unclear language fails to communicate.

Good interviewing requires the skill to avoid biased responses. Interviewing is interaction, and whatever affects the interaction between the interviewer and the interviewed person affects the answers obtained. Differences in sex and race are an example, as when women interview men and whites interview blacks. Men are not always likely to be frank with women interviewers on matters that men typically do not share with women. Blacks might not be candid with whites on some matters of race. Also, people of lower social status sometimes tell a higher-status interviewer only what they think the interviewer wants to hear.

Survey research is the most widely used mode of social research in American sociology. In almost all cases, furthermore, the survey employs a sampling of the population to be studied. It is sampling techniques that make practical the undertaking of surveys on a nationwide basis.

A more limited sample, however, may better serve the purpose of a particular study. When sociologist Gary Marx wanted to study the mood of blacks during a period of militant protest, to get at their feelings about racial progress as well as their attitudes about whites, about Jews, and about violence and demonstrations, he developed a sample survey tailored to these concerns.[15] His study first carried out a sample survey of blacks in four key cities—New York, Chicago, Atlanta, and Birmingham—and balanced that with a sample survey of blacks in metropolitan regions outside the South. Thus, he focused on *urban* blacks, and particularly on Northern ones, at a time when such places were the location of militant protest and rapid racial change.

Experimental Research   Sometimes sociologists do what psychologists more often do—they conduct an experiment. Under carefully controlled conditions the experimenter tests the effect of a stimulus on a test group. The basic intent of experiments is to isolate the relationship between two factors from all the distorting influences to be found in the natural environment.

One strategy is to use the artificial environment of a laboratory in order to rigidly delimit the factors that will influence the results. A great deal of small-group research is carried out this way. A small group is brought together and given a task to perform, and the researchers, often from behind one-way mirrors, or in other unobtrusive ways, observe and record the activity. The laboratory allows for the most rigorous exclusion of confounding influences, but its very artificiality limits the kinds of sociological problems that can be studied.

Most small-group experiments involve innocent, even trivial kinds of behavior. Occasionally, however, there are social experiments that involve more significant, even potentially harmful behavior, and then such studies often become controversial. Such were the studies on obedience conducted by Stanley Milgram.[16]

Milgram utilized thousands of volunteers from all walks of life in a study which made the voluntary participant a "teacher" in what was presented as a test of the effects of punishment on learning. Each teacher worked with a student, whom he or she was led to believe was another volunteer but who in fact was a member of the experimental team.

The student was strapped in a chair and wired with electrodes. The teacher was seated before a shock board labeled from 15 volts ("slight shock") to 450 volts ("danger—severe shock") and was instructed to give increasingly higher volts for wrong answers.

As the voltage in the shocks increased, the students complained; by 285 volts they were screaming and pleading to be released. Most students then asked the white-coated experimenter what to do; they were instructed to continue. Some did not, but two-thirds of them obeyed orders and continued to press the shock button to the limit of 450 volts. The shock board was a fake and the screaming students were acting, but the volunteers did not know this.

Milgram's experiment provided sobering evidence of the capacity of ordinary people to obey what they believed to be legitimate authority, even when it meant inflicting considerable pain on others.

Experiments in Natural Settings   But sociologists are more likely to conduct experiments in natural settings, rather than in laboratories. Here they usually use two groups, the *experimental* one, which is subjected to the experimental stimulus, and a *control group,* which is not. A sociologist, for example, might want to test the effect, say, of an environmental message on a particular group. The first step would be to arrange to have an experimental group exposed to the message —a book or pamphlet, or a movie—and a control group not exposed. A *pretest* of both groups would first measure some relevant attitudes on environmental issues, and a *posttest* on both groups would then measure any effect of exposure to the message.

The Case Study   Instead of a survey or a series of experiments, another researcher may choose to do a *case study,* a fairly detailed analysis of only one instance: one family, one community, one riot, one school or factory. A case study cannot claim representativeness, but if not much is known, one detailed case may offer a rich source of questions and ideas for further work. Social scientists never assume, anyway, that one study of any kind is going to accomplish it all; one study always builds on what went before and contributes to future work. Many case studies are undertaken as fieldwork.

Fieldwork   There is a long tradition in sociology (and, of course, in anthropology) of *fieldwork:* gathering data by direct observation in natural situations. Some sociologists choose to be *participant-observers,* taking part in the social life of some group or community to make observations from the inside. What is found out by this means often would not be easily (perhaps never) revealed by interviews or questionnaires.

Where the researcher is a *nonparticipant* observer, the goal is to observe from close-up long enough so that the observer's presence is not a disturbing factor. Skilled fieldworkers not only observe what people do, they learn what they *mean* by what they do as well. In this way, a social group is studied from the inside, and we learn the shared understandings and meanings that make what people do understandable in human terms. (See "Observing the Police by Participant-Observation.")

There are a number of outstanding fieldwork studies in sociology, in each case providing interesting analyses of different aspects of American life. Back in the 1930s, William Whyte was a participant-observer of the street-corner life of young males in an Italian neighborhood in Boston.[17] Some thirty years later Elliot Liebow, who is white, managed to "hang out" with black males in Washington, D.C., and, by gaining

acceptance, constructed a rich description of their lives.[18]

Another fieldwork study, which had great influence on sociological thought, was Erving Goffman's detailed observation of life in a mental hospital.[19] Goffman spent months observing close-up the depersonalizing treatment of patients in a totally controlling institution, wherein people lose control of their lives and are then less capable of once again becoming self-controlled and responsible.

Documentary Research   Some sociological problems do not lend themselves either to sample surveys or to fieldwork, particularly when events occurring over a period of time are an important aspect of the study. Then, sociologists may look for *documentary* evidence. Good libraries have more than books; they are a significant resource of documents: official records and reports, the Census, congressional hearings, annual reports of government agencies and corporations, and the like.

When sociologist Daniel Bell set out to forecast the coming shape of postindustrial society, he looked for evidence of significant trends in a wide variety of social and economic documents, including the Census. From a rich body of such materials he extracted evidence of new trends in occupations, such as the continued increase in professional and technical occupations; the decline of manufacturing in the United States and the rise of a service economy; and the political subordination of the corporation to a society in which social planning will rationally control future development.[20]

Among these documentary sources, the United States Census is worth special mention. Since 1970, the Census has been continuously collecting basic information about the American people and has provided social scientists with one of their most useful and most frequently used sources of data for social research. Materials from the Census will be quoted frequently throughout the chapters of this book, and many of the tables presenting quantified data will be drawn from Census documents.

Historical Research   A great deal of documentary material provides evidence of social trends, of patterns of social development and change in society over time. This is the kind of material the historian uses in

OBSERVING THE POLICE BY PARTICIPANT-OBSERVATION

Sociologist Jerome Skolnick spent some twelve weeks in direct observation of detectives in preparing a prize-winning study of urban police work.* Here are some of his comments on his participant observation of city detectives.

Under direct observation, detectives were cooperative. They soon gave permission to listen in to telephone calls, allowed me to join in conversations with informants, and to observe interrogations. In addition, they called me at home whenever an important development was anticipated. Whenever we went out on a raid, I was a detective so far as any outsider could see. Although my appearance does not conform to the stereotype of the policeman, this proved to be an advantage since I could sometimes aid the police in carrying out some of their duties. For example, I could walk into a bar looking for a dangerous armed robber who was reportedly there without undergoing much danger to myself, since I would not be recognized as a policeman. Similarly, I could drive a disguised truck up to a building, with a couple of policemen hidden in the rear, without the lookout recognizing me.

At the same time, I looked enough like a policeman when among a group of detectives in a raid for suspects to take me for a detective. (It twice happened that policemen from other local departments, who recognized that I was not a member of the Westville force, assumed I was a federal agent.) Even though I posed as a detective, however, I never carried a gun, although I did take pistol training on the police range. As a matter of achieving rapport with the police, I felt that such participation was required. Since I was not interested in getting standard answers to standard questions, I needed to be on the scene to observe their behavior and attitudes expressed on actual assignments.

One problem that this sort of research approach raises is whether an observer's presence alters the normal behavior of the police. There is no certain control for this problem, but I believe the following assumptions are reasonable. First, the more time the observer spends with subjects, the more used to his presence they become. Second, participant-observation offers the subject less opportunity to dissimulate than he would have in answering a questionnaire, even if he were consciously telling the truth in response to standardized questions. . . . Third, in many situations involving police, they are hardly free to alter behavior, as, for example, when a policeman kicks in a door on a narcotics raid.

Finally, if an observer's presence does alter police behavior, I believe it can be assumed that it does so only in one direction. I can see no reason why police would, for example, behave *more* harshly to a prisoner in the presence of an observer than in his absence. . . . Thus, a conservative interpretation of the materials that follow would hold that these are based upon observations of a top police department behaving at its best. However, I personally believe that while I was not exposed to the "worst," whatever that may mean, most of what I saw was necessarily typical of the ordinary behavior of patrolmen and detectives, *necessarily*, because over a long period of time, organizational controls are far more pertinent to policemen than the vague presence of an observer whom they have come to know, and who frequently exercises "drop-in" privileges. If a sociologist rides with police for a day or two, he may be given what they call the "whitewash tour." As he becomes part of the scene, however, he comes to be seen less as an agent of control than as an accomplice.

Notes

* Jerome H. Skolnick, *Justice Without Trial: Law Enforcement in Democratic Society* (New York: Wiley, 1966) pp. 35–37.

carefully reconstructing the social events of some ear-lier time. Sample surveys and field studies, in turn, provide observations only of the present. Until re-cently, in fact, sociological researchers largely ignored historical materials. But no longer is that so, and no longer can any sharp line be drawn between good so-cial history and good historical sociology.

The reason for this lies in a renewed emphasis in sociology on understanding the present as the out-come of social trends and developments of the past. We cannot understand our present society unless we understand the changes over time which gave it its particular shape. Nor can we anticipate future trends unless we see them as extensions of, or changes in, trends which have been developing over time. A soci-ological perspective, in short, which ignores the past can never do more than *describe* the present. To *un-derstand* the present we must know what happened in the past.

This emphasis on a historical perspective reflects the fact that society is never fixed in its forms, but is always changing. To understand society we must un-derstand how it has been changing, and how those changes have produced a present-day society that dif-fers from past society. To do that, we must be capable of standing back and taking a longer view. If we stand too close to the trees, we may not see the forest.

A recent fine example of historical research in soci-ology is Theda Skocpol's comparative study of the French Revolution of 1787–1800, the Russian Revo-lution of 1917–1921, and the Chinese Revolution of 1911–1949.[21] Dissatisfied with existing sociological theories of revolution, which, she observed, were based on how political protest and change were sup-posed to occur in liberal-democratic and capitalist so-cieties, Skocpol decided to undertake a comparative historical analysis of these three world-shaping revolu-tions in order to develop a more adequate theory.

From her detailed analyses of these three large, complex sets of events, she learned that they occurred in countries that lagged behind in economic develop-ment; that these revolutions produced new states, more centralized, bureaucratic, and internally power-ful than before; and that peasants and workers were more directly incorporated into national politics. But she also came to understand that no universal theory of revolution was possible, for the causes of revolution vary with historical and international circumstances.

The Problem Chooses the Method All these ways of gathering data—sample surveys, fieldwork, experi-ment, documentary and historical studies—are useful and necessary in sociological research. It is a principle of scientific research that the method employed is de-termined by the needs of the study. What kind of data to gather, and how to gather it, are decisions to be made on the basis of what needs to be known. The problem determines the method, not the other way around.

Theory: The Effort to Explain

Sociological research begins and ends with theory. It begins with the effort to define a problem, a theoreti-cal statement or question of what needs to be known. It ends when the researcher generalizes from the data to make a theoretical statement and then relates the study's findings to existing theory, providing further confirmation or requiring modification.

Generalizing from facts and constructing theories which explain facts are quite natural to the human mind. Scientists did not invent this, but they do insist that scientific explanations be constructed *logically* and always be capable of being tested *empirically*.

We generalize first when we sum up some data: For example, whites on the average earn more income than blacks do (see "Averaging the Data"). Such a statement, however, needs to be explained. One ex-planation might be that education *correlates* closely with income—high education, high income; low edu-cation, low income—and that whites achieve more education than blacks do (see "Correlation: How Things Go Together"). So, better-educated whites qualify for better jobs more often than blacks do.

While this might seem to explain the facts, it also raises another issue: *Why* do whites achieve more education than blacks do? Here we find some compet-ing theories. Most sociologists favor a theory of dis-crimination: whites possess and use the power to dis-criminate, so that educational discrimination gives them more of the jobs requiring more education. But there are others who insist that *aspirations* for educa-tion differ significantly between the races, as well as among ethnic groups and social classes (and why this is so poses another interesting problem).

Each of these attempts to theorize rests on the no-tion that blacks earn less than whites because, on the

AVERAGING THE DATA

The most common way to summarize data is to calculate *central tendencies,* or what we commonly call *averages.* There are three ways to do this: mode, mean, and median.

The *mode* is the number that occurs most frequently in a series. If, for example, the grades in a sociology class of 40 students ranged from A to D, but 24 students received a B−, that would be the modal grade, the grade most frequently given. It might or might not be close to the mean or median, however, depending on how all the grades were distributed.

The *mean* is the most familiar average; it is computed by adding a series of figures and dividing by the total number in the series. An exam, for example, might be graded on a scale of 0 to 100; when the instructor adds up the students' scores and divides by the number who took the test, the result is the arithmetic mean.

In some cases the *median* will be a more useful average than the mean. Suppose, in the above example, that the mean score was 84 but that most students had scores below that. A few very high scores can pull up the mean (just as a few very low scores can pull it down). A more representative figure might then be computed by finding the test score that was in the very middle of the series of scores, where half the scores are above it and half are below it. If, in our example, that turned out to be 76, that might be more useful to the instructor than the mean of 84.

average, they are less educated. But it is also a fact that, when whites and blacks of the same educational level are compared, white still earn more. Such a fact lends greater support to a theory of discrimination.

Furthermore, these efforts to construct a theory draw upon data about the present: income and educational levels, social aspirations, etc. But one could ask: How did these differences between the races come about? Was it always this way? And if whites have the power to discriminate, where did this power come from? Answering these questions brings in the long history that began in slavery and continued through court-sanctioned segregation until 1954. Any theory about black and white differences today has to take into account the history of the long-established and the changing-but-still-unequal social relations between the races.

These brief examples perhaps will make the point: sociologists are interested in more than facts. They not only want to know *what* is so, they also want to be able to say *why* it is so. The first requires them to be *empirical* and constantly seek out facts; the second requires that they generalize from these facts and be *theoretical*.

Objectivity: A Norm for Scientific Work

To study the rich and complex flow of social life without letting passion and prejudice get in the way is no easy task. Yet that is exactly what the scientific method demands of the social scientists. They must be impartial observers of social life, not partisans or propagandists. That is what it means to be objective.

Social scientists become objective when they can discipline their thinking so as to reduce the possible bias and distortion in observation and analysis produced by their attitudes, emotions, values, like and dislikes. Anyone is capable of being more objective in one situation, less so in another. Experimental psychology has taught us, for example, that if we are emotionally involved in something (or someone), or intensely prejudiced about it (or them), or if we have interests at stake, then our social perceptions (what we see and don't see) will be strongly affected. Our feelings will keep us from seeing the reality others can see.

For social scientists objectivity is a *norm,* a standard by which they are to be judged and which they strive hard to attain. In doing research, some useful techniques have been devised to make objectivity more likely. A scientific sample, for example, ensures that a small group is representative of its population. A biased sample would lead to invalid inferences. As we have already noted, sociologists have learned much about designing questionnaires and conducting interviews so as to avoid the obvious pitfalls of distorted responses.

While long experience enables researchers to guard against the obvious sources of bias, that alone is never sufficient. A more general principle for ensuring objectivity is used in all science, and the social sciences are no exception. This is the requirement that any scientific work be open to public examination by competent students of the field. Scott Greer calls this the "norm of publicity."[22] Whatever personal bias is present in the work should be noted and challenged by others who hold no such bias.

This tells us that objectivity is sustained, then, not primarily by individual objectivity, but by institutional practices, such as public scrutiny. Another practice is replication of studies to see if other researchers can get the same or similar results.

Bias as Perspective   Like all human beings, social scientists share the values and assumptions of their society, often of their social class. Contemporary American sociologists are professional, educated, middle-class people, and they share the assumptions and values to be found among such people. Not all of these can be guarded against when doing social research. Bias in research now becomes the *collective bias* of the community of scholars. The norm of publicity will not suffice in this case.

As long as American sociologists were confined to a sociological community that was almost exclusively American, few of them knew how to break out of a limited American view of the world. But now sociology is more and more an international community. The

---

CORRELATION: HOW THINGS GO TOGETHER

That high and low education relate closely to high and low income is one of hundreds of such observations that can be found in the sociological literature, many of which will be cited in this book. A great deal of sociological research seeks to establish such relationships.

In doing so, sociologists make use of a statistical measure called the *correlation coefficient*. A correlation of zero means that two variables have no consistent relationship. A correlation of 1.0 means a perfect *positive* relationship; an increase in one variable is always associated with a corresponding increase in the other. A *negative* or *inverse* relationship, in turn, means that an increase in one variable is associated with a corresponding decrease in the other, as, for example, the *higher* a person's social status, the *less* likely is he or she to be charged with a crime, or convicted if charged, or imprisoned if found guilty.

Sociologists do not find perfect correlations among social data; instead, they find stronger or weaker ones. In the relationship between education and income, for example, factors besides education affect a person's income: sex and race (white males earn more than blacks and females of equal education); or the nature of the occupation (physicians earn more on the average than other professionals); or the size of the business (large corporations generally pay better salaries for similar work than do small firms). Education will only account for some limited amount of the variation from low to high income.

Recognizing that fact, most researchers will combine the several factors they hypothesize that will explain most of the variation in the dependent variable by using a *multivariate technique*. Even then most social research yields only weak to modest correlations, telling us that the factors that affect a single variable are often numerous as well as difficult to measure accurately.

American-ness of American sociologists is subject to check by European and Third World sociologists. American sociologists, for example, have often seemed to assume that social life is normally carried on in an individually competitive environment characteristic of a capitalist society, but sociologists in socialist societies can point out the limitations of such an assumption.

Furthermore, though most American sociologists still do their research in American society, more and more such work is deliberately *comparative* and contains some data drawn from societies other than this one.

All of this increases the potential for an objective, cross-cultural, cross-national sociology. None of it is a guarantee, however, But even recognizing the problem of collective bias presses sociologists to find ways to break through the closed minds that everyone suffers as a consequence of sharing membership in particular social groups.

The Obtrusive Observer   These complex issues have led some social scientists to argue that social science cannot reach the level of objectivity that natural science can, because the social scientists are part of the very thing they analyze. But physical scientists now recognize that even they do not escape the problem: The method of observation always affects the phenomenon being observed; the observer is always an obtrusive observer.

There can be no avoidance of the fact in any science; scientists can only confront the issue and take account of it. Kai Erikson summed it up well:

> Recent critiques of sociology, then, focus attention on something we have really known for a long time—that the sociological enterprise, for all its internal consistencies and balances, nevertheless rests on a soft substratum of human biases and assumptions. This is inconvenient, perhaps, but inescapable; and we can only take what comfort we can from the fact that the older and more confident sciences have known it for years and have learned to regard it as a natural condition of their work.[23]

SUMMARY

Sociology is *the study of society.*

Why is there society? Because (1) the human organism can neither survive nor develop into a person without prolonged association with others, and (2) human survival requires the cooperative social labor of human beings to create an enduring organization of social life.

Sociology began in response to the vast social changes which transformed the European world *from agrarian to industrial,* and created a world too large and complex to be familiar through personal daily experience.

The *origin* of sociology is in the effort to formulate a theory of this new industrial society and to observe and describe the lives of people in new urban environments.

The *sociological perspective* focuses on collective, shared social life from the smallest group to the largest structure. Mills's distinction between private troubles and public issues is one way to see the connection between the personal world of the individual and the larger social structure.

Sociologists are concerned both with the *empirical* and *theoretical* aspects of their study. The empirical is concerned with the gathering of *data.* Theory begins with making certain assumptions about the ''real'' world, poses questions, and then selects and organizes those social facts that answer the question.

There are three major theoretical orientations. The *functional* perspective emphasizes how each part of society contributes to its overall organization. Some functions are *manifest,* that is, people recognize and intend the consequences of their actions; but many others are *latent,* for people often do not recognize or intend the consequences.

The *conflict* perspective emphasizes that conflict and change are a constant feature of all human societies. This leads sociologists to focus on power, domination, and inequality.

From the *interactionist* perspective, social interaction is the basic process from which all group life emerges, and it is through their interaction that human beings construct, maintain, and change social life.

The *uses of sociology* are viewed differently by different sociologists:

1. Some think it most useful simply *by developing into a science.*

2. Others see in it a *practical use* for established groups and organizations, by helping them solve their problems and improve managerial and administrative control over citizens, employees, and consumers. This includes an *ideological* use, that is, providing "ideological ammunition" for various interest groups.

3. Others see the usefulness of sociology for *social reform,* which seeks changes in the practices and policies of the dominant groups and organizations to resolve various social problems.

4. Still others see in sociology a *critical use,* which requires sociology to serve no power or established interest but to be a *humanistic* and *liberating* study striving to understand the world in order to change it.

There are *six steps in doing research:* (1) defining the problem; (2) reviewing the literature; (3) formulating hypotheses and testing *variables;* (4) choosing a research design; (5) collecting data; and (6) analyzing and interpreting the results.

The *major methods* of research are surveys, the case study, experimental, fieldwork, documentary, and historical.

Sociological research begins and ends with *theory,* which is the process of generalizing from facts to construct an explanation. Sociologists want to know *what* is so, and *why.*

Objectivity is the basic norm of science; it is a discipline of thinking so as to reduce the possible bias and distortion in observation and analysis produced by one's attitudes, emotions, values, likes, and dislikes.

Objectivity requires that all scientific work be open to public inspection. The collective bias of a community of scholars can only be guarded against by communication with an ever wider range of scholars, as when the "American-ness" of scholars is checked by European and Third World scholars.

NOTES

[1] C. Wright Mills, *The Sociological Imagination* (New York: Oxford University Press, 1959; paperback edition, 1974), p. 8.

[2] *Ibid.,* pp. 5 and 7.

[3] Paul F. Lazarsfeld, William H. Sewell, and Harold L. Wilensky, *The Uses of Sociology* (New York: Basic Books, 1967), p. x.

[4] *Ibid.,* p. xiii.

[5] Mills, *op. cit.,* p. 80.

[6] *Ibid.,* p. 80.

[7] *Ibid.,* p. 81.

[8] *Ibid.,* p. 81.

[9] Robert S. Lynd, *Knowledge for What?* (Princeton, N.J.: Princeton University Press, 1939; paperback edition, 1966), p. 191.

[10] For a fuller discussion of humanist sociology, see Alfred McClung Lee, *Toward Humanist Sociology* (Englewood Cliffs, N.J.: Prentice-Hall, 1973).

[11] Alvin W. Gouldner, "Anti-Minotaur: The Myth of a Value-Free Sociology," *Social Problems* 9 (1962):205.

[12] See Nicholas Pastore, *The Nature-Nurture Controversy* (New York: King's Crown Press, 1949).

[13] Joseph A. Kahl and John M. Goering, "Stable Workers, Black and White," *Social Problems* 18 (Winter 1971): 307.

[14] See, for example, Walter C. Reckless, "The Use of the Death Penalty—A Factual Statement," *Crime and Delinquency* 15 (January, 1969): 43–56.

[15] Gary Marx, *Protest and Prejudice: A Study of Belief in the Black Community* (New York: Harper & Row, 1967).

[16] Stanley Milgram, *Obedience to Authority: An Experimental View* (New York: Harper & Row, 1973).

[17] William Whyte, *Street-Corner Society: The Social Structure of an Italian Slum* (Chicago: University of Chicago Press, 1943).

[18] Elliot Liebow, *Tally's Corner: A Study of Negro Streetcorner Men* (Boston: Little, Brown, 1967).

[19] Erving Goffman, *Asylums: Essays on the Social Situation of Mental Patients and Other Inmates* (Chicago: Aldine, 1961).

[20] Daniel Bell, *The Coming of Post-Industrial Society: A Venture in Social Forecasting* (New York: Basic Books, 1973).

[21] Theda Skocpol, *States and Social Revolutions: A Comparative Analysis of France, Russia, and China* (New York: Cambridge University Press, 1979).

[22] Scott Greer, *The Logic of Social Inquiry* (Chicago: Aldine, 1969), pp. 6–7.

[23] Kai T. Erikson, "Sociology: That Awkward Age," *Social Problems* 19 (Spring 1972): 433.

SUGGESTED READINGS

Scott Greer, *The Logic of Social Inquiry.* Chicago: Aldine, 1969. A useful introduction to social research.

Philip E. Hammond, ed., *Sociologists at Work: Essays on the Craft of Social Research* New York: Basic Books, 1964. A collection of informative essays by sociologists on how they actually carried out their research.

Alfred McClung Lee, *Toward Humanist Sociology.* Englewood Cliffs, N.J.: Prentice-Hall, 1973. A very readable plea for sociology to be humanistic.

Robert S. Lynd, *Knowledge for What?* Princeton, N.J.: Princeton University Press, 1939; paperback edition, 1966. The renowned classic argument for a value-relevant sociology.

John H. Madge, *The Origins of Scientific Sociology.* New York: The Free Press, 1962. An analysis of the classic research projects in sociology.

C. Wright Mills, *The Sociological Imagination.* New York: Oxford University Press, 1959. An impressive case is made for a sociology concerned with human values.

Part 2

THE STUDY OF SOCIAL LIFE

TWO

INTERACTION
The basis of society

Often, to learn new ideas people have to unlearn old ones. So it has been in the study of society. The development of sociology includes a long effort to free us from older ideas that explained human behavior solely in terms of instincts or by such factors as geography, climate, or race.

In studying society, sociology starts with the simple but fundamental idea that neither individual conduct nor the organization of society can be explained by any nonsocial factor. Person and society in all their human variety emerge from human interaction.

To get from the simple matter of *interaction* between any two persons to the complex reality of society, however, requires some other concepts. *Social role, social relation, and social structure* are the basic concepts necessary to understand how social life takes the organized form we call society. This chapter will concentrate on exploring these basic units of sociological analysis.

INTERACTION: SOCIAL AND SYMBOLIC

If we set out to observe social life, what do we see? We see people acting: talking, playing, working, arguing. When persons act, they do something that they and others understand and give a name to: "eating dinner," "taking a test," "writing a paper," "reading a book," "watching TV," "playing baseball," "making love," "borrowing money," "going to work."

To name it is to identify it, separate it out from the stream of ongoing activity. One act is marked off from another by the language shared by members of the society. By knowing the language, each of us knows what the act of, say, taking a test, is and what it means.

By not knowing the language we do not know what the act is or means, even though we observe it directly. If we came upon a group of crouching young men and asked, "What are they doing?" And someone said, "Shooting craps," we would then understand their actions if we knew what dice were and how they were used in a game of chance. Otherwise, their actions would not make any sense to us. Any action seems strange when you do not understand what it means to the actors involved. Only when we understand the meanings the actors give to their actions do we understand what they are doing.

Social Interaction

These social acts, which we observe and interpret, are not isolated bits of activity; rather, each is somehow connected with other social acts in a continuous stream of human activity. Social life is carried on through constant social *interaction* among people.

Social interaction is the process by which two or more persons are acting toward and responding to one another at the same time.

A conversation between two or more persons is a simple example of interaction. Each person speaks to the others—here again, a common language is necessary—and at the same time responds to what the others are saying. Furthermore, each person takes account of the others. To "take account" is to define the others as having a particular meaning for the actor (the other is a friend, teacher, salesperson; he or she is friendly or impersonal; he or she is important, influential, or not) and then act toward the other person on the basis of how he or she has been defined.

Interaction Is Symbolic   The interaction that goes on in a simple conversation is not just people emitting sound but expressing some shared meanings through gestures and words, in short, through *symbols.* Each actor must understand and respond to the others' gestures and words in a like manner; in short, they must "speak the same language." When this occurs, there is communication; interaction is always a communicative process. (Language and other symbols are the realm of *culture,* which we examine in the next chapter.)

Signs and Symbols

It is not a new idea that human beings live with and through symbols, and that language is our most basic symbolic process. But only within this century has the importance of our symbolic capacities become a firm pillar of our assumptions about being human.

Signs   Acknowledging that there are impressive similarities between animal and human behavior (and that in some important ways humans *are* animals), the anthropologist Leslie White insists there is nonetheless a basic difference: animals do not enter into the human world—the symbolic world.[1] Animals, agrees White, can be taught to respond to a vocal command, and any kind of vocal sound can be used for such a purpose. Here we are dealing with *signs,* not symbols. A sign is "a physical thing or event whose function is to indicate some other thing or event."[2] Some signs occur in nature, such as dark clouds and wind signifying a coming storm; others are human-made, such as a traffic signal.

Animals can learn very complex sign systems, and animals (including human ones) can be conditioned to respond in set ways to contrived signs. White, however, makes the significant point that although a dog can learn appropriate signs, it is only a person who *"can and does play an active role in determining what value the vocal stimulus is to have. . . ."*[3] In short, a dog only passively *learns* signs, but a person can *create* signs.

Symbols   When signs are conventional, that is, human-made, they are *symbols.* Symbols are all those objects (including words) for which human beings have a set of shared meanings and values. Symbols always signify something, but not always a particular, specific event, like dark clouds signifying coming rain, or like a traffic signal telling us to stop or go. Thus, the "sign" of the cross is not a form to signify any particular event or action (though its origin is in the crucifixion of Jesus Christ), but a symbol to represent the *meanings* and *values* of the Christian faith. Symbols come into being only when objects (including words) are assigned a set of meanings and values (see "The Symbolic World").

One of the major philosophers of this century, Ernst Cassirer (1874–1945), saw in symbol-creating the distinctiveness of what is human. "This new acquisition," he said, "transforms the whole of human life. As compared with other animals, man lives not merely in a broader reality; he lives, so to speak, in a new dimension of reality."[4]

Symbolic Interaction

When interaction proceeds through the communication of meanings by language or other symbol-using processes, it is *symbolic interaction.* Persons in social interaction communicate meanings by their verbal behavior, as well as by conventionally defined (thus symbolic) gestures, such as winking or thumbing one's nose. These gestures, according to George Herbert Mead, become *significant symbols* when they are *conscious* gestures by one actor which are then responded to by a second actor.[5]

Defining the Situation   By the use of symbols actors define the situation in which interaction occurs, for it never occurs in a vacuum; there is always a larger context in which interaction takes place. For example, people conversing over dinner may be guests invited to dinner at another's home; or they may be business persons carrying out a business transaction in an ex-

THE SYMBOLIC WORLD

The world we live in is rich with symbols, some ancient and honored, some new, but always in use; and when used, they sometimes fade out, they change in meaning, new ones replace old ones. Here are some familiar symbols of Western culture.

1. *Political* symbols: the *flag* of any nation; the *hammer* and *sickle* of world communism; the Nazi *swastika;* the *donkey* and the *elephant* of the two American parties.

2. *American national* symbols: The American flag; the 4th of July; Memorial Day; George Washington, Abraham Lincoln; Bunker Hill; Boston Tea Party; Gettysburg Address; Declaration of Independence; the Constitution; the Bill of Rights.

3. *Colors* are symbols: *red* (blood) for courage (but red is also communism's symbolic color); *yellow* for cowardice; *black* for darkness, fear, and evil, for mourning; *white* for innocence and purity (the white bridal gown).

4. *The animal kingdom:* doves for peace; hawks for war and aggressiveness; sparrows are insignificant but belong in God's kingdom; eagles for strength and majestic courage; foxes for cunning; lions for strength (king of the jungle); jackals for low, dishonest action; snakes for treachery and deceit.

5. *Physical gestures* are symbols: the military salute; the handshake; waving good-bye or hello; thumbs up; thumbs down; thumbing your nose; shrugging your shoulders; smiling or frowning; the two-fingered "V" sign; winking; raising an eyebrow.

pensive restaurant, with one of them paying the bill and putting it on an expense account, or yet again, they may be members of a family exchanging news about what each did that day.

"Conversation over dinner," then, takes place in different social situations, and this has consequences for the actors' conduct. Friends at dinner may engage in serious discussions, feel able to express themselves freely, and even dare to disagree, while remaining friends. Businessmen intent on a transaction, however, are likely to avoid serious subjects (besides the business deal) and stick to sports or shoptalk. In a family context, conversation will not only be an exchange of news but a frank sharing of feelings and sentiments, perhaps a parent's reprimand of a child, or other matters of family business.

In each of these instances social interaction goes on in particular kinds of social situations. And it was the kind of social situation it was because it was *defined* that way by the actors in the situation. What each situation "really" was, was a matter of definition by the actors involved.

All of this leads to the idea that "if men define a situation as real, it is real in its consequences," which is what W. I. Thomas (1863–1947) meant by *the definition of the situation.* Thus, if actors define a situation as hostile and threatening, they will act to defend themselves, perhaps to be hostile, too. To point out that objectively they were wrong may be true but irrelevant for the purpose of understanding their actions.

This conception of social interaction as a symbolic process rooted in a language of shared meanings — and language, too, is created through interaction — is basic to all the social sciences. Even individual persons cannot be understood without referring to the social interactions significant in their life-experiences. In seeking to study society, sociology builds upon the concept of social interaction but it focuses upon those interactions that occur with regularity. These stable and persistent interactions we call *social relations.*

ROLES AND RELATIONS

To get married is to enter into a social relation; to make friends with someone is, also. To hold a job puts one into a social relation with an employer or supervi-

Conversation over dinner in the intimate atmosphere of the home provides an opportunity to talk freely.

sor; to enter college, into social relations with teachers and other students. The list is extensive and covers most of what anyone of us does in a day. The larger part of our individual activities, in short, involve us in social relations with others.

Many social relations demonstrate the *authority,* and hence the inequality, built into society: employer to employee, teacher to student, parent to child, team coach to player. Few social relations, in fact, are relations among equals, even when they are warm and affectionate, as in a family.

Most of the social relations we become involved in occur because we belong to social groups and organizations. In that case, social relations locate us in a *social position* (sometimes called a *social status*) in those groups: a son or daughter in a family, an executive of a business firm, a secretary in a government office, a chairperson of a committee. The occupants of these positions interact with the occupants of other positions

—a wife with her husband, a doctor with patients, an employer with employees. In these interactions there are mutual *expectations* about how each will and *should* act toward the other. A *social role,* then, defines the action "expected" by the actors who occupy social positions.

Roles and Role Expectations

Roles in real life are not like roles in a play or film, where an actor learns his lines as the author wrote them and then acts out the part on cue as directed. The language of "actor" and "role" are borrowed from the theater and provide a useful analogy, as long as it is not taken literally. In interacting with others, we are not acting out roles which have already been prepared for us in advance. (Even though it sometimes may seem that way, as when an older person admonishes a younger one: "Act your age.") Real life is closer to improvisational theater.

A useful conception of role is that offered by the sociologist, Ralph Turner, who suggests we might think of a role as *consistency in orientation*.[6] What Turner means by this is that a role does not require of us any specific conduct; instead, it suggests that we interact with "friends" in a manner consistent with what friendship means to us and to them.

Two people who are friends expect of each other what they could never expect of anyone else. So do members of a family. "That's what a friend is for"— this old cliché suggest one should expect more from friends than from others. Yet there is no author's script to specify *exactly* what friends are supposed to do for each other. Over time, as relationships develop among people who are friends, they work out more specific expectations.

But how far can this be carried? Can we be expected to help a friend do something dishonest, or to escape the clutches of the law? In some situations and groups there would be such an expectation, and a strong one, too. But in many other cases it would be much more uncertain. Thus, there is almost always this element of uncertainty in role expectations. "I thought you were my friend," someone says to another when the help asked for has been refused.

Where Roles Get Specific   In a large and complex society like the United States, any role expectation could only be stated very generally, and even then with many exceptions. Yet, most of us experience quite specific role expectations every day. This is so because the roles in which we interact are tied to specific groups, and our belonging to these groups subjects us to the specific expectations of conduct upheld in the social relations of that group. In particular families, communities, and ethnic and religious groups, a person learns that there are specific ways he or she is expected to act toward others. Social classes, too, develop specific role expectations.

Because roles become specific only in specific social groups, the same social role can differ considerably from group to group. When a woman marries a corporation executive, the role expectations of wife which she encounters differ considerably from those encountered by a woman who marries a blue-collar worker. In marrying a corporation executive, a woman expects to be a gracious hostess for social entertaining; a skilled, amicable participant in many social functions; and perhaps to take an active public role in charitable or other socially useful (but noncontroversial) activities. The wife of a factory worker encounters no similar role expectations.

When people share specific role expectations,

The female executive and the mother respond to quite different role-expectations.

when, that is, they know what behavior to expect of others and what behavior is expected of themselves in social situations, they can then interact in a stable and orderly fashion. Each person's behavior meshes smoothly with that of others in like situations. The creation of shared role expectations, then, is the first step in organizing social life.

Role-Set Up to this point we have spoken as if there were but one role associated with a social position, but that is not so. A student, for example, finds himself in a relation with fellow students, which invokes one set of expectations, and in a relation with professors, which brings forth somewhat different expectations. In turn, interacting with administrators and other rule-enforcers manifests still other expectations; and even quite different expectations may emerge from interacting outside the university, as, for example, with the local police. For students, then, there is not one role but a *role-set,* a differentiated set of role-expectations to orient themselves toward the other actors in the several different relations in which, as students they become involved.[7]

Role-Change Roles, and the expectations which define them, are not fixed forever in some traditional form. For one thing, as we already noted, there is always something uncertain, even ambiguous, about some aspects of social life; as a consequence roles are continually being redefined and altered in social interaction. As people act out their social roles, they also continuously redefine and remake them.

We can sometimes see changes in role-expectations acted out in successive generations. Many young women today support one another in defying some traditional expectations that were compelling for their mothers, such as those about not becoming well-educated, having children, not training for a profession, getting married, and particularly about not living with a man before marriage or without expectation of marriage. In interacting among themselves and with young men, these young women are creating new expectations for their roles and, incidentally, for male roles, too. When a young college-educated woman marries and also pursues a full-time professional career, both she and her husband are changing the traditional role-expectations for wife and husband.

Role-Conflict Different and changing role expectations often create strain and tension for individuals when these roles are not merely different but also contradictory.[8] The individual cannot meet one role expectation without violating another. A foreman, for example, becomes a "man in the middle" when management expects him to be the front rank of managerial authority in organizing and controlling the work situation, while the workers expect him to be a "good guy" who sympathizes with their problems and speaks up for them and their interests.[9] Being a leader of workers and also a representative of management, then, is *contradictory.*

Often such a contradiction is never resolved but simply lived with, though not without psychological cost to the individual. The strains and tensions can flair up in such symptoms as headaches, excessive drinking, and difficulties in relating to others. Sometimes management may try to alleviate the situation by adopting a "human relations" ideology and having supervisory people display concern for the problems and dissatisfactions of the workers. The intent is not to eliminate the foreman's role conflict but to use this display of concern for the workers *instrumentally,* as a way to reduce personal dissatisfactions in order to maintain high levels of productivity.

When the foreman's conflicting roles are plainly evident to the workers, the way is set for a change to eliminate this particular contradiction. Under collective bargaining, the foreman can be defined as the representative of management only; a new role, that of shop steward, is then created to speak for the workers.

Role-conflict usually occurs whenever there is social change. A new generation, for example, may find itself in conflict with the more established and traditional role expectations of the older generation. The changing feminist perspective is a current example of new role definitions by younger women (and many young men, too) in conflict with that of much of the older generation, both women and men.

Roles, Positions, and Persons

Wife and mother, and teacher and principal, are roles that clearly link role expectations to positions in such social groups as family and school. But there are other social roles not so easily connected to any particular social position. They may, instead, be identified in people's minds as a personality type, such as "peacemaker," but in fact they are social roles, though anchored to no particular social position.

When tension and conflict disrupt social relations in a group, for example, one member may act as a peacemaker mediating between contending factions and persons. In a family a mother may mediate between a stern father and his rebellious children for the sake of family peace. In large organizations, however, the necessary role of peacemaker becomes a well-defined social position—mediator, ombudsman, grievance officer, or arbitrator—provided with the resources and authority needed to act to maintain peace, or at least working relations. (The idea of "antagonistic cooperation" probably best describes social relations in large organizations, where members have unequal power and reward.)

Former pro football coach John Madden was long noted for his emotional outbursts at officials, but such an outburst in return would not fit the role of game official.

An aggressive, combative person, or one who readily takes sides or finds fault, may be a poor risk to serve as mediator for a group. When mediator becomes an official position, qualifying for it requires individuals with certain skills and also with patience and self-discipline. Mediators who easily "blow their stacks" are not likely to succeed in such a role.

Another role, which is not anchored to a social position, is that of the "life of the party," the outgoing extrovert who enjoys being the center of attraction and can perform well to amuse others. In school the class "clown" may do the same. There are usually no positions to accommodate these roles; there are only situations in which these roles are appropriate.

Within small groups, such as committees, sociologists who conduct social experiments have identified two roles that are not tied to any specific position. One is the *task-centered* role, wherein the role-taker supplies ideas but also disagrees and criticizes. The other is the socially supportive role of the person who tries to build agreement, is supportive of others, and breaks tension with humorous remarks. This second role is much like that of mediator.

Within large organizations, too, there are roles that are not formally defined and assigned to any particular position. A familiar one is that of the "gopher," usually taken by younger, lower-ranking persons who are sent on errands. They "go for" coffee and doughnuts, or perform other services for people with more rank. Making coffee in the office is often another instance of this.

Still another is the "mother" role in the office, that of the woman who finds that others (mostly male) turn to her for support and sympathy and to whom they bring their troubles. (See the discussion in Chapter 12 of this and related "role-traps" experienced by women breaking into previously all-male roles in corporations.)

A role that has been the focus of feminist concern is that of the secretary who finds herself assigned tasks unrelated to her skills and responsibilities. She finds herself with the role of "office wife," asked to attend to personal matters, to do things such as shopping, and in similar ways to meet needs that are not the formally specified tasks of her job.

From Roles to Groups Understanding social roles and social relations enables us to grasp the idea that social life is an organized and relatively stable process. Roles and relations are basic units—the building blocks—of a *social group*.

The Social Group

When there is persistent interaction among the same people, and they build and develop social relations into a stable pattern, and when they also identify to some extent with one another, they are a group. A group can be defined as *a plurality of persons sharing a common pattern of interaction.*

Groups vary in size from very small to very large, from informal, loosely organized ones, to large, rationally controlled organizations. Here are the types of groups most commonly identified in sociological analysis:

The primary group is a small group, like a family, marked by intimate face-to-face interaction, reasonably long duration (people can then know each other well), and is the group in which close personal relations are sustained.

The peer group is an important kind of primary group, one which emerges spontaneously from among individuals who are equal in social status to one another. Children in play form a peer group; the high school cliques of adolescents are' peer groups; workers on the job and soldiers in war form peer groups. These small intimate groups (as we shall demonstrate in Chapter 5) provide their members with support and understanding in facing a larger, impersonal world, while yet being a form of control over the behavior of the individual.

The formal group emerges when groups grow in size. Once groups grow beyond a small handful of members, social relations cannot easily be personal and intimate. The larger the group, the more is this so. When this happens, the roles and positions of the group are officially and explicitly designated, duties are formally assigned, and definite rules govern social interaction. The activities of all members are organized so as to lead efficiently to achieving goals. (We shall examine formal groups in detail in Chapter 5.)

The *community* is a quite different kind of group, ranging from the small village to the large city. Community means the organization of social relations within a geographic locality. In small communities of the past there was a strong sense of community—a "we-feeling"; while this is hard to sustain in large communities, there is still often civic pride and strong local identity. (See Chapter 8 for a full discussion of community.)

Society is the largest of social groups, one which includes these others. When a human population inhabits a territory on a relatively permanent basis, and within that territory sustains and carries on a set of activities by which social life is fully organized, there is a society. (Society is the concern of Chapter 6.)

From the smallest group to the largest, the most intimate to the most formal, groups exist when social interaction leads to stable patterns of social relations—a social structure. A group is not the same as a social structure; rather, a group *has* a social structure.

SOCIAL STRUCTURE

In the dictionary definition *structure* means the arrangement or interrelations of the parts that make up a whole. Bricks and boards do not make a building until they are put together in some arranged manner, according to a design. Similarly, the notes of the musical scale must be arranged in some creative order by a composer to make a musical composition.

In these examples the concept of structure is not difficult to grasp, for it materializes before our eyes. We can see the parts arranged into some logically connected system. But *social* structure is an abstract concept, less easy to "see." It expresses the idea that people interact in roles that are related to one another in some systematic way.

The family, for example, includes (as a minimum) the roles of mother, father, daughter, son. But to make these several roles into a family, there must be some consistency in the way they relate to one another. The roles of father and mother, for example, must include all the necessary parental responsibilities and tasks, whether these are divided up by a more traditional conception of the sex roles, or more equally, as often happens now. Who does what, and who has authority for making which decisions—these must be worked out so that what is *expected* of each member of the family does not contradict what is expected of the others. Social structure, then, combines social roles into a consistent system of social interaction.

What some sociologists call social structure, others may call social organization or social system. In each case the concept conveys the same idea: that social roles and relations are organized into relatively stable and persistent patterns.

Complex Structures

Simple structures combine a small number of roles and relations, but in the modern world structures grow ever larger and, consequently, more complex. When that happens, social structures are marked by an increasing *division of labor,* by an increasing *hierarchy,* and by more centralized *authority.*

Division of labor As structures become more complex, there is an increasing specialization of social roles. The tasks which must be accomplished are broken down into a number of smaller, more specialized ones and then assigned to different people, so that each one performs only a limited function; this process is *role-allocation.* The role of the mediator we examined above serves here as an example. In the family the mother may from time to time mediate between father and children. But in a larger structure, the mediating task may be assigned to a person or to a subgroup to do that and nothing else. The structure of any large corporation or government agency is striking evidence of a division of labor which creates a great number of narrow, specialized jobs.

Hierarchy Larger structures are more *hierarchical* than small ones. Social positions within them are ranked from top to bottom; rewards, prerogatives, and privileges are then carefully allocated according to rank. Such ranking has powerful influence on how people interact with one another. It becomes easier to interact within ranks than across ranks, that is, with social equals than with those in inferior and superior positions. In some cases, as in the military, those of high rank (commissioned officers) and those of low rank (enlisted men and women) may not even be allowed to "fraternize" with one another. Separate off-duty officers' clubs keep the more privileged ranks apart from the enlistees. Even where no actual rule forbidding interaction exists, as is true of most civilian organizations, it nonetheless becomes expected and the common practice. This is reenforced, of course, when spatial separation (shop and office, as well as separate dining facilities) keeps people physically apart even when performing their duties.

Authority The effect of hierarchy on interaction is further emphasized by the fact that large structures tend to concentrate authority at the top. People in the top social positions give orders and decide policy; those below take orders and carry out policy.

In effect, then, larger social structures, by further dividing the labor, by increasing hierarchy, and by concentrating authority, greatly restrict, constrain, and inhibit social interaction.

Structure: Stability and Change

Structure provides relative stability in the organization of social life—that much should be evident from what has been said. Structures, however, are only *relatively* stable and integrated, some more so, some less so. There is never a perfect integration of roles.

Some strain and tension, therefore, appear in any social structure. There are always role conflict, contradictions in group objectives, hostile as well as cooperative relations, struggles for power, and disagreement over the rights of various social positions.

The idea of a social structure does not deny the fact of change, nor does it assume a social life without conflict. Peace and harmony never prevail unchallenged, and a social structure is not based only on consensus about how life should be organized. On the contrary, coercion, force, and power are common characteristics of social structures; disagreement and discord are always present, though they may often exist below the surface. On the surface social structures appear to be more stable and harmonious than in fact is the case.

A social structure, therefore, is never static and unchanging; instead, it is always undergoing change and conflict is always present. We will round out our brief review of the concept of social structure by looking at conflict and change as being as typical of social structure as is stability.

SOCIAL CHANGE AND SOCIAL CONFLICT

Change and conflict are closely connected, for there are few changes that are not resisted by some who feel that they lose something of value—prestige and position, wealth and property, opportunity and privilege—by changes. Change is so pervasive in modern society that we are often taught to view it as *progress.* Yet what is progress for some—an improvement in their life situation—may not be progress for others. And what is progress from one perspective—an increase in the material prosperity of a society—may also come at a social cost, such as increased power for a property-controlling class, or a decrease in the capacity of people to control their own lives.

Modern ideology teaches us to accept most change as progress, without asking: progress for whom? at whose expense? But that same ideology teaches us that conflict is *dysfunctional,* that is, it disrupts and damages the social structure. Conflict is deplored as not only harmful but as unnecessary.

But if we are to grasp the importance of conflict and change for the study of society, we must set aside simple-minded notions that change is always for the better and that conflict is always destructive. We must look more closely at how change and conflict alter the very structure of society.

How Change Comes About

Social change can happen quickly and unexpectedly. It can also grow slowly and cumulatively. When that happens it may build up to a critical point where change *then* seems to come quickly. Change can be planned and intended, or it can be the unplanned consequence of other developments. For our purposes, let us view social change as coming about (1) through cataclysmic events; (2) as the unplanned consequences of other developments and processes; (3) as planned changes, though always with unplanned consequences; and (4) through social conflict.

Cataclysmic Events   Such disruptive events as natural disasters (floods, earthquakes, and plagues) as well as humanly created ones, such as wars and depressions, usually bring social change in their wake. A dramatic instance is the bubonic plague which swept Europe in the fourteenth century and quite literally wiped out one-third of the population. During that same period increasingly severe winters ended the growing of cereal grains in Iceland and of grapes in England. Human settlements were abandoned. Famine and depopulation were common. These natural conditions, combined with a crisis in the system of agricultural production and distribution, contributed substantially to

the decline of feudalism as Europe's basic form of human society. Capitalism and a new form of human society emerged.[10]

Wars, too, are significant sources of change. For one thing, any nation that loses a war rarely goes unchanged. At the most, it can cease to exist and become a colony of the victor, or it can be divided up among other nations. Poland was for a long time partitioned among Prussia, Austria, and Russia. When Japan surrendered in World War II, the old imperial-military structure was swept aside, and a new social structure, modeled in significant ways after the United States, was put into its place.

But war often has significant internal effects on a nation, even when it "wins." Militarization puts enormous power in the hands of the military, which it may not fully relinquish, and the controls of the population deemed necessary in war may not fully disappear afterward. War, then, may lessen democracy within a nation.

Depression, too, changes a society. To cope with the unemployment, the bankruptcies, and the suffering, and to prevent social unrest from becoming violent, governments and dominant classes are forced to institute welfare measures which then become permanent. During the Great Depression of the 1930s in the United States, the federal government, among other measures, developed unemployment insurance, social security for retirement, public housing, and measures to save farmers from bankruptcy. At the same time, workers organized into unions in the big industries, like automobile, electrical and steel. A new coalition of classes and racial and ethnic groups came together in the Democratic Party, which then became the dominant political party in the United States. These changes, brought about in response to the Depression, were lasting changes in the North American social structure.

World War II followed the Depression in the United States, and these two cataclysmic events thoroughly changed the basic social relations of the North American people. From the Depression came a welfare society; from the war, a warfare state. National expenditures for domestic welfare and then for war and the preparation for war (symbolically labeled national defense) became the two central concerns of federal government. The basic political-economic structure of the United States now differed radically from what it had been in the 1920s.

Unplanned Changes The necessary response to cataclysmic events produces quite intended changes, such as new welfare measures and the development of defense industries (a military-industrial complex), but the full range of consequences is not foreseen or intended. For example, the unrest created by extended unemployment in the Depression led to a wave of union organization, ending the long dominance of the nonunion "open shop" in most basic industries. Also the growth of liberal programs for social welfare had several unintended effects: the growth of vastly enlarged federal bureaucracy; the development of more refined forms of federal taxation to finance such programs; and ultimately the emergence of a truly dominant national government, far more powerful and far more controlling of resources than state and local governments.

Perhaps one of modern history's most striking examples of unplanned change is the urbanization of modern populations, the growth of great cities in place of village and countryside. Not only was this urbanization unplanned, but most cities grew in an unplanned manner.

A change in basic demographic trends—in birth and death rates, for example—is another case of unplanned change which has enormous impact on society. After World War II a "baby boom" gave the United States a significantly larger youth generation, required a massive expansion of schools and colleges, and made the cultural climate and the market for mass consumption more focused on the young.

Now the birthrate has declined again, school populations are declining, teaching jobs decreasing, and the established social services are giving more attention to other age groups, particularly those over 65 years of age, who are increasing in numbers.

A related kind of unplanned change is the increase in the Spanish-speaking population in the United States. Illegal but persistent immigration of poor people from Mexico has so increased this population that many social scientists believe that, in another decade or so, the Spanish-speaking minority will outnumber the black population. Already this has brought other changes: the controversy over bilingualism in education, the changing pattern of minority politics, and the increase in Spanish votes in the political arena.

These examples are cases of specific and limited unplanned changes which, nonetheless, force changes to be made in social structure. If we take a longer, historical look, however, we recognize that, as such unplanned changes keep occurring over a long time, there is a *cumulative* effect on society, a gradual buildup of changes that, at some critical point, may lead to the emergence of new social structures.

Evolutionary theories of social change view gradual change in society as just such a cumulative process, though always marked by certain crucial turning points. The invention of big-game hunting about 100,-000 years ago, according to sociologist Roberta Ash Garner, was one such turning point, with others to follow; from roughly 6000 B.C., "change becomes rapid and markedly cumulative."[11]

Karl Marx's conception of revolution was also based on an evolutionary development of society, with capitalism as the latest but not the last change in the basic structure of society.[12] He theorized that under capitalism the *forces* of production (technology and the organization of work to use this technology) would continue to develop and change, but at some critical point further development would be hindered by the *social relations* of production (private ownership of the productive forces and the oppressive relations between a property-owning and a wage-earning class). The consciousness of this contradiction would then produce a revolutionary change.

Planned Changes A great deal of social change in the modern world, however, is quite planned and intended, though the full consequences of those changes are not. The introduction of new technology, for example, may be intended to increase production among the same number of workers, or perhaps allow the employer to get by with fewer workers, or perhaps allow him to employ semiskilled machine operators when before he had to hire skilled craftsmen. Such changes may lead to the gradual and unforeseen elimination of the class of skilled workers, and the growth of a semiskilled working class.

The introduction of new technology is one example of change by *innovation* and *diffusion*. Sociologists have been interested in how the planned innovation of new technology, new techniques and practices (for example, a new form of crop rotation), or new scientific inventions (drugs, hybrid corn) are successfully diffused throughout a society.

Successful diffusion requires that there be a small group who will take the risk involved in making a change; these *early adopters* may see economic ad-

The onset of the Great Depression in the 1930s subjected many people's lives to unplanned changes. This World War I veteran set out from California, accompanied by wife and children, with an old car and $2.75, to demonstrate in Washington, D.C., for a bonus.

Others tried any way they knew how to earn a living, including selling apples.

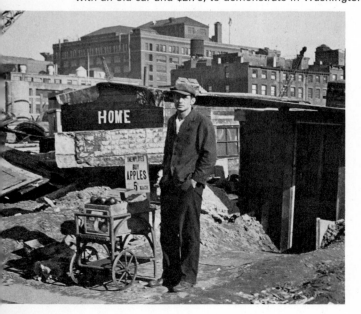

vantage for themselves in such a change and also can afford a loss if it fails.[13] Such innovators are more often the already economically advantaged, as, for example, large landowners, who are also educated and more favorable to science and technology, in contrast to poor peasants cultivating small plots. Innovations are successfully diffused when they support the interests and values of those most ready to adopt such changes, but they will be resisted if they are perceived to require change in established values and ways of living, or if they threaten economic and class interests.

Social Policy   The development of social policy is another significant example of planned change. New social policies in civil rights, for example, have altered the old patterns of discrimination and racial privilege to bring about new social relations between racial groups in the society. "Equal opportunity" and "affirmative action" are changing the sexual composition of many once male-dominated occupations and professions. (As we shall see later, change through social policy usually comes after much conflict and struggle.)

In modern societies, policy-making has now become a major governmental activity, central to the further development of that society. But in most cases, policy-making is a planned and controlled process from which most of those whose lives are affected by the policy changes are excluded.

Most social change is a complex combination of the planned and the unplanned, the cataclysmic and the gradual. While the Great Depression of the 1930s, for example, was a sudden collapse of the economy, some of the social changes introduced, such as social security, were likely to have come anyway, if more slowly. The Depression created a climate of urgency where it became possible to develop policies of planned change. This enabled the federal government to introduce programs to cope with unemployment, hunger, and bankruptcy. If we can say that one of the unplanned consequences of the Depression and of World War II, which soon followed, is the enormous growth of governmental bureaucracies, we need also note that such growth of governmental programs and policy-making was the deliberate political program of American liberals. They intended to develop a federal responsibility for social problems, and so they sought change by planned programs. Whether anticipated or not, increased bureaucracy and greatly enlarged government followed.

Social Conflict

Too often conflict is viewed as disruptive and undesirable, as *destructive* rather than *constructive* (see "The Functions of Social Conflict"). But social conflict is always present in social life; it is a fundamental feature of human society and merely to deplore it is to miss its significance as a force for social change.

Conflict is struggle over values or over scarce resources, in which two contesting groups each seek to impose their values or their claims on resources over those of the other. To do so, each seeks to maintain or to change the social structure in terms of his or her values or interests.

Such a conception of conflict and struggle does not necessarily imply violence, although violence can occur. Most of the time conflict takes nonviolent form.

The Roots of Conflict   Conflict does not occur because people are unreasonable or uncooperative or too selfish, or because they are unwilling to live civilly and decently with others. Nor is it true that conflict would be unnecessary if people better understood one another or communicated more effectively. The idea that conflict is unnecessary is an assertion found frequently in a society in which dominant groups try to pretend that there is no legitimate basis for social conflict.

Conflict is real, not imaginary, because it is rooted in real social differences in society. Differences of class and status, of wealth and opportunity, are the roots of social conflicts of *material interests,* where scarce resources are unequally shared. Increased wages for the worker, for example, may be at the expense of increased profits for the employer. A shift of the tax burden from corporate to personal, or vice versa, is another. A struggle over rent control pits renters' interests against those of property-owners. A struggle over utility rates within a regulatory agency puts into conflict the interests of consumers of energy, who want low rates, against the utility's investors, who want higher dividends, and the utility management, who want to accumulate capital for investment. Or take the now common conflict over protecting clean water and air against polluting industries. Here profits and jobs are often in conflict with a community's interest in its citizens' health.

Class Struggle   In any society where dominant classes own and control the land, factories, or ma-

THE FUNCTIONS OF SOCIAL CONFLICT

In opposition to the common notion that conflict is always and only *destructive,* George Simmel, a gifted and insightful European sociologist, argued that conflict can be positive in its functions for social groups.* Positive outcomes of conflict, he pointed out, can offset negative ones. Some examples of these are:

Clarifies issues. Conflict may "clear the air" by making it evident what protesting groups want and what price others may have to pay to achieve a resolution of long-standing resentments and tensions. It may also make clear that two groups have an unresolvable conflict of interest that can only lead to further problems.

Conflict may clarify and sharpen other matters, too: the extent and limits of authority; the boundaries of groups, including their physical boundaries; the distribution of rights and privileges for various categories of members. The conflict over equal rights for blacks and women, for example, often has this latter function.

Unifies group. Conflict against an external *threat* to a group is unifying in its *internal* effect. Members can put aside other differences and reaffirm their common values and interests. Solidarity and morale increase. On the other hand, such a situation decreases the tolerance of deviation; loyalty to the group is more closely measured.

Induces change. Since conflict needs to be resolved, the outbreak of conflict brings about those changes in relations and in values and attitudes that enable a group to resolve the conflict.

Notes

* See George Simmel, *Conflict and the Web of Group Affiliations,* trans. Kurt H. Wolff (New York: The Free Press, 1955); a brilliant rendering of Simmel's theory of conflict is in Lewis A. Coser, *The Functions of Social Conflict* (New York: The Free Press, 1956).

chinery, social struggle will put one class into conflict with another. Marxians have always emphasized and viewed this as the fundamental struggle in society. But it would be a mistake (one Karl Marx did not make) to see class struggle as always violent and revolutionary in intent. The struggle of workers to organize unions and to get a larger share for themselves is class struggle—but not necessarily one with a conscious intent to change the basic structure of property relations. So, too, the struggle of landless peasants to own some land may require breaking up the huge estates of rich landowners, but those peasants also insist on retaining the system of private ownership of land. Class struggle can also be evident in less dramatic ways, as in the struggle over taxes, over welfare measures, and over economic security.

The Struggle Over Values But not all conflict is class struggle; people also struggle over *values.* The struggle over abortion often brings into conflict people who hold strongly to different moral positions which really cannot be compromised. Material gain and loss can be, for these are relative matters, but values are more likely to be held as absolutes. For example, if abortion is defined as the unjustified taking of a human life—as murder—then there are no grounds for compromise.

Similarly, civil libertarians hold individual liberty to be an "inalienable" right of every person, thus, a basic, uncompromisable principle. The liberties of all persons are to be protected, even if some of them, like fascists, do not believe in those rights, or if others—bigots and authoritarians—believe in those rights only for themselves, but not for others such as lower classes, racial minorities, and political demonstrators.

Moral differences over sexual behavior, over the licensing of gambling and drinking, over legislation about drug use, bring more traditional conceptions of moral conduct into sharp conflict with newer ones, and painful disagreements about what should and should not be permitted or tolerated. Indeed, one further dimension of this now is the debate on just how much individual behavior should be regulated by the state, regardless of what that behavior might be.

There are many cases in which both material and value interests are at stake in the same struggle. This is so in struggles over civil rights, for example, where both the value of equal rights and equal opportunity, and the material interests of minorities in improving their educational and job status, are at stake. The feminist movement struggles not only for the right of women to equal status with men, but for the opportunity for women to gain jobs and income once largely beyond them.

What some groups or classes strive to gain, others resist their getting. Employers refuse to pay higher wages, and workers strike; blacks feel they are denied equal rights and protest by demonstrations.

The most familiar explanation of this is that conflict arises from a struggle over *scarce resources;* since so much of what is valued is only in finite supply, the more some get, the less others can have. The statement is true enough, yet it gives us less than adequate explanation. For one thing, it applies most obviously to the conflict over material interests, less so over conflicts about values. But it does not get to the roots of conflict.

"Life Is Not Fair"   The scarcity of material resources on which people depend is not inherently or necessarily a source of conflict. It depends, rather, on how these resources are distributed, on what share each one gets and how any dividing up is defended as legitimate. Conflict will be avoided *if* at least the minimal needs of all are met and *if* the pattern of distribution is considered to be fair.

But few human societies beyond the most simple readily achieve any genuine consensus on this. In most societies it is too evident that inequality in social power produces an inequality in sharing the rewards of social life. Those who control the society's economic resources take a greater share for themselves.

Wealth and privilege accrue to power; social classes get unequal shares of what society has to offer.

Those who get an unequal share of wealth and power usually also get an unequal share of prestige and respect. The more powerful often show no respect, even contempt, for others, particularly those racially and ethnically different. Their identity as a separate people may be threatened by those who would like to change them into something else. Thus, all racial and ethnic minorities, like all colonial peoples, suffer not only from a smaller share of wealth and power; they may even be denied the right to continue their own way of life, to live by their own values. The various American Indian tribes, for example, long dishonored by white Americans, are struggling now to escape a degrading, impoverished existence. Now acknowledged as Native Americans, they are struggling to retain and revive the Indian way of life and its ancient values. In this way, material interests and values become joined together in defining the terms of a social conflict.

Despite all the efforts to justify unequal shares, it is probably impossible to dispel the idea that "life is unfair," as President Carter asserted in defending his position on abortion. People will feel unfairly denied, or even oppressed and coerced, by the set of institutional arrangements existing in their society. In whatever way open to them, they will struggle to change it, to get a "fairer" share. How they do that can take different forms.

The Forms of Social Conflict

In the struggle to change the structure of society, or to resist such a change, conflict takes various forms. It may be more open and violent, it may be muted because strongly suppressed, it may flow through legitimate forms of political action, or it may move into illegitimate channels. Here are some common forms of conflict.

Social Movements   A strong sense of unjust suffering readily provides the rationale for a social movement. The civil rights movement, the feminist movement, the environmental movement, the antiwar movement were all powerful forces for social change from the 1960s until the present and are thus basic to recent history. In earlier times, it was the labor movement, the

"Life is not fair." An elite and privileged British couple at the races at Ascot pay little notice to the homeless man who scrutinizes them so intently.

movement against slavery (the abolitionists), the suffragettes' movement (the early feminists struggling for the vote for women), the Progressive movement for democratic social reform. From the early nineteenth century, in Europe and the United States, the struggle for socialism has been a continuing movement, far stronger in Europe than in the United States. (In Chapter 19 we will examine social movements in more detail.)

Civil Politics In modern democratic societies there is an effort to bring conflict into the political institution, to get people to work "inside the system" instead of "outside." It is a principle of liberal politics that all classes and groups should have access to the political process and should be encouraged to pursue their goals through conventional political means. This ideology of civil politics seeks to control and restrain conflict by absorbing it into the struggles of political parties and elections, into pressure groups and organized interest groups, and, basically, into a politics of modest goals and compromise. It claims that the political structure of democratic society can respond adequately to the claims and demands of those for whom life has too often been unfair, that all conflicting interests can be accommodated and justly settled. It sees conflict as a basis of gradual reform, but not as a basis for more radical alteration of the social structure.

An ideology of civil politics also encourages the legitimation of specific forms of conflict, while putting other forms outside the bounds of acceptable action. The legalization of trade unions and the requirement for collective bargaining ''in good faith,'' for example, is an attempt to contain labor-management conflict within manageable bounds, to avoid violent strikes, and most of all to offset the possible development of a revolutionary movement of the working class.

Consistent with such an ideology, various kinds of social mechanisms for *conflict resolution* have been developed to deal with different groups and interests in conflict with one another. These include mediation and arbitration, and hearings before panels and commissions authorized to make decisions to settle disputed claims while yet protecting the established legal rights of both parties to the conflict. Even court suits and judicial actions may be a mechanism for resolving conflicts, as when federal judges order school boards to institute busing plans in order to desegregate racially imbalanced school.

Riots and Rebellions   That any conflict even exists may be long denied until suppressed resentments reach a breaking point, and, having no more legitimate outlet, burst forth in riot and rebellion. The spontaneous, unplanned riot is a likely form for a powerfully rebellious statement by an oppressed class, even in quite dictatorial societies. Twice in recent years Polish workers have violently rebelled against the Communist government over food prices, in both cases forcing policy changes, in one instance bringing about a change in the internal power structure of the Communist system. In the 1960s most sociologists viewed race riots as just such unplanned rebellions. Once a riot occurs, the basis of conflict cannot be denied.

Violent expressions of civil disorder have been frequent throughout American history. From the 1740s to the 1790s, debtor farmers undertook a series of often violent rebellions to protest economic exploitation and political exclusion at the hands of merchants, shippers, and planters.

> In state after state, civil disobedience of hated laws was followed by intimidation of, or physical attacks on, tax collectors and other law enforcers, by the closing down of courts to prevent indictments and mortgage foreclosures from being issued, by the rejection of halfway compromises proferred by Eastern legislatures, and finally by military organization to resist the state militia.[14]

From 1870 to 1930 labor violence marked the struggle of working men in the coal fields of Pennsylvania, on the railroads, at steel plants and textile mills, in the mining and timber industries of the West, and finally in automobile and other mass production industries during the 1930s.

The 1960s brought yet another phase in the violence of Southern civil rights marches, Northern urban rebellions, campus protests against the Vietnam war, and eventually a major rebellion against the conduct of a war and the drafting of youth for service in that military conflict.

Revolution   A revolution is the ultimate form of struggle against the prevailing social structure, one in which the intent is to alter the society's institutions and create a whole new social order based on a radically different set of principles. Yet revolutionary movements only sometimes succeed; in an unequal power struggle they often fail. However, the effort of dominant classes to ward off revolutionary efforts may lead them to make reforms which, though far less than revolutionary, are much more than they would otherwise have done.

When social conflict so radicalizes oppressed classes that they adopt revolutionary goals and values, little compromise is possible (or even deemed desirable). What is at stake now are thoroughly opposed conceptions of basic interests, justified in quite irreconcilable ideologies of what a good society would be like.

Structure, Change, and Conflict

A structure of social relations brings relative stability to social life. Social life has an organized pattern to it, people know what to expect of one another in different social situations, and the routines of everyday life have an understandable meaning and significance.

But that same social structure is ever changing and is fraught with conflict, only latent and suppressed in some cases, plainly evident in various forms of conflict in others. The structure of a human society is, in part, a matter of consent and shared values, and in part, a matter of power and coercion. There are always some groups for whom life in their society is an oppressed existence. Societies vary, of course, in how widely shared and genuine is their consensus of values. They also vary in the extent to which coercion and power are built into the social relations of groups and classes, but in no society beyond the most primitive are they absent.

For the student of society, then, the need is to pay attention to the elements of structure, of change, and of conflict which are present in any society, and, in order to do that, to try to understand the degree and form of consensus and shared values, on the one hand, and the element of power and coercion, on the other.

SUMMARY

Social *interaction* is the basic process of social life. Those more persistent and stable social interactions, *social relations*, are the concern of sociology.

Because interaction proceeds through language and other symbols, it is symbolic interaction. Through symbols we define situations so as to define appropriate conduct; this *definition of the situation* says: "if people define a situation as real, it is real in its consequences."

A social *role* defines what people "expect" of one another in social relations. A role is not a script to follow but a consistency of expectations people in a social relation share. There are always some aspects unspecified and uncertain.

Role conflict occurs when there are contradictory expectations for social roles; this happens when social relations change, and may continue unless further change removes the contradictions.

Roles and relations are the building blocks of *social structure*, which is the stable pattern of social relations that gives shape and form to a group or society. Modern social structures grow larger and more complex, marked by an increasing division of labor, an increasing hierarchy, and more centralized authority.

The social order provided by a stable structure of social relations, however, is never static and unchanging, but instead is always marked by social *change* and by social *conflict*. Change comes about both by planned processes and as the unplanned consequences of other actions; it also comes about in the wake of cataclysmic events, both natural and human.

Much social change also comes about through social conflict. The roots of conflict are in different *material interests* and *values*, which in turn have their sources in the inequality of an "unfair" social life.

Social conflict occurs in varied forms, such as *social movements, civil politics, riots and rebellions,* and *revolution.*

NOTES

[1] Leslie A. White, *The Science of Culture* (New York: Farrar, Strauss, 1949; paperback edition, Grove Press, 1958). See particularly Chapter 2, "The Symbol: The Origin and Basis of Human Behavior."

[2] *Ibid.,* p. 27.

[3] *Ibid.,* p. 29.

[4] Ernst Cassirer, *An Essay on Man: An Introduction of a Philosophy of Human Culture* (New Haven, Conn.: Yale University Press, 1945; paperback edition, Doubleday, 1953), p. 43, paperback edition.

[5] George H. Mead, *Mind, Self, and Society* (Chicago: University of Chicago Press, 1934), p. 80.

[6] Ralph Turner, "Role-Taking: Process Versus Conformity," in Arnold M. Rose, ed., *Human Behavior and Social Processes* (Boston: Houghton Mifflin, 1962), pp. 20–40.

[7] See Robert K. Merton, "The Role-Set: Problems in Sociological Theory," *The British Journal of Sociology* 8 (June 1957): pp. 110–111.

[8] See William J. Goode, "A Theory of Role Strain," in his *Explorations in Social Theory* (New York: Oxford University Press, 1973), pp. 97–120.

[9] Donald E. Wray, "Marginal Men of Industry: The Foreman," *American Journal of Sociology* 54 (January 1949): 298–301.

[10] See Roberta Ash Garner, *Social Change* (Chicago: Rand-McNally, 1977), pp. 318–320, and Immanual Wallerstein, *The Modern World-System: Capitalist Agriculture and the World Economy in the 16th Century* (New York: Academic Press, 1974), pp. 34–37.

[11] Garner, *op. cit.,* p. 8.

[12] For a brief introduction to Marx's ideas, see T. B. Bottomore, ed., *Karl Marx: Selected Writings in Sociology and Social Philosophy* (New York: McGraw-Hill, 1964).

[13] Everett Rogers, *Diffusion of Innovations* (New York: The Free Press, 1962).

[14] Jerome Skolnick, *The Politics of Protest* (New York: Simon and Schuster, 1969), p. 11.

SUGGESTED READINGS

Peter Berger and Thomas Luckmann, *The Social Construction of Reality.* Garden City, N.Y.: Doubleday, 1966. An examination of our humanly created reality as both objective and subjective.

Randall Collins, *Conflict Sociology: Toward an Explanatory Science.* New York: Academic Press, 1975. An impressive effort to place social conflict in the center of sociological analysis.

Lewis A. Coser, *The Functions of Social Conflict.* New York: The Free Press, 1956. An insightful use of Simmel's idea that conflict is both functional and dysfunctional for society.

Roberta Ash Garner, *Social Change.* Chicago: Rand McNally, 1977. A stimulating, radical treatment of social change.

Louis Schneider, *Classical Theories of Social Change.* Morristown, N.J.: General Learning Press, 1976. A scholarly review of how social theorists have thought about social change.

Arnold M. Rose, ed. *Human Behavior and Social Processes.* Boston: Houghton Mifflin, 1962. An interesting set of papers by sociology's leading symbolic interactionists.

Culture implies all that which gives the mind possession of its own powers; as languages to the critic, telescope to the astronomer.

Ralph Waldo Emerson

Three

CULTURE

If human beings make tools and shelter in order to survive, they also make *symbols* and these are the stuff of culture. Culture is the term social scientists use to refer to the system of symbols by which meaning and significance can be understood, shared, and expressed among a people.

Culture is an ordered system of symbolic meanings and understandings.

It is hardly more than a century since anthropologists—who are supposed to be the experts on comparing the world's peoples and cultures—were saying that the people of Old Europe and their descendants of the New World possessed *culture,* while most of those they had conquered or exterminated were *savage;* the one people were called *civilized,* the other *barbaric.* Such claims suited those conquerors who would mindlessly destroy lives and annex the homeland and property of their victims.

These distinctions about the earth's people are no longer made by anthropologists. All people, without exception we now know, have a culture.

THE IDEA OF CULTURE

To understand the idea of culture we must start again from the point of departure we used before, namely, that human beings are not genetically programmed for survival but must of necessity create the conditions of their own existence. As workers and makers, human beings assure their biological survival and at the same time construct a social life.

But they do more than this, for they are not merely workers and makers, however skilled and sophisticated they seem to be compared to other animals. They are more than intelligent and creative beavers, always working, always doing something. They are creatures unlike (as far as we can tell) any other on earth in that they need to find a *meaning* in all they do, to confer a *significance* on all their activities. Human beings need to live within a system of meanings; they must find a significance to their life that includes but also goes beyond the survival demand of eating, working, and sexually reproducing.

Biologists and others like to point out that being *social* is not exclusively a human attribute and that most animals display social behavior. They nurse, feed, and protect their offspring; they live together in families, packs, herds, or some other group. They also display forms of dominance and submission. But they do not express this social behavior *culturally* through a system of symbols. This cultural realm is peculiarly human.

Culture includes the language, the philosophy, the religion, the values and ideologies to be found among a people. It also includes its science, its political beliefs, its moral codes, its forms of art and recreation. Culture provides the basic form of the many ceremonies and rituals of social life such as weddings, funerals, and commencements.

But culture also is found in the most mundane details of everyday life. The way we cook food and the way we furnish our homes, for example, are modes of culture. So are the dietary standards we follow, whether these are required by medical knowledge or religious beliefs. Everybody eats, but some people must not eat pork and other people become vegetarians.

The Artifacts of Culture

Some sociologists include within the concept of culture the many material objects produced by human knowledge and skills: tools, buildings, clothing, food, means of transportation, and the like. However, in this discussion we choose to follow the current trend in anthropology and to limit the concept of culture to symbolic meanings. Material objects are the *artifacts* of culture, objects produced by human labor. As material objects their primary cultural meaning is their usefulness.

But they also possess other meanings, too. We use clothing, for example, to keep warm but also to conceal parts of the body that should not, according to our culture, be in public view. Who people are, furthermore, is often symbolized by their dress: the judge's robes, the nurse's white dress, the police officer's uniform. People dress differently for work or school, for the beach or a party, or for a wedding or a funeral; there are ways of dressing that signify the meaning of each of these occasions and are therefore "appropriate" dress.

Culture and Social Structure

Though culture, like society, has its origins in social interaction, it should not be confused with society or with social structure. According to anthropologist Clifford Geertz:

> Culture is the fabric of meaning in terms of which human beings interpret their experience and guide their action; social structure is the form that action takes, the actual existing network of social relations. Culture and social structure are then but different abstractions from the same phenomenon.[1]

Culture: The Social Heritage That culture is peculiarly human should now make clear to us its origins: like the tools and skills by which we assure our survival, and like the social relations from which we construct a society, a culture is humanly made. We do not get it genetically; we develop it from our interaction with one another over time—over many lifetimes—

By the ceremonial dress of these children, modern, Western-dressed Japanese signify that they have not forgotten their social heritage.

and transmit it by *learning* from one generation to the next.

Because culture is learned and transmitted from one generation to the next, social scientists call culture our *social heritage.* The intent is to emphasize that we socially inherit a culture, whereas our physical characteristics are biologically inherited.

Yet to emphasize that culture is a social heritage, while true enough, can be misleading if we allow ourselves to forget that, culture, like social structure, changes over time. New experiences, challenges, and opportunities, as well as new problems and troubles, lead people to discard some aspects of a culture and create new ones. A culture is not only inherited from past generations, it is continuously recreated by succeeding generations.

LANGUAGE AND CULTURE: THE SAPIR-WHORF HYPOTHESIS

The idea that we construct and define reality through language has been a powerful if still controversial idea since the work of Edward Sapir and Benjamin L. Whorf, going back some fifty years. The "Sapir-Whorf hypothesis" states that, as a speaker of a particular language, we interpret the world through the unique grammatical structures and categories of that language. Sapir said that "the worlds in which different societies live are distinct worlds, not merely the same world with different labels attached."*

Whorf studied the Hopi Indian language and compared it to European languages.** Each language, he asserted, embodied a model of its world. "Standard European Average" has, for example, a model of time as past, present, and future—an endless flow—while the Hopi language has no such concepts of time and space, for its structure offers a different model of the universe—a model, according to Whorf, that would make it intuitively easier for the Hopi than for any European to grasp Einstein's theory of relativity.

In the spirit of the Sapir-Whorf hypothesis, anthropologist Dorothy Lee examined the language of the Trobriand Islanders.† She found that *change* and *becoming* are foreign to their thinking, and Trobriand Islanders are concerned only with *being*. Each object, person, or event is examined in terms of itself alone, not in contrast, and is grasped timelessly. There is not a historical past, nor a separate mythical reality for the Trobrianders, but history and myth are forever present, participating in all current being, giving meaning to all current activity. For the Trobriander, life is expressed as a changeless whole, and the Trobriander expects and wants this year to be the same as last year.

The Sapir-Whorf hypothesis has been seriously challenged by the linguist Noam Chomsky, who argues that the deepest structures of syntax (sentence structure) and the basic linguistic design are the same for all languages.‡ The difference between Hopi and European, from this perspective, are differences of "surface structure," that is, of ways of expressing a thought, but not of differences of thought.

The Symbolic Order

Symbols, as we saw in Chapter 2, are all those objects (including words), human-made, for which human beings share a set of meanings. But to confer meaning on objects and events requires that they be given recognizable form; that is, named and categorized. The simple perception that rain follows hard wind and dark clouds would not be mentally possible for us unless we could name and categorize "wind," "clouds," and "rain." That requires words, as well as sentence structure in which a thought can be clearly communicated; in short, a language. Language is a basic part of culture and also is essential to the further development of culture.

Language Though the capacity to speak is found universally in all human beings, a language must still be created. It is the primary means of human communication; without it we cannot be human. With it human beings have moved far beyond the level of animal existence to create a new form of social reality organized around the human capacity for symbolizing.

Through language we can do more than name and categorize objects that are already present in the environment—like wind, rain, and trees. We can also name and identify "invisible" objects such as *friendship* and *marriage*. We could not mentally conceive of such things except through the symbols provided by language, and they could not then exist for us unless we had the words for them. In his classic *Mind, Self, and Society*, George Herbert Mead (1863–1931)

What is at issue here is what our human nature owes to biology and what to culture. The Sapir-Whorf hypothesis is essentially a claim that human beings construct their social existence, including their language, and that different peoples at different times and places have done so in quite different ways. Chomsky's work, in turn, begins from a different assumption, that the capacity for language is genetically programmed and that at birth a child possesses an innate capacity to use language, though it must learn *a* language. How much language, and by implication culture, is genetically coded and how much it is learned and created is then once more in dispute.

The Sapir-Whorf hypothesis was developed at a time when social scientists stressed the diversity and relativity of cultures—no two cultures, it was felt, were alike—and when it was assumed that each newborn infant begins with a blank slate consisting only of *capacities* to learn and develop but lacking any built-in design for cultural structure and content. In arguing that the capacity for language is genetically programmed, Chomsky challenged that basic assumption and suggested, instead, that there is a basic, underlying innate structure, at least of language, which all humans share. If it is true of language, it may be true of other aspects of social life as well.

The long-standing and still unresolved issue of what it is about human beings that is biologically derived and what is culturally learned takes a new turn from this recent work in linguistics. The answer arrived at, if one ever is, will go a long way in shaping our conception of what it means to be human.

Notes

* Edward Sapir, "The Status of Linguistics as a Science," *Language* 5 (1929): 207–214.
** Benjamin L. Whorf, *Language, Thought, and Reality* (Cambridge, MA.: MIT Press, 1956).
† Dorothy Lee, "Being and Value in a Primitive Culture," *Journal of Philosophy* 46 (1949): 401–415.
‡ Noam Chomsky, *Aspects of a Theory of Syntax* (Cambridge, MA.: MIT Press, 1965).

pointed out that things, like the "friendship" noted above, could not exist "except for the context of social relationships wherein symbolization occurs."[2] He goes on to say:

Language does not simply symbolize a situation or object which is already there in advance; it makes possible the existence or the appearance of that situation or object, for it is part of the mechanism whereby that situation or object is created.

What Language Does Without language our human skills and capacities would be impoverished. That becomes plain to us when we realize that (1) we perceive through language and (2) that we think through language (see "Language and Culture: The Sapir-Whorf Hypothesis").

Perceiving. Language provides the spectacles by which we "see" the world. Walter Lippman once said: "First we look, then we name, and only then do we see." In short, language *organizes* our perceiving process; it identifies, selects, and also omits. What we do not have a word for may not be seen. Without the concept of *neurosis,* for example, we would never see neurotic behavior, only somebody's erratic actions, if we even noticed them at all. Words are the tools of our perception.

Thinking. We do more than perceive with the aid of language, we *think* with language. To think is to speak, and there is neither thinking without speaking nor speaking without thinking. Without the grammatical ordering of words into coherent sentences, thought is vague and rudimentary. Plato had Socrates say: "When the mind is thinking, it is talking to itself." Yet, it was only a century ago that this ancient insight became fully understood and accepted. In 1887, when Max Muller, a pioneering student of language, delivered his famous dictum: "No thought without words," it became controversial just because that idea was not obvious, but since then it has become accepted without serious dispute.

(We hope it is understood here that "speaking" is not confined to those of us who can make vocal sounds. The small number of *mutes* who cannot give sound to words can still, in the sense meant here, "speak," that is, put words into coherent sentences; therefore, they can also think.)

Symbols and Reality

All of us know that we live in a "real" world, one which really exists and is not a hallucination. What we less readily recognize is that our "real" world is a symbolic order which human beings constructed in their social relations. What is "real" is not the raw sense impressions and perceptions that bombard our several senses of seeing, hearing, feeling, tasting, and smelling. Instead these raw sense impressions become real for us only as they are named and identified by language. By means of language we sort them out, order them, make sense of them.

The sounds of a summer night, for example, are for most modern persons the sound of a *natural reality,* that of wind and animals. But in an earlier time every sound was acutely recorded as evidence of evil spirits, of ghosts, for the darkness of night was the habitat of evil. For some of us in a city the night may be dangerous because it is the habitat of street criminals. In these cases people are in different "realities."

In these modern days—to provide another example—someone's bizarre and "unreal" behavior will likely be perceived as evidence of mental stress or even illness, of being "really sick." But in an earlier time it would be defined differently—that the person was possessed of the devil, bewitched. In these cases different symbolic systems give us different "realities" from the same raw sense data.

THE ELEMENTS OF CULTURE

The cultural dimension is pervasive and inclusive; there is no aspect of social life that is not also cultural. It is useful, however, to make a distinction between two categories of cultural elements: the *cognitive* and the *normative.*

Cognition: The Known World

Much of what we understand as culture includes the *cognitive,* the world of known facts available as a store of practical knowledge. Even the most technologically simple people know a great deal about nature and about how to manipulate it. Whether they hunt or fish or gather, or some combination of these, they know a lot about plants and animals; and they possess considerable skill in turning this knowledge to practical use.

The evolution of human societies was made possible by the growth of cognitive elements: knowledge of how to domesticate animals, and of how to grow crops, fell trees and turn them into lumber for building, and refine and develop tools. Over long centuries this led to the Industrial Revolution and then to the advanced technology of today.

In modern life the cognitive elements of culture include such common knowledge as, for example, how to drive a car, change a tire, or cook a hamburger, among the vast array of other ordinary skills and practices that are so necessary in everyday life. But they also include a great deal of specialized knowledge, like that which marks almost any occupation, such as the applied knowledge and skills of the plumber, the engineer, the physician, the lawyer, the accountant, the computer analyst, and so on.

There has also grown a more theoretical knowledge, *science,* which can abstract from practical techniques in order to build conceptions, not just of what works and how, but *why* it works. Science seeks to develop a conception of abstract principles that lie behind observations of successful practice and knowledge of natural process and mechanical technique.

The growth of these cognitive elements of culture has had enormous impact on social structure. A new technology, for example, often changes social structure in ways never anticipated or intended, as when the earlier development of large machinery required that it be located in factories, not in homes, and so had a powerful effect on the structure of the family (see Chapter 13).

To focus on these cognitive elements of culture emphasizes how *practical* culture is, that it is a large collection of skills, practices, and techniques. From this perspective culture is an *adaptation* to environment, a cognitive body of knowledge and techniques by which human beings make possible their own physical survival.

Norms and Values

Culture is not the same as social interaction. But no social interaction goes on without being guided, or at least influenced, by culture. Culture brings a moral sense to social interaction, to guide it and limit it, to set rules to follow. This morally directive function of culture is provided by *norms* and *values*.

Norms In any society or group there are rules of conduct which tell us what "should" be done in social situations. There are *norms*. Norms are not all of equal importance in any group; they vary considerably in how seriously they are taken and in what kind of reaction they bring when they are violated. A pioneering sociologist, William Graham Sumner, once made a distinction between *folkways* and *mores* to focus attention on this matter of the relative seriousness of norms to the group.[3]

Folkways. These are norms not viewed as crucial to the group's welfare, though they are customary in a group; that usually means they are traditional, long-established, and accepted as the right way. Such matters as polite manners, ways of greeting people, and correctness of dress are all folkways.

To violate the folkways does not bring serious punishment, but it may get you ridiculed or gossiped about. It may reflect on your upbringing or lead someone to ask: "What's the matter, don't you know any better than that?" To have good standing in a group leads anyone to conform to the folkways; you try to show you "learned your manners" in childhood. Still, those who deliberately persist in violating folkways are not likely to suffer too severely. Sometimes they may even gain by building a reputation for being different, independent, or nonconformist.

Mores. Those norms that people regard as crucial for the welfare of the group are mores. Here violation is a serious matter and some kind of group-enforced punishment will follow. It is one thing not to dress according to the usual demands of a situation, but it is quite another thing to violate group standards about the rights of persons to their lives and property. To sexually molest children or to murder another person violate the mores in this society and probably almost all others.

Among the strongest mores are *taboos,* those forbidden behaviors the violation of which is shocking and offensive. Eating human flesh is a common one, though cannibalism does exist as a practice in some primitive societies. The *incest* taboo, however, is universal; all known human societies prohibit mating or marriage between parent and child and between brother and sister.

Some mores are put into a written code, with specified punishments for violations, and social agencies are created by governments with authority to enforce them and punish violators; then mores become *laws.* Even in *preliterate* societies, however (which have no written language), strongly held mores prevail and violation brings punishment.

There are times and circumstances when what standards are to be included within the mores is in serious dispute, for example, the opposition to abortion from those who believe that killing an unborn fetus is murder and violates the right to life. In opposition to that position are those who just as strongly believe that it is the right of *every* woman to decide for herself to abort or not, and that the state has no authority to forbid the practice of abortion.

Norms Change Like the interactions and social relations they regulate and guide, social norms change as new situations and problems develop for a group. Folkways, by their nature, change more readily than mores. The relaxation of dress standards is an example.

Because mores are the moral standards intensely held and because they define the social action thought to be crucial for the meaning and identity of a group, for its very way of life, they are especially resistant to change. Efforts to make changes can then produce intense conflict within the group, or, more likely, between groups in a society. In the United States the struggles about abortion, as we noted, as well as about the punishment of drug offenders, amnesty for Vietnam draft-evaders, and the acceptance of homosexuality are pertinent examples.

Values Norms are reasonably clear; they state the do's and don'ts of social life. But values are always more general and abstract and their relation to the specific actions of individuals is never direct and obvious. Values are conceptions of what is good, true, and beautiful, of what is desirable to achieve. They provide standards by which choices can be made among pos-

CONTRADICTIONS IN VALUES: A CASE OF LIFE AND DEATH

It is common and expected that people will come to the aid of others in dire need or personal danger, especially so for members of their own family. They may, for example, give blood on more than one occasion, or even give a kidney for transplant. Here moral obligation to family and kin, or even the moral requirement to help others in need, is a powerful value which takes precedence over personal interest.

As long as people readily and voluntarily give of themselves for others, no contradiction between the moral obligation to help others and the rights of the individual is apparent. Yet such a contradiction exists in American culture.

In 1978 a court case in Pennsylvania made it evident that individual rights (even seemingly selfish ones) do not yield to the traditional demand to sacrifice for others. An asbestos worker, suffering from a fatal form of anemia, had asked a court to require that his cousin, who was the only known compatible donor, to give 21 ounces of life-saving bone marrow. Without it, he had only one chance in five of living as long as a year. The cousin refused to do so voluntarily, claiming that there was a risk for him in such a medical undertaking, and that he was not legally obligated to do so.

The judge upheld this person's right to refuse to help, even though, the judge said, "I have condemned someone to death to be carried out by fate." The precedents of American common law, noted the judge, uphold the sanctity of the individual and therefore the law cannot compel anyone to give aid or to take action to save another person's life.

MAJOR VALUES IN AMERICAN SOCIETY

An impressive effort to identify the major values and cultural themes of American life has been carried out by sociologist Robin Williams, Jr.* He worked out fifteen such "value-orientations." They are not all consistent with one another, nor can they all be said to characterize all Americans.

1. *Achievement and Success.* Personal achievement, especially occupational achievement, in a competitive process brings the rewards of success: wealth and prestige.

2. *Activity and Work.* Americans are an active, doing people, always busy, and work—"directed and disciplined activity in a regular occupation"—is the most highly valued form of activity.

3. *Moral Orientation.* Americans tend to see the world always and in every way in moral terms, feeling it necessary to make moral judgments of all situations and all personal conduct as right or wrong, good or bad.

4. *Humanitarian Mores.* Americans have long demonstrated a capacity to respond sympathetically to the plight of unfortunate people, spontaneously to provide aid when disaster strikes, to engage in numerous community projects to help others, and to side with the underdog.

5. *Efficiency and Practicality.* The activism of Americans leads them to value highly efficient and practical action: to emphasize invention, expansion, "getting things done." Engineers are admired, poets are ignored.

6. *Progress.* A faith in progress means an optimism about the future, a looking ahead

not back ("history is bunk," said Henry Ford), a willingness to change, a belief in the perfectibility of the common man.

7. *Material Comfort.* A high level of material comfort proclaims the superiority of the "American standard of living."

8. *Equality.* The persistent theme of equality means equality of opportunity, and equality of formal rights and obligations; it also is exhibited in the ways individuals relate to one another.

9. *Freedom.* To be free is to be unrestrained by powerful groups or authority; to be free is to possess freedom of speech and press. It also means freedom to choose one's church, one's residence, one's occupation.

10. *External Conformity.* Despite personal independence and "rugged individualism," Americans display considerable uniformity in speech, manners, dress, grooming, recreation, and political ideas. There is a standardization of individuality.

11. *Science and Secular Rationality.* Science is rational, functional, disciplined, active; it requires systematic diligence and honesty. It fits an engineering civilization, for it has practical utility and encourages efficiency.

12. *Nationalism-Patriotism.* Americans are nationalistic, elevate loyalty to country and its life-ways—"Americanism"—to a supreme virtue; "un-American" is an epithet for disallowed deviance, thus encouraging conformity.

13. *Democracy.* The belief in democracy is a commitment to majority rule, representative government, but also reserves certain "inalienable rights" for the individual.

14. *Individual Personality.* There is a value placed on the development of individual personality and an aversion to invasion of individual integrity.

15. *Racism and Related Group-superiority Themes.* A pervasive and powerful counter current to many of the above is the assignment of value and privilege to individuals by virtue of race or a particular group membership.

A number of these values are basic to an industrial and capitalist society: achievement and success, activity and work, efficiency and practicality, material comfort, and science and secular rationality. These are the values challenged by the counterculture, and they are now less dominant in the value-orientations of a newer, more affluent, generation.

Note also that the values of humanitarian mores, freedom, democracy, and individual personality conflict with such other values as external conformity, nationalism-patriotism, and race and group-superiority themes.

Notes

---

* Robin M. Williams, Jr., *American Society: A Sociological Interpretation,* 3d ed. (New York: Knopf, 1970), pp. 438–504.

sible alternatives and by which specific courses of action can be judged.

For Americans, *democracy* is a value; at times, therefore, a certain action can be chosen over another because it is more democratic. *Efficiency* is also an American value, and it, too, can be used to select one line of action over another. But it doesn't follow that what is democratic is also efficient; indeed, too often

efficient actions seem that way because they involve fewer people in deciding about them and are therefore less democratic, perhaps not democratic at all.

In the same society, then, values come into opposition in particular situations and may, indeed, be contradictory (see "Contradictions in Values: A Case of Life and Death"). Robin Williams's analysis of dominant American values (See "Major Values in American

Society'') offers several examples of values that often clash with one another in specific situations: Freedom of choice clashes with external conformity; equality of opportunity conflicts with the assignment of value and privilege by virtue of group membership.

Norms, Values, and Interaction   In any society, because of the constant application of norms in daily interaction, people are likely to be more aware of norms than of values. They are more conscious of do's and don't's, the statements of ''you should,'' ''you must,'' ''you can't,'' and the statements that say, ''Thou shalt, thou shalt not.'' Values, in contrast, are more general principles and always need to be interpreted for application to a specific situation.

While norms are clearly instrumental in guiding social interaction, and values are basic in choosing alternate modes of action, it would be an exaggeration to say that norms and values *determine* how people act. They do not, for what happens in social life is much more complex. Culture does not provide, through its norms and values, a blueprint that is then simply followed by people.

The blueprint theory of society does not fit the facts of social existence. Societies as we know them are highly active and dynamic, filled with conflict, deceit, cunning. Behavior in a given situation tends to be closely related to that situation, to be strongly affected by individual interests, to be unpredictable from a knowledge of norms alone. Far from being fully determinative, the norms themselves tend to be a product of the constant interaction involving the interplay of interests, changing conditions, power, dominance, fraud, force, ignorance, and knowledge.[4]

In social interaction people constantly use norms to decide what they (and others) should do. However, in situations in which these norms operate, other things also affect what happens: an individual's self-interest, for example. Helping a friend, we noted before, may be a powerful norm; but if it means losing a job, that may produce a conscious sense of limits on how much that norm can govern behavior. It may lead someone to invoke another norm: it's right to protect one's job since ''I have a family to feed.'' In a society that emphasizes individualism as a value, individual self-interest and individual rights are often used as normative reasons for not calling the police or testifying in court: ''I don't want to get involved,'' or, ''You have to look out for Number One.''

SOME ASPECTS OF CULTURE

Understanding the cognitive and normative aspects of culture is basic to understanding culture. But there are two other aspects of culture that need at least brief attention: the integration of culture and cultural relativism. Then we can turn to the issue about how culture is affected by the complexity of modern society.

The Integration of Culture

If culture is, as we defined it, an ''ordered system,'' then it is surely more than a grab bag of cultural items. When anthropologists have studied preliterate and peasant peoples, they tell us that in these small societies the various elements of culture hang together by an internal logic. For example, religious beliefs, kinship values, and technological knowledge are integrated with little friction or tension.

But modern cultures are expected to be less well integrated. The relatively rapid rate of social change and the complexity and size of the social structure produce many inconsistencies and strains.

This contrast between the well-knit traditional culture and the less-integrated modern one is familiar in modern social science, but this view of more traditional cultures as ''seamless webs'' may very well be exaggerated. At least as distinguished an anthropologist as Clifford Geertz thinks so. He tells us that ''patterns counteractive to the primary ones exist as subdominant but nonetheless important themes in, so far as we can tell, any culture.''[5]

But beyond this sort of natural counterpoint there are also simple, unbridged discontinuities between certain major themes themselves. Not everything is connected to everything else with equal directness; not everything plays immediately into or against everything else . . .

Cultural discontinuity, and the social disorganization which, even in highly stable societies can result from it, is as real as cultural integration.[6]

Cultural Relativism

To offset the intolerance and limited understanding people have shown for other cultures, there is the argument for *cultural relativity*. It asserts that all human cultures are equally legitimate and each has an essential integrity; each culture developed by the human struggle to create a symbolic life in circumstances limited by the natural environment. Different as they are from one another, no one culture was to be preferred. Indeed, our preferences—and, of course, each of us has preferences—merely provide evidence that our values and choices have been shaped by our own culture. From the perspective of cultural relativism, then, human conduct in a society has to be judged only by the cultural standards of that society, not by the standards of another.

We are *ethnocentric* when we judge other peoples and cultures by the norms and values of our own. What we know and accept we believe to be best; what is different and strange we often judge as unworthy and inferior. Indeed, ethnocentric persons judge their own ways as not only right and superior, but often as "natural," with the implication that what is culturally different may be unnatural.

As a way of opposing the narrowness of ethnocentrism, cultural relativism can be liberating. It frees us from the ignorance—and the arrogance—of thinking that the ways of our culture are the best or only worthy ways human beings can devise for living. It teaches us about the varied ways to be human that have been created and elaborated, valued and defended, throughout eons of human evolution.

Yet cultural relativism has its problems, too. Does it mean that we can make no moral judgments outside of our own society? Does it prevent us from passing judgment on slavery, race genocide, military dictatorship, and the torture of political prisoners? Are we to judge concentration camps and gas chambers, on the one hand, and fair trials and right to political dissent, on the other, as simply different but in no way inferior to the other? Only the morally indifferent could live by such a position. Cultural relativism was never meant to uphold any such indifference to the cruelties and oppressions to be found in so many societies.

On a worldwide basis there is now a clearly growing acceptance of an egalitarian value: That all persons are equally human, and that science has effectively denied those once common judgments of a natural inferiority that would warrant some people's being treated as less than human. If the treatment of the Jews during the Holocaust is the outstanding example of behavior impossible to justify by cultural relativism, so also is the torture and execution of political prisoners (indeed, the very idea of their being *political* prisoners), the harsh racial practices of countries such as South Africa, the genocide of a people, like the Cambodians, by starvation and political mistreatment and manipulation, and the inferior position to which women are still bound in many societies, including the Islamic.

What culture relativism does do, however, is force us to recognize that each society provides a different way to be human and each has values of its own. We are narrow indeed if we fail to see any value in cultures other than our own. But any effort at an unprejudiced exploration of human culture will also reveal to us the many ways in which human societies, *including our own,* deny respect and personal development to some in that society.

SUBCULTURE AND LIFE-STYLE

In peasant communities, in African and American Indian tribes, indeed, in all small traditional societies, there seems to be but one homogeneous culture. But in large, complex societies there is much more variation in how the culture is learned, used, and expressed among various subgroups of the society. Social complexity, then, is accompanied by cultural complexity. It is then that we find it useful to speak of *subcultures*.

The Subculture

There is so much variation in modern societies that probably no class or group carries out and exemplifies the culture of that society completely or most typically. All groups and classes vary somewhat in the manner in which one can see the culture operate in their daily lives and activities. It would be unproductive to speak of each of these as a subculture. It *is* useful to think of a subculture when we are looking at groups that vary substantially from the main patterns of the culture. These groups vary because of their distinctive history and origins, which they steadfastly maintain, or because they are people involved in quite deviant life-styles. A *subculture is the distinctive norms, values, and life-styles of a group which still shares in the total culture of the society.*

Ethnic subcultures   These originate in the persistence of the immigrant group to maintain its group identity and at least some of its old-country ways over generations, while yet adjusting to and adopting some of the cultural attributes of the larger society.[7] Ethnic subcultures have been prominent in the development of the United States, and some still remain. Over time, however, ethnic subcultures often lose much of their group identity and cultural distinctiveness as succeeding generations become increasingly "Americanized."

Yet the assimilation of ethnics into the society has not been a process so thorough as to absorb all the immigrant's cultures into a single culture; the famed *melting pot* has not yet melted away all ethnic distinctiveness in American life.[8] Millions of people in the United States still find in their ethnic origins a source of valued identity, even after more than one generation.

The case of the French in Canada poses an interesting issue. While they may be thought of as a subculture from the perspective that says Canada is primarily an English-originated culture, it is also the case that the French occupy a distinct region of Canada, the province of Quebec, and in that region they are the overwhelming majority. There, many *Québecois* do not see themselves as a subculture, but instead as a nation within a nation, denied their own nationhood.

In the United States the Civil War was fought to prevent Southerners from undertaking a similar separation from the rest of the United States and setting up a nation of their own. Though the outcome of the war ended that historic effort, it did not end the Southern sense of being a people apart. Indeed, the very defeat suffered in the "War Between the States" kindled long and persistent memories, symbolizing in that war a meaning for the South it was never to have in the North and the West.

Are southerners, then, a subculture? Certainly, a strong case can be made for a southern regional subculture, much like an ethnic one, based on the distinctiveness of its history and a strong sense of being a different people.[9] History, tradition, and a collective identity would support such an interpretation.

Yet even as we note the possibility, the southern way of life may be receding before the powerful thrust of the dominant culture. No longer do southerners move north for economic opportunity; instead, northern people follow the flight of manufacturers who move south with their plants, looking for cheaper labor and less taxes to pay. Furthermore, the "moderniza-tion" of the South by the movement of new plants there has also brought a new middle class of corporate executives down from the North. The southerners no longer monopolize their own territory. The invasion of northern capital on a new scale may finally end a historic way of life, incorporating it into the dominant American pattern. There will be a loss in the cultural variety of American society.

Isolated Groups

Social and physical isolation can also maintain a subculture. The Amish and the Hutterites provide obvious examples in the United States.[10] Here, strong religious differences from the main traditions of Christianity form the basis for a rejection of the more modern culture. Such self-imposed isolation protects such groups from the "corrupting" influence of modern society.

Physical and social circumstances may create a relative isolation that may not necessarily be self-imposed. Such is the case for the rural isolation of the mountain people of Appalachia, the Appalachian whites whose poverty and lack of education have often made them seem like a disadvantaged minority.

Isolation can be largely social rather than physical (though it can be both, of course); such has been the fate of black Americans from the time of slavery through a segregated existence until today. The black people in the United States are undeniably American in their culture, for African heritages are very largely lost. (One of the reasons Alex Haley's *Roots* has been such a stunning success is that it traced the roots of one black family to long-lost African origins.) Yet blacks were long denied equal status in American society and were segregated into communities of their own. The historic result was to produce what is perhaps the most powerful and influential subculture within the United States, one which expresses the experiences of a people long socially isolated because of race, economically exploited for their labor; a people made in America yet never equally accepted.

Such a culture has produced a unique life-style. It has its own internal variations as in the contrast between the rural south and the urban north, and it has given to the main culture a great deal in language and popular culture. Jazz, for example, and the blues are notable cases of musical creativity in the black subcul-

Ethnic celebrations are evidence of the many flourishing subcultures in the United States.

These Hutterite women and children are members of a subculture sustained by a self-imposed isolation.

ture, from which white popular culture has borrowed much.[11] The overwhelming presence of black performers in popular music is testimony to how much that music has its origin in black culture.

COUNTERCULTURE AND ALTERNATE LIFE-STYLE

What distinguishes a *counterculture* from other subculture is this: it *counters,* that is, opposes or goes against the dominant culture. The idea of a counterculture is not new, for there have been others before this time. But the specific label, "counterculture," came into use only in the 1960s.

The Origins of Counterculture

Apparently the first modern counterculture appeared in France in about the 1830s, offering a *bohemian* life-style to oppose the conventional bourgeois one.[12] It was created by young artists and intellectuals and was intended to develop a counter-personality to capitalism's ideal person, the bourgeois, whose life exhibited sobriety, discipline, respectability, conformity, logical reasoning, and a practical and acquisitive conduct which gave priority in life to work and money-making.

In the early twentieth century Greenwich Village in New York City provided both a place for and a symbol of bohemian life transplanted to the United States. Here artists and writers could live on the margins of respectable society, "liberated" from the conventional patterns of middle-class life. Though the bohemian life-style declined in the 1930s and 1940s, a victim of the Depression and World War II, it reappeared again in the 1950s in the person of the *beats,* only to be replaced by the *hippies* in the 1960s.

The bohemian counterculture was confined to a relatively small circle of largely artistic persons and rarely touched the lives of the masses of people, even within the middle class. But in the 1960s, for the first time in history, the bohemian spirit spread among masses of young people in Europe and the United States. Only a small minority of American youth, however, were fully caught up in its life-style, though an increasingly larger circle of other youth were influenced by it. The most conservative and conventional youth were not involved in it; many liberal youth were not because they were anxious to be active in the mainstream of American politics. Black youth, whose cause led them in a different direction, also were not involved. But perhaps most fundamental was a class difference. Countercultural youth were more likely to be middle class than working class, more likely to be college youth than working youth.[13]

The counterculture of the 1960s originated from some basic, material developments in American society, developments that created a need for new values and cultural change. Perhaps the first of these was the emergence in massive numbers of a new generation of youth—the product of the postwar "baby boom"—segregated from adult life by extensive participation in higher education, and raised in a historically new environment. Richard Flacks sums up that youth-shaping environment:

By the middle of the twentieth century, the American society was qualitatively different from the society that had given birth to the cultural framework of capitalism. The family firm has been supplanted by the giant corporation, the free market by the "welfare-warfare" state, and the entrepreneur by the manager and the bureaucrat. Technology had created a superabundant economy in which the traditional virtues of thrift, self-denial, and living by the sweat of one's brow seemed not only absurd, but actually dangerous to prosperity. Technology seemed to promise not only an abundance of goods, but a world in which hard physical labor could be eliminated.[14]

Yet new cultural values were slow to come forth. People still preached the old ethic of work and self-denial, but leisure was becoming a more significant activity; life-style rather than occupation was becoming the way to express to others one's sense of self-worth. And consumption was so basic to mass production that people had to be encouraged not to be thrifty and self-denying.

Culture versus Counterculture

American culture is a vast, complex, and often inconsistent pattern of values and themes, and the counterculture opposed only some of those values and themes. If, therefore, we try to look below surface manifestations to find what was most basic to it, we are likely to discover viewpoints embracing different emphases and interpretations.

Theodore Roszak, in what is probably the most influential interpretation, emphasized the counterculture as a basic opposition to the *technological* domination of modern life.[15] He saw it as in opposition to the engineer's values of *efficiency* and *practicality.* More basically, he understood it to be a fundamental challenge to *science* and the kind of *rational* mentality science demanded. Such a counterculture also rejected the values central to the life-style that a technological society nourished: striving and success, devotion to work, and material comfort. A culture that gave priority to these values necessarily suppressed others: playfulness, human community, a sense of sacredness, love and beauty.

Philip Slater, in turn, saw in the counterculture the first expression of a new culture.[16] The old culture, he argues, is based on the core belief of *scarcity:* that human gratification is in short supply. Based on this, the old culture chooses, among others, property rights over personal rights, technological requirements over human needs, competition over cooperation, producers over consumers.

The counterculture, however, sees only plentifulness in modern society:

The new culture is based on the assumption that important human needs are easily satisfied and that the resources for doing so are plentiful. Competition is unnecessary, and the only danger to humans is human aggression.[17]

A culture that assumes scarcity also assumes the necessity of inequality, the postponement of gratification, and the self-discipline to avoid overstimulation.

This, asserts Slater, leads to self-restraint, and coldness in personal conduct, and a cultural emphasis upon quietness and muted colors: "Clothes must be drab and inconspicuous, colors of low intensity, smells non-existent. Sounds must be quiet, words should lack emotion."[18]

The counterculture can be understood as an effort to develop a life-style in opposition to this: "Psyche-delic colors, amplified sound, erotic books and films, bright and textured clothing, spicy foods, 'intense' (i.e., Anglo-Saxon) words, angry and irreverent satire —all run counter to the old patterns of understimula-tion."[19]

Both these interpretations of the counterculture, by Roszak and by Slater, whatever their differences of emphasis, saw the roots of the counterculture in its op-position to those values that have long been dominant and controlling in American life. The counterculture, then, was an effort to find a radically new way to be human.

In looking for that way, the youth who created the counterculture did not invent it out of nothing or out of some foreign cultural material. Like the rest of us they were "products" of American society. The countercul-ture, Slater argues, picked up themes secondary in the dominant culture and gave them priority.[20]

When countercultural youth spoke about being *authentic* (unhypocritical), and argued for community, for the right to "do your own thing," and for human equality, they were not bringing forth new values. They were, instead, trying to give primacy to values that had been overshadowed by other, sometimes op-posed values. In that sense they were reaffirming values which all Americans recognize and accept, but values which did not have strong support in existing institutions.

Contradictions in the Counterculture

Like the culture it opposed, the counterculture also displayed inconsistency and even apparent contradic-tion. In its brief flowering it continued to change and to be expressed in a different manner. But the changes that occurred never did resolve three basic dilemmas that beset the counterculture from the beginning: about technology, about politics, and about individu-alism versus community.

Antitechnology—Maybe?   From the outset the counterculture, as Roszak has properly emphasized, made a strong critical case against the technological domination of our lives in twentieth-century America. Such an attack helped to create a consciousness about technology that still exists; a concern as to whether we need to be so attached to technology in all its manifes-tations, all its products and gadgets. But it was easier to make the case in principle than it was in actual prac-tice:

> Any large-scale assault on technology would produce a host of defenders even from within the attacking armies— each rushing to place some prized possession on the en-dangered appliance list. Most nature lovers, who dream of living in the wilderness after all the nasty bulldozers and jets and factories have been magically whisked away, fail to notice that their fantasy includes a stereo or a blender or a Ferrari. Americans are hopelessly enmeshed in equip-ment and won't escape it in the lifetime of anyone now liv-ing.[21]

In a mechanical age it is difficult to live without de-pending upon mechanical things. The early counter-cultural life-styles, while rejecting some mechanical ad-ditions to their lives, took up others and built them into their very existence. For one thing, they became highly dependent on the supply of electricity and on electronic circuits. Without them there could not be electric guitars, hi-fi's, and the amplifiers so basic to a musical style. They also developed a drug culture as one aspect of consciousness-raising, and for this they were fully dependent on a chemical technology that made so many drugs available in powder and pill form.

Politics and Antipolitics   Throughout the 1960s and early 1970s many young people saw themselves as both politically radical and countercultural. The poli-tics of radical change, however, requires a disciplined commitment to future goals, and thus a postponement of gratification; it also requires a concern with power— how to get it and use it. It demands hard work, organi-zation, and a task-oriented life-style.

For many in the counterculture, politics required too much discipline, too much commitment to dull work and to often routine tasks. They could not be po-litical and at the same time undertake, as Slater noted, "the cultivation of inner experience, psychic balance, or enlightenment. Heightening sensory experience, committing oneself to the here-and-now, and attuning oneself to the physical environment are also sought,"[22]—these, too, undercut any effort, even any interest, in politics.

There was, then, a basic dilemma never solved. On the one hand, the counterculture was an effort to make a radical break with the values and life-style of the main culture, to devise another way to be human. On the other hand, those who went into politics found it impossible to be truly countercultural. Even a radical politics shares values with the old politics—about getting power and building organization—and is thus "corrupted."

Individual and Community   Perhaps even more fundamental, however, was the dilemma, even the sheer confusion, posed by the never resolved conflict between an unrepressed individualism and a new community. On the one hand was much talk about cooperation instead of competition, and about building new communities—communes—based on cooperation and equal sharing.

Yet, on the other hand, the struggle to get out from under conformity to old cultural ways produced a heightened emphasis on individualism. Few seemed to realize that individualism was no new value but, indeed, perhaps the old value most basic to industrial society. In its most extreme form, it became "do your own thing," a slogan which clearly put self (and self-interest) before anything (or anyone) else.

The contradiction between these two was often apparent in the effort to construct communes that would provide an institutional base for a new cultural life. Too often they soon failed. "New culture enterprises often collapse because of a dogmatic unwillingness to subordinate the whim of the individual to the needs of the group."[23]

What Happened to the Counterculture?

What flowered and spread so quickly in the 1960s seemed soon to lose appeal and die away in the 1970s. The counterculture, apparently, is now but an interesting footnote to the cultural history of the United States. That raises two questions: What happened to it? Did it produce any lasting effects?

The inability of the youthful adherents of the counterculture to solve the problem of politics and their failure to build enduring communes are two basic reasons. If the counterculture were to succeed, it had to effect changes in society and it had to build its own organizational base. It could not do either.

But there were other reasons, too:

1. By their seemingly bizarre conduct, countercultural youth often failed to communicate to others what their new pursuits were about. Some of them, for example, carried new forms of life-style to such an excess that adults, and even many young people, reacted against it. The use of drugs, for example, which were supposed to expand consciousness and release the imagination from the symbolic confines of an old culture, often simply destroyed minds. While conventional people may have carried personal hygiene to a ridiculous point with their mass consumption of perfumes and lotions, deodorants and mouth washes, hair rinses and shampoos, many countercultural youth reacted against that to a point where they denied the simple, health-sustaining value of cleanliness. This produced the stereotype of the smelly, unwashed hippie and so deflected an understanding of the counterculture from what was basic to what others mistakenly saw as typical.

2. Much of what originated in the counterculture was appropriated by the entrepreneurs of popular culture and commercially exploited, often for fat profits. Rock concerts made promoters and performers rich; in time they provided engagements before large audiences in concert halls and arenas, even stadiums. But what was critical in the music was often muted and made harmless, to be more acceptable to commercial radio and to be attractive to larger audiences of young people who were not fully countercultural.

Drugs, too, which countercultural youth had introduced to the middle class, were expropriated for an enormously profitable drug traffic, not international in its scope. New criminal entrepreneurs created and expanded a clientele among various segments of American society: college youth; young American soldiers at bases in Korea and Germany; disadvantaged ghetto youth; urban street people from everywhere; and even avant-garde upper-middle-class "swingers," always seeking new thrills for their fashionable life-styles.

3. Perhaps most crucial of all, a greater tolerance for many of the innovations and creations of the counterculture developed, and they were absorbed into

Communes such as this agricultural one in New Mexico flourished in the 1960s.

In the 1970s, a return to more traditional values had occurred. This couple appears to have blended both youthful and middle-class values.

popular culture. This was true for new styles for men's hair; it was also true for new musical forms. The dominant culture absorbed the countercultural emphasis on more color in clothes as well as on informality of dress style.

What had once been countercultural, then, became part of a larger and even more varied American culture. The counterculture ceased to be radically different from the rest of the culture, and the line between the hippies and their counterculture and the rest of American youth (and adults, too) became less clear.

Yet this very success of the counterculture in getting its innovations accepted was also its failure. What was accepted was always first made acceptable by being diluted and modified into less extreme form. The critical and countering intent of the counterculture was removed. In being absorbed even partially, the counterculture was tamed and made harmless to the culture it once opposed and to which it was supposed to be an alternative.

Lasting Effects?   Did the counterculture contribute anything of lasting benefit (or harm) to the dominant American culture? Did it affect how Americans act and think?

Perhaps its most basic effect was to encourage many people to liberate themselves from conformity to one dominant cultural style of what was fashionable in everyday life; it reemphasized the idea of choice in defining one's own life. People dared to dress more informally, to cultivate new forms of leisure activity, to enter into new modes of sexual relations, and to develop new conceptions of their roles and relations with others.

"Do your own thing" became a rallying cry and a new standard for all kinds of people who once felt oppressed by a lack of life-choices. Though not by intention, the counterculture contributed to a widening of cultural choice and so made possible a greater plurality of life-styles for Americans.

Yet that, as Philip Slater made so clear, could hardly be called its intention. Indeed, what the counterculture here did was to give renewed spirit and meaning to the most basic value of the old culture, that of individualism. In doing that it only further weakened the possibility of creating community, the cooperative sharing and mutual concern for one another which, if properly developed, reduces the exaggerated emphasis upon the individual and the individual's "rights."

Nonetheless, the counterculture now comes into more adequate sociological perspective for us. It was a brief, confused, sometimes exotic attempt to develop new cultural values and life-styles that were not only new but which challenged and opposed the old ones.

POPULAR CULTURE AND MASS CULTURE

While ethnic subcultures are all around us, and while a counterculture from time to time emerges and recedes and emerges again in new forms, the place of culture in modern society cannot be fully understood unless we give attention to the form in which it now dominates everyday life, that of popular and mass culture.

High, Folk, and Popular Culture

Our daily lives are so surrounded and invaded by popular culture—by music from radio and hi-fi; by comedy and crime drama and "soap operas" from TV; by comic books and comic pages and sports pages—that we cannot conceive of life free from it, and probably do not want to. (Nor do the producers of popular culture want us to, either.)

Yet only in industrial society, which comes relatively late in human history, has there been such a form of culture. Prior to that there was *high* culture and *folk* culture. The distinction between the two comes from the distinction between a small, literate elite, an upper class, which encouraged and sustained a serious art, and a nonliterate mass of ordinary people who created their own culture out of the concerns and values of their daily lives: their songs; their stories told by one generation to the next; and their forms of play in a life which allowed but little time for recreation.

High culture is the classics of literature and the great traditions of art and sculpture. It was produced (in almost all cases) by single artists working within established art forms and within the framework of their culture. It was serious; what it had to say about life could challenge and even disturb the listener-looker-hearer. It could entertain but it was not simply an entertainment. It could be difficult and demand the full commitment of a person's mind and senses.

Folk culture, too, gave expression to the serious and significant in life. A folk people sang and rhymed and talked: about birth and death, man and woman, child and adult, the seasons and the earth; of justice and cruelty, and of fate and destiny. They also danced and played games on those ceremonial occasions when they could spare themselves from daily labor: at weddings and wakes, at the celebration of harvest, on religious holidays.

Folk culture was shared in by everyone and commonly participated in, for a folk people entertained themselves; they were their own composers and musicians, dancers and story-tellers. Within the traditional folk village, the communal relationships shared by all were the source of all cultural expression and individual development.

But neither high nor folk culture as it once existed exists now. Folk culture, in fact, probably does not exist at all anywhere in the Western world, and little of it anywhere else. What happened? The industrialization of the world brought people together in new roles in new social localities—it uprooted and destroyed their ancient ways of living—and in the process destroyed old cultural forms, particularly the folk culture.

The social changes brought about by industrialization have been going on for better than a century now, but it has only been since World War II that we can observe the full effect of industrial capitalism on human culture. For one thing, mass production has provided a mass of consumer goods for all but the poorest, and it has reduced (though not yet eliminated) the burden of necessary labor, therefore giving people more time for leisure. The movement of people from country to city, and from city to suburb, is evidence of one kind of uprooting mobility, as is the movement of whole generations into education and occupations unavailable to the generations before them. The mass media necessarily plays a large part in this process as folk culture recedes, and the media promote and distribute a mass culture.

The result is clear and plain to see—a historical transformation in human culture unlike anything before:

As society becomes fully industrialized, popular culture becomes the most universally shared type of culture and

colors most aspects of individual and social life. High and folk culture retain only marginal influence on private and social life.[24]

Technology and Popular Culture

The growth and spread of popular culture is bound up with the development of a technology for communication, beginning, historically, with the printing press. In the nineteenth century the struggles of the working classes established the right of their children to an education. The spread of literacy among the masses of ordinary people then combined with the development of printing presses capable of producing inexpensive papers and books to hasten the growth of popular culture.

That same inexpensive printing, however, also made possible the growth of real education and knowledge among workers. A more politically educated working class participated in politics, developed unionism, and many of them learned and took seriously the ideas of socialism. The potential of popular culture as a source for expressing working-class dissent and even for developing revolutionary aspirations still seemed very much a possibility in the nineteenth century.

Most of the other technological developments so crucial to the growth of popular culture came about in the last decades of the nineteenth and early years of the twentieth century: the invention of the motion picture and the phonograph record, and later the radio. Television burst with stunning impact on the social landscape only after World War II. Familiar to us as it is, and dominating our lives as it does, it has only been around for about thirty years.

In whatever form technology provided, the mass media became big business which mass produced for mass tastes. While the industry did not, at the outset, create those tastes, they have sought to shape them, to direct them, and to exploit them. What most distinguishes mass culture from popular culture then, is that mass culture is manufactured and mass produced. It is tailored to the tastes of mass audiences, but those mass audiences are also carefully cultivated and developed. Huge investments and vast potential profits mean that great care is taken to shape and cultivate the mass of consumers whose daily purchases make mass culture a basic aspect of consumption in a capitalist society.

Popular Culture and Mass Culture

The scholarly critics who debate the qualities of this culture speak sometimes of popular culture, sometimes of mass culture. Both terms are used, and often interchangeably. Does it make any difference?

It does, because the two terms convey different emphases and interests among those trying to make sense of this cultural material. "Popular" comes from the Latin word for "people" and means common to the people, accepted by the people, or liked by the people. A popular culture, then, is a culture commonly shared by the people; it is not a culture of the elite.

But the meaning of "popular" also implies that popular culture comes *from* the people, from the common experiences of their lives. A recent book, *The History of Popular Culture,* depicting the daily lives of people from the days of Greece and Rome to the present, treats popular culture in just that way: the culture of and by people in their everyday life.[25]

Most popular culture today, even if it is a culture *of* the people, is not *from* the people. Instead, it is manufactured and marketed by a culture industry. When this emphasis is made, the term *mass culture* seems more appropriate. A mass culture is one that cuts across and includes a range of social classes and groups. The television soap operas, for example, attract an audience of twenty million that ranges from welfare mothers to middle-class housewives to college students.

Consumer Culture

When we think of mass culture, we usually think of movies and television, rock concerts and disc jockeys, baseball and football games, and all the other entertainments which we are asked to look, watch, and listen to. But no adequate conception of mass culture can be restricted to the mass entertainments. Mass culture also includes fashions and fads in clothes and home furnishings; the backyard patios and station wagons of suburban ranch homes; the latest in jewelry and bodily adornment for both male and female; and so much else.

Americans are always anxious to save work and time, and industry continually offers a never-ending stream of new commodities proclaimed to save time and labor: electric can openers and electric shavers; prepared foods and premixed drinks (no one makes anything from "scratch" anymore); zippers and wash-and-wear garments; power mowers for suburban lawns and power tools for suburban householders—the list goes on and on. This, too, is mass culture; it is where mass production and mass consumption meet in the shaping and defining of new modes of living in American society.

Just as much as these commodities, mass culture includes the mass-consumed products bought everyday in drugstores, discount stores, and supermarkets: the cigarettes and pain-killers, mouthwashes and deodorants; all those little things we believe to be so essential to our daily existence. In this daily consumption, furthermore, our tastes and habits are interwoven indelibly with products whose brand names have become a part of mass culture: McDonald's hamburgers ("we do it all for you"); Kentucky fried chicken; Coca-

The elaborate, suburban shopping mall is the most recent manifestation of the consumer culture.

Cola ("the real thing"); Pepsi-Cola ("the Pepsi generation"); and this gem: "Chevrolet—like baseball, hotdogs, and apple pie."

Mass culture, then, is also a *consumer culture.* American industry recognized some time ago that the genius of mass production could not be translated into profits unless there was also mass consumption. As workers—white-collar and blue-collar—the American people first became a modern labor force for mass production. But it was also necessary that they become mass consumers of that which their labor produced.

Advertising and Consumption   It was through advertising that the connection between mass production and mass consumption was made. Businessmen advertising their wares is hardly new, but modern advertising as we know it is a creation only of the last fifty years. It developed in response to a social crisis in modern capitalism: the evident inability to convince workers that the jobs offered by modern capitalism were worthy of their respect and loyalty. "The factory had not been an effective arena for forging a predictable and reliable work force."[26]

A number of different defenses and changes were thought up, but of these, the development of a sophisticated advertising industry which would incorporate the workers into the consumption patterns of modern society was the most significant. It promised to control the workers, since nothing else had, and also to meet the need for mass consumption. The business community understood the larger meaning of the social change being devised.

Beyond standing at the helm of the industrial machines, businessmen understood the social nature of their hegemony. They looked to move beyond their nineteenth-century characterization as captains of industry toward a position in which they could control the entire social realm. They aspired to become captains of consciousness.[27]

American capitalism would offer workers shorter hours and more pay—that idea was fundamental to the new ideology of consumption as it was spelled out by Edward Filene, a pioneer of the consumer movement and himself a Boston department store merchant. (While all this was worked out in the 1920s, it did not in fact become the practice then; wages stayed low and the forty-hour week did not become law until

the late 1930s. It was only after World War II that American workers, both white-collar and blue-collar, earned enough money and had enough time to share in the fruits of the consumer society.)

Captains of Consciousness   The advertising system that developed was not content merely to hawk the wares of industry. It sought, instead, to use advertising as an instrument of social change. First, it had to break the conservative, austere model of the sensible person in a society of scarcity—being thrifty, doing without—else mass consumption was not possible. People had to understand it was necessary to be in debt; the new consumer economy could not function with thrifty people who always paid cash.

Beyond that, advertising set out to change values, and no dimension of social life was beyond its effort. It set itself up as teacher and modernizer; it undertook to change family life and child-rearing, to reduce paternal authority, to uphold the ideal of being young, and to change thoroughly the modern woman as wife, mother, and homemaker. Stuart Ewen offers this revealing quotation from Edward Filene, made in 1931:

. . . since the head of the family is no longer in control of the economic process through which the family must get its living, he must be relieved of many ancient responsibilities and therefore of many of his prerogatives . . . Women . . . and children are likely to discover that their economic well-being comes not from the organization of the family but from the organization of industry, and they may look more and more for individual guidance, not to their fathers, but to the *truths* which science is discovering.[28]

The family was not sacred to business. While others (sociologists included) lamented the loss of family unity, advertising subtly attacked its authority and cultivated in its place the consuming *individual* who seeks to meet her or his needs in the marketplace of consumption.

All of this reached maturity in the 1950s, when television gave to advertising its most potent medium, one which no home could dare to be without. It effectively combined mass entertainment with mass consumption. Through it, modern industry moved from its location in production to the heart of consumption, penetrating into the family and the individual personality, intent on creating a new national personality suited to the needs of American capitalism.

Popular versus Mass Culture

Behind the disputed choice of words—*popular* or *mass*—lies a more basic conflict over the meaning of such a culture. Those who argue that it is debasing and destructive take popular/mass culture to be a massive threat to the idea of a truly free society and genuinely autonomous human beings. Those who defend it deny it is any such threat, and some even see positive virtues in it. This is a much more difficult matter to decide than that of high and low taste, but no sociological understanding of the place of culture in social life can ignore the issues involved.[29]

How anyone decides on these issues is much more a matter of one's values than of objective evidence. We cannot offer here a resolution of the issue, only a short summary of what is a difficult problem. The arguments about mass culture boil down to three basic charges and denials.

The Commercialization of Culture   Mass culture is manufactured culture, and like any manufactured commodity made for sale on a mass market, it is mass produced in some standardized form—that is one basic charge against mass culture. In the words of one critic, Dwight MacDonald:

Mass culture is imposed from above. It is fabricated by technicians hired by businessmen; its audiences are passive consumers, their participation limited to the choice between buying and not buying. The Lords of *kitsch,* in short, exploit the cultural needs of the masses in order to make a profit and/or to maintain their class rule—in Communist countries, only the second purpose obtains.[30]

Herbert Gans, in turn, insists that while mass culture is indeed standardized, stereotyped, and produced by formula, high culture is not entirely free from these, either.[31] A more familiar response is to insist that the market responds to consumer demand, which is quite diversified, and that mass culture does offer a variety of fare to suit different tastes. This is the "freedom of choice" argument, one which business and advertising constantly repeat.

The business of mass culture and of consumer culture, however, concentrates upon only the large (that is, mass) markets of consumers, for only these are profitable. Jeffrey Schrank, for example, reports that what was once the Top 40 or even Top 60 songs played on radio stations is now that in name only; no more than ten or fifteen songs are played per week.[32] There may be limits to how much the mass production of mass culture can limit the range of cultural offerings, but the diversity of mass tastes is nonetheless affected by the commercial control of mass culture.

Mass Culture and the Individual   Perhaps most of the critics of mass culture have spent their rage against what they believe to be its worst effect: that it dehumanizes, brutalizes, stupifies, dulls the imagination, and weakens the critical faculties. It trivializes life and suggests that there can always be happy endings, easily identifiable "good guys" and "bad guys," and obvious "right" and "wrong." It offers us escapism but no opportunity to come to grips with the most basic issues of life.

But these critics, according to Herbert Gans, exaggerate the effects of mass culture on people's lives and underestimate the capacity of people to discount the efforts to persuade and influence them. Only the poor and the children, he reports, cannot effectively discount and are therefore more influenced than the rest of us—but don't we all start out as children? Few people, he asserts, take the media at face value, use it to solve problems, or even use it as a description of reality.[33]

But if it is difficult to accurately assess the effect of mass culture on human personality, it is not difficult to see how mass culture deliberately limits the range of ideas and perspectives offered. Mass culture stays away from "controversial" material. That does not mean pornography; that means ideas and depictions critical of the established order of society. Each of us possesses different, even conflicting attitudes, and mass culture tends to reinforce the conservative and uncritical ones, diminishing our more critical capacities.

Gans acknowledges that mass culture has emphasized middle-class culture and attitudes at the expense of working-class and lower-class cultures, and by doing so has increased middle-class cultural and political power.[34] Gans also says that people respond selectively to what they see and read, according to their values, so that the mass media work to reinforce "already existing attitudes and behavior, rather than to create new ones."[35]

Mass Culture and Mass Society   Take the above issue one step further. The effect of mass culture, its critics charge, is to destroy the basis for independent thought and critical political action, which paves the way for corporate domination in culture and politics as in the economy, at the worst producing a totalitarian society. Individual autonomy, freedom, and democratic practices are threatened by a mass culture.

Again, Herbert Gans argues that the evidence supports no such dire possibility. Instead, he claims, the very sources of independent thought and action—the family and peer groups, and voluntary associations—have proliferated even as have the mass media. Though the state can in emergencies take over the mass media, Gans insists that the role of the media can only be "the reinforcement of existing social trends."[36]

Yet even Gans recognizes that corporate domination in the mass culture is threatening, as in this comment, chilling when you realize it comes from a defender of that culture:

In America, television and the other media are controlled by commercial institutions, which are more interested in maximizing profits than in political control—except when media content becomes too critical of free enterprise. Even so, they are likely to support the media's democratic role only as long as it supports their profitseeking, and when they or their advertisers become antidemocratic, the media's democratic role is restricted.[37]

Gans, furthermore, may be underestimating the intent of corporate leadership to use the consumption of mass culture and of mass-produced commodities to control consciousness and to create a mode of cultural domination. The aspiration to be "captains of consciousness" means just that: to control the conscious choices people in this society make about how to live as human beings.

Aspiration and intent, however, are not achievement. Stuart Ewen tells us that the captains of consciousness, while dominating the production of culture, have nonetheless found a growing resistance to their control.[38] The refusal to be rendered passive and mute by mass culture is still strongly evident. It is evident most of all in the consumers' movement, which is now the critical and reforming voice in the consumer culture. It is evident whenever a counterculture emerges from among the young. It is evident in any new form of political dissent. It is evident in the environmental movement and among those who pose the issue of the *quality of life* as too important to be left to corporate capitalism and the consumer culture. It is evident in the growing movement of parents to limit the new demonstrably negative effect of television on children. It is evident in feminism and in the many ways in which people seek to escape the confining and smothering effect of conventionally stereotyped roles.

All that is popular culture is not mass culture. Many of these resistances and new developments are popular; they come from people, not from corporations or advertising agencies or TV producers. Where they prove to be broadly popular, however, the producers of mass culture will attempt to take them over and profit from them. They will turn them into cultural commodities, packaged anew and smoothed out to remove their critical intent. And they often succeed in this. But they have not yet quite become captains of consciousness.

SUMMARY

Culture is an order system of symbolic meanings and understandings. It is humanly created through social interaction and is transmitted over generations.

Symbols are all those objects (including words), human-made, for which human beings share a set of meanings. Through language we construct symbolic orders and those are our "real" worlds.

The elements of culture are: *cognition,* the world of known facts available as a store of practical knowledge; and *norms* and *values.* Norms are rules of conduct, and are both *folkways*—norms not crucial to the welfare of a group—and *mores,* norms defined as crucial and the violation of which will bring punishment. Values are abstract conceptions of the good, true, and beautiful; of what is desirable to achieve.

____In small societies the various elements of a culture are *integrated* into a well-knit whole, but the cultures of large complex societies are not.

Cultural relativism is an argument for the integrity of all cultures and that human conduct is to be judged only by the cultural standards of the society in which it occurs. But cultural relativism is not intended as justification for the cruelty and oppression found in many societies.

Subcultures are the distinctive norms, values, and life-styles of a group that still shares in the total culture of the society.

____A *counterculture* emerges when a group or segment of society comes into opposition to at least some dominant values.

____*Popular* and *mass* culture has largely supplanted folk and high culture in industrial societies. Popular culture has become commercialized and mass produced and is now corporate-dominated; it is mass culture. There is a persistent debate over whether mass culture debases taste, is a threat to a free society, and reduces the capacity for independent thought. Mass culture does avoid critical ideas and depictions, yet there is also resistance to its influence.

(NOTES

[1] Clifford Geertz, *The Interpretation of Cultures* (New York: Basic Books, 1973), pp. 144–145.

[2] George Herbert Mead, *Mind, Self, and Society* (Chicago: The University of Chicago Press, 1934), p. 78; quotation, p. 80.

[3] William Graham Sumner, *Folkways* (Boston: Ginn, 1906).

[4] Judith Blake and Kingsley Davis, "Norms, Values, and Sanctions," in Robert E. L. Faris, ed., *Handbook of Modern Sociology* (Skokie, Ill.: Rand McNally, 1964), p. 464.

[5] Clifford Geertz, *The Interpretation of Cultures* (New York: Basic Books, 1973), p. 406.

[6] *Ibid.,* p. 407.

[7] For the persistence of ethnicity, see Daniel P. Moynihan and Nathan Glazer, *Beyond the Melting Pot* (Cambridge, Mass., M.I.T. Press, 1963).

[8] Andrew W. Greeley, *Ethnicity in the United States* (New York: Wiley, 1974).

[9] See Lewis M. Killian, *White Southerners* (New York: Random House, 1970).

[10] See, for example, John A. Hostetler, *Hutterite Society* (Baltimore: Johns Hopkins Press, 1974).

[11] See Ortiz M. Walton, *Music: Black, White, and Blue: A Sociological Survey of the Use and Misuse of Afro-American Music* (New York: William Morrow, 1972).

[12] For a fine analysis of the creation of the bohemian, see Cesar Grana, *Bohemian versus Bourgeois* (New York: Basic Books, 1964).

[13] See Richard Flacks, *Youth and Social Change* (Chicago: Markham, 1971), pp. 47–56.

[14] *Ibid.,* p. 22.

[15] See Theodore Roszak, *The Making of a Counter Culture* (Garden City, N.Y.: Doubleday, 1969), p. 31.

[16] See Philip Slater, *The Pursuit of Loneliness,* rev. ed. (Boston: Beacon Press, 1976), pp. 122–123.

[17] *Ibid.,* p. 114.

[18] *Ibid.,* p. 115.

[19] *Ibid.,* p. 115.

[20] *Ibid.,* p. 119.

[21] *Ibid.,* p. 127.

[22] *Ibid.,* p. 124.

[23] *Ibid.,* p. 128.

[24] Ernest van den Haag, "Of Happiness and of Despair We Have No Measure," in Bernard Rosenberg and David Manning White, eds., *Mass Culture: The Popular Arts in America* (New York: The Free Press, 1957), pp. 504–536; quotation from p. 508.

[25] Norman F. Cantor and Michael S. Werthman, eds., *The History of Popular Culture* (New York: Macmillan, 1968).

[26] Stuart Ewen, *Captains of Consciousness: Advertising and the Social Roots of the Consumer Culture* (New York: McGraw-Hill, 1976), p. 18.

[27] *Ibid.,* p. 19.

[28] *Ibid.,* p. 131.

[29] These issues have been explored in detail in two noted collections: Rosenberg and White, *op. cit.;* Norman Jacobs, ed., *Culture for the Millions* (Princeton, N.J.: Van Nostrand, 1961). Two recent books, both more favorable than not to popular culture, are: George H. Lewis, ed., *Side-Saddle on the Golden Calf* (Pacific Palisades, CA.:

Goodyear Publishing, 1972); Herbert Gans, *Popular Culture and High Culture: An Analysis and Evaluation of Taste* (New York: Basic Books, 1974).

[30] Dwight MacDonald, "A Theory of Mass Culture," in Rosenberg and White, *op. cit.,* pp. 59–73; quotation on p. 60.

[31] Gans, *op. cit.,* pp. 21–23.

[32] Jeffrey Schrank, *Snap, Crackle and Popular Taste:*

The Illusion of Free Choice in America (New York: Delta, 1977), p. 167.

[33] Gans, *op. cit.,* 30–43.

[34] *Ibid.,* p. 32.

[35] *Ibid.,* pp. 47–48.

[36] *Ibid.,* p. 46.

[37] *Ibid.,* p. 47.

[38] Ewen, *op. cit.,* pp. 187–220.

SUGGESTED READINGS

Norman S. Cantor and Michael S. Wertman, eds, *The History of Popular Culture.* New York: Macmillan, 1968. An interesting collection of essays on popular culture through the ages.

Stuart Ewen, *Captains of Consciousness: Advertising and the Roots of the Consumer Culture.* New York: McGraw-Hill, 1976. A brilliant analysis of one dimension of mass culture.

Herbert Gans, *Popular Culture and High Culture: An Analysis and Evaluation of Taste.* New York: Basic Books, 1974. A thoughtful sociological analysis of popular culture and high culture in democratic society.

Clifford Geertz, *The Interpretation of Cultures.* New York: Basic Books, 1973. A leading anthropologist explains culture as the "fabric of meaning" by which we interpret experience and guide our behavior.

Cesar Grana, *Bohemian versus Bourgeois.* New York: Basic Books, 1964. A fine historic analysis of the antiindustrial origins from which came the counterculture.

Theodore Roszak, *The Making of a Counter Culture.* Garden City, N.Y.: Doubleday, 1969. An interpretation of the counterculture that has not yet been surpassed.

Jeffrey Schrank, *Snap, Crackle, and Popular Taste: The Illusion of Free Choice in America.* New York: Delta, 1977. A readable analysis of how popular taste is deliberately shaped by producers and advertisers.

Philip Slater, *The Pursuit of Loneliness,* rev. ed. Boston: Beacon Press, 1976. A provocative critique of the dominant American culture.

Ortiz M. Walton, *Music: Black, White, and Blue: A Sociological Survey of the Use and Misuse of Afro-American Music.* New York: William Morrow, 1972. An analysis of how cultural forms created with a segregated subculture are borrowed and used within the dominant culture.

A separate individual is an abstraction unknown to experience, and so likewise is society when regarded as something apart from individuals.

Charles Horton Cooley

Four

SOCIALIZATION
The person in society

No society exists apart from individuals, nor do individuals exist apart from society. That rather obvious point is another way of saying that some conception of human nature and of the relation of the individual to society is, therefore, necessarily built into sociological study.

HUMAN NATURE AND HUMAN BEING

There is an old argument in the social sciences about how we become a human being.

One position is that we inherit our most fundamental characteristics; *biology,* therefore, is the determining factor. Our genes, it is argued, have most to do with determining our behavior.

An opposing position is that we do not inherit our nature but that it is nurtured and developed in interaction with others—we are socialized, and it is *culture* that is the determining influence on human behavior and personal characteristics.

Until the earliest years of this century most social scientists in the United States believed strongly in the role of biology in determining our basic nature. What social scientists believed was even more thoroughly maintained in the dominant white population. Then

there developed a heated and prolonged argument contesting these claims about the determining function of biology.

This challenge to biological determination advanced a quite different argument about human nature, one which asserted that people acquired their characteristics and attributes by being nurtured in a culture, that is, by being socialized. In time a new definition of how to become a human being emerged, one which gave full emphasis to the place of culture and vigorously denied that the biology of the human organism had any place at all in shaping the human being. The biological determination of an earlier day was replaced by a cultural determination.

Biology and Culture

We do not yet know all there is to know about the function of biology and culture in shaping the human being. Both are involved, of course, so that the earlier arguments built up about either biological or cultural determination are equally one-sided.

One thing we do know is that human beings are not organized through *instincts,* which are inborn mechanisms for responding to situations in the environment. Instead, they must *learn* how to cope and be effective.

We also know that the human being undergoes a long period of childhood dependence, for there is much to learn. But this gradual social maturation is accompanied by a gradual physical maturation, so that the biological organism is capable of learning some things at a later time that simply could not be done earlier. Learning to walk and talk cannot come at birth, for example, while the onset of puberty in both males and females requires new patterns of learning about sexual conduct and sexual relations.

Once social scientists thought that the need to be social, to interact with others and to want human company was entirely learned as a consequence of this prolonged childhood dependence. But now there is the conception that the human infant is biologically programmed to be social. They suckle, grasp adults, and cling in such a way as to increase contact, and snuggle down into a person's arms. To be sure, this need to interact physically with others is given cultural form that varies from one society to another.

Yet biology does more than contribute an organism to be shaped by cultural forces. The biological endowment of human beings both limits what is culturally possible (though there is an impressive variety of types of human beings) and also affects cultural patterns. Languages, for example, are cultural material, and within different cultures there are different languages. But it now seems that all human beings are neurologically organized for speech. Our *capacity* for speech, then, is biologically determined, but it is up to people to create a specific language.

Biology and culture, then, do not make separate contributions to the development of the human being; instead they interact with one another. Within limits, culture gives distinctive shape and form to the biological organism, so that in specific societies at particular times in history the biological material is shaped into typical models of man and woman. That same biological material can be shaped quite differently in another society and at another time in history. Shaping the human organism into typical persons in a particular society is the function of socialization.

SOCIALIZATION

Socialization is the basic process by which the human organism becomes a person and a functioning member of society and by which such persons are continually integrated into groups by acquiring as their own the norms, values, and perspectives of such groups. It is, therefore, a process essential for individuals, else they could not become human. It is also a process essential for society, for it could not persist without continually socializing new members.

A society cannot exist unless there are people who are capable of performing its roles and carrying out necessary social activities. But such people do not come ready made; they have to be produced.

At birth the human organism knows nothing and can do nothing to meet its own needs; it is totally dependent on others. Its social characteristics develop slowly, and they do so only when and if the individual interacts with others and shares the experience of living in society. We *become* human, it seems, only by being in society.

But since any human infant would die if not cared for by others, we are all in society from birth. How do we know, therefore, that one becomes human only by being in society?

Feral Children

Some evidence to answer that question might come from the rare cases of *feral* children, who survived physically even though they were cut off from the socializing influence provided through human contact. Over the centuries there have been many myths about children raised by animals in the wilderness, going back at least to the Roman myth of Romulus and Remus who, left to die as infants along the Tiber River, were raised by a she-wolf. However, lack of systematic observation of these few cases gives them no scientific credibility.

Two actual, credible cases reported by sociologist Kingsley Davis, however, are at least approximations of the feral child. These were cases of two young girls who had missed the first six years of normal socialization.[1] Because they were illegitimate, they had been hidden in dark rooms and attics and never allowed normal human company. When discovered, both were unable to speak, and they had no "mind," as we know the term, to think or reason.

One of the girls—Anna—could not walk or talk and had been seriously neglected; her abdomen was bloated and her legs were skeletonlike. She was found lying on her back, limp and apathetic, expressionless and seemingly indifferent to everything around her. She could not feed herself, wash herself, or do anything at all for herself. She was believed to be deaf and possibly blind (she was not) and perhaps to be feeble-minded (she may have been).

In the next four and a half years—before she died of hemorrhagic jaundice—Anna made considerable progress. For one thing, she learned to walk well and to run fairly well, though clumsily. She could wash her hands and brush her teeth and was clean about her clothes. She loved a doll, and she could build with blocks and string beads. She talked mainly in phrases, repeated words, and tried to carry on a conversation. At the time of her death, she had reached the development of a normal two- or three-year-old child.

The other case of extreme isolation, a girl named Isabelle, had lived her first six years in contact only with her deaf-mute mother. As a result she communicated only in gestures and made strange, croaking noises. She displayed fear and hostility toward strangers, especially men, and was pronounced feeble-minded and uneducable.

Despite such judgments, specialists worked with Isabelle and, after a slow start, she demonstrated a remarkable progress for one deprived of human contact for so long. In a little over two months she was putting sentences together. By the time she was eight and a half years old, she had reached a normal level for her age. In two years she had covered the stages of development that normally require six. In time, she entered school and functioned as a normal child.

Isabelle's greater recovery may be explained by the more skilled attention she received after being discovered, as well as by the fact that she had more friendly contact with another person, her mother, in those early years. Anna may even have been feeble-minded. In either case, however, there is vivid testimony to what isolation from human contact means for normal personality development.

Social Deprivation

Such cases as these are very few. But there is a larger body of evidence about children who have been deprived of the care usually given by loving mothers. The issue here is not only *physical* care—feeding and bathing and diapering—but *emotional* care as well: paying attention to them, talking to them, cuddling them.

A noted and often cited study by René Spitz examined a hospital where a group of children—all under three years of age—were fed and clothed adequately but, because of too few nurses, given very little personal attention.[2] No one talked to them, carried them around, or cuddled them. The human results were devastating: within two years fully a third of the children had died and the rest were mentally retarded.

Spitz compared this case with that of the nursery of a women's prison, where the nurses' care was supplemented by the mothers, and each child received personal attention. Not one of the children in the nursery died, and they learned more proficiently than did the others how to walk, sit, and talk. The conclusion seemed to be clear: loving attention is as essential as food for the human infant.

A series of studies by William Goldfarb came to a similar conclusion.[3] He discovered that early child care, even when physically adequate, produces apathy and lack of emotional response if it is not given with personal attention. These socially deprived children fail to develop physically, mentally, and socially. Furthermore, improved mothering later on can rarely reverse the consequence of such early deprivation.

In order to develop normally, then, the individual needs to interact with *caring* persons. That does not have to be the child's mother. But it does have to be someone who will "mother" the child.

Such evidence as this becomes of renewed importance at a time when so many women who are mothers also are working, and when the demand for day-care for the children of working mothers has become a political issue. How early in life children can be safely left to the adolescent baby-sitter or the understaffed day-care facility is a real issue for many young parents, and an issue to which child-care specialists are giving renewed attention.

Becoming a Person

No matter how lacking in personality are newborn infants, loving parents care for them and treat them as valued individuals. They engage the infants in interaction from the beginning of their lives.

Through this interaction the new human being begins to learn and share in the culture. The early learning of language, furthermore, enables the child to participate in more complex social interaction. George Herbert Mead, who did pioneering work on socializa-

The effective socialization of each new human being requires much loving care.

tion, stressed the crucial role of language in this process.[4]

Mead started from the fact that interaction and communication exist for animals even without language. Each newborn human also interacts with others before learning any language. Through this interaction the child learns the meaning of facial expressions and voice tones, for example, and soon knows when another is pleased or angry. The learning of *gestures*—frowning, pointing, and the like—forms the basis for learning language.

The child already knows the meaning of many objects and events—food, milk, spoon, high chair, getting washed, taking a nap—before learning the words for them. Once language is a part of the socialization process, however, it makes possible ideas about behavior. Now the child can *think,* for to learn a language is to acquire a mind. Then the developing human can reflect upon others' action toward itself and about the meaning of its own actions toward others.

(In Chapter 3 we pointed out the importance of language as a basic aspect of culture in making us human, and in giving us a mind. We quoted Max Muller: "No thought without words." We are here returning to that point again in a somewhat different context, but the basic principle still applies: the creation of language as symbol is basic in making us human. Learning a language is a basic step in the humanizing of the individual; without it one cannot become truly human.)

Taking the Role of the Other   We all notice how readily children imitate adults, but for Mead this became a significant step in their socialization. By taking the role of the other, according to Mead, children learn how to respond to objects around them.

At first the child takes the role of a *particular* other—usually its own mother or father. In its play it reenacts what it has observed, often reversing roles by taking its parent's role and having a doll or another child (or even an imaginary one) play its own role. In short, it acts out how its mother acts toward it. Observe, for example, how a small child scolds a doll, using the words and voice tone of its mother.

But when children reach the state of development where they can enter into organized games with other children—roughly about the age of eight—they must then take into account the expectations of all the other participants, not merely some particular other. In playing games such a baseball, Mead says, there are fixed roles, such as pitcher and batter, and a basic set of rules—one has to run the bases in order and touch each of them; no shortcuts. These roles and rules provide some general expectations controlling the actions of all the participants.

Children learn these roles and rules through participating in the game. They learn what anyone is supposed to do in a particular situation—throw the ball to first base, for example—and they learn what is "fair" and "not fair."

In taking part in a game, therefore, children learn a generalized set of expectations and attitudes shared by all the participants—what Mead calls the *generalized other.* The social attitudes of a group now organize and direct the behavior of the child.

By practicing an adult task, these two small girls are taking the role of the other.

Internalization Through the social interaction of the play group the child learns not only what to expect and demand of others—"everybody gets a turn," for example—but comes to expect and demand the same of itself. The social attitudes of the group are now its own. What was once something external has now been *internalized*. Most importantly, what others expect of the child, the child now expects of itself.

Prior to internalization, society is experienced by young children as an *external* process, something "out there" that controls and constrains their actions, that compels them to do some things and not to do other things. Socialization and the development of the self internalizes what was external.

The Emergence of Self There are two important things to note about this. First, the child now has, in ordinary terms, a *conscience*. It can respond morally to its own actions and thought and judge itself as it perceives it would be judged by the group. When this happens, the growing human being can feel guilty, ashamed, mortified, embarrassed, or also proud or

THE FUND OF SOCIABILITY

Any socialized person has a continuing need to interact with others, a need to be *sociable*. Separated from friends and family we are lonely. This observation led sociologist Robert S. Weiss to hypothesize a *fund of sociability:* "individuals require a certain amount of interaction with others, which they may find in various ways."* They may have fewer, more intense relationships, or more but less intense ones. The loss of one relationship, as by divorce, suggested Weiss, could be compensated by increased sociability with others.

But Weiss and a colleague studied men and women who met in an association called Parents without Partners, and their findings did not support the hypothesis. Though belonging to Parents without Partners proved useful to these divorced parents, it did not diminish their sense of loneliness. This was even true when good friends were made.

This led Weiss next to study married couples who had recently moved to Boston from some distance away, where they were out of contact with old friends and family. The wives, it appeared, suffered from lack of friends with whom they could share the concerns of their daily lives. Their husbands, even when they tried, simply could not function as friends.

It seemed apparent that friendships do not provide the functions ordinarily provided by marriage, but marriage does not provide the functions provided by friendship. There seem to be different kinds of relationships providing different functions.

Weiss and his associates then worked out a theory of functional specificity of relationships: "individuals have needs which can only be met within relationships, that relationships tend to become relatively specialized in the needs for which they provide, and as a result individuals require a number of different relationships for well-being."† Weiss suggests five categories of relationships.

1. *Intimacy,* a relationship in which individuals can express their feelings freely and without self-consciousness. It requires trust, understanding, and ready access. Marriage provides such a relationship, and so can friendship.

2. *Social integration,* a relationship in which participants share similar concerns or are striving for similar objectives. People help one another, exchange information and ideas, do

pleased with itself. The capacity for self-judgment means the individual now has a *self* which has developed through the individual's social interactions with others.

Secondly, the socialized individual now has become a member of society, expecting of itself what others would expect of it. The social norms that control conduct have now been internalized, so that social control becomes self-control. Society is now inside the human being. This is the way in which a society produces the human beings necessary to carry on that society.

One of the first steps in developing a self occurs very early, when the child is first able to discriminate among its surrounding objects. At some quite early point the new human being knows that the world outside is made up of separate and distinct objects and soon learns to tell one from another. A baby can tell mother and father from strangers long before she or he knows the words or understands the social relations.

But while other persons become objects to the child, the child is not as yet an object to itself. The child is conscious of others but not yet conscious of itself.

The self grows and develops from this gradual process of becoming aware of and responding to oneself, even as one responds to others. To be able to respond to oneself, to approve or disapprove of oneself, re-

favors for one another. Among women (wives), he says, this function is provided by friends; among men by relations with colleagues, as well as by friends. A sense of isolation and boredom occurs when such a relationship is absent.

3. *Opportunity for nurturant behavior,* a relationship in which adults take responsibility for the well-being of a child. Weiss says that, based on his experience, men seem more able to act as foster fathers than women do as foster mothers. The absence of this function produces a sense of life as unfulfilled, meaningless, and empty of purpose.

4. *Reassurance of worth,* a relationship that proves an individual's competence in some role. Men and women who work find this reassurance in work relations, and some men find this in family life, too. Women who do not work outside the home look to their relations with husband, children, and acquaintances for recognition of their competence in managing a home and family. A loss here results in decreased self-esteem.

5. *Assistance,* a relationship of providing services or making resources available, is basic to kin relationships, but also to neighboring and friendships. Its absence produces a sense of anxiety and vulnerability.

These are tentative generalizations, derived from one piece of research, and in no sense definitive. But they point up a significant relationship between the person and society. Once the human organism has been socialized, Weiss tells us, and a self has emerged, there is a continuing need to interact with others. This much has often been stated before, but what Weiss's work adds is the recognition that just any relationship cannot be substituted for another. Different relationships meet different kinds of needs, and Weiss's categories are one effort to specify what these might be.

Notes

* Robert Weiss, "The Fund of Sociability," *Trans-action* 6 (July–August 1969): 36–43. Reprinted in Morris L. Medley and James E. Conyers, eds., *Sociology for the Seventies: A Contemporary Perspective* (New York: Wiley, 1972), pp. 68–77, and also in John W. Kinch, *Sociology in the World Today* (Reading, Mass.; Addison-Wesley, 1971). Quote from p. 37.

† Weiss, *op. cit.,* p. 38.

quires that one is able to look at oneself from the outside, as would another person.

The Looking-Glass Self Charles Horton Cooley called this process the *looking-glass self.*[5] He suggested that we all undergo a process of imagining how we appear in the eyes of others. Cooley said that:

so in our imagination we perceive in another's mind some thought of our appearance, manners, aims, deeds, character, friends, and so on, and are variously affected by it.

A self idea of this sort seems to have three principal elements: the imagination of our appearance to the other person; the imagination of his judgment of that appearance; and some sort of self-feeling, such as pride or mortification.[6]

Our conceptions of ourself are then shaped by what others have indicated they think of us, and in responding to what others think, our own self-development is greatly affected. The self we develop is a *social self,* a product not only of social interaction but of the social values and attitudes of the group we have come to share and internalize. (See "The Fund of Sociability.")

Self and Society: The Uncertain Fit

This process of socialization lets us see how society "gets into" the person. There seems, then, to be a fit between society and individual. Some social scientists stress this cultural fit between person and society, as in this quote from anthropologist Ruth Benedict:

> Most people are shaped to the form of their culture because of the enormous malleability of their original endowment. They are plastic to the moulding force of the society into which they were born.[7]

According to this view, the human being is passive material that can be shaped into any form desired or required by society. The sociologist Dennis Wrong calls it an *oversocialized image,* one in which the individual is seen as nothing but the *role-player,* so thoroughly socialized by society that there is a complete internalization of norms.[8] This presumably produces a high consistency between person and society.

But no such person and no such society exists. The reality of the relationship between society and person is different. If socialization works so perfectly, why is there violence and conflict? Why is there dissent and deviance? And why do so many people feel coerced and forced by society? Clearly, the relationship between self and society is not a smooth fit. There is a quality in all persons that resists the expectations of society.

How to account for the lack of good fit between self and society has led social scientists to pursue two major lines of explanation. One emphasizes how the nature of society produces the contranormative actor, while the other focuses on the nature of human beings.

The Contranormative Actor   In any large and complex society, there must always be norm-violating (*contranormative*) action just because the norms of such a society are always inconsistent and contradictory.[9] Consequently, the process of socialization also produces inconsistencies and conflicts rather than an easy, smooth fit in the relation of the individual to society. Only in an idealized folk society, from this perspective, could we expect a perfect fit between self and society. Probably no such society now exists, and perhaps it never did. Modern societies are far too complex and changing to be other than inconsistent and contradictory. That, in turn, always produces contranormative action by individuals.

Robert Merton has approached the issue in another way.[10] He points out that violation of the norms will occur whenever people cannot be sure of achieving goals in a legitimate manner. They will then be tempted to go after them illegitimately. In the United States, for example, the pursuit of "success" in life can be valued so highly that some persons will cheat or steal in order to beat out others. Cheating on exams in college in order to get a higher score on a test, in order to get a better grade, in order to have a better chance to get into a medical school or other professional or graduate programs, is a fairly common example.

For those at the bottom of society, success through individual competition may not even be possible, because of ethnic, racial, and class discrimination. In such cases, success in society may be sought in illegitimate ways, such as becoming rich and powerful through the criminal rackets.

Even sociology's classic literature gives us no reason to assume that the individual is other than a *contranormative* actor. Émile Durkheim, a major figure in the founding of sociology, insisted that crime is "normal," not "pathological," because no society could ever totally enforce its norms. To try to do so, he argued, would make society so repressive as to lose the ability to change and to adapt to new circumstances.

> Where crime exists, collective sentiments are sufficiently flexible to take on a new form, and crime sometimes helps to determine the form they will take. How many times, indeed, it is only an anticipation of future morality—a step toward what will be.[11]

What Durkheim meant can be illustrated by the example of bootlegging and running "blind pigs" and "speakeasies," places where liquor could be bought and consumed in a society that forbid it. These were criminal acts during the time when the Prohibition Amendment was the law of the land. But in time these criminal activities were replaced by quite legal liquor stores, bars, and cocktail lounges. Similarly, in some states, the numbers racket has been partially replaced by legal track-betting and now by state lotteries.

Social life, therefore, is always normatively regulated, and norms are internalized by the individual and enforced by society—but never fully. The *oversocialized* individual does not exist in the real world. But neither does its opposite: a collection of free and unregulated creatures each pursuing are individual self-interest without regard or concern for others. The relation between self and society lies somewhere between these two extremes.

The Natural Human Being The concept of the contranormative actor is an attempt to argue that the explanation for a less than perfect fit between self and society is a consequence of the nature of society — its internal inconsistencies and contradictions. But another position is that human nature is also a basic factor.

This explanation begins with the observation that the human organism is never a *passive* object on which society carries out its socializing influences. Instead, the organism is always an *active* agent in its relation to society. Even the newly born infant acts and reacts; it cries and kicks and asserts itself. The smallest child will *resist* things being done to it; it will spit out food, pull away, or otherwise try to do what it wants to do.

From the outset of life, then, the individual is an active participant in its own socialization. The human being is not simply clay, which can be molded in any form desired in society, or an empty vessel into which can be poured any cultural content desired.

Two of the names most noted for describing how we become human — George Herbert Mead and Sigmund Freud — have both recognized the active, resisting, asserting aspect of the organism. Both have clearly insisted that the human being is always *social* but not determined in *every* way by society.

In describing the emerging self, Mead distinguished between two aspects of it that he called the "I" and the "me." The "me" is the socialized side, made up of internalized attitudes; it is society inside the person. But the *I* is there, too, as an aspect of the self. It is a spontaneous, creative, often impulsive side, a *self-interested* side that takes into account the *me* but is not entirely controlled by it.

In this way, Mead did not grant to society any complete victory over the person. He recognized an aspect of each person's self that is not fully socialized, so that the conduct of any person can never be totally explained as conformity to the norms of society.

Freud, too, distinguished aspects of the self. He called *superego* what the organism internalizes from society. Against this, he posed the *id,* powerful biological drives and "instinctual endowments," including the sexual, which made of the human being an aggressive creature capable of being exploitative of others: *Homo homini lupus* (man is wolf to man), he said.[12] Between these two was the *ego,* a reality-oriented sense which mediated between the instinctual drives on the one hand and society's socializing force on the other.

Freud's image of the human being is that of an aggressive animal, held back and repressed by social controls. Civilization is then essentially an unpleasant but necessary repressive structure imposed on only partially socialized organisms. This view, which is a pessimistic one, emphasizes too much the sheer force of biological instincts and drives to satisfy most social scientists today.

Nonetheless, we cite both Mead and Freud to point out the falsity of the image of the oversocialized person. The human being is always a *social* creature but the molding process of society, which we call socialization, never works like some mechanical process manufacturing objects according to a set of specifications. By socialization society produces persons, but those persons from the beginning of their life actively share in their own human production. They *resist* and they *assert* and the person they become, the self they develop, is in some way an outcome of the interaction between other persons as agents of society and their own self-interested organisms.

The Agents of Socialization

To be socialized adequately in any society, the newborn organism must be involved in persistent social interaction, and this requires social groups which have a particular responsibility for their care and development. These groups are society's *socializing agents,* and the family is the most obvious one.

The Family as Socializing Agent In all societies there is some form of the family that takes responsibility for the care and nurturing of the very young. Such a group does more than meet the needs of the dependent child. It provides — partly unconsciously and informally, partly consciously and deliberately — instruction in moral conduct and in socially needed skills. The family, therefore, becomes the representative of society's general standards and expectations of conduct.

The Family as Primary Group The family is the most significant *primary group* in the socialization of the child. Charles Horton Cooley developed the concept of the primary group from observations of his own children in the family situation. Cooley defined primary groups as "characterized by intimate, face-to-face cooperation and association."[13] Within the primary group the new human being is loved and wanted. It is here that there is the "mothering" so necessary for human development. Only those who are loved and cared for in primary groups can grow up and be able to love and care for others.

As Cooley saw it, the organism acquires a human nature within the primary group. By this he meant the internalization of those "sentiments and impulses" that separate the human from the animal and are, he felt, universally characteristic of human beings. The primary group is the cradle of human morality and ideals, for it fosters a sense of decency and worth that becomes part of the human being for the whole of it existence.

The Peer Group   While family is the first and therefore the most primary of the primary groups, in time the socializing individual moves into more frequent interaction with others. This takes place in the *peer group,* which is the play group for the small child and the teenage gang or clique for the adolescent. As the word *peer* suggests, it is a group of those who are formally equal, unlike the family, where there is parental power and authority.

The highly particular expectations and demands of the family, backed by parental authority, are now replaced by the generalized demands and expectations of the peer group. (In Mead's language, the generalized other replaces the particular other.) The peer group provides the individual with significant experiences in learning how to interact with others, how to be accepted by others, and how to achieve status in a circle of friends.

The School   Since, from an early age, children spend much of their day in school, that organization cannot help but be a socializing agent. For one thing, school provides the opportunity for many primary groups to be formed, for school brings together children of the same age. The formation of adolescent cliques is one of the more significant features of social interaction in the high school.

In an earlier period there was often a greater consensus between the school and the family on basic values, so that the school served to *reinforce* the values and norms already transmitted to children by the family. In such cases, the family invariably backed up the school, even on the matter of punishment. Older adults who went to school under such circumstance have often recalled that if a boy got spanked in school as a punishment, when he told his father, he got spanked again.

Parents also backed up and supported the socializing influence of the school even when its values were different. This occurred when the school was viewed by parents as the opportunity for their children to get an education and get ahead in the world. They looked to the school to teach the child values and skills which they could not.

But in some circumstances the agreement and mutual support of family and school may not be sustained. Middle-class school teachers, for one thing, may uphold models of behavior and teach social values that are incongruent with those practiced in the family and the neighborhood by lower-class and working-class children. If the school succeeds, the socializing influence of the family is weakened. This, however, may be the very process that "fits" a lower-class child for entrance into a middle-class world. But if it does not succeed, the conflict between two modes of socialization may unfit the child for success in school. Here is where we find so many school dropouts; early in life they were socialized to a basic set of values and a lifestyle that were incompatible with those of the school.

While the school teaches essential skills and knowledge, as well as dominant social values, it also teaches the young how to fit readily into the bureaucratic structure of society. It does this by teaching them to get along cooperatively with others and to comply with authority. The students who "survive" high school and college by acquiring credentials and graduating have been socialized to a pattern of action which fits the demands of bureaucratic world of work. This is the "hidden" agenda of the school.

(In Chapter 10 we shall investigate further the place of the school in the socialization and training of the young in a society.)

Class and Socialization

In complex societies families are located in different social classes and that makes for differences in how children are socialized. Children of privileged and upper-class families are not going to be socialized in the same manner as children of families at the lowest class level.

The adolescent peer group is an important agency of socialization.

Social scientists have for a long time tried to show how differently the family socializes infant and child within different social classes. In the 1940s research seemed to show that middle-class mothers followed a rather rigid, inflexible schedule of feeding an infant, attempted toilet-training early, and tried to establish early attainment of habits of cleanliness.[14] By the 1950s, however, new research seemed to suggest just the opposite. Now the middle class appeared permissive and less demanding in its child-rearing practices.

The apparent contradiction of these findings is removed when we recognize, as Urie Bronfrennbrenner pointed out, that middle-class child-rearing practices have changed over time.[15] Middle-class parents tend to follow professional advice on child-rearing, particularly that of such authorities as Arnold Gesell and Benjamin Spock. Changing advice brought about changing practices.

Lower-class mothers in the ghettoes, in contrast, seemed to proceed flexibly without a rigid schedule and to allow greater freedom for impulsive and even aggressive behavior. But the stable working-class family (not to be confused with the lower class) usually made strong demands on its children, but it also gradually adopted the child-rearing practices of the middle class.

In more recent work sociologist Melvin Kohn tied socialization to the characteristics of middle- and working-class occupations.[16] He found that the occupation —which absorbs so much of a man's time and energy —affects his conception of what kind of an individual his children should be. And his wife seems to share that idea.

Many working-class jobs are routine, repetitive, and closely supervised. Typically, this leads the worker to value conformity to external authority. He then emphasizes that his children should learn obedience. Many middle-class occupations, in contrast, require initiative and independent judgment. An important dimension is the ability to deal with people or, in other cases, with abstract ideas. Men who work in these kinds of jobs want, not obedience, but autonomy and independence in their children. They emphasize that their children should learn to control their own behavior, rather than having it controlled by someone in authority.

Comparing middle class and working class in this way, however, lumps together many subclasses and varied occupations, for middle and working class are broad, inclusive categories. Middle class, for example, could be further divided. A study doing just that compared families of the "old" middle class of independent businessmen and self-employed professionals with families of the "new" middle class of salaried executives and professionals employed in large organizations.[17]

It seems that the new middle-class parents teach their children the importance of adjustment, security, and getting along with others. This is consistent with the newer child-training literature. The old middle-class parents instilled in their children a more active and manipulative approach to life. The child learned how necessary it was to develop strong aspirations and to strive hard for educational and occupational goals. These were the values found in the professional child-training literature of forty years ago. (Since the professionals in child-training change their ideas from time to time, we are not suggesting here that the newer child-training ideas, apparently followed most by the new middle-class parents, are in fact superior. Our concern is only that these differences affect the socialization of children.)

Different social classes face quite different life situations. Parents are likely to try to teach their children what they think it requires to cope with the situations common to their social class, for that is what they know best from experience. That being so, we can expect to find that different social classes socialize their children in different fashions.

Role Acquisition

The social roles that children learn at an early age are basic elements of socialization. Internalizing demands and expectations of these roles shape the developing self. Through early role-taking, especially roles of sex and class, children develop the general pattern of attitudes and values characteristic of their own sex and class. In such a way, a society reproduces itself. Since we have looked at class, let's look at sex roles.

Sex Roles The origin of sex roles seems to lie in the once primitive conditions in which superior male strength, on the one hand, and the confining nature of childbearing and child care for women, on the other, enabled males to achieve dominance over women. While these conditions have long since disappeared, the dominance of males and consequent division of sex roles and self-formation have not. At least not yet.

What this means is evident enough: girls and boys are socialized to fit different kinds of social roles. Girls have long been raised to want to fill the social roles which women have always filled: being mothers, first of all; being always secondary to men; and filling only those other roles that are consistent with the female self, such as teacher or nurse.

Societal expectations toward the sexes differ remarkably, and these expectations are soon internalized. The long dominant and traditional sex stereotype of the Western world says that "women are essentially nuturant/expressive/passive and men instrumental/active/aggressive."[18] Until recently, as a consequence women have *learned* to be less aggressive, not to compete, and to think of themselves as less intelligent and capable than males. In school girls start out learning faster than do boys. They learn to speak sooner and to read and count sooner. But in high school (again, until recently) boys caught up with girls in verbal tests and went well ahead of them in math.[19] Though more girls graduated from high school, fewer went on to or graduated from college.

When children first learn to read, and even before, they are exposed to contrasting conceptions of male and female. A study of picture books to which the American Library Association awarded prizes for "excellence," for example, showed to preschool children images of a basically male world.[20] Females were not even present in a third of the books; in the total sample examined, males outnumbered females by a margin of eleven to one. Furthermore, boys were seen as involved in varied and often adventurous activities as leading and initiating, while girls were passive, and were followers and watchers. While boys learned to do many things, girls were more likely to be presented as helping their mother in domestic tasks.

During adolescence both girls and boys become more aware of their adult status, and family, school, and peer group increase the pressure to be either "feminine" or "masculine." The conceptions of what is feminine and masculine narrow considerably in adolescence from what they were at an earlier age. While the ten-year-old girl can be a "tomboy," the sixteen-year-old girl cannot.

It is in adolescence that the role-models offered by adults begin to reveal themselves in the maturing young person. An adolescent girl knows what a woman is and does from observing her mother, other female relatives, female teachers and nurses, and of course, actresses and performers in movies and television. Until very recently, she had little opportunity to observe women in significant and prestigeful roles in society, such as senators and judges, scientists and corporation presidents.

Furthermore, in adolescence the family exercises a sharper, less equal control over girls than boys. As Jo Freeman noted, "Girls receive more affection, more protectiveness, more control and more restrictions. Boys are subject to more achievement demands and higher expectations."[21] The boy is being prepared to be active in shaping his world, the girl to accept being modeled by it.

That, at least, is how it has been and, to some extent, still is. But the world is changing toward a more equal division between the sexes and to fewer sex-role distinctions. Now the socialization experiences of young women no longer teach them to want only traditional sex roles or to see themselves as inherently less capable than males. (In Chapter 12 we will return to this issue.)

Adult Socialization

Most people once assumed that socialization in early years formed the character structure of a person into a firm and definite model that would not change much throughout life. But socialization is a continuing process. Indeed, in modern societies continuing socialization during the adult years is essential, since a person's life situation may change rapidly. As a result, the early agents of socialization can provide little specific preparation for many later roles.

Going from hometown and high school to a distant college, or to a job in a factory, or into the armed services requires further socialization. Learning an occupation is always more than acquiring skills and knowledge; it means the growth of an *occupational personality*. The beginner absorbs new attitudes and values toward the situation in which work occurs and learns new ways in which to relate to people. From this the beginner gains a new self-image, an occupational identity.

Throughout adult life, furthermore, there is continuing socialization to new roles and new situations, such as getting married, becoming a parent, then becoming a grandparent and a retired person. Talking to others who have done the same provides some readiness, some knowledge of what to expect, in short, an *anticipatory* socialization.

The adult couple whose children have married and moved away, leaving an "empty nest," for example, must adjust to a new life situation. In studying a sample of urban middle-class couples, Irwin Deutscher found that this change in their life situation did not appear to be particularly difficult and only a few had problems adapting.[22] There was sufficient anticipatory socialization for almost all of them. They had accepted the inevitability of the situation, and had been prepared by such earlier experiences as the departure of children for college or military service.

Resocialization

There are some circumstances in which a new socialization experience comes after childhood and makes a sharp break with an individual's past. Early socialization is undone, and a person's way of life is abandoned for a radically new and different one. This transformation of the person in a short period is *resocialization*. Religious conversion is a notable example of resocialization. Recruitment into certain kinds of social groups is yet another example. So is "brainwashing," a process of coercive thought control, which first received public attention in the United States when it was practiced on captured American soldiers by the Chinese during the Korean War.

Military and religious groups are the prime examples of the kind of groups that carry out resocialization after the recruitment of new members. These groups require a commitment to a way of life and a standard

This ordination of priests is a ceremony marking the completing of a resocialization experience.

of personal conduct radically different than that found in conventional life, yet they must recruit their new members from among conventional people.

To begin their resocialization of the individual, such groups start with isolating the new recruit from conventional society. This gives the new group sole access to the individual. Its socializing influences cannot then be offset by countervailing exposure to the larger society.

A common technique by such groups is to strip the individual of all overt symbols of prior status. The recruit's clothes are taken away and a uniform, unlike anything worn in civilian life, is supplied in its place. The head may be shaved to remove whatever symbolic significance hair style may have had.

Deliberate humiliation and degradation are often included in the early stages of resocialization. The intention is to remove all sense of self-esteem and self-respect acquired from the individual's past life. Past status is suppressed to make way for a new status. Basic training in the Marine Corps utilizes this extensively. The low status of first-year students in military academies often includes harassment by older cadets, petty sanctions and rules, and few, if any, privileges.

Stripping away old identities precedes the effort to build new ones. This involves removal from society, special techniques of relearning, and close involvement with a peer group. Peers support and reward one another and provide close support through a group solidarity built up by sharing a common experience. They have suffered the same debasement and humiliation and have undergone together the same personality reconstruction that is the core of their resocialization.

Here, for example, is how a sociologist describes the resocialization of young civilians into cadets at the United States Coast Guard Academy:

The new cadet, or "swab," is the lowest of low. The assignment of low status is useful in producing a correspondingly high evaluation of successfully completing the steps in an Academy career and requires that there be a loss of identity in terms of pre-existing statuses. This clean break with the past must be achieved in a relatively short period. For two months, therefore, the swab is not allowed to leave the base or to engage in social intercourse with non-cadets. This complete isolation helps to produce a unified group of swabs, rather than a heterogeneous collection of persons of high and low status. Uniforms are issued on the first day, and discussions of wealth and family background are taboo. Although the pay of the cadet is very low, he is not permitted to receive money from home. The role of the cadet must supersede other roles the individual has been accustomed to play. There are few clues which will reveal social status in the outside world.[23]

Since a commitment to a new identity is being deliberately created, the effectiveness of the process must be constantly tested. Passing a series of tests is necessary if one is to be a priest or a military officer, for example. The basic issue is not skill or knowledge, though that is obviously involved, but thorough socialization into and commitment to a role and its life-style.

In this process strong sanctions may be invoked; resocialization always occurs in groups with unquestioned authority over their recruits. These strong sanctions are part of the relearning process. They can be the harsh discipline common to the military, or enforced isolation, or techniques of humiliation before peers.

But rewards are also used in resocialization. They can be the promise of membership in an elite group, high social status, or the promise of eternal salvation.

Resocialization is the standard and continuing process of some groups in society, like military and religious ones. Normal socialization will not produce priests and military officers. But there are other important instances of resocialization in modern society.

Many of the new religious sects, some Christian, some not, use techniques of resocialization when recruiting young people into their ranks. The Hari Krishna is one example. More recently, there has been much controversy over some new Christian sects, such as the "Moonies," particularly because of their apparent attempt to get their recruits to reject their parents and family as one part of their new commitment. Parents have gone to court to try to get their children back, even when this meant young people over the age of 18, and some have utilized a forced "brainwashing" process to try to reverse the resocialization.

SOCIAL CONTROL

When individuals internalize the norms and values of society, they are able to exercise self-control. Yet no society can rely entirely on socialization and self-control. There are always laws and customs and ways to enforce them; *external sanctions* reinforce internalization. Even small groups can place pressure and demands on individual members as the price for acceptance by the group. All of this is *social control.*

But punishments and threats of punishments are not the only way to reinforce self-control. Individuals may be induced through *rewards* to undertake an activity of value to the society. They may, for example, be willing to submit to rigorous training and hard work for some future reward, whether that be winning a championship or getting into medical school.

Punishment as Social Control

Punishment that controls behavior can range from the mildest rebuke to the ultimate penalty—death. While only a political authority can legitimately deprive a person of life—though organized crime does it illegitimately—many social groups resort to ostracism or isolation, cutting off an offending person from social interaction with others. Large organizations may remove a person from membership: a company fires an employee; a school expels a student. Lesser penalties can be suspension, a fine, or demotion. Political authority can use fines or jail sentences.

Informal Controls   Even the smallest group, or the most loosely organized, manages to effect social control. *Ridicule,* for example, is often effective because it threatens to damage the group's respect for the individual. A person's personal reputation and good standing in the group may be at stake. This is why *gossip* is such an *effective control mechanism. To avoid being gossiped about, the individual must avoid conduct that, if gossiped about, would damage his or her reputation in the community. "What will the neighbors think?" controls the conduct of those who, in fact, do care what the neighbors think.

In the small rural community and cohesive neighborhood of the past, informal controls such as gossip worked well because people lived entirely among those before whom their conduct was always visible. There was no place to hide or conceal activities from others. The anonymity and impersonality of the city, however, made this kind of control less effective. In the city the law had to take over from these informal controls.

Yet even for many urban people the neighbors still do count. But now "neighbors" may mean fellow church members, fellow employees, or even bosses. What somebody thinks of you counts; and much social control depends on that.

Reward as Social Control

Rewards are a familiar aspect of social life. Trophies and championships reward outstanding individual and team performance. High grades and scholarships reward academic excellence. Gold stars send small children proudly home to show their parents their good papers. Remove these, and the activity itself, even if valued, may not induce as concerted and sustained an effort.

The belief in "rags to riches" in American life has been a powerful myth leading generations of Americans to believe that sustained effort on their part would be rewarded with personal success, *if* they also had ability and moral character. This is the *Horatio Alger myth,* the story of the poor but hard-working boy who eventually reaches the top.

After a century the Horatio Alger myth was not survived intact. When success must increasingly be found in organizational careers, what becomes valued is the capacity of individuals to work well with others, to get along cooperatively. Relations with others becomes as

Awarding a coveted trophy is a form of positive social control; it induces a sustained effort in a valued activity.

important as hard work and ability. *Personality* is the term that symbolizes this new aspect. Without an acceptable "personality" an individual has less chance to succeed. Being successful in a career today usually requires education and training, as well as "personality" and a willingness to work hard.

The lure of rewards as a significant social control can also be deliberately used by political authority to harness human talent and shape individual aspirations. During the Cold War climate of the 1950s, for example, the federal government adopted a policy to encourage the development of scientific and technological talent. It was feared that Soviet Russia was getting ahead of us. Federal grants subsidized programs to steer large numbers of talented youngsters into careers in science. What then seemed at one level to be the personal decision of many young people to puruse science as a career was in fact the consequence of deliberate efforts to induce just such an outcome.

Freedom and Social Control

To dwell on the mechanisms of social control, whether punitive or rewarding, puts emphasis on how the group demands conformity by the individual. It seems to deny the freedom and individuality that we ordinarily take to be such important values in American culture.

Achieving social control in a large, complex society, however, is much more difficult than in a small group, a fact some people see as a problem and others see as a guarantee of individual freedom. However, now there are new electronic techniques for eavesdropping on private conversations, which becomes a new means for controlling behavior. The storing up of information in computers—data banks—about an individual's income, income tax, and credit records, academic and occupational histories, and records (if any) of arrests, charges, and convictions, offers a new potential means of controlling behavior.

New technologies of communication and information-storing, whatever their other uses, are also possible instruments of social control. Look how each one of us carries around small cards which are keys to stored-up information about our past and present activities: driver's license, social security card, student and/or employee I.D., and bank credit cards. Today the issue of the right of individual privacy has turned to this matter of the records of individuals, of who has the right to have access to them, and the purposes for which they can be used. Attempting to protect individual rights of privacy in a society of computerized records kept by huge bureaucracies is now a new frontier in the continuing battle for individual civil liberties.

Controlled Worlds Imaginative minds have often created visions of society in which control over the person is thorough and complete. In *Brave New World* Aldous Huxley designed an antiutopian society in which individual human beings are biologically manufactured to specification and socialization is so effectively carried out that there is never any problem of social control.[24] People are designed to have only those abilities, emotions, and aspirations required to perform social roles already programmed and planned.

Based on biological engineering, Huxley's conception of a controlled, freedomless future, however chilling, seemed unlikely back in 1932. But in the 1970s the science of biology moved a little nearer to effective genetic control, and Huxley's science-fiction nightmare of over forty years ago no longer seems beyond achievement. It creates almost undreamed of problems about the ethics of social control for free societies. The freedom of geneticists to experiment with genetic material, for example, became by 1977 a national controversy over the need for adequate guidelines to protect the rest of us against possible genetic accidents.

What Huxley imagined in biological terms B. F. Skinner put forth in psychological terms. Skinner wrote *Walden Two,* a science-fiction novel about a utopian society in which socialization is perfected to eliminate the emotions of fear, hate, and envy in completely controlled environments.[25] Skinner has become world-renowned for advocating a technique of psychological reinforcement that will make people fit culturally desired standards. Another of his works *Beyond Freedom and Dignity,* has aroused enormous controversy for its outright advocacy of instituting behavioral controls over individuals.[26]

Both Huxley and Skinner, and others, too, point to the possibilities of controlling human beings by a powerful science, biological in the one case, psychological in the other. Despite impressive advances, however, science is not able as yet to prescribe for society's leaders and ruling institutions the behavioral mechanisms for fully effective control of people. Even though many scientists aspire to such an achievement, others oppose it. At stake here is a fundamental problem: how science is to be used in the complex issue of freedom and control in modern society.

INDIVIDUALISM, IDENTITY, AND ALIENATION

While in any human society there are individual differences, in modern society there is much greater development of the uniquely individual character of each person. The great French sociologist, Émile Durkheim, observed that a society with little division of labor was one in which "individuality is nil," but that where the division of labor was greater, "the more specialized the individual, the more personal his activity." Durkheim's telling point was: "Individuality arises only if the community recedes."[27] By this he meant that individuality grows only as the *folk* society we spoke of earlier—small, homogeneous, with little division of labor—gives way to the larger, more differentiated and culturally heterogeneous society.

Individuality, then, is a *fact* in modern society, but it is also a *value*. Being a unique individual with a mind of one's own is respected. However, in American society, there are some ambivalence and inconsistency here, for there are both the value of *individual personality* and the value of *external conformity*. As sociologist Alfred McClung Lee notes:

To the nervous amusement and even grave concern of many friendly European students of the United States situation, we vaunt our personal independence, our respect for "individualism," and our opposition to "authoritarianism" and then, without appearing to realize our inconsistency, rationalize our conformism. In terms of our behavior, we hold conforming to be one of our highest virtues.[28]

But the issue goes well beyond the apparent inconsistency between individuality and conformity. For the past third of a century a pressing concern has been the impact of vast and powerful social organization on human beings, on the potential loss of individuality before the fact of a conformity-demanding social structure. The common argument is that modern society forces a loss of identity for the individual, that one becomes a face in the crowd, a number on an IBM card. The increasingly more organized and bureaucratic development of modern society, it is now feared, is destroying the very individuality which modern society first created.

Individuality and Organization

It is in the growth of large, bureaucratic structures that the contradiction between individualism and the demands of society seem most apparent. It has led to the idea that a new type of person was needed by bureaucratic structure, one who excelled in relating well to others and who accommodated easily to diverse situations. Not individual, self-motivated performers but cooperative teamworkers now seemed to be the new requirements for human personality. To some important degree, individuality gave way before the demand for conformity to the work situation in large organizations.

Sociologist David Riesman first set forth this idea in his influential book, *The Lonely Crowd*.[29] Riesman argued that a highly urbanized society, organized through large bureaucratic structures, needs a highly flexible, continually socializing type of person. Such a personality type is particularly sensitive to the demands and expectations of the immediate situation and responds readily to the cues about what others expect in behavior.

Riesman called this new personality type *other-directed*. The other-directed personality type is socialized early to be particularly dependent on the peer group, to be well liked and accepted, and to make those adjustments in personal conduct that will ensure acceptance by peers. Parental values internalized in early childhood have less to do with a person's conduct in social interaction than does his or her readiness to respond to peers and to the larger contemporary world to which such a person is oriented through peers.

This other-directed type, according to Riesman, is now to be found among the urban, college-educated, bureaucratically employed middle classes. These are the people who manage and administer the corporations and public agencies which organize so much of modern life. The "new class" family mentioned earlier, which socializes its children to get along well with peers, provides support for this conception of a new pattern of personality development.

Riesman's work was interpreted by many as describing a decline in individualism in American society. But Riesman intended no such idea. Instead, he was describing what seemed to him to be a new way in which society constructed a "mode of conformity." Nonetheless, his work provided the basis for an extended discussion about the threat of large-scale organization to individualism.

A popularization of his ideas by William Whyte brought the phrase, "organization man," into the American vocabulary as an unflattering term for upwardly mobile men in large organizations whose career aspirations led them to overconform to the social world.[30]

Yet much of this literature was a cry of alarm based on error and myth. First, there was a romanticized reading of history, mistakenly attributing a rugged individualism as a normal aspect of life in American society, which it never was. Secondly, there was reliance on a romantic mythology about the freedom and individualism to be found in small-scale social worlds and the loss of those qualities through the growth of social structure. But small organizations are no more free or less conformity-demanding than larger ones.

A great deal needs to be known about how individuals adapt to large, complex social structures before we can adequately balance out what combination of gains and losses are inherent in the growth of social structure.

Social Identity

While conformity as a threat to individualism is one way to examine the relations between the individual and modern society, another is in terms of *identity*. Each of us carries around a self-identity, an image about ourself built up from membership and roles in social groups and grounded in our most and also least successful social experiences. Our personal identities are built up in life through attachments that grow and are valued, through membership in groups into which we are born, and by choices from among whatever options are open to us.

Ascribed Identity   No one has a completely free choice in establishing an identity. To be male or female is basic to personal identity, as it is to be black or white. Such identities are *ascribed*—that is, assigned at birth. Membership in an ethnic or religious group—being Irish or Polish, Jewish or Catholic—is also an ascribed identity.

Some people can by choice escape and change an

ethnic or religious identity. They can consciously discard the clues that others use to establish another's identity in their minds—speech, mannerisms, group memberships, and loyalties. The immigrant of the second generation who looks for *role models* in people outside the ethnic group and tries hard to imitate them is an example.

Because skin color is so easily visible and also unchangeable, racial identities remain ascribed. Nonetheless, blacks who are in fact racially mixed sometimes cannot be distinguished from darker complected whites and can then, if they choose, pass from black to white status. *Passing* remained available only to a small number of people socially identified as black, and was utilized only as long as being black was persistently a negative identity in the United States. The increase in black pride and positive self-identity—"black is beautiful"—in recent years has probably decreased the desire to pass even among the few who could carry it off.

Sex is even more fixed as an ascribed identity. One is born biologically male or female, with appropriate genitalia. In growing up each individual is then socialized to culturally prescribed roles, behaviors, and feelings defined in a particular culture as "natural" for men and women. Yet in all cultures it has been evident that some individuals do not as easily as others learn to be typically male or female. In American culture, we noted earlier, girls can be "tomboys" up to a certain age, usually about puberty. After that, they were pressured hard into being appropriately feminine. While little tomboys can be tolerated and even appreciated, little boys who resist the demands of masculinity are "sissies," and that is not tolerated.

Yet in the modern world ascribed identity is never the whole of any person's identity, as it would be for a peasant or an aristocrat in a medieval society. To a large extent modern people choose their identities from among some range of options, though not all options are equally available to everyone. These identities are *achieved*.

Occupation as Identity   Occupation has long been the most significant *achieved* identity in modern society. For those in highly rewarded occupations, involvement in work is often their central life-interest; they pursue a career. But for most others, who work at jobs that are not highly rewarded or even well regarded, work does not become their central life-inter-

est, even though work itself will be a valued activity. This has been true for a long time for most blue-collar workers, for example.[31] For them work is a means to an end, not an end in itself. A person has to earn a living.

Work and occupation for many, perhaps most people, is a small factor in establishing their identity. Instead, they try to build their self-identity from involvement in social groups outside the world of work —the neighborhood, the church, their ethnic group, a bowling league, an amateur sports team, and from the satisfying peer-group relations and social recognition to be gained from such involvement. For such people, the problem of identity is one of trying within their own circles to find the personal recognition and respect that will offset the *negative identity* which class or group position in society at large assigns them.

Negative Identities

In a society organized into social classes, where some people have high rank but most people do not, to be an ordinary person is to be a nobody. It is to have a negative identity. Recognition and respect are only accorded those who possess the signs and symbols of status.

Sociologist Herbert Gans described life in a community of working-class second-generation Italians in Boston, where life was largely contained within the family and the ethnic neighborhood.[32] The job in the hostile outside world provided a living, but these "urban villagers" refused to get deeply involved in a class position which brought little reward as measured in terms of freedom and dignity.

More recently, these ethnic neighborhoods have been broken up, in part by the movement of the next generation to the suburbs, in part by urban planning and renewal problems that have torn up old neighborhoods to build new highways or expensive high-rise apartments in an effort to renew the city. They no longer provide an effective haven for those who do not have the options to move into the ranks of positive identity.

So much emphasis is put upon being mobile in the United States, in going to college, getting a better job, and being a "success," that those who do not do so are made to feel inferior and a failure. Even though such people recognize that, quite objectively, the options to being mobile were not theirs, they cannot easily escape a feeling of being unworthy and responsible for their own fate. And the dominant ideology encourages that attitude.

There is then much pain for those who do not make it into the ranks of the successful. They suffer the *hidden injuries of class* so movingly described by Richard Sennett and Jonathan Cobb.[33] They bear the emotional wounds of those who can find nothing in the culture's reservoir of symbols that will lead others to accord them respect. They get less credit for their own achievements and capabilities than they deserve, but so powerful is the cultural thrust to respect only the symbols of occupational success, that they, too, have doubts about themselves.

These people whom Sennett and Cobb described so sympathetically were not the poorest and most deprived. They were "ordinary" Americans, both blue-collar and white-collar, of average income, but with no college education, thus with no serious prospects of ever being a "success." Though they are not seriously deprived materially, they are deprived of dignity and respect. This is how Sennett and Cobb describe a Greek immigrant who has become a janitor in a middle-class apartment house:

It is difficult for Ricca Kartides, even as he creates some measure of material security in his life, to feel that his quantitative gains translate into the emotional sense of independence and assuredness he wants from these material improvements. He sees himself as receiving the ultimate form of contempt from those who stand above him in society: he is a function, "Ricca the janitor," he is a part of the woodwork, even though he makes $10,000 a year, owns a home, drives a car, and has some money in the bank for his children's education. He feels vulnerable and inadequately armed, but what has he done wrong?[34]

There are many others who suffer even more from negative identities. Being poor, for example, is a negative identity in the United States. Being on welfare is even more so. Being a school "dropout" or having too little formal education is also. A nonwhite in the United States, who experiences prejudice and discrimination in daily life, knows only too well what it means to be negatively identified by others. Put in these terms, women's liberation is a struggle to create a more positive identity for women, first in their own minds, subsequently in men's.

People always try to build self-respected identities out of the only roles and memberships available to them. That was the significance of the once stable ethnic neighborhood. It provided a small world in which a person could be respected and walk among equals with dignity. The decline of these neighborhoods leaves people more than ever exposed to the judgments of high and low occupational rank as the only way to confer respect. "The creation of badges of ability requires the mass to be invisible men."[35] It becomes harder than ever to find other forms of dignity and respect.

Sennett and Cobb found that the workers they interviewed in Boston understood that their old ethnic neighborhoods were disappearing, no longer able to offer them a secure, however small, world of positive identity from which to shield themselves against the harsher judgments of American society. Now, though not by any conscious choice, they are being integrated into the larger society:

For the people we interviewed, integration into American life meant integration into a world with different symbols of human respect and courtesy, a world in which human capabilities are measured in terms profoundly alien to those that prevailed in the ethnic enclaves of their childhood. The changes in their lives mean more to them than a chance, or a failure, to acquire middle-class *things.* For them, history is challenging them and their children to become "cultured," in the intellectual's sense of the word, if they want to achieve respect in the new American terms; and toward that challenge they feel deeply ambivalent.[36]

Identity Crisis

The widespread existence of negative identities in American society, and the problems of so many ordinary citizens in establishing self-respected identities, are not, however, given much attention by sociologists. Instead, they have focused on the search for viable identities among middle-class people; it is here that the concept of *identity crisis* comes into use.

Erik Erikson first developed the concepts of identity and identity-crisis in studying the complex process of coming of age in modern society.[37] But the concern for identity came into widespread use during the 1960s as a way of analyzing the difficulties experienced by upper-middle-class youth in accepting the career-oriented identities for which a college education is essential. They did not want to join the "establishment" so readily open to them. They did not want to commit themselves to the social roles through which they were expected to pursue a rewarding adult career. They experienced an *identity crisis,* a difficulty in knowing what socially recognized identities would allow them to become the person they want to be and to live in accordance with their values.

To some extent probably most youth in modern society face an identity crisis as part of coming of age, for identities and roles must be chosen for adult life. Each generation faces new circumstances, and only a few people inherit the specific statuses of their parental generation. Most youth must choose an occupation, at least seek a job; only some get to *choose* a career.

Women and Identity   Women, too, have been struggling with the problem of their identity. The feminist movement is basically a challenge to the historic identities for women established in earlier forms of society. Many women have experienced a personal crisis in accepting the society's definition of them as persons and in the allocation to them of a set of traditional roles: wife, mother, homemaker; or occupational roles subordinate to those which men occupy.

In these cases of identity crisis, many people have undergone the pain and anxiety of wondering how they fit into society, of whether they can or should continue in the same life-roles, and of anguishing over the poor fit between their self-image and their occupational image, between the person they want to be and the roles allocated to them or within their reach.

Alienation

People who cannot readily accept their established social identities, and those who suffer the hidden injuries of class, are among the many whose relation to society is one of *alienation*. Alienation is both an objective *condition* of one's existence and a subjective *feeling* about social life.

People are in fact alienated when the humanly constructed social world, or aspects of it, is beyond the reach of their power or their understanding; when, in effect, society is a *thing* that controls them rather than the other way around. Karl Marx first made the concept of alienation a central one by brilliantly describing the alienation of the industrial worker. (See the discussion in Chapter 17.) The worker, said Marx, does not feel he belongs to his work, or that he fulfills himself as a creative human being, or that the product of his labor is his, or that in work he even belongs to himself.

The root of the concept of alienation is the word "alien," which means something strange and not belonging to one. Most social scientists have defined the concept of alienation psychologically as an attitude; a feeling of being powerless and without control over the significant forces of one's life; a feeling of not even understanding the workings of society and its institutions; and a feeling of self-estrangement, that is, of a loss of interest or involvement in such necessary activities as work or citizenship.

The best-known example of this is the work of Melvin Seeman, who developed five dimensions of alienation as psychologically experienced by the individual:[38]

1. *Powerlessness* is experienced when an individual realizes that one cannot control one's own destiny in the society to which one belongs.
2. *Meaninglessness* is experienced when the individual no longer understands events occurring in the social world, no longer knows what to believe, or no longer believes that satisfactory predictions of outcomes can be made.
3. *Normlessness* is experiencing the inability to achieve socially acceptable and desirable goals in ways acceptable in that society or in the individual's social group.
4. *Isolation* is experienced when the individual places a low value on the goals and beliefs that are most highly valued in that society.
5. *Self-estrangement* is experienced when there is a loss of pride or interest in work or other activity; these activities, no longer valued in themselves, become only necessary means (such as income) to other ends and rewards.

A sense of alienation as the experience of one or more of these feelings is not uncommon in the relation of individuals to modern society. To feel powerless and also to experience meaninglessness are a common fate for masses of people in large, complex societies with unequal classes and social power. Such societies seem neither controllable nor understandable by the political and economic modes of action available to ordinary people despite the existence of democratic institutions. (For that reason we shall later examine *political* and *economic* alienation.)

It is then that people realize how few are any such modes of action controlled by other than powerful elites, and perhaps not even by them. Then alienation is no longer an issue primarily about the *feelings* of individuals, but an issue about *conditions* in society which produce such feelings.

SUMMARY

Socialization is the process of interaction whereby the organism becomes human and acquires a nature by internalizing the culture. The *self* emerges in socialization when one learns to be conscious of oneself as a social object and to respond to oneself with approval and disapproval. Socialization requires gesture and language (communication), and *taking the role* of the other.

There is always an uncertain fit between self and society, for the inconsistent and contradictory norms of society produce *contranormative* action. The real individual is not an *oversocialized* person. Furthermore, the individual does not passively accept socialization but actively participates in it and affects it.

The family and, later, peer groups are the primary *agents of socialization. Schools* are also, and *social class* effectively differentiates socialization.

Through *role acquisition,* children internalize demands and expectations to shape the developing self; *sex roles* are a primary example.

Adults undergo continuing socialization when they are socialized to new roles in new situations. They also undergo *anticipatory socialization.*

Resocialization is a radical transformation of the person in a short period, when early socialization is forcibly abandoned and a new self emerges.

Social control relies on more than socialization and self-control. Social groups enforce norms by a variety of means, from rebuke to death. Peer groups can exercise effective control just because individuals value acceptance by their peers. Both *punishment* and *rewards* are means of social control. Powerful controls in modern life threaten individual freedom.

Individuality is a fact in modern society, but it is also a value; however, it is countered by pressures to *conform.* The *other-directed* personality type is a mode of conformity fitting the demands of bureaucratic life.

Group memberships significant to us are the source of our *identity.* Some identities are *ascribed,* some *achieved.* Negative identities are assigned to people who cannot escape disadvantaged or minority status.

Youth often face an *identity crisis,* a difficulty in knowing what combination of roles so fit their character that they can participate in society in ways that allow them to become the persons they want to become and to live in accordance with their values.

For the individual, the condition of *alienation* in modern society produces a feeling of powerlessness, meaninglessness, normlessness, isolation, and self-estrangement.

NOTES

[1] Kingsley Davis, *Human Society* (New York: Macmillan 1949), pp. 204–208.

[2] René Spitz, "Hospitalism," *The Psychoanalytic Study of the Child* 1 (1945): 53–72; "Hospitalism: A Follow-up Report," in *ibid.* 2 (1946): 113–117.

[3] See, for example, William Goldfarb, "The Effects of Early Institutional Care on Adolescent Personality, "*Child Development* 14 (1943):213–225; "Effects of Psychological Deprivation in Infancy and Subsequent Stimulation," *American Journal of Psychiatry* 102 (1945): 441–447.

[4] George Herbert Mead, *Mind, Self, and Society* (Chicago: University of Chicago Press, 1934), esp. chaps. 2 and 3.

[5] Charles Horton Cooley, *Human Nature and the Social Order* (New York: Scribner's, 1902), pp. 103–184.

[6] *Ibid.,* p. 104.

[7] Ruth Benedict, *Patterns of Culture* (Baltimore: Penguin Books, 1946), p. 232.

[8] Dennis Wrong, "The Oversocialized Conception of Man in Modern Sociology," *American Sociological Review* 26 (April 1961):183–193.

[9] For a review of the literature supporting this argument, see Judith Blake and Kingsley Davis, "Norms, Values, and Sanctions," in Robert E. L. Faris, ed., *Handbook of Modern Sociology* (Skokie, Ill.: Rand McNally, 1964), pp. 456–484.

[10] Robert K. Merton, "Social Structure and Anomie," in his *Social Theory and Social Structure,* rev. and enlgd. ed. (New York: The Free Press, 1957), pp. 131–160.

[11] Émile Durkheim, *The Rules of Sociological Method* (New York: The Free Press, 1950), p. 71.

[12] Sigmund Freud, *Civilization and Its Discontents* (New York: W. W. Norton 1961), p. 58.

[13] Charles Horton Cooley, *Social Organization* (New York: Scribner's, 1909), p. 23.

[14] Allison Davis and Robert J. Havighurst, "Social Class and Color Differences in Child-Rearing," *American Sociological Review* 11 (February 1946):31–41.

[15] Urie Bronfenbrenner, "Socialization and Social Class Through Time and Space," in E. E. Maccoby, T. M. Newcomb, and E. L Hartley, eds., *Readings in Social Psychology* (Holt, Rinehart, and Winston, 1958), p. 400.

[16] Melvin Kohn, *Class and Conformity* (Homewood, Ill.: Dorsey Press, 1969).

[17] Daniel R. Miller and Guy Swanson, *The Changing American Parent* (New York: Wiley, 1958).

[18] Jo Freeman, "The Social Construction of the Second Sex," in Scott G. McNall, ed., *The Sociological Perspective* (Boston: Little, Brown, 1977), p. 119.

[19] Roger Brown, *Social Psychology* (New York: The Free Press, 1965).

[20] Lenore J. Weitzman, Deborah Eifler, Elizabeth Hokada, and Catherine Ross, "Sex-Role Socialization in Picture Books for Preschool Children," *American Journal of Sociology* 77 (May 1972): 1125–1150.

[21] Freeman, *op. cit.,* p. 126.

[22] Irwin Deutscher, "Socialization for Postparental Life," in Arnold Rose, ed., *Human Behavior and Social Processes* (Boston: Houghton Mifflin, 1962), pp. 506–525.

[23] Sanford M. Dornbusch, "The Military Academy as an Assimilating Institution," *Social Forces* 33 (May 1955): 317.

[24] Aldous Huxley, *Brave New World* (Harper & Row, 1932).

[25] B. F. Skinner, *Walden Two* (New York: Macmillan, 1948).

[26] B. F. Skinner, *Beyond Freedom and Dignity* (New York: Knopf, 1971).

[27] Émile Durkheim, *Division of Labor in Society* (New York: The Free Press, 1947), p. 130.

[28] Alfred McClung Lee, *Multivalent Man* (New York: George Braziller, 1966), p. x.

[29] David Riesman, with Nathan Glazer and Reul Denny, *The Lonely Crowd* (New Haven, Conn.: Yale University Press, 1950).

[30] William H. Whyte, *The Organization Man* (New York: Simon and Schuster, 1956).

[31] See Robert Dubin, "Industrial Workers' Worlds: A Study of the 'Central Life Interests' of Industrial Workers," *Social Problems* 3 (1956): pp. 131–142.

[32] Herbert Gans, *The Urban Villagers: Group and Class in the Life of Italian-Americans* (New York: The Free Press, 1962).

[33] Richard Sennett and Jonathan Cobb, *The Hidden Injuries of Class* (New York: Knopf, 1972).

[34] *Ibid.,* p. 50.

[35] *Ibid.,* p. 68.

[36] *Ibid.,* p. 18.

[37] Erik Erikson, *Childhood and Society* (New York: W. W. Norton, 1950), pp. 227 ff., and "The Problem of Ego Identity," in Maurice Stein, Arthur Vidich, and David White, eds., *Identity and Anxiety* (New York: The Free Press, 1960).

[38] Melvin Seeman, "On the Meaning of Alienation," *American Sociological Review* 24 (December 1959): 783–791.

SUGGESTED READINGS

Charles Horton Cooley, *Human Nature and the Social Order* New York: Scribner's, 1902). Cooley's perceptive analysis of the "looking glass self" in socialization is found here.

Erik Erikson, *Childhood and Society* (New York: W. W. Norton, 1950). An early, still perceptive analysis of the problem of identity and identity crisis as an aspect of coming of age in modern society.

Sigmund Freud, *Civilization and Its Discontents* (New York: W. W. Norton, 1961). Freud's conception of the relation between the individual and society is here sketched out.

Aldous Huxley, *Brave New World* (Harper & Row, 1932). Still an impressive antiutopian account of biological control and thoroughgoing socialization in creating an unfree society.

George Herbert Mead, *Mind, Self, and Society* (Chicago: University of Chicago Press, 1934). Here is Mead's classic analysis of human socialization.

Jean Piaget and Barbara Inkhelder, *The Psychology of the Child* (New York: Basic Books, 1969). Piaget's theory of how a child develops cognitively is here concisely stated.

David Riesman, with Nathan Glazer and Reul Denny, *The Lonely Crowd* (New Haven, Conn.: Yale University Press, 1950). A classic interpretation of the modern person as "inner-directed."

Richard Sennett and Jonathan Cobb, *The Hidden Injuries of Class* (New York: Knopf, 1972). A sensitive analysis of how class position deprives individuals of dignity and respect.

The division of labor is found in all social groups, large and small.

there are designated differences of rank that unequally allocate rewards, prestige, and authority.

Social Controls Social groups exercise control over their members in a number of ways. As we saw in Chapter 4, members are socialized to the groups norms and values, and they internalize their own group's expectations of behavior.

But groups do not depend only on socialization, and this is more so in the larger group. Sanctions —both rewards and punishments—are invoked. Even small groups can bring strong pressure to bear on a member; ridicule and ostracism are effective as informal controls. Large organizations, in turn, reward through increased material benefits, promotion to a higher rank, while punishing by fines, demotions, and other losses for the person, and by expulsion from the group.

Membership: Belonging to a Group People in social groups are conscious of belonging together in common membership. In formally organized groups who belongs is indicated by membership rosters and appropriate insignia (cards, badges, pins, even uniform or dress). Even in small, informal groups, conferring recognition on one person as belonging and another as not belonging may by done by the way people are addressed or by the conversations in which they are included. There are always obvious ways of inclusion and exclusion in any group. No human group ever has any difficulty in letting an individual know whether or not he or she is "one of the group."

Membership in a group may be defined by rules and formal criteria, or it may simply be by an informally established consensus. In either case membership defines the social *boundaries* of the group. It establishes who belongs now, and who might belong in the future. Thus, a neighborhood club may include only those who reside in some neighborhood, but new neighbors in the future might be included, and it is even possible that the physical dimensions of the neighborhood might be redefined.

Integration and Unity   Social groups, from the smallest to the largest, persist over time only when members feel bound to the group and have reasons to belong. There is nothing to guarantee that a group will go on forever—and none ever has. When an ethnic group worries that the marriages of its youth to outsiders will weaken the group, then group members are conscious that the persistence of the group is not assured. This is also the case when a church worries that it is not reaching youth and is not recruiting enough young people into the ranks of the clergy.

Yet there are also situations in life in which the breakup of social groups is accepted as natural and inevitable, as, for example, the high school cliques that disband after graduation, and the peer groups in the army that break up with demobilization. Every family group breaks up eventually; the maturity of children and the death of parents are inevitable.

Groups persist, however, if they carry on activities that people value and need. When that is so, belonging to a group and sharing in its activities can develop a strong sense of group unity and an individual sense of loyalty to the group.

Disunity and Conflict   The unity of any group and the loyalty of its members does not happen just because it is a group. Unity exists to a greater or lesser degree; it is strong or it is weak. There are good reasons for some groups to be poorly integrated, verging on disunity, and to be in conflict. For one thing, since the members of any one group usually belong to other groups as well, no one group may command a total loyalty or a full commitment from any individual. The diversity of background found among the members of a political party, for example, might include farmers and workers, blacks and whites, city-dwellers and suburbanites, homeowners and renters, and Catholics, Protestants and Jews, all of whom have some different political goals. Such diversity makes a strong sense of unity and shared purpose harder to achieve.

Large groups often suffer a weak sense of belong-

ing among their members if they place only a utilitarian value on membership in the group. This often happens when members are the employees of a particular organization, and hold a job because they need a job, not because they value the organization. The same thing occurs when highly mobile and ambitious professionals accept employment for a time in a particular university or corporation in order to advance their personal careers and leave it as soon as a more attractive opportunity occurs.

Social groups, then, vary considerably in the degree of unity and consensus they possess. While some groups have very loyal members and are strongly unified, others are only weakly so, have a turnover of members, and may experience a great deal of internal conflict. The difficulties of disunity and conflict can be the fate of a group of any size, as witness those families that always seem to be quarreling and fighting. In fact, however, these difficulties are more likely to be the problems of large groups.

Goals   It is not particularly useful to look for the goals of a small, informal group, for goals are conscious, stated objectives to be attained by coordinating the efforts of group members. The meaning of a small peer group for its members is in the value these members find in warm, supportive social relations; no other goal or purpose is required. But goals are an important component of larger groups, especially those organized to pursue a given objective: to sell a product, win an election, or provide a service.

Groups carry on particular kinds of activities and usually agree on what these are and on how they are to go about them. But this consensus of goals and procedures is not easy to achieve, again particularly in large groups, and disagreements may bring about internal conflict. Members of a union may disagree on whether to strike; a political party is torn apart by conflict over issues of social policy; a civil rights group may fight over whether to support some particular form of legislation. Changing conditions and changing memberships bring demands for new modes of action, while old members hold to traditional goals and actions; the results can only be internal conflict.

While these components are common to all social groups, there are still significant differences among them. We now turn to an examination of the small primary group and its function in a world of large groups.

THE PRIMARY GROUP

Though the basic trend of modern life is toward the domination of social life by large organizations, small groups still remain necessary units of social life. Among the small groups found in society, the *primary group* is crucial in the understanding of social life.

As we saw in Chapter 4, Charles Horton Cooley first defined the primary group as a small intimate group within which is found the kind of social relation that permits socialization to occur. The family and the peer group of children are the obvious examples. The concept of primary group, then, gets at two things: a type of social relation and the type of group within which such a relation is sustained.

The Primary Relation

The primary relation between human beings is probably best exemplified by the idealized one between mother and child, between lovers, between the closest of friends. It is one of love, of close affectional attachment, of emotional involvement, and it is never viewed as merely something useful or as a means to get something else; instead, it is valued for its own sake.

Such a relation between individuals is necessarily *personal,* not impersonal. It is a relation between particular persons who know well and care deeply for one another. Each person is interested in the other *as a person,* not as an agent or as a role-player in social groups. The primary relation, therefore, involves the whole person in all of his or her human uniqueness.

One consequence of this is that the primary relation is *diffuse.* The relation binds two people to each other "for better or worse," as the marriage vow says, and for all dimensions of life, not just some specific one. The obligation that such caring produces is not limited in scope or in kind. In this sense it differs sharply from the inpersonal and *contractual* relation between employer and employee, whose obligations to one another are limited and specific (and often legally spelled out).

Primary-Group Characteristics

What is the kind of group that makes possible and best sustains the primary relation? There are three basic conditions for a group to be primary: small size, face-to-face interaction, and reasonably long duration.

Size A primary group must be small enough for each person to be a unique personality to one another. As a group increases in size, interaction ceases to be between whole persons, but instead is between agents and role-players. When persons cannot know each other fully, only limited and selected aspects of each self are brought into interaction with the other.

Being small, then, is a necessary condition for a group to be primary, but small size alone is not sufficient to produce the primary relation. There are many small groups that are not primary; the numerous committees that one finds in large organizations are probably the most obvious example.

Face-to-Face Interaction Almost always, primary relations depend on the close physical proximity of face-to-face interaction. Yet, like small size, such face-to-face interaction does not guarantee the relation will be primary. Face-to-face interaction occurs everyday when people ride a bus or shop in a store, yet these interactions are superficial and short-lived, not enduring or with deep meaning. Neither is likely to respond to the other as a unique person. Like size, face-to-face interaction is a necessary condition for a primary group but is not in itself sufficient.

Duration The development of primary relations in a group cannot occur when interaction is infrequent and sporadic. It must be frequent and durable. Primary relations develop among people who interact frequently over an extended period of time. The longer people interact face-to-face, the more intimately do they become related to one another; the better they know one another as whole persons, the more they become attached and emotionally involved with one another.

PEER GROUPS

One kind of primary group found widely throughout society is the *peer group.* Unlike the family, the peer group is not institutionalized by society. Instead, it emerges spontaneously from among social equals who to some extent share the same life conditions.

"Peer" means equal in status. Adolescents form peer groups, for they are equal in an age-defined status. Workers in a factory form a peer group, for they are equal in a work-defined status.

The peer group, we saw earlier, is an agent of childhood socialization. But in modern society, peer groups are important in another way. They develop within large organizations: among adolescents in school, soldiers in the army, workers in a factory, and the like. Studies of peer groups within such organizations have focused on two related problems: (1) social control and power and (2) integration.

Social Control and Group Power

The power of the peer group over the work situation was first discovered in a pioneering study by Elton Mayo and his associates at the Hawthorne plant of Western Electric.[1] In these studies, Mayo, a psychologist, interested in determining what incentives or conditions of work increased worker productivity, had been experimenting with various physical and psychological influences on the individual worker. He explored every possible influence on worker productivity and job satisfaction.

It was only after years of research that Mayo discovered that small networks of interpersonal relations —peer groups—had far more influence on work behavior than did all the other many factors he and his groups had been studying for almost a decade. The discovery of the previously unrecognized peer group changed the whole social scientific conception of the relation of the person to large organization.

Social Control   The ability of the peer group to control individual work behavior was made impressively evident by one of the Hawthorne studies, that of the Bank Wiring Room.[2] Fourteen workers were engaged in an interrelated production for which management had specified how work was assigned, how it was to be done, and at what rate. But the work group developed a spontaneous pattern of interaction, including its own norms to govern work. Workers helped one another and exchanged work assignments, even though this was forbidden. They changed considerably the pattern of work organization first imposed by management.

Most important of all, the peer group developed a consensus about output of work; each worker was then governed by the group's norms, not management's. These norms allowed less output than man-

agement wanted; from management's point of view, therefore, the peer group was responsible for restricting output.

Furthermore, the group was very effective in handling the individual who was tempted to stray from the norms of the group and increase his output. In this study, as in many other factory studies, the "rate-busting" worker met the hostility of the group. By ridicule, harassment, ostracism, and even physical violence, they brought the individual into compliance with the group's standards.

On their own group initiative, then, workers will restrict output by setting their own production norms and will also quite effectively control one another. Nor can such group restrictions be easily seduced by managerial efforts to provide individual inducements and rewards for maximizing individual effort. Such inducements as piecework, bonus payments, and the like have encountered serious resistance among workers, who will not allow production standards to exceed what they regard as a "fair day's work," if they can help it.

(Whether they can help it is often a matter of the degree of supervision imposed by management, the way work is organized, and even by the nature of the prevailing technology. The production line in automobile and other forms of manufacturing, for example, allows management to control the levels of productivity by regulating the speed at which the line moves. Yet even here workers resist what they regard as "speedup," an issue that has on more than one occasion produced a militant form of peer-group response, that of the unauthorized work stoppage—the "wildcat" strike.)

Group Power as Worker Control   To see group-imposed norms controlling production only as restriction of output is to accept a managerial interpretation, not a sociological one. Equal emphasis must be given to the fact that these work groups emerge naturally and spontaneously among those who share the same life situation and environmental conditions—in this case, workers in a factory—and that work restriction is a collective and cooperative effort to achieve a level of control over the circumstances of the job, something that could not be done by the individual alone.

By imposing their own standards, workers are seeking some small expression of group power in behalf of their own interests—as they conceive them. Their peer group is an emergent adaptation to the circumstances of being fully controlled on the job. Without the intervening peer group, the individual stands alone within the larger organization; isolated individuals are unable to resist organizational demands as effectively as they can when they are part of a group.

Integration

When first becoming part of a large organization, the individual often feels alone and insecure—a stranger, uncertain about everything. New college students and newly drafted soldiers, for example, can feel homesick even when surrounded by many others. Being lonely is a *social* and *psychic,* not a physical, state of affairs.

But if a peer group takes the new person in and "shows him or her the ropes," the entrant learns the way around and soon feels more "at home." The transition to new roles in a new group is eased. For college students or soldiers the feeling of homesickness abates as new primary relations integrate them into the organization.

But if such primary relations do not develop, if the individual, by choice or not, is a "loner," then his or her performance is likely to be poorer than that of others and personal well-being will suffer. Such persons often suffer a sense of personal disorientation that may very well produce emotional disturbances. It may also lead to withdrawal from the organization, to quitting college, or to going AWOL in the armed services. At worst, it can lead to violent conduct against others or against self—suicide.

This is what Durkheim told us about integration in his great study, *Suicide.* When people are integrated into a group, it sustains them against personal troubles. When not, they suffer in some way. In modern society—where most groups are large, impersonal, and poorly integrated in any normative sense—peer and other primary groups are essential for this integrating and sustaining function.

Peer Groups in War   When the peer group integrates the individual into the larger organization, it then is not opposing that organization but is functioning to support it. And large organizations may not be able to operate effectively if they lack such peer-group support.

A series of studies on American, German, and Soviet soldiers during World War II provided evidence for such a sociological argument.[3] The emergence of a set of primary relations among conscripted soldiers served, however unintentionally, to tie the individual soldier into the larger military structure and to sustain him in the face of difficult demands for soldierly performance. The existence of satisfactory primary relations with peers, in fact, was basic to soldier's being able to act effectively in combat and to withstand the strains and stresses brought on by fatigue and danger.

Both American and German soldiers were subjected to a great deal of propaganda about the aims of the war for their respective nations, the meaning of the conflict, and the idea of great causes at stake. Yet not such propaganda, but a sense of loyalty and obligation to a few others with whom they shared hardship and danger was the decisive influence on them. Furthermore, the primary relationship of comradeship was more important to individual morale than all the efforts to convince conscripted soldiers about the national and international importance of what they were doing.

In fact, the German army fought effectively and seemed to maintain combat morale until the very end, despite American efforts at psychological warfare intended to weaken their resolve to fight on, particularly when the war was obviously going against them. Like his American counterpart, the German soldier was bound into primary ties of enduring comradeship, and his loyalty held him to the task of combat and sustained his morale.[4]

It was much the same with Soviet soldiers. Their ability to endure combat, according to Edward Shils, "drew relatively little sustenance from any attachment to the central political and ideological symbols of the society in which they lived."[5] Instead, support came from other sources, of which one was "the morale of the small unit, i.e., the mutual support given by members of the group to each other . . ."[6] (See "Primary Groups in the Vietnam War.")

These studies of men in combat are striking examples of the importance of the primary group for sustaining the individual and providing emotional support and security. But the lessons hold true in all large organizations and in circumstances less personally threatening than those of combat.

Peer Groups and Subcultures

When peer groups develop among enlisted men in the army, among workers in a factory, among blacks in the urban ghetto, or among students in the university (to take a few examples from many possibilities), this larger body of peers provides an extended net-

PRIMARY GROUPS IN THE VIETNAM WAR

The idea that primary relations are essential to maintain morale among combat soldiers in war was developed by observations during World War II. However, an American sociologist, Charles C. Moskos, Jr., spent a lot of time with front-line combat soldiers during the Vietnam War, and his observations led him to doubt that primary groups were as significant as had been claimed.*

In a war in which soldiers' morale was particularly difficult to sustain, Moskos argued for the significance of three basic issues: the Army's system of rotation; the necessary and pragmatic value of primary relations; and a latent ideology.

Rotation

Begun during the earlier Korean War, the rotation system was one which asked a soldier to serve a specific, limited time in an overseas assignment, after which he was rotated out and back to the United States. During the period Moskos was observing soldiers in the Vietnam combat, the period for rotation was one year. Few men in a unit had the same rotation schedule.

As Moskos noted:

The rigid turnover of personnel hinders the development of primary relations, even as it rotates out of the unit men who have attained fighting experience.

. . . Overall, the rotation system reinforces a perspective which is essentially private and self-concerned.

Moskos, in fact, attributed to the rotation system the most important influence in hindering primary relations among combat soldiers:

If substantive differences do exist, particularly between World War II and the wars in Korea and Vietnam, much of the variation could be accounted for by the disruptive effects on unit solidarity caused by the introduction of the rotation system in the latter two wars.

The Value of Primary Relations

Despite the disintegrative effect of rotation on group solidarity, primary relations among combat soldiers do exist and are basic to their ability to perform well. But Moskos interpreted primary relations as existing only because they had survival value for the individual soldier:

. . . The fact is that if the individual soldier is realistically to improve his survival chances, he must *necessarily* develop and take part in primary relationships. Under the grim conditions of ground warfare, an individual's survival is directly dependent upon the support—moral, physical, and technical—he can expect from his fellow soldiers. He gets support to the degree that he reciprocates to the others in his unit. In other words, primary relations are at their core mutually pragmatic efforts to minimize personal risks.

Latent Ideology

Moskos also quarreled with the idea that no ideological commitment was a motivating influence on the soldier. Vietnam soldiers, even as soldiers in previous wars, refused to take seriously the official ideology for being in Vietnam, and, furthermore, expressed contempt and hatred for Vietnam, the Vietnamese people, and especially the Vietnamese army.

Yet, Moskos asserts,

Primary groups maintain the soldier in his combat role only when he has an underlying commitment to the worth of the larger social system for which he is fighting.

Although soldiers did not express patriotic sentiments, they nonetheless, Moskos insists, believed "in the legitimacy, and even superiority, of the American way of life."

When Moskos interviewed front-line soldiers, he found that most of them (twenty-two out of thirty-four) emphasized the material comforts to be found in the United States: paying jobs, automobiles, consumer goods and leisure activities.

Put in another way, it is the materialistic—and I do not use the term pejoratively—aspects of life in America that are most salient to combat soldiers.

Notes

* Charles C. Moskos, Jr., "Why Men Fight," *Trans-action* 7 (November 1969): pp. 13–23.

work of peer relations. Among such peers there is a shared sense of sympathy over common status and common problems and also a "grapevine," a communication network that allows for a wider sharing of norms and information.

The sense of "we" that so closely identifies one peer with another, and which Cooley regarded as an indicator of the primary group, flows out from the smaller and more intimate peer group to the larger network of peer relations. If the relationships of this larger network cannot be so intimate, or even face-to-face, they develop, nevertheless, in a perspective of sympathy and identification ("they're people like us"). This, in turn, enables individuals to view them as extensions of their primary relations, as interactions with others who share the same fate and life circumstances. In the past, neighborhoods and communities were just such larger and somewhat more extended "we-groups," more primary than secondary, even though all persons in them could not engage in face-to-face interaction.

But neighborhoods and communities in modern society are not usually extended we-groups. They can be in some instances, and the stable ethnic neighborhood, where it still exists, is a good example. Such were the "urban villagers" that Herbert Gans discovered: an Italian neighborhood of second-generation working-class people.[7] Here was a subculture both ethnic and working class, providing the interaction network from which peer groups emerged. Each peer group was formed from among people who shared the same values. Social class and ethnicity combined to be a major source of identity formation, and also to provide a subcultural basis for peer groups.

The peer relations that people often cannot find any longer in neighborhood or community may be found in shared status in large organizations. This is true of soldiers in the army, students in college, workers in a factory. In the same way the sense of having "brothers" and "sisters" develops among members of ethnic and racial groups, or social classes, when social movements emerge within their ranks.

Peer Groups and Adolescence

The importance of peer groups in relating individuals to society is vividly evident when we examine the status of adolescents. Adolescence is an uncertain and insecure status found only in modern society, where preparing for adulthood is lengthened, partly by the demand for longer years of education, partly because an advanced technology does not need the young coming into the labor force at an early age.

In their extended and uneasy transition to adulthood, adolescents find in primary relations among peers a sympathetic context for ready acceptance of one another and for a sympathetic sharing of the problems of growing up. Their peer groups, as we saw earlier, are agents for a continuing socialization over the prolonged gap from childhood to adulthood, modifying and sometimes contradicting socialization by the family.

Through peer groups the adolescent discovers a way to come to grips with the larger society, to resist and challenge it, even rebel against it. This would not be possible for the individual alone. The sustaining support of peers and the emotional ties of primary groups are necessary elements in generating an adolescent subculture.[8]

Peer Groups and Resistance

Peer groups among adolescents in school and among workers in a factory have this in common: each reveals a subculture of *resistance* to the official authority and work standards of the organization in which they are lowest in status and power. In each case the peer group is the core element in generating a perspective that expresses the meaning of being in subordinate status in a situation over which the individual has little control.

It is by a network of peer relations that subordinate persons in large organizations can take back some control over their own life circumstances. Workers will impose their own production norms and will restrict output to less than management wants, as we have seen. Adolescents, in turn, find means for having adult-forbidden experiences (sex, alcohol, and smoking, for example), for resisting the work and study values that are official for the school, and for developing a set of their own values centering around personality development and identity-formation. In the process they often create styles and fads that repel and bewilder adults.

The Importance of Peer Groups

It should not be thought, however, that all peer groups are created under conditions of subordination and so become agents of resistance. Peer groups exist among all segments of, and at all levels in, society. That is so because peer groups perform a number of basic functions in society.

We can sum up our own analysis of peer groups by noting that peer groups *socialize* the individual from childhood on, including adolescent socialization, and the continuing socialization of adulthood; *integrate* the otherwise isolated individual into the larger group—its morale and unity depend on this; and *enable* those of lower status and power to develop a *subculture of resistance* to authority and power and to gain some limited *control over their life conditions*.

In the basic trend from small to large organization the function of the peer group takes on a particular significance in relating the individual to the ever-enlarging society. It becomes increasingly an agent for adult socialization and a means for integrating the person into the large, impersonal structure. But equally important, it becomes a means for acting effectively against established power, a source of resistance and self-control, without which the dominating control of large organization over the individual would go unchallenged.

SMALL GROUPS WITHIN LARGE GROUPS

Significant as peer groups are, they are not the only small groups to be found within large ones. There are also those small groups that are deliberately created by large organizations as an efficient means to carry out some important activity. When organizations grow large, there is always some delegation of task and authority to small units: committees, boards, panels, juries, and the like.

These task groups are often involved in *making decisions*: they decide among alternatives, make or at least recommend policy, choose candidates or applicants, or in some other fashion decide among a range

The working committee within large-scale organization is now the common form of the small group.

of possible choices or actions for the larger organization. They are thus crucial components of the larger organization, yet they are in themselves quite small groups.

Observing how a small task group makes its decisions is exceptionally difficult to do, for only rarely can a social scientist share in the process or even observe what goes on. As a result, social scientists have substituted the study of small groups under laboratory conditions. Their primary interest has been in the *forms* rather than the *content* of social interaction; that is, in *how* the group interacts, not in what it interacts about. Though such study of small groups is recent—practically all research comes after 1950—Georg Simmel suggested its value more than fifty years ago.

Small Groups in the Laboratory

Research on small groups under carefully controlled laboratory conditions began in American sociology in the 1940s. In 1947 Robert Bales and his associates at Harvard University began an influential series of experiments on how people interact in small group situations.[9] Each group was given a task to carry out, consisting of a set of facts about a problematic situation and a request to review the facts and make a recommendation for action.

Bales and his associates worked out a set of categories for observing the interaction, distinguishing between remarks that elicited responses, responses to these remarks, whether they were positive or negative, or whether they were questions or suggestions. (Note that they were only interested in how the interaction went on, not in what it was about.)

A further breakdown of these observations produced twelve interaction categories:

A.	Positive reactions	Shows solidarity
		Shows tension release
		Shows agreement
B.	Problem-solving attempts	Gives suggestion
		Gives opinion
		Gives orientation
C.	Questions	Asks orientation
		Asks opinion
		Asks suggestion
D.	Negative reactions	Shows disagreement
		Shows tension increase
		Shows antagonism

Instead of the common conception of a small group as consisting of a leader and several followers, Bales and his associates developed the conception of two complementary leaders: an *idea person,* who initiates problem-solving attempts but who also disagrees more with others and shows more antagonsim to others, and a *best-liked* person who offers responses that are positive. Such a person as the latter is supportive, and makes humorous remarks that release group tension. The best-liked person also asks more questions.

These, then, are two complementary roles. The *idea* person concentrates more on the task at hand

and is more aggressive, while the best-liked person concentrates more on the social-emotional problems in the group's interactions and plays a more passive and consensus-seeking role.

The researchers discovered, moreover, that there were high participators who talked a lot and were primarily problem-solvers, while *low* participants specialized in positive or negative responses or questions; this latter category included the well liked. The researchers furthermore found it useful to distinguish between those who were high in activity—they talked a lot —but were not contributing much to problem-solving. They were using the situation to achieve prominence in the group, but the group usually recognized the difference between them and the real problem-solvers.

On the basis of this, Bales suggests five types of roles in small groups:

1. The *good leader,* the rare type who is both well liked and a problem-solver.
2. The *task specialist* who is high on activity and task ability, but who is less well liked.
3. The *social specialist* who is well liked, but ranked less high on activity and task ability.
4. The *overactive deviant* who is high on activity, but relatively low on task ability and likability.
5. The *underactive deviant* who is low on activity and problem-solving and not well liked.

The Range and Limit of Small Group Studies

This innovative work by Bales and his associates set the stage for many different studies of small groups that illuminate the nature and consequence of social interaction.[10] Many of these studies were particularly concerned with the functions of small groups in large organizations.

Valuable as these studies have been, however, and rich and suggestive in their findings, there are still serious limitations on the controlled study of small groups under experimental conditions. In many such studies the groups are together only for a short time, have come together for only the research purpose, and the task itself is of no consequence to the individuals involved. There is no set of shared understandings built

up over time among the participants, and there are no binding commitments and ties. Thus, artificial and real groups differ in ways that limit the scope and significance of small-group research.

In large organizations small groups often make decisions that have consequences for the organization as a whole, as well as for the individuals and the subgroups within it. The meetings of a small group, then, can be an arena of struggle for contending factions with different objectives, and for individuals whose career aspirations may be at stake. Often there is a *hidden agenda* of covert objectives that shapes the character of the social interaction that goes on. Furthermore, the ability to control the appointment of individuals to task-oriented small groups within large organizations is one index of power within that structure. Laboratory studies can only with difficulty tap these aspects, if at all.

The Significance of Small Groups Despite the steadily increasing size of social groups, small groups remain a basic feature of modern society. Yet the significance of small groups has been altered and redefined by the persistent increase in the scale of social organization. Indeed, the importance of the peer group, we saw, is largely in terms of its capacity to *integrate* the individual into a larger organization, or to enable the individual to *resist* being integrated and fully controlled. Small groups such as committees, in turn, are necessary units for the efficient functioning of all large organizations.

THE CONSEQUENCES OF THE BASIC TREND

At one time the normal activities of everyday life were carried on within the localized and usually more personal relations that the small scale of organization made possible. Much of this is now a thing of the past. While a lot of the social interaction that goes on everyday still occurs in small groups, there are differences.

A second and related difference is that the small, local group is now often a unit within a larger one. The local social security office, the corner gas station, the neighborhood supermarket, the nearby American Legion post, the headquarters of a local union—these

The small corner store and the large supermarket are together one example of the basic trend from small to large organization.

are but a few examples of what is a dominant feature of modern life: that the small groups of the immediate environment, wherein the routines of everyday life go on, are no longer separate and independent groups, but instead are units of large, controlling organizations, often nationwide in scope.

One difference is that the small groups of the past have often grown into or been replaced by larger ones. The mom-and-pop corner grocery has given way to the supermarket; the small firm of fifty or so employees has moved into a new plant housing ten to one hundred times as many people under one roof; the local dry-goods store has grown into the modern department store. Even at the local level the scale of social organization has grown.

These differences do not mean only that social groups have expanded to include more people. They also have more units and divisions—they are more complex in structure—and cover a wider geographical area. That is what is meant by the basic trend from small to large organization.

Sources of the Basic Trend

There is nothing new or recent about this trend from small to large social groups; it has been a feature of modern society since the onset of the Industrial Revolution. Furthermore, even though modern society has been developing in form and character for almost two centuries, and its distinctive features have been recognized and analyzed throughout the twentieth century, the trend continues unabated.

But what produces such a basic trend? There are three historic and closely interrelated factors that account for it:

1. *Industrialization.* The revolution in the reshaping of society we have learned to call the Industrial Revolution began with the introduction of industry technology, the reorganization of work into larger units to accommodate to those new techniques, and the recruitment of workers from among agricultural people. Like the agricultural revolution of some six thousand years ago, the industrialization of society again set in motion the organization of larger social units of human population: this time factories instead of small shops, cities instead of villages, and more of the *nation-building* process already under way in Europe.

2. *Urbanization.* The growth of urban populations has always accompanied industrialization. Cities grow to immense size, concentrating great numbers of people at one geographical locality. The familiar experience of living in a small community of people like oneself, with whom one interacted daily on a personal basis, gave way to a process of living in close proximity to strangers, with whom interaction could only be impersonal.

3. *The Rise of the Nation-State.* The nation is a political structure that unites populations larger than the tribal and village structures of the past, breaks down local barriers to trade and commercial development, and integrates a population under a central government. Indeed, a modern society is by definition a *national* society.

This transformation of society by industrialization, urbanization, and nation-building into a form we now call "modern" continues into the present; it is not yet a completed chapter in human history. The basic trend from small to large organization is a continuing feature of that transformation. From it, in turn, there are inevitable consequences for the structure of social life. Many of these consequences will be examined in the remaining chapters, as they bear upon specific aspects of society, but there are several broad and encompassing ones which deserve our considered attention here, in order to more fully comprehend the sociological significance of the basic trend.

The Decline of Local Autonomy

As social groups enlarge and become more complex, they seek a greater control over all the activities carried on within their boundaries. The result is increasing centralization and concentration of power at the top. Large social groups pull control over resources and over the organization of people away from small, local groups. There is a flow of resources and power upward that diminishes the local autonomy and independence that once was at least a partial reality.

For over fifty years now American sociologists have been exploring the effect of industrialization and urbanization on community life in the United States. In reviewing such classic studies as Robert Park's pioneering exploration of city life in Chicago, Robert and Helen Lynd's analysis of how industrialization reshaped a small midwestern city (Muncie, Indiana), and William Lloyd Warner's study of the effect of corporate ownership over local factories in Yankee City, a New England town, sociologist Maurice Stein notes that:

> There is one underlying community trend to which all three of the studies refer. That is a trend toward increased interdependence and decreased local autonomy. Park referred to the process as urban or metropolitan dominance. . . . Lynd noted the parallel phenomenon of dominance by centers of technological diffusion so that Muncie came to depend increasingly on Hollywood and New York for its entertainment, as it did on Detroit for industrial advance in the automotive plant. Warner dealt with this specifically in his discussion of the impact of absentee ownership, by which Yankee City shoe factories became the lowest echelon in a chain of command reaching upward to New York City.[11]

Yet large numbers of Americans have kept alive the idea that small town and rural life still is a self-governed, autonomous way of life, a grass-roots democracy, and a haven of true individualism. Sociologists Arthur J. Vidich and Joseph Bensman made a detailed study of one small, rural town in upper New York state to put just such ideas to the test.[12] They discovered that the residents of Springdale do, indeed, believe that their small town is superior to city life, a place where traditional moral values are lived up to among neighborly "folk" who know and appreciate each other as persons, and who use the designations "friend" and "neighbor" when speaking of others in the town.

But the reality is something else, and Springdalers know it and are thus ambivalent about the larger society. They respect the great institutions of American society and take pride in its military might and industrial productivity. They also know that urban and metropolitan society is technically and culturally superior:

> . . . almost everyone goes to the city for shopping or entertainment; large numbers of people are dependent on the radio and television; . . . Springdalers clearly realize how much of local life is based on the modern techniques, equipment and products which originate in distant places.[13]

What Springdalers realize less fully, however, is how much they have lost political independence. The reality is what Vidich and Bensman call a "political surrender"—an acceptance of political decision-making at more distant centers of government. Springdale has entered a state of dependence in relation to distant government:

> As a consequence of this pattern of dependence, many important decisions are made for Springdale by outside agencies. Decisions which are made locally tend to consist of approving the requirements of administrative or state laws. In short, the program and policies of local political bodies are determined largely by acceptance of grants-in-aid offered them—i.e., in order to get the subsidy specific types of decision must be made—and by facilities and services made available to them by outside sources.[14]

What Vidich and Bensman document so fully about one small town is no less true for larger ones, even great cities. When resources and power flow from the local level upward, the dependency of local units on distant centers for a share of resources reduces their capacity for independent action. This is also true of social organizations besides communities —school systems, labor unions, political parties, corporations, churches, civic organizations, charities, and universities. When there is a decline of local autonomy, people develop a reduced sense that they can control the decisions which shape everyday life.

The Impersonalization of Social Interaction

Increasingly the interaction that occurs in everyday life is no longer between peers, or between people who know each other well, but among persons who interact impersonally and who are agents of some larger system. As employees, customers, sales clerks, and the like, we interact with a large body of people we do not know personally. While personal relations of the primary-group kind remain significant in modern life, they have gradually been removed from many spheres of daily interaction, to be replaced by impersonal relations.

In the effort to account for impersonalization of social interaction, social scientists have focused on two contrasting aspects of contemporary social life: the city and the bureaucracy.

The City: Strangers in our Midst The sheer quantitative increase in people gathered within the limits of a city produces a qualitative change: the city becomes composed of people who are largely strangers to one another; it is then an arena of impersonal relationships.

In his renowned essay, "The Metropolis and Mental Life" (1918), the German sociologist, Georg Simmel, elaborated the psychic and interpersonal consequences of this for the urban dweller.[15] The sheer variety and constantly changing environment of the city presses upon the city dweller a constant barrage of stimuli and impressions. Each one cannot be responded to seriously or with full attention, nor can each one arouse excitement and surprise, else social life would be chaotic and the individual would be mentally and emotionally exhausted. It is as protection, then, from such disturbances to one's capacity to function daily, that the city dweller adopts a protective attitude, one which, Simmel says, places the head before the heart, lessening the likelihood of responding emotionally. The metropolitan dweller is therefore *blasé, indifferent,* and *reserved:*

This mental attitude of metropolitans toward one another we may designate, from a formal point of view, as

reserve. . . . As a result of this reserve we frequently do not even know by sight those who have been our neighbors for years. And it is this reserve which in the eyes of small-town people makes us appear to be cold and heartless. Indeed, if I do not deceive myself, the inner aspect of this outer reserve is not only indifference but, more often than we are aware, it is a slight aversion, a mutual strangeness and repulsion, which will break into hatred and fight at the moment of a closer contact, however caused.[16]

The Bureaucratization of Social Life When social groups increase in size in the modern world, they become more *bureaucratic.* We will explore in a later chapter what that means; here we need only to note that large organizations create a body of specialized roles, each with a specific, often narrowly defined function, and ranked below one another in degrees of authority. All of this is directed by an administrative staff whose task is the control and coordination of the entire organization. In a bureaucracy, relationships are intentionally designed to be impersonal, for personal feelings must not prevent the social actors from interacting effectively with others in the organization in carrying out their assigned tasks.

Large-scale organizations match increased size and scope of organization with increased hierarchy and power. There are more ranks within the organization, more levels of authority and decision-making further removed from the levels below. Authority, therefore, is not only more concentrated, it is more remote and impersonal for most persons. "They" decide—and nobody is sure who "they" are. Decisions come down, not under the signature of a known person, but under the imprimatur of "management" or "administration."

The city and bureaucracy, then, are different environments, but they are the environments of residence and work common to most modern people. Each in its own way produces an impersonalized human existence to an extent unimagined a century ago.

The Loss of Community

With bureaucratization and increased size comes a decline in the traditional small groups that once organized everyday life. What also declines, however, is the loyalty and commitment to the group that often marked social relations in these traditional groups, as well as the unity of a traditional culture. Large, imper-

Large-scale organization brings about bureaucratic and impersonal processing of people.

sonal groups are not "family" or "community," and they cannot easily pretend to be.

As a consequence, people are often only loosely connected to large organizations. Their relation is not rooted in an inherited status and moral obligation; instead, it is contractual and instrumental—limited in obligation and seen as useful (a job; a customer), but not a moral commitment. Bureaucracies, in short, are not causes for which people readily make sacrifice.

But society, too, is affected by this decline in moral obligation. Émile Durkheim sought to analyze this condition as being a consequence of modern society's division of labor. The increasing specialization of roles, he felt, provided people with different experiences and ways of living, and this leads inevitably to individualism. But that also makes more difficult the maintenance of common bonds, the very sense of belonging together and of sharing common norms. The result is *anomie,* Durkheim's term for a condition in which social norms no longer effectively control individual be-

havior and there is no effective social regulation. It then produces the worst aspect of individualism, what today we would recognize by such a phrase as "looking out for number one."

To stress the decline of moral obligations and social regulation in modern society is one approach. Another is to emphasize that such a society, as a product of specialization and increased size, is increasingly remote and abstract from the perspective of individual experience. According to sociologist Anton C. Zijdervald, societies become more abstract as they increase in size:

If a rural community modernizes and grows into a big industrial metropolis, it will become abstract. Face-to-face relationships will shrink into a few friendships based on the individualistic principle of privacy and difficult to maintain because of social and geographic mobility. For the rest, they will be replaced by anonymous roles imposed on man by a rationally organized society in which efficiency rates higher than the human dimensions of life.[17]

Society becomes an abstract entity, from Zijdervald's perspective, when the individual confronts it as "the system" or "the establishment," that vaguely defined "they" who decide at remote levels beyond that of the individual's concrete, daily experience. When its coercive controls reach down into anyone's personal life, however, then society is concrete; "but it evaporates into an awareness of loss of meaning, reality, and freedom when modern man tries to keep this coercion under control and evade the sense of absurdity and inauthenticity."[18]

The abstract, remote nature of modern society, according to Zijdervald, produces a constant protest; people seek to bring a personal, moral meaning back into their lives in an immediate, concrete way. The counterculture we described in Chapter 3 is one vivid example of such a protest, as is the effort at decentralized neighborhood control in large cities (see Chapter 8). The new religious movements, which have been so appealing to some middle-class American youth, providing them with a personal meaning for their existence that they could not find otherwise, is also evidence of this protest against a remote, abstract society, lacking any meaning but rational efficiency, no longer possessing the moral bonds that unite people in a concrete, immediate communal existence shared and understood at the immediate interpersonal level of life (see Chapter 15).

Judging the Basic Trend To emphasize that the basic trend from small to large groups has these three consequences—the decline of local autonomy, the impersonalization of social interaction, and the loss of community—creates at first glance an image of modern society that is largely negative. Our analysis seems to have forced us into an implied value-judgment *against* the trend from small to large. Is that justified? The consequences of the trend are real enough, but the value problem posed for us is much more difficult to assess.

From Small to Large Groups: The Value Problem

Small towns are supposed to be warm and friendly, big cities cold and impersonal. Such a myth still flourishes today even as it has over the past century. According to such a myth, the growth of large and impersonal groups is viewed as dwarfing the individual and thus subverting individuality. Conformity and the stifling of creativity are widely viewed as the inevitable outcome of the eventual dominance of society by bureaucratic structures.

Yet such a perspective distorts what we know sociologically about the significance of size in social groups for the individual and for society. To speak of the warmth and personal relations of the small community is to stress but one side of the coin.

The small community or any other small human group also exerts greater social control and "invades" the personality to a much greater extent. The small group exposes the private individual to the others; the more intimate the relationship, the less there is that is secret or entirely a private matter. The more people know about what we think and feel, the greater is the pressure to think and feel as they do.

The greater formality and impersonality of secondary (that is, *not* primary) relations protect persons against an invasion by others of the privacy of their thoughts and feelings. Role-playing in a complex society may very well mean that we don "masks" behind which our genuine selves are concealed. But this also serves to protect these intimate feelings from an exposure that might bring attack if they are deviant from the group's perspective. The problem of human individuality and group size, then, is much more complicated than the oversimplified generalization that bigness in organization threatens individuality.

If the relation between group size and individuality is complex, no less so is the relation between group size and other social values. An increase in the scope of organization, in fact, promotes some other social values, among which are diversity, personal freedom, greater choice and opportunity, as well as organizational efficiency and effectiveness. Greater productivity and higher standards of living, so essential for choice and opportunity, are based upon organizational efficiency. Even impersonality has its functional value; for a larger number of people to interact efficiently in accomplishing some useful task requires some degree of impersonality.

At the same time, as we have seen, an increase in size tends to concentrate power in the hands of fewer persons at the top and to reduce local autonomy. Within social groups, furthermore, increased size leads to bureaucratization. In both cases large groups take control of a greater share of resources and develop the power to organize large aggregates of people and make far-reaching decisions. Even as they are increasingly removed from the level of everyday life, their actions nonetheless dominate the basic processes of a society.

There is a paradox, then, in the contrast between the small and the large in human groups, between the primary and the secondary. Although a world without the primary would be cold and humanly unbearable, a world that is only primary would seem small and confining to any person expecting to exercise the individual choice and personal freedom so prized in modern society. It is part of the historic record that we became freer and more individualistic when societal development "liberated" some individuals from the small and confining world of kinship and village. Cities have always been more diverse and freer than small, traditional villages. Yet that same process has created a bureaucratization of life and a concentration of power that now seem to threaten not only individuality, but the capacity of people in small, local groups to make decisions and control the pattern of their lives.

The Emerging Global Structure

The trend from small to large which we have been describing is defined as one from the small community to the nation-state, from local groups to national ones. Until recently it made sense, sociologically, to see the trend in such terms, but no longer. The last half of the twentieth century, at least, has been a period of developing *global* structures: *a world system* is emerging beyond the level of national systems.

The basic trend does not stop at national boundaries, but extends beyond them into larger regions. Economic regions organized cooperatively, such as Europe's Common Market, or consortiums of nations producing for a world market, such as OPEC, or the multinational corporations producing and distributing goods for world markets, not national ones, are each an example of how this new trend is reaching beyond national boundaries and creating new social processes, new bases of concentrated power, new forms of control over resources that are then not controllable at the national level.

Such a system is developing in economic organization well before it has done so in political organization, and that produces problems. Yet that is not a deterrent to the global structure's coming into being. World market systems organized by multinational corporations, in partnership with the larger industrialized nations of the capitalist world, are altering the social and cultural patterns of most peoples and nations. A new order of

world dimension is on the horizon, bringing into being new social forms even larger and more remote from the patterns of everyday life. And it will also bring new forms of social conflict, new forces for social change.

A Final Note   From small to large group is an unmistakable and perhaps irreversible trend in modern society. The consequences of this trend are many, and we have briefly described several of them. These consequences are more than a *quantitative* change, as measured by numbers of people in groups; they are also *qualitative* changes in social interaction and in social groups.

Such qualitative changes have consequences for the lives of all of us on the planet Earth, given that these are global trends. Scholars, political leaders, scientists, journalists, and social critics have added one voice to another in trying to make some assessment of what is good or bad about these changes, and especially of what values are gained or lost in the transition to some new pattern of social relations.

Sociology can contribute to that assessment by a sober and objective analysis of modern society, its institutions and class structure, its population characteristics and trends, as well as the social issues which create efforts at social change. Such an analysis will be the concern of the remaining chapters.

McDonald's on the Ginza in Tokyo—a striking example of the global trend in mass consumption and the consumer culture.

SUMMARY

The basic trend is from small groups to large ones in the modern world. Larger groups tend also to command a greater share of resources, possess more power, and dominate the basic activities of society even as they become remote from everyday life.

A *group* is a plurality of persons sharing a common pattern of interaction. Its *basic components* are: roles and norms; division of labor; social controls; membership; integration; and (sometimes) goals.

The *primary* group is small, with face-to-face interaction, and of reasonably long duration. It makes possible the *primary relation,* which is a close, personal one and is of value for its own sake. Family and peer groups are the most notable cases of primary groups.

The *peer* group—a primary group of social equals—is significant for its functions for the larger society. These are: effective *social control* of individual conduct; *socialization* of the individual from childhood on, including adolescent socialization and the continuing socialization of adults; *integration* of the otherwise isolated individual into the larger group—its morale and unity depend on this; and enabling those of lower status and power to develop a *subculture of resistance* to authority and power and to gain some *limited control over their life-conditions.*

Within large organizations small groups are necessary units for carrying out delegated tasks. The study of these groups under laboratory conditions has focused on how people interact to solve problems and accomplish tasks, dividing labor between *task specialists* and *social specialists.*

The basic trend now means that *many of the small groups of everyday life are often units of larger organizations, no longer separate and independent.* Even those that are have become much larger.

The major consequences of the trend for modern society are: the *decline of local autonomy,* as larger groups concentrate power at the top and remove from the local level the capacity for independent action; the *impersonalization of social interaction,* particularly through the concentration of people in the city and the bureaucratization of social life; and the *loss of community,* which means that people are no longer as closely attached and as loyal and committed to their social groups, but view their participation as limited in obligation and instrumental (useful for another purpose, like a job).

Small groups are idealized over large ones, which distorts a complex *value problem.* Small groups tend to be warm and personal, yet often more controlling. Large groups are more impersonal and concentrate power at the top, yet they create conditions for greater personal freedom and individuality.

The basic trend from small to large group now extends beyond the nation-state; there is now an emerging *global structure.*

NOTES

[1] See Fritz Roethlisberger and William J. Dickson, *Management and the Worker* (Cambridge, Mass.: Harvard University Press, 1947).

[2] *Ibid.,* Part IV.

[3] Samuel A. Stouffer and others, *The American Soldier: Combat and its Aftermath,* Studies in Social Psychology in World War II (Princeton, N.J.: Princeton University Press, 1949), vol. II. See also Edward A. Shils, "Primary Groups in the American Army," in Robert K. Merton and Paul F. Lazarsfeld, eds., *Continuities in Social Research: Studies in the Scope and Method of "The American Soldier"* (New York: The Free Press, 1950), pp. 16–39.

[4] Edward A. Shils and Morris Janowitz, "Cohesion and Disintegration of the Wehrmacht in World War II," *Public Opinion Quarterly* 12 (1948): 280–315.

[5] Edward Shils, "Primordial, Personal, Sacred, and Civil Ties," *The British Journal of Sociology* 8 (June 1957): 141.

[6] *Ibid.,* p. 141.

[7] Herbert Gans, *The Urban Villagers: Group and Class in the Life of Italian-Americans* (New York: The Free Press, 1962).

[8] For a study of the importance of cliques in high school in governing action and affecting values and goals, see James S. Coleman, *The Adolescent Society* (New York: The Free Press, 1961).

[9] Robert F. Bales, *Interaction Process Analysis: A Method for the Study of Small Groups* (Cambridge, Mass.: Addison-Wesley, 1960). For a summary of subsequent research, on which the following discussion is based, see Robert F. Bales, "Task Roles and Social Roles in Problem-solving Groups," in Eleanor Maccoby, Theodore Newcomb, and Eugene Hartley, eds., *Readings in Social Psychology,* 3d ed. (New York: Holt, Rinehart and Winston, 1958), pp. 437–447.

[10] For a review of small group studies see Theodore Mills, *The Sociology of the Small Group* (Englewood Cliffs, N.J.: Prentice-Hall, 1967).

[11] Maurice Stein, *The Eclipse of Community* (Princeton, N.J.: Princeton University Press, 1960; Harper Torchbook paperback edition, 1964), pp. 107–108 in paperback edition.
The classic works are Robert E. Park, *Human Communities* (New York: The Free Press, 1952); Robert and Helen Lynd, *Middletown* (New York: Harcourt, Brace, 1929); and *Middletown in Transition* (New York: Harcourt, Brace, 1937); and William Lloyd Warner, *The Social System of the Modern Factory* (New Haven, Conn.: Yale University Press, 1947).

[12] Arthur J. Vidich and Joseph Bensman, *Small Town in Mass Society* (Princeton, N.J.: Princeton University Press, 1958).

[13] *Ibid.,* p. 79.

[14] *Ibid.,* p. 100.

[15] Georg Simmel, "The Metropolis and Mental Life," in Kurt Wolff, ed., *The Sociology of Georg Simmel* (New York: The Free Press, 1950).

[16] *Ibid.,* p. 415.

[17] Anton C. Zijdervald, *The Abstract Society: A Cultural Analysis of Our Time* (Garden City, N.Y.: Doubleday, 1970; Anchor Books paperback edition, 1971), p. 55.

[18] *Ibid.,* pp. 49–50.

SUGGESTED READINGS

James S. Coleman, *The Adolescent Society* (New York: The Free Press, 1961). An analysis of the importance of cliques in the lives of high school youth.

Herbert Gans, *The Urban Villagers: Group and Class in the Life of Italian-Americans* (New York: The Free Press, 1962). An interesting study of an ethnic neighborhood as a persisting community in a large city.

Eliot Liebow, *Tally's Corner: A Study of Negro Street-Corner Men* (Boston: Little, Brown, 1967). A study of a peer group among poor black males.

Robert and Helen Lynd, *Middletown* (New York: Harcourt, Brace, 1929), and *Middletown in Transition* (New York: Harcourt, Brace, & World, 1937). Two classic studies of how industrialization affected a community.

Theodore M. Mills, *The Sociology of Small Groups* (Englewood Cliffs, N.J.: Prentice-Hall, 1967). A useful analysis of the research on small groups.

Maurice Stein, *The Eclipse of Community* (Princeton, N.J.: Princeton University Press, 1960). An analysis of community studies that reveals how sociologists documented the decline of local autonomy.

Arthur J. Vidich and Joseph Bensman, *Small Town in Mass Society* (Princeton, N.J.: Princeton University Press, 1958). Two sociologists probe into the illusion and reality of life in a small town in the United States.

William F. Whyte, *Street-Corner Society: Structure of an Italian Slum,* rev. ed. (Chicago: University of Chicago Press, 1955). The classic study of peer groups in an ethnic community.

Anton C. Zijdervald, *The Abstract Society: A Cultural Analysis of Our Time* (Garden City, N.Y.: Doubleday, 1970). An interesting analysis by a European scholar of the consequences of the trend from small to large scale in modern society.

Part 3

SOCIETY AND GROUPS

What is society, whatever its form may be? The product of men's reciprocal action. Are men free to choose this or that form of society? By no means.

Karl Marx

Six

SOCIETY

Sociology is the study of society—that we said early on. In the last two chapters we have been laying a foundation on which that study can proceed. Now it is time to make clear what it is we are talking about when we say "society."

THE CONCEPT OF SOCIETY

In trying to understand what something is, it is often useful to break it down into its basic elements. The basic elements of society are three: *population, territory, and social organization.*[1]

Population. A society has a population, while groups and organizations have members. The difference is simple but basic: in Leon Mayhew's phrase, the societal population is "the self-perpetuating inhabitants of a territorial area."[2] By mating and reproduction a population reproduces itself.

Note that we are dealing here with a population, not necessarily a *people.* Whether or not the population of a society shares a culture and views itself as one people is something to be determined by observation of the actual case, not something to be taken for granted. As we noted before, the French in Canada are a distinct people but they are also only part of the population of a larger national society, even though many of them wish to be separate.

Territory. A self-perpetuating societal population inhabits a given territory on a relatively permanent basis. Such a territory is the largest within which mating is common and residence is relatively permanent.

Social Organization. A societal population in its territory is involved in complex processes of social interaction. It carries on a set of activities—economic, political, educational, and so on—that organizes social life. These several social activities each become a partly independent structure of social relations with their own specific characteristics. Yet they also overlap with each other and link together and share much in common, for they are activities carried on by the same population.

These components give us a definition: *Society is all of the systems of social interaction carried on by a population* within a specified territory.

The Nature of Society

This definition of society does not assume in advance that a society is highly integrated and culturally united. It can be, of course, but often it is not. Culturally different peoples may share the same society. They may even participate in common activities in a reasonably workable way. The world today abounds in such societies; so much so that it is difficult to find a society with a population that shares but one culture.

While a society can absorb and contain culturally different peoples, it nonetheless suffers strain and conflict for doing so. This becomes particularly apparent when the cultural differences are differences of language or religion (and sometimes both). The strife in Northern Ireland between Catholics and Protestants, and in Canada between French-speaking and English-speaking peoples are examples frequently in the news.

(In both of these cases, of course, the differences of religion and language are matched by differences of class and wealth; if this were not so, the conflict symbolized in religion and/or language would be less severe.)

Among the new nations of Africa, the original tribal identities, which distinguish one African people from another, still persist and even flourish. However, the new national boundaries do not coincide with the original tribal territories and, as a result, most African nations contain more than one tribal people. Some tribes have even been divided by boundaries cutting across their ancient tribal lands. As a consequence, tribal loyalties are the basis for intense struggles for power within these newly developing societies. These new societies, in effect, are still emerging out of old tribal ones.

Societal Boundaries Most of us—social scientists included—hold the idea that a society is a relatively self-sufficient, self-contained structure with well-marked boundaries that both separate it and insulate it from the surrounding environment of other societies. From this perspective, a society is but the largest system of social interaction, within which all other groups, organizations, and institutions are but subunits. But such a conception is no longer adequate in the modern world, however reasonable it might once have seemed.

Take, as a case in point, the huge multinational corporations like General Motors, Exxon, or ITT. Are these business organizations subunits of the American economy? Their business is worldwide, they produce and sell everywhere, they own facilities in many countries, and in some cases they earn more profits abroad than they do in the United States. In no way, then, does a conception of a self-contained *American* economy in a self-contained *American* society describe reality. Such giant corporations may have their "home" in the United States, but their corporate activity is neither contained within nor controlled by the United States. In the world today, therefore, societies cannot be viewed as self-sufficient and self-contained.

Several crucial activities of modern society—economic production, technological development and use, scientific research and development—flow easily across societal boundaries. Furthermore, the trained managers, technicians, and scientists involved in these activities also move readily from one society to another. The mobility of goods and technology is matched by the mobility of the world's most highly trained personnel.

By these activities such forms of modern culture as scientific and technological knowledge also flow into and across societies. Modern ideologies do also, and no society in the world is exempt from the influence of one or more ideological currents: capitalism or socialism, for example, in one variant or another; managerial ideologies; technological ideologies; ideologies about what is modern, and so on.

Mass culture, too, penetrates almost all societies. Wearing jeans and listening to rock music on records or radio become the aims of millions of young people in many societies. American movies and television programs are seen the world over, and Hilton hotels and even McDonald hamburgers can be found all over the globe. Now European football—soccer to us—a truly worldwide sport, is finding acceptance in the United States.

THE DEVELOPMENT OF COMPLEX SOCIETY

Human societies have been developing in form and structure for thousands of years. While it is not our task to review that long history here, it *is* useful to have some conception of what that process was.[3]

Though the time span, by human perspective, is very long, the historic record is quite clear: human societies have become increasingly more complex in their organization and also larger in size. If we ignore all the extraordinary variation and diversity in human societies known to archeologists and historians, we can account for this evolutionary process from the time of wandering bands to today's modern industrial society as an evolution of forms of society distinguished from one another by four basic processes:

1. Improved *technology* for production of food, clothing, and shelter.
2. Increased *population* and expansion into a larger territory.
3. Greater *specialization* of groups and roles and a greater *differentiation* of occupations, classes, and other groups in the organization of society.

Horticultural Societies

When primitive people learned to cultivate the soil, about ten thousand years ago, the way was set for the emergence of a more complicated form of society, though one still primitive in character. The digging stick, and later the hoe, permitted the planting of seeds and the harvesting of crops.

Now some time could be devoted to activities other than tilling the soil. In some societies, such as that of the Zuni Indians of New Mexico, a great deal of time was devoted to ceremonial activities, while other horticultural societies spent much time and energy in war. In either case, there were new specialized roles: priests and warriors. There was also a modest economic specialization, with some people designated to specialize in the production of the now greater range of goods made for daily use: weapons and tools, but also pottery and utensils.

These were larger societies than those of the hunting and gathering stage. Such increased size of society led to a necessary political organization, with headmen or chiefs as full-time political leaders, something not possible for hunting and gathering people.

Horticultural societies gradually improved in technology. The hoe replaced the digging stick, terracing and irrigation developed, as did fertilization, and there was also the development of metallurgy and the manufacture of metal tools; axes and knives especially. These technological advances made possible the further enlargement of society, both in expansion over a greater geographical area and by increased density— a larger population could be sustained in the same geographical area. The settled village, relatively permanent and enduring, was now fundamental to social life.

Agrarian Societies

If the horticultural society began to emerge with the invention of the digging stick, and later the hoe, it was the invention of the plow, harnessed to a domesticated animal, that set in motion the evolution of agrarian society some five to six thousand years ago. A wide range of technological developments greatly increased the productivity of society, accompanied by increases in the territory occupied and the size of the occupying population. This led to the growth of governing systems, with armies and ruling classes (warfare was a common activity in agrarian societies). The political

American-made popular culture is found all over the world. Here in Paris a display in front of a movie theater advertises a Marx brothers film made in Hollywood.

4. Increasing *centralization* of control in order to manage and coordinate an increasingly complex society.

Hunting and Gathering Societies

The most primitive form of human society was that of hunting and gathering. Lacking all but the most simple tools, hunting and gathering peoples grouped together in small, usually nomadic bands—nomadic because they had constantly to move on to find more edible plants and more animals to hunt.

For such people, life was an existence lived close to the subsistence level, with little surplus food ever available. Since they could not store or preserve food, life often went quickly from feast to famine.

Each group was small, probably averaging about fifty persons. They were self-sufficient, having little contact with any other people, so that each small band or tribe lived largely by itself, depending solely on its own resources.

Long before the emergence of industrial societies, cities developed as the organizing centers of agrarian empires. Here, high in the Andes Mountains in Peru, are the remnants of what was once such a center for the great empire of the Incas.

extension of control over wide territories even led to the development of great empires.

But perhaps most important as a characteristic of agrarian societies was the emergence of the *urban community*. Cities emerged as coordinating and controlling centers for agrarian societies, producing the historic contrast between rural and city life, between farmer and peasant, on the one hand, and artisan and merchant, on the other. Indeed, the advanced technology produced a surplus that made possible an extensive trade and commerce, and the emergence of classes of artisans and merchants. The cities also housed a ruling class, as well as administrators, and religious and military leaders.

Within the class of artisans increasing specialization produced a vast increase in the number of different crafts, perhaps as many as 150 to 2,000 in the larger cities. When one adds to this the many other kinds of occupations—officials, soldiers, priests, merchants,

servants, laborers—it becomes clear that the urban centers of agrarian societies had produced a notable diversity of occupations.

Though these cities were the controlling center of agrarian societies, they were never more than a minority of the entire population. Between the twelfth and fifteenth centuries in Europe, for example, the urban population was probably never more than 10 percent of the total. For any agrarian society, the limits of the technology required that the large majority of the population live in rural villages and be directly engaged in the tilling of the soil. Only with the coming of industrial society was that changed.

Industrial Societies

Over the last two hundred years, advances in technology and changes in economic organization have altered the agrarian form of society beyond recognition, and brought about industrial society.

What first marks industrial society is its enormous technological advance, which permits the use of far more diversified raw materials, quite different sources of energy, far more complex and efficient tools, and, as a consequence, an enormous increase in the production and consumption of material goods. The industrialization of society, in fact, has vastly increased the standard of living of industrial populations.

It has had other consequences, as well: the destruction of local markets systems through integration into larger ones; the growth of large corporations to produce goods and employ large staffs; an even more intensive specialization of labor, producing thousands of occupations where before there were merely hundreds; and an increase in the size of cities as well as the steady increase in the proportion of the total population living in cities. Industrialization *urbanizes* the population.

The growth of societies with such large and diversified populations has a further political consequence: it means the emergence of the modern *nation-state,* a political entity that takes on more and more functions of service and control.

There are many other changes in society involved in the transition from agrarian to industrial society: in community, in family, in life-style, in politics, and in culture. Much of what sociology is about is an effort to understand how thoroughly industrialization has altered human society over the past two hundred years, what forms and modes of life it makes available, and what in turn it has put beyond the possibility of experience for today's people. It is concerned with understanding what has happened to reshape human society, what society is now like, and what directions of change seem now to be in the making.

In industrial society an advanced technology controls the mass production of almost all consumer goods, including food. In this scene chickens are being processed before shipment to the supermarket.

SOCIAL INSTITUTIONS

Fundamental to the analysis of society is the understanding of social institutions. There are two different ways to speak of institutions. One begins with the idea of an *institutional norm* and defines an institution as a complex of such norms. Institutional norms are supported by strong group consensus, and sanctions for violation are imposed by enforcing agencies, for they are *obligatory.* They are, indeed, what Sumner meant by the *mores.*

A second conception of institution stresses the social acts which the norms govern, thus suggesting *institutional roles and relations.*

These two ways to define institutions are not incompatible. One calls institutions the norms that govern action; the other calls institution the action itself. An institution is clearly composed of both norms and actions. But we still need to know something else: why some activities are institutionally normative and some are not.

It is conventional to designate such major patterns as the family, the economy, and politics as social institutions. But this is misleading, for not every kind of familial, economic, and political activity is institutionalized. What is basic is that some activities are more important than others for the maintenance of society. Each societal population devises ways to produce goods and feed itself, to govern and regulate its ways of living, and to educate the young to carry on social life.

But if it is important that these activities are carried out, it is equally important *how* they are carried out. It is here that we get closer to the idea of an institution. In a capitalist society there are legal contracts and private property; in modern society marriage is monogamous and bigamy is forbidden; in a political democracy the citizens possess the right to vote and only the legislature the citizens elect can enact laws. Within the framework of economy, family, and politics, each of these specific actions—making contracts, owning property, marrying, voting, and enacting laws—are *legitimate* actions, morally and legally sanctioned and supported. They are institutions.

Social institutions have two components: (1) established practices and actions, and (2) the norms that make these practices and actions the legitimate ones. That second component tells us something important about institutions and about the organization of society. The varieties of human experience make it clear enough that there is more than one way of carrying out these important activities: property need not be privately owned, and marriage need not be monogamous. But while different societies choose different ways, any one society chooses only one way and makes it the only legitimate way for it, morally and legally.

Seeing an institution as composed of norms and actions gives us a definition: *an institution is a normative system of social action deemed morally and socially crucial for a society.*

If we were properly technical, we would not call the whole range of economic or political activities institutions, but, perhaps, *institutional spheres,* for only some of these activities are institutionalized.[4] Selling a used car or writing a letter to your congressman are not institutionalized actions, but the right of private property is, and voting in an election is also.

With that warning, then, the institutions of society are:

1. *Family.* Every society develops a social arrangement to legitimize mating and the care and socializing of the young.

2. *Education.* The young must also be inducted into the culture and taught the necessary values and skills. In preindustrial societies this is accomplished largely within the kinship system, but in modern societies a separate system of education develops.

3. *Economy.* Every society organizes its population to work, to produce, and to distribute material goods.

4. *Polity.* Every society develops a governing system of power and authority, which ensures social control within a system of rights and rules, protects and guarantees established interests, and mediates among conflicting groups.

5. *Religion and Science.* In past societies there was always a sense of sacredness about their life-ways, which then was a powerful integrating and cohesive force. Religion gave cultural expression in symbol and rite to this sense of the sacred. But in modern societies religion performs this integrating function but weakly, if at all.

The legitimation that religion once provided, science now does, though not in exactly the same way. But it is science that claims to possess the only valid knowledge, and which then legitimizes a wide range of practices and actions in modern society.

Institutions: Consensus and Coercion While it is proper to emphasize that institutions are the *legitimate* way to carry out necessary social activities, it would be wrong to create the impression that they originated only through common agreement and are supported by an unchallenged moral consensus. The historical record would support no such interpretation. Complex societies were shaped in processes of ecological expansion; in the struggles for control of territory and populations, victorious groups imposed their institutions on others. Many people became Christian, for example, through "conversion by the sword." Conquest and coercion have had as much to do with the establishment of social institutions as have consensus.

MODERN SOCIETY

While human society has taken many forms over thousands of years, and has become more complex, now we inhabit a modern society. It is that form of society that interests us the most.

The gradual emergence of what we now call modern society was a complex process of social disruption and change that altered old institutions beyond recognition and gave them radically new forms. It was a turbulent historical process, marked often by violence, revolution, and class struggle. Eventually, it changed the whole world.[5]

Whatever else it is, modern society is an *industrial society.* The recognition of this fact is perhaps the first (and therefore now the oldest) idea in understanding how modern society differs from what went before. Those scholars who insist that we define modern society as basically an industrial society point out that it is the demands and consequences of industrial production which most basically influence the structure of modern society.

Industrial societies emphasize industrial production of goods and thus give priority to whatever will maximize that production. That gives them some features in common, however else they differ in cultural traditions: the same technology; similar technical and scientific knowledge; and the same effort to provide the necessary technical training; the same job classifications and skill-rankings, which in turn shape the structure of occupations and occupational rewards. Industrial societies strive for technical and productive *efficiency,* and so for them the "rational" course of action is always determined by cost-accounting: they strive to get more for less.

In industrial society technical occupations increase at the expense of nontechnical ones, and the distribution of wages and salaries among occupations is fairly similar. In such a society, management and administration emerge as major functions and as major occupations of authority and prestige. There is increasing specialization and, furthermore, the separation of the economic system from the family and from religion; home and work place are no longer the same.

The Master Trends But modern society is more than an industrial structure; it is the outcome of a number of *master trends* that have been going on for several hundred years. They include the following:

1. *Capitalism.* The emergence of capitalism began as far back as the thirteenth century in medieval Europe. It developed into a powerful, tradition-destroying system of privately owned production for profit, which enormously increased material productivity, reshaped the class structure, and fundamentally altered the basic institutions of society.

2. *Industrial technology.* The development of mechanized processes vastly increased the production of goods, shifted the base of work from agriculture to industry, and raised the material level of the population. Capitalism exploited technology to create wholly new factory systems of industrial manufacturing and many new specialized occupations. The development of this industrial system is what is meant by the *Industrial Revolution.* It is this system that makes a society into an *industrial society.*

3. *Urbanization.* The transformation of society by capitalism and industrialism then shifted the population from predominantly rural to predominantly urban locations. While cities

are not new, only in modern society has most of the population lived in urban areas.

4. *The Nation-State.* The ecological expansion created by industrial capitalism brought the nation-state into being as the politically controlling unit, extending national loyalties into more diverse human populations than ever before.

5. *Bureaucracy.* The need to administer larger units of population brought about by ecological expansion, particularly with people from diverse cultural origins, brought into common use the bureaucratic form of organization, particularly in the economic and political spheres. Again, modern society did not invent bureaucracy, but it has made it a basic feature of its structure.

6. *Science.* Scientific knowledge is the most valued knowledge in modern society. It makes possible the control and exploitation of nature, and the harnessing of varied forms of energy. From such knowledge technological advance is assured.

7. *Mass education.* Modern society requires, at a minimum, the literacy of all its population. Beyond that, it requires mass education to train the population in industrial techniques and skills, to build commitment and loyalty to the nation-state and its institutions, and to produce a highly trained scientific and technological class.

Folk and Modern Society

While these master trends describe the processes that made modern societies out of premodern ones, they give us only a basic outline of such a society. They are of little help in enabling us to understand what modern society has to offer in ways to live a human life.

For over a hundred years now many people have been trying to understand modern society and to make some judgment on its merits. Their concern was not a disinterested one, either; they wanted to judge how the quality of life was affected by industrialization, particularly in the change from small-scale communities to large societies. When, in the nineteenth century, a young German sociologist, Ferdinand Toennies,

drew a sharp and provocative contrast between *Gemeinschaft* (Community) and *Gesellschaft* (Society), a passionate debate about modern society was underway that has not yet run its course.[6] While other scholars were to introduce other terms for a basic contrast between modern and premodern, his formulation remained the best known and most influential. It was an American anthropologist, Robert Redfield, however, who more recently introduced the term, *folk*.[7] (We shall say *folk* and *modern* in this discussion.)

The concepts, folk and modern, do not describe any real society. They are an effort to select a few basic elements which are most typical of a number of similar societies; thus folk and modern are *social types*.

These are the basic elements most commonly selected and discussed by Toennies and others:

1. *Size.* Folk societies are typically small; the primitive or peasant village compared to the great industrial city is the relevant contrast. Its basic components are small; family and kinship and small local groups are the basis of the individual's social relations. Interaction is thus face-to-face among familiar persons.

    In the modern society large-scale organizations dominate modern life and social interaction is increasingly impersonal.

2. *Kinship.* Kinship is the social basis of a folk society. It is a cooperative group for meeting most needs and functions, including the economic. Kinship obligations are binding and family ties are close and secure.

    In modern society kinship declines in functional importance, as do its obligations. Other, more specialized agencies assume tasks once carried out by kin groups: schools, welfare agencies, business firms, old-age homes, hospitals, and the like.

3. *Division of labor.* The folk society lacks mechanization and science; consequently, it has little specialization in occupations or economic functions. Tasks may be divided among men, women, and children—by sex and age—but there is only a limited number of tasks to perform, and most members know and understand these and share in the skills and competencies.

Modern society, in contrast, develops an extensive and complex division of labor. There is a separate organization for almost every particular function or activity. Furthermore, *within* large organizations there is extensive specialization. (A publication of the United States government lists 21,741 separate occupations.)[8]

4. *Culture.* Since there is a limited division of labor, the people in a folk society share a common body of practical knowledge, as well as common standards of conduct. Their culture is *homogeneous,* that is, commonly shared by everyone. A folk culture is also more cohesive and integrated, and there is more adherence to established customs.

    Since modern society operates through a large number of various subgroups, it displays a more diverse, less consistent and less integrated culture. There are subcultures, deviant cultures, and even countercultures. Because people in modern society engage in so many different activities, there is less knowledge in common, more specialized and limited beliefs, skills, and knowledge.

5. *The sacred.* A sense that much in life is sacred is basic to folk society. Long-established traditions, accepted without question, produce a deep sense of reverence for the ways of the group. Many objects are invested with sacredness in folk society and are kept away from the ordinary and profane, often by ceremony and ritual. Among villagers in Yucatan studied by Redfield, for example, the field in which maize (corn) is grown is *zuhuy.* "Everything that is protected from or is not exposed to the contamination of the ordinary, the earthly, the profane, is *zuhuy.*"[9] Maize growing in the field is *zuhuy,* guarded over by unseen gods, even the Virgin. It is even called "by the same word, *gracia,* used to denote the spiritual essence of offering made to the gods."[10] Only when prepared for eating or when sold in the market is it called by the ordinary word for maize (ixim).

In modern society, by contrast, the realm of the sacred shrinks. Modern society maximizes the practical and useful. Furthermore, the rational mind of science encourages skepticism about practices not based on tested procedures. Science also develops attitudes that welcome new practical ideas and new technical knowledge. In modern society, in short, the dominant place once accorded religion is replaced by the primacy given to science, its methods, and its practical application.

The Folk-Modern Comparison: Is It True?

Comparing folk and modern as social types has provided some useful perspective on what modern society is, but it is a biased perspective, nonetheless. It is biased because it compares the two types of societies in terms of the positive attributes of one of them: folk society as a cohesive community, small and personal, with strong kinship and a deeply shared culture, capable of providing deep roots and a strong sense of belonging. Modern society is described as lacking these. The comparison, then, is in terms of what a folk society *is* and a modern society *is not.*

Whether intended or not, this perspective on folk society has romanticized it, presenting it as being secure, harmonious, integrated with nature, cooperative, with a deep reverence for life.[11] This idyllic image is rooted in the old notion of primitives as noble savages —even though here the primitives were peasants— and civilization as the loss of dignity and serenity, which presumably comes naturally to simple, "uncivilized" people. It is an exaggerated contrast, but one that provides an important and influential criticism of modern life as cold and impersonal, manipulative of people, materially greedy, and lacking deep roots.

But a great deal of fieldwork tells us that real primitives and peasants are not the noble creatures they have been made to appear in so much romanticized literature. From an anthropological point of view the primitive is neither noble nor debased, neither a savage nor nature's ideal human uncorrupted by civilization. The primitive is simply human in her or his own particular way.

So, too, are peasants. Oscar Lewis, for example, restudied the same three villages in the Yucatan that Robert Redfield had visited seventeen years before. He found that they were not the idyllic communities Redfield had pictured; instead, he found them to contain discord; criminal behavior; politically generated violence; poverty; oppression; and interpersonal relations marked by fear, envy, and distrust.[12]

The image of a folk society is often quite unlike the real communities that social scientists discover in field-work. Its members are often authoritarian, parochial, suspicious of the stranger, and intolerant; in short, highly ethnocentric.

If folk society offers a deeply rooted life, it also binds the person to it without options or much individual choice. If it provides a sense of belonging and a clearly established personal identity, it may also demand uncritical adherence to established ways of life. The "other face" of folk society is a denial of the individualism, freedom, and personal choice so prized in modern life and at least partially made possible.

On the Other Hand But if the contrast between folk and modern society is a flawed one, that does not give us reason to discard it. It does express an important notion, developed over a hundred years ago and still relevant: that modern society has sacrificed, or at least weakened, some basic human values, such as those of community, of close personal relations, and of family and neighborhood and other small groups. No matter what its other achievements, the primacy and importance taken from these have made modern society a crippled, if still impressive, achievement in human organization.

Mass Society

Many of the arguments made in contrasting folk with modern society are also made by those who characterize modern society as steadily becoming a *mass society*. This is a critical and pessimistic perspective on modern society, which sees capitalism, industrialism, and the market economy as having burst forever the small, closely-knit communities of the past.[13]

There are two different emphases in this perspective, though both draw upon the same conception of historical development, namely, the emergence of modern society as a national society organized centrally by a nation-state. One is a *psychological* analysis about what happens to *individuals* in such a society; the other is a *political* analysis about what happens to social *groups*.

The Individual in Mass Society By the emergence of modern society, according to this perspective, individuals were freed from the constraining traditions and primary obligations of the past. But when family and

community decline as groups significant in controlling life, the limited and specialized groups that take their place cannot provide the same sense of belonging, the same quality of personal relations, the same secure grasp of one's personal identity. The very process of relating to others becomes more difficult. Most social relations are superficial and impersonal, involving no deep commitment or emotional attachment; others are primarily manipulative, with people constantly trying to use each other for their own ends. One's status is never secure, and one has to prove oneself with others in each new situation.

In such conditions, neither individualism nor freedom are personally rewarding, and, as Erich Fromm once demonstrated in a powerful analysis of this condition in Germany (which led to Hitler and Nazism), people seek to "escape from freedom."[14] They do so by looking for something secure: another form of group therapy, a fan-worshipping idolization of a mass-cultural celebrity, a commune, involvement in any new fashion or fad, or the security offered by an authoritarian religious cult or political movement.

The Group in Mass Society The political perspective on groups in mass society, according to sociologist William Kornhauser, sees primary and other smaller, local groups as *isolated* from the national centers of authority and decision-making. From local community to nation-state, and from primary group to organizational headquarters, is a large jump, and what is needed is a level of intermediate organization, one that can provide the links that give the individual a sense that participation at the level of everyday life ties in significantly with the larger social structure. Kornhauser offers the example of a person's relation to work and occupation. While there can be satisfaction in work itself, still the sense of fellowship and control over the conditions of work are equally important for the existence of occupational attachments.

It is precisely these latter sources of interest and participation in work that require independent groups for their realization. Informal work groups supply some basis for fellowship and control at work, but with the growth in scale and complexity of the factory, office, and work institutions generally, they are insufficient. Therefore, all kinds of formal work associations, are needed.[15]

When, Kornhauser notes, they fail to develop, or when they, too, grow out of the reach of their members and are not capable of giving the individual a sense of participation and control,

   . . . people are less likely to find the whole sphere of work an interesting and rewarding experience. Consequently, people may cease to care about their work, though of course they continue to work, despite their alienation from their jobs.[16]

If people's social relations are superficial, not rooted and secure, if their sense of belonging and group responsibility are weak, then they are vulnerable to manipulation by mass media, either in the form of propaganda for the benefit of political elites, or in the form of mass culture, which entertains but does not educate. Such a people are then vulnerable to a manipulative control by those who dominate the powerful bureucracies of modern society as well as the agencies of mass communication. In that, say the critics of mass society, is the real possibility of totalitarian control and the end of free society.

There are, in turn, defenders of modern society against these charges; they deny that modern society is or is becoming a mass society bound to end in totalitarianism. Instead, according to them, modern society finds strength in its *pluralism:* its variety of groups and subcultures which offsets the possibilities of mass control, and which offers unlimited opportunities for people to find rewarding social relations in keeping with their personal choices. Thus, Daniel Bell says:

   If it is granted that mass society is compartmentalized, superficial in personal relations, anonymous, transitory, specialized, utilitarian, competitive, acquisitive, mobile, and status-hungry, the obverse side of the coin must be shown, too—the right to privacy, to free choice of friends and occupation, status on the basis of achievement rather than ascription, a plurality of norms and standards, rather than the exclusive and monopolistic social controls of a single dominant group.[17]

Bell's defense is a balancing act; he acknowledges the criticisms of mass society, but in turn points to what he sees as its virtues. However, the critics of mass society would not deny the existence of these virtues; the question would be whether they are sufficient to provide the sense of secure social relations that any viable society must provide its people.

The argument for mass society may be criticized in the same way that the folk-modern comparison was: by its selective concentration on some few though important aspects. It becomes a thoroughly negative por-

trait. Its proponents refuse to look for the offsetting developments, the still possible creative actions and satisfying social relations of which human beings in modern society are still capable. Whether they are of sufficient quality to prevent the future's being that of a mass society remains to be seen.

Like the folk-modern contrast, the concept of mass society, though perhaps one-sided, nonetheless constantly reminds us that modern society has a darker side. It has been unable to sustain (or re-create) a strong community, well-integrated around commonly shared values or provide people with well-rooted and cherished social identities. These values have been sacrificed on behalf of an enormous material growth, constant social change, and increasing social and individual opportunities.

The dilemma of modern life is that we want and need, on the one hand, a community of shared values and a well-rooted social identity, and, on the other, growth and change and increasing individual opportunities. But modern society cannot offer both in any equal proportion. That, perhaps, is the lesson we learn from these critiques of modern society.

The concept of mass society is not a description of American society or any other specific society; neither is it a statement of what modern society actually is nor of what it necessarily will become. Mass society is an abstract type, and actual societies will only in some greater or lesser degree approximate a mass society. It does provide a diagnosis of some *tendencies* in large-scale modern societies which can undermine freedom and individuality unless checked.

Bell's critique, then, does not disprove the concept of a mass society; it merely indicates some of the values which can counteract the potential for its development. Kornhauser, in turn, stresses the need for a high degree of autonomy of social groups, extensive self-government, and the participation of individuals in several such self-governing systems.[18]

BEYOND MODERN SOCIETY

Modern society is not the last phase in the development of human society; it is only the most recent. While much of the world is still struggling to become modern, those societies that best represent what modern society is are already moving into a *postmodern future.*

Modern society has a *history;* it emerged in Europe through a process of social change and reached its high point in the first half of the twentieth century. But social change goes on, and now new seers and prophets emerge to tell us what new forms of society the indicators of change point to.

On that matter there is no agreement. Given different values, and different conceptions of the forces of historical change, scholars have different, even conflicting, images of what the future holds and of what human society will be like by the year 2000—and that, please note, is less than two decades away and well within the working lifetime of today's college students.

Though attempting to foresee the future is at best a tricky business, there is no lack of prophets. Some are exponents of doom and disaster; others are almost pollyannaish in proclaiming the ability of such societies as the United States to continue along its present path, only bigger and better. A future of more of the same seems unlikely now, though a future that is ultimate disaster is no longer unthinkable. Nuclear holocaust cannot be dismissed as impossible, and a world polluted to a point beyond livability is not entirely unlikely, either, given the stubborn persistence of some antiecological interests.

But our concern here is not to review the business of forecasting the future, but to focus upon the idea that modern society has already begun to reach its historical end. *Some* new form of society is coming over the horizon, or even, perhaps, several new forms.

As we move into postindustrial society, according to Daniel Bell, such blue-collar workers as these seen leaving work will decline as a proportion of the labor force.

The Postindustrial Society

Perhaps one of the more interesting efforts to map out social trends observable in the present and then to think out what major changes in the structure of society they will lead to, is Daniel Bell's *The Coming of Post-Industrial Society*[19] It is an analysis built upon *tendencies* and "the meaning and consequence of those tendencies if the changes in social structure that I describe were to work themselves to their logical limits."[20] There is no guarantee, Bell is quick to inform us, that these tendencies have to work to their logical limits. Social conflict or war may disrupt these trends and produce quite different results.

The postindustrial society that Bell sees emerging by the year 2000, and already partly in place, is not a utopia. It will suffer from its own social problems and contradictions. But neither will it be the human disaster foreseen by the critics of mass society. According to Bell, the modern society now nearest to being postindustrial is the United States—and it is primarily the United States that he uses in discussing the trends leading to the postindustrial future. However, Western European societies, Japan, and the Soviet Union are also become postindustrial.

Though the change into postindustrial society is a complex and intricate process, Bell tells us that we can more easily understand it if we examine five dimensions that give basic meaning to the idea of such a society and the changes that are bringing it about. These are as follows:

The Service Economy[21] In a postindustrial society the majority of the labor force no longer finds work in agriculture or manufacturing but in services: trade, finance, transport, health, recreation, research, education, and government. When most of the world has not even yet become industrial, only the United States has begun to move into a service economy. According to Bell, the United States:

is the first service economy, the first nation, in which the major portion of the population is engaged in neither agrarian nor industrial pursuits. Today about 60 percent of the United States labor force is engaged in services; by 1980, the figure will have risen to 70 percent.[22]

The Preeminence of the Professional and Technical Class[23] In an industrial society the blue-collar occupations dominate, and the semiskilled worker is the largest single category in the labor force. But since 1956 in the United States white-collar occupations have outnumbered blue-collar ones; by 1970 the margin of white-collar over blue-collar was more than five to four.

But more crucial for the trend to postindustrial society is an even more rapid growth in professional and technical occupations. Their growth as a whole has been twice that of the average labor force, while the growth of scientists and engineers has been triple that of the working population as a whole.

The significance of this is not merely in growth and decline of occupational categories, or in the increasing importance of a university education, but in the emergence of a new class structure. The professional and technical class will be, according to Bell, the "heart" of postindustrial society.

The Primacy of Theoretical Knowledge[24] The specifically defining characteristic of the new society, says Bell, is *knowledge:*

Industrial society is the coordination of machines and men for the production of goods. Postindustrial society is organized around knowledge, for the purpose of social control and the directing of innovation and change; and this in turn gives rise to new social relationships and new structures which have to be managed politically.[25]

But the knowledge deemed so crucial is *theoretical* knowledge, not merely practical knowledge; thus, the central importance of science and scientists. Once, technological development came from inventors who knew nothing of the scientific principles behind their tinkering. But now technological advance follows from scientific theory; new industries like computers, electronics, optics and polymers are science-based and dependent primarily on theoretical work prior to production. Theoretical knowledge increasingly becomes the "strategic resource" of society.

Though the theoretical knowledge of which Bell speaks is primarily that of the natural sciences—physics, chemistry, and biology—it is not restricted to that. The use of a mathematically refined *economic* theory to rationally manage the economy is, by Bell's outlook, an indication of what will be typical in the postindustrial society: the use of theoretically grounded knowledge to develop technology *and* to guide social policy and direct social change.

If it is theoretical knowledge that becomes so central, then assuring an adequate number of scientifically trained professionals becomes a major problem for such a society. That necessarily becomes a concern of government policy. Since it is only in universities that such training can take place, and since universities also provide the resources for much of the basic research needed to advance theoretical knowledge, universities then become central organizations in the structure of postindustrial societies.

The Planning of Technology[26]   In the postindustrial society, in order to maintain productivity and higher standards of living, new technology can be planned and utilized. In the past, technological advance often had destructive consequences; fertilizers, for example, increased agricultural production but polluted rivers; DDT as a pesticide saved crops but destroyed wildlife and birds. The introduction of technology was uncontrolled because innovators were only interested in a specific result.

But in the postindustrial society, Bell believes, *technology assessment*—measuring all possible effects of any new technology—will be required before any new technological innovation can be put to use. Any harmful side-effects can be known in advance. This means a controlling role for government in regulating the activities of corporations in marketing new scientific and technological innovations. More importantly, this means a society in which the planned advance of technological change is conscious and deliberate; postindustrial societies, according to Bell, may be able to plan and control technological growth.

The Rise of a New Intellectual Technology[27]   If machine technology has been the symbol of industrial society, then a new intellectual technology will symbolize the postindustrial society. It emerges in response to the problems that come from increased size and complexity of human organization and is, in effect, an effort to manage the large-scale systems in which most of us are unavoidably involved.

This new technology is primarily based on the computer, and involves the use of a new set of mathematical tools that can handle a large body of facts rapidly and accurately and chart out a rational course of action in the management of large-scale society. To do this, all risks and costs of any line of action, or any proposed social program, can be assessed beforehand, so that a "best" solution can be made of the choices of-

fered. What is best?: "one that either maximizes the outcome or, depending upon the assessment of the risks and uncertainties, tries to minimize the losses.[28]

If the computer seems to control the decisions to be made, it is systems analysis that provides the theory that controls the computer. And that brings into central decision-making roles a new group of *technocrats,* the experts in systems analysis, who seek to reduce all decision-making to a technical process.

But postindustrial society, Bell argues, is not going to be *technologically determined,* that is, it is not going to be a society in which technology decides and people then adjust as best they can. While a new technocratic elite of the scientifically trained will enter into the structure of power, they will not alone be decisive in making basic decisions of policy.

Bell asserts that "no matter how technical social processes may be, the crucial turning points in a society occur in a political form. It is not the technocrat who ultimately holds power, but the politician.[29] But as the indispensable experts of the postindustrial society, the technicians cannot be discounted. "The politician," says Bell, "and the political public, will have to become increasingly versed in the technical character of policy, aware of the ramified impact of decisions as systems become extended."[30]

This, then, is postindustrial society: a service society based on science and advanced technology. But these five dimensions, which outline for us the basic characteristics of postindustrial society, leave unstated, or at best implied, some other very significant features of such a society. Here are five:

1. Postindustrial society will give us more bureaucracy, not less.

2. It will increase the centralization of controls and decision-making. Indeed, the whole apparatus of intellectual technology is to devise a control system for ever larger areas of social life. Decisions will increasingly be made technically, at the top of large social systems, not by democratic processes.

3. Increasing bureaucratization and increasing centralization of control puts more power into the hands of professionals—scientists, engineers, systems analysts, and the like—and these professional experts then claim a competency to act contrary to popular attitudes and values in making decisions. Bell acknowledges that *professionalism* clashes with *populism* when people advance claims for more rights and greater participation in the society.

THE POSTINDUSTRIAL SOCIETY AS AN ALTERNATIVE FUTURE

Though Daniel Bell has carried out the most systematic effort to describe and define the postindustrial society, he did not originate the effort, nor even coin the term, *postindustrial.* That was done by a French sociologist, Alain Touraine.*

As a conception of the near-future, the concept of postindustrial society is an alternative to both the Marxian conception of *revolution* by the working classes against capitalism and the liberal conception of gradual piecemeal *reform* of capitalism in the direction of a welfare state. These two conceptions of what the future might and should be have dominated European and American social theory for over a century. The concept of a postindustrial future is, then, an attempt to break loose from the monopoly of thought commanded by orthodox Marxian and liberal theories.

The postindustrial thinkers agree with liberal theorists that there will not be a working-class revolution to overthrow capitalism and install a socialist society. But they do not share the liberal inability to conceive of a radically transformed future. Instead, they perceive a gradual, yet revolutionary change in the basic character of industrial-capitalist society to produce a new order, which, while retaining much of what already exists, also radically alters the shape of the social classes, the culture, and the institutions of the present society.

Notes

* Alain Touraine, *The Post-Industrial Society,* trans. Leonard F. X. Mayhew (New York: Random House, 1971, original French edition, 1969).

If the struggle between capitalist and worker, in the locus of the factory, was the hallmark of industrial society, the clash between the professional and the populace, in the organization and in the community, is the hallmark of conflict in the postindustrial society.[31]

4. The organization of postindustrial society does not resolve but only continues the contradiction between culture and social structure as this has developed within capitalism in this century. Capitalism, by its very success in providing more material goods and more leisure time, has destroyed forever the Protestant ethic: dedication to work, frugality and saving, industriousness and self-denial. In the realm of consumption and private life, this ethic no longer applies, especially for the younger generation. But in the organization of work the system continues the long-established demand for prudent conduct, hard work, and a commitment to career and success. One requires self-discipline; the other seeks play and pleasure.[32]

There is as yet no emerging moral system to override these conflicting values of the social structure and the self-enhancing culture, no "transcendent ethic," as Bell calls it. The lack of such a moral system then becomes the basic cultural contradiction of late capitalist society, carried on unresolved into the postindustrial society. Postindustrial society may maximize efficiency, service, and technological development, but this achievement does not inspire people and does not provide meaning and purpose to human life. Such a lack will challenge its very existence.

5. A service society no longer is primarily engaged in manufacturing, but its population does not cease to consume manufactured goods. Manufacturing necessarily goes on elsewhere in the world. Multinational

corporations export machinery, technical know-how, and capitalist investment into countries where wages are cheaper, and then bring back both the goods manufactured and the profits earned.

That process invites an observation and a question. The observation is that postindustrial society depends not only on an interdependent world economy, which is obvious enough, but also on some industrial societies *not* becoming postindustrial. A service society is a controlling society, one which owns a great deal of the world's technology and the capital that makes industrial production possible. But those other dependent, controlled societies are a necessary part of the total picture. Clearly, all the world cannot aspire to be postindustrial; it is, in effect, a privileged position in the world.

The question then becomes: can that privileged position be maintained? Even such a distinguished economist as Paul Samuelson wonders:

> Suppose that economic equilibrium did dictate our becoming a service economy, living like any rentier on investment earnings abroad . . . Can anyone really believe that in the last three decades of the twentieth century the rest of the world can be counted on to permit the continuing flow of dividends, repatriation of earnings and royalties, to large corporations owned here?[33]

Since the answer is unmistakably no, we can expect to see conflict between the privileged postindustrial nations and the rest of the world, a struggle between haves and have-nots, one which makes the post-industrial future so uncertain.

This does not mean it is the United States against the rest of the world. While the United States is now the first postindustrial society, it will not be the only one. As we noted before, several others are sufficiently developed to move into such a future, according to Bell: Japan, the Soviet Union, and those of Western Europe.

Other Futures, Another Society

For Daniel Bell, postindustrial society is the outcome of trends already apparent in industrial society. What makes his image of postindustrial society so persuasive for so many is that he bases it on these trends which he can empirically demonstrate. Just pursue these trends to their logical outcome and you have de-

scribed the future. It is, after all, a reality already partly here.

The coming of a postindustrial society, therefore, depends on the uninterrupted *continuity* of several powerful trends, some of which have been going on throughout this century. But is there any assurance that these trends will continue undisturbed? There is not; Bell pointed out that social conflict could destroy the likelihood that the trends work themselves to their logical limits.

There are other ways of thinking about the future of society which do not assume continuity but see *discontinuity*—a disturbance and conflict—as shaping the changes that will bring about a new form of society. Those who think in this fashion base their analysis not primarily on social trends but on social *contradictions* and the conflict and struggle they bring about. From such conflict and struggle emerge new forms of society. This emphasis upon contradictions and conflicts challenges the idea that the model of the future must be that of a postindustrial society gradually emerging from present trends and continuing indefinitely into the future.

The Fiscal Crisis   One contradiction leads to a fiscal crisis. In capitalist society government (the state) has a twofold task: (1) maintaining or creating the conditions for successful capital *accumulation,* in order that the economy may grow and expand through constant investment in profitable pursuits; and (2) maintaining the *legitimation* of the system by seeking always to create social harmony among contending classes and groups.[34]

These two tasks contradict one another. A state that invokes policies to help corporate capitalism accumulate capital does so at the expense of other social classes and so risks their loyalty and support. But a state that does not assist in capital accumulation risks drying up the source of its own tax revenue, the profitability of a healthy economy.

Modern states in capitalist societies find themselves forced to expend ever larger sums of money for welfare measures: income subsidies to the poor, social insurance, assistance for the aged, medical care, and the like. There is also the need to maintain and expand the educational system, for an advanced capitalist society requires a better educated labor force. These are expenditures which, on the one hand, keep the peace by reducing suffering and hardship, and on the other hand are social investments in the reproduction of a more highly trained labor force, which is necessary for modern capitalism.

Yet meeting these necessary and growing expenses requires greater tax revenue, which means higher taxes, which in turn reduces the profitability of corporate capitalism. A further source of social expenditure, necessary to maintain capitalism in a sometimes hostile world, is the military. The state, then, becomes a welfare-warfare state requiring huge budgetary expenditures that are essential to the survival of corporate capitalism yet hamper the accumulation of capital. There is, therefore, a growing strain between state expenditures and state revenues, a *fiscal crisis,* for state expenditures tend to grow more rapidly than the means of financing them. In the United States the cost of social security now exceeds its revenue despite increased rates, yet the state dare not reduce its modest payments to the retired and those looking toward retirement without risking serious political repercussions.

Culture versus Economy   In modern life the young and the affluent have come to expect and demand a worthwhile and rewarding life, an experience of self-development and fulfillment. For those who reach the pinnacle of managerial and professional success, this may very well be found in established careers. But even for many of those, and certainly for most others, the demands of the system for discipline and commitment to an organizational role contradict the desire for self-realization, now so strong an element of modern culture.

Bell, as we noted above, recognized this as perhaps the fundamental conflict in industrial society.[35] For some radicals and even some Marxists who no longer believe in a working class destined to revolt against capitalism, the demand for revolutionary change may emerge instead among the young and better-educated.

The Haves versus the Have-Nots   The United States, and other societies becoming postindustrial, maintain economic domination over those societies whose industrial production provides the cheap goods for mass consumption that ensures their high standard of living. The multinational corporations and the American military extend American influence and power to every corner of the globe.

But such dominating power is always resented and resisted. Even Daniel Bell acknowledged that postindustrial America may in time become involved in a new form of "class struggle," one between the rich nations and the poor nations, where the extremes of wealth and poverty are so striking. Bell called this a problem for the twenty-first century, but in fact it is a problem that is already here.

State Capitalism and State Socialism   Postindustrial society is too rational and planned to allow corporations to remain unregulated. Rather, their pursuit of their own particular interests becomes subordinated by the state to an overall plan of development and economic growth. Postindustrial society is a form of state capitalism.

By contrast, elsewhere in the world, state socialism prevails. By the conventional Marxist agenda, the socialist state should proceed to abolish privilege, inequality, and social classes, and create the conditions for the emergence of a truly *communal* society in which all persons are equal to one another in their opportunity to realize their full potential as human beings. They would live in cooperation and mutual support, not in competition and exploitation. Such a society will no longer require the governing power and control of the state and it will wither away.

So goes the Marxist script. But twentieth-century reality is one of socialist states, such as the Soviet Union, which show no signs of withering away, in which social classes and privileged elites exist, and in which the state holds all power. This dismaying reality produces a crisis in Marxism about the possibility of creating an egalitarian society through socialist revolution.

The recognition that both state capitalist and state socialist societies can be postindustrial (as Bell claims), with powerful regulating states and huge bureaucratic structures, is the source of renewed belief that if the future society is to be decently livable, it must be decentralized. *Small is beautiful.*[36] Bureaucracy must be replaced by small, communal structures, without sacrificing the potential benefits of advanced technology. The ages-old trend toward society larger and more complex is to be reversed.

What all this says is clear enough: many perceptive minds recognize that ours is a time of transition, and that a new form of society is probably not far off. But what it is likely to be and what it might be—on that there is no consensus.

THE GOOD SOCIETY

Over many centuries thoughtful people have taken the measure of human society, not by comparing one actual society to another, but by constructing some conception of what society could or should be. They have compared the existing to the possible, the *real* to the *ideal*. This construction of imaginary utopias has long been a significant way to think about society.

Most social scientists want only to examine real societies, not ideal ones, for they regard a consideration of the utopian as unscientific. Yet such considerations intrude into their analyses. The folk-modern comparison so long important to sociology was based upon a conception that society should be a deeply rooted community. Also, the vast amount of social scientific literature examining the relation of the individual to society never escapes consideration of what would be better or even ideal.

One reason why social scientists cannot escape utopian ideas is because these ideas are widely held in modern society. Its population has come to expect and demand more; or at least its younger, better-educated, and more affluent have. The demand for equal opportunity for women and minorities, or for more self-fulfilling and psychically rewarding jobs, for example, are expectations-based, however unconsciously, on some conception of what ideally society could and should offer its inhabitants.

The capacity for thinking utopian seems to vary with changing circumstances. The nineteenth century was a century of confidence in the possibilities of human progress, and so utopian ideas flourished and many actual utopian experimental communities were created.

But the twentieth century has been more pessimistic. Two devastating world wars, the Great Depression, and the rise of both fascist and communist totalitarianism, do not seem to invite utopian fantasies of some ideal society of the future. Instead, we have had *dystopian* images, those of frighteningly repressive societies dominated by those who control a powerful technology. George Orwell's novel, *1984,* is perhaps the outstanding example of this kind of literature.

In the twentieth century the literature of science-fiction has replaced older forms of both utopian and dystopian literature. Science-fiction reflects the modern interest in the enormous possibilities of science and technology and its promised capacity to free us from an earthbound existence. Science-fiction writers can utilize more freely than other artists the unfettered human imagination to create images of society, both possible and sometimes desirable, if certain conceptions of scientific development are assumed. However indirectly, much of this literature is then a critique of existing society.

What Is the Good Society?

From the days of ancient Greece, when Plato described his ideal *Republic,* to the latest in science-fiction utopias, the concept of the good society has been a fertile image in the human mind. It has always been a historical product, reflecting conditions and situations as people lived them. In the modern world, where science, technology, and large-scale organization are basic factors of social life, the concept of the good society reflects both the hopes and fears that these particularly modern features arouse in people.

If we extract from a vast and varied literature, we can offer the following as the basic concerns of those who have tried to define what the idea of the good society means for modern people.

Communal   The good society is *communal*. It is a community, rather than a bureaucracy or an aggregate of unrelated people. This means that social life is based upon a consensus of values and ideals about how society should be organized and how we should live our lives. Each of us feels that we *belong* and are bound to enduring social relations with people we love and respect. People care and cooperate.

The loss of the communal dimension to society was what the folk-modern analysis was all about. In folk society people put down roots in a commonly shared and respected way of life; in modern society they were uprooted and mobile, strangers in their own land, without anchorage and often feeling lonely and unloved.

The interest several years ago in building *communes* outside the established structure of society was only the most recent effort to recreate community. In modern society people seek community in many ways: in churches and neighborhoods, in lodges and civic clubs, and in social movements. But these are, at best, communities of those selected to be together by

Science-fiction has long given us images of some future society by building upon the possibilities of an advanced technology, especially one which can reach beyond the earthbound confines of our present existence. Now a developing space technology is taking some steps in that direction.

shared characteristics, rather than communities built among those who share the same condition of life.

Controllable In the past people felt that the conditions of their existence were largely beyond their control. Limited knowledge and a limited technology gave but a limited control over nature, and human existence was necessarily one of scarcity and unending labor. The poverty and suffering of most human beings was accepted as inevitable. The fear of the unknown, the uses of magic, the ever present threat of disaster, even the concept of punishing gods (or God) in religions were expressions of this experience of limited control.

Now, in modern society, science and technology have much diminished these fears of uncontrollable natural forces, yet modern people still do not feel they control the conditions of their lives. Now it is not na-ture but society that seems uncontrolled, or even in control.

The enormously impressive achievements of science and technology have not reduced *alienation*, that feeling people have of being powerless in the face of what is their own creation: society. The poet Emerson expressed it in these words:

Things are in the saddle,
And ride mankind.[37]

Part of the matter is the enormous scale of human organization. An economy of world markets, a great nation-state, and huge controlling bureaucracies do not give anyone, even those in advantaged positions, the feeling that the social world is humanly controllable. And the vision of postindustrial society, as Bell made clear, promises only to extend these, not to reduce them.

For modern people, a utopian image of a good society tends to emphasize the capacity of human beings to have a rational control over the circumstances of their lives. Bell warned that conflict between professionals as experts and the populace would be common in postindustrial society. *Decentralization* and *self-government* become goals for social change, designed to bring the social world down to human scale and within the reasonable control of those who must live in it. But it is a goal ridiculed, or even denounced, in turn, by those committed to the continuity of trends in modern society which will make postindustrial society seem even more uncontrollable by the majority of people.

Self-Fulfillment   More and more in modern society increasing numbers of individuals demand the opportunity for a fulfilling and rewarding life, free of demeaning drudgery and boring routine. They expect to be able to realize their full potential of abilities and skills.

Once it was common to think that only an elite, a naturally gifted minority, could achieve such self-fulfillment and personal self-development. But in the modern world it is no longer easy to sustain such notions of a few who deserve the privilege of self-realization while the rest labor in drudgery to make that possible.

Ancient Athens, long greatly admired as the source and creator of a marvelous culture, was such a society. A small elite of men lived full and rewarding lives, giving over much time to things cultural and civic, to public matters as well as private ones. But they could do so because they lived off the labor of the majority of people in that society, people who had no such opportunities to do other than carry out their assigned tasks. Such was the lot of the majority in glorious Athens: the artisans, the slaves, and the women.

In times past, when technology was primitive and scarcity unavoidable, the most utopian conceptions of society included a slave or proletarian class who labored that others might live well. This was always justified by the idea that humanity came in two categories: those few who had ability and the rest who did not; the elite and the masses. While such an idea is by no means abandoned—it lives on partly in the idea of meritocracy, as we shall see later—there is no scientific basis for building a society on any such division of humankind. In a society in which more leisure and education are within the grasp of the majority, the need for self-fulfillment as a human being is no longer a privilege of the very few. That is why it becomes one major criterion of the good society.

Nonetheless modern society has difficulty meeting this widespread demand. There are several reasons for this. For one thing, even if a service society exports much of its unrewarding labor to be done elsewhere, there are still dirty and lowly tasks which are also necessary: somebody must still collect the garbage, clean the toilets, and take care of the bedpans. There are also still jobs that are dangerous and fatiguing: down in coal mines and in foundries, for example. And there are more and more jobs that are so routinized and undemanding of anyone's mental faculties that they numb the mind with boredom. The simple, routine nature of these jobs makes for productive efficiency, but they deny any human aspiration for self-realization on the job.

The Ideal and the Possible   The concept of the good society operates at two levels, the *ideal* and the *historical*. The ideal is simply a statement of what human society is at its best: a community ordered by the values of justice, equality, and liberty. At the historical level, the good society is the historically possible approximation, the nearest and best given the limitations of knowledge and technology.

Even the best of minds can differ about what is historically possible now or in the near future, over what it is reasonable to strive for and to hope for. But the concept of the good society, which is always utopian in some sense, provides one further way in which human beings can examine the societies in which they reside. It tells us one very important thing: that our values and our ideals for the potentiality of humankind are never restricted to the historically limited society in which we reside. Our ideas can always transcend reality. Human beings will always construct conceptions of futures better than the present one. It is the task of a critical sociology to assist in the necessary task of measuring the real against an ideal in terms of the humanly possible.

MEASURING SOCIETY

Human societies are large, complex, and ever-changing structures. Getting the measure of them, that is, analyzing and assessing them, is always a difficult task. There are, however, at least two ways in which some assessment of society can be made: the evolutionary and the comparative. Both of these we have touched upon briefly in this chapter.

The evolutionary development of society from more primitive to complex forms, as we have seen, culminated in a modern society which was capitalist, industrial, and urban. That evolutionary process we can expect to go on, and the usefulness of Daniel Bell's notion of postindustrial society was that it suggested how a new form of society would evolve in the near future out of trends in the present society.

Karl Marx, too, used an evolutionary conception of the development of human society. This development led to capitalist society, which was then to be followed by a new form, a socialist society that would create the conditions, he argued, for the creation of a community of truly free and equal individuals. (That, by the way, was his meaning of communism, not what is meant by the term today as a consequence of the society created by the Russian revolution.)

The comparison of folk and modern society is but one effort to be comparative. There are many other ways, including the comparison of developed with underdeveloped (or dependent) societies, or of one particular society, say the United States, with another which is basically similar, say Germany, or with one which is both like it in some ways and quite different in others, say the Soviet Union. A disciplined comparison of societies is a method for bringing out basic features that might not be so evident if we just examined one society. Comparing the United States to some other society, or comparing the United States today to what it was at some earlier time, is a way of bringing out its distinctive features.

Lastly, comparing the real society with an image of the good society provides another point of analysis. In particular, it enables people to ask whether the real as it really is, is all that is possible; or whether it is reasonable to hope and struggle for something better.

SUMMARY

Society is all the systems of social interaction carried on by a population within a specified territory.

Human societies have developed over long centuries by improved *technology,* increased *population* and expanded *territory,* greater *specialization* and increased *differentiation* of occupations and classes, and increasing *centralization* of control.

From the primitive form of small *hunting and gathering* tribes, there came in turn *horticultural* societies, *agricultural* societies, and now *industrial* societies.

Social institution is a normative system of social action deemed morally and socially crucial for a society. The institutions of society are *family, education, economy, polity,* and *religion* and *science.*

Modern society is an industrial society characterized by these *master trends:* capitalism, industrial technology, urbanization, the nation-state, bureaucracy, science, and mass education.

The contrast of *folk-urban* society emphasizes how modern society has lost the rootedness, tradition, kinship, homogeneous culture, and sense of sacredness in life once presumed typical of small, preindustrial (folk) societies.

The concept of *mass* society also interprets modern society as having destroyed the small, closely-knit community of the past, producing in its place superficial social relations and an easily manipulable population. However, defenders of modern society deny this gloomy assessment and see virtues in the *pluralism* of groups and subcultures.

Both folk-urban and mass society concepts, while one-sided, point to what values have been lost or made more difficult in modern society.

Modern society will in time be succeeded by some new form. Bell's idea of a *postindustrial* society organized primarily around advanced knowledge and technology, a service economy, and dominated (but not controlled) by a new professional and technical class, is one influential image of the future.

Other critics emphasize conflict and contradiction within present society as producing changes in the shape of society. These include the contradiction for the state in supporting capital investment while yet supporting welfare measures, leading to a *fiscal crisis*. Other perspectives emphasize the contradiction between a discipline demanded of the economy and the pleasures and self-fulfillment sought in the culture; the conflict between the *have-not* nations and the post-industrial ones; and the emergence of *state socialist* and *state capitalist* societies.

Historic image of the *good society* compares real and imagined societies by such criteria as *communal, controllable,* and *self-fulfillment.* Two other ways to measure society are by *evolutionary development* and by *comparison* of one society to another or by one society to different historic periods in its development.

NOTES

[1] The following discussion draws upon Leon Mayhew, *Society: Institutions and Activity* (Glenview, Ill.: Scott, Foresman, 1971).

[2] *Ibid.,* p. 21.

[3] Some useful sources are Gordon V. Childe, *Man Makes Himself* (New York: Mentor Books, 1951); Walter Goldschmidt, *Man's Way: A Preface to the Understanding of Human Society* (New York: Holt, Rinehart and Winston, 1959); Fred Cottrell, *Energy and Society* (New York: McGraw-Hill, 1955); and Otis Dudley Duncan, "Social Organization and the Ecosystem," in Robert E. L. Faris, ed., *Handbook of Modern Sociology* (Chicago: Rand McNally, 1964), pp. 36—82.

[4] The term is from Mayhew, *op. cit.,* p. 33.

[5] See Karl Polyani, *The Great Transformation: The Political and Economic Origins of Our Time* (Boston: Beacon Press, 1957).

[6] Ferdinand Toennies, *Community and Society,* trans. and ed. Charles Loomis (East Lansing: Michigan State University Press, 1957).

[7] Robert Redfield, "The Folk Society," *American Journal of Sociology* 52 (January 1947): 293—308.

[8] U.S. Employment Service, *Dictionary of Occupational Titles,* 3d ed. (Washington, D.C.: Government Printing Office, 1965).

[9] Robert Redfield, *The Folk Culture of Yucatan* (Chicago: The University of Chicago Press, 1941), p. 120.

[10] *Ibid.,* p. 121.

[11] Émile Durkheim's formulation of *mechanical and organic* solidarity is an exception to this. See *The Division of Labor in Society,* trans. George Simpson (New York: The Free Press, 1947).

[12] Oscar Lewis, "Tepoztlán Restudied: A Critique of the Folk-Urban Conceptualization of Social Change," *Rural Sociology* 18 (1953): 121—134.

[13] For discussion of mass society, see Robert Nisbet, *The Quest for Community* (New York: Oxford University Press, 1953); William Kornhauser, *The Politics of Mass*

Society (New York: The Free Press, 1959); and Daniel Bell, "America as a Mass Society: A Critique," in his *The End of Ideology* (New York: The Free Press, 1960).

[14] Erich Fromm, *Escape from Freedom* (New York: Holt, Rinehart and Winston, 1941).

[15] Kornhauser, *op. cit.,* p. 76.

[16] *Ibid.,* p. 76.

[17] Daniel Bell, *The End of Ideology* (New York: The Free Press, 1960), p. 29.

[18] Kornhauser, *op. cit.,* pp. 229—230.

[19] New York: Basic Books, 1973.

[20] *Ibid.,* p. 14.

[21] *Ibid.,* pp. 14—15 and Chap. 2.

[22] *Ibid.,* p. 15.

[23] *Ibid.,* pp. 15—18 and Chap. 3.

[24] *Ibid.,* pp. 18—26 and Chap. 3.

[25] *Ibid.,* p. 20.

[26] *Ibid.,* pp. 26—27 and Chap. 4.

[27] *Ibid.,* pp. 27—33 and Chap. 5.

[28] *Ibid.,* p. 31.

[29] *Ibid.,* p. 360.

[30] *Ibid.,* p. 365.

[31] *Ibid.,* p. 129.

[32] For Bell's discussion of this issue, see *ibid.,* pp. 475—480.

[33] Quoted in *ibid.,* p. 486.

[34] This is the argument of the influential study by James O'Connor, *The Fiscal Crisis of the State* (New York: St. Martin's Press, 1973).

[35] Bell has elaborated this problem in his *The Cultural Contradictions of Capitalism* (New York: Basic Books, 1976).

[36] See E. F. Schumacher, *Small Is Beautiful* (New York: Harper & Row, 1973).

[37] Ralph Waldo Emerson, *Ode to W. H. Channing.*

SUGGESTED READINGS

Daniel Bell, *The Coming of Post-Industrial Society* (New York: Basic Books, 1973). A provocative, controversial effort to discern the future to the year 2000.

Daniel Bell, *The Cultural Contradictions of Capitalism* (New York: Basic Books, 1976). A follow-up study that stresses how capitalism has created two incompatible cultures.

Gordon V. Childe, *Man Makes Himself* (New York: Mentor Books, 1951). A well-recognized analysis of social evolution.

Fred Cottrell, *Energy and Society* (New York: McGraw-Hill, 1955). A thoughtful sociological account of how the technological harnessing of energy has contributed to social evolution.

Erich Fromm, *Escape from Freedom* (New York: Holt, Rinehart and Winston, 1940). A classic work establishing the psychological responses of mass society.

William Kornhauser, *The Politics of Mass Society* (New York: The Free Press, 1959). An exploration of the political meaning of mass society.

Leon Mayhew, *Society: Institutions and Activity* (Glenview, Ill: Scott, Foresman, 1971). A brief but highly instructive effort to update sociology's central but often neglected concept, society.

Robert Nisbet, *The Quest for Community* (New York: Oxford University Press, 1953). A thoughtful, learned analysis of the renewed concern for community in the modern world.

Karl Polyani, *The Great Transformation: The Political and Economic Origins of Our Time* (New York: Holt, Rinehart and Winston, 1944; paperback, Boston: Beacon Press, 1957). A classic analysis of the origins of modern, industrial society in Europe.

Robert Redfield, *The Folk Culture of Yucatan* (Chicago: The University of Chicago Press, 1941). The most influential study of folk society in recent social science.

Ferdinand Toennies, *Community and Society,* trans. and ed. Charles Loomis (East Lansing: Michigan State University Press, 1957). This great classic established the basic contrast of folk and modern.

Alain Touraine, *The Post-Industrial Society,* trans. Leonard F. X. Mayhew (New York: Random House, 1971). A French socialist and leading sociologist advances a much more critical conception of postindustrial society than does Bell.

. . . the great modern state is absolutely dependent upon a bureaucratic basis.

Max Weber

Seven

BUREAUCRACY IN MODERN SOCIETY

In the modern world, ever larger organizations rise to dominate the social landscape, commanding a greater share of the social resources, ever greater social power, and proving to be effective mechanisms for organizing large aggregates of people in the pursuit of social goals.

THE NATURE OF LARGE ORGANIZATIONS

Large organizations are not all alike. Political parties, business firms, voluntary civic groups, governmental agencies, hospitals, prisons, universities, and armies are all large organizations; yet all are different from one another in the goals they pursue and in the kind and amount of resources they command. If they are all large, however, they are not equally so, for what is large can be anything from a department store or a social service agency to the General Motors Corporation or the Department of Defense.

Although variations in size and in purpose distinguish large organizations from one another, what is probably most common to them is a tendency to move forward *formalization* and then *bureaucratization;* these terms will be defined later on. It is these de-

velopments in modern organizations that will be the concern of this chapter.

Goal Specificity

Formal organizations are constructed for the pursuit of relatively specific objectives. It is goal-specificity that makes it possible for organizations to build a *rational* structure, that is, one in which activities are organized so as to lead efficiently to a previously defined goal. The more clearly and precisely an organization defines its goals, the more able is it to construct a rational structure.

Goal specificity is a matter of degree, not an all or nothing matter. Some organizations are more specific than others about their goals. Universities, for example, are often less specific than a business firm or a governmental agency. Undergraduate education, graduate training, and research are three valued activities in a university, but which should have precedence over the others, or what balance should be sought among them, is often an unsettled matter. Thus, where to put resources, what kind of teaching load to assign to the faculty, and how large a class size typically for undergraduates, may be matters of dispute within the university.

If the goals of bureaucratic organization are specific, however, they are not unchangeable. Even in such organizations as business firms, specific goals first established are subject to change over time, as circumstances change and as different groups within the organizations reshape goals to suit their particular interests.

In changing circumstances, too, goals may become too costly, or even unattainable. In some cases full success in attaining a goal may no longer justify putting so much of the organization's resources into it. When Dr. Jonas Salk developed a successful vaccine for polio, for example, the nationwide organization devoted to raising funds for the fight against polio—the National Foundation for Infantile Paralysis—was no longer justified. But organizations do not disappear for such reasons. The self-interest that many people have in an organization leads them to develop new goals and activities to enable the organization to continue. The National Foundation, for example, took up other childhood diseases and birth defects to which it could easily adapt an already existing medical services program and its nationwide "March of Dimes" fund-raising program.[1]

Formalization

The structure of an organization is "formal" when its positions and relations among them are officially and explicitly designated, independently of the characteristics of the persons who might occupy the positions. It is possible to draw a diagram of a formal structure, to picture it as a series of *offices* which rank above and below one another on a chart of organization. Office-holders perform specialized functions and are governed by written rules and regulations. Like goal specificity, formalization is a matter of degree; some organizations have formalized their structures more thoroughly than have others.

Bureaucratization

Formalization makes the rules, the authority, and the functions of office explicit. *Bureaucratization* carries this one step further; it is the development of a specialized administrative staff whose task is the control and coordination of the formal structure of an organization. What the owner-manager of an enterprise once did himself (and still does in small organizations)

is now subdivided among a number of specified functions, such as personnel, sales, production, research, advertising, and the like. Thus, when organizations grow in size, administering them requires a separate staff:

> In an organization that has been formally established, a special administrative staff usually exists that is responsible for maintaining the organization as a going concern and for coordinating the activities of its members.[2]

THE ORIGINS OF BUREAUCRACY

If we were to ask why bureaucracy is so pervasive in the modern world, an adequate answer can be either *historical* or *functional*.

The Emergence of Bureaucracy

Bureaucracy is not a new thing; some degree of bureaucracy was characteristic of great empires of the past. When control of long frontiers for defense or of waterways for subsistence was necessary, the complex administrative task generally brought into being a body of administrative officials and some methods for administering in routine and stable fashion, so that there was an accountability of these officials to the emperor.[3] For this reason, bureaucratic structures existed during the Roman Empire, and in civilizations such as the Chinese, the Byzantine, and the Egyptian.

Though bureaucracy in some ancient forms has existed outside of a money economy (where payment was in kind), Max Weber showed that the emergence of a money economy facilitated the development of bureaucracy; it permitted the payment of salaried officials who could count on the security of their position and thus on an opportunity for a career.[4] Such officials were dependent on the organization and on their superior, yet were independent enough to carry out assigned functions and to exercise judgment and expertise in doing so.

Yet, while bureaucracy existed in many premodern societies, it was *seldom* the dominant mode of organization it has become in modern society. The development of capitalism and the modern state, two major components in the development of modern so-

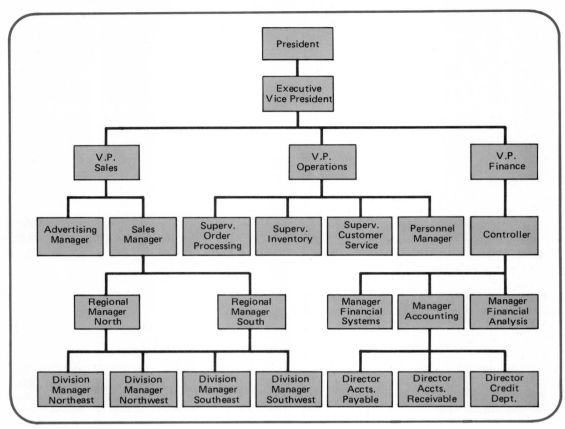

FIGURE 7.1
A typical business organization chart.

ciety, stimulated the growth of bureaucratic organization. The rational calculation of economic risks required not only a money system and a rational system of accounting, but also a political system that was not arbitrary and disruptive. Stable control of the economic and political conditions under which business flourished, then, demanded a rule of stable and accountable law and a system of officials who could be counted on to enforce law and ensure stability. According to Weber, "the great modern state is absolutely dependent upon a bureaucratic basis. The larger the state, and the more it . . . it becomes a great power state, the more unconditionally is this the case."[5]

The Functional Meaning of Bureaucracy According to this historical view, the bureaucratic form of so-

cial organization grew as certain social conditions encouraged its development. It thus provides historical evidence for the functional argument, namely, that bureaucracy is a response to a problem in social organization. Whether it be a factory, an army, or any process of organizing and administering the work of a fairly large and diversified number of people, those who seek to carry it out have to face a basic problem: what is the organizational form by which the efforts of so many people can be effectively coordinated into a common, productive effort? Bureaucracy is an indispensable aspect of modern society because it provides an efficient means for a stable and routinized administration of large and complex structures.

According to Max Weber, bureaucratic organization has grown because of its purely technical superiority over other forms of organization. He goes on to note that bureaucracy compares with any other form of organization "exactly as does the machine with the nonmechanical mode of production."[6] Bureaucracy, it seems, develops fully in any society which places foremost value on efficiency and effectiveness of administration. No previous society has equaled modern society's priority on the need to administer efficiently (see "Max Weber (1864–1920: The Rationalization of Social Life").

FORMAL STRUCTURE

The effort to coordinate efficiently the actions of many people toward a single objective leads to the development of *formal* structure. We call it formal, following Weber, whose classic formulation of the components of bureaucracy is still the basic one. Weber specified these components.

1. Each person in a bureaucratic organization occupies an *office,* which exists as an explicit definition of duties and functions, separate from the person who holds the office. The office, therefore, does not belong to any person; no one has a special claim upon it by virtue of inherited position, special rank, or privilege. Rather, claimants for the office are those who possess explicit qualifications based upon defined duties and functions. This separation of office from person frees the organization from dependence on any particular person, and provides a condition whereby individuals become dispensable and replaceable actors in the organization.

2. The relationships in a formal structure are relations among offices, not among persons, hence are *impersonal.* This ensures cooperation among persons who must interact to carry out their assigned duties; their personal feelings for one another can be subordinated to the demands of the office. The spirit of impersonality is one of detachment and distance, enhancing the capacity to render rational and objective judgments, uninfluenced by likes and dislikes of particular persons.

3. In a bureaucracy the norms are spelled out, generally in written and codified form, in quite explicit sets of *rules* and *regulations.* The rules are specific, in that they apply to quite definite situations and circumstances, but are also general, in that they formally apply to all (or at least all office holders within the scope of the rule) in an impersonal manner.

4. Bureaucracy develops a high degree of *specialization* of function and areas of *technical* competence. The selection of personnel for office then comes to be made in terms of technical and professional qualifications. This makes important the development of tests and other measures of technical achievement, by which the qualified can be certified. Any college student is aware of how much his or her life is governed by various kinds of tests.

5. A bureaucracy has a hierarchy of offices, with a chain of command and a centralization of authority and major decision-making within a management or administration. Thus, bureaucracy makes explicit the location of authority and the range and limits of the exercise of authority for any office. Each person in a bureaucracy is responsible *to* someone above him or her and is responsible *for* the actions of those under his or her authority. (See Figure 7.1.)

The Formalization of Organization

These several points provide a conception of the formalization of organization. It is rendered explicit and unambiguous and thus highly rational; indeed, it can be put down on paper by reducing it to a chart of organization that defines offices, codifies rules, specifies the flow of authority and the extent of responsibility, and indicates the technical competences that provide qualification for office.

Such an organization has distinct advantages over a more traditional one. For one thing, a formal organization does not depend upon the sentiments that the members hold toward one another; it even discourages those positive sentiments that might interfere with professional discipline and objective judgment. The organization becomes independent of any particular person and can replace anyone and continue to function. A large formal organization is unlikely to be disrupted by the loss of even its top-ranking officer.

Authority, Rewards, and Communication

The analysis of formal structure in large organizations has often focused particularly on three issues: authority, rewards, and communication.

MAX WEBER (1864–1920): THE RATIONALIZATION OF SOCIAL LIFE

In Max Weber's analysis, bureaucracy becomes sociologically significant, not only because it is increasingly dominant in modern life but also because its very dominance signifies the increasing *rationalization* of modern life. For Weber, a world grown more rational is the most significant development in the history of the Western world. A rationalized world is one less spontaneous, less mysterious, more subject to rule and procedure. It is a world moving away from custom and emotion, disregarding these to base action upon criteria related to the efficient attainment of objectives.

As Weber made clear, the rationalization of life proceeds in a number of different directions, but bureaucratic rationalization constitutes a major one. It is, though, by no means the only one; science, for example, is another. It may be that science and bureaucracy are the most significant of the rationalizing forces at work altering the world.

Science strips the world of much of its mystery, and sometimes unintentionally, of much of its charm. It contributes significantly to a "disenchantment with the world"—and here Weber was quoting Friedrich Schiller. It treats the world as a natural process that proceeds by rules of nature. The more man-as-scientist penetrates into nature, the more nature becomes known and unmysterious, and much of the workings of natural process become quite matter-of-fact.

Bureaucracy is a rationalizing force because it seeks to order its own world in a systematic fashion, within a clearly defined set of rules and procedures applying to all possible situations. In short, it seeks to reduce the world to a calculated and predictable pattern, controlled by criteria that logically relate means to ends.

Bureaucracy proceeds in the most efficient manner, not, therefore, necessarily in a customary manner. It is ever ready to discard tradition, it tries to repress the claims of sentiment, it abhors passion, and it ignores aesthetics. It has a place for the engineer but not the poet. Bureaucracy encourages matter-of-factness in thinking, seeing the world as a set of facts and things to be handled, manipulated, and treated.

When bureaucracy proceeds so rationally, it contributes significantly to rationalizing the world. Increasingly, the matter-of-fact attitude, the treatment of the world as an environment of objects and things which behave according to natural rules and are thus manipulable and controllable, constitutes a secular rationality that is now an inherent part of modern thinking, not merely scientific thinking. We are all living in a rationalized world.

Authority Formal organizations are designed so that, consistent with the hierarchy of positions, some positions have authority over others. In order that the occupant of each position will be able to carry out his tasks, sufficient power is provided in the form of control over resources—an adequate budget, access to personnel—and also control over people in subordinate positions by the capacity to reward or sanction.

Weber notes that hierarchy in office and "graded authority means a firmly ordered system of super- and subordination" by which lower offices are supervised by the higher ones.[7]

But this "firmly ordered system" of graded authority needs to be viewed as legitimate by participants in the system, else the exercise of decision-making at any given point will be challenged and orders will not be obeyed. Authority is always *delegated* downward in formal organization, so that each position operates with the authority allocated it from above.

But there has to be an ultimate source of legitimation of authority. That lies in charters, articles of incorporation, constitutions, bylaws, and legal statutes. The president of a corporation has his authority delegated by the board of directors, which draws its authority from the incorporation papers and the legal statutes governing corporation structure and the rights of private property.

Universities differ from corporations and other bureaucracies in that the faculty, which nominally ranks low on the university's chart of organization, nevertheless claims and exercises authority independently of the president and the chain of command. This is authority over curriculum and other academic matters and is usually delegated directly to the faculty by the board of trustees.

Rewards One consequence of ranked positions in formal organizations is an unequal distribution of rewards. Salaries range upward from that of the night watchman to the president. Other rewards—designated parking spaces, private offices, private secretaries, executive bonuses—may be available only to some upper level of ranks.

Such an unequal distribution of rewards, it is claimed, functions to attract talented people and to serve as an incentive to people to be productive. But the intricately complex differentiation within formal organization often makes the reward system a source of discontent. It is not easy to get agreement on the criteria by which rewards should be distributed.

Sometimes this may be because nonrational criteria enter in; women, for example, may be paid less because they are women, not because they are less productive. At the same time, note that it may be efficient—thus rational—for a corporation to take advantage of the weaker, more vulnerable position of women in the labor market in order to buy competent service more cheaply. Such efficiency may be rational from one perspective, but is hardly based on a rational conception of reward by merit.

In other cases, it is because credentials are claimed to be indicative of a greater capacity to perform with more ability or skill, when to many without a college degree it may not be obvious that the "college boys"

are doing more, only that they get more money because they went to college.

Finally, an organization does not necessarily attempt to provide equity in distributing rewards; it may only pay what it needs to get trained people and keep them in the system. This may mean that at one time it may be able to get secretaries and production workers cheaply, but pay dearly for engineers or research chemists.

Communication No complex organization can function effectively—or indeed at all—unless it has assured channels of communication. A pioneering student of organization, Chester Barnard, has made the existence of formal communication networks the central focus of his conception of organization.[8] Channels of communication, he says, must be known to all participants, each member should have access to the formal channel of communication, the lines should be as short and direct as possible, and those communicating should make use of the appropriate line of communication, not bypassing any link. Ideally, each member will have access to what he or she needs to know but will not be overburdened with extraneous information.

But effective communication in a hierarchy often proves to be difficult. For one thing, information flows more easily downward than it does upward, and the middle levels often block or distort communication between top and bottom. Furthermore, Barnard's principle that each should have access to what he or she needs to know is subject to interpretation; upper levels may believe that lower levels need to know only orders—what to do—and some occasional propaganda from the top, while those in lower levels may feel they need—and have a right—to know more.

As a consequence, informal and extralegitimate channels of communication in organizations—"grapevines," "scuttlebutt," "rumor mills"—operate in the absence of effective formal communication. Someone calls a strategically placed friend to find out "what is going on" or a secretary tells another secretary who tells someone else, and so on. In some cases these informal channels may contribute to the effectiveness of the organization by making possible quick and efficient communication not possible by formal means, or by encouraging a sharing of information among those who have similar tasks and responsibilities. But when these channels transmit inaccurate information, particularly at times of change and tension, they inhibit the effectiveness of the organization.

INFORMAL STRUCTURE

In his pioneering studies Max Weber focused on the formal processes that make bureaucracy a rational system, while leaving relatively unexamined the spontaneous and unplanned action that can be observed in any large organization. What actually goes on in large organizations, then, is only partially explained by a theory about formal structure. This other aspect of organization—"bureaucracy's other face"—is what sociologists conveniently call *informal structure*.

The Emergence of Informal Structure

However impersonal bureaucracy is supposed to be, the people who work in an organization interact frequently with some others; they come to know each other as persons, not merely as officeholders. As a consequence, they build a complex network of social relationships that are not formally prescribed; indeed they may violate some of the formal sanctions of the organization. Thus, as friends, they may "cover" for one another when they take time off that is not allowed, or they may provide one another with information about what is going on, creating informal gossip channels that circumvent the slower and less informative official channels. They invoke friendship as a way to get favors from others or to get information or ma-

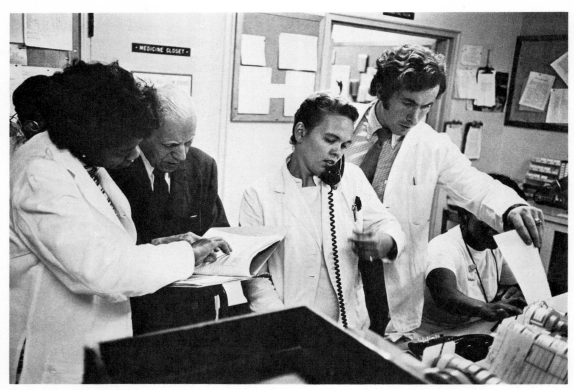

Modern professionals, such as these physicians and nurses, now often practice their trained expertise within large, bureaucratic organizations, such as hospitals.

THE BUREAUCRATIC PERSONALITY

The tension between administrators and professionals suggests that professionals adapt less easily than do administrators to the demands of authority and hierarchy in bureaucratic organization. The administrators and managers of bureaucratic organization—the "bureaucrats"—have long been viewed as timid and conforming individuals, unimaginative and uncreative, lacking initiative and flexibility, carefully following rules even when the result makes no sense. But is this mere stereotype or an accurate portrait?

Social scientists have accepted an influential essay by Robert Merton which argued that the psychological consequences of efficiency, rationality, and predictability in bureaucratic organization must of necessity produce "overconforming" officials.[18] There has been little actual research to test this model of the bureaucratic personality, however, and what there is has been inconsistent.

A study in metropolitan Detroit that compared salaried "bureaucratic" families with self-employed "entrepreneurial" families found that bureaucratic parents emphasized to their children the importance of adjustment to society, security, and getting along with others, while entrepreneurial parents instilled in their children a more active and manipulative approach to life, with an emphasis on strong aspirations and hard striving toward goals.[19] Here was support for the idea of a conforming bureaucratic personality.

Organization and Person

A world more bureaucratic, it would then seem, demands a more appropriate type of person, one who fits the role-needs of large-scale organizations and their competitive, impersonal environments. Sociologist David Riesman suggested that by mid-twentieth century just such a type of person had emerged in the United States: the *other-directed* individual.[20]

During the nineteenth century, the typical personality type was better defined as *innerdirected*. This was a person socialized in childhood into values and moral standards gained largely from the family, who then uses these standards to guide and control his or her behavior throughout the changing circumstances of adult life. A failure to conform to internalized standards produces *guilt.*

But in the twentieth century a new type of society, highly urbanized and incorporating people into large-scale organizations, demands a highly flexible, continually socializing type of person. This is the other-directed type found particularly among the urban, college-educated, bureaucratically employed middle classes.

The character of the other-directed person is especially sensitive to the expectations of peers in the immediate situation. Such a person readily responds to the cues about what to say or do that are expertly detected in the behavior of others. An other-directed individual is highly dependent on peer groups, and is socialized to be well liked and accepted—to "get along" with others and to "relate." Indeed, the need to be liked is basic to the other-directed personality. For direction and guidance, then, the other-directed person turns not primarily to parental values internalized in childhood, but to conformity to peer expectations and to the larger organizational world to which he or she is oriented through peers. A failure to conform to peer expectations produces *anxiety,* not guilt.

The Organization Man   Some years later, William Whyte gave popular expression to this concept of the other-directed person in business by the phrase, "the organization man."[21] Whyte studied middle-level corporate executives, their wives, and their suburban lives as evidence of a vastly conforming trend in modern, middle-class life. Indeed, "organization man" entered the American vocabulary, like the somewhat older term, "company man," as an unflattering name for upwardly mobile men in large organizations whose career aspirations led them to overconform to the social world.

William Whyte (and others, too) thought they were describing a decline in individualism in the United States. The organization man had presumably replaced the rugged individualist. The less free, more conformity-demanding bureaucratic structure had replaced the smaller social worlds of the past in which freedom and individualism flourished. But this interpretation is largely a romantic misreading of history. Rugged individualists there may have been, but they were not the typical person in those earlier days of our history. And small organizations, we have already

Business suits and briefcases are the trademark of the "organization man." At places such as Park Avenue in New York City they can be seen in abundance.

seen, are not freer and less conformity-demanding than large ones.

The Personality Market

Another equally critical view of the relation between bureaucracy and personality is C. Wright Mills's concept of the "personality market." The vastly increased need for white-collar skills and services, which is also one consequence of the change from small, local business firms to large ones, has created a situation where one's personality, as well as one's trained skills, becomes a commodity which one "sells" on the labor market. This is particularly true for those bureaucratic functions dealing primarily with sales, personnel, advertising, and public relations.

There are three conditions for a stabilized personality market. First, an employee must be part of bureaucratic enterprise, selected, trained, and supervised by a higher authority. Second, from within this bureaucracy, his regular business must be to contact the public so as to present the firm's good name before all comers. Third, a large portion of this public must be anonymous, a mass of urban strangers.[22]

What Mills is pointing to is bureaucracy's need for a pseudopersonal relation to substitute for the real thing. The salesperson's "friendly" smile; the tactful, courteous manners displayed to clients and customers; the deliberate use of a "pleasing" personality to sell something or otherwise do business—this is the marketing of personality, the "selling" of yourself as if your own personality were a packaged commodity to be advertised and sold.

The conscious recognition that personality could be a marketable commodity perhaps began with Dale Carnegie's book (first published in 1936 and a best-seller for many years) *How to Win Friends and Influence People,* which meant how to win friends *in order* to influence people. From then until now a long series of best-selling "success" manuals, Dale Carnegie seminars, various courses and training programs, and charm schools, have promised an easy formula for success in dealing with others in the bureaucratic, corporate world.

As a consequence, notes Mills:

. . . the requirements of the personality market have diffused as a style of life. What began as the public and commercial relations of business have become deeply personal: there is a public-relations aspect to private relations, including even relations with oneself. . . . The sales personality, built and maintained for operations on the personality market, has become a dominating type, a pervasive model for imitation for masses of people, in and out of selling.[23]

The Gamesman   A newer study by Michael Maccoby suggests that these types were replaced in the 1970s, in at least some cases, by a new type, the *gamesman.*[24] Maccoby and his associates interviewed 250 corporate executives, plus their wives, children, and secretaries, in twelve large firms. These twelve were innovative and growing corporations in such high-technology fields as weaponry, electronics, and data processing.

Like the organization men, the gamesmen were team players, but with a difference. Their success was measured by their ability to organize teams that win in competition within the corporation and also in competition between the corporation and a rival in the corporate world.

According to Maccoby's perspective, the organization men came into being in the quieter atmosphere of the 1950s, but the turbulent 1970s brought the gamesman on the scene. They were willing risk-takers in an unstable environment. Intelligent and quick to learn, they cared for and were concerned about the welfare of co-workers—up to a point. They knew that unhappy workers were not likely to be creative, but they did not feel they could waste time on others' personal problems unrelated to the goals of the team. Many of them, furthermore, recognized legitimate social concerns about safety, quality, and environmental impact, but unless they and their competitors were restrained by governmental regulations, they ignored these issues.

In the often exciting world of innovative technology, the gamesmen are the successful ones, but their gamesmanship nonetheless takes a personal toll. They are winners who ignore losers and who avoid a deep personal involvement with colleagues. As a consequence, they gradually dry up their emotions and reduce their capacity for warmth and love. Some of them painfully recognize the loss they and their wives and children incur because they do not become genuinely devoted to other human beings. They often seem unable to grow beyond the adolescent notion that life is always a game and to outgrow the self-centered interest in scoring another victory.

Not all those whom Maccoby interviewed were gamesmen, however. There were still the organization men so prominent in the 1950s, and there were also the worst of rugged individualists, *jungle fighters,* intent on dominating and controlling. No one type of personality, then, exists today in the corporate structure. Furthermore, if Maccoby had studied executives in other types of corporations—banking or steel or oil, for example—or if he had studied executives in television or administrators in the university, perhaps other types than the gamesman would have been the most prominent.

Comparing Bureaucrats and Nonbureaucrats   A recent study by sociologist Melvin Kohn went at the issue in another way: he compared bureaucratically employed men with nonbureaucratically employed ones, and he, too, got findings that did not fit an image of a timid and conforming bureaucrat.[25] Based on interviews with over 3,000 employed males, Kohn argued that:

Men who work in bureaucratic firms or organizations tend to value, not conformity, but self-direction. They are more open-minded, have more personally responsible standards of morality, and are more receptive to change than are men who work in nonbureaucratic organizations.[26]

These findings contradict the predominant image of the bureaucratic personality. Kohn asserted that bureaucrats are more highly educated than nonbureaucrats, and that this one factor makes considerable difference. But not all the difference. There are also differences in the bureaucratic conditions of occupational life:

These are, principally, that the employees of bureaucracies tend to work at substantively more complex jobs than do other men of comparable educational level, but under conditions of somewhat closer supervision; to work under an externally-imposed pressure of time that results in their having to think faster; to work a shorter week; to work in company of, but not necessarily in harness with, co-workers; to face greater competition; to enjoy much greater job protections; and to earn more than other men of similar educational background (even when in jobs of comparable occupational status).[27]

The variation in types of persons dominant in large, bureaucratic organizations, then, dispels any notion that bureaucratic structure produces only one bureaucratic type of person. The fit between organization and personality is obviously more complex and varied, and is not yet fully understood. A great deal more needs to be known about how individuals adapt to large, complex structures before we can adequately balance out what combination of gains and losses for individuality are implied by the emergence of bureaucracy.

BUREAUCRACY AND SOCIAL POWER

Bureaucracy by design and intent is not democratic. To say that is not merely to criticize but instead to observe that a significant issue in modern society is the relation of bureaucratic structure to the distribution and exercise of power.

The hierarchical nature of bureaucracy has always concentrated authority at the top. This is so even when, for reasons of efficiency, considerable authority may be decentralized to subordinate units of the organization, and when the professional expert may enjoy considerable autonomy in the performance of his functions. Accordingly, a complex and efficient organizational apparatus is controlled by its top administrators, who are in a position to exercise power relatively independently of those to whom they are nominally responsible, such as trustees, directors, or elected cabinet officers.

When bureaucrats are full-time career officials of government agencies and their superiors are elected or appointed cabinet officials, these latter are often at a severe disadvantage in carrying out policy that the former oppose. The career officials' control of the organization enables them to offer considerable resistance to new policies. When a socialist party in an agrarian province of Canada came to power, for example, conservative career officials effectively subverted the efforts of the newly appointed cabinet officers to carry out a reforming program.[28] The cabinet officers depended so much on the bureaucratic machinery, as well as the knowledge and skills of the bureaucrats, that they were unable to overcome the resistance of the bureaucrats to political innovations.

This suggests that bureaucracy is often a conservative force in resisting social change because a combination of power, based upon control and competency, and an ideological orientation may lead bureaucrats to favor a particular social policy. However, the opposite effect can also be achieved. By appointing new officials who have a different political ideology but the same professional competence, bureaucracy can be a powerful force for social change.

Bureaucracy and Totalitarian Power

Historical scholarship has provided evidence of the importance of bureaucratic structures in the rise to power of totalitarian groups. Stalin, for example, used his strategic position as secretary of the central committee of the Bolshevik Party and the control of the party machinery that this gave him to consolidate his power within the party structure and to defeat and destroy his opponents.

Totalitarians have long recognized the importance of organizational bureaucracy as an instrument of power. Philip Selznick, for example, documented the Bolshevik technique of capturing power within an organization to use it as a weapon in the struggle for power.[29] In this process, the offices of secretary and treasurer are more useful to hold than that of president, since through them the money and the appointed staff positions of the organization can be controlled.

Perhaps the most painstaking and impressive examination of the relationship between bureaucracy and the consolidation of totalitarian power is Franz Neumann's superb analysis of the way in which the Nazis used bureaucracy in building a totalitarian power structure in Germany.[30] When the National Socialist (Nazi) Party seized power in Germany in 1933 there was already in place a powerful governmental

The authority to make policy in a large organization is usually concentrated in the hands of a few top officers or directors—and, as yet, they will typically be white and male.

bureaucracy. This bureaucratic administration of the German state was strengthened and enlarged, even as the party gained control of it. It did that by three means: *expulsion* of Jews and other "unreliable elements"; *indoctrination* of government personnel; and *monopolization* of all new positions.

The party itself became a huge bureaucratic machine, with party offices paralleling governmental ones, even to one for foreign affairs. Most of its top leaders, furthermore, held top governmental positions, so the two bureaucracies were interlocked.

But the process did not stop there. "National Socialism must necessarily carry to an extreme the one process that characterizes the structure of modern society, bureaucratization."[31] A basic aspect of Nazi control was to destroy every independent group that stood between citizen and state—trade unions, political parties, churches, and civic organizations—then to create in their place a system of autocratic bureaucracies that sought to organize and control all areas of life: work, family, culture, athletics, youth, recreation. There was, says Neumann:

. . . a huge network of organizations covering almost every aspect of human life, each run by presidents and vice-presidents and secretaries and treasurers, each employing advertising agencies and publicity men, each out to interfere with, to act as the mediator in, the relations between man and man. . . .

What National Socialism has done is to transform into authoritarian bodies the private organizations that in a democracy still give the individual an opportunity for spontaneous activity.[32]

Bureaucracy and Democracy

Even in democratic societies those who control large bureaucratic organizations constitute an elite of power, for large and efficient organizations are significant instruments of power, whether they are labor unions, political parties, corporations, trade associations, civic organizations, or governmental agencies. According to Peter Blau and Marshall Meyer:

. . . bureaucracies create profound inequalities of power. They enable a few individuals, those in control of bureaucractic machinery to exercise much more influence than others in society in general and on the government in particular.[33]

In modern society, bureaucracy and democracy at best live in tension with one another, for they are two very different human systems. Bureaucracy is a system for the efficient organization of human action for explicit goals, and it uses human beings as experts who know better than anyone else how to carry out specialized tasks. Democracy, in turn, is a system for governing by the participation and consent of the governed; achieving the consent of the governed requires that dissent be allowed and indeed freely expressed in order that consent by a majority be freely attained.

The unintended but nonetheless real effect of the proliferation of bureaucracies in modern societies, then, is to contribute to the creation of a social world of large organizations. Each is hierarchical, authoritative, highly organized, and rationally planned, and each manned by administrative and technical experts with professional qualifications for what they do, for the judgments they render, and for the decisions they make or at least strongly influence. Such a world, however unintentionally, is not democratic. This concentration of power in bureaucratic organization has far-ranging implications that were not anticipated in a democratic theory, the basic ideas and values of which have their roots in the small-scale world of the eighteenth century.

Yet bureaucracies are not entirely antidemocratic (and antiequalitarian) in their influence. For one thing, they make use of rational employment policies that accept all who qualify, regardless of such ascribed status as sex or race.[34] Furthermore, equal treatment under law (or rule or regulation) and objective and equal treatment of all according to some objective criteria are values that bureaucracies readily accept in principle.

To be sure, large organizations by no means always practice these values. But attainment of such values is not contrary to rational bureaucratic functioning. If public bureaucracies, like the police and the schools, were to treat all citizens equally, regardless of class or race, such neutral practice would strengthen democracy. This does not usually happen because influential groups in the community maintain their privileged positions within organizations against the rational criteria of the bureaucratic process, as when white males control these organizations.

BUREAUCRACY IN A POSTMODERN SOCIETY

Whatever may be the moral stance we take toward it, the fact remains that we live in an "organizational society." The working lives of most of us are absorbed in large, bureaucratized organizations. The significant economic, political, and civic activities that shape decisions for the future are made largely by and through these organizations. The theory of formal organization that began with the work of Max Weber stressed the hierarchical control of routinized work processes in highly centralized organizations. The moral response to that was to see pervasive bureaucracy as a threat to the freedom of the individual by promoting the bureaucratic conformity of "organization men," as well as being a threat to democratic process.

But as is so often the case, reality moves ahead of theory. In recent years a number of innovations and developments in organizational structure have challenged existing theory. It seems that bureaucracy in postmodern society will not be what we now know bureaucracy to be.

Some of the changes are readily apparent now. Professional autonomy and expertise, for example, force modification in hierarchical controls and achieve greater freedom of movement and decision-making on the job. We can expect this trend to increase. Greater technical competence on the part of people in bureaucratic structures will require greater modification to accommodate to their professional work patterns. More and more, people will be recognized as competent, self-regulating individuals who can be entrusted to do a job without close supervision.

Furthermore, technological developments move large organizations away from the model of the routinized production line, whether in factory or office; routine work is increasingly mechanized, requiring fewer but better-trained people on the job who can and must assume greater personal responsibility for what goes on at the point of production. Automation only maximizes this process.

Not the least factor in the new form of organization is the resistance of more educated people to being treated like "organization men." Michel Crozier, one of Europe's foremost students of organization, insists that a more "sophisticated" people in a more "complex culture" are a basic factor in the evolution of organization in modern society.[35] From his perspective, this has another consequence; the power of experts is to be reduced, not strengthened. Managerial power will be less a technical power—that of the expert—and more a political and judicial power; administrative success will depend more on the human qualities of leadership than on scientific know-how or on being the "boss."

These predictions about bureaucracy in postmodern society are about changes in the internal structure of formal organization. They herald new forms that will be more livable for a better educated, more professionalized work force. If this is to be so, then bureaucracy may more successfully integrate individuals into the organization, individuals who can build strong

commitments to a career in the organization and to its objectives.

But in a society more, not less bureaucratized, the problems of the relation of bureaucracy to democracy remain difficult and unresolved. On that matter there are essentially two positions emerging in the relevant literature. One argues that bureaucracy is a necessary feature of modern society, though not beyond reform; a second position argues for a fundamental commitment to the debureaucratization of society.

Is Bureaucracy Necessary?

The argument that bureaucratic organization is necessary is based upon the argument that it is an instrument by which modern society undertakes tasks of

Bureaucratic organization seems to be changing from one in which orders move down a chain of command to one in which management strives to coordinate and control, which makes necessary more meeting together in small groups.

large dimension and accomplishes them efficiently. The gathering of human skills and technical resources into a single highly rationalized organization permits the effective exploitation of opportunities for technological development, for scientific advance, and for the mass production and distribution of resources that create an affluent society.

The abolition of large-scale organization, it is argued, would require a return to small communities, to a simpler and less productive technology, to lowered standards of living, and indeed to many of the conditions that prevailed in the nineteenth century. It seems unlikely that the moral deficiencies and human problems of bureaucracy—real and compelling as these are—are going to induce a modern people to forgo the obvious advantages of organization for a return to some romanticized version of a simpler life. Thus, the dilemma of bureaucracy versus democracy:

Even if we could turn back the clock of history and abolish bureaucracies, we would be reluctant to do so because of having to surrender the benefits we derive from them. Some authors have concluded that modern society's need for bureaucratic methods spells the doom of democracy. But why interpret a historical dilemma as a sign of an inescapable fate? Why not consider it a challenge to find ways to avert the impending threat? If we want to utilize efficient bureaucracies, we must find democratic methods of controlling them lest they enslave us.[36]

Bureaucracy with a Human Face   Those who insist on the necessity of bureaucracy, however, have been able to offer very little on the matter of how to save democracy from bureaucratic subversion. Instead, they have suggested the possibility of a less authoritarian organization, as we noted above, with more autonomy for its professional staff—bureaucracy with a human face. That is the futurist vision offered by sociologist George Berkley, for example, who speaks of it as becoming a "loose, amorphous, and sprawling affair."[37] Management is to be less a matter of authority and control, more a matter of coordination and support.

Such an approach, however, focuses only on the *internal* nature of bureaucracy, on the relation of its individual members to the processes of centralization, hierarchy, and authority. It does not confront the more basic issue, that of the power of bureaucratic organization in a democratic society.

Participation and Self-Government

For some time now, particularly in European industrial societies, there has been developing both theory and practice committed to the idea that there is an alternative to bureaucratic domination. It is a conception of democratic participation applied to all forms of organization in society, including especially those of the economic sphere.

The most notable form is that of workers' participation and self-management in industrial enterprises. Developments in Sweden, Yugoslavia, Holland, France, and Norway have in each case moved toward a greater involvement of workers in the decision-making process of the organization and thus toward a decentralization of authority.[38]

There are a variety of theories and practices now existing and in contention, but the most antibureaucratic among them call for the full democratization of decision-making and a full sharing in civic responsibility by the members of all the organizations of society, and, consequently, of society itself. Carole Pateman expresses the ideal in this way:

For a democratic polity to exist it is necessary for a participatory society to exist, i.e., a society where all political systems have been democratized and socialization through participation can take place in all areas. The most important area is industry; most individuals spend a great deal of their lifetime at work, and the business of the workplace provides an education in the management of collective affairs that is difficult to parallel elsewhere . . . If individuals are to exercise the maximum amount of control over their own lives and environment then authority structures in these areas must be so organized that they can participate in decision-making.[39]

As modern society moves into postmodern forms we can expect two significant developments. One will be the further extension of the bureaucratic form of organization throughout the world, whether it be capitalist or socialist, democratic or totalitarian. There is coming into being, in Henry Jacoby's phrase, "the bureaucratization of the world."[40]

But there is also coming into being a struggle against bureaucracy, one that begins with the denial of the claim that bureaucracy is necessary and unavoidable. Doing away with the bureaucratization of human organization, however, requires a radical democratization of existing society, one that would radically transform existing capitalist and socialist societies. It would seek, instead, to decentralize large organizations, to extend participation in decision-making to all members or citizens, and to develop fully the individual's capacity to share in authority and to assume a civic responsibility. More than bureaucracy is at stake in such a struggle; it is the very shape of society.

It is worth noting, furthermore, that this struggle against bureaucracy has not had its greatest impetus and development in the United States. The United States has, instead, provided the fullest development of a positive, sociological theory of bureaucracy, developed from Weber but lacking his own moral position against it. From such sociological theory, in turn, has come the academic specialization of administrative and management theory, a process that builds upon the assumptions of the naturalness, the rightness, as well as the necessity of bureaucratic structure.

The struggle over bureaucracy has reached only an incipient stage—and more in theory than in practice. But it seems evident enough now that postmodern society will be an arena of struggle in which bureaucracy will be one point of battle.[41]

SUMMARY

Formal organization is characterized by *goal-specificity;* by *formalization* and by *bureaucratization.*

A formal structure has these components: (1) positions are explicitly defined as offices; (2) social relationships are impersonal; (3) norms are explicit rules and regulations; (4) a high degree of specialization of function with utilization of criteria of technical competence; and (5) a formalized hierarchy of offices and a centralization of authority.

Authority in organization is delegated downward but is always ultimately legitimated.

A system of *rewards* is used to assure adequate recruitment and to encourage productivity, but disagreements over criteria can make rewards a source of discontent.

Clear channels of *communication* are essential for effective organization. Where formal communication is inadequate, informal "grapevines" provide needed information.

Formal organizations have also an *informal* structure. Interaction among peers leads people to know each other as persons and so to act in ways other than officially prescribed. They help one another to get around red tape, and they resist being mere agents of the organization.

Professionals create problems for organizational authority by demands for *autonomy* in work and by efforts to promote *professional* goals at the expense of organizational goals.

The conception of a bureaucratic personality as a person conforming closely to rules, timid and unimaginative, is not fully supported by social research. In large corporations the "organization man" may have been replaced with the "gamesman." A great deal needs to be known about how individuals adapt to large, complex structures before we can fully understand the relation of individuality to bureaucracy.

Bureaucracy is a source of power in society, and power accrues to those who manage bureaucratic organizations. All totalitarian societies have utilized bureaucratic structure to centralize power. Bureaucracy and democracy are in tension because the first is an efficient organization for achieving explicit goals, and the latter is a system for governing by the participation and consent of the governed. The proliferation of bureaucratic organizations is then a threat to democratic practice, though such rational practices of bureaucracies as equal treatment of all supports democracy.

In postmodern society, bureaucracy will spread while also allowing its well-trained members greater autonomy and responsibility. However, there is also emerging a basic challenge to bureaucracy in the form of efforts to decentralize and to create self-governing organizations.

NOTES

[1] See David L. Sills, "Voluntary Associations: Instruments and Objects of Change," *Human Organization* 18 (Spring 1959): 17–21; reprinted in John N. Edwards and Alan Booth, eds., *Social Participation in Urban Society* (Cambridge, Mass.: Schenkman, 1973), 173–179. See also David Sills, *The Volunteers* (New York: The Free Press, 1957).

[2] Peter M. Blau and Richard W. Scott, *Formal Organizations: A Comparative Approach* (San Francisco; Chandler, 1962), p. 7.

[3] See Karl Wittfogel, *Oriental Despotism* (New Haven, Conn: Yale University Press, 1957).

[4] Hans Gerth and C. Wright Mills, eds. and trans., *From Max Weber: Essays in Sociology* (New York: Oxford University Press, 1946), Chap. 8, "Bureaucracy," pp. 196–244, esp. pp. 204–209.

[5] *Ibid.,* p. 211.

[6] *Ibid.,* p. 214.

[7] *Ibid.,* p. 197.

[8] Chester Barnard, *The Functions of the Executive* (Cambridge, Mass.: Harvard University Press, 1938).

[9] For a discussion of colleague control in group medical practice, see Eliot Friedson, *Professional Dominance: The Social Structure of Medical Care* (New York: Atherton Press, 1970).

[10] According to sociologist Roger Krohn, scientists are more closely regulated and less autonomous than physicians; see his *The Social Shaping of Science: Institutions, Ideology, and Careers in Science* (Westport, Conn.: Greenwood, 1970).

[11] See William Kornhauser, *Scientists in Industry: Conflict and Accommodation* (Berkeley: University of California Press, 1962); and Simon Marcson, *The Scientist in American Industry* (New York: Harper & Row, 1960).

[12] Melville Dalton, "Conflicts Between Staff and Line Managerial Officers," *American Sociological Review* 15 (June 1950): 342–351.

[13] Charles Perrow, *"The Analysis of Goals in Complex Organizations,"* *American Sociological Review* 26 (December 1961): 854–855.

[14] *Ibid.,* p. 859.

[15] *Ibid.,* p. 862.

[16] Ruth Leeds, "The Absorption of Protest: A Working Paper," in W. W. Cooper, H. J. Leavitt, and M. W. Shelly II, eds., *New Perspectives in Organizational Research* (New York: Wiley, 1964), pp. 115–135.

[17] William J. Haga, George Graen, and Fred Dansereau, Jr., "Professionalism and Role Making in a Service Organization: A Longitudinal Investigation," *American Sociological Review* 39 (February 1974): 122–133.

[18] Robert K. Merton, "Bureaucratic Structure and Personality," in Robert K. Merton, et al., eds., *Reader in Bureaucracy* (New York: The Free Press, 1952), pp. 361–371.

[19] Daniel R. Miller and Guy E. Swanson, *The Changing American Parent* (New York: Wiley, 1958).

[20] David Riesman, with Nathan Glazer and Reul Denny, *The Lonely Crowd* (New Haven, Conn.: Yale University Press, 1950).

[21] William H. Whyte, *The Organization Man* (New York: Simon and Schuster, 1956).

[22] C. Wright Mills, *White-Collar* (New York: Oxford University Press, 1951), p. 183. For a similar conception of personality, the "marketeers," see Erich Fromm, *Man for Himself* (New York: Holt, Rinehart and Winston, 1947).

[23] *Ibid.,* p. 187.

[24] Michael Maccoby, *The Gamesman* (New York: Simon and Schuster, 1976).

[25] Melvin L. Kohn, "Bureaucratic Man: A Portrait and an Interpretation," *American Sociological Review* 36 (June 1971): 461–474.

[26] *Ibid.,* p. 465.

[27] *Ibid.,* p. 469.

[28] Seymour M. Lipset, *Agrarian Socialism* (Berkeley: University of California Press, 1949).

[29] Phillip Selznick, *The Organizational Weapon* (New York: McGraw-Hill, 1952).

[30] Franz Neumann, *Behemoth: The Structure and Practice of National Socialism* (New York: Oxford University Press, 1942).

[31] *Ibid.,* p. 367.

[32] *Ibid.,* p. 369.

[33] Peter M. Blau and Marshall W. Meyer, *Bureaucracy in Modern Society,* 2d ed. (New York: Random House, 1971), p. 166. This is one of the few studies of bureaucracy that contains any discussion of its relation to democracy. See Chap. 8.

[34] *Ibid.,* pp. 164–165.

[35] Michel Crozier, *The Bureaucratic Phenomenon* (Chicago: University of Chicago Press, 1964).

[36] *Ibid.,* pp. 167–168.

[37] George E. Berkley, *The Administrative Revolution: Notes on the Passing of Organization Man* (Englewood Cliffs, N.J.: Prentice-Hall, 1971), p. 24.

[38] See Benot Abrahamsson, *Bureaucracy of Participation: The Logic of Organization* (Beverly Hills, Cal.: Sage Publications, 1977).

[39] Carole Pateman, *Participation and Democratic Theory* (London: Cambridge University Press, 1970), p. 43.

[40] Henry Jacoby, *The Bureaucratization of the World,* trans. Eveline L. Kanes (Berkeley: University of California Press, 1973; paperback edition, 1976).

[41] Some conception of the struggle against bureaucracy can be gained from these sources: Abrahamson, *op. cit.;* Pateman, *op. cit.;* and Jacoby, *op. cit.;* as well as C. George Benello and Dimitrios Roussopoulos, eds., *The Case for Participatory Democracy* (New York: Viking Press, 1971); Kenneth A. Megill, *The New Democratic Theory* (New York: The Free Press, 1970); and Murray Bookchin, *Post-Scarcity Anarchism* (Berkeley, Cal.: The Rampart Press, 1971).

SUGGESTED READINGS

Chester I. Barnard, *The Functions of the Executive.* Cambridge, Mass.: Harvard University Press, 1938. A pioneering study by an experienced executive that stresses communication.

Morroe Berger, *Bureaucracy and Society in Modern Egypt.* Princeton, N.J.: Princeton University Press, 1957. A study of the problems of bureaucracy in a society still traditional in many ways.

George E. Berkley, *The Administration Revolution: Notes on the Passing of Organization Man.* Englewood Cliffs, N.J.: Prentice-Hall, 1971. A review of changes in organizational theory and practice presumably heralding a postbureaucratic era.

Peter M. Blau and Marshall M. Meyer, *Bureaucracy in Modern Society,* 2d ed. New York: Random House, 1971. A brief survey of the study of bureaucracy by a foremost student, including a chapter on democracy and bureaucracy.

Peter M. Blau, *The Dynamics of Bureaucracy.* Chicago: University of Chicago Press, 1955. Blau's renowned study of bureaucracy in social service agencies.

Michel Crozier, *The Bureaucratic Phenomenon.* Chicago: University of Chicago Press, 1964. An influential French study that predicts the transformation of bureaucracy to less authoritarian forms.

Hans Gerth and C. Wright Mills, eds. and trans., *From Max Weber: Essays in Sociology.* New York: Oxford University Press, 1946. Herein is Weber's famous pioneering essay on bureaucracy.

Alvin Gouldner, *Patterns of Industrial Bureaucracy.* Glencoe, Ill.: The Free Press, 1954. An oft-quoted study of bureaucratization processes in a mine and a factory.

Seymour M. Lipset, *Agrarian Socialism.* Berkeley: University of California Press, 1950. A study of how entrenched bureaucracy can resist political change.

Franz Neumann, *Behemoth: The Structure and Practice of National Socialism.* New York: Oxford University Press, 1942. Still a superb study of the political and economic bureaucratization of Germany under the Nazis.

Max Weber, *The Theory of Social and Economic Organization,* trans. A. M. Henderson and Talcott Parsons. New York: Oxford University Press, 1947. Another source of Weber's writings on bureaucracy.

City air makes people free.

Medieval saying

Eight

URBAN STRUCTURES

One of the oldest forms of social group is that created by human aggregates clustering within a geographical area, a social arrangement that varies from the smallest village to the gigantic metropolis. It is this form of social group that we have long called *community*.

The concept of community has usually meant two things: first, the organization of social life within a geographical locality; and, secondly, closely knit social relations and a strong social unity—a "we-feeling." The small village of premodern times—the village as folk society—provided the model of what was meant by community.

But this historic form of community has largely been replaced by the city. The folk community of preindustrial life has given way to the encompassing *urban structure* of modern life. While the city is also located within a geographical locality, it does not exhibit the closely knit social relations and the strong social unity that once defined the community.

For some, the passing of traditional village life and the emergence of the modern city mean an inevitable decline of community; the city, they believe, cannot truly be called a community. This, in turn, leads others to look instead, for the qualities of community—unity and a sense of belonging together—in other forms of social organization: in religious groups, social movements, ethnic and racial groups, professional organizations, and the like.

But whether or not the city deserves to be called a community, it nonetheless stands out as a prominent feature of modern society. Urban structures now incorporate most of the population in modern societies the world over. Furthermore, even in the sprawling urban locality, people develop sentiments of belonging and attachment that they do not do for bureaucratic structures.

It may be too soon, then, to deny that the city can be a modern version of community. But, in any case, the city is a fundamental component of modern society; for that reason, it needs to be examined sociologically for what it is. And it needs to be analyzed in terms of its still promising potential as a form of community.

URBANIZATION

For most of human history, the largest part of humanity lived in small bands for hunting and gathering, and after that in localities no larger than the rural village. No longer is this so; the Industrial Revolution broke through the ancient pattern of human settlement and created industrial cities of size and scope not dreamed of before.

In Europe this began some three centuries ago, with the movement of vast numbers of peasants to cities and factory towns, where they became urban workers. This was a tremendous uprooting process, in which former peasants lost any sense of being located in a stable and traditional community, organized around kinship, religion, and a common life.

In the United States, in turn, the rapid pace of industrialization after the Civil War converted the nation into an industrial society in a few decades, and set in motion a rapid urbanizing process. Americans became city people in large numbers in a short period. By now, about three Americans out of four are urban and more than half live in metropolitan areas of over 100,000 population. Furthermore, the trend continues to run strongly in that direction. The continued industrial and technological transformation of modern society promises only further urbanization of its population.

The Rise of Cities

Cities are not anything new. According to historical records as well as archeological evidence, people have lived in cities for three or four thousand years. But usually only a small part of a society's population inhabited the city, the majority living an agrarian life in the surrounding countryside.[1]

Cities could not emerge, however, until certain specified conditions made it possible for them to do so. For one thing, there had to be a sufficient surplus of food and other resources to enable a small segment of the population not to engage in direct, food-producing activities. At first, this segment was probably a priesthood, which became in time an administrative and political elite. Second, there also had to be a level of tech-

nology and of social organization that enabled the city to have sufficient control over the countryside in order to ensure its own existence. Armies and bureaucracies came to be essential units in the social organization that made the city possible. Peasants, it should be understood, did not willingly yield up any surplus; cities were built by forcefully expropriating a surplus from the countryside.

Medieval Cities   The growth of cities never occurred at an unbroken pace. In Europe, for example, the fall of Rome brought an urban decline for several centuries. Cities did not become significant again in Europe until the restoration of trade and commerce about the tenth century. Then cities grew up around the walled towns that served as administrative centers and defensive strongholds for the feudal aristocracy. Gradually an urban population of artisans and merchants built the great medieval cities that produced a distinctly urban culture and way of life.[2]

Throughout the Middle Ages, however, these cities were small by present standards and grew slowly. For example, Florence in 1388 had a population of 90,000 and Venice in 1422 had 190,000. London in 1377 had only 30,000, but by 1801, as the major city of the most industrialized nation in the world, it had 865,000 inhabitants.

The Urbanized Society

Prior to 1850 there were large industrial cities in the western world, yet no society had so concentrated

Walled medieval cities grew up as trade centers and defensible areas to house the local aristocracy.

its population in cities to an extent sufficient so that society could be considered urbanized. Even by 1900 probably only Great Britain was an *urbanized* society. But now all industrial societies are urbanized, and there is an accelerating world trend toward global urbanization.

The growth of an urban population in the world is greater than population growth in general. According to United Nations data, it has grown in the following manner:

- 1800   5.1 percent
- 1850   6.3 percent
- 1900   13.3 percent
- 1950   28.7 percent
- 1975   39.2 percent
- (projected)   2000   47.9 percent[3]

As Table 8.1 shows, however, there is much greater urban concentration in the more industrially developed nations.

Urbanization in the United States   The United States has been an urbanized society for only a few decades. According to the first census in 1790, only one person in twenty (5.1 percent) lived in an urban

place. From the Civil War on, however, the urban population grew steadily:[4]

- 1860   19.8 percent
- 1870   28.2 percent
- 1900   39.7 percent
- 1920   51.2 percent
- 1950   59.0 percent

The turning point had arrived in 1920; by then more than half the population of the United States lived in urban places.

As it turned out, the census figure of 59.0 percent urban population was an undermeasurement. By redefining *urban* the Census Bureau increased the 59.0 to 63.7 percent (see "Measuring the Urban Population"). By 1960, under the new definition of urban, the proportion reached 63.9 percent, and by 1970 it was 75 percent.

World Urbanization   This rapid urbanization is hardly unique to the United States; several nations, in fact, are even more urbanized. In 1977 the following nations had the most highly urbanized populations:[5]

- Belgium   95 percent
- West Germany   92 percent
- Australia   86 percent
- Sweden   81 percent
- New Zealand   81 percent
- Denmark   80 percent
- Netherlands   77 percent
- Canada   76 percent
- United States   73 percent
- France   71 percent

TABLE 8.1
Growth of Urban Population in Less Developed and More Developed Regions, 1800—2000, by Percentage

	Less Developed	More Developed
1800	4.3	7.3
1850	4.4	11.4
1900	6.5	26.1
1950	15.7	53.6
1975	27.2	69.3
2000 (projected)	39.0	80.1

Source: *Population Bulletin of the United Nations, No. 8-1976, United Nations, 1977, Table 10, p. 33.*

THE METROPOLITAN AREA

The movement of people from rural to urban areas is continuing, but now it is accompanied by a shift from city to suburb. The urban population now

MEASURING THE URBAN POPULATION

Until 1950 the U.S. Bureau of the Census defined *urban* as all places of 2,500 or more incorporated as municipalities. But this had become an inadequate definition. Because of the growth of an urban fringe around central cities that remained unincorporated, yet had the density and social characteristics of an urban place, the urban population was underenumerated.

A new definition of urban, then, includes all incorporated places of 2,500 or more, as before, but adds two new categories: (1.) the densely settled urban fringe around cities of 50,000 or more, and (2.) unincorporated places of 2,500 or more people outside of the urban fringe.

The *urban fringe* is defined as continuously built-up areas outside of major cities which have a density of about 2,000 persons per square mile.

As a consequence of this new definition, the 59.0 percent considered urban in 1950 by the old definition became 63.7 percent. Seven and a half million people were added to the urban category—and subtracted from the rural one—by this redefining process.

DEFINING THE METROPOLITAN AREA

In 1950 the redefinition of urban residence led the U.S. Bureau of the Census to create several new categories by which to measure the urban concentration of the population:

1. *Urban area* includes the central city plus all the contiguous areas with densities of about 2,000 inhabitants per square mile.

2. The *standard metropolitan statistical area* includes one or more cities of 50,000 or more, the one or more counties in which they are located, and any adjoining counties that by certain social and economic criteria are dependent on the central city (or cities).

3. The *standard consolidated area* is composed of contiguous standard metropolitan statistical areas. At present, two are designated: one for "New York-Northeastern New Jersey" and one for "Chicago-Northwestern Indiana."

spreads out from the city into a hinterland, formerly but no longer rural, frequently larger in physical area than the central city, and sometimes equal to or even surpassing the central city in population.

The term, *metropolitan,* refers to a concentration of urban population distributed among a central city and a complex of smaller satellite cities and villages surrounding it. This is the *metropolitan area,* measured by the Census Bureau as *standard metropolitan*

statistical area (SMSA). (See "Defining the Metropolitan Area.")

We need only go back as recently as 1950 to find graphic evidence of the growth of metropolitan areas (see Table 8.2). The largest gain in population since 1950, however, has occurred in metropolitan areas but *outside* central cities, that is, in the suburbs. In 1950, 36 million people, almost one-fourth of the population, lived in the suburbs; while 50 million, or

	1950	1960	1970	1977
TABLE 8.2 Population in Metropolitan and Nonmetropolitan Areas, United States, 1950–1977, by percentage				
Metropolitan	57	66.7	73.9	73.3
Nonmetropolitan	43	33.3	26.1	26.7

Source: For 1950: Conrad and Irene Taeuber, *The Changing Population in the United States* (New York: John Wiley and Sons, 1958), p. 140; for 1960 and 1970: U.S. Bureau of the Census, Census of Population, 1970, vol. 1, *Characteristics of the Population,* Part A, Section 1, p. 34; for revised 1970 figures and for 1975 estimate: U.S. Bureau of the Census, *Current Population Reports,* Series P-25, no. 810, "Estimates of the Population of Counties and Metropolitan Areas, July 1, 1976, and July 1, 1977," (1979) Tables 6 and 7.

one in three, lived in a central city. By 1970, the suburbs had 12 million more people than the central cities; and more than one-third (37.2 percent) of all Americans lived in a suburb.

The movement to the suburbs was greatest in older cities, including these larger cities: Detroit, Los Angeles, Philadelphia, San Francisco, Boston, Pittsburgh, St. Louis, Washington, D.C., Cleveland, Newark, Buffalo, Cincinnati, and Kansas City, Missouri. In some of these areas the suburban population had become as high as three out of every four persons in the metropolitan area. By 1970 the metropolitan areas with the highest proportion of people living outside the central city were:

- Newark   79.4 percent
- Boston   75.8 percent
- Miami   72.5 percent
- Pittsburgh   71.8 percent
- St. Louis   67.0 percent
- Detroit   61.9 percent

This rapid increase in the suburban population would be even greater, except that newer cities in the Southwest (what is now called the Sunbelt) gained considerably. Table 8.3 records this decline in the population of older cities, and Table 8.4 the increase of the population in the fastest growing cities, all of which are in the Southwest.

From 1950 to 1970, then, there were two major shifts in population in the United States. The first was a continuing shift from rural to urban, as the metropolitan population grew at the expense of the nonmetropolitan one. In second was the rapid movement, especially in the older urban areas of the North, from the central city to the suburbs.

Since 1970, however, there is some indication of a change. While older northern cities continue to decline, the suburban population, apparently, is moving even farther out, beyond the limits of the metropolitan region itself. Table 8.2 documents a small proportionate increase, instead of a loss, in the nonmetropolitan population.

Such a new movement, however, which is a continuance of an unregulated urban sprawl, may be checked by other factors: the increasing cost of energy and of new suburban housing may limit this particular movement throughout the 1980s. Some urban experts think that these energy and inflation factors may help to slow the decline of the central city's population, as well.

The Emergence of Megalopolis This massive shift of population to suburbia has created an enormous urban sprawl, as well as a steady development along metropolitan corridors that result from the high-speed expressways that link one metropolis to another. The result is often that the farthest reach of one metropolis touches the next in an unbroken urbanized spread that swallows up once rural and isolated areas.

TABLE 8.3
Population Decline in Selected Cities, 1960–1975

City	1960 Population	1970 Population	Percent Decrease	1975 Population	Percent Decrease
Boston	697,197	641,071	08.1	636,725	0.7
Buffalo	532,790	462,768	13.1	407,160	12.0
Chicago	3,550,404	3,366,957	05.2	3,099,091	5.1
Cincinnati	502,550	452,524	9.8	412,363	9.0
Cleveland	876,050	750,902	14.3	638,793	14.3
Detroit	1,670,144	1,511,482	09.5	1,335,085	11.8
Pittsburgh	604,332	520,117	13.9	458,651	11.8
St. Louis	750,026	622,236	17.0	524,964	15.6

Source: U.S. Bureau of the Census, *County and City Data Book, 1977* (Washington, D.C., Government Printing Office, 1978), Tables 4 and A-4.

TABLE 8.4
Population Increase in Selected Cities, 1960–1975

	1970	1975	Increase	Increase
	Population (in thousands)	Population (in thousands)	1960–70	1970–75
Austin, Texas	255	301	37.2	17.7
El Paso, Texas	322	385	16.5	19.7
Houston, Texas	1,253	1,326	33.6	5.9
Phoenix, Ariz.	589	664	34.1	12.9
San Jose, Cal.	461	555	125.9	20.5
Tucson, Ariz.	267	296	25.6	10.9

Source: U.S. Bureau of the Census, *County and City Data Book, 1977* (Washington, D.C., Government Printing Office, 1978), Tables 4 and A-4.

This unending urban sprawl that melds one metropolis into another is *megalopolis*, the superurbanized space. The most advanced case of megalopolis in the United States is on the Atlantic seaboard, running south from Boston through New York to Washington, D.C., into northern Virginia. In Texas, Dallas and Fort Worth are gradually linking up with Houston and San Antonio.

THE DECLINE OF LOCAL AUTONOMY

One significant consequence of urbanization—concomitant with the rise of the modern nation-state, the market economy, and bureaucratic associations—

is the decline of local autonomy. The extent of local autonomy in the eighteenth and nineteenth centuries has probably been overstated, but nevertheless the rural community approximated in some ways a localized society. Few modern communities can do so. The modern nation moves increasingly toward centralized political controls, and modern government penetrates into even the smallest of communities in many ways. Local independence of action is increasingly limited, and local resources are increasingly inadequate compared to the richer resources of the nation-state. (The "political surrender" of Springdale, the small town in upstate New York discussed in Chapter 5, is evidence again of this point.)

As a result, local government has only circumscribed powers and increasingly assumes responsibility for only a small range of services—streets, sewers, garbage collection, and zoning, for example, as well as fire and police protection. It does more than this only when the local situation is desperate—as when the closing of a local factory results in a vigorous industrial development program—or where federal or state government prods and encourages and assists—as in school consolidation and urban renewal.

Politically, local communities in the United States are not, and never have been, separate and independent governments; their powers are granted by state government. Local school systems have increasingly been subject to the controls and standards of state boards of education. The local economy, in turn, is absorbed into a national market, and its local enterprises are frequently the branch plants of large firms whose headquarters are elsewhere.

Perhaps the most telling point is that, with few exceptions, cities large and small are no longer able to meet the necessary costs of local services (including education), let alone provide the finances to renew and redevelop the community. Local communities, in short, have become increasingly dependent on state and federal revenues, for they no longer control sufficient resources of their own.

The program of federal revenue-sharing, by which some proportion of the tax revenue that flows into Washington is then returned to local communities, is now a permanent source on which many cities necessarily depend. Without it they could not provide an adequate level of local services.

This dependency on federal and state revenue is most acute for older cities, particularly those in the East and North. Many of them are in debt and without financial aid could not avoid bankruptcy. New York City and Cleveland both reached the edge of bankruptcy in the 1970s, and only federal assistance in New York's case prevented it from occurring. Other cities have faced a similar threat and often have avoided bankruptcy only by cutting community services. Financial solvency has then been avoided by a decline in the quality of community services and by dependency on higher levels of government.

The same has been true of education. Cities as large as Cleveland and Chicago, as well as a number of smaller ones, have recently reached a point of insolvency in which only some infusion of state funds have kept the school doors open and teachers on the job.

Local communities are also dependent on large corporations for their economic health. The effort to attract new plants, and even to keep established ones, often compels communities to compete against one another by offering tax-breaks by building a new plant with local revenues, or otherwise sacrificing some degree of local resources for corporate benefit. These large corporations, in turn, are able to play off one community against another when choosing to relocate a plant or invest in a new one.

Even when the local community is a city of considerable size, then, it does not possess the power and resources to give it a significant dimension of autonomy. Instead, it is a structure dependent on, and largely shaped by, the decisions and policies of the federal and state governments, as well as the large corporations, for these are by now the dominant forms of political and economic power in modern society.

URBAN ECOLOGY

Of all the forms of social organization, community by definition is locality-based; accordingly, the shape and form of community are influenced by the physical environment and by existing technology. The location of communities as well as the distribution of people, functions, and services in their physical space are both matters of the *ecology* of the community.

Small villages became in time towns and cities when their strategic location linked them into larger systems of trade and exchange. Thus communities located at seaports or on navigable rivers grew into cities, while villages in the hinterland remained small. The coming of steam power and railroad opened up further opportunities for locating urban sites, but even here water routes still played an important part.[6]

In the Middle Ages, fortified castles ringed by walls were built on high land; such a location was more defensible from military attack. When trade was renewed and flourished again, by the tenth century, merchants found it safer to locate close to the protective walls of these castles, and from such locations many medieval cities grew.[7]

The Uses of Urban Space   Every community, no matter how small, locates different activities and functions somewhere within its available space. How that process occurs is what urban ecology is largely about. For example, in earlier industrial cities, when workers walked to and from work, residential and industrial areas could not be far apart. As a consequence, workers lived in close-in neighborhoods which suffered all the possible pollutional consequences of early industry; only the middle class was able to reside farther from industry.

Commuting by railroad and the later development of the electric streetcar freed people from close-in residence and permitted in time a greater separation of residence and work; residential neighborhoods could be located farther from industry. The coming of the automobile accelerated this process of residential patterning and made possible an even greater separation of work and residence.

Observing these processes a half century ago led sociologists to develop an urban ecological model for understanding how urban space was used. According to this model, the competition for space in the city produces a segregation of people and facilities. At the center of the city is the principal business district (frequently called "downtown"), which centralizes in a relatively small space major commercial and financial functions. These processes of *segregation* and *centralization* produce areas inhabited by specific categories of people—the poor, the wealthy, the immigrants, the minorities—as well as areas used for specific functions: factory districts, shopping areas, theater districts, and the like.

The Concentric Zone Model   The first urban ecological model was developed by Ernest Burgess; it viewed the city as a series of concentric circles, each circle being a different zone of functional use of space determined by the competition for space among various economic groups (see Figure 8.1).[8]

Other American sociologists have developed other theories, though Burgess's has remained the best known. Homer Hoyt suggested *sectors* instead of zones; a more complicated *multiple nuclei* model has been developed by Chauncey D. Harris and Edward I. Ullman. Each of these models differs from Burgess's theory only in the idea that the consequences of competition for space are too simply represented by a concentric zone model.

The Growth of the City

Whether too simple or not, the value of Burgess's theory was its effort to explain the *growth* of the city. According to Burgess, the city grew out from its centers, pushing out to its periphery as population grew and demands for space increased. The theory implicitly recognized that areas and neighborhoods aged, leading to physical deterioration. As a result, original residents or business users of the area moved out to newer areas where land was not yet used up and often was cheaper. Left behind were old and worn-out areas and left behind also were those categories of people who could not successfully compete for the newer areas.

As time goes on, a middle-class area of fine, large homes ages, and the economic value of the latter declines. At some point a social group of lower economic status begins to move in—*invasion*—and when they have become the dominant residential group, *succession* has occurred. In this way an area may change from white to black, or from an older immigrant group to a newer but economically poorer one.

Those who move in the face of invasion form new areas farther out; the movement to the suburbs is one index of invasion and succession having reached the point where the central city has used all its available land space. The search for new space, particularly by the economically affluent, now frequently goes on almost entirely beyond the city limits.

The City and the Market   Burgess's concentric zone model—and the others, too—was based upon a basic proposition: that the city grew and took shape as the unplanned outcome of economic competition for

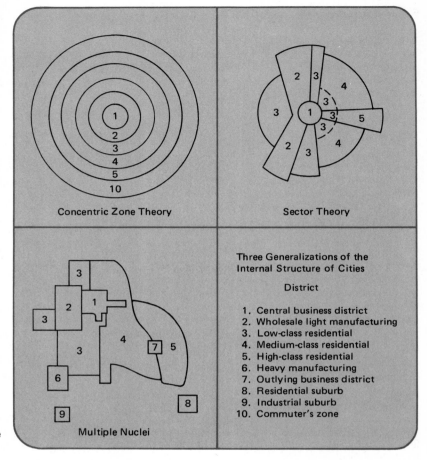

FIGURE 8.1
Three generalizations of the
internal structure of cities.

space. The capitalist rule of supply and demand seemed to prevail here as much as it did in the production and distribution of goods. The inference is that, in a capitalist society, the capitalist market determines the growth and ecological structure of the city.

Yet these market processes are never alone or always decisive for shaping the city. In a study of Boston, for example, Walter Firey found that high-status families chose to remain in such older, prestigious residential areas as Beacon Hill; thus noneconomic values can also influence the use of land in the city.[9] Such considerations, for example, as a desirable view, scenery, an elevated or commanding site, a spacious area, or a comfortable distance from "nuisance" activities are mentioned by Alvin Boskoff as some of the

major reasons for retaining land use that defy market criteria.[10] Upper-middle-class residents of Chicago, for instance, have maintained residence in a particularly desirable lake-front area, replacing old large homes over time with high-rise apartments.

Yet even here, it should be noted, economic factors are present. The groups which can seem to make an exception to market processes can do so only because they also have economic means. The people who stayed on Beacon Hill, like the people who have maintained lake-shore residence in Chicago, possess the higher income and the political influence necessary to protect their stake in an urban neighborhood.

The ecology of an urban community, then, is a dynamic process of adjustment and accommodation among competing claims for a limited land use. What prevails in a community at a given point in its history is a compromise among market factors, on the one hand, and status and other symbolic considerations, on the other.

Yet, despite the effect of symbolic values in preserving and revitalizing old areas of a city, by and large *in the United States* it is market processes that are dominant. Nonetheless, there is something distinctly American about this process. In other capitalist societies, in Europe and Latin America, the city has not developed in the fashion we have been describing for the United States. Instead, the middle-class residential areas remain close to the center of the city and the working class and the poor live farther out.

It is primarily in the United States that market forces have produced a situation in which the older cities are deteriorating and efforts to save them have up to now seemed futile. Burgess and others who understood the market process, which governed city growth earlier in this century, did not, however, seem to anticipate what the outcome would look like half a century later. In order to assess that more adequately, we must first look at urbanism and at the development of the suburban community.

URBANISM

The decline of the small, rural community and the growth of large cities as the common mode of life for most people in modern society thrust into public consciousness the issue of what life was like in cities. The sociological view on *urbanism* until very recently was quite consistent with the view held both in popular and academic literature, in folklore and in intellectual analysis.[11] The city was viewed negatively, while the small town of the past was romanticized. Rural life, it was claimed, maintained sturdy virtues, while city life eroded moral character.

Urbanism as a Way of Life

The sociological version of urbanism was developed over several decades of urban studies, most notably of Chicago. The image of the urban community implicit in these studies was made plain by Louis Wirth in an influential essay, "Urbanism as a Way of Life,"

whose very title became a common phrase.[12] He defined the city as "a relatively large, dense, and permanent settlement of socially heterogeneous individuals."[13] Thus he postulated three characteristics: size, *density,* and *heterogeneity,* and then proceeded to derive the characteristics of urbanism from them.

Size   The relatively large *size* of the modern city, according to Wirth, produces a wide range of social differences, and such diversity weakens the bonds of kinship and neighborliness, as well as the sentiments generated within a folk tradition. Most daily relationships become impersonal, superficial, transient, and segmental.

Density   The city, according to Wirth, concentrates large numbers in a limited space, and the resulting *density* produces diversification and complexity. The physical closeness of people who are not tied by bonds of sentiment produces competition, aggrandizement, and mutual exploitation. Movement throughout the congested city brings frictions and irritation, and close contact among unrelated people brings about reserve and increases the likelihood of loneliness.

Heterogeneity   The *heterogeneity* of the city is its diverse people, different each from the other in so many ways. Wirth credits this difference with fragmenting group memberships and loyalties, since each individual associates with a number of groups, but each group is related to only a segment of the individual's personality (as parent, taxpayer, worker). City people move often, even within the city; group membership changes, and organization is hard to maintain. The typical city dweller is not a stable, long-residing neighbor.

This overwhelmingly negative view of the city takes as its standard the small rural community of the past; the characteristics of urbanism are derived by measuring the city against that model. The social diversity and contrasting life-styles of the city are only deplored. An appreciative conception of the city as freer than the village, with a wider range of social choices for the individual, is ignored when the reference point is the traditional, tightly integrated folk community.

Furthermore, Wirth's essay summarized a tradition of sociological observations made largely during a period of very rapid growth, when an incessant flow of migrants into the city brought together people without families and not yet into occupations and more stable life-styles. Even then, however, there were areas of stable family residence. But it was the residential instability of in-migrant areas, says Herbert Gans, which produced heterogeneity, not the other way around.[14] From instability, not size and density, came those negative aspects of urban life.

The imagery that Wirth and others gave us, then, is historically specific. When the city is viewed at a later period, and when the most stable as well as the least stable areas of city life are included in the analysis, it appears as a more coherent and reasonable place for human beings to live and work.

Reassessing Urbanism

Recent sociological research on the city has even more thoroughly reassessed and challenged the negative conception of urbanism as a way of life which Wirth gave us, particularly on the issues of primary relations and the urban neighborhood.[15]

Primary Relations   While it is true that a large proportion of any person's social relations in the city are necessarily impersonal, nonetheless, urban people do find satisfying primary relations in the city.[16] If the neighborhood seems no longer a significant basis, they find other sources. They develop friendships out of acquaintances made within their profession or occupation, their place of work, their membership in church, labor union, fraternal lodge, business organization, or political party. The wide range of urban interest groups provides the context within which some urban people sort out those congenial few who form a small circle of primary relations.

The Urban Neighborhood   The urban neighborhood, however, is still a source of primary relations for many, particularly where stability of residence prevails. There some residents develop closer and more intimate relations with some other neighbors. This occurs more in neighborhoods of single-family homes than in apartment house areas, and more in homeowner neighborhoods than in rental areas. It is also more characteristic of working-class and lower-middle class neighborhoods than of upper-middle-class ones. It is most evident in ethnic neighborhoods.

The Ethnic Neighborhood   Established ethnic neighborhoods often constitute small social worlds of culturally homogeneous people; they are urban *villages,* such as Herbert Gans found in an Italian working-class area of Boston.[17] Their way of life is based on primary groups and kinship within the structure of the ethnic group; it lacks the anonymity and secondary group relations which Wirth emphasized, and it is weak in the frequency and influence of formal organizations. Its members possess an in-group outlook that makes them suspicious of people and activities outside their own group. Thus their lives are characterized by a great deal of isolation from others, even though they live in close physical proximity. This pattern of urban villagers prevailed in American cities in Wirth's day even more than now. While in significant decline, it nonetheless persists.

More recently, Gerald Suttles has studied a poor area of Chicago and outlined the strategies by which residents of slum and near-slum neighborhoods order their relations in such a way as to preserve peace and maintain some decent order.[18] Four different ethnic groups, each with its own internal structure and lifestyle, share the same area. The neighborhood street-corner groups and social clubs protect group interests and keep boundaries intact. People rarely cross these boundaries, which are based upon ethnic solidarity, upon sexual and territorial segregation, and upon age-grading.

Order in the City   But such a social order cannot always be successfully maintained under conditions of change and deterioration in the central city. James Q. Wilson argues that "it is the breakdown of neighborhood controls (neighborhood self-government, if you will) that accounts for the principal concerns of urban citizens."[19] And it is this same concern, he says, that leads a majority of Americans (except blacks) to say they prefer small towns and suburbs, where there is a greater social homogeneity and where local government can reinforce the informal neighborhood sanctions.

More and more, cities are places where people are unable to maintain the sense of community, defined by Wilson as a desire for the observance of standards of right and seemly conduct in the public places in which one lives and moves, those standards to be consistent with—and supportive of—the values and life-styles of the particular individual.[19]

Older neighborhoods, usually economically poorer and often yet an ethnic village, can still be found not far from the cental business district. From this East Boston neighborhood a resident can see the towering office buildings of downtown Boston.

This inability to maintain community in the city is particularly true for affluent white people, who retreat into well-protected high-rise apartments; for poor white people, often elderly, who cannot escape to safer areas; and for blacks.

Stable neighborhoods and effective social controls are not incompatible with the diversity of city life. They are, however, difficult to maintain in the face of physical deterioration, and are further eroded by economic and political neglect, as well as racial and ethnic tensions. Below some minimum level of economic support and of adequate social services, then, any urban neighborhood is likely to drift into the condition of a slum.

But if such a minimum of economic and social support is assured, stable neighborhoods can persist amidst urban heterogeneity, thriving on the cultural di-versity only the city can offer. The effort to revive dying cities, we shall see later, depends on understanding how social order can be built in the diverse and heterogeneous city, a perspective that is largely absent yet from most contemporary images of the city.[20]

THE SUBURBAN COMMUNITY

Suburban residential development is not new; in the early 1800s English industrialists moved their family residences out of such industrial cities as Manchester and Liverpool in order to escape the filth and fetid air. Residence beyond the city limits for the more prosperous of the city's industrial and financial leaders was a well-developed pattern in the United States before the turn of the century.

At first, suburban residence was limited to upper-income people who could afford the private transportation and the time spent in travel. With the growth of railroads, suburban communities sprang up along railroad lines. Probably through the 1920s most suburban residents commuted by train to the city. With the growth of motor transportation and the mass consumption of automobiles, suburban communities were no longer confined to railroad lines, and a much larger space around the periphery of the city became potentially available for residential development. With car and bus available to a much broader stratum of people, so too was the opportunity for suburban residence.

In the United States, suburban development accelerated rapidly after World War II. There were a number of economic factors to account for this; (1) the Depression decade of the 1930s followed by a war produced little new housing; (2) then, postwar prosperity and delayed marriage for servicemen produced a pent-up demand for new housing. These circumstances were propitious for a great increase in the construction of new housing.

But why did this occur in suburban areas? Why not in the city?

By the end of World War II most larger American cities had exhausted their available land space and population potential. Additional population and housing growth had no alternative but to spill into the area surrounding the city. Then, too, the construction industry was now ready to change from individual, handcraft construction to the mass construction of homes. Only outside the central city was there sufficient land available for this.

To this point, then, we can explain the growth of suburbs by such factors as: (1) the development of modes of transportation; (2) the demand for and supply of new housing; and (3) the exhaustion of land space in the central city. These constitute the social conditions, primarily economic and ecological, which account for the growth of suburban residential communities at a greatly accelerated rate in the United States since World War II.

Such an explanation would be sufficient if the movement from central city to suburb were only residential. But, in fact, industry, too, has long been moving out of the central city. As early as 1900 a process of

industrial decentralization was underway. It merely accelerated after World War II. There were technical reasons for this move, such as new assembly-line production, which required new, low, spread-out factories, instead of multistoried ones, and the larger amount of land required was cheaper outside the city. But problems of rising city taxes and increasing costs associated with urban location, and, perhaps more importantly, the effort to find an isolated atmosphere more suited to control over its labor force, also gave industrialists reason to move out of the city.[21]

Industry has led, not followed, the move to suburban location. But that does not tell us who in the population *can* and who *does* move to the suburbs.

Who Goes Suburban?

Who does go suburban, then? The young, the more economically secure, the socially mobile—these find suburban living more accessible and most cogenial to their interests and values. Obversely, suburbia excludes the poor, the older, and the social minorities, and these people constitute in turn a significant segment of those left behind in the movement out of the city. This tells us, in objective terms, what the selective process is which sorts out the urban population for suburban residence.

The mass construction of housing in suburban developments means that the suburb is no longer a symbol of upper-class status. Yet this "democratization" of suburbia has not gone so far as to make it equally accessible to all economic levels. Although blue-collar workers have joined white-collar workers in moving to the suburbs, and large metropolitan areas now possess working-class suburbs, suburban residence, nevertheless, remains most economically accessible to middle-income people. Even then, middle-class blacks have usually been blocked in efforts to find suburban housing. Now there is evidence of a modest though steady movement of middle-income blacks to the suburbs.

Suburbia as Anticity Suburbia pulls people to it because of what it has to offer, but the city frequently pushes them out, as well. People flee the city to escape its noise and congestion, its dirt and untidiness, its crowdedness and decaying housing. But the city is more than physically unattractive to many people; it is often socially unattractive as well. It possesses slums and slum dwellers; poor whites and poor blacks recently arrived from the rural South, whose less-educated children are viewed as threatening the academic levels of the city's public schools. Poor schools and slums, racial conflict and large relief rolls, juvenile gangs and criminal violence—these are some of the negative symbols of the city that lead people to seek the suburban life.

Much of the movement to the suburbs, then, is an effort—individual by individual, family by family—to escape urban blight and to shed social responsibility for the larger and more difficult problems of American cities. It is an attempt to create small enclaves isolated from the problems of urban-industrial existence, while enjoying its amenities and advantages.

Family Life and the Suburb

The first postwar expansion of the suburbs in the 1950s was accomplished largely by the construction of large subdivisions of single-family homes. Social observers then tended to see a connection between the new suburbs and a renewed emphasis on family life. In an earlier study—for example, Wendell Bell—argued that a child-centered family life is chosen by suburbanites as a value over other possible alternatives.[22] In the suburbs higher than average economic status, a decline of ethnic identification and clusterings, and a strong familistic orientation apparently marked a distinctive suburban life-style.

More recently, Richard Sennett has argued that this is the basic factor explaining the existence of suburbs as homogeneous communities, more important than the economic and ecological factors that made the suburbs possible. According to Sennett, ". . . people who now live in suburbs value their home settings because they feel that closer family ties are more possible there than in the city center."[23] This leads, he says, to a simplification of the social environment; wide swatches of houses of the same socioeconomic level are separated from wide swatches of commercial development, particularly the suburban shopping center. "People desire this simplification because it permits the intensity of family relations to gather full force."[24] The assumption behind this, Sennett notes, is that the family might be weakened if its members were exposed to a richer, more diverse social condition.

Sennett finds in this a basic malaise of modern life, a fear of the richness of urban society, stemming from the fact that "suburbanites are people who are afraid to live in a world they cannot control."[25] Thus the impulse to simplify life by living in relatively more isolated, homogeneous environments for family life.

Sennett is not the first to emphasize homogeneity as a defining attribute of suburbia: the intentional selection (and restriction) of people alike to one another to reside in the same community. From this has been built up a myth about suburbia that at best only partly captures an ever-changing reality.

Suburbia: Myth or Reality?

The myth about suburbia has been an unflattering image of affluent, status-conscious America in its new

The movement of middle-class people to the suburbs brought about the invention of the enclosed shopping mall for an affluent clientele.

residential life-style. Suburbia, so goes the myth, has developed a hyperactive social life, which includes both intensive neighboring with a loss of personal and family privacy, and an active organizational life that reflects every conceivable kind of shared interest in the community.

All of this is possible, the myth says, because the suburbanites are a very homogeneous people: (1) they are about the same age; (2) they are at about the same point in family cycle with children about the same age; (3) they have similar education and jobs, and (4) their social aspirations and values are the same. Such a pervasive similarity then produces a "classless" community—really a one-class community. It also results in a similar life-style that suggests conformity in values and behavior.

Yet all this may be more myth than reality.[26] Perhaps the starting point is the discovery that the suburban community is not exclusively middle class. There are now numerous blue-collar suburbs, and many large middle-income suburban developments attract a range of social classes.

Herbert Gans, for example, carefully documented the variation from working class to lower-middle class to upper-middle class among residents of the same suburban community; as well as the variation in aspirations, life-styles, family-styles, political orientations, and degrees of community involvement to be found within it.[27] The apparent excessive homogeneity of people in any one suburb is more likely in the early years of its existence, and less so as time goes on and there is more movement in and out.

That suburbia presumably demands conformity and a common life-style from its inhabitants once promoted the idea that it turns city Democrats into suburban Republicans. But Berger found that automobile workers who had moved to a new suburb continued to vote Democratic.[28] Gans, in turn, has documented in even greater detail that politics, family patterns, and life-style were not thoroughly altered by the movement to Levittown. Furthermore, the workers and lower-middle-class of suburbia are not mobile; they know it, and do not absorb the life-styles of executives and professionals. Most of the workers that Berger studied did not belong to any organization besides a union, though Gans found a large number of civic organizations operating in Levittown.

Furthermore, the presumably suburban life-style turns out on close inspection to be a *middle-class* life-style, evident among middle-class people whether they reside in the suburb or in the city. In one study, for example, H. Lawrence Ross compared the life-styles of upper-middle-class apartment dwellers, some of whom lived in the central city, others in the suburbs.[29] He found no significant differences between the two. What differences there are between city and suburb are more likely to be explained as differences of class and ethnicity than place of residence.

The Newer Suburbia   The social changes of the 1970s produced a newer suburbia alongside the older one of single-family residences. This change was most strikingly evident in the rapid construction of "luxury" apartments and town-house complexes intended for working couples and single adults. Whole residential complexes where a child is not to be seen have now become common in the suburbs.

Indeed, the suburbs can no longer be viewed only as child-centered communities. In 1977, according to a recent study by the Bureau of the Census, 43 percent of the families in the suburbs had no children under 18 living at home, a figure only slightly below that of 47 percent for city dwellers.[30] Furthermore, about one suburban child in nine was living in a family maintained by a woman with no husband present (compared to one in five in the city).

THE METROPOLIS

The steady movement of population, particularly white and affluent, to the suburbs has brought into being a large metropolitan area of separate suburban communities surrounding the central city. This area is not an integrated community, yet it is more than simply a geographical area.

Such a development has set in motion a struggle to unify the metropolis, even to create metropolitan government by uniting suburbs and city into a sprawling supercity. If successful, it would take from the suburbs what autonomy and independence they now have.

The Unity and Disunity of the Metropolis

For some purposes, the metropolitan area can be (and is) treated as a functionally integrated community. It is a single trading area: one or more daily newspapers serve its population; large department stores deliver to the suburbs and establish branch stores there; supermarkets, drugstores and banks operate a chain of branches throughout the area. The services basic to an interacting and interdependent population are also provided on an area basis: water and sewage, electric power, gas, public transportation, and telephone. So also are cultural activities, hospitals, and various social services. For many significant purposes the metropolitan area is organized as a single interdependent system.

Politically, however, the metropolitan area is not one community but many. It is fragmented into numerous small political subdivisions that makes it difficult to develop a shared responsibility for metropolitan-wide problems—water, sewage, expressways, and similar services.

But the effort to create a single metropolitan government is a cause that attracts as yet only a small, though influential, number of civic leaders, urban professionals, and corporate executives. To these proponents of metropolitan unification, the political subdivisions of the metropolitan area are an irrational structure based only upon petty jealousies and parochial interests. Political scientist Robert Wood expressed their opinion as:

> A theory of community and a theory of local government are at odds with the prerequisites of contemporary life and, so far theory has been the crucial force that preserves the suburb. There is no economic reason for its existence and there is no technological basis for its support.[31]

The heavy value on "community" and on "local" government, says Wood, prevents rational metropolitan organization. "If these values were not dominant, it would be quite possible to conceive of a single gigantic metropolitan region under one government and socially conscious of itself as one community.[32]

Yet, despite what Wood says, there is reason for the persistence of separate suburban communities. The ideology (or theory) that suburbanites hold utilizes some hallowed American traditions about local independence and grass-roots democracy to defend the political existence of independent suburban communities, however inefficient they may be. Undoubtedly, suburbanites take seriously their own myth about independence and grass roots.

But this ideology, if taken at face value, conceals group interests. At the present time, for example, suburbs are selective about who gets in; they have managed to erect quite firm barriers against racial minorities and poor people. The more economically advantaged suburbs now maintain the best public school systems, and their academically excellent high schools offer the best access to the more preferred colleges and universities.

Suburbanites know that they have a real stake in the existence of a separate suburb. The myth they perpetuate rings the bell on some hallowed values, but their interests are in the economic and social advantages that the selectivity of the suburb makes possible. When Robert Wood says, "There is only the stubborn conviction of the majority of suburbanites that it ought to exist, even though it plays havoc with the life and government of our urban age," he ignores the real social interests of suburbanites that are served by not having political unification of the metropolis.[33] For some time to come, there is not going to be a single metropolitan government.

But that fact should not obscure the forces that press toward unification. For one thing, the proponents of unification are influential in the professions having to do with government and public service, and they have significant allies in corporate executives, foundation officials, and federal government executives—all of whom are committed to the rational and efficient organization of the large American metropolis.

A crucial factor in the pressure for metropolitan unification is the commitment of many large corporations to such an objective. Many corporate executives see their own interests as hurt by the fragmentation of local government in the metropolis, particularly in terms of attaining a rational tax structure and in planning to expand or relocate plants. Furthermore, corporate headquarters are often still in the central city, even though the factories may be in the suburbs, and corporations stand to lose financially by the city's deterioration. As one student of urban planning notes:

> Some corporate leaders complain about the lack of metropolitan regional planning and appear to be increasingly in favor of regionalized political structure. Thus a struggle may ensue between suburban subclasses militant in their desire to preserve their local public-sector autonomy and large capitalist interests pushing for planned, rationalized, metropolis-wide government.[34]

It is also worth noting that the struggle to decrease or even eliminate the property tax—the major source of revenue for local government—will further weaken local government and, among other things, contribute indirectly to metropolitan unification.

One possible outcome of this struggle is a compromise that will allow the fiction of local independence and identity to remain, with perhaps some power retained over local schools and over decisions about who gets to live in the suburbs, while relinquishing effective control over necessary services to separate metropolitan authorities, such as a water and sewage authority, and a road-building authority, a metropolitan transportation authority, and the like. In time, there may be a suburban version of the myth that Vidich and Bensman found in Springdale, a myth of being an independent community preserving a preferred lifestyle but in fact contradicted by the societal and bureaucratic penetration into the local community.[35]

THE CRISIS OF THE CITIES

When urban experts say there is an "urban crisis," they mean specifically the decline of central cities. It is the other side of the growth of suburbia. The movement of primarily white and affluent people to the suburbs leaves the central city with a burdensome share of the poor, the elderly, and the racial minorities.

But business, too, has moved out of the city. Shopping malls have taken most retail trade to the suburbs, and factories have relocated beyond the city limits. Both people, as homeowners and taxpayers, and capital, as the source of jobs and investment, have been abandoning the city.

In pointing this out, we can more easily see *what* happened, less easily understand *why* it has happened. The process is a complicated one in which several different factors interact on one another.

We need to begin with a historical reminder: that cities grew from small towns because they provided the setting for mobilizing an industrial economy. "Above all, cities are a social and physical device for creating the cohesive, ordered environment necessary for combining labor and capital effectively."[36] But if cities were to exist as a necessary component of the economy, they, in turn, required a great deal of social investment in a physical and social infrastructure; in streets, sewage, and a water system; in public transportation; in police and fire protection; and in schools. From this came municipal government and urban politics.

Furthermore, the city is not only a necessary organizing unit for capital. It is also a place where people live, and people organize a city to express their human needs and cultural values. To the necessary infrastructure, they add social amenities: parks, museums, libraries, and the like, and the variety of residential neighborhoods. In a capitalist society, these are largely provided by the public sector, as is most of the physical and social infrastructure.

As cities grow and prosper, however, the social costs of the services and amenities provided through the public sector also rise. The necessary taxes now reduce the profits of corporations as well as the incomes of middle- and upper-income residents, who increasingly feel they are receiving a lesser share of public expenditures. This is made worse by rising land prices in the crowded city and by the increasing need to replace and improve aging components of the infrastructure. Thus, the motivation to look elsewhere, beyond the city boundaries, for a place where social costs of urban services might be less.

Why People Leave the City   The movement of people from city to suburb, we saw earlier, began with the pent-up demand for new housing, and the availability of much more cheaper land outside the city for the mass construction of housing. At the same time, the congestion, the physical deterioration of older areas, the often dirty air, led people to look outside the city for a physically better environment. In time, the departure of whites for the suburbs altered the proportion of blacks to whites and increased racial tensions. In the flight of the middle-class to the suburbs, the quality of city schools declined. These two factors only gave further reason for whites to leave for the suburbs.

In addition, the costs that a city incurs to provide basic services rise steadily, and so, necessarily, do its taxes. For the more affluent whites, the movement to the suburbs includes an effort to find a community of people like themselves, in which the costs of municipal services are less and the services are primarily for them, not for other social classes, as is true in the city.

Why Corporations Leave the City   For corporations, too, the city over time has meant rising costs of production. Technological changes have often meant it was cheaper to build a new type of plant in the suburbs rather than seek to remodel an older one in the city.

Like the middle class, corporations often wanted to avoid the social problems of the city, and the tax burden that these reflected. No less so, a large corporation often saw in a small suburb the prospect for a greater voice and influence in affecting tax rates than it had in the city, where a politically active working class could counter corporate demands in the struggle over services and the city budget.

By locating in developing cities, and congregating a large labor force there, corporations had in fact helped create a working-class environment which in time they could not readily control. Large working-class neighborhoods provided a basis for working-class political power to which urban political leaders had to give serious attention.

For corporations, the removal of the work place from the city was intended to reduce the militancy and political potency of workers and thus to increase the social control of capital over its labor force.[37]

The Future of Central Cities

While people and business continue to abandon the older central cities of the United States, there is yet considerable effort to halt their decline and find ways to revive them. Even as middle-class people continue to move out, corporate investment in new office buildings, civic arenas, and even hotels goes on. There are clearly contradictory forces at work.

For about three decades now, federally funded urban renewal has been a means by which cities have attempted ambitious projects of urban renewal. Slum areas close to the central business district have been cleared away, and the recaptured area has been used as a new commercial area or as a new residential area, planned to entice upper-middle-class professional and managerial people back to the center of the city. But as yet, there is no strong evidence that these efforts are going to succeed.[38]

The Inner City The renewal of the city is primarily a renewal of the *inner* city, the area beyond the central business district that includes transient residential areas, slums, and racial ghettoes. In many cities the inner city now extends for miles, and its present devel-

opment suggests that it may someday include the entire central city, and perhaps even the older suburbs. What is not inner city—the outer city—is much like the suburbs in social character, so that, as Herbert Gans observed, the real distinction in urban life is not between the central city and the suburbs but between the inner city and the outer city, regardless of where corporate boundaries may fall.[39]

In the contrast of inner and outer city are two social worlds, two collections of compatible life-styles. Gans sees several types of people who are inner-city dwellers. One of these is the *cosmopolites,* those students, intellectuals, writers, musicians, and artists, and some other professionals, who find in the city a compatible cultural atmosphere. Another is the "ethnic villager" (the resident of an ethnic neighborhood). There are also two groups of disadvantaged who cannot escape the city: the *deprived,* the very poor and the nonwhites, and the *trapped,* those usually older or otherwise disadvantaged people who are left behind when a neighborhood changes in economic and perhaps racial or ethnic composition.

The Black Inner City As suburbia developed from the movement of a white population out of the city, the central city, and particularly its inner core, became increasingly black. In Washington, D.C., blacks were a majority of the population as far back as 1960.

As blacks become an actual majority in some older central cities, there is a potential for black political power. In 1967 black political leaders were elected mayor in Gary, Indiana, and in Cleveland, Ohio. In the 1970s a black became mayor both in Detroit and Atlanta. Here was a significant political consequence of white exodus from the central city: the emergence of black voting majorities in central cities. In a very real sense, then, the future prospects of the city are interwoven with the future prospects of race relations in American society. The "urban crisis" and the "racial crisis" are not issues that can be resolved independently of one another.

Death by Decentralization A basic assumption behind much of the effort to revitalize the city is that it constitutes the organizational center of the metropolitan area. However, the movement out of the city, evident to anyone who studies census statistics and maps, call such an assumption into question. The central city may no longer be central, either geographically or

When the middle class leaves for the suburbs, older people with limited resources are among those left behind in the inner city.

functionally. Corporate capitalism may no longer require the degree of centralization that once gave the central city its dominance. A powerful process of decentralization threatens the future of the older American city, despite all urban renewal efforts.

Yet what the central city will finally become is by no means clear. There is more than one future evident in already existing trends and policies.

The City as Reservation   One possibility is continued decline, until all who can have left the city, and only those without economic and political resources remain. The city, in Norton Long's term, becomes a "reservation," a confinement of the poor and unemployed, the people on welfare, the poorly educated, the racial minorities, and the neglected elderly.[40]

To keep the city from exploding in violent protest, a portion of the national revenue is funneled to the city's bureaucracies and politicians to maintain control over the reservation's natives. Such revenues permit the growth of a municipal bureaucracy that presents itself as being concerned for the plight of the urban downtrodden, but which in fact does nothing to alter the oppressive environment which the city has become.

Around it will flourish a spreading metropolitan area, uneasy about the city but not anxious to do anything for it, and trying hard to insulate itself from the people confined to urban decay. More and more suburban residents will have less reason than ever to travel into the center city for jobs, shopping, services, or entertainment; it will become a no-man's land for the middle class.

The Reintegration of the City   There is, however, still an enormous investment in the central city to be protected and maintained: office buildings and department stores, banks, and theaters. There are also museums, libraries, civic centers, and universities in the central city, and little likelihood that any suburb could marshal the resources to replace these. For financial and cultural reasons, then, there is reason to try to rebuild and renew the city, to reintegrate the older cities into the productive urban complex.

A program as ambitious as this can only be accomplished by a partnership of corporate capital and state and national government. A program of subsidies is combined with new ways to allocate taxes and to shift the fiscal burden to higher levels of government, namely, metropolitan and state. This, in turn, is linked to a streamlined reorganization of government and ef-ficient budgetary controls to provide jobs, restore the city's resource base, and make it once more a productive and profitable unit for capital investment. Sociologist Richard C. Hill calls this the State Capitalist City.[41]

Yet, as Hill notes, the price the city and its dependent population pay is political impotence—a loss of control over the city's fiscal resources, and more importantly, over deciding the future form and character of the city. Fiscal control and managerial authority are assumed by state and metropolitan government.

This, of course, requires that metropolitan government be made a reality and metropolitan fragmentation be ended. The suburbs would lose their status as independent communities. Many corporate executives, we saw earlier, have supported metropolitan reorganization. For them, the removal of the costly burden of the reservation city and the threat of urban rebellion it represents require that its separation from the suburbs be ended.

As yet, however, this program has had only limited success in ending urban decay and reintegrating the city. Its program for reorganizing the metropolitan area into a single government has mostly failed.[42] Its political coalition of the city's disadvantaged population, large corporations, and the federal and state governments may be fragile; its opposition, in turn, is formidable.

There would seem, then, to be only two alternatives for the future of the aging central city: either it becomes a confining reservation for an unwanted population, or a combination of corporate and governmental forces brings about its revival and reintegration into the national economy, but at the loss of its independence and self-governing ability. If there is any other possible future for the city, it would seem to be in the realization of it as a community.

The redevelopment of old urban centers often locates glittering new high-rise buildings near decaying structures, as in this contrast of Detroit's Renaissance Center (Ren-Cen) with old commercial structures.

THE FUTURE OF COMMUNITY

Modern society now is urban society, its population concentrated in huge metropolitan areas. The small communities of the past are probably forever *in* the past.

If this is so, what are the prospects for community? The question does not ask simply about locality: the trends in urbanization and metropolitanization tell us about how people are to be distributed in space. Rather, the question asks about *community,* that historic sense of common identification that makes a locality always more than a place on a map, that makes it a social group that arouses a strong sense of personal identification.

There is no common conception of what is the future of community in the United States at the present time. Different people want different things. Yet locality, as place of residence and work and of family life, remains a basic fact of human existence. In that sense there will continue to be some kind of community.

But what is not obvious or clear as yet is what forms community will take. One powerful trend in the shaping of community is the segregation of homogeneous populations. The early suburban development perhaps did that best, but so did the ethnic neighborhood and the black ghetto. More recent cases are the student ghetto around a university, the retirement communities of older people, and the huge apartment complexes of people without children.

But there is also the effort to renew the city, to create there local government and thus vital local political life. It seeks to combine the diversity and challenge of the large city with a smaller, more controllable scale of organization.

Each of these experiences of community in the urban complex—suburb, ghetto, ethnic neighborhood, neighborhood organization—provides some measure of the problem of achieving community in modern society. Each is an experience from which to learn. None seems to provide the fully satisfactory model for community in a society moving rapidly from modern to postmodern.

Perhaps these examples are too much influenced by the city and metropolis as they now are and as they have evolved over the past century. Small adjustments may not be enough. What may be needed is a radical rethinking of what the city at its best has been as a livable community and what it takes to recreate that in a new time under new circumstances.

As our society becomes more urbanized, we have less an idea of what city life can be. As Murray Bookchin observes:

> Paradoxically, we live in a world marked by rampant urbanization—but one that lacks real cities. As the once clearly demarcated cities inherited from the past are devoured by the expanding metropolis, the city begins to lose its definition and specificity, as well as its function as an authentic arena for community and solidarity. The city disappears in the great urban belts which spread across the land.[43]

Perhaps there is one generalization that can safely be drawn from the urban experience in the twentieth century: that the search for community is an effort to develop some localized dimension of manageable social and political size in the face of the large-scale (and often bureaucratized) organization that is the hallmark of modern society; and that such a confrontation between the possibilities, values, and disabilities of small and large is most likely to occur in the urban metropolis. Here is where community will be created for the many, not the few, if it can be created at all.

(SUMMARY

Urbanization is a worldwide process correlated with industrialization. It has brought about the decline of the autonomous, local community.

Wirth saw "urbanism as a way of life" as a consequence of *size, density,* and *heterogeneity,* and from this produced a negative image of the city. This image has been somewhat redressed by recent work.

Urban *ecology* relates people to land in a competitive process. Burgess's concentric circles represented zones of differing land use to explain city growth. Competition for space is a rational-function process of market values, modified somewhat by symbolic values, such as status.

The *suburbs* have been more accessible for the young, the economically secure, and the mobile, while less so for the poor, the elderly, and the minorities. Suburbia has been explained as an escape from the city and an effort to create a secure, homogeneous environment in which to raise children.

Metropolitan areas are a single entity for many service functions, but are politically fragmented. The rational appeal to unite for efficiency is rejected by suburbanites who see in their separate localities the preservation of interests.

Efforts to renew the city may not succeed. The inner city and the *outer city* (not always the same as city and suburb) are two contrasting social worlds. The concentration of blacks in the central city means that inner city and outer city may in time signify black and white. Furthermore, the decentralization of population, services, and industry makes possible the future abandonment of the central city.

Abandonment of the city by the economically productive would make the city a "reservation" for confining the unwanted segments of the population.

The struggle to renew the city offers two alternatives: a program of corporate and government investment and reorganization to reintegrate the city into the economy, but at the loss of its independence; and the development of local neighborhood organization leading to an emphasis upon decentralization and local control and ownership of necessary resources.

The future of community in this urbanized society is as yet unclear. Probably no one form of community will do for all. But the search for community now is an effort to develop manageable and decentralized community in the urbanized setting.

NOTES

[1] See Gideon Sjoberg, *The Preindustrial City; Past and Present* (New York: The Free Press, 1960), and R. M. Adams, *The Evolution of Urban Society* (Chicago: Aldine, 1966).

[2] For a classic analysis of medieval cities, see Henri Pirenne, *Medieval Cities; Their Origins and the Revival of Trade* (Princeton, N.J.: Princeton University Press, 1925; Anchor paperback edition, 1956). See also Max Weber, *The City,* trans. and ed. Don Martindale and Gertrud Neuwirth (New York: The Free Press, 1958; paperback edition, Collier Books, 1962).

[3] *Population Bulletin of the United Nations,* No. 8-1976, United Nations, 1977, Table 9, p. 32.

[4] For a discussion of urban growth in the United States, with the above and additional data, see Donald J. Bogue, "Urbanism in the United States, 1950," *American Journal of Sociology* 60 (March 1955: 471—486.

[5] U.S. Bureau of the Census, *World Population: 1977: Demographic Estimates for the Countries and Regions of the World* (Washington, D.C.: Government Printing Office, 1978).

[6] For a discussion of how industry and technology determine the location of community, see William H. Form and Delbert C. Miller, *Industry, Labor and Community* (New York: Harper & Row, 1960), Chap. 2.

[7] See Pirenne, *op. cit.*

[8] Ernest W. Burgess, "The Growth of a City: An Introduction to a Research Project," in Robert Park, Ernest W. Burgess, and Roderick D. Mackenzie, *The City* (Chicago: University of Chicago Press, 1925), pp. 47—62.

[9] Walter Firey, *Land Use in Central Boston* (Cambridge, Mass.: Harvard University Press, 1947).

[10] Alvin Boskoff, *The Sociology of Urban Regions* (New York: Appleton-Century-Crofts, 1962), p. 108.

[11] See Morton and Lucia White, *The Intellectual versus the City* (Cambridge, Mass.: Harvard University Press and M.I.T. Press, 1962; paperback edition, New York: Mentor Books, 1964).

[12] Louis Wirth, "Urbanism as a Way of Life," *American Journal of Sociology* 44 (July 1938): 1—24.

[13] *Ibid.,* p. 1.

[14] Herbert Gans, "Urbanism and Suburbanism as Ways of Life: A Re-evaluation of Definitions," in Arnold Rose, ed., *Human Behavior and Social Processes* (Boston: Houghton Mifflin, 1962), pp. 306—323.

[15] For a cogent discussion of these issues, see Scott Greer, *The Emerging City: Myth and Reality* (New York: The Free Press, 1962).

[16] See, for example, Morris Axelrod, "Urban Structure and Social Participation," *American Sociological Review* 21 (February 1956): 13—18, and Nicholas Babchuk, "Primary Friends and Kin: A Study of the Association of Middle-Class Couples," *Social Forces* 43 (May 1965): 483—493. Both papers are reprinted in John N. Edwards and Alan Booth, eds., *Social Participation in Urban Society* (Cambridge, Mass.: Schenkman, 1973).

[17] Herbert Gans, *The Urban Villagers,* (New York: The Free Press, 1962).

[18] Gerald D. Suttles, *The Social Order of the Slum: Ethnicity and Territory in the Inner City* (Chicago: University of Chicago Press, 1968).

[19] James Q. Wilson, "The Urban Unease: Community vs. City," *The Public Interest* 12 (Summer 1968): 28.

[20] For an insightful discussion of this issue specifically applied to New York City, see Jane Jacobs, *The Death and Life of Great American Cities* (New York: Random House, 1961).

[21] For a discussion of the reasons for industrial decentralization, see David Gordon, "Capitalist Development and the History of American Cities," and Patrick J. Ashton, "The Political Economy of Suburban Development," in William K. Tabb and Larry Sawers, eds., *Marxism and the Metropolis: New Perspectives in Political Economy* (New York: Oxford University Press, 1978).

[22] Wendell Bell, "Social Choice, Life Styles, and Suburban Residence," in William Dobriner, ed., *The Suburban Community* (New York: Putnam, 1958), pp. 225–247.

[23] Richard Sennett, *The Uses of Disorder: Personal Identity and City Life* (New York: Knopf, 1970; paperback edition, Vintage Books, 1971), pp. 69–70.

[24] *Ibid.,* p. 70.

[25] *Ibid.,* p. 72.

[26] See Bennet M. Berger, "The Myth of Suburbia," *Journal of Social Issues* 17 (1961): 38–49.

[27] Herbert J. Gans, *The Levittowners: Way of Life and Politics in a New Suburban Community* (New York: Pantheon, 1967).

[28] Bennet M. Berger, *Working-Class Suburb* (Berkeley: University of California Press, 1960).

[29] H. Lawrence Ross, "Uptown and Downtown: A Study of Middle-Class Residential Areas," *American Sociological Review* 30 (April 1965): 255–259.

[30] U.S. Bureau of the Census, *Social and Economic Characteristics of the Metropolitan and Nonmetropolitan Population, 1977 and 1970* (Washington, D.C.: Government Printing Office, 1978), Table 7, p. 44.

[31] Robert C. Wood, *Suburbia; Its People and Their Politics* (Boston: Houghton Mifflin, 1958), p. 18.

[32] *Ibid.,* p. 18.

[33] *Ibid.,* p. 18.

[34] Ann R. Markusen, "Class and Urban Social Expenditure: A Marxist Theory of Metropolitan Government," in Tabb and Sawers, *op. cit.,* p. 107.

[35] Arthur Vidich and Joseph Bensman, *Small Town in Mass Society* (Princeton, N.J.: Princeton University Press, 1958).

[36] John H. Mollenkopf, "The Postwar Politics of Urban Development," in Tabb and Sawers, *op. cit.,* p. 119.

[37] See David Gordon, in Tabb and Sawers, *op. cit.,* pp. 48–51.

[38] For sociological analysis of urban renewal, see Scott Greer, *Urban Renewal and American Cities* (Indianapolis: Bobbs-Merrill, 1965); and Peter H. Rossi and Robert Dentler, *The Politics of Urban Renewal* (New York: The Free Press, 1961).

[39] Gans, "Urbanism and Suburbanism as Ways of Life," pp. 635ff.

[40] Norton Long, "The City as Reservation," *The Public Interest* (Fall 1971).

[41] Richard C. Hill, "Fiscal Collapse and Political Struggle in Decaying Central Cities in the United States," in Tabb and Sawers, *op. cit.,* pp. 230–232.

[42] See John C. Bollens and Henry J. Schmandt, *The Metropolis* (New York: Harper & Row, 1970), Chap. 11.

[43] Murray Bookchin, *The Limits of the City* (New York: Harper & Row, 1974), p. viii.

SUGGESTED READINGS

Bennet Berger, *Working-Class Suburb* (Berkeley and Los Angeles: University of California Press, 1960). A study which demonstrated that moving to the suburb did not give workers middle-class values.

Murray Bookchin, *The Limits to the City* (New York: Harper & Row, 1974). A radical, libertarian critique of urbanization as the destruction of urban community.

Herbert Gans, *The Levittowners: Way of Life and Politics in a New Suburban Community* (New York: Pantheon Books, 1967). Perhaps the best study about what the American suburb has become as a community.

Milton Kotler, *Neighborhood Government: The Local Foundations of Political Life* (Indianapolis: Bobbs-Merrill, 1969). An argument for the possibility of decentralizing the city politically.

David Morris and Karl Hess, *Neighborhood Power: The New Localism* (Boston: Beacon Press, 1975). An exploration of the idea of social power located in city neighborhoods.

Lewis Mumford, *The City in History* (New York: Harcourt, Brace & World, 1961). A classic treatment of the rise of the city and its contribution to human development.

Richard Sennett, *The Uses of Disorder: Personal Identity and City Life* (New York: Knopf, 1970; paperback edition, Vintage Books, 1971). An insightful critique of suburban homogeneity and a plea for the city as diversity, not sameness.

William K. Tabb and Larry Sawers, eds., *Marxism and the Metropolis: New Perspectives in Urban Political Economy* (New York: Oxford University Press, 1978). A collection of essays that brings a Marxist perspective to bear on the city in the United States.

Morton and Lucia White, *The Intellectual versus the City* (Cambridge, Mass.: Harvard University Press and M.I.T. Press, 1962; paperback edition, New York: Mentor Books, 1964). A historical analysis of the anticity bias that has been prevalent for so long in American thought.

Part 4

STRATIFICATION

The golf links lie so near the mill
That almost every day
The laboring children can look out
And see the men at play.

Sarah N. Cleghorn

Nine

SOCIAL CLASS

In any human society, people rarely, if ever, accept all others as social equals. Instead, they build into the very structure of society inequalities of material goods and social opportunities that set some off from others in persistent distinctions of higher and lower ranks. Some are rich and some are poor, some are privileged and others are not; a few are admired, most are not, and some even are despised.

In the most basic sense, then, the *stratification* of society means its division into a series of levels, or strata, ranking one above the other by virtue of the unequal distribution of certain social assets, such as material rewards, privilege, opportunity, and power. However much modern people may profess a belief in equality, inequality is built into the structure of modern society.

INTERPRETING INEQUALITY

It has always proved difficult to discuss stratification without either justifying it or attacking it. Most theories of stratification have been explanations of why there must be inequality in society. Sociologists would assert, however, that the intention of their analysis is not to justify or condemn stratification but to examine the conditions under which various forms of stratification occur.

Justifying Inequality

There are a number of different ways by which inequality has been justified, but they tend to fall into two main perspectives: those that base their argument on inherent differences in human nature; and those that base it, instead, on the requirements of society.

Inherent Inequality In ancient Greece Aristotle defended slavery on the ground that some people are naturally free and others are not. Many times since then the existence of social inequality has been explained in terms of human nature—some people are presumed to be *biologically* superior to others, which is then supposed to justify *socially* established differences of wealth and privilege. Thus, inequality in social positions is presumed to reflect inequality in human nature.

The argument had wide currency in American society throughout the first decades of this century. It was used to assert the superiority of whites over blacks and Anglo-Saxons over more recent immigrant groups from southern and eastern Europe, and thus to justify various forms of segregation and discrimination. Today such biologically based arguments have generally been rejected as scientifically invalid, as racist, and as politically reactionary.

Inequality by Merit The most influential argument now is that which first endorses equality of opportunity, then argues that the more *qualified* people should occupy the "better" positions in society and thus get more reward than the less qualified. This is a *meritocracy*, a society based on assignment of position and greater social reward for those presumed to be more qualified. The term was first coined by British sociologist Michael Young.[1]

The proponents of meritocracy agree that in fact equal opportunity is not yet true of any modern society. But they advocate social measures to make it possible, including various testing measures to sort out the naturally more able from the less able, and to allow the more able to obtain more education.

Despite the emphasis on equal opportunity, the basic theme of meritocracy is inequalitarian for two reasons. First, it accepts the unequal rewarding of social positions as justified. Secondly, it assumes that, even after equal opportunity is achieved, there will still be differences in demonstrated ability; that is, there will be the qualified, the less qualified, and the unqualified. What the advocates of meritocracy want to achieve is a close fit between position and person—the most qualified persons in the most demanding positions receiving the most reward.

The Functional View

Another sociological version of the inequalitarian argument asserts that in every society there are some positions that are of the greatest importance for society and that require the greatest amount of training or talent.[2] To ensure that these important positions are filled by qualified persons, there must be inequalities in the distribution of such social rewards as income, status, and power. According to this functionalist perspective, stratification is the "unconsciously evolved device by which societies insure that the most important positions are conscientiously filled by the most qualified persons."[3]

Unavoidably, such a sociological defense of inequality aroused controversy. Some sociologists, for example, pointed out that it is difficult to prove that the greatest reward goes to the most qualified to perform the most needed functions. This led to a modification of the functionalist argument to stress only that there had to be sufficient inequality in reward to ensure that people would undertake the longer and more arduous training required of the more demanding positions.

According to this modified argument, jobs like garbage collecting are lowly rewarded because they require little skill, even though the work is essential for the community. Yet this still leaves many material differences of social reward unexplained.

Like the meritocracy argument, functional theory supports greater reward for the professionally qualified in societies in which the professions are expanding.

Both arguments are justifications for inequality which are particularly appealing to professional classes.

The Equalitarian View

A contrary thesis—that inequality is neither just nor necessary—has persisted as a counterargument over the centuries. In the transition from medieval to modern society the scholarly work of such men as John Locke and Jean-Jacques Rousseau undercut such ideas as the divine right of kings (which declared that kings ruled because God sanctioned them to do so) and made more acceptable the democratic principle that sovereignty rests in the people. Much of the effort in the eighteenth century was to destroy the justification for legal inequality. Equality before the law became a principle of democratic society.

The Marxian View   In the nineteenth century a powerful critique of inequality was offered by Karl Marx. For Marx, the private ownership of the means of production—land, tools, and machinery—created an oppressive class system, divided between exploitative owners and exploited workers. Human freedom and equality were not possible until the control and direction of the means of production were shared among all who did the productive work. Only then could exploitative class relations be abolished. In sharing in goods and participating in necessary work, Marx believed, "from each according to his ability, to each according to his need."[4]

A Conflict Perspective

In contemporary sociology, partly in opposition to the functional conception of stratification, a *conflict* perspective has emerged, deriving support from the writings of C. Wright Mills and German sociologist, Ralf Dahrendorf, and, more basically, from Karl Marx.[5] Conflict theorists see society as an arena of combating groups struggling over the distribution of scarce goods, a struggle in which social power is the significant key to their distribution. These theorists emphasize the significance of conflicts over group interests, as well as the coercion of one group by another. It is the more powerful, therefore, who get most of the scarce goods, and the associated privileges and opportunities. Justifications of inequality are then but convenient rationalizations by those who get the most.

The struggle over the distribution of scarce goods often produces class conflict; here farm workers and their supporters march to mobilize public support for their demands for a larger economic share.

The existence of inequality has been a persistent feature of social life, and explaining that inequality has often seemed either to justify or to condemn it. It has proved to be difficult, if not impossible, to do otherwise.

CLASS AND STATUS

Two issues persistently occur in discussing stratification as a general feature of all human societies. One of these is the extent to which the system of stratification in a society is relatively open or closed; that is, whether or not people must remain in the class into which they were born. The other is the issue of whether there is a single basis for stratification, or instead several dimensions on which social ranking occurs.

Open and Closed Systems

A comparison of class in modern society with such systems as *castes* and *estates* is usually made to contrast *closed* systems in the historic past or in still preindustrial societies with the presumed *open* system of modern society.

Caste The concept of *caste* refers to the permanent, relatively rigid form of social stratification developed over long centuries in India.[6] Each caste is usually an occupational category closed off to one another so that individuals cannot in principle change their caste designation (though in practice the principle is sometimes violated). Since castes are *endogamous* (marriage occurs only within the caste) intermarriage is not available as a way of changing caste position. Individuals are born into their caste; this alone determines their membership.

Neither economic nor political organization alone could provide the almost complete separation of the castes from one another. But the Hindu religion provides a supernatural explanation and thus sanctifies and justifies the order of castes. Caste imposes duties and obligations on each person; no matter how lowly and menial such duties are, the Hindu religion provides a sacred basis for observing caste patterns and for not violating the provisions and rules of caste order.

Industrialization in India has put a severe strain upon the ancient caste system, though it has not yet eliminated it. Though new occupations and professions require new sets of relations, the caste system has shown a remarkable capacity to adapt to social changes of considerable scope. As modernization continues in India, a modified system of caste may yet survive, at least for a long time, as an adaptation to a more modern society.

Estate   In contrast to caste, the *estate* was a series of social classes in medieval Europe rigidly set off from one another and supported by custom and law, but not, like caste, sanctified by religion.[7] A hereditary, landowner aristocracy was the upper class of the estate system, with the upper levels of the clergy closely associated. The lower class were the peasants, who worked the land. These two classes made up the basic class structure of feudalism.

The slow growth of trade and commerce during the early Middle Ages, and the growth of cities, brought two other classes into existence, occupying a position between the aristocracy and the peasants: the merchants and the craftsmen.

Though movement upward in status was never forbidden by religion, both custom and law tended to keep people in their estates of birth. What made this so was a technologically simple agricultural economy. An agrarian system with a large number of peasants and a relatively low level of productivity did not permit much expansion of occupations or much opportunity for individuals to move from one social level to another. This was reinforced by customs associated with inheritance of status and property and with laws that established the particular rights and privileges of each social level.

Class   In contrast to caste and estate, a class system is *open* in that its social strata are not reinforced and made rigid and fixed by religion or law, or even to the same extent by custom. Furthermore, moving up in class position is valued and encouraged. Yet the contrast with castes and estates often leads to exaggeration of the openness of class systems. Inheritance of property and class differences in educational opportunities signify that class systems are only relatively open.

From Caste and Estate to Class   Contrasting class with caste and estate points up the fact that each form of stratification has emerged in and is a significant part of the social structure of historically quite different types of society. As the world modernizes such older systems of stratification as caste change radically or even disappear as the estate system has; a modern class system comes to be the dominant form of stratification. To this point, we have only linked class to industrialization and to the occupational structure. We need now to examine more closely the concept of social class.

Social Class

The fact that class is somehow related to economic organization leads some people, particularly Americans, to define class simply in terms of income. However, income alone does not adequately define class. Often skilled workers and even unionized, semiskilled workers in the large, mass-production industries earn as much as, if not more, than many people in white-collar occupations. Many white-collar and blue-collar incomes overlap. Income does not sufficiently set apart people whose relation to the productive process is quite different.

Many social scientists have specified the *source* of income as a criterion of class: The combination of what people do in the division of labor (occupation) or of what they own (property), as well as what they earn (income), can provide an adequate and revealing conception of stratification in economic terms. This concern constantly takes sociologists back to the writings

This scene of members of the British royal family at a public event provides us with an example of still existing high social status transmitted by family inheritance, a pattern largely outmoded by the advent of modern society.

of Karl Marx and Max Weber to understand what social class is.

Karl Marx on Class Marx's analysis of class begins with the recognition that the members of society are divided into economic strata, each stratum being made up of those who share a similar function in the organization of economic production. The division of labor, based upon the existing technology, creates a set of social relationships among people as workers. This necessary cooperation in the division of labor separates people into different functions—such as peasant and landlord, worker and owner-employer—and provides the basis for the existence of social classes.

Marx believed that the participation of individuals in the productive process provides them with crucial life-experiences, which shape their beliefs and strongly influence their actions. At the same time those who share similar positions have similar experiences, and so come to have similar attitudes and beliefs, a process fostered by frequent communication and interaction with one another. Furthermore, they share in time an awareness of economic interests, and of conflict and disagreement with other classes over the distribution of wealth. One of Marx's definitions of class says much of this:

In so far as millions of families live under economic conditions that separate their mode of life, their interests and their culture from those of the other classes, and put them into hostile opposition to the latter, they form a class.[8]

This "hostile opposition" is, for Marx, a necessary aspect of social class. In uniting to do "common battle" against another class, a stratum of workers or peasants becomes a social class. Otherwise, as Marx saw it, they are in individual competition with one another.

While it is common to assert that Marx viewed economic factors as determining how people act, his conception of class, in fact, is *political*. A social class, in his conception, exists only insofar as an economic stratum is aware of and is prepared to struggle for its economic interests against another class: ". . . the struggle of class against class is a political struggle."[9]

Max Weber on Class Max Weber, like Karl Marx, asserts that the economic organization of society is the basis of social class. People are in the same *class situation,* Weber says, when their occupation or their ownership of property gives them a similar chance, however large or small, to obtain some of the things valued in a society: material goods, physical health, education, travel, leisure, and exposure to a wide range of highly prized social experiences. Some people have goods to sell to others, and it is this which determines their *life-chances*. Other people sell their skills or labor on a labor market to available employers. Still others, such as professionals, offer highly valued and relatively scarce services to a clientele. Each of these constitutes a different "class situation." For Weber, a class is a collectivity of people who share a common set of life-chances as these are determined by property, occupation, and income. His specific definition is:

> We may speak of a "class" when (1) a number of people have in common a specific casual component of their life-chances, in so far as (2) this component is represented exclusively by economic interests in the possession of goods and the opportunities for income, and (3) is represented under the conditions of the commodity or labor markets.[10]

Weber recognized the varied ways in which the possession of property and of goods by those who "do not necessarily have to exchange them" gave them an advantage in the market over those who have to sell their goods to survive or who had no goods but only their "services in native form." Weber sounded not too different from Marx when he said: " 'Property' and 'lack of property' are, therefore, the basic categories of all class situations."[11]

For both Marx and Weber, then, social classes are outcomes of unequal social reward that are successfully claimed by various economic strata for their participation in the productive processes of the society.

The Multidimensionality of Stratification

Social class as economically based stratificiation does not exhaust the forms which stratification takes, though it is the most important. Of all major students of stratification, Weber best took account of the complexity of stratification in suggesting such forms as *class, status,* and *party.*

Status Groups As distinct from class, according to Weber, status refers to the ranking of social groups by *prestige* and *honor*. A *status group* may be said to exist when a number of individuals occupy a similar position in the prestige ranking of their community, and when they recognize each other as equals and interact regularly with one another. They form friendship circles, dine together, belong to the same organizations, encourage the intermarrying of their children, and otherwise exhibit a common *style of life.*

Religious and Ethnic Status Religion and ethnicity provide criteria not only for status in the community but also in society. The Jews, for example, are a people whose ancestry and traditions go far back in time; they have a specific identity, and they are more culturally homogeneous than many ethnic groups. Jews develop an organizational and community life that parallels that of other middle-class groups. They create their own associations and clubs, their own welfare organizations, indeed, all the forms of social life in a typical community. This not only gives them a sharp sense of separate identity and status, it also gives others a conception of the Jews as a separate status group.

While higher status frequently goes to those who established a community, or at least are long settled there, low status equally often goes to those people who are the most recent arrivals in the community, especially if they enter at a low economic level. This was usually the case with the great mass of immigrants who came to the United States from eastern and

SOCIAL CLASS AND LIFE CHANCES

Max Weber's concept of *life-chances* refers to the opportunity to acquire the valued material and nonmaterial rewards of society. Such life-chances, Weber pointed out, are unequally distributed among social classes. Besides income, other rewards include the chance for health and well-being. Here are some examples:

1. *Health.* The chance for a long and healthy life is not one that comes out equally in any society, but particularly the United States. (That is because every other industrial society has provided a national health system to pay for medical care for all.)

A longer life expectancy is correlated with social class—the higher the class, the longer one will probably live. Exposure to toxic and carcinogenic materials, for example, is a risk of many working-class occupations. Occupations with high risks of accidents at work are also working class. It is also true that better-educated people know more about medical care, nutrition, and habits of health.

2. *Mental Health.* What is true for physical health is equally true for mental health. People of lower classes have a better than average chance of becoming a patient in a mental hospital. Furthermore, those of higher classes are likely to receive better treatment; more frequently such advantaged people are treated at private hospitals and given psychotherapy, whereas the less advantaged are sent to public institutions where care is less adequate and sometimes is almost nonexistent.

3. *Education.* The chance for higher education declines as one goes down the class structure, despite much financial aid and publicly subsidized universities. This is partly a matter of financial resources, partly a matter of better educational opportunities for the advantaged to acquire academic skills and motivations. The wealthy have better schools than the nonwealthy.

4. *Criminal Conviction and Imprisonment.* The chance to escape imprisonment for criminal activities, or even to escape conviction, improves as one moves up the class ladder. The lower classes do not necessarily commit more crimes; they are simply less favorably treated in court, while white-collar offenders are better treated. The system of justice, in terms of arrest, conviction, and severity of punishment, treats differently people from different social classes.

In addition, the lower classes live in neighborhoods where crime rates are high. As a consequence, they are more often the victims of robbery and violence.

These few examples suggest that the chances to live longer and in better health, to retain one's sanity, to get a good education, and to stay out of prison are better for those of higher class position.

Notes

SOURCES: Evelyn M. Kitwanger and Phillip H. Hauser, *Education and Income Differentiation in Mortality, United States, 1960* (Chicago: University of Chicago Population Center, 1967); August B. Hollingshead and Frederick C. Redlich, *Social Class and Mental Illness* (New York: Wiley, 1958); Christopher Jencks and Others, *Inequality: A Reassessment of the Effect of Family and Schooling in America* (New York: Basic Books, 1972); S. M. Miller and Pamela Roby, *The Future of Inequality* (New York: Basic Books, 1970); Oscar Ornati, *Poverty amid Affluence* (New York: Twentieth Century Fund, 1966).

southern Europe after 1880. Relatively unskilled at first, largely from rural, peasant backgrounds, speaking little if any English—they clustered in immigrant colonies in America's rapidly growing industrial cities and soon constituted ethnic status groups that ranked low in the community.

Racial Status   When we speak of Jews and European immigrants, we have reference to *cultural* criteria for distinguishing one status group from another. But *racial* criteria for status also enter into the issue. Race is a biological factor, and when race becomes a criterion for status the members of the society *evaluate the biological differences in terms of superior or inferior.* This means that they impute to race social differences (such as mental ability or moral character), even though these differences cannot be supported by scientific evidence. But if people *believe* that such differences exist, they act accordingly; thus, the social consequence is to create a ranking of racial groups.

When criteria of status are racial, religious, and ethnic, and when those who rank low by such criteria are looked down on by others and are denied the life-chances according to others, we have *minority status* and *minority groups* who suffer from *prejudice* and *discrimination.* Obversely, those who rank high by such criteria, such as white, Anglo-Saxon Protestants (WASPs), are advantaged. In either case, a common status situation, like a common class situation, affects people's life-chances. (The inequality that comes from racial and ethnic status will be examined in Chapter 10.)

Status and Class   Though it is useful to distinguish status from class, the two are always interlinked; status is never independent of class. Low status is usually associated with lower-class position, and high status groups usually hold higher-class positions, though the relation may not be perfect. On the other hand, people in the same social class may be in different status groups: middle-class whites and blacks, Jews, Protestants, and Catholics, for example.

In the upper class, established families of old, inherited wealth often constitute a "high society" status group which is closed off to less "cultured" new money—the *nouveaux riches.* However, the latter's children may be able to achieve social acceptance, because they can be educated to the life-style of an upper-status group, and because, unlike their self-made fathers, they did not have to work themselves up from a lower social level.

In preindustrial societies, the distinction between class and status is less evident. Where there is little mobility from one social class to another, and thus where the same set of families occupies a particular class level from one generation to the next, the social interaction among them develops a commonly shared style of life. Peasants, artisans, merchants, and aristocrats in medieval society not only existed in different class situations, each also exhibited a common style of life, quite different from other classes. In such cases, then, class and status merge into a single pattern of stratification.

Under conditions of relatively rapid social change and social mobility, class and status diverge, and people in the same class situation may belong to different status groups. Weber recognized this when he observed:

> When the bases of the acquisition and distribution of goods are relatively stable, stratification by status is favored. Every technological repercussion and economic transformation threatens stratification by status and pushes the class situation into the foreground.[12]

Furthermore, focusing on both class and status as different dimensions of stratification makes more sense in understanding stratification in some societies than in others. Thus, Frank Parkin, a British sociologist, claims that:

> This "multidimensional" view of the reward system is perhaps useful in analyzing societies like the United States which are highly differentiated in terms of race or ethnicity, religious affiliation, and sharp regional variations (especially between north and south) as well as by social classes. But in societies like Britain and many other European countries, multiple cleavages of this kind tend to be rather less marked, so that the multidimensional model would seem to be less applicable.[13]

However, white English people and nonwhite Pakistanis and West Indians have come into open, violent conflict in recent years, suggesting that Weber's distinction between class and status may now be quite applicable to the British situation.

Party   Why does Weber put party with class and status in his forms of stratification? For Weber the three are linked because each is a basic aspect of social power. Parties, Weber observed, are structures organized to acquire property and thus to achieve domination. They may recruit followers from either classes or status groups, and thus be concerned with representing class or status interests in political struggles. What is more usually the case is that they draw from both classes and status groups, rather than from one or the other exclusively.

Nonetheless, sociologists rarely deal with parties as an aspect of stratification. Instead, it is Weber's distinction between class and status that has been incorporated into sociological analysis.

Community, Status, and Social Class

In the United States, the work of a social anthropologist, W. Lloyd Warner, has greatly influenced the American study of social stratification, particularly his study of Yankee City, which was the real community of Newburyport, Massachusetts.[14] Warner and his associates studied how prestige was distributed in Yankee City and other small cities and towns, combining both economic and noneconomic criteria in defining a series of "classes."

Warner developed a sixfold classification by taking the familiar terms—upper, middle, and lower—and dividing each into an upper and lower. Thus, there is an upper-upper class, composed of the community's elite of long standing, its old ruling families of high prestige, and a lower-upper class of rising families with newly won wealth, eager to win social acceptance. (In some of the small midwestern towns studied, there was only a single upper, thus a five-class system.) The upper-middle class constitutes the established business and professional people, and the lower-middle class is made up of varied white-collar occupations, small businessmen, and skilled workers. The upper-lower is composed of skilled and other workers who are "respectable" though poor and hardworking, whereas the lower-lower includes the most economically depressed whose way of life is not respected by other members of the community.

SOCIAL CLASS IN INDUSTRIAL SOCIETY

As a consequence of the Industrial Revolution in Europe, two distinctly new roles emerged. One was that of the capitalist *entrepreneur,* who put up the cap-

ital for an enterprise. Consequently, he had ownership of the machinery and materials that went into the production of goods, and so, too, of the finished commodities. These he sold for profit on the market. He combined in his person the functions of managing and owning the business.

The contrasting role was that of the *worker.* He was employed to operate machinery by which goods were produced, and he was paid a wage for his work. He did not own the machinery he operated. He was an employee, and he was property-less in the sense that the tools of production belonged not to him but to the entrepreneur.

The industrial process under capitalism with its private ownership of property, therefore created two basic social classes—a *middle class* and a *working class.* (The property-owning class was called middle class because, when it emerged, there was still an upper class of landowning aristocracy.)

Under early industrialism these classes were rather clearly separated. One earned profits, the other wages; one class was self-employed and employed others, the other was employed. Wages were relatively low, and a considerable difference in standard of living separated the two classes. The ownership of property, specifically the tools of production, and the independent status of self-employment, as well as the authority inherent in being an employer, became the symbols of middle-class prestige and respectability.

But as industrialism advanced, as large industrial organizations replaced the many smaller family enterprises, as individualistic, competitive capitalism of the eighteenth century became twentieth-century corporate capitalism, a modification of class structure occurred.

The Middle Classes

With the growth of large-scale enterprise over the last eighty years, a wide range of new, white-collar positions were created. These technical and administrative positions are salaried, and the individuals are employees. Thus, they are not middle-class in the nineteenth-century sense of the term; they do not derive income from profit nor own the business. Yet they are not in the same stratum as wage-earners. Their positions often require considerable training and, as highly specialized persons, they operate with less supervision or direction than do workers. In their mana-

THE VOCABULARY OF CLASS
IN THE UNITED STATES

In the United States there has never developed any stable vocabulary of class, any agreed-upon set of terms by which Americans can identify themselves and others. When simply asked what class they belong in, most Americans use terms like average, moderate, and the like—anything but upper and lower. And many cannot think of any appropriate term.

The most frequently cited evidence for this "middling" view of class by Americans is a Gallup poll, which asked a national sample of Americans if they thought they were upper, middle, or lower class. The results:*

- Upper Class   6 percent
- Middle Class   88 "
- Lower Class   6 "

However, when psychologist Richard Centers added *working class* to the other three terms, the results were as follows:†

- Upper Class   3 percent
- Middle Class   43 "
- Working Class   51 "
- Lower Class   1 "
- Don't know   1 "
- Don't believe in
  classes   1 "

These data from national polls go back almost three decades. Has there been any change since then? A recent study, done in 1964, showed the following:‡

- Upper Class   2.2 percent
- Upper-middle Class   16.6 "
- Middle Class   44.0 "
- Working Class   34.3 "
- Lower Class   2.3 "
- No classes exist   0.6 "

Some decline in working-class identification and some increase in middle-class identification seems to have occurred since the 1940s, perhaps reflecting actual shifts in occupational patterns since that time.

Notes

* George Gallup and S. F. Rae, *The Pulse of Democracy* (New York: Simon and Schuster, 1940), p. 169.

† Richard Centers, *The Psychology of Social Classes* (Princeton, N.J.: Princeton University Press, 1949), p. 77.

‡ Robert W. Hodges and Donald Tremain, "Class Identification in the United States," *American Journal of Sociology* 73 (March 1968): 535–547.

This self-employed shopkeeper in his small, old-fashioned store is the classic example of the old middle class, in contrast to the corporate employee of the new middle class, one among many in a large organization.

gerial capacities, they exercise authority over others. Furthermore, their compensation exceeds that of workers, often several times over. Consequently, sociologists have found it useful to recognize an *old* middle class and a *new* middle class.[15]

The Old Middle Class The old middle class is made up of those whose relation to property is one of ownership, who operate their own individual or family enterprises, and whose income is derived as profits from the ownership and operation of such a business. In addition, old middle class includes the "free" (self-employed) professionals, who "hang out their shingle" and conduct a private practice in law, medicine, dentistry, and the like. Their income is derived from the fees paid them by their clients.

The New Middle Class The new middle class, in turn, covers a wide range of salaried, white-collar positions. The salaried manager or executive, the technical

specialist, and the salaried professional make up this class. A combination of skills and specialized knowledge are necessary for these middle-class occupations, some of which are professionalized, most of which are specialized and skilled.

But not all of them are, and there lies the problem. *White-collar* and *middle class* are terms used interchangeably, even by sociologists. What was once a useful way of distinguishing between the middle and the working class—calling one white-collar, the other blue-collar—no longer accurately describes the complicated reality of modern class structure.

Upper- and Lower-Middle Class So wide is the range of class positions in the new middle class that it covers everything from a vice-president to a corporate lawyer, an engineer, a draftsman, to a file clerk. The fact that these are all "white-collar" jobs is not reason to define them as being in the same social class.

Sociologists recognize this and make a distinction

between an *upper*-middle and a *lower*-middle class. The first is composed of salaried professionals and executives; the second is composed of the more routinized clerical and semitechnical jobs, which do not require the skills and advanced education of professionals, nor the managerial authority of executives.

Increasingly, as we shall see in Chapter 16, these lesser white-collar positions cannot be distinguished from working-class jobs in income, in education, and in skill-level; they are similar, also, in often being closely supervised and lacking any authority. They are at the bottom of the ranking order of the employing organization. Indeed, like the working class, the people in these positions have turned increasingly to collective bargaining in order to promote their job security and increase their material rewards. It is among such positions that labor organizing has made its greatest gains in recent years.

If we ignore the color of shirts and collars we could argue that the range of modern clerical jobs—book-keeper, secretary, stenographer, cashier, bank teller, file clerk, telephone operator, office machine operator, payroll and timekeeping clerk, typist (and now word processor), as well as postal clerks and mail carriers, stock clerks, shipping and receiving clerks, among others—constitute the *growing* working-class occupations. That is what Harry Braverman has argued in his revealing study of work and occupational change in the twentieth century.[16]

Braverman also cites data from the Department of Labor on the earnings of full-time workers to show that the *weekly* wages of clerical occupations are less than those of all blue-collar workers; only service workers earn less.[17] More recent data, as reported in Table 9.1, support that observation.

Class and Occupation   Occupation alone does not distinguish between old and new middle class. For example, two different persons might be accountants. But if one operates his own accounting business, he is a small businessman of the old middle class; whereas the other, who is employed at a salary, is not. Their occupation is the same, but their class position is different. Similarly, a lawyer with an independent practice is old middle class, but a salaried lawyer working for a corporation or a large law firm is a salaried professional of the new middle class.

The old middle class has been declining

TABLE 9.1 Weekly Earnings of Occupational Categories, 1977	
White-Collar	
Professional and Technical	$277
Managers and Administrators	302
Salesworkers	225
Clerical	167
Blue-Collar	
Craft Workers	259
Operatives (except transport)	171
Transport Operatives	231
Laborers	181
Service Workers	142
Others	
Private Household Workers	59
Farm Workers	127

Source: U.S. Bureau of the Census, *Statistical Abstract of the United States: 1978* (99th Edition), Washington, D.C., 1978, p. 423.

throughout this century, while the new middle class has been expanding relatively rapidly. In 1977, only 8.4 percent of employed persons in the United States were self-employed, and that figure drops to 7 percent if farm-owners are exempted.[18]

The Working Classes

Since the worker in modern industry never was self-employed, the distinction between old and new, as in the middle class, does not apply. There are, however, several working classes.

Perhaps the basic working class, under industrial conditions, has been that of semiskilled occupations directly involved in operating the machinery of industrial production. This broad stratum of blue-collar workers has been organized in mass unions in the United States since the 1930s; in Europe even earlier.

But there is also a class of workers, such as tool and die workers in industry and skilled craftsmen in the construction trades, whose high skills bring better wages and working conditions. They are the "cream" of the working class. Often, they are organized in craft unions.

Below these classes, there is a class of unskilled laborers, employed in small factories and in service industries, whose wages are low (often the federal minimum or just above that), and who lack job security, for their areas of small-firm employment are not usually organized by unions. There is also a shrinking class of domestic servants, still a form of employment for a large number of women, mostly black. In the agricultural area, farm laborers, including migratory workers, constitute another kind of lower working class.

These unskilled and underemployed—in whose ranks are what is now called *the working poor*—suffer by comparison with the other working classes in social power (they are not usually organized), in income, and in job security. Their ranks are now increased by the addition of many dispossessed by mechanized agriculture (and mechanized mining in Appalachia) from rural America; a disproportionate number of them are black. (We will return to this issue for a closer look in Chapter 11.)

Is There an Upper Class?

The assertion that the working class and the middle class were the two basic classes to emerge from industrial capitalism seems to imply that no upper class exists. The term originally applied to a landed aristocracy, a ruling class whose wealth was derived from the ownership of large agricultural estates in an agrarian society, and whose power enabled it to monopolize the functions of political management and decision-making. Capitalism and industrialism seriously undercut the privileged position and entrenched class power of the aristocracy. Land became subordinate to industry as a source of wealth and democratic revolutions overthrew the ruling aristocracy.

Since then, the term upper class has had no consistent meaning. Some would argue that historically the upper class passed out of existence. Others apply the term to those who are simply the wealthiest. An upper class, if one exists, ought to be distinguished from upper-middle class by income, by power, by privilege, by style of life, and by function in the division of labor. Does such a class exist in the United States?

Some sociologists describe an old upper class of families of great wealth, usually of income derived from extensive investments and property holdings, not

from occupations. Upper-class families are characterized by a distinctive and exclusive life-style, based upon family wealth, family lineage, and unique patterns of socialization.[19]

More recently, C. William Domhoff culminated several years of research on high status and social power to sketch out a portrait of a national upper class, cohesive on the basis of in-group interaction and common life-style:

. . . I believe it can be argued that the upper class is more cohesive than any other level of the American social hierarchy. Its smaller size, greater wealth, different sources of income (stocks and bonds), different schooling, different leisure activities, and different occupations, not to mention its complicated web of intermarriages, are evidence of this statement.[20]

But Domhoff's conception of an upper class is more than just a class of great wealth and exclusive life-style. It is also, he says, a governing class,

by which I mean a social upper class which owns a disproportionate amount of the country's wealth, receives a disproportionate share of the country's yearly income, contributes a disproportionate number of its members to governmental bodies and decision-making groups, and dominates the policy-forming process through a variety of means. . . . The governing class manifest itself through a power elite which is its operating arm.[21]

An upper class, then, is a class of dominant wealth and power. Based as it is on the ownership of capitalist property, and given its ability to exercise a dominant influence on the operations of government and national policy, such an upper class is surely, as Domhoff says, a governing class; it is, most basically, a *capitalist* class.

Summarizing Social Class

Our discussion to this point has identified the major categories of social class to be found in all industrial-capitalist societies, including American society. Here is a summary of them:

Upper class: a class with dominant, inherited wealth, not accumulated from salary but from ownership of capitalist property; it is a *capitalist* class.

Upper-middle class: the salaried professionals, as well as executives and administrators of corporate and public organizations of modern society; but also the self-employed professionals and the owners of substantial independent businesses belong here, too.

Lower-middle class: a broadly inclusive category of "white-collar" positions more routinized and supervised, clerical and semitechnical in nature, which, in fact, might also be defined as working class.

The *working classes:* a *skilled* class of craftsmen is one working class; another is a semiskilled class of machine operatives; yet another is an unskilled class, often irregularly employed, who are the *working poor* and often called a *lower* class.

These are broad, basic categories, which in the middle ranges—lower-middle and working class—overlap, and where any particular occupational category belongs can be an issue of dispute. Nor does income fall neatly into these categories. There is both overlap, on the one hand, and a considerable range of income possible *within* a given class. Professionals, for example, can range from incomes barely above the working class to amounts above $100,000.

SOCIAL CLASS IN COMMUNIST AND CAPITALIST SOCIETIES

The most familiar sociological analyses of class emphasize the nature of class structure under *industrialism,* largely ignoring any differences that might occur between communist and capitalist societies, both types of which are industrial. Usually, the point is made that, despite ideological claims of Marxism, there have developed structured inequalities in communist societies much like those in capitalist societies.

Such a broad similarity, however, may obscure some differences between the two types of societies that are worth noting. Frank Parkin, a British sociologist who has examined this issue, begins with laying out what he believes to be the basic reward system of advanced Western capitalist societies, as follows:[22]

- Professional, managerial and administrative
- Semiprofessional and lower administrative
- Routine white collar
- Skilled manual
- Semiskilled manual
- Unskilled manual

Parkin then looked for a significant "break" in the reward hierarchy and argued that "in Western capitalist societies this line of cleavage falls between the manual and nonmanual occupational categories."[23] This is so, Parkin insists, even though there is an overlap in the *incomes* of the lesser white-collar occupations with the more skilled manual workers.

What Parkins means by a break in the reward hierarchy is the line that separates those who are better rewarded from those who are poorly rewarded. This means such things as:

better promotion and career opportunities; greater long-term economic security, and, for many, guaranteed annual salary increases on an incremental scale; a cleaner, less noisy, less dangerous, and generally more comfortable work environment; greater freedom of movement and less supervision, and so forth.[24]

It is this, Parkins asserts, which generally distinguishes manual from nonmanual work in capitalist societies. But in communist societies, while differences of income and other rewards are considerable, the pattern is not identical with that of capitalist societies.

Class Inequality in the Soviet Union   The Soviet Union has not maintained a consistent position on the matter of class and equality. The Russian Revolution in 1917 brought about a period of greater equalization of rewards as well as of social opportunities. But in the early 1930s Stalin attacked "equality-mongering" and declared greater material incentives and privileges had to be offered as a stimulus to get people to learn skills and assume responsibilities in building an industrial society. From this development, the Soviet Union built a complex and highly differentiated reward structure; in the 1940s further changes in taxes favored the better paid and further increased inequality.

After Stalin's death, however, some of the trend to greater inequality was reversed. The minimum level wage was raised; other workers were granted raises so as to *reduce* differentials among various skilled categories. The income tax became more progressive, easing the burden on lower income groups.

Inequality in Eastern Europe   In the communist societies of eastern Europe, the fluctuations between equalitarian and inequalitarian trends have not been as sharp as in the Soviet Union, but similar reactions have occurred. After an early period of socializing property and reducing class differentials of reward, similar campaigns against "equality-mongering" appeared in the 1950s, producing greater inequality among the range of occupations, so that Parkin could say: "It is certainly the case that in eastern, as in western, Europe the occupational reward hierarchy tends to correspond to the hierarchy of skill and expertise."[25] However, here, too, increasing inequality was halted by government action, and by the 1960s blue-collar workers had been put into a more favorable position.

Blue-Collar and White-Collar in Communist Societies

In these communist societies "highly skilled or craft manual workers enjoy a higher position in the scale of material and status rewards than do lower white-collar employees."[26] In Yugoslavia, for example, in 1961 skilled workers on the average earned about 25 percent more than office staff, while the latter earned about 35 percent more than unskilled laborers. Indeed, by 1964 manual workers earned better incomes than did lower white-collar workers in Bulgaria, Hungary, Czechoslovakia, and the Soviet Union; only Poland was an exception.[27]

Such differences have affected the distribution of occupational prestige. Skilled workers have a higher social standing in these countries than do the routine white-collar positions. The overall reward hierarchy, then, according to Parkin, in contrast to capitalist societies, runs as follows:[28]

- White-collar intelligentsia (professional, managerial, and administrative positions)
- Skilled manual positions
- Lower or unqualified white-collar positions
- Unskilled manual positions

On the basis of this, Parkin claims that the reward structure of these societies does not break between manual and nonmanual as clearly as it does in Western capitalist societies. Instead, "the most obvious break in the reward hierarchy occurs along the line separating the qualified professional, managerial, and technical positions from the rest of the occupational order."[29]

BLUE COLLAR/WHITE COLLAR: CLASS AND OCCUPATION

The transition from an agricultural to an industrial society radically altered the class structure of modern society. But what of the future? A postmodern society will clearly affect occupations and also social classes, though just how is not easy to perceive. There are two major trends, however, that are basic to any conception of the direction that stratification will take in even the near future: the trend in the occupational base of the working class, and the trend in the group of a new technical/professional class.

Trends in Class Structure

Since the class structure of industrial society is a direct product of its division of labor, anything that is likely to alter the division of labor will influence social class. Technological developments that eliminate occupations and create new ones change the division of labor and thus the class structure. In part the emergence of new middle-class positions, for example, arises from the development of new professional and technical fields; these are most likely to be salaried positions, requiring considerable training, in large public and private organizations.

Throughout this century in the United States, from 1900 to 1977, there has been a dramatic shift away from farm occupations to urban occupations, and from blue-collar to white-collar occupations (see Table 9.2). In 1900 only 17.6 percent of all workers were white-collar; but in 1956 the percentage had surpassed those in blue-collar jobs, and the proportion increases steadily. By now, almost half of the employed are in white-collar jobs, while blue-collar jobs have remained a fairly stable proportion of all jobs.

The greatest change has occurred in farming. In 1900 more people were in farm jobs than in any other category. By 1950 this was down to 12.4 percent. Since then it has continued to decline rapidly, so that now less than 4 percent of the labor force is in farming.

There seems to be no reason to assume any change in this basic trend in at least the near future. Therefore, if the trend continues unchanged, there will be a substantial decline in the working class as it has been historically defined.

TABLE 9.2
Percentages in Major Occupational Groups, 1900–1979, in the United States

	1900	1950	1970	1979
White-collar Workers	17.6	37.5	48.3	51.3
Blue-collar Workers	35.8	39.1	35.3	32.7
Service Workers	9.0	10.9	12.4	13.3
Farm Workers	37.5	12.4	4.0	2.6

Source: For 1900 data, Bureau of the Census, *Historical Statistics of the United States, Colonial Times to 1959,* p. 74; other from *Statistical Abstracts of the United States, 1979,* p. 418.

The fate of the working class in industrial society has long been a matter of wide discussion and debate, in part because of the Marxian belief in the working class as the agent of revolutionary change. There have been two arguments against this Marxian position: first, that the working class will decline in numbers to become too small a class to be the revolutionary force against capitalism. The second is that workers have gained so much, they have lost their once militant class consciousness and have become more like the middle class in attitudes and life-style.

Studies of workers in Europe as well as in the United States seem to support the idea that industrial workers no longer possess the militant class consciousness so evident in the nineteenth century and even in the 1930s. Certainly, violent class struggles have declined in the Western industrial nations, replaced by unions and collective bargaining. This, in turn, has suggested that due to sharing in society's affluence, workers are no longer distinguishable from the middle class.

But sociologist James Rinehart has taken a hard look at the available data and has come to the conclusion that the working class's becoming middle class is more myth than reality.[30] Herbert Gans, too, we saw in the previous chapter, found that in a suburban community working class and middle class were different in values and life-styles, as well as in political attitudes and in civic participation.[31]

However, some of this confusion can also be attributed to the fact that many blue-collar occupations earn as much income as do many white-collar ones. This does not make them middle class; instead it raises a question about how middle class are these white-collar jobs.

Is There a New Working Class?

Many social scientists, in both Europe and the United States, have recently been speaking of a "new" working class, white-collar rather than blue-collar. A new range of occupations are defined as working class, even though they are no longer manual, blue-collar jobs; these jobs are technical functions in a highly technological society, are found in large organizations, and do not possess any managerial authority; instead they are subject to supervision and control as much so as blue-collar jobs and are often as routinized.

According to social critic Michael Harrington, this new class is coming to be a significant force in American social life:

The new stratum on which we focus is not based upon property or employment in the private corporation. Its members work, for the most part, in public, or semipublic sectors—education, health, social services, defense and defense-related industries, aerospace—and are therefore dependent on federal political decisions for their economic well-being. They also tend to be employed by large organizations and often, for all their educational attainments, they are subordinate participants in a hierarchical system.[32]

It is this publicly based position that orients them to white-collar unionism and to politics, according to Harrington—and white-collar unions have been the fastest growing unions in recent years.[33]

There is yet much debate and disagreement among both European and American scholars over this new working class, and about whether it will be a progressive political force or not. But the emergence of a large and steadily growing white-collar aggregate of technically trained people in administratively subordinate positions seems now to be a basic trend. Combined with the decline of farmers and farm laborers, as well as blue-collar workers, this trend suggests a major

According to Michael Harrington and other analysts, this schoolteacher is better defined as an example of the new working class.

change in this society's occupational and class structure, as well as in the occupational and class basis for democratic politics.

The New Professional Class

While some sociologists are concerned with the development of a new *working* class, others see emerging in modern society a new *professional* class of persons highly trained in science, in modern technology, and in various highly specialized professions.

The emergence of such a class is a basic proposition of Daniel Bell's conception of postindustrial society. Such a society, he says, is a "knowledge society"; innovation increasingly comes from research and development, which in turn is made possible only by science and technology. Bell defines the new class as made up of four components: scientific; technological (applied skills: engineering, economics, medicine); administrative; and cultural.

While Bell specifies an inclusive range of occupations in the new class, his specific focus is clearly on scientists and engineers, on economists and mathematicians, for these are the possessors of the specialized knowledge on which the new technology is founded. It is their knowledge, says Bell, which is the information base for the economy today.[34]

More critical thinkers have also noted the emergence of this new class. Michael Harrington, for example, says:

. . . there is a new stratum in the American social structure; its members are characterized by college or graduate or professional education and *relatively* well-paid occupations, often in a new technology sector, with *some* opportunity for nonroutine work.[35]

While a wide range of thinkers on both the Right and Left have acknowledged the emergence of this new stratum, the issue which divides them, however, is what implications follow from its existence.[36]

Is the New Class Political? The issue is not the set of occupations which marks off the new class from other, particularly lesser classes, but whether its members share a common set of attitudes and values and are then able to act collectively as a political force. If they cannot become a political force in their own right, then, however indispensable their function and however much they gain in reward and privilege, they remain servants of power. But if they can, are they of the left or right, for or against capitalism, progressive or reactionary?

It is just this basic issue which divides all those who recognize the importance of the new class, and which provides the basis for most discussions. Bell believes that it will not be a class capable of taking political power, and that it will not fundamentally shape the future society nor be its ruling class.[37]

Harrington, too, believes that these new professionals are not now involved in making the basic choices of society and are not a ruling class. In fact, he says, "It is, like every other class, internally ambiguous and even contradictory, and only a minority of its members are politically active."[38] The new class, he says,

. . . is not inevitably and inherently on the Left or the Right. It has tendencies toward *both* liberal elitism *and* a democratic politics of alliance with working people and the poor. Which of these tendencies will prevail is not a question that can be settled theoretically. It will be decided politically.[39]

Yet this new class is bound to be a significant participant in the struggles that will shape the future, if for no other reason than that its members are highly skilled and knowledgeable and carry out necessary technological and administrative functions in society. They are, in short, in a strategic position to make a difference, and their *collective* judgement (if they can make one) about what is possible and desirable for all of us in society can be decisive in determining what the future of society will be like.

Classes Old and New

A sociological concern for the rise of new social classes and the decline of old ones is more than an effort to describe new forms of class structure in modern society. Marx taught us that classes are always potentially more than simply categories of people in similar occupations who share the same condition of life. When conscious of common interests, and mobilized for action, they become a political force, even, possibly, an agency of revolution.

A change in class structure always implies a shift in relations of power and a possible challenge to dominant values and modes of thought. What a new class might become as a political force and what new forms of class struggle it might engage in could be decisive for the future of society.

SOCIAL MOBILITY

How people are recruited for the class positions of society opens up a complex and often controversial issue, that of social mobility. If each social class transmits its property and position to the next generation within its own ranks, then each social stratum is *closed* and there is no mobility. If, instead, there is no such transmission by mechanisms of inheritance, then the system is *open* and there is social mobility.

Industrial societies are usually categorized as open in contrast to the caste and estate systems. But such openness is relative, and the contrast with caste and estate systems may unwittingly exaggerate. In open

systems expectations and aspirations of mobility are developed, and a claim is made, at least in the United States, about *equality of opportunity,* namely, the equal chance to be mobile. *But, there is not and never has been an equal chance for individuals in all social classes to be mobile.*

Structural Mobility

What makes mobility a reality is a change in occupational structure, enlarging the range and proportion of middle- and upper-level occupations while reducing the proportion of lower ones. By first moving peasants into urban occupations and later increasing white-collar occupations, the transition from an agrarian to a industrial economy provides social mobility not imagined before. Mobility created by changes in the occupational structure of the society is *structural* mobility (sometimes called *forced* mobility).

But social change does not stop at the transition from agricultural to industrial society. Rather, advanced industrial countries move beyond the predominance of manufacturing occupations to develop the *tertiary* branch of the economy: trade, transportation, communication, and personal and professional services. At the same time agricultural employment declines both proportionately and absolutely, while manufacturing declines proportionately. This change increases white-collar and middle-class occupations.

These developments, rather than individual effort, primarily account for social mobility. This is true, furthermore, of any industrial society, whether that society is capitalist or socialist.

The Soviet Union, for example, has undergone rapid industrialization since the Russian Revolution in 1917. In the process, millions of peasants have been shifted to urban occupations, and higher education has increased considerably as a necessary means to train large numbers of people for varied technical and professional fields. The industrialization of the Soviet Union simply created a great stratum where it had not existed before.

Mobility and the Family

The family is the social unit through which an individual is placed into the class structure. Through the family the child can inherit property, occupation, educational opportunity, life-style, family connections, even titles and legal privileges. In nonindustrial societies, this may constitute the major process for locating individuals in the social structure. In industrial societies inheritance processes do not guarantee transmission of social status by kinship to nearly the same extent, but such societies still do not eliminate inheritance as a significant process.

Family and Education   Even where the family cannot transmit property to the next generation, it nonetheless seeks to maximize the social chances of its children. Middle-class people seek preferred educational opportunities for their children, to teach them what they believe to be the attributes of successful people, to provide them with the necessary credentials, and in other ways to increase their children's chances of being mobile.

For the nonpropertied classes, particularly, education is a necessity in the mobility process. Educational opportunities have never been equally open to all economic levels, though the growth of public education to the university level has widened the chances for an education and made it no longer the narrow class privilege it once was.

In the nineteenth century individuals gained entrance into the middle class by accumulating some modest capital; in the twentieth century a college education more and more becomes the "social capital" necessary to make one's way into the middle class. Differences in the ability of families to make a college education possible, financially and culturally, is now as crucial as accumulating and transmitting property once was.

Family and Life-Style   In other ways, too, families of higher social status improve the mobility chances of their children. Having fewer children, for example, increases the chances of a family to do more for the children it does have; in all industrial societies the upper economic levels have fewer children than do those of the lower economic levels.

But perhaps more importantly, upper-status families improve the mobility chances of their children by their very life-style. A child of a professional person is exposed to the cultural atmosphere and a pattern of attitudes and values appropriate to and expected of someone at that class level. In subtle ways they are prepared for a professional or an equivalent occupa-

tion by their childhood socialization. Such a child has a distinct advantage over the child of a factory worker.

Inheriting Occupational Level   Studies of social mobility seem to indicate that most people are not mobile, and that what mobility does occur is not usually from top to bottom, but instead a small movement from one level to the next. In one of the recent studies, for example, the authors report that 30 percent of the men in the sample had "inherited" their father's occupational *level* (though not necessarily the same occupation). Most of the others usually moved only to an adjacent or near-adjacent category.[40] Furthermore, they note, such inheritance is especially marked for sons of professionals; 40.4 percent of the professionals in their national samples were the sons of professionals.[41]

The most extensive effort to measure social mobility was undertaken by sociologists Peter Blau and Otis Dudley Duncan, who gathered information on 20,000 American males. By comparing the education and occupation of fathers and sons, they found that 37 percent of the men in white-collar jobs were the sons of blue-collar workers.[42]

Note, however, that Blau and Duncan assume that a shift from a blue-collar occupation to a white-collar one is always upward mobility. But our earlier discussion about what is lower-middle class and what is working class questioned whether all white-collar occupations were necessarily middle class. Based on skills and incomes, many of them could be labeled working class.

The available facts tell us therefore that social mobility is real enough, but that there is undoubtedly much less of it than the myths about equal opportunity would have one believe.

Social Mobility in Europe and America

Americans readily believe that the chance to be mobile is greater in the United States—"the land of opportunity"—than in any European society. Furthermore, Europeans seem also to believe this. But that does not necessarily make it so. A study by sociologists Seymour Lipset and Reinhard Bendix undertook to find out.[43]

Lipset and Bendix divided their data into a simple manual-nonmanual distinction for a number of industrial countries—existing data did not permit a more refined breakdown. Their carefully computed index of total vertical mobility showed little difference from one industrial country to another.

More recently, Lenski has computed a similar manual-nonmanual index based on data from a variety of sources.[44] He lists the United States as first with a mobility rate of 34 percent, but five other countries are close behind: Sweden, 32 percent; Great Britain, 31 percent; Denmark, 30 percent; Norway, 30 percent; and France, 29 percent.

Social mobility, then, is fairly similar in industrial societies. Perhaps the most basic finding is that most manual workers' sons move largely into the more modest white-collar positions while mobility into the upper, elitist levels of occupations is most possible for those who start halfway up the scale.

Social Mobility in Communist Europe

How does social mobility in the Western industrial (and capitalist) societies compare with that of eastern Europe? Because of difficulties in getting comparable data, few sociologists have dared to make any comparisons. But Frank Parkin has sought out data from communist societies and attempted some comparison.[45] From a quite subtle discussion we can abstract two basic points. One is that the dominant class of managers and professionals, like such classes in capitalist societies, is able to transmit competitive advantage to their own children.

The other point is that, though privileged classes assure high position for their children, there is nonetheless much social mobility for peasants and manual workers in these societies. The increase in white-collar positions as a consequence of industrial expansion has provided in eastern Europe a level of mobility for those lower in occupational rank that exceeds that in the United States and Europe. Parkin cited a 1963 study of Hungary, for example, that showed that 77 percent of managerial, administrative, and professional positions were filled by men and women of peasant and worker origin, and that 53 percent of doctors, scientists, and engineers were from such families.[46]

Furthermore, argues Parkin, this *fact* of social mobility has encouraged high aspirations among the working classes: ". . . parents' ambitions for their children are pitched much higher in socialist than in

capitalist society."[47] This is true to such an extent that the numbers of aspiring young people is greater than the number of higher positions to fill.

It does not follow that such mobility will continue indefinitely into the future. Once a new, dominant class comes into being and its own children have distinct advantages in the recruitment for upper positions, and once the period of rapid change in the occupational structure is over, what then? Parkin acknowledges that whether the openness of the socialist system can be maintained over the long run is a crucial issue for which no answer is now available.

Coping with Limits on Mobility

What do people do in a modern society when they cannot be mobile? One possibility is to define oneself as a failure, as lacking what is required for success. But this is very self-punishing and most people hedge in assuming that it is entirely a matter of their own deficiencies.

Alternatively, individuals can lower their aspirations by expecting and being satisfied with much less than they once hoped for. They lower their aspirations to fit the modest gains in status they can realistically accomplish. Some people also come to believe that chance plays an important part. The only difference, they believe, between themselves and a more mobile person is a "lucky break."

Other people recognize their own nonmobility as fact, but transfer their unrealized aspirations to their children. Sociologist Eli Chinoy found this among automobile workers, who knew they were not going to escape from factory work or move up in the factory hierarchy, but who maintained strong hopes that their children would make it into middle-class occupations.[48] In this way, they were able to keep alive in themselves a belief in opportunity in America.

Alternate Routes to Mobility   Between those who are mobile and those who are not is a quite different category: those who are mobile but not in the conventional way. They have not moved up in the structure of conventional business and professional occupations. Yet movie or television stars, recording and concert rock music performers or professional baseball or football stars, are also mobile. So is any person who has achieved high political office, or one who has become a high-ranking labor leader.

Popular entertainment, professional athletics, politics, and labor is each an avenue for career mobility in American society. A successful entertainer or athlete can attain wealth and public fame. Through labor and politics, another can attain power. Through popular entertainment, professional athletics, and politics, then, some individuals may be able to win social acceptance from the more conventional high-status people and so ensure middle or upper status for their children. Labor leaders often transfer middle-class status to their children.

Social mobility in these ways does not require the usual certificates of education and professional training, though it may require long years of hard work, practice, and accumulated experience. For those who have ability and ambition but lack formal training, a career in one of these ways can provide mobility not otherwise possible. This explains why so many successful people in these fields come from lower-status backgrounds, particularly from minority groups.

THE PERSISTENCE OF INEQUALITY

This society is like all other modern societies in that no matter how much it changes, inequality persists. It is also like all other modern societies in that its commitment to equality is limited and specific.

Throughout all its history American society has made a commitment to only two limited forms of equality: equality of opportunity and equality before the law. Its practices, of course, have been far short of its ideals, so that neither of these two limited forms has been made real. The recent struggles for racial and sexual equality provide evidence of that.

The Equal Chance to be Unequal

What is basic to equality of opportunity and equality before the law is that each is, in principle, a commitment to the idea that all persons in society should get an equal chance to compete against one another. But, in competing against one another, some will get further ahead and others will fail. The result, in short, is inequality, for equality of opportunity and equality before the law are both efforts to ensure an equal chance to be unequal.

This idea, of course, is the principle of *meritocracy*; it is the idea that unequal status and reward are "fair" if everyone had an equal chance to compete for unequally rewarded positions. It takes for granted that all positions in society can be fairly rewarded by an unequal distribution of reward.

Unequal Wealth   It has been a widely held conception that there has been a more equitable distribution of wealth in the United States since the reforms instituted by the New Deal during the 1930s. This is not so. There is today as great an inequality in the distribution of wealth, if not greater, than there was fifty years ago (*see* Chapter 11).

Class Is Inequality   The concept of equality contradicts the concept of social class, for class, by definition, is a structure of inequality. That is why, no matter how much Americans may proclaim a belief in equality of opportunity, the very existence of social classes is a system for distributing life-chances unequally. A genuinely equal society could only be a classless society.

Equality in Communist and Socialist Systems

Marx believed that true equality could be achieved and social classes abolished in a future communist society in which the productive forces had so advanced as to eliminate scarcity. Only then was equality possible. But communist revolution has come, not in the most industrially and technologically advanced societies, but in industrially undeveloped societies, where scarcity has remained a basic fact of life. The result has been, not a classless society, but new classes in a new society.

In the Soviet Union and other communist countries, there are those who earn much higher than average incomes. In addition, they receive such privileges as access to automobiles and country homes—comparable to the expense-account benefits of capitalist societies.

In several western European capitalist countries, socialist parties control the government. But, according to Frank Parkin, while this has produced a strong system of social welfare, it has not produced any major pressure to equalize income. "After thirty-five years of socialist rule in Sweden, income differentials between working-class and middle-class occupational groups are no narrower than in western societies ruled by *bourgeois* governments."[49]

More significantly, according to Parkin, these socialist parties in western Europe have since the 1950s abandoned their long-standing commitment to *egalitarian* socialism in favor of *meritocratic* socialism; that is, a commitment to equality of opportunity for the individual, and competitive pursuit of unequally rewarded positions. Meritocratic socialism would not eliminate rich and poor. There is, therefore, in both the western capitalist and eastern European communist societies, no political party any longer committed to equality among the social classes.

Classlessness, it would seem, is an idea whose time has not yet come.

Class and Inequality   In this chapter we have reviewed the basic issue of social class as the fundamental unit of stratification. But there is much more to say. The next chapter takes up one matter basic to social class, the unequal distribution of material reward, namely, wealth and poverty. After that we will broaden the analysis of stratification by looking at race and ethnicity as bases for social inequality, and then at sex.

SUMMARY

Social stratification is the inequality of status found throughout social structure, though it varies in form from one society to another. An inequalitarian view accepts stratification as right and natural, even necessary. An equalitarian view believes stratification is both unjust and unnecessary.

Caste is a rigid form of stratification sanctioned by religion, while *estates* are rigid forms of stratification enforced by law and custom but not by religion. *Classes* are relatively open strata, not fixed by law, custom, or religion.

Karl Marx saw classes as economic strata politically organized, engaged in struggle against the oppression of dominant classes.

Max Weber sees stratification as multidimensional: *class,* as economic strata; *status* groups, as noneconomic bases for prestige; and *parties,* as groups contesting for power.

W. Lloyd Warner called classes the prestige rankings of the community's status groups.

Status, in contrast to class, is evident in such things as the status of old, settled families; the glamour status of "star" performers; and status based on religion, ethnicity, and race. In times of economic stability, stratification by status is preeminent and class and status tend to merge. But in situations of change, class becomes prominent again.

Under capitalism there emerged two basic classes: a *middle class* of owner-operators and a *working class* of employees. In time a *new* middle class of salaried employees developed and became more numerous. With the demise of aristocracy, the existence of an *upper class* has been argued pro and con, though recent work has provided some documentation of an upper class of very wealthy families of inherited income and extensive property ownership, a *capitalist* class.

There is an *upper-middle* class of salaried professionals and executives and administrators, as well as self-employed professionals and the owners of substantial independent businesses.

The *lower-middle* class is a broad category of "white-collar" positions more routinized and supervised, clerical and semitechnical in nature, which might also be defined as working class.

The *working* classes are a *skilled* class of craftsmen; a *semiskilled* class of machine operatives; and an *unskilled* class who are the working poor and are often called *lower* class.

Despite ideological claims, communist societies also have social classes. In the communist states of eastern Europe, in contrast to capitalist societies, skilled workers rank above and are better rewarded than those holding routine white-collar positions.

The basic trend affecting class structure has been from farm to urban occupations, and from blue-collar to white-collar.

Working-class people have been viewed as less class-conscious, an *embourgeoisement* due to affluence. But this has been exaggerated; working-class people continue to differ from middle-class people in values and political attitudes, in life-style and civic participation.

With the decline of blue-collar workers, some social scientists see a new working class coming into being, a class of white-collar, technical jobs, most in public employment, providing the basis for white-collar unions.

Other social scientists are concerned about the emergence of a *new professional* class, particularly engineers and scientists. Because this class will be so strategic in the movement to a postindustrial future, its attitudes and politics are important; but so far there is no definite political character to this new class, either of the Right or the Left.

Social mobility is less a matter of individual aspiration, more a matter of change in occupational structure that increases middle-class positions. Family affects mobility by its process of social inheritance and by providing better social chances for its children.

There is only a small difference in the degree of mobility between the United States and European nations, despite common belief to the contrary. Even people who are not mobile often believe in opportunity, taking satisfaction in very modest gains and transferring aspiration to their children. For those who aspire but cannot make it conventionally, there are alternate routes: athletics, entertainment, politics, and labor unions.

In communist Europe industrial expansion has made much social mobility possible for peasants and workers, but privileged classes also assure high position for their children.

Inequality persists in both capitalist and communist societies. In the United States the commitment is to equality of opportunity and equality before the law, both limited forms of equality, rather than to the full equality that would require a classless society.

NOTES

[1] Michael Young, *The Rise of the Meritocracy, 1870–2033* (London: Thames and Hudson, 1958; Baltimore: Penguin Books, paperback edition, 1961).

[2] Kingsley Davis and Wilbert Moore, "Some Principles of Stratification," *American Sociological Review* 10 (April 1945): 242–249.

[3] Kingsley Davis, *Human Society* (New York: Macmillan, 1949), p. 367.

[4] Karl Marx, *Selected Writings in Sociology and Social Philosophy,* ed. T. B. Bottomore and Maximilien Rubel (New York: McGraw-Hill, 1964), p. 258.

[5] See C. Wright Mills, *The Power Elite* (New York: Oxford University Press, 1965), and Ralf Dahrendorf, *Class and Class Conflict in Industrial Society* (Stanford, Cal.: Stanford University Press, 1959).

[6] See Edmund R. Leach, ed., *Aspects of Caste in South India, Ceylon and North-West Pakistan* (Cambridge: Cambridge University Press, 1960); and M. N. Srivinas, *Caste in Modern India and Other Essays* (Bombay: Asia Publishing House, 1962).

[7] See Henri Pirenne, *An Economic and Social History of the Middle Ages* (New York: Harcourt, Brace, 1937).

[8] Karl Marx, *The Eighteenth Brumaire of Louis Bonaparte, Karl Marx and Friederich Engels: Selected Works* (Moscow: Progress Publishers, 1968), p. 172.

[9] Karl Marx, *The Poverty of Philosophy* (New York: International Publishers, n.d.), pp. 145–146.

[10] Max Weber, "Class, Status, and Party," in Hans Gerth and C. Wright Mills, *From Max Weber: Essays in Sociology* (New York: Oxford University Press, 1946), p. 181.

[11] *Ibid.,* p. 182.

[12] *Ibid.,* p. 194.

[13] Frank Parkin, *Class Inequality and Political Order: Social Stratification in Capitalist and Communist Societies* (New York: Praeger Publishers, 1971), p. 17.

[14] See W. Lloyd Warner, *Social Class in America* (New York: Harper & Row, 1960). For a summary of the Yankee City studies, see his *American Life, Dream and Reality* (Chicago: University of Chicago Press, 1962).

[15] See C. Wright Mills, *White Collar* (New York: Oxford University Press, 1953).

[16] Harry Braverman, *Labor and Monopoly Capital* (New

York: Monthly Review Press, 1974), Part IV, "The Growing Working-Class Occupations."

[17] *Ibid.,* pp. 297–298.

[18] Employment and Training Administration, Department of Labor, *Employment and Training Report to the President,* Washington, D.C., 1979.

[19] See E. Digby Baltzell, *Philadelphia Gentlemen: The Making of a National Upper Class* (New York: The Free Press, 1958).

[20] G. William Domhoff, *The Higher Circles: The Governing Class in America* (New York: Random House, 1970), p. 97.

[21] *Ibid.,* p. 109.

[22] Parkin, *op. cit.,* p. 19.

[23] *Ibid.,* p. 25.

[24] *Ibid.,* pp. 25–26.

[25] *Ibid.,* p. 147.

[26] *Ibid.,* p. 146.

[27] *Ibid.,* p. 144.

[28] *Ibid.,* p. 147.

[29] *Ibid.,* p. 149.

[30] James W. Rinehart, "Affluence and the Embourgeoisement of the Working Class: A Critical Look," *Social Problems* 19 (Fall 1971): 149–162.

[31] Herbert Gans, *The Levittowners: Ways of Life and Politics in a New Suburban Community* (New York: Pantheon Books, 1967).

[32] Michael Harrington, "Old Working Class, New Working Class," *Dissent* (Winter, 1972): 159–160.

[33] The fastest-growing union is the American Federation of State, County, and Municipal Employees; 40 percent of its membership is white-collar, including engineers, scientists, and medical technicians.

[34] See Daniel Bell, *The Coming of Post-Industrial Society* (New York: Basic Books, 1973), Chap. 3.

[35] Michael Harrington, "The New Class and the Left," *Society* 16 (January/February 1979): 27.

[36] For a discussion of the new class and its significance, see B. Bruce-Biggs, *The New Class?* (Edison, N.J.: Transaction Books, 1979).

[37] Daniel Bell, "The New Class: A Muddled Concept," *Society* 16 (January/February, 1979): 23.

[38] Harrington, *op. cit.,* p.28.

[39] *Ibid.,* p. 29.

[40] Elton F. Jackson and Harry J. Crockett, Jr., "Occupational Mobility in the United States: A Point Estimate and Trend Comparison," *American Sociological Review* 29 (February 1964): p. 6.

[41] *Ibid.,* Table 1, p. 7.

[42] Peter Blau and Otis Dudley Duncan, *The American Occupational Structure* (New York: Wiley, 1967).

[43] Seymour M. Lipset and Reinhard Bendix, *Social Mobility in Industrial Society* (Berkeley: University of California Press, 1959).

[44] Gerhard Lenski, *Power and Privilege* (New York: McGraw-Hill, 1966), p. 411.

[45] See Parkin, *op. cit.,* pp. 137–159.

[46] *Ibid.,* p. 155.

[47] *Ibid.,* p. 156.

[48] Eli Chinoy, *Automobile Workers and the American Dream* (New York: Random House, 1955).

[49] Parkin, *op. cit.,* p. 121.

SELECTED READINGS

E. Digby Baltzell, *Philadelphia Gentlemen: The Making of a National Upper Class.* New York: The Free Press, 1958. A sociologist who is upper class describes what the upper class is like.

T. B. Bottomore, *Classes in Modern Society.* New York: Pantheon Books, 1966. A short, critical review of the literature on social classes in modern society.

G. William Domhoff, *The Higher Circles: The Governing Class in America.* New York: Random House, 1970. Domhoff pulls together varied data to prove the existence of an American upper class.

Seymour M. Lipset and Reinhard Bendix, *Social Mobility in Industrial Society.* Berkeley: University of California Press, 1959. An effort to compare social mobility in the United States with social mobility in Europe.

Gaetano Mosca, *The Ruling Class.* New York: McGraw-Hill, 1969. A classic work claiming that human society is always divided between the rulers and the ruled.

Frank Parkin, *Class Inequality and Political Order: Social Stratification in Capitalist and Communist Societies.* New York: Praeger Publishers, 1971. A British sociologist examines and compares the inequality of class in both capitalist and communist societies—and finds both basically committed to inequality.

Richard Sennett and Jonathan Cobb, *The Hidden Injuries of Class.* New York: Knopf, 1972. A sensitive, penetrating exploration of the psychic and moral injuries of loss of dignity and feelings of unworthiness experienced by ordinary workers in a status-conscious society.

E. P. Thompson, *The Making of the English Working Class.* New York: Pantheon Books, 1964. A great piece of historical scholarship on the shaping of a working class in an industrializing society.

Ten

WEALTH, POVERTY, AND THE WELFARE STATE

One of the enchanting songs sung by Tevye in *Fiddler on the Roof* is "If I Were a Rich Man." Dreaming of being rich has long been a fantasy for millions of people.

Yet the rich have never been popular as a class, and the stereotype of them in popular literature is one of self-indulgence, meanness, and selfishness, and of enriching themselves at the expense of other people.

Poverty, in turn, has sometimes been viewed as a virtue, but only when it is a matter of choice, as when monks take vows of poverty. Like the rich, the people who are poor have rarely been pictured as having any positive qualities. Sometimes they are viewed as a class of people without ability and capable of only the most unskilled labor. More often they are viewed as lacking in moral virtues—as lazy and irresponsible and without ambition—and therefore to be blamed for their own poverty. Often, too, they are seen as untrustworthy, likely to commit criminal acts.

These views are *stereotypes*, popular but distorted images of rich and poor held by those who are neither rich nor poor. Though these images are not accurate, they do serve a function for those who hold them. They provide moral justification for the middling position of those who have avoided poverty while not becoming wealthy.

Too much wealth, the stereotype implies, corrupts people, for it is wealth far beyond what is rightfully earned by industrious effort. Too little, in turn, according to the stereotype, signifies people who are unable or, more likely, unwilling to earn their way by hard work. By such thinking, the working class and the middle class assert their own deserving status over those who have too much and those who have too little.

Yet if such people persistently despise and dread being poor, they are ambivalent toward the rich. They envy such wealth and would not refuse to be rich if the opportunity occurred. But lacking that wealth, they suspect that the wealthy have become rich, not so much by hard work and ability, but more by luck, illicit conspiracy, and an opportunism unchecked by any moral scruples.

At the same time, the experience of the working class in capitalist societies has taught them (and others) an important lesson: that being in economic need is too often the undeserving fate of people who are unable to control the economic circumstances of their lives. From this, in time, came the social reforms that led to the formation of the welfare state. These reforms are a modest effort to provide a secure level of material existence for all and to redistribute wealth.

WEALTH AND THE WEALTHY

While there is a multitude of poor, there are far fewer who are rich. From the social-scientific literature we can learn a great deal about the poor but only a little about the rich. The rich possess the means to keep their lives private and free from sociological scrutiny, while the poor are studied and reported on by an army of investigators.

There is no governmental definition of wealth as there is of poverty. Wealth, furthermore, is hard to measure. Income is duly reported to the Internal Revenue Service, but *wealth* and *income* are not the same. For the very wealthy, earned income, such as salary, is but a small part of their accumulated holdings of property.

Laws and tax rates change, but the wealthiest segment of the population remains little affected. The gap between the wealthy and the rest of the population changes very little over time.

Trends in the Distribution of Wealth

There is a persistent claim that tax laws and social policies in industrial societies have been taking from the rich and giving to the poor, that is, equalizing the wealth.[1] In the United States, the trend toward white-collar occupations and rising productivity, as well as social reforms instituted in the 1930s, created a widely shared conception that wealth was now more evenly distributed than it had been in the years before the Depression.

But available evidence for the United States supports no such claim. There is an enormous gap between the very rich and those of average income, and that gap has only been slightly modified throughout the twentieth century. There is as great an inequality in the distribution of wealth, if not greater, than there was in the 1920s.

The concentration of wealth in the hands of a tiny minority is impressive. According to Robert Lampman's authoritative study, the wealthiest one percent of the population owns about 80 percent of all publicly held corporate stocks; about all (tax-exempt) state and local government bonds; about 40 percent of all federal bonds; 36 percent of all mortgages and notes; and about 30 percent of the nation's cash.[2]

More recent evidence provides further support for the argument that a small minority owns most of the wealth in the United States. Take, for example, these two observations:

The upper 5 percent of the population owns more than half of the national wealth.[3]

A mere one-half of one percent of the population owns at least one-third of the national wealth.[4]

A recent government document observes that the richest one-fifth of the population owns more than three-fourths of the national wealth, while the poorest one-fifth owns barely anything at all.[5] The distribution of wealth in the United States, as reported by this source, offers a striking lesson in material inequality in the world's leading industrial society:

- Top Fifth   76.0 percent of wealth
- Fourth Fifth   15.5 percent of wealth
- Middle Fifth   06.2 percent of wealth
- Second Fifth   02.1 percent of wealth
- Lowest Fifth   00.2 percent of wealth

Note that three-fifths of the population—that's 60 percent—owns less than 10 percent of the national wealth, while the upper 40 percent of the population owns over 90 percent of the wealth.

In terms of personal money income (including money-in-kind expense accounts) the top 20 percent of families has received over 40 percent of such income since World War II. The bottom 20 percent, in turn, has received but 5 percent of the total (see Table 10.1).

The distribution of money income in 1977, as presented in Table 10.2, reveals how modest a share of the national income most Americans receive. More than one-fourth of all families (27.5 percent) earned less than $10,000, while half earned $16,009 or less, the median figure. At the other end, slightly over one in five (22.4 percent) earned over $25,000, and a mere 2.6 percent exceeded $50,000 in income.

Nor does the federal income tax serve to redistribute wealth. It is a complicated and largely regressive instrument of national taxation through which, in general, poor people and people of average income pay

The extremes of wealth and poverty in the United States are made graphically evident by this contrast of housing: the mansion set back on beautifully landscaped grounds compared to Harlem's ugly stone and brick slums.

out a higher *proportion* of their income in taxes than do wealthy people. It is possible for a person of considerable wealth to pay little or no taxes in a given year (see "Who Pays the Taxes?").

These data—and much more—document the enormous disparity in material rewards. A more progressive tax structure does have an effect on income distribution in some (but not all) European countries, but considerable disparity remains.

Even in the Soviet Union and other Communist countries, there are those who earn much higher than average incomes. In addition, they receive such privi-

leges as access to automobiles and country homes—comparable to the expense-account benefits of capitalist societies.

In several Western European countries, socialist parties control the government. But, according to Frank Parkin, while this has produced a strong system of social welfare, it has not produced any major pressure to equalize income. "After thirty-five years of socialist rule in Sweden, income differentials between working-class and middle-class occupational groups are no narrower than in western societies ruled by *bourgeois* governments."[6]

TABLE 10.1
Percentage Share of Aggregate Income by Each Fifth of Families and by Top 5 Percent, 1950–1977

Percent	1977	1970	1965	1960	1955	1950
Lowest Fifth	5.2	5.4	5.2	4.8	4.8	4.5
Second Fifth	11.6	12.2	12.2	12.2	12.3	12.0
Middle Fifth	17.5	17.6	17.8	17.8	17.8	17.4
Fourth Fifth	24.2	23.8	23.9	24.0	23.7	23.5
Highest Fifth	41.5	40.9	40.9	41.3	41.3	42.6
Top 5 Percent	15.7	15.6	15.5	15.9	16.4	—

Source: U.S. Bureau of the Census, Current Population Reports, Series P-60, no. 118, "Money Income in 1977 of Families and Persons in the United States" (Washington, D.C.: Government Printing Office, 1979), Table 13, p. 45.

TABLE   10.2
Money Income of Families
in the United States, 1977

Income Category	Percent Earning
Up to $4,999	9.4
$5,000– 9,999	18.1
$10,000–14,999	18.4
$15,000–19,999	17.7
$20,000–24,999	13.9
$25,000–49,999	19.8
$50,000 and over	02.6
Median Family Income:	$16,009
Median for Whites	16,740
Median for Blacks	9,563
Median for Spanish Origin	11,421
Mean Family Income	18,264

Source: U.S. Bureau of the Census, *Current Population Reports,* Series P-60, no. 116, "Money Income and Poverty Status of Families and Persons in the United States: 1977 (Advance Report), 1978, Table B, p. 2.

More significantly, according to Parkin, these socialist parties in Western Europe have since the 1950s abandoned their long-standing commitment to *egalitarian* socialism in favor of *meritocratic* socialism; that is, a commitment to equality of opportunity for the individual, and competitive pursuit of unequally rewarded positions. Meritocratic socialism would not eliminate rich and poor. There is, therefore, in both the Western capitalist and Eastern European communist societies, no political party any longer committed to material equality among the social classes.

THE SYSTEM OF POVERTY

It is an embarrassment to American claims of affluence and opportunity that so many people are still poor. Unlike earlier times, the poor are no longer visible to the rest of the population as they once were. Many of them, and particularly black people, are now confined to inner-city poverty areas or to rural pockets hidden from view from the great expressways (see "Where Do the Poor Live?").

Because of this, during the 1950s many people, even social scientists, believed that there were no longer any substantial number of Americans who were poor. But in the early 1960s a widely read book by Mi-

TABLE   10.3
Number and Percent of Persons Below Low-Income Level,
1959, 1964, 1974, and 1977, by Race

Years	Number Below Low-Income Level (thousands)			Percent Below Low-Income Level		
	Total	White	Black	Total	White	Black
1977	24,720	16,416	7,726	11.6	8.9	31.3
1974	24,260	16,290	7,747	11.6	8.9	31.4
1969	24,147	16,659	7,095	12.1	9.5	32.2
1964	36,055	24,957	11,098*	19.0	14.9	49.6*
1959	39,490	28,484	10,475	22.0	18.1	55.1

* Blacks and other races not separated this year. In other years, other races included in totals.
Source: U.S. Bureau of the Census, *Current Population Reports,* P-60, no. 119, "Characteristics of the Population Below the Poverty Level: 1977" (Washington, D.C.: U.S. Government Printing Office, 1979), Table 1.

WHO PAYS THE TAXES?

All of us, it is agreed, should pay our fair share of taxes. But what is a fair share? In the United States "fair share" is defined philosophically as a *progressive tax system;* those who earn more are to bear a larger burden of the taxes by paying their taxes at a higher rate.

But is that the way the system actually works? At first glance, it seems to; the federal income tax is a series of graduated tax rates from no taxes for the lowest income to a maximum of 70 percent for those with incomes over $200,000.

In reality, however, that is not the way it works. Various provisions of the tax laws provide the so-called "loopholes" which largely benefit the rich; substantial portions of their income are subject to lesser tax rates or are even subject to no taxes at all.

Capital gains, that is, income derived from assets used for investment, is the most significant of these tax advantages for the wealthy. Only 40 percent of the income derived from investment is subject to taxation. That means that under recent legislation the tax on capital gains income can only reach a maximum of 28 percent instead of the income tax maximum of 70 percent.

Tax-free state and municipal bonds are the other major forms of tax breaks for the wealthy. In order for states and cities to borrow money at lower interest rates, the federal government exempts from income taxes the interest earned on such bonds. This is a form of investment favored by the wealthy; as we saw above, the wealthiest one percent of the population owns most of these bonds.

There are other tax advantages, too; for example, there are tax exemptions on more than one-fifth of the income earned from the production of oil, gas, and minerals.

Regressive forms of taxation, in turn, force middle- and lower-income people to pay a proportionately larger share of their income in taxes than do wealthy people. The property tax is regressive, the federal payroll tax (Social Security) is also, and one of the most regressive forms of taxation is the sales tax.

Many corporations now reward top executives by means other than straight salary, to enable them to avoid the highest tax rates. Profit sharing, deferred-compensation plans, and stock options, that is, the privilege of buying corporation stock at less than market value and then realizing a gain that is then taxable as capital gains, are some of the alternatives used.

In these and other ways, then, the American system of taxation, progressive in philosophy, is regressive in practice, allowing the wealthiest segment to escape the obligation of bearing their "fair share" of taxes.

chael Harrington pointed to an "other America" of urban and rural poor.[7] The urban riots of that decade made it even more evident that the poor were still very much with us.

How Many Are Poor?

Those who insist that poverty is on the decline in the United States point to a considerable change since 1947. Using the 1962 poverty figure of $3,000, "we find that between 1947 and 1963 the proportion of families in poverty dropped from 32 percent to 19 percent (in 1962 dollars)."[8] Since then, the number of Americans in poverty has continued to decline, although throughout the 1970s the rate of poverty has changed very little (see Table 10.3). By the end of the 1970s one of every nine Americans was still poor.

WHERE DO THE POOR LIVE?

As Michael Harrington observed almost 20 years ago, the poor are still with us but they are often out of sight. They do not get to live anywhere they might choose.

According to recent census figures, the poor are located primarily in central cities and secondly in small towns and rural areas. They are least likely to live in the suburbs.

In 1976 almost four in ten of all poor (38.0 percent) lived in central cities, but more than half of all black poor (54.9 percent) did so.

Not only are poor blacks, to a greater extent than poor whites, confined to central cities, but they are far more likely than whites to be found in what the Bureau of the Census calls a *poverty area,* what others call the *inner city* or the *ghetto.* Almost two of every three poor black persons in central cities (63.7 percent) are located in such poverty areas, compared to less than one-third (30.7 percent) of comparable whites.

This greater concentration of blacks in poverty areas, which makes them so much less visible to middle-class whites, holds true for all poverty areas, rural as well as urban. Two-thirds of all poor blacks (66.9 percent) live in poverty areas, while less than one-third of whites (30.5 percent) do so.

Notes

SOURCE: U.S. Bureau of the Census, *Current Population Reports,* Series P-60, no. 115, "Characteristics of the Population Below the Poverty Level: 1976" (Washington, D.C.: U.S. Government Printing Office, 1978), Table C, p. 6; Table D, p. 7.

A Profile of the Poor

Who the poor are today is quite different from those called poor in an earlier period. In the nineteenth century, and until after the depression of the 1930s, working-class people were the poor. But in the years since World War II, that is no longer the case. The nature of poverty has undergone considerable change.

It is quite apparent that changing conditions of the American economy can make some people poor while it makes others affluent. Changes in technology, for example, often displace workers by abolishing their jobs, while creating other, better paying ones for people more technically trained. This happens to both rural and urban workers; large numbers of blacks, for example, were displaced by mechanization from such jobs as picking cotton, sending them into cities to look for work.

Loss of job by technological change is but one factor in accounting for the poor. Those who are poor are those least likely to have opportunities in the job market. This lack of opportunity clearly affects certain categories of people more than others: the nonwhites; the uneducated and untrained; those families with a female head; the elderly; families headed by youthful, untrained males; and people on farms (see "A Profile of the Poor").

Poor Whites and Blacks In absolute number there are a lot more poor whites than blacks, some 16.4 million compared to 7.7 million in 1977; this is a ratio of almost 7 to 3 (see Table 10.3). That means that almost seven in ten of the poor were white, while more than three in ten of the poor were black.

But whites outnumber blacks in America almost 9 to 1, which means that the *proportion* of blacks who are poor is much higher than it is for whites. Thus, the

HOW POOR IS POOR?

Throughout the 1960s there were both confusion and controversy about how many Americans were poor. What level of income defines anyone as poor is clearly a relative matter, both because of a persistently increasing cost of living, and because of variable situations: what an elderly couple can get by on would be inadequate for a family of five with three school-age children.

In 1964 the federal government adopted a poverty index developed by the Social Security Administration. This index of low income was based upon a nutritionally adequate food plan designed by the Department of Agriculture, and it took account of such factors as family size, sex of the family head, number of children under 18 years old, and farm-nonfarm residence. Annual revision in the index was based upon price changes of the items in the economy food budget.

This poverty index was modified in 1969.* Annual adjustments in the levels of income were based on changes in the Consumer Price Index rather than merely the cost of food in the economy food plan. Furthermore, in 1964, the farm level had been established as 70 percent of the nonfarm level, on the assumption that farm families produced for their own use about 30 percent of their food budget. This came to be regarded as inadequate measurement, and thus the farm level was redefined to 85 percent of the nonfarm level.

For 1977 the poverty level for a nonfarm family of four with a male head was $6,191. (At the 125 percent level it was $7,739.) For a family of seven or more, the poverty level was $10,216. For a couple age 65 it was $3,666.†

The official poverty level necessarily increases along with the constant inflationary increase in the cost of living. Here are some figures for selected years:‡

- 1963 $3,128
- 1965   3,223
- 1970   3,968
- 1975   5,500
- 1976   5,815
- 1977   6,191

Notes

* U.S. Bureau of the Census, *Current Population Reports,* Series P-23, "Revision in Poverty Statistics, 1959 to 1968" (Washington, D.C.: U.S. Government Printing Office, 1970).

† U.S. Bureau of the Census, *Current Population Reports,* Series P-60, no. 119, "Characteristics of the Population Below the Poverty Level, 1977" (Washington, D.C.: Government Printing Office, 1979), pp. 204–206.

‡ *Ibid.,* Table A-1, p. 204.

A PROFILE OF THE POOR: 1977

One of every nine Americans (11.6 percent) is poor.

Race

One of every eleven whites (8.9 percent) is poor.
Almost one of every three blacks (31.3 percent) is poor.

Education

Almost four in ten of the poor (37.4 percent) have an elementary education or less.
More than six in ten (61.8 percent) of the poor 22 years of age and over have not finished high school.

Age

One in seven (14.1 percent) of persons 65 years and older is poor.
Almost three in ten (27.1 percent) of black persons 65 years and older are poor.
Almost one in five (19.4 percent) of families headed by a person under 25 years is poor.

Sex

Almost one in three (31.7 percent) of families headed by a female is poor.
Over half (51.0 percent) of families headed by a black female are poor.
Almost one in four (24.0 percent) of families headed by a white female is poor.

Family Size

While one in every eight families (12.9 percent) is poor, almost one third (30.6 percent) of families with five or more children under 18 years is poor; more than four in ten (42.9 percent) of families with six or more; and almost half (47.9 percent) of families with seven or more.

Farms

While less than 4 percent of Americans are in farming, one in six (17.1 percent) of all persons on farms is poor.
Almost four in ten (39.3 percent) of all black persons on farms are poor.

Notes

SOURCE: U.S. Bureau of the Census, *Current Population Reports,* P-60, no. 119, "Characteristics of the Population Below the Poverty Level: 1977" (Washington, D.C.: U.S. Government Printing Office, 1979).

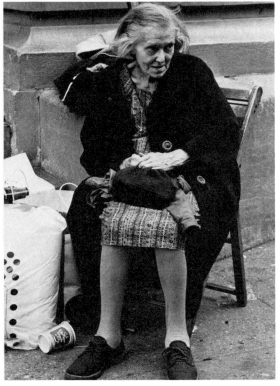

Poverty in the United States is the unwanted fate of quite different people in different places: black children in the rural South; a rural family in Maine; urban dwellers in an older northern city; and a lonely bag lady in New York City.

almost 70 percent of the poor who are white is less than 10 percent of all whites (8.9 percent), while the 30 percent of the poor who are black accounts for almost one of every three blacks (31.3). The chance of being poor is obviously much greater for a black than for a white.

Age and Poverty   Age is related to poverty in two ways. Older people, particularly those over 65 years of age, are often without adequate savings to keep pace with rising living costs, and they are at a severe disadvantage in finding employment in a labor market that uses age as a criterion for employment—the older you are, the more difficult it is to obtain employment. Although increases in Social Security and now Medicare have lifted many aged people from the bottom levels of poverty, such assistance has still left a large number who fall short of levels of adequacy and comfort.

But it is not merely the older who suffer disproportionately from poverty. Children, too, make up a disproportionate share of the poor, for many more large families than small ones are poor. Furthermore, young families headed by males up to the age of 25 are a disproportionate segment of the poor. This is even truer if the head of the family is a female. In these cases young people who have left school and married early lack the skills to find regular employment or to find any employment outside of the lowest-paying jobs.

These categories, then, are the beginning of a profile of the poor. Also concentrated among them are the functionally illiterate, those whose education has been so meager that for all practical purposes they *are* illiterate. In addition, they lack marketable job skills.

The Changing Poor

Since 1959, poverty, as measured officially by the federal government, has declined from 22.0 percent to the 1977 level of 11.6 percent (see Table 10.3). That overall decline, however, obscures several changes within the subgroups who are poor that has altered considerably the profile of the poor from 1959. For one thing, whites in poverty have decreased more rapidly since 1959 than have blacks, at an approximate rate of four to three.

One important factor is that since 1959 the number and proportion of families in poverty headed by males, both black and white, decreased in number by

over 50 percent, while poor families headed by white females have increased slightly, and those headed by black females have increased by about one-third. As a consequence, by 1977 more than one-third of all poor families (36.2 percent) were headed by a woman; these were less than one-fourth of the poor in 1959.

These and other internal shifts in the poverty group therefore suggest that whites have more readily escaped poverty than have blacks, and that young families, particularly those headed by females, will become a larger part of the total poor population. Such shifts suggest that what is emerging is a "hard-core" of poor people harder to raise above the poverty level.

The poor people who find themselves in one or another of these categories are not there by choice. But they are not able to choose to be anywhere else.

The Near-Poor

Everyone who is not poor by the government's standard is not necessarily affluent, or even comfortable. The poverty rate set by the government is so low that many families and persons not officially in poverty are nonetheless living on a low income, and are poor in fact if not by government decree. There is, consequently, a large category of *near-poor*, people who are only a little above the official poverty level.

The Census Bureau has given us some measurement of this by recording all those who fall within a poverty rate of 125 percent of the official level. Table 10.4 shows how the number of families who are poor increases by using this method. Note, particularly, the high proportion of female-headed families in poverty by this measurement.

The poor and the near-poor, it seems, are not distinct populations but overlapping ones. Many people move back and forth between these two categories from year to year. A study of 5,000 American families carried out by economists at the University of Michigan (the Panel Study on Income Dynamics) discovered that only about one person in five (22 percent) defined as poor in 1975 had been poor in every one of the preceding nine years.[9] This means, they asserted, that only about 3 percent of the population can be considered "persistently poor." They are most likely, the study found, to be headed by a person 65 years old, or by one with little education, or by a black, a female, or a disabled person.

TABLE 10.4
Percentage of Families in Poverty by Official Standard and by 125 Percent of Official Standard, 1977

	Official Low-Income Level	"Near-Poor": 125 Percent of Official Level
All Families	9.3	13.5
White Families	7.5	10.6
Black Families	30.5	37.2
Families with white female head	31.3	40.1
Families with black female head	51.0	62.0

Source: U.S. Bureau of the Census, *Current Population Reports,* Series P-60, no. 119, "Characteristics of the Population Below the Poverty Level, 1977" (Washington, D.C.: U.S. Government Printing Office, 1979).

The Poverty Trap

The poverty in which several million American families find themselves is sustained and reinforced by a set of conditions that are beyond the scope of the individual to alter. Obviously, the poor are poor because they have little money, but they also have few prospects for significantly increasing their supply of money. They are unemployed or underemployed, or they are employed in low-paying jobs; there are both welfare poor and working poor. But a changing labor market needs less and less the relatively unskilled or low-skilled labor which the poor can provide. They are in effect marginal to the needs of the economy.

Nor are the poor organized or otherwise able to exercise power. They are in no position to force a redistribution of income that would eliminate their poverty. Without power, they are unable to change the circumstances of their lives, or to fight effectively the landlords, merchants, politicians, social workers, educators, and others whose practices only ensure a continuation of their poverty.

Housing is one of the major expenses of life that raises particularly difficult problems for the poor. Slums by definition are areas of inadequate housing, and the United States Census records that substandard housing still exists in substantial numbers in American cities. The numerous "inner cities" are large areas of deteriorated and still deteriorating housing. The poor either accept inadequate housing, or else they pay comparably more for housing than anyone else. If they do that, they sacrifice clothing, medicine, or other important consumer items.

While the poor can purchase adequate housing only at a serious sacrifice of life's other necessities, most of their consumer purchasing is also done at a disadvantage. Slum merchants also exploit the poor. Sociologist David Caplovitz has documented the fact that the poor pay more for goods of poorer quality than does any other group of people in the city.[10] They are victims, in the first place, of an inability to get around enough to do comparison shopping. More to the point, they have little cash on hand, and their credit is nonexistent in most stores in the community.

But there are merchants who specialize in selling on credit to the poor and manage to make it a profitable enterprise. The poor are as hungry as other Americans for such durable goods as furniture, television sets, and radios. This creates a set of circumstances in which their effort to share in the affluent society's consumption patterns makes them vulnerable to effective economic exploitation. Their desire for consumer goods only increases their entrapment in the world of poverty.

In addition, the poor must accept the quality of schooling that the community makes available to their children. And that schooling is inferior. The children of the poor, therefore, perpetuate the lack of education of their parents and, in a technological and affluent society, this perpetuates poverty. To say that the poor fail to complete an education is not to criticize them. It is simply to state a fact of great importance. Put another way, a body of professional educators consistently fails to educate the children of the poor in a satisfactory fashion.

The structure of poverty is not only a network of disadvantages in housing, consumption, and schooling, it also takes a personal toll in physical and mental health. Chronic ill health plagues the poor, and they are more susceptible to contagious diseases. A slum environment inevitably threatens health standards. Yet medical care is provided only grudgingly.[11]

Furthermore, the poor suffer more from emotional difficulties. But they get little attention from psychiatric facilities until they reach that serious point where they are disruptive in their relations with others and must be hospitalized.[12]

On Understanding Poverty

The poor have rarely been viewed favorably by other social classes. Most of the time they have been looked down upon unsympathetically and blamed for their own plight. Throughout the long development of industrial society, and even before, the dominant middle-class image of the poor was a morally critical one. Furthermore, the rapid pace of industrialization within the past 150 years did little to change the perspective expressed originally in the Elizabethan Poor Laws, adopted during the reign of Queen Elizabeth I in England (1558–1603). These laws were based on the assumption that any condition of personal dependency was the fault of the individual and an indication of a morally defective character.[13]

In the nineteenth century scientific explanations joined moral ones in condemning the poor and dependent as inherently inferior. Thus the poor suffered a double stigma: They were viewed as both genetically inferior and morally unfit. Such definitions of why the poor were poor were easily attached to blacks, given the persistence of racist ideologies in the United States.

But such interpretations of genetic and moral unfitness were also attached to the immigrants from Eastern and Southern Europe at the turn of the century. The ending of open immigration in the 1920s was hastened by dire warnings of the danger of allowing such "inferior" people to come in large numbers into the United States.

Although details may vary slightly over time, this middle-class perspective on poverty has changed but little over the last several centuries. The claim that the poor lack the qualities of moral responsibility and individual initiative, as well as personal pride and independence, allows the middle class self-satisfaction about its own primary virtues. Therefore, so goes the ideology, the plight of poor people is their own fault, a consequence of genetic and moral defects.

Much remains of this perspective even today. Now it is likely to be directed specifically at those on welfare, particularly at blacks. Some Americans still seem to believe that people on welfare are lazy, prefer welfare to work, are uneducated because they are stupid, are given to criminal behavior, and have loose morals so that they produce illegitimate children.

Blaming the Victim But this historically conservative view now has competition. There is another perspective, one that rejects all racist and genetic arguments as unscientific and reactionary. Instead, it is asserted, poverty is a consequence of social and cultural conditions. The poor are made that way by conditions in the society. Yet the new, liberal ideology, according to psychologist William Ryan, still blames the victim for his condition, though much more subtly.

The new ideology attributes defect and inadequacy to the malignant nature of poverty, injustice, slum life, and racial difficulties. The stigma that marks the victim and accounts for his victimization is an acquired stigma, a stigma of social, rather than genetic, origin. But the stigma, the defect, the fatal difference—though derived in the past from environmental forces—is still located *within* the victim, inside his skin.[14]

Ryan's thesis is that middle-class liberals, backed by social-scientific research, still see the poor person as basically inadequate and incompetent, though not at fault. But now he or she is uneducated or "culturally deprived" or unmotivated for achievement, or lacking in occupational skills. These defects, then, must be corrected by changing the victim.

The poor person is to be changed by being made more like the middle class: presumably educated, responsible, hard-working, skilled, or whatever other flattering attributes the middle class assigns to itself and regards as the basis for its "success." This is arrived at,

Ryan notes, by first identifying a social problem (poverty), then determining how the victims (the poor) differ from others, and defining the differences as the cause of the social problem.[15]

By that logic, the poor are poor because they are uneducated. This fails to grasp the idea that the poor are uneducated because they are poor. There is a vast difference between these two concepts.

Trying to change the victim therefore becomes a program of action that shifts the target from the basic causes of the problem—racism, unemployment, low income, poor schools—to the victims themselves. We are asked, says Ryan, to ignore continued discrimination against black people, the gross deprivation of services to the poor, the heavy stresses endemic in their life. "And almost all our make-believe liberal programs aimed at correcting our urban problems are off target; they are designed to change the poor man or to cool him out."[16]

The Culture of Poverty Myth

The liberal mythology for blaming the victim has been supported by social scientists through a theory of a *culture of poverty,* a term first developed by Oscar Lewis on the basis of his sympathetic portraits of poor people in Mexico. He characterized such a culture as:

. . . a strong present time orientation, with relatively little ability to defer gratification and plan for the future, a sense of resignation and fatalism based upon the realities of their difficult life situation, a belief in male superiority which reaches its crystallization in *machismo* or the cult of masculinity, a corresponding martyr complex among women, and finally, a high tolerance for psychological pathology of all sorts.[17]

The culture of poverty theory makes much of childhood socialization and, indeed, tends to overemphasize the profound effects of the early years. Thus, Lewis again:

Once the culture of poverty has come into existence it tends to perpetuate itself. By the time slum children are six or seven they have usually absorbed the basic attitudes and values of their subculture. Thereafter they are psychologically unready to take full advantage of changing conditions or improving opportunities that may develop in their lifetime.[18]

Deferred Gratification   The poor are often accused of being spendthrift, of squandering any resources that might come to them, and of not postponing pleasure for the sake of saving. In the language of the psychologist, they do not *defer gratification,* a presumed inability that according to some social scientists, makes the poor so unlike the middle class.

But perhaps too much emphasis has been put on this one characteristic—or so some social scientists now believe.[19] For one thing, the ability to defer gratification until some future time, to plan for a future and save for it, to forgo pleasure in the present for the sake of one's future is hardly an accurate description any longer of middle-class people. They now buy on time, go into debt, complain of not having enough income, and sometimes moonlight. Increasingly, middle-class women enter the labor market to bring home a second paycheck because the family's life-style exhausts the primary one.

A comparison of the middle classes and the poor on the matter of deferred gratification can only be valid if it is assumed that the objects deferred are equally valued, if deferment imposes the same loss or suffering or pains of denial, and if there is the same probability of achieving the gratification in the future. But the poor may not place the same value on that for which the middle class defers; it may cost the lower class much more to make such a deferment, given its lesser resources, and it may realistically have much less confidence in its ability to attain it.

In similar fashion, presumed differences between middle-class culture and a lower-class culture of poverty on such matters as sexual behavior, child-rearing, aspirations for children, and attitudes toward law-abiding behavior do not differentiate the poor from others sharply. Sociologist Hylan Lewis, for example, found that lower-class parents differed little in values and attitudes from the middle-class parents, but were less able than middle-class parents to act consistently with those values.[20]

All those who are poor cannot be forced into a single cultural model. Even Oscar Lewis, who invented the concept, claimed that only a minority of poor fitted the culture of poverty. There is enormous phychological and cultural variation among people who happen to be poor.

This is not to say that the poor are simply like other people. Poverty is a destructive condition with a strong impact on people. Sociologist Hyman Rodman has suggested that members of the lower class share the dominant values but that circumstances do not permit

The middle class now spends much of its income for desired consumer goods, and goes into debt to do so. This lineup of pleasure boats at a marina on Fire Island, New York, exemplifies the unwillingness of the middle class to practice deferred gratification.

them to live by all these values, so they *stretch* them to take account of the severe limits a life of poverty imposes on them.

They do not maintain a strong commitment to middle-class values that they cannot attain, and they do not continue to respond to others in a rewarding or punishing way simply on the basis of whether these others are living up to the middle-class values. A change takes place. They come to tolerate and eventually to evaluate favorably certain deviations from the middle-class values. In this way they need not be continually frustrated by their failure to live up to unattainable values. The resultant is a stretched value system with a low degree of commitment to all the values within the range, including the dominant, middle-class values.[21]

What Rodman and others have argued is that poor people have no choice but to adapt to the unrewarding, even threatening conditions of poverty, and much of their behavior can be accounted for in this way. The

poor have behaved as they have, not from a radically divergent cultural perspective, but out of the force of circumstances and lack of alternatives. In that sense, much of their behavior is *adaptive* to the circumstances of poverty, deprivation, and powerlessness.

Sociologist Lee Rainwater makes this observation and then says:

. . . If lower class culture is to be changed and lower class people are eventually to be enabled to take advantage of "opportunities" to participate in conventional society and to earn their own way in it, this change can only come about through a change in the social and ecological situation to which lower class people must adapt.[22]

The Welfare Poor

One of the significant discoveries coming from the new concerns for poverty is how little welfare has done

THE MYTHS OF WELFARE

Myths about welfare seem to be so deeply imbedded in the dominant culture that simple contrary facts are difficult to accept. Among the more prominent myths are these:

1. *The poor are able to work but are lazy and shiftless.*
   FACT: Almost all the payments by Aid to the Families of Dependent Children (AFDC), the society's major welfare program, go to children and their mothers, not to adult males.
   Furthermore, the poor do work a great deal, when they can, though many work at federal minimum wages, which as a full-time wage would provide an income well below the poverty level for a family of four.
2. *Cheating is rampant among welfare seekers.*
   FACT: Cheating is difficult to measure, but some experts believe that only 5 to 10 percent of those on welfare receive money for which they are not eligible, and that almost half of that is due to bureaucratic error. While other experts think that dishonesty may account for a little more, all agree that welfare cheating is no more frequent than cheating on the income tax or on expense accounts.
3. *Once people become poor, they remain poor.*
   FACT: The poor population is fluid, with people constantly rising above the poverty level while others fall below it. Only a small proportion of the poor persist in poverty.
4. *Poor blacks leave the South, where welfare benefits are low, for cities like New York and Detroit, where benefits are much higher.*
   FACT: Blacks who migrate to the North are less likely to be on welfare than blacks who were born in those cities, according to a study by the Bureau of the Census of six northern cities with large black populations.

Notes

SOURCE: *The New York Times,* May 22, 1977.

to alter the depressed status of the poor. The present structure of welfare was created in the 1930s and is little changed since then, even though the prevailing assumption of the Depression—that people were only in temporary need of help until the Depression ended —no longer fits the reality of poverty now.

Furthermore, all the poor do not benefit from welfare. The permanently unemployed have exhausted unemployment benefits, and, being jobless, are not paying into Social Security. The millions who are employed at low wages—the working poor—do not qualify for any welfare benefits, except eligibility for public housing. (In 1977, according to the Census Bu-

reau, one in five of the poor [20.2 percent] worked full-time.)

Perhaps the major source of welfare assistance has become AFDC (Aid to Families with Dependent Children), which provides minimum support for families lacking a male head and breadwinner. The local public welfare rolls constitute the last resort for those who qualify for nothing else.

Welfare is immensely unpopular as social policy among both the working and the middle classes. The poor, we noted earlier, are blamed for their own plight —today, even as they were in the past. With so many black people on welfare, it is even more unpopular with whites. However inaccurate it is, the prevailing white American stereotype of welfare is the black AFDC mother raising several illegitimate children (see "The Myths of Welfare").

Yet those in power who so dislike welfare seem to be unable to do away with it. In a significant study Frances Fox Pliven and sociologist Richard A. Cloward demonstrate that relief performs two important functions: (1) it prevents or at least moderates disruption and rebellion on the part of the poor, and (2) it maintains a pool of cheap labor by periodically pushing people off relief into low-paying jobs and by making relief as demeaning and unpleasant as possible to its recipients.[23]

Public welfare is a vast, bureaucratic, controlling apparatus, operated by middle-class professionals. If the poor become dependent upon it, the apparatus does nothing to remove that dependency. And many poor people have no alternative but to be dependent on it for food, clothing, shelter, and medical care. None of these necessities are offered without red-tape and an invasion of people's lives—a demeaning experience—and none are offered in any quantity or quality comparable to what middle-class people can readily buy. Welfare is not a *solution* to poverty—it was never intended to be—but a custodial process that discourages independence, self-reliance, and self-respect, those attributes the poor are so often accused of not possessing.

The inadequacies of public welfare in the United States, however, are somewhat unique to this society where the welfare state is less effectively developed than it is in a number of European societies. In all industrial societies a welfare state has developed systematically throughout the twentieth century and is now a basic feature of all these societies.

THE WELFARE STATE

What is now called "the welfare state" began in the nineteenth century in European capitalist societies. It started as a set of social reforms intended to provide a reasonable degree of economic security for the working class. Once under way the programs grew and expanded, and became deeply embedded in the social expectations of the population, until the welfare state became a fundamental aspect of every modern society.

Any understanding of the welfare state must recognize that the word "welfare" is meant in a broad and inclusive sense. In the United States, welfare often means only assistance for the most impoverished. But in its broader meaning it refers to a wide range of social services developed and organized by government for its working population, its children, and its elderly. According to sociologist Harold Wilensky,

Dominating the "welfare and health" category are three expensive programs: pensions, death benefits, disability insurance; sickness and/or maternity benefits or health insurance or a national health service like Britain's; and family and child allowances. Also included are the less expensive programs of workman's compensation, and related labor market policies; "public assistance" or "social assistance" including miscellaneous aid to the handicapped and the poor; and benefits for "war victims."[24]

The programs of the welfare state, then, are not primarily charity for helpless and dependent people, but services regarded as a right for a broad range of social classes. Wilensky defines it this way:

The essence of the welfare state is government-protected minimum standards of income, nutrition, health, housing, and education assured to every citizen as a political right, not as charity.[25]

Welfare and Economic Level

The expenditure of public funds for social services is, not surprisingly, highest in the richest nations, lowest in the poorest ones. This is not only true when measured by dollars (or equivalents) spent, it is also true when measured as a percentage of the national wealth. The richest nations spend (and can afford to spend) *proportionately* more than do poor ones, for it is they who have an economic surplus to distribute.

Wilensky ranked 64 nations from richest (the United States) to poorest (Upper Volta) and grouped them in quartiles. The richest 16 nations spent an average of 13.8 percent of Gross National Product (GNP) for social services; the second sixteen spent 10.1 percent of their GNP; while the third and fourth groups of sixteen, all very poor nations, spent 4.0 and 2.5 percent of GNP, respectively.[26]

This pattern of expenditures holds true whether the nations are communist or capitalist, more democratic or more authoritarian. A study by Frederick Pryor, for example, which compared seven communist and seven capitalist countries, found that these countries were identical in their public expenditures for health and welfare, and that between 1956 and 1962 they converged in their expenditures for education.[27]

More Welfare, Less Welfare

While it is the case that rich nations spend proportionately more than the poor ones for the services of the welfare state, it does not follow that they are all equally generous in funding social services. Quite to the contrary. Some of them spend considerably more than do others, so that there is much more welfare for the population in some of these nations than in others.

Wilensky found that the United States was not among the big spenders. In 1966 it spent less (7.9 percent of GNP) than did any of the other top 25 nations, except Japan. Those spending the highest proportion of GNP on social services were:

- Austria   21.0 percent
- West Germany   19.6 percent
- Belgium   18.5 percent
- France   18.3 percent
- Netherlands   18.3 percent

In contrast, those which spent the least were:

- Hungary   8.8 percent
- Iceland   8.7 percent
- Israel   8.3 percent
- United States   7.9 percent
- Japan   6.2 percent

The Soviet Union ranked among the lesser spenders, at 10.1 percent of GNP, but still ahead of the United States.[28]

Resisting the Welfare State

How can we explain the fact that the United States, though richer, has been much less willing to support social services than any industrial society of Europe? As Wilensky notes:

It is true that the United States is more reluctant than almost any other rich country to make a welfare effort ap-

propriate to its affluence. Our support of national welfare programs is halting; our administration of services for the less privileged is mean. We move toward the welfare state, but we do it with ill grace, carping and complaining all the way.[29]

Yet Wilensky insists that strong opposition to the welfare state is not an American peculiarity. Instead he looks for factors that both promote and hinder its development. Those factors may, in the past and even yet in the present, have been strong in the United States, but they are not peculiar to any one society.

For one thing, the welfare state is better developed in those societies that first originated the idea of social services and have had longer experience with it. It is also stronger in those industrial societies where there is a strong working class with traditions of worker participation in the administration of welfare programs, such as Germany, France, Belgium, and Austria.

Modern societies use individual competition as a means of allocating people to occupations, and in doing so help breed an ideology of economic individualism. This is the idea that everyone has an equal opportunity for education and jobs, that everyone has the obligation to work hard and try to get ahead, and that if they do not, it is at least partly their own fault. This ideology is particularly strong in the United States, but it is also evident in other industrial societies. Wherever it is present, it is a source of resistance to the development of the welfare state.

Wilensky identifies three other basic structural features which account for the variation in expenditures for social services among rich countries:[30]

1. When the national government has more centralized authority, as in France, Italy, and the Netherlands, it can override local political levels and this promotes welfare spending;

2. A growing middle mass of citizens, with more educational opportunities, more occupationally mobile, and socially distant from the poor, is a strong factor in hindering welfare spending. This probably applies to the United States more than to any other industrial society.

3. Where there is an extensive system of *private* health and welfare benefits—hospitalization, sick leave, pensions, and the like—

which benefits mostly the employed and better-paid, and which supplements public benefits, support for spending more for *public* benefits is lessened.

Welfare as Redistributing Income

In many European countries where socialist values have been influential, the social services are a means to redistribute income, to give the poor and the working class more by taking from the more affluent. As a result, taxes are much heavier in European countries, but a more generous range of social services is offered.

One major distinction between the United States and other industrial nations is the *family allowance*. The United States stands out from other modern societies in providing support payments only to parents who do *not* work. In other industrial societies all families are provided a monthly grant for each child. In Belgium, for example, in 1976 each family got $36 for its first child under 16, $57.25 for the second, $78.40 for the third, and $80 for the fourth and following. A family with four children, then, would receive a monthly stipend of $251.65, or $3,020 a year.[31]

The philosophy of the family allowance is to assure a minimum income for families with children, and to compensate for the fact that wages paid workers do not take family size into account. A person with no children, one child, or six, gets the same wage or salary. A program of family allowance, then, is a policy of some moderate redistribution of income.

Whether the welfare state in capitalist societies redistributes wealth in any significant way is an issue widely argued. Some critics of the welfare state argue that it is not, because the taxes to finance the social services are generally regressive, that is, these taxes take proportionately more from those of lesser income than they do from the more wealthy.

But Wilensky, in contrast, argues that as a whole the effect is substantially egalitarian. More to the point, he claims that the short-run payment "is overwhelmingly progressive while the financing is only mildly regressive, with a net balance clearly favoring the poor."[32]

However, he acknowledges that what holds in the long run cannot be easily determined. Britain's National Health Service provides an example. It is used most intensively by the old, the young, and the poor. But the material inequalities of British society produce better health for the upper-income half of the population.

The poor die young—before they can contract the chronic diseases that dearly cost national health schemes. The more affluent citizens live to a riper age, chronically collecting health services paid for by the life-long taxes of the deceased poor. A program that is highly progressive at a cross-sectional moment may be highly regressive in the life-time of the particular generation.[33]

The Growing Welfare State

Whatever may be the criticisms of the welfare state, or the degree of political opposition, it nonetheless continues to grow and expand. For one thing, the richer countries are, the more they yield to pressures to broaden the coverage of more of the population against more risks: job-injury, sickness or pregnancy or both, old age, invalidism and death, reduced standard of living because of family size (family allowances), and unemployment.

Perhaps the one factor that most increases welfare expenditures is the proportion of older people in the population. "The aged are the main current beneficiaries of the two most expensive programs—pensions and health insurance. They are also a prime beneficiary of public assistance or social assistance."[34]

The innovation of Medicare in the United States in 1964 is one major factor in a sharp increase of expenditures for social welfare in the decade from 1966 to 1976. As a proportion of GNP, expenditures went from 7.9 percent to 20.6 percent. This put the United States much closer to the leaders in welfare spending

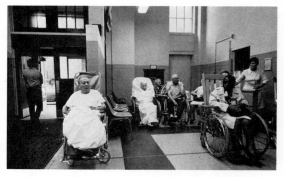

Providing adequate medical care for the elderly is a major expense of welfare in all industrial nations.

in Europe, despite the greater ideological resistance to welfare in this society.

A comparison between 1966 and 1976 spending makes clear, not only that the United States now comes closer to European nations in welfare expenditures, but that expenditures in general in major industrial nations increased proportionate to GNP (see Table 10.5).

While the United States still lags behind West Germany and Great Britain, it has come almost even with Sweden, a noted leader in the development of the welfare state, and has substantially surpassed Canada, even though that society has a family-allowance program.

THE FUTURE OF INEQUALITY

The belief in equality has always been tempered in philosophy and moderated in practice; in short, a lot of talk but little action. Though equal opportunity is a widely acknowledged right, the effort to make it real— to reduce inequalities in life-chances between blacks and whites, rich and poor—still lacks an effective politics of equality in the United States.

One reason is that the dominant value-system of American society does not—verbal pretensions aside —proclaim belief in the principle of human equality. Rather, there are specific beliefs in *equality of opportunity* and *equality before the law.* Neither of these values is systematically practiced, so that reality violates even these beliefs.

It seems unlikely that equality of opportunity and equality before the law can be made real in a society where property, income, and education are unequally distributed. The advantaged classes and groups protect and justify their advantages. An emerging meritocracy in both communist and capitalist societies, may in fact herald the new form that stratification will take and with it a new rationalization for inequality.

TABLE 10.5
Expenditures for Social Programs as a Proportion of Gross Nation Product, for Selected Nations, 1966 and 1976

	1966	1976
West Germany	19.6	32.0
Sweden	17.5	21.1
Great Britain	14.4	28.0
Canada	10.1	13.0
United States	7.9	20.6

Sources: For 1966 data, Wilensky, *op. cit.,* Table 4, pp. 122–124. Wilensky drew his data from ILO, *The Cost of Social Security, 1964–66* (Geneva, 1972), pp. 317–323. For 1976 data, *The New York Times,* August 7, 1977.

A meritocracy, with its certified inequalities, can exist side-by-side with the welfare state, and undoubtedly will in the near future. The social services of the welfare state will serve to limit the expansion of inequality in the meritocracy, but only to limit it, not to eliminate it.

If that is the case, the struggles among groups and classes with unequal shares in the rewards of society will go on, though in new forms. Inequality is a basic patterning of human societies, a basic source of ideologies about how life should be organized and how people differ from one another. It is also a basic source of group and class struggle, and thus fundamental to the politics of any society.

However inevitable and natural inequality may seem to be, though, the ideal of equality as a perspective on what society might be and as a source of criticism for the institutional inequities of any society, remains. If a postmodern society will generate a new form of inequality, such as meritocracy, it will also generate new dreams of human equality.

SUMMARY

Millions of Americans are still poor, despite the country's affluence. These disproportionately include: the nonwhite; the poorly educated; the elderly; the young, untrained worker; and families headed by females.

welfare is not for the poor

it is an exclusive system for the young and old

The poor are trapped in a set of structural conditions beyond individual control: poor housing, exploiting merchants, and inferior education, with a consequent physical and mental toll.

Middle-class explanations of poverty still blame the poor for being poor—*blaming the victim*—but while some employ older ideas of genetic inferiority, others utilize a *culture of poverty* theory.

In the United States public welfare has done little to change the condition of the poor, and is immensely unpopular with the middle class.

The *welfare state* is a broad and inclusive system of social services for the working population, and children, and the elderly—not merely for the poor—and is offered as a right, not charity.

The richer industrial nations spend proportionately more for social welfare than do other nations. Among them, the United States, until recently at least, has been one of the nations that lagged behind in developing its social services.

Despite some resistance, the welfare state continues to expand as the range of services is increased for ever larger segments of the population.

The United States lacks an effective politics of equality. In part this is because most Americans believe, not in equality per se, but specifically in *equality of opportunity* and *equality before the law,* even though both are violated in practice.

The new form of inequality emerging in both communist and capitalist societies is a *meritocracy.*

NOTES

[1] See, for example, Gerhard Lenski, *Power and Privilege: A Theory of Stratification* (New York: McGraw-Hill, 1966), pp. 338–345.

[2] Robert Lampman, *The Share of Top Wealth-holders in National Wealth* (Princeton, N.J.: Princeton University Press, 1962), p. 8ff.

[3] Herbert Gans, *More Equality* (New York: Pantheon, 1973).

[4] Ferdinand Lundberg, *The Rich and the Super-Rich* (New York: Bantam Books, 1969), p. 11.

[5] Executive Office of the President, Office of Management and the Budget, *Social Indicators, 1973* (Washington, D.C.: U.S. Government Printing Office, 1973).

[6] Frank Parkin, *Class Inequality and Political Order: Social Stratification in Capitalist and Communist Societies* (New York: Praeger Publishers, 1971), p. 121.

[7] Henry P. Miller, *Poverty: American Style* (Belmont, Cal.: Wadsworth, 1966), p. 115.

[8] Michael Harrington, *The Other America* (New York: Macmillan, 1962).

[9] *The New York Times,* July 17, 1977.

[10] David Caplovitz, *The Poor Pay More* (New York: The Free Press, 1963).

[11] See Anselm Strauss, "Medical Ghettoes," *Trans-action,* May 1967, pp. 7–15.

[12] See Frank Riessman, Jerome Cohen, and Arthur Pearl, eds., *Mental Health of the Poor* (New York: The Free Press, 1964).

[13] See Harold Wilensky and Charles N. Lebeaux, *Social Welfare and Industrial Society* (New York: Russell Sage Foundation, 1958).

[14] William Ryan, *Blaming the Victim* (New York: Random House, Vintage paperback edition, 1972), p. 7.

[15] *Ibid.,* p. 8.

[16] *Ibid.,* p. 25.

[17] Oscar Lewis, *The Children of Sanchez* (New York: Random House, 1961), pp. xxvi–xxvii. For a telling critique of the idea of a culture of poverty, see Charles A. Valentine, *Culture and Poverty* (Chicago: University of Chicago Press, 1968).

[18] Oscar Lewis, "The Culture of Poverty," *Scientific American* 215 (October 1966): 7.

[19] See S. M. Miller, Frank Riessman, and Arthur Seagull, "Poverty and Self-Indulgence: A Critique of the Non-deferred Gratification Pattern," in Louis A. Ferman, Joyce L. Kornbluh, and Alan Haber, eds., *Poverty in America* (Ann Arbor: University of Michigan Press, 1965), pp. 285–302.

[20] Hylan Lewis, "Child Rearing Among Low-Income Families," in Ferman, Kornbluh, and Haber, *op. cit.,* pp. 342–353.

[21] Hyman Rodman, "The Lower-Class Value Stretch," *Social Forces,* December 1963, p. 209.

[22] Lee Rainwater, "The Problem of Lower Class Culture and Poverty-War Strategy," in Daniel P. Moynihan,

ed., *On Understanding Poverty* (New York: Basic Books, 1969), p. 251.

[23] Frances Fox Pliven and Richard A. Cloward, *Regulating the Poor: The Function of Public Welfare* (New York: Pantheon, 1971).

[24] Harold L. Wilensky, *The Welfare State and Equality: Structural and Ideological Roots of Public Expenditures* (Berkeley: University of California Press, 1975), p. 2.

[25] *Ibid.,* p. 1.

[26] *Ibid.,* Table 1, p. 19. These data were from 1966.

[27] Frederick L. Pryor, *Public Expenditures in Communist and Capitalist Nations* (Homewood, Ill.: Irwin, 1968), pp. 282–285.

[28] Wilensky, *op. cit.,* Table 4, pp. 122–124.

[29] *Ibid.,* p. 32.

[30] *Ibid.,* Chap. 3.

[31] *The New York Times,* August 7, 1977.

[32] *Ibid.,* pp. 91–92.

[33] *Ibid.,* p. 96.

[34] *Ibid.,* p. 26.

SUGGESTED READINGS

Herbert Gans, *More Equality* (New York: Pantheon, 1973). A leading sociologist argues the possibilities of more equality within the established institutional framework of American capitalism.

Michael Harrington, *The Other America* (New York: Macmillan, 1962). The still relevant and highly readable study that "rediscovered" poverty.

Oscar Lewis, *The Children of Sanchez* (New York: Random House, 1961). A provocative and compassionate work that first developed the concept of the *culture of poverty.*

Ferdinand Lundberg, *The Rich and the Super-Rich* (New York: Bantam Books, 1968). A fascinating analysis of the nature and sources of great wealth in this society.

S. M. Miller and Pamela Roby, *The Future of Inequality* (New York: Basic Books, 1970). A thorough sociological examination of the sources of inequality in American society, with suggestions for tentative goals for the near future.

Frances Fox Pliven and Richard A. Cloward, *Regulating the Poor: The Functions of Public Welfare* (New York: Pantheon, 1971). A brilliant, prize-winning study of how public relief programs function to control the poor.

William Ryan, *Blaming the Victim* (New York: Vintage Books, 1972). A searing, provocative, and highly influential critique of how the middle class blame the poor for their poverty.

Charles A. Valentine, *Culture and Poverty* (Chicago: University of Chicago Press, 1968). A critique of the idea that there is such a thing as a culture of poverty.

Harold L. Wilensky, *The Welfare State and Equality: Structural and Ideological Roots of Public Expenditures* (Berkeley: University of California Press, 1975). A thorough analysis of the welfare state, its growth, and its pattern of expenditures among industrial nations.

The problem of the twentieth century is the problem of the color line.

W. E. B. Dubois

Eleven

RACIAL AND ETHNIC INEQUALITY

Inequality in society takes many forms, but none has commanded more public attention, nor aroused more social controversy, in the United States in recent years than the inequality signified by *race* and *ethnic* status and by *poverty*. That the poor and the minorities are overlapping categories only compounds the issue.

While the understanding of racial and ethnic minorities overlaps with understanding poverty, the issues are not identical, and in this chapter we give consideration to racial and ethnic minorities.

RACIAL AND ETHNIC MINORITIES

Some members of society, by virtue of their racial or ethnic status, are blocked from full and equal participation in all phases of social life—and this makes them a *minority*. Minority as a status, then, must be distinguished from minority as a numerical proportion. It is true that in the United States whites are the numerical majority and blacks the numerical minority.

But in the Republic of South Africa, the dominant whites are the numerical minority and the subordinate blacks are the numerical majority. There the numerical minority is dominant and in control, while the numerical majority is in a subordinate status. The same situation existed until recently in Rhodesia, now the Republic of Zimbabwe.

Sociologically, a minority group is *not* primarily defined by its number. Louis Wirth provided a useful definition:

We may define a minority as a group of people who, because of their physical or cultural characteristics, are singled out from the others in the society in which they live for differential and unequal treatment and who therefore regard themselves as objects of collective discrimination.[1]

Types of Minority Groups

What are the types of groups that most frequently become organized into majority-minority relations? An examination of the historical record tells us that dominant social groups have defined minority groups in terms of a very few criteria, of which the two most im-

In recent years American Indians have been militant in their struggle to remain a distinct people. In such demonstrations as this one they have gained support from sympathetic whites.

portant ones have been *racial* and *ethnic*. (For clarification of these terms, see "The Meaning of Race and Ethnicity;" For other criteria for being a minority, see "Are There Other Minorities?")

The creation of racial and ethnic minorities in the United States was one consequence of the historic struggle to shape a new nation, to settle a vast continent, and, in time, to make a modern industrial society. The dispossession of Indians, the enslavement of Africans, and (later) the open invitation to eastern and southern Europeans to immigrate in great numbers are in each case a historic event by which a white, English-speaking people asserted their dominance over the society and denied to others an equal status.

Indians The Indians were already here when the first white settlers arrived from Europe (which is why today they are often called Native Americans). As the indigenous people, native to the land, they were pushed out of their long-settled areas and gradually dispossessed of the lands they claimed. To take their land was often to take their way of life and destroy a culture.

Indians were never slaves (though efforts were made, unsuccessfully, to enslave them), but in the nineteenth century they were forcefully expelled from their lands, killed off in large numbers in armed conflict, and finally penned up in reservations under conditions of extreme poverty and deprivation.

The status of Indians in the United States has been different from that of any other minority. Until 1871 the federal government entered into treaties with Indian tribes, treating each one as a nation. But these treaties were often violated, and military conflict with the Indians reduced their numbers and took increasingly larger shares of their tribal lands.

After 1871, when the Indians were made wards of the federal government, efforts at forced assimilation only further destroyed tribal culture, deprived them of

ARE THERE OTHER MINORITIES?

Louis Wirth's definition of minority can include more than racial and ethnic groups. Religion has frequently been a basis for minority status.

During the 1970s a new interest in the problems which beset groups and categories other than racial and ethnic led to a conception of them as suffering from discriminatory treatment. In that sense they could be defined as minority groups. Perhaps the most important are the following:

Women, who demand equal opportunity in jobs and education, and who struggle against sexual inequality in all aspects of life. The feminist movement is perhaps the most basic and potentially revolutionary of all present minority struggles (see Chapter 12).

Homosexuals, many of whom have now come into the open and defined their homosexuality as a "sexual preference" which they demand be seen as a choice equivalent to that of heterosexuals.

The *elderly,* who have discovered that *age* is frequently a basis for neglect and discriminatory treatment.

The *physically handicapped,* who have found that there is often little or no provision made to enable them to function in education and employment, when only small adjustments would offset their disabilities.

THE MEANING OF RACE AND ETHNICITY

What is properly meant by "race" and "ethnicity" is often a matter of some confusion, especially when these terms are used to designate minority groups. A little clarification may be helpful.

Race

Contrary to common sense, *race* is not a significant category in the scientific effort to understand differences among human beings. The world's more than four billion people possess a number of physical characteristics by which they differ: skin color, hair texture, and distinctive nose, lip, and eyelid forms, among others. These physical differences have evolved over the last 50,000 years through adaptation to differences in environment.

Because human inbreeding has gone on constantly throughout history, there are no pure races. While anthropologists have defined three major categories of the human species (Caucasoid, Mongoloid, and Negroid), millions of people are so mixed in biological ancestry that they simply cannot be readily located in any one of these three.

More important to scientists has been the effort to specify what are *not* the characteristics of race. Such attributes as intelligence and skill; such moral qualities as honesty, trustworthiness, and ambition—these do not distinguish one race from another. Neither does temperament, criminality, or artistic ability.

The category of race, then, is not scientifically important, but it is sociologically important because people believe that races are real and that people of different races possess different characteristics. Furthermore, they act on their beliefs. Despite its lack of scientific credibility, we deal with race because in the modern world it remains a significant category of human belief and action.

Ethnicity

Ethnicity refers to *cultural* features distinctive of a people, such as language, place of origin, and heritage. These dimensions of culture give to a specific population a collective identity as a *people*.

While ethnicity may sometimes be referred to as *nationality,* not all ethnic peoples have had a nation of their own. Indeed, throughout the world, ethnic groups can be found struggling for the right of nationhood. By their cultural distinctiveness they are a people with or without a national identity.

It is common to use the term *ethnic* to refer to a people who are racially the same as the society's dominant groups but differ in culture. It should be clear, however, that a people who are defined racially may also, by virtue of cultural heritage and a separate existence, be an ethnic group. This is true of American Indian peoples, for instance.

much of their land holdings, and further reduced their numbers. The Indian population, estimated to be between 700,000 and one million when white Europeans first arrived on the North American continent, steadily declined to a low of 237,000 in 1900.

In 1934 Congress asserted the right of Indians to be Indians and to retain their tribal identity and organization, encouraged their self-government, and sought to assist them economically. Even this policy, however, shifted back around 1950 to an encouragement of assimilation.

But the Indian people have resisted being assimilated into the majority culture, and in recent years there have been even stronger expressions of their intention to remain a culturally distinct people. Against this, however, is a still powerful pressure to get them to give up their Indian-ness and to assimilate.

Throughout all this the Indians have been the poorest and least educated of all Americans. According to the 1970 Census, the median years of schooling for those 25 years and older was only 9.8, compared to a national average of 12.1; only 33 percent had graduated from high school, compared to 52 percent nationally. Their rate of unemployment was four times the national average and 38.3 percent lived below the poverty level, compared to a national rate of 13.7 percent.

Yet despite poverty, poor education, and discrimination, the Indian people have strengthened their sense of their own cultural identity and have grown steadily as a population. In the 1970 Census there were 792,730 of them, more than triple what there had been in 1900. Most Indians still live on reservations or in rural areas, but about one in seven has now relocated to urban areas, where usually they enter as the least skilled, the poorest, and most poorly housed minority.

Mexican-Americans (Chicanos) The Spanish colonization of what is now Mexico began before 1600 and soon extended into what later became the southwestern United States: Texas, California, New Mexico, Arizona, and Colorado. From that colonization came the *mestizo*—a mixture of white Spanish and native Indian population. Mestizos now compose about 60 percent of the Mexican population.

In the 1840s an expanding United States went to war with Mexico, and by 1848 Mexico ceded all territory north of the Rio Grande River. The large Mexican population already there, in what they regarded as their own territory, then became economically and politically subordinate to the invading "Anglos."

Since 1900 Mexicans from Mexico have come into the southwestern United States in large numbers, some legally, some illegally. They have come mostly to take low-paying jobs, to live in segregated communities, and to be treated more like a lower *caste* than simply a lower *class*.

While the Mexican-American population remains concentrated in the five southwestern states—Arizona, California, Colorado, New Mexico, and Texas—it has now spread northward and eastward, and mostly to cities. The image of the Mexican family as migratory pickers of fruits and vegetables is no longer accurate; 80 percent of them now live and work in urban areas. Communities of Mexican-Americans have emerged in Los Angeles, San Francisco, Denver, Dallas, Houston, Kansas City, Chicago, Detroit, Toledo, and Buffalo.

Large numbers of Mexicans migrate illegally from Mexico each year, and while many are caught and returned, some more than once, many others remain. Their illegal status makes them vulnerable to exploitation by employers looking for cheap labor, for they are not able to gain the protection of the laws on minimum wages and working conditions without revealing their illegal status.

Puerto Ricans Like people of Mexican origin, Puerto Ricans are Spanish in culture and language. Puerto Rico is a small island in the Caribbean on which the Spanish first made a European settlement; as in Mexico, they produced a racially mixed population. The United States gained control of Puerto Rico in 1898 in the settlement of the Spanish-American War.

In 1917 Puerto Ricans became citizens of the United States by an act of Congress, and in 1952 the Commonwealth of Puerto Rico was created. Though Puerto Rico is internally self-governing, the commonwealth relationship is based on common citizenship, common defense, a common market, and a common currency. Not all Puerto Ricans accept commonwealth status. There is a small group which seeks independence, and there is a larger group which wants Puerto Rico to become the fifty-first state in the union.

New York City has been the port of entry for Puerto Ricans coming to the mainland, and most have settled there. Of the 1,319,309 Puerto Ricans who had migrated by 1970, almost two of every three (63.2 percent) had settled in New York City. The others went to urban areas in the Northeast and Midwest; 95 percent of Puerto Ricans live in urban areas.

Spanish Origin The Bureau of the Census has always had difficulty enumerating Mexican-Americans and Puerto Ricans, not always distinguishing among those who speak Spanish or who have a Spanish surname. Now, the Bureau identifies people of "Spanish Origin" and separately counts Mexicans, Puerto Ricans, Cubans, and Central and South Americans. Table 11.1 gives the Spanish-Origin population as of 1979.

Mexican-Americans and Puerto Ricans, as Table 11.1 shows, make up 75 percent of the Spanish-Origin population; it is these two groups that constitute the disadvantaged minorities. They are both growing populations steadily increasing their proportion of the total American population. That is largely because they have a higher birthrate and are younger populations; the median age of those of Spanish Origin is 22 years compared to 30 years for the non-Spanish population. Immigration from Mexico, both legal and illegal, adds to that population, and migrants are usually younger. In 1976 persons of Spanish Origin were 5.5 percent of the population.

The Bureau of the Census always notes that persons of Spanish Origin may be of any race and so does not list them as nonwhite. But the minority status of Mexican-Americans and Puerto Ricans is based upon a perception of them as nonwhite and, accordingly, they have been treated as such.

TABLE 11.1
Persons of Spanish Origin in the United States, 1979

	Number (in millions)	Percent of Total
Total	12,079	100
Mexican	7,326	60.6
Puerto Rican	1,748	14.5
Cuban	794	6.6
Central and South American	840	7.0
Other	1,371	11.4

Source: Bureau of the Census, Current Population Reports, Series P-20, no. 347 "Population Characteristics, Persons of Spanish-Origin in the United States: March, 1979," Washington, D.C.: Government Printing Office, 1979, Table 1, p. 4.

Black Americans   The importation of Africans as slave-labor for the large plantations of the South made of race a moral and political issue from the time of the American Revolution until the present. Even after the abolition of slavery, blacks remained a source of cheap labor in a rural, southern economy until 1900, when they began to move north to cities and to another type of segregated existence.

Since the depression of the 1930s blacks have been disproportionately located in central cities, disproportionately employed in low-paying jobs, and have suffered a disproportionately high rate of unemployment.

Black Americans are the largest minority group in the United States; in 1976, the 24 million blacks were 11.5 percent of the American population. Blacks are increasing in number faster than are whites, though not at as fast a rate as are people of Spanish Origin. Their median age in 1978 was 24.3, compared to 30.6 for whites.

The origin of these minorities in the United States can be traced back to basic formative processes in the making of the nation. Indians were driven from the land they had long occupied and finally penned up in reservations; Mexican-Americans lost control of a territory they first settled and became a lower caste of cheap labor; and blacks entered the society as slaves to meet a demand for cheap labor in an expanding plantation economy. These events were a long time ago, but the consequences of minority status constructed then—a superior status for whites, an inferior status for nonwhites—has remained even until now as the basic contradiction of this society's claim to equality of opportunity.

Asian-Americans   Chinese and Japanese first migrated to the West Coast of the United States in the nineteenth century, the Chinese in the 1850s, the Japanese in the 1880s. Both experienced much racial hostility, were often the objects of violent acts, and suffered much discrimination, including systematic attempts legally to exclude them. The Chinese were excluded from immigrating in a series of congressional measures in 1882, 1892, and a permanent one in 1904. This act was repealed in 1943.

Though the Japanese also experienced much racial hostility, they were never legally excluded. But in 1922 the Supreme Court ruled that Japanese could not become citizens, citing the first naturalization act of

Most Chinese and Japanese live on the West Coast. Perhaps the best-known place is San Francisco's Chinatown.

1790, which made citizenship available "to any alien, being a free white person." This was later used as a reason to keep Japanese from owning or leasing land.

During World War II all Japanese on the West Coast were interned for the duration by the military in relocation centers and were forced to dispose of their property at considerable loss. Years later this forced internment was admitted to have been unconstitutional and a partial financial restitution was made by the federal government.

In 1970 the Census listed 432,002 Chinese, 40 percent of whom lived in California, and 373,983 Japanese, 64 percent of whom lived on the West Coast. These 800,000 Asian-Americans, despite a heritage of racial hostility and discrimination, have both retained a commitment to their group identity and have largely married within their group. Yet they have succeeded well in the American system, for their values encourage industriousness and education.

According to the 1970 Census, both groups have attained a higher level of median education than that of the total population's 12.1 years: 12.4 for the Chinese; 12.5 years for the Japanese. Both have attained white-collar jobs at a rate exceeding that of the rest of the population.

Despite these achievements, however, both Chinese and Japanese are not as economically successful as whites who have the same amount of education. (This is also true of blacks.) Here may be evidence that discrimination still exists for Asian-Americans.

The Immigrants

From 1890 on, until war broke out in Europe in 1914, a great mass of immigrants from Eastern and Southern Europe—Poles, Italians, Hungarians, Slovaks, Greeks, and others—entered the United States. They did so, not merely because they wanted to seek better economic opportunities than were offered in their own lands, but because the rapid growth of industry in the United States created an enormous demand for unskilled factory labor, far more than could be met by migrants from America's own rural areas.

European immigrants became the major source of cheap, unskilled labor in a rapidly expanding industrial economy. "By 1912, some 60 percent of the miners and some 58 percent of the iron and steel workers were foreign-born, and an additional 15 to 20 percent were their native-born children."[2]

These newer Americans were visibly different by virtue of their cultural patterns and life-styles. They spoke a language other than English, they dressed differently, and their customs and ways of life contrasted sharply with dominant customs and life-styles. When they clustered together in ethnic ghettoes, they perpetuated for several generations a life-style that made them culturally visible. Even when their use of English, as in the next or later generations, was not noticeably different, their names were identifiably ethnic, whether Hungarian, Polish, or Italian.

Simply being culturally different, however, does not make an ethnic group a minority. But poor immigrants who worked at low-paying jobs and who were the object of extensive discriminatory practices, as well as much prejudice toward "foreigners," became minority groups.[3]

The status of ethnic groups changed, however, with industrial and occupational change. As a group, they took advantage of changes in the division of labor to move into more rewarding occupations, and to increase their standard of living. Unions helped, too, by providing higher wages and greater job security.

There were other factors accounting for this group mobility. Political machines and the expansion of municipal government opened up civil service jobs controlled by City Hall. After World War II the expansion of education brought members of these groups into schoolteaching and other professions, and into expanding corporate and governmental bureaucracies.[4]

From the days of political bosses and machines, ethnic groups have used the political process to accumulate wealth and position and then to use it for the benefit of group members: municipal contracts let to one of their own group, choice political and judicial appointments, and the like.

This group mobility has been viewed by historians and sociologists as hastening the process of assimilation and acculturation, and therefore of a gradual decline in the existence of these immigrant groups and of their ethnic identity.[5]

The idea of America as a "melting pot" has long had strong support as a major value in American society, with the goal of gradual absorption of varied ethnic groups into the major cultural pattern. What has been a goal to many has seemed also to be a historical fact: the old ghettoes disappeared and the younger generation seemed to lose much of their ethnic identification.

But sociologists may have been too ready to write off ethnic groups as no longer a significant part of American social life. When Nathan Glazer and Daniel Moynihan studied ethnic groups in New York City they found them to be very much "alive" yet. An identification with ethnic groups was still quite meaningful to many people. Ethnic groups, furthermore, were significant units of the political structure of New York City.[6] Even among white people of European origin, ethnic identity is still very real (see Table 11.2).

The Jews as Minority Group   The Jews are one of the Western world's most persistent minority groups. They have existed for centuries in various societies, taking on some of the characteristics of the host society, yet always remaining a group apart as much by choice as by the prejudices of the dominant group. They have maintained over centuries a culture which

TABLE 11.2
Major Ethnic Groups in the United States, 1973

Origin	Population (in millions)	Percent of Total Population	Percent High School Graduates
English, Scottish, and Welsh	26.0	12.6	70.4
German	20.5	9.9	63.9
Irish	12.2	5.9	60.1
Italian	7.1	3.5	54.1
French	3.9	1.9	53.7
Polish	3.7	1.8	54.9

Source: U.S. Bureau of the Census, *Statistical Abstracts of the United States: 1979* (Washington, D.C., Government Printing Office, 1979), p. 33.

has sustained them through the vicissitudes of mistreatment and persecution.[7]

In Europe, in the Middle Ages, the Jews were often restricted to a limited set of occupations, and their presence in cities was often tolerated only on condition that they lived separately. This frequently meant in a walled-off part of the city—the first meaning of *ghetto.*[8] If the ghetto was segregation enforced by gentiles, it was also a form of protection; Jews were safe from molestation behind the walls.

In smaller towns and cities of Eastern Europe, Jews were often the target of violence, the scapegoats of others' class and group frustrations. Often they were the victims of a *pogrom* (an organized massacre or violent attack), and were literally driven out and forced to move on. These *pogroms* were responsible for the emigration of Russian Jews to the United States in the nineteenth century.

Jews are at present about 3 percent of the population in the United States and are largely concentrated in New York City and other large urban areas, mostly in the North. Present trends indicate that the Jewish population is growing more slowly than is the rest of the population.

What is historically significant about Jews in both Europe and the United States is their refusal to give up their identity. They have persistently resisted being assimilated, or even accepting the goal of assimilation.

Instead, most Jews have always taken a position in favor of *pluralism*—a situation in which culturally distinct groups can maintain their separate identities and pursue their group interests without suffering from discrimination—in short, to be an *ethnic* group but not a *minority.*

The idea of cultural pluralism is not new; it was worked out by philosopher Horace Kallen over a half century ago, challenging the idea that ethnic groups should be pressed to assimilate into a homogeneous "melting pot."[9] This position did not become the nation's dominant philosophy or social policy, however, but recent events have made it more attractive. Now many blacks, Indians, Chicanos, as well as Jews and traditional European ethnic groups seem to want to retain their group identity while not being denied their equal rights in a democratic society.

Rediscovering Ethnic Groups

The idea that the end of immigration meant the absorption of ethnics into the dominant culture has been a powerful belief for several decades. It was sustained throughout the 1950s and 1960s despite contrary evidence from social scientists. Sociologist Gerhard Lenski first challenged it in his study of racial and religious affiliation in Detroit.[10] Though not explicitly concerned with ethnicity, he found significant cultural and political differences among blacks, white Protestants, Catholics, and Jews. Then came the Glazer and Moynihan study of the continuity of ethnicity (and race) in New York City. It made a strong case for the idea that the "melting pot" had not yet eliminated ethnic groups as still viable bases for political action.

The more theoretical work of sociologist Milton Gordon helped clarify the issue.[11] Gordon distinguished among variants of assimilation. *Acculturation* —absorbing the dominant Anglo-Saxon culture— was the first form of assimilation and clearly the one most in evidence. But absorbing the dominant culture did not necessarily lead to *structural* assimilation, that is, the movement of ethnics into social positions in the groups and communities controlled by the dominant Anglo-Saxons.

Furthermore, acculturation did not mean a conscious *identification* with the majority group and a rejection of ethnic origins. As political scientist Michael Parenti points out, even when ethnics move to suburbia and no longer share a common residential neighborhood, they still often retain ethnic cohesion and identity.[12] Among ethnics of whatever social class, movement from the original ethnic neighborhood and the emergence of American-born generations do not usually lead to the disintegration of the group but to new adjustments in minority organization.[13] *Even when most of the life-styles assume an American middle-class stamp, these in-group social patterns reinforce ethnic identifications and seem to give them an enduring nature.* Today identifiable groups remain not as survivals from the age of immigration but with new attributes, many of which were unknown to the immigrants. In short, changes are taking place in ethnic social patterns, but the direction does not seem to be toward greater assimilation into the dominant Anglo-American social structure.[14]

The persistence of ethnicity is now widely recognized. There is even some sympathy for the working-class ethnics who remain in the central city, caught in the midst of racial conflict and struggling to preserve their way of life against any and all encroachments, including that of blacks. Many of these white ethnics, left behind in an old section of the central city, are poor and share in all the disadvantages that low income always brings.[15] They lack education and their children are being poorly educated in inner-city schools. They are, economically and socially, little if at all better off

than blacks—and feel threatened by black gains and forgotten and ignored by liberal middle-class whites, who seem to them to be concerned exclusively with the problems of black people.

What seems to be happening is this: the white ethnics who are largely of southern and eastern European origin (and are largely Catholic or Orthodox) have begun to move steadily into better-paying occupations, though for most there remains a gap between them and white Protestants in education and income. However, they have not discarded their ethnic identity; instead, it has been revitalized in recent years.

EXPLAINING MINORITY STATUS

Explanations of why minorities exist often employ such concepts as *prejudice* and *discrimination*. Yet this often confuses the issue as much as it clarifies it. For one thing, these are negative terms, and most people deny that they are prejudiced or that they discriminate. In addition, these are emotionally loaded terms, so that their use in objective discussion becomes difficult. Lastly, the two terms are often used interchangeably, though in fact they have different meanings.

Basically, prejudice refers to negative beliefs, attitudes, and feelings, while discrimination has reference to behavior, specifically, to unequal treatment of persons by virtue of their race or ethnicity. Thus, to refuse a person a job or admission to a college solely because of his or her race, even when the individual has the required qualifications, is to discriminate.

Does Prejudice Cause Discrimination?

The folklore and common sense of our culture tell us that prejudice causes discrimination. This is an argument so basic to an American perspective, and seemingly so obvious to many, that too few have ever questioned it. Yet, to the social scientist, it does not follow that *every* act of discrimination is a consequence of a person's prejudicial attitude.

To say that prejudice causes discrimination is to say that *attitude causes behavior.*[16] But a prejudicial attitude can cause discriminatory behavior only if the prejudiced person is free to act solely as he or she would wish. This is only rarely the case for anyone. In any organized society, each person must on most occasions act in ways that are expected, even demanded, and does not have the choice of acting out personal prejudices. Does this mean there can be prejudice without discrimination and discrimination without prejudice? The answer, of course, is yes.

Prejudice without discrimination occurs when a prejudiced person cannot discriminate even if one would want to. An employer who cannot refuse to hire because of race, an admissions director who cannot deny admission to a student because of race, a restaurant owner or manager who cannot refuse to serve anyone because of race—these are all instances where an individual's prejudice does not lead to discrimination. Law or custom or official policy can prevent any such discriminatory behavior.

Discrimination without prejudice, in turn, occurs when individuals discriminate because that is required by law or common practice, not because they are prejudiced. Such is the case, for example, when a white couple refuse to sell their home to a black couple because of neighborhood pressure and realtors' practices, not because of any prejudice of their own.

In short, discrimination has to be explained in terms of group processes and structure as well as the culture of the group, rather than solely, or even primarily, in terms of individual attitudes. Whether people do or do not discriminate is more a matter of their acting consistently with expectations of the situation than of acting out their own attitudes. Nor can we overlook the use of social power to support or countervail law, policy, or custom.

Minority Status and Social Power

To explain discrimination in terms of law and social policy, even of custom, requires that one social group be able to control and define law and custom and social policy in order to dominate the other. And this requires that it have *social power*. To be a dominant group and to confine a minority group to a subordinate position within the social structure—"to keep them in their place"—requires the dominant group to have the instruments and mechanisms of power necessary to sustain its dominant position. Whites can discriminate against blacks in employment, for example, only if whites control the distribution of jobs.

It is this process of discrimination that creates a minority group. The very act of discriminating—in jobs, housing income, social services, and education—is the social process by which a racial or ethnic group is converted into a minority group. The mere holding of prejudicial attitudes by one group toward another does not make of the recipient group a minority; it merely indicates the existence of group hostility. Thus blacks develop attitudes of resentment and hostility toward whites, but whites do not become a minority because of this.

The Function of Prejudice

If prejudice does not cause discrimination, what (if anything) does it do? One function of prejudice is to provide a rationale or justification for discriminatory behavior. The late Ruth Benedict, for example, argued that racial beliefs and prejudices came *after* the onset of the slave trade, specifically in response to the attacks upon it as inhuman and un-Christian.[17] Racist beliefs emerged, she argued in effect, to justify already existing behavior.

When the differences between a dominant and subordinate group are racial, then myths about racial inferiority and superiority will constitute the core of the justifying prejudice. Then it is more than attitude; it is a set of culturally developed beliefs about how one group is superior to another and thus deserving of its advantaged position. Furthermore, it makes use of *stereotypes* of both the dominant and subordinate groups. Stereotypes are culturally based images of a category of people, attributing to them a uniformly common set of characteristics; for subordinate groups, the stereotypes are negative and deny positive characteristics. Thus, when whites hold a stereotype of blacks as lazy, less intelligent, and given to criminal behavior, they also hold a stereotype of whites as ambitious, intelligent, and law-abiding. A negative image of the subordinate group is accompanied by a flattering self-image by the dominant group of itself, one that justifies its being dominant, indeed, makes it seem natural that it would be.

When this constitutes a firm social belief, it provides a perfectly logical basis for discriminatory behavior by the dominant group. It feels justified in sustaining inequalities in educational opportunity, for why extend equal educational chances to people you believe to be unequal in ability? It feels justified in denying voting rights, for why extend the franchise to people you believe do not have the intelligence to understand the political process? It feels justified in discriminating in employment, for why extend job opportunities to people you believe not to be capable of holding a job demanding skill and ability?

From a scientific perspective such beliefs may have no validity. Yet they will persist anyway, as long as they function to justify one group's discriminations against and domination over another.

The Function of Discrimination If the function of prejudice is to justify discriminatory behavior, what, then, is the function of discrimination? What does discrimination *do*? What a group does when it discriminates against another group is to set up social mechanisms by which it denies equal access to the rewards of society. It makes race or ethnicity a major determinant in the distribution of life-chances.

The Structure of Discrimination

The key to minority status, we have seen, is the capacity of one group to impose discrimination upon another. Though discrimination can and does take many forms, there are a few modes of discrimination that are significant, even crucial, because the entire structural arrangement of dominant-minority relations depends upon them. They are the key to the advantages and privileges that discrimination gives to the dominant group.

Economic Discrimination in the economic sphere is primary; by such means a dominant group controls jobs, land, credit, and investment. Discrimination in *employment* has understandably received most attention in a society like ours in which most people are employees, not self-employed.

Economic discrimination is the crucial process in allocating whites and the nonwhite minorities unequally throughout the occupational structure, and thus also throughout the class structure. If discrimination did not operate in the allocation of jobs, then one could expect that racial groups would be distributed proportionately throughout the occupational structure. But in the United States, we find that nonwhites are underrepresented in the better-paying occupations, overrepresented in the rest, and earn substantially less income than do whites (see Tables 11.3 and 11.4). Based on Census and Department of Labor data for 1976, Harrell R. Rogers, Jr., has computed the actual representation of nonwhites in occupations as a proportion of an expected representation if there were equal chances (and measured as 1.00):[18]

- professional and technical workers   .71
- managers, officials, and proprietors   .38
- clerical workers   .86
- sales workers   .38
- craftsmen and foremen   .68

TABLE 11.3 Occupation by Race and Spanish Origin, 1978					
			Spanish-Origin		
	White	Black	Mexican	Puerto Rican	Other
White-collar	51.8	36.2	18.5	26.2	36.4
Blue-collar	32.9	38.2	63.1	52.3	47.8
Service	12.3	24.1	11.3	19.8	14.9
Farm	3.0	2.4	6.9	1.7	1.2

Source: U.S. Bureau of the Census, *Statistical Abstracts of the United States: 1979* (Washington, D.C.: Government Printing Office, 1979), pp. 33 and 416.

	Under $10,000	$10,000 to $14,999	$15,000 to $19,999	$20,000 to $24,999	$25,000 and over	Median
TABLE 11.4 **Income of Families by Race and Spanish Origin, 1977**						
White	24.5	18.6	18.4	14.6	23.8	$16,740
Black	52.1	18.0	12.8	8.2	9.0	$ 9,563
Spanish Origin	42.4	22.7	15.6	9.6	9.7	$11,421

Source: U.S. Bureau of the Census, *Statistical Abstracts of the United States: 1979* (Washington, D.C.: Government Printing Office, 1979), p. 449.

In contrast, nonwhites are overrepresented in other, less rewarding occupations:

- operatives (semiskilled)   1.38
- private household workers   3.60
- other service workers   1.75
- laborers   1.79

This means, for example, that for every 100 nonwhite professional and technical workers one would expect to find if there were equal chances, there are in fact only 71; correspondingly, there are only 38 managers, officials, and proprietors. In contrast, there are 138 semiskilled workers, 179 unskilled laborers, and 360 private-household workers instead of the 100 that would be expected if nonwhites had equal opportunity.

Education   In an industrial society, the quality of one's education is increasingly significant for an individual's life-chances. Perhaps nowhere has equal opportunity come to be asserted more than in the sphere of education. Effective discrimination in education relegates any minority to inferior positions in the class structure. It makes the practice of economic discrimination easier. Indeed, little if any overt discrimination need be practiced in assigning jobs if the educational process has consistently educated the dominant group well and the minority group poorly. In short, educa-tion, probably more than any other factor, affects people's chances to compete for occupational status. As Table 11.5 ahows, blacks and people of Spanish Origin still lag well behind whites in educational achievement.

Politics   Denial of political rights to a minority is a denial of political power. As long as free elections exist, minority groups can translate their grievances and demands into political goals. Nor do they need to possess greater numbers to do so. Rather, they can make a difference in otherwise close elections, providing the margin by which one party or the other, one candidate or the other, wins. Given freedom to vote, therefore, a minority group can mobilize its members behind a determined leadership and learn to exercise genuine political power. The elimination of other forms of discrimination—jobs, schools, housing—can then become significant goals for which such political power is effectively exercised.

In societies such as the Republic of South Africa, the dominant but numerical minority of whites has written a constitution that gives full citizenship only to whites, and denies it to blacks. In the United States, the passage of the Fifteenth Amendment to the Constitution in 1870 guarantees the political rights of citizenship to all regardless of race. Thus, white control of the political process has had to resort to more devious devices, especially in counties in the South where blacks were a numerical majority.

The most conspicuous consequence of residential segregation is the concentration of black people in large central cities.

TABLE 11.5
Percentage of Persons 25 Years and Older by Years of Schooling Completed, 1978

	4 years of High School	1 to 3 years of College	4 years or more of College	Median years Completed
All races	36.1	14.1	15.7	12.4
White	37.0	14.4	16.4	12.5
Black	29.0	11.4	7.2	11.7
Spanish-Origin	24.6	9.2	7.1	10.2

Source: U.S. Bureau of the Census, *Statistical Abstracts of the United States: 1979* (Washington, D.C.: Government Printing Office, 1979), p. 145.

To prevent blacks from voting, a wide range of techniques have been used. One was the white primary—restricting the Democratic Party's primary to whites on the supposition that parties were merely private clubs. In the once one-party South, the primaries were the real election. There was also a poll tax (a tax to vote), which discouraged the poor, both white and black, from voting. A more sophisticated and even more dishonest technique has been a literacy requirement, or a requirement to demonstrate some familiarity with the Constitution and the American system of government. White election officials could then fail even educated blacks while passing semieducated poor whites. By court decisions and legislation, and by vigorous federal enforcement under President John Kennedy, these practices have been severely reduced and the participation of blacks in the electoral process in the South has increased rapidly, changing the southern political process considerably.[19]

Nonetheless, blacks do not yet vote in the same proportion as do whites. But people of Spanish-Origin are even less involved in voting; they are substantially behind both whites and blacks in this regard, as Table 11.6 makes evident. This is particularly the case for Mexican-Americans in the Southwest, who have only begun to challenge the political domination of white Anglos that for so long has kept Mexican-Americans powerless.

Housing Discrimination in housing is primarily a matter of residential segregation. The restriction of blacks

TABLE 11.6 Political Participation in 1978: Percentages Who Reported They Were Registered and Voted		
	Reported Registered	Reported Voted
Total	62.6	45.9
White	63.8	47.3
Black	57.1	37.2
Spanish-Origin	32.9	23.5

Source: U.S. Bureau of the Census, *Statistical Abstracts of the United States: 1979* (Washington, D.C.: Government Printing Office, 1979). p.

to specific residential areas, and their exclusion from most of the residential neighborhoods of the community, particularly the more desired ones, is a pattern of segregation not legitimized in law since the Supreme Court in 1947 ruled as unconstitutional the practice of *restricted covenants*. (These were clauses in deeds to property restricting sale to whites only, sometimes to gentiles only.)

Nonetheless, residential segregation has been effectively carried on by a series of practices worked out

Because of segregated residential patterns, large numbers of children are still in all-white or all-black classrooms.

by realtors, home-financing institutions, property-owners associations, and political officials.[20] Within large northern cities in the last two decades, however, white movement to the suburbs has broken some of the resistance, making a wider range of housing available to blacks. In turn, however, suburban communities have sought to exercise the racial restrictions once so successfully practiced within the central city.

Perhaps the most significant consequence of racially segregated housing is segregated schooling. Once segregation in schooling was regarded as *de facto*, that is, not legally required, but the unplanned consequences of other restrictive practices. But in recent court cases the National Association for the Advancement of Colored People (NAACP) has sought to demonstrate that there have been deliberate efforts to draw neighborhood boundaries in such a way as to preserve all-white schools. School busing, the most controversial attempt to end segregation in schooling, is an effort to assign pupils on a basis other than residence, on the assumption that residential segregation, particularly between white suburbs and black inner-cities, is a pattern that will remain for some time.

Each of these major patterns of discrimination relates to the others. Segregation in schooling is associated with differential equality in education, and with differential bases of financial support for the education of white and of black children. Residential segregation, in turn, makes that possible. Differences in education provide quite different capabilities in the competition for jobs.

None of these forms of discrimination can be practiced except as whites possess the power to do so: to control property and land values and access to housing, to control political office, to control jobs and credit —in short, to control the economic, political, and educational resources of the society.

Institutional Racism This control of the several institutions of American society by whites to the disadvantage of nonwhites has been called *institutional racism*. Black activist Stokely Carmichael and political scientist Charles Hamilton gave this concept prominence in their widely read book, *Black Power;* and then social activist Louis L. Knowles and political scientist Kenneth Prewitt explored it in some detail.[21]

Carmichael and Hamilton note that most whites would not do anything as savage as bombing a black church and killing five black children, as was done in Birmingham, Alabama. But when in the same city "five hundred black babies die each year because of lack of proper food, shelter and medical facilities," they claim, "that is a function of institutional racism."[22]

Basically, whites assume a "white" superiority and a set of prerogatives that go with it. Some whites base their assumption upon notions of racial (genetic) superiority; others base it upon assumptions of cultural superiority. What they do not often recognize, however, is the subtle workings of advantage for whites when such assumptions and the prerogatives they justify are built into the very functioning of the institutions.

Getting a job or getting admitted to college, for example, depends on meeting some job requirements. Even if race is consciously banned as a requirement, an even competition between blacks and whites is not immediately created. Past workings of other institutions, such as education, have produced differences in the quality of learning, of job training, of opportunities for various significant experiences. All this will give whites an advantage over blacks. (In the same manner, males have an advantage over females, middle class over working class.)

The practices of social institutions are never equal toward those they serve, and so the distribution of benefits is not, either. When such differences affect whites and blacks to the advantage of whites, this is institutional racism.

RACE AND RACISM

Even though the collapse of European colonialism has reduced (though not eliminated) white domination of nonwhite peoples in Africa and elsewhere, the fact of race has become strikingly significant in the structure of world affairs in the twentieth century. It is a source of internal conflict of major proportions throughout the world, including some major industrial societies, such as the United States.

Beliefs about racial superiority are not an invention of Western peoples; they have appeared from time to time elsewhere, even in Africa prior to the coming of white colonialists. Nonetheless, there is a pattern of racist belief peculiar to the Western world, perhaps the most pervasive and powerful racist ideology the world has known. Although its roots go back to the slave trade, according to sociologist Pierre L. van den

Berghe, Western racism emerged as a distinct ideology only around the 1830s and 1840s and reached its peak between 1880 and 1920.[23] It has since entered a period of decline, but it remains alive and cannot be expected to disappear for three or four more decades.

The emergence of Western racism, says Van den Berghe, requires the presence of racially distinct groups, different enough so that at least some of their members can be readily classifiable. But these visible group differences must overlap with differences in status and culture and a situation of established inequality. These conditions most likely occur when groups come into contact through migration, when one group invades another people's territory and enslaves it, or when one group "imports" another group as slaves or as an indentured alien group. Yet, even then, the prevailing ideology is not always racist; it may only proclaim the cultural superiority of the dominant group.

Explaining the origins of Western racism, according to Van den Berghe, must take into account three main factors:

1. Racism provided a rationalization for capitalist exploitation of the New World and of colonial expansion in Africa, in particular the exploitation of non-European, nonwhite people, including systems of slavery.
2. Racism fitted with the new Darwinian theories in the biological sciences, which made notions of the racial superiority of white people over nonwhite people seem scientific.
3. Ideas of equality and freedom could only be violated (and they were) to justify slavery and the exploitation of colonial peoples if some distinction were drawn between *humans* (who were entitled to be free and equal) and *subhumans* (who were not).

The end of slavery as a legal institution did not end racist ideology; indeed, in the United States, as Van den Berghe noted, its peak was from 1880 to 1920. It was only after the 1920s that scientists came to reject racist theories and that social scientists came to develop explanations of race relations that were not based upon presumed racial differences.

Political action for civil rights in the United States was directed to providing equal rights and equal treatment for blacks, as for all minorities; to end various discriminatory practices; to eliminate racial segregation; and to achieve racial integration in politics, in jobs, in education, and, eventually, in housing. Probably most minorities also accepted these goals.

In the twentieth century, black intellectuals thought, through the race issue, to arrive at quite other conclusions than did white intellectuals about the future of black people in the United States.[24] This literature, however, received but scant attention from white intellectuals and social scientists until the black revolt in the 1960s made it apparent that there was no longer a taken-for-granted agreement between blacks and liberal whites on the future of race relations in the United States.

The rejection of the goal of integration in a new mood of militancy and separatism by some blacks, particularly youthful ones, confronted sociologists in the 1960s with a major sociological problem: how do we explain race relations in the United States? It seemed that the events in the real world of racial conflict might not any longer fit the prevailing model of explanation that had dominated sociological thought for several decades—the *assimilation* model. From this crisis of theory alternate models emerged. Let us examine some of them briefly.

The Assimilation Model

The experience of most European immigrants in gradually assimilating themselves into American life provides a model to explain the gradual change in the status of blacks and Spanish-Origin minorities. Immigrants first clustered in urban ghettoes, experienced destitution and discrimination, and were controlled in various ways—politically and economically—by other groups. In time they built up communities, gained a political base, and reduced the disadvantages that beset them. They experienced some mobility and a great deal of acculturation.

Applying the assimilation model to blacks means looking upon them as an ethnic group, and like other ethnics, as immigrants. In this case, though, their migration was not from Europe but from the rural south. Since blacks went north only after most European immigration, they are therefore the newest immigrants and so also the lowest group in status. But presumably they too will create communities out of their ghettoes, gaining enough political power in time to reduce the discriminatory power of dominant groups.

But there has been serious disagreement, not over the thinking of blacks as ethnics but over the comparability of their experience with earlier generations of Èuropean immigrants. The *Report of the National Advisory Commission on Civil Disorders* (known as the Kerner Report) suggested that there were several factors that made it impossible for blacks to follow the path of earlier immigrants.[25] For one thing, the maturing corporate economy no longer needed the unskilled labor that immigrants once offered. Hence, it now did not need the unskilled black worker.

Further, the *Report* argued that racial discrimination—the racism of white Americans—far exceeded the discrimination experienced by European immigrants—"a bar to advancement unlike any other."[26]

The *Report* cited other reasons, such as the decline of political machines that once gave immigrants economic help in exchange for political support. Basically, the *Report* argued that the 1960s and 1970s did not offer blacks the opportunity for a long, hard climb out of ethnic poverty and discrimination:

> The immigrant who labored long hours at hard and often menial work had the hope of a better future, if not for himself then for his children. This was the promise of the "American dream"—the society offered to all a future that was open-ended; with hard work and perseverance, a man and his family could in time achieve not only material well-being but "position" and status. . . .
>
> What the American economy of the late 19th and early 20th century was able to do to help the European immigrants escape from poverty is now largely impossible.[27]

The idea that black people, through hard work and perseverance, can follow the earlier immigrants into the main stream of American economic life, has been a widely held belief, even by some social scientists. Yet the *Kerner Report* makes it clear that the objective conditions for such a way to get ahead simply does not exist any longer. If blacks are to "make it" into the mainstream, other ways to advance must be developed.

The Economic Class Model

Because of changes in the economy—a more advanced technology and a reduction in unskilled jobs—many blacks have become an *underclass* of impoverished and unusable labor. The future only promises more of this, as further technological development reduces even more the need for unskilled labor.

This perspective places economic factors as basic to any understanding of race relations, and emphasizes the location of the majority of black Americans, Mexican-Americans, and Puerto Ricans in a lower class of the unemployed or underemployed. What employment is available is most often in the competitive sector of small businesses, where the workers are unorganized, wages are low, and there are none of the other fringe benefits that go to workers who are employed by large corporations and are protected by strong unions through collective bargaining.

The Colonial Model

The idea that blacks (and Mexican-Americans) could be viewed as a colonized people, instead of an immigrant group or an underclass, came originally from the writings of several black scholars. It got wider recognition when Stokely Carmichael and Charles Hamilton publicized the concept of *internal colonialism*.[28] Then sociologist Robert Blauner took it up as a serious sociological argument.[29]

It violates common understanding for most Americans to speak of colonialism except in terms of establishing domination by a colonizing nation over the geographical territory of a conquered people, typically different in race and culture. The land and labor of the colonized people are exploited, and the colony comes under the economic and political control of the colonizing nation.

Obviously, this does not seem to fit the American case. As Blauner notes, "Classic colonialism involved the control and exploitation of the majority by a minority of outsiders. Whereas in America the people who were oppressed were themselves originally outsiders and were a numerical minority."[30]

But this argument, Blauner insists, misses the major point: that the concept of *colonization* captures the common experiences of racially subjugated people in America and elsewhere, and is applicable even when there is not a colonial *system*. There are four basic aspects to colonization. First, it begins with the *forced* entry of the colonized people into the dominant society, in contrast to the *voluntary* entry of immigrants. Second, the colonizing power seeks to control, transform, even destroy the values and life-style of the colonized people. American slave-holders, for example, separated tribal members in order to weaken all cultural and organizational ties among the slaves. Thirdly, the colonizers closely administered and controlled the colonized people, giving them an experience of being constantly managed and manipulated by outsiders. Finally, colonization employs racism to justify the domination and control of one people by another.

The colonial model points out some crucial differences between blacks and the white immigrants from Europe into the United States. First, unlike blacks, European immigrants came voluntarily. Secondly, their ghettoes usually lasted only one or two generations, whereas the black ghetto persists. Though some few individuals escape it, most do not. Thirdly, and perhaps more crucially, white ethnics in a generation or less were able to develop ownership of their own stores and residences, and also to enter the social structure so that much local control was exercised by people from their own group.

But for blacks, and also for Mexican-Americans, this has never been so.[31] Their segregated communities have remained under white control and ownership. Whites own the residences and stores, and whites control the jobs. The schools have been run by whites, as have the social-work agencies and the political parties—and white police patrol the segregated streets. Blacks are thus relatively powerless because they control no significant resources, economic or otherwise.

To sociologists like Blauner, the colonial model makes more understandable the struggle of blacks and Mexican-Americans to control their own communities and to construct an independent political bloc that can press for action to meet the distinctive needs of each community. None of this makes sense if one assumes that assimilation is proceeding for them as it did for white immigrants. But community control and a political bloc are but two ways to seek liberation from colonial status.

These three models—assimilationist, economic-class, and colonial—are in each case an effort to explain race relations in the United States. And each assumes that change toward racial equality will necessarily come in a different way:

The *assimilationist* model is the most optimistic, for it assumes that by virtue of hard work and individual effort racial minorities, like immigrants before them, will surely make their way into the mainstream of American life, as long as all legal barriers are removed.

The *economic-class* model assumes that racial minorities will only advance by means of a class strug-gle in which they will necessarily unite politically with all other economically disadvantaged groups and classes.

The *colonial* model necessarily puts the emphasis on separate black and Mexican-American struggles to gain independent political power in order to liberate their people from colonial domination.

In the early 1970s there was vigorous discussion among black leaders and intellectuals over which of these models, or others, best fit the immediate and long-run political situations blacks faced: over whether race was more important than class, or the reverse; whether the blacks should integrate or go a separate way of development; or whether blacks should work within the present system or press for radical change. (See "Race or Class: Which Is More Significant?")

But, in fact, the civil rights movement made little further progress in the 1970s, and has often split hopelessly over strategies and goals. Economic recession has made progress in jobs more difficult. As a result, the effort to effect civil rights action through law and court decisions, pressed under the symbol of *affirmative action*, has received greater attention as a program for racial progress, but also as a source of division between blacks and whites.

AFFIRMATIVE ACTION

The most fundamental significance of the 1954 Supreme Court decision on school desegregation was that it removed Constitutional support for legal forms of segregation. Equal treatment for all, regardless of race, became the basic law of the land.

But discrimination is more than a legal matter; it is a social and cultural process as well, deeply rooted in basic assumptions and practices of the society. The act of removing the legal barriers to equal treatment, therefore, did not significantly change attitudes and practices. Those who had thought it would were sorely disappointed. They had expected great changes; the results in improved education and jobs for blacks, however, were modest.

In time it became evident to the leaders of the civil rights movement that changing the law was only a necessary first step in providing equal opportunity for all minorities; something further had to be done. From that conviction came *affirmative action*.

RACE OR CLASS: WHICH IS MORE SIGNIFICANT?

The success of many black Americans in entering into professional and managerial positions, even while an impoverished underclass persists, creates unanticipated consequences, such as the growth of new class divisions among blacks and conflicts of class interests between the successfully mobile and persistently poor.

William J. Wilson, a black sociologist at the University of Chicago has used this change to develop a new conception of the place of blacks in American society. He has developed a highly controversial argument that race is of "declining significance" for the life-chances of blacks and that it is now their class position which most affects their fate.*

Wilson describes a black middle class which, he says, encounters no hostility in entering the white corporate structure. Being black no longer holds back the talented and educated, so that the qualifications of class, not the stigma of race, determine the chances of blacks for privilege and position.

Wilson is fully aware of the continued poverty and unemployment of masses of black people, but here too he feels that what is primarily needed is a social policy attacking inequality on a class, not a racial basis.

Those who disagree with Wilson acknowledge the reality of black gains but deny that race is now of such little importance. They stress the Bakke case as evidence of a continuing difficulty of making affirmative action effective and legally secure. They also stress the continuing dependence of racial minorities on effective legal enforcement of equal opportunity as a necessary counter to continuing white prejudice.

Wilson's critics also point to the still large gap in income and occupational position between blacks and whites in the middle class, and express the fear that recession may erode these gains.

The value of Wilson's work is not that it offers a definitive explanation of what is happening to blacks (it doesn't), but that it puts a necessary focus on the changing interaction of class and race in American society. Sociological analysis now needs to develop a more adequate account of the dynamics of class in changing the relation of blacks and whites to one another and of effecting the life-chances of both. Race has not suddenly become unimportant in American society, but its significance has changed as blacks have changed their relation to class structure.

Notes

* William J. Wilson, *The Declining Significance of Race* (Chicago: University of Chicago Press, 1978).

What Is Affirmative Action?

There are those who argue that, in principle, the government has no business doing anything beyond acting *against* discrimination. It should not promote equal opportunity, according to this perspective; it should only prevent or prohibit actions of racial discrimination.

Such a principle gives minorities the *legal right* to compete equally, but it does not give them the social or cultural skills and attributes to do so. Past discriminations often leave them at a disadvantage when competing with dominant group members for jobs, for grades, or for entrance to professional school.

It is this discrepancy between legal right and socially developed ability that is the basis of affirmative action. From the perspective of affirmative action, it is not sufficient simply *not* to discriminate; it is necessary to *do* something, to *affirm* equal opportunity by specific action. Affirmative action means a conscious, deliberate effort to seek out and find minorities for equal opportunities in such basic areas as jobs, education, and housing.

While affirmative action can take many forms, it has become controversial when it takes the forms that its opponents call "quotas" or "reverse discrimination." What to the proponents of affirmative action is a justifiable means to provide equal opportunity, is to others an act of racial preference that is as discriminatory as the discrimination it seeks to replace.

The opponents of such forms of affirmative action have wide public support. In a survey conducted by the Gallup Poll in March 1977, a national sample of adults was asked this question:

Affirmative action has made it possible for blacks to attain training and jobs once denied them.

AFFIRMATIVE ACTION: BAKKE AND WEBER

Creating a program of affirmative action, which will give special assistance to minorities without violating the rights of the majority, has proved to be difficult and legally complicated. Two decisions by the U.S. Supreme Court provided some conception of what is and is not legally acceptable, without removing all the confusion and uncertainty.

The Bakke Case

Allen Bakke was a practicing engineer who, in his midthirties, decided to change careers. His efforts to get into a number of medical schools, however, brought only rejections (probably, in most cases, because of his age). He then chose to sue one of the schools to which he had applied—the University of California at Davis—on the grounds that its program of setting aside 16 places for minorities in the entering class violated his rights because it allowed admission to individuals who were less qualified than he. After a series of decisions and appeals, Bakke won admission to medical school by a decision of the Supreme Court in June 1978.

In deciding the case for Bakke, the Court revealed a wide range of conflicting conceptions of affirmative action and no clear majority in regard to all of the issues raised by Bakke's suit. The nine justices issued six different opinions. Through the swing vote of one justice, the Court managed to make two 5–4 decisions:

1. Justice Lewis F. Powell joined four other justices in voting to order Bakke admitted to medical school. The four justices, in an opinion written by Justice John Paul Stevens, claimed that the case could be readily decided on the basis of Title VI of the Civil Rights Act of 1964, which forbids anyone to be excluded from participation in any program receiving federally financed assistance.

Justice Powell, in voting with the others to create a majority, based his decision on a more constitutional issue, namely, the clause in the Fourteenth Amendment to the Constitution, which guarantees the equal protection of the law for all, regardless of race. On that basis, he said, Bakke had suffered discrimination.

2. Justice Powell then joined the four dissenting justices in voting that race and ethnicity could and indeed had to be taken into consideration in admissions programs. He disagreed with Justice William Brennan, whose minority opinion asserted that past decisions by the Supreme Court and federal regulations had established that "race-conscious action is not only permitted but required to accomplish the remedial objectives of Title VI." But he did claim that "the State has a substantial interest that legitimately may be served by a properly devised admissions program involving the competitive consideration of race and ethnic origin." But, he asserted, "the assignment of a fixed number of places to a minority group is not a necessary means toward that end." He offered the affirmative action program at Harvard University as a model. At Harvard, race or ethnic background is a "plus" factor in considering an applicant for admission, but such applicants are still compared competitively to others.

What these two decisions seemed to say was that a quota system was contrary to law, but that special consideration of race and ethnicity was valid; affirmative action still had a legitimate place in the policy of the government.

The Weber Case

A year later, in June 1979, the Supreme Court ruled again, this time on a company training program that specifically set aside a number of positions for blacks. In 1974 the Kaiser Aluminum and Chemical Corporation and the United Steel Workers of America had entered into an agreement for a training program at Kaiser's steel mill at Gramercy, Louisiana. For the 13 positions in the training program, seven were reserved for blacks, six for whites.

A white worker at the plant, Brian F. Weber, filed suit against his employer when he was rejected for one of the white positions, while two blacks with less seniority were accepted. He charged that Kaiser's affirmative action program violated the ban on racial discrimination in employment specified in Title VII of the 1964 Civil Rights Act.

After the Bakke decision, supporters of affirmative action feared that any program which involved a numerical plan—"fixed numbers"—would be outlawed by the Supreme Court, and in this manner would eliminate thousands of company job-training programs. But that was not how the Court was to decide.

By rejecting a literal reading of the law, a bare majority of five justices ruled that Kaiser's affirmative action program was within the intent of the law: to improve the lot of those who had for so long been excluded. But consciously and deliberately the majority who so ruled made a narrow decision, one not intended to have broad application. Constitutional guarantees of equal protection under the law (the Fourteenth Amendment) was not an issue, the majority ruled, because the program was a voluntary one between private parties—a company and a union—involving no federal or state funds or programs.

While the principle of affirmative action has been upheld by these decisions, its application to the many diverse situations in education and employment is still being worked out in administrative practices, with more Supreme Court decisions yet to come.

Some people say that to make up for past discrimination, women and members of minority groups should be given preferential treatment in getting jobs and places in college. Others say that ability, as determined by test scores, should be the main consideration. Which point of view comes closest to how you feel on this matter?[32]

The results were striking. Eighty-three percent of the sample opposed "preferential treatment" and only 10 percent favored it. Even nonwhite minorities were opposed, though not by such a margin; 64 percent opposed, 27 percent favored.

Furthermore, affirmative action has been challenged in the courts, and the Supreme Court decision in the renowned Bakke case in 1978 seemed to put an end to any system of quotas. Yet the Supreme Court has been careful to assert that affirmation action in some form has a valid place, and that race can be taken into account in determining admissions (see "Affirmative Action: Bakke and Weber").

In large part now affirmative action takes the form of *goals* rather than *quotas*. No specific numbers are assigned (that would be a quota), but an effort is made to find ways to increase the number of minorities so as to reach a states goal in a given period of time.

THE FUTURE OF RACE RELATIONS

For almost twenty years after the Supreme Court decision of 1954, white and black people struggled, sometimes even violently, over the terms and conditions of relations between the races. A civil rights movement rose to give force and vision to demands that the old ways of segregation and discrimination give way to equal treatment and opportunity.

And there was a great deal of social change. By legislation and court decisions the federal government became committed to equal opportunity as the law of the land, to be required, not only of all agencies of the federal government, but also of state and local governments and private enterprise.

By the end of the 1970s there was clear evidence of sweeping change of remarkable progress in moving toward racial equality; but there was also substantial evidence of lack of progress.

The Racial Progress

Since the civil rights struggles of the 1960s racial progress has been real and substantial, to an extent that is irreversible. The days of legal segregation are gone and the struggle for *legal* equality has succeeded. The struggle for *social* and *economic* progress, in turn, is less impressive, but there are substantial gains. The evidence of racial progress includes the following:

1. Perhaps as much as 30 percent of urban blacks have made substantial economic gains in jobs and income and have escaped the confines of the black ghetto. They have moved to better housing in the city, some even to the suburbs. (Between 1970 and 1977, according to the Bureau of the Census, blacks in the suburbs have increased by 34 percent.)

2. Blacks have increased substantially as students in universities, and as college graduates, and also as members of the professions. (The education of blacks will be analyzed in Chapter 14.)

3. By the end of the 1970s there were over 4,500 black elected officials, compared to less than 500 in 1968. (But that is still less than one percent of all elected officials, whereas blacks are 11.5 percent of the population.)

The Lack of Progress

Yet the progress that has marked this period of social change is only part of the record; there is also much lack of progress. Consider the following:

1. From 1968 to 1978, unemployment doubled among blacks, reaching a level of 14 percent. Among black youth in many inner-city ghettoes, it is as high as 40 to 50 percent. And almost one-third of the black population is still below the official poverty line; 19 percent of Mexican-Americans and 39 percent of Puerto Ricans are, also.

2. Despite federal programs of urban renewal, most older central cities contain many square miles of abandoned houses and stores, rubble-strewn streets, burnt-out and vandalized property, vacant commercial blocks, and continuing decay of urban neighborhoods. For poorer blacks, decent housing, let alone a livable neighborhood, is still difficult to attain.

3. There has been a steady increase in the number of black families headed by a female, yet black women generally earn only 61 percent of what black males earn. According to the Bureau of the Census, by 1977 35 percent of all black families were headed by women without husbands.

4. Central city schools have declined in quality, and there is a persistent disparity in the quality of education between black inner-city schools and suburban schools.

5. Despite the mandate for equal education, blacks and Hispanics are concentrated in the poorer-quality urban schools in segregated patterns. There are large black majorities in the largest cities. Nonwhites in public schools range from a high of 96 percent in Washington, D.C., to 84 percent in Detroit, 75 percent in Baltimore, 70 percent in Chicago, and 62 percent in Philadelphia. (The education of minorities will be examined in Chapter 14.)

Conflicting Perceptions of Racial Change

This evidence of both progress and lack of progress in ending racial inequality in the United States has produced predictably different perceptions about racial change among white and black Americans. Whites tend to emphasize the progress, while more blacks are discouraged with the lack of progress.

During the 1970s there was a decline in the optimism of black people about future racial progress, and a growing sense that white Americans are less concerned about what happens to blacks. Consider the following:

In 1968, 63 percent of blacks felt that much progress had been made in the preceding ten or so years, but in 1978 only 45 percent of northern urban blacks felt that way.[33] Forty-four percent of these same blacks felt that whites did not care whether blacks made any progress, compared to only 33 percent who felt that way in 1968.

In 1968, 49 percent of blacks thought that there was "real hope" for eventually ending prejudice and discrimination, but by 1978, 53 percent of northern urban blacks thought the situation would always be the same, while only 33 percent believed it would eventually be ended.

The increasing pessimism of blacks shows up, also, in differences between blacks and whites in assessing racial progress for blacks. For example, two-thirds of urban northern whites in 1978 said that blacks had made a lot of progress over the past 10 or 15 years in removing discrimination, compared to 45 percent of blacks who said the same thing; 51 percent of blacks believed that little change had occurred.

While whites do not deny that some prejudice and discrimination still exists, most believe that blacks are more readily being hired and promoted than they were ten years ago. But approximately half of urban northern blacks believe that many blacks still are denied jobs, promotions, and housing because of race.

Who Is Right? Who Is Wrong?   How can we account for these conflicting perceptions? Are whites simply wrong in assessing progress for blacks? Or are blacks so pessimistic they cannot see that progress?

The answer is not that one is right and the other wrong, but that each is perceiving and thus emphasiz-ing a part of a total process. There is progress for some, a lack of progress for others.

As we noted above, perhaps 30 percent of black Americans have achieved economic gains sufficient to remove them from the bottom of the economic system. They have gained education, white-collar jobs, a better income, and better housing. But an even larger number of blacks have made no such progress, and many of them have no prospects of ever doing so.

If there is a significantly growing black middle class, there is also a black underclass with no prospects for a better future. The specter of a class of permanently un-employed, sustained on welfare, and living unproduc-tive lives, now haunts the nation.

Beyond Civil Rights

The struggle for civil rights for racial minorities has now completed an historic phase. There no longer is any question that racial discrimination in jobs, school-ing, and housing is illegal, and beyond that, that some form of affirmative action is legitimate social policy.

But even affirmative action will not do more than expand the opportunities for those minorities who can "make it" into the system. The majority who cannot will remain an impoverished, wasted class of people, unless and until the struggle goes beyond civil rights to economic justice.

SUMMARY

Minority designates a *status,* not a quantity—a status of domination and control by a major-ity (dominant) group. The power to discriminate by one group over another creates a minority.

Racial and ethnic groups have been two of the more important types of minority groups. For the United States, the historical process of shaping a new nation and settling a vast continent by white settlers from Europe created basic racial and ethnic minorities: the Indians by dispos-session and conquest; the blacks by enslavement; Mexican-Americans by military victory over Mexico; and the European immigrants by an open invitation to immigrate at a time of industrial expansion.

Once thought to be disappearing by virtue of assimilation, *ethnicity* is now rediscovered as a still meaningful identity for many. While there has been cultural assimilation—*acculturation*—there has been less *structural* assimilation.

Prejudice is the attitudinal aspect of minority status, *discrimination* the behavioral. The rela-tion of prejudice to discrimination is often confusing; it is not that prejudice causes discrimina-tion, but that prejudice *justifies* discrimination.

Discrimination is the process by which one group is able to deny to another equal access to the rewards of society.

The most significant forms of discrimination are economic, educational, political, and housing.

Institutional racism refers to the discriminatory practices within the institutions—particularly the educational, economic, and political.

Racism in the Western world, according to Van den Berghe, is distinguished by three factors: a rationalization for capitalist exploitation by Europeans and colonization of the non-European, nonwhite peoples; a Darwinian theory that gave to racial superiority a scientific claim; and a distinction between humans and subhumans in order to justify slavery and exploitation and the violation of ideals of equality and freedom.

There have been three basic models for explaining race relations in the United States:

1. The *assimilation* model, which sees blacks as only the latest of immigrant groups, which will then assimilate and move up economically, as have other ethnic groups (but changed conditions made this model doubtful in the 1970s).

2. The *economic-class* model, which views blacks as largely an economically obsolescent underclass.

3. The *colonial* model, based on the idea that the enslavement of black Africans created an internal colony, marked by the fundamental characteristics of the colonizing process: forced entry, as by slavery; the destruction of the original culture; close control; and racism.

While some believe that the government should do no more than act against discrimination, others believe that that is not enough to eliminate generations of discrimination and disadvantage. *Affirmative action* is the attempt to do more in forms of special consideration and preferential treatment.

When that preference takes the form of *quotas*, opponents have charged "reverse discrimination." The Supreme Court in the Bakke case ruled out quotas in education while upholding the principle of affirmative action; in the Weber case they accepted quotas when voluntarily arranged between private parties and when no federal funds or programs were involved.

A large majority of all segments of the public have expressed opposition to "preferential treatment" in public opinion polls.

Blacks and whites have conflicting perceptions of racial progress because there has been real progress, in particular, creating a new middle class of upwardly mobile blacks; but there is also a lack of progress, threatening to leave the society with a permanently unemployed underclass.

NOTES

[1] Louis Wirth, "The Problem of Minority Groups," in Ralph Linton, ed., *The Science of Man in the World Crisis* (New York: Columbia University Press, 1945), p. 347.

[2] Oscar Handlin, *America: A History* (New York: Holt, Rinehart and Winston, 1968), p. 696.

[3] A Pulitzer Prize-winning history of these immigrants to American society, including an excellent study of the development of ethnic communities, is Oscar Handlin, *The Uprooted* (Boston: Little, Brown, 1951).

[4] For a detailed review of such changes in one city (New York), see Nathan Glazer and Daniel P. Moynihan, *Beyond the Melting Pot* (Cambridge, Mass.: The M.I.T. Press and Harvard University Press, 1963).

[5] For a discussion of how sociologists and others have used the concept of assimilation, see Milton M. Gordon, *Assimilation in American Life: The Role of Race, Religion, and National Origins* (New York: Oxford University Press, 1964), esp. Chaps. 3 through 6.

[6] Glazer and Moynihan, *op. cit.*, pp. 301–310.

[7] For a study of Jews in American society, see Nathan Glazer, *American Judaism* (Chicago: University of Chicago Press, 1957), and Marshall Sklare, ed., *The Jews: Social Patterns of an American Group* (New York: The Free Press, 1958).

[8] For an understanding of the origins of the ghetto, and a detailed study of the Chicago ghetto of the 1920s, see

Louis Wirth, *The Ghetto* (Chicago: University of Chicago Press, 1928).

[9] See Horace Kallen, *Culture and Democracy in the United States* (New York: Boni & Liveright, 1924).

[10] Gerhard Lenski, *The Religious Factor* (New York: Doubleday, 1961).

[11] Gordon, *op. cit.*

[12] Michael Parenti, "Ethnic Politics and the Persistence of Ethnic Identification," *American Political Science Review* 61 (September 1967): 717–726.

[13] *Ibid.,* p. 722.

[14] *Ibid.,* p. 721.

[15] For a highly readable account of the social life and problems of one such area (Kensington in Philadelphia), see Peter Binzen, *Whitetown: U.S.A.* (New York: Random House, 1970)

[16] The outstanding work on prejudice is still Gordon Allport, *The Nature of Prejudice* (Cambridge, Mass.: Addison-Wesley, 1954; paperback edition, New York: Anchor Books, 1958).

[17] Ruth Benedict, *Race: Science and Politics* (New York: Viking, 1940), Chap. 7, "A Natural History of Racism."

[18] Harrell R. Rodgers, Jr., *Racism and Inequality: The Policy Alternatives* (San Francisco: W. H. Freeman, 1975), p. 89 (data from Table 2).

[19] For a detailed analysis of black voting in the South, and its impact on Southern politics, see Donald R. Mathews and James W. Prothro, *Negroes and the New Southern Politics* (New York: Harcourt, Brace & World, 1966).

[20] For an excellent analysis of how this has been done in one city (Chicago), see Rose Helper, *Racial Policies and Practices of Real Estate Brokers* (Minneapolis: University of Minnesota Press, 1969).

[21] See Stokely Carmichael and Charles V. Hamilton, *Black Power: The Politics of Liberation in America* (New York: Random House, 1967); and Louis L. Knowles and Kenneth Prewitt, eds., *Institutional Racism in America* (Englewood Cliffs, N.J.: Prentice-Hall, 1969).

[22] Carmichael and Hamilton, *op. cit.,* p. 4.

[23] Pierre L. van den Berghe, *Race and Racism: A Comparative Perspective* (New York: Wiley, 1967), p. 15.

[24] See Francis L. Broderick and August Meier, eds., *Negro Protest Thought in the Twentieth Century* (Indianapolis: Bobbs-Merrill, 1965); and Harold Cruse, *The Crisis of the Negro Intellectual* (New York: Morrow, 1967).

[25] New York: Bantam Books, 1968.

[26] *Ibid.,* p. 279.

[27] *Ibid.,* p. 282.

[28] Carmichael and Hamilton, *op. cit.,* Chap. 1.

[29] Robert Blauner, "Internal Colonialism and Ghetto Revolts," *Social Problems* 16 (Spring 1969): 393–408.

[30] *Ibid.,* p. 395.

[31] For the application of colonialism to Mexican-Americans, see Joan W. Moore, "Colonialism: The Case of the Mexican-Americans," *Social Problems* 17 (Spring 1970): 462–473.

[32] *The New York Times,* May 1, 1977.

[33] The data in this section are from *The New York Times,* February 25, 1978. The 1968 data reported there were from the Survey Research Center of the University of Michigan; the 1978 data were from a New York Times/CBS Poll.

SUGGESTED READINGS

Pierre L. van den Berghe, *Race and Racism: A Comparative Perspective* (New York: Wiley, 1967). An influential work in carrying the study of racism beyond the analysis of individual attitudes.

Robert Blauner, *Racial Oppression in America* (New York: Harper & Row, 1972). A series of critical essays on understanding racism, here is Blauner's influential essay on internal colonialism.

Stokely Carmichael and Charles Hamilton, *Black Power* (New York: Random House, 1967). A compelling analysis of the problems blacks face, by a militant black activist and a black social scientist.

Harold Cruse, *The Crisis of the Negro Intellectual* (New York: Morrow, 1967). The crises of black intellectuals in assessing America is analyzed historically by a black intellectual.

Vine Deloria, Jr., *Custer Died for Your Sins: An Indian Manifesto* (New York: Macmillan, 1969). A mordantly witty analysis of the condition of the Indians and their relations with white Americans.

Nathan Glazer and Daniel P. Moynihan, *Beyond the Melting Pot* (Cambridge, Mass.: The M.I.T. Press and Harvard University Press, 1963). An important study that makes it clear that ethnicity still survives.

Milton Gordon, *Assimilation in American Life: The Role of Race, Religion, and National Origins* (New York: Oxford University Press, 1964). A fine analysis of assimilation and cultural pluralism in American life.

National Advisory Commission on Civil Disorders, *Report of the National Advisory Commission on Civil Disorders* (New York: Bantam Books, 1968). The Kerner Report, which analyzes the causes of the riots of the 1960s.

William J. Wilson, *The Declining Significance of Race* (Chicago: University of Chicago Press, 1978). Wilson's provocative thesis is that class, not race, is now more important for blacks.

Twelve

SEXUAL INEQUALITY

Women are half the human race, yet the division of labor between the sexes was humankind's first act of social domination, and the inequality it produced has endured throughout all history and has been reproduced in all human societies.

Sexual inequality is deeply rooted in the myths and values of culture, in the social roles accorded each sex, and in the long-lasting conception of what is masculine and what is feminine. It is, moreover, sanctified in religious teaching:

> For a man . . . is the image and glory of God; but a woman is the glory of man. For the man is not of the woman, but the woman of the man. Neither was the man created for the woman, but the woman for the man. (1 Cor. 11).

Such judgment is not only Christian; in Judaic and Moslem teachings, too, women's inferiority to man is affirmed.

Some feminists and some social scientists find it useful to consider that women are a minority, like blacks and Hispanics. Yet there is a difference, too, because of both their numbers and their roles. It is not only that women are not a numerical minority; neither are they a suppressed majority held in their "place" by a small ruling elite.

More to the point, men and women live in intimacy and bondage to one another through the act of sexual reproduction and the expression of sexuality. Also, by birth and marriage, women share with men their class and ethnic status.

The feminist demand for equality implies consequences far deeper than that of equal access to the positions of the class structure. In this chapter we shall examine the bases for sexual inequality and the efforts of women to achieve an equality with men in this society.

SEX AND GENDER

Every effort to explain sexual inequality is in some way or other based on a conception of differences between the sexes. These differences, it is usually claimed, make it "natural" that men should dominate.

But such claims often confuse what it is that women and men derive from nature and what they acquire from culture. They confuse, that is, the biology of *sex* with the cultural attributes of *gender*.

The Biological Difference

If one were to look for biological differences to explain male domination, what would one look for? It is women who bear children and nurse them, and this is a primary biological difference between women and men. Bearing children has consequences for what women can and cannot do, at least to being sometimes constrained and limited in their social and economic activity. But that is not reason for male domination.

The most obvious case for the biological superiority of males probably lies in the evidence of greater height and weight, and in the musculature (the body's muscular system) which men possess. Men, in short, are physically stronger than women when strength is measured by muscle power.

But males are not stronger than females when strength is measured in other ways. They start life with less capacity than women to survive physically. More of them are stillborn, and more of them die in the first year of life; more males are born malformed, and more suffer injuries at birth. They are less resistent than females to diseases, and they cannot bear pain as well. In short, if men are larger and stronger, women are more durable.

Nature has recognized this lesser capacity in males and made up for it by having more males than females born; in the United States the ratio is about 106 to 100. However, by the time these males and females are in their midtwenties, they are equal in number.

A review of a great range of research in human biology and in psychology provides very little evidence that there are fixed, determined behavioral propensities in either males of females.[1] It is not biology that creates such clear differences between how women and men act, and it is not biology that requires that males be dominant over females. Instead, the available evidence from primate studies, from studies of human infants, and from the studies of adult hormones shows "that biology constrains but does not determine the behavior of the sexes, and that differences between human males and females reflect an interaction between our physical constitutions and our patterns of social life."[2]

Nature and culture interact in most complex ways to shape men and women into the human beings they actually are.

Gender: The Cultural Difference

Social scientists have long insisted that it is culture, not biology, which primarily determines human personality and the organization of social roles. As we saw in Chapter 4, human beings become persons and de-

velop a self through *socialization.* The concept of socialization discredited those theories that had used biology to claim the natural inferiority of some races to others. Yet, somehow, this same idea was not as readily applied to the sexes.

Until very recently, instead, social scientists used a *biosocial* explanation of the differences between the sexes. They believed that social roles appropriate to each sex were determined by two basic biological facts: that men are physically stronger than women and that women alone bear children. That also, they felt, accounts for the existence of "masculine" and "feminine" personalities appropriate to these roles.

The idea went like this: men, being stronger, undertook the more strenuous tasks, like hunting and fighting enemies, while women, limited by childbearing and child care, performed simpler tasks nearer the home. Anthropologists, in fact, have often made a great deal out of this separation of sexual tasks in early humans and credited the male specialty of hunting with being a significant turning point in human evolution, one from which "our intellect, interests, emotions, and basic social life" are derived as "evolutionary products."[3]

Sociologists, in turn, have updated this idea for a time when men no longer hunt for a living. Men have been defined as *task specialists,* who organize practical activities and provide for the material needs of the family, while women are seen as *socioemotional specialists,* who provide warmth, love, and emotional support.[4] Two specialized roles—one instrumental, the other expressive—are thus presumed to be linked to the biological characteristics of the sexes.

It would be apparent to any woman that this is a singularly male view. There are obviously numerous task specialities associated with the caring for children, preparing food, and maintaining a house. Housework may be unpaid labor, but it is a set of tasks which require work and organization.

But even the original idea—that man the hunter is the provider—hardly stands up to careful scrutiny. For one thing, hunting big animals was an irregular, uncertain activity, insufficient to meet the daily needs for food. That required small-game hunting and gathering, that is, foraging and collecting the food available in nature. The early peoples who were hunters were also gatherers. Hunting alone was insufficient and survival depended on the collecting of vegetable foods by women.

Woman: Provider and Laborer   With the evolutionary advance to agricultural societies, the contribution of women to providing food increased. A recent analysis of verified ethnographic data revealed, for example, that in all known subsistence societies women contributed substantially to food production. In nearly 45 percent of 862 societies surveyed, women accounted for more than 40 percent of the food produced.[5]

That is not all. In many societies women have been traders and have operated the local market. In some African societies, such as the Yoruba, women may control much of the food supply, trade in distant markets, and accumulate cash. In Haiti, about one person in fifty is a market trader and most of them are women. So are most of the peasants who come to the market to buy and sell. In the Jewish ghettoes of Eastern Europe, strong, self-confident women possessed enormous influence on the affairs of the community, controlled the family's finances, and often ran the family business. The historical and anthropological record, then, simply denies any sharp distinction between instrumental and expensive sex roles.

Furthermore, while the greater strength of men may have led them to be hunters and warriors, this has not spared women from burdensome labor. The capacity of sturdy peasant women for backbreaking toil is legendary. In some regions of the world, such as sub-Saharan Africa, the labor required to raise crops is considered women's work. It is women in such societies who most often are the ones to haul wood and carry water; and it is women who walk with burdens on their heads while their husbands ride on the backs of animals.

Prior to the industrial age women's work substantially complemented the men's in providing suste-

In many parts of the world women are the traders and run the markets. This woman in India sells bread and is bargaining with a customer.

nance; in some cases women were the economic providers. In any case, they were never spared burdensome labor.

Perhaps only as hunter and warrior have men had roles from which women were fully excluded. Women, in turn, have most often cared for the children they bore, though in many cultures men have also shared in child care, or even assumed a greater responsibility for the training of young boys. Again, it is only in industrial society, where work and home are separated, that the men's absence from home puts the burden of child care so exclusively on women.

Sex and Temperament

A corollary of sex-role differentiation is the idea that men and women have basically different personalities, each being appropriate to their role. To be "masculine" is to be more assertive, aggressive, achieving, and possessing. To be "feminine" is to be passive, compliant, gentle, and emotionally warm.

It was the remarkable Margaret Mead who first told us that this was simply a cultural *stereotype,* and that real men and women in different cultures did not necessarily fit these masculine and feminine models. Her classic fieldwork among three New Guinea tribes provided us with compelling evidence to destroy forever any notion of personality that fitted only one sex.[6]

Among one tribe, the Arapesh, Mead discovered that the women were quite "feminine"; they were gentle, warm individuals. But so were the men. Both sexes, in fact, disapproved of aggressive behavior; both men and women cared for children.

In startling contrast was a neighboring tribe, the Mundugumor, a cannibalistic and head-hunting people. The men were fierce, aggressive, and violent. But the women were very much like the men. They seemed to dislike their necessary maternal fate of being pregnant and nursing children.

A third tribe, the Tchambuli, however, possessed both masculine and feminine sex roles, except that they were reversed. The energetic, working women were traders and were the economic providers for the family. The men, artistic and specializing in rituals, took care of the children.

Such variability in the temperaments associated with sex is not confined to tribes in New Guinea; it has been found elsewhere in the world. What we Westerners take to be the "nature" of men and women is evidently not universal. Margaret Mead made the point clearly:

> If those temperamental attitudes which we have traditionally regarded as feminine—such as passivity, responsiveness, and a willingness to cherish children—can be easily set up as the masculine patterns in one tribe, and, in another, be outlawed for the majority of women as for the majority of men, we no longer have any basis for regarding aspects of such behavior as sex linked.[7]

There is, it seems, no one conception of what is feminine or masculine that holds true across all cultures; there is no universal type of male or female. In every society, instead, cultural standards prescribe what is ideally male or female—and even then there is considerable variation in the actual distribution of these ideal attributes in the men and women of that society. Whatever is the appropriate personality and temperament for men and women in any society, it is acquired in the process of being socialized into a culture.

Socialization and Sex Roles

Why is it that we wrap a male infant in a blue blanket, and a female infant in a pink one? At the beginning of a child's life, we signal to ourselves and others that here is, not simply a new life, but a new male or female. Even before a child has any awareness of it, its socialization into a sex role has begun. It starts in infancy in the family, and is carried on in school; and it is supported by the mass media and developed in peer groups.

Children learn their gender identity (their cultural conception of their sex) and the appropriate sex roles well before they know anything about the biology of sex. By the age of three, apparently, children have established a firm conception of what they are, even if they are still uncertain about all the behavior and attitudes that go with being so.

Family   In the family the child learns this in so many different ways. Children learn it directly and forcefully, as when mother or father says, "Girls don't act like that," or "Boys don't cry." But they learn more of it indirectly, by the toys provided: dolls for girls, trucks, guns, and bats and balls for boys; by the forms of behavior encouraged or even tolerated: a boy is "just being a boy" if he gets mud all over himself, while a girl is expected to stay clean; and even by the way they are talked to and played with: girls are handled gently, while boys are more likely to be tossed around roughly. All the subtle cues of tone of voice and "body language"—how a child is held, for example—communicate conceptions of gender even before language skills have been developed.

School Schools, in turn, offer a more organized environment for learning sex roles. Textbooks, for example, show adults in roles traditionally linked to sex: women as teachers, nurses, librarians—and mothers; boys as doctors, lawyers, policemen—and fathers. Such *stereotyping* of the sexes reinforces the conceptions children develop early about what their gender allows them to do.

But schools provide gender training in other ways, too. They do so when they teach courses and offer activities segregated by sex: shop for boys, home economics for girls; football for boys, cheerleading for girls.

Mass Media The message is further reinforced by the mass media. Whether it is soap opera or commercials, daily television offers stereotyped conceptions of sex roles. Women are either "sex-objects" in commercials directed to men, or are dutiful, energetic housewives preferring one brand of detergent or canned soup over others because of their devotion to their family's needs.

Peer Relations Children in peer relations contribute strongly to their own socialization into gender. Since George Herbert Mead's work on socialization (see Chapter 4 again), we know that the child's world of play and games contributes significantly to their personality development. Sociologist Janet Lever has demonstrated significant gender differences in how

Socialization in activities defined as appropriate to one's sex begins at a young age.

BOYS AND GIRLS: THE GAMES THEY PLAY

The games that children play, it seems, differ by sex in ways which protect and reinforce the traditional sex-role division of American society. That is what sociologist Janet Lever discovered when she studied in detail how 181 fifth-grade children, aged 10 to 11, spent their time in play.* The children were divided evenly between suburb and city, and all of them were white and middle class.

There were six differences between boys and girls in play:

1. *Boys play outdoors far more than girls.* Boys engaged in team sports played outdoors, and went farther from home to do so. Girls preferred more activities—like playing with Barbie dolls or board games—best played indoors.

2. *Boys more often played in larger groups.* This difference, too, reflects the choice of activities—outdoor team sports and indoor doll-playing—but even when outdoors, girls played in smaller groups.

3. *Boys' play occurs in more age-heterogeneous groups.* Because boys' games sometimes require more players than are available at one age level, younger boys are allowed to join in the game—for example, boys of ages 9 to 15 or 16 playing ice hockey.

4. *Girls play more often in predominantly male games than boys play in girls' games.* Some girls, depending on their ability, played regularly on boys' baseball or basketball teams. Boys often played girls' games like hopscotch or jump-rope, but only as "teases."

5. *Boys play competitive games more often than girls.* This may be because a game like baseball is challenging and boys had much more skill to develop, while girls had reached the ceiling of skill in such activities as jump-rope; they grew bored sooner and turned to other things. But it was also the case that boys settled their quarrels more effectively and rarely allowed a dispute to interrupt a game except briefly. Girls, less experienced in handling such disputes, often quit playing when a dispute broke out.

What do these sex differences in children's play signify for adult roles? Boys, it would seem, are better prepared for work roles; they learn to be more independent, develop organizational skills, and learn to operate in rule-bounded events and to adjudicate disputes. They also become more skilled in situations demanding group interdependence and cooperative skills.

Girls, in turn, are more likely to develop socioemotional skills, function better in small, intimate groups, and are less competitive.

If this is so, the child's world of play and game helps to perpetuate different abilities for the sexes, which then serve to reinforce traditional sex roles.

Notes

* From Janet Lever, "Sex Differences in the Games Children Play," *Social Problems* 23 (April 1976): 478–487.

boys and girls play, with important consequences for their development as masculine and feminine persons (see "Boys and Girls: The Games They Play").

✳But Socialization Isn't All

Despite all the effect of deliberate socialization and gender training, it does not follow that boys and girls internalize completely the stereotyped model of being masculine and feminine. While some boys turn out closer to the masculine stereotype, others vary from it, some to quite an extent. While some girls, too, are close to the feminine stereotype, others vary considerably. There is at least substantial overlap between the sexes on most measurable attributes.

Maccoby and Jacklin's thorough analysis of the research on sex differences led them to conclude that there is far less difference between the sexes in social behavior, intellectual abilities, and motivations than has been assumed. Only four differences, they found, are really well established by the research: girls have greater verbal ability; boys possess more mathematical skill, are superior in visual-spatial ability, and are more aggressive.[8]

Other long-claimed differences between the sexes are not borne out by careful research. Girls, for example, do not seem to be more social than boys, or to be less motivated to achieve. Neither do they seem to have less self-esteem.

The findings, furthermore, did not support the idea that boys are more analytic, or that they are better at tasks that require more abstract reasoning instead of rote learning. It also may be, as the stereotype has it, that boys learn to be more competitive and dominating than girls, and that girls, in turn, learn to be more compliant and nurturing; but there is simply not enough evidence from existing research to provide answers.

We can get another perspective if we observe how men and women behave on the job. It has often been asserted that women have limited aspirations for advancement and that they create sociable peer groups (instead of competitive relations) on the job; also, that they seek more satisfaction outside of work and dream of escaping. But according to Rosabeth Moss Kanter, who studied women and men in corporations:

If women sometimes have lower aspirations, lesser involvement with work, and greater concern with peer group

relations—so do men in positions of limited or blocked mobility.[9]

The differences between men and women may often be more a consequence of their placement in social structure than of early socialization. That women occupy more of the lower positions, have less opportunity for advancement, and are more often the object of discrimination may do more to account for differences between them and most men than observations of early training in family and school.

We have something to learn from this. Women, by virtue of giving birth to and caring for children, may in fact develop differently than do men. Working in unpromotable jobs may shape their attitudes and behavior. The persons they become, therefore, are a consequence of the roles assigned them and of their place in social structures; it is not inherent in the biology of sex.

SEXUAL DOMINATION

That women may be different from men in some observable ways does not necessarily imply that they are inferior; they may, in fact, merely be different. Nonetheless, sex *differences* are always linked to the issue of sexual *domination*. And men, it would seem, always dominate.

Always? Have women ever ruled in any society? Have they ever, in some society somewhere, sometime, been the equal of men?

Domination: Men Over Women

The prevailing assumption in social science is that the answer to the above questions is a clear NO. Male domination seems to be a *universal* feature of human society. Such a presumption is based on evidence of three kinds: modern, historical, and archeological.

Modern evidence comes from an examination of all known contemporary societies, including still-existing preliterate ones which anthropologists have carefully observed. *Historical* evidence derives from all known records of literate peoples. *Archeological* evidence comes from the reconstruction of what prehistoric societies must have been like, based on the physical evidence which archeologists dig up.

Both the historical and contemporary evidence—

particularly the contemporary—give scant support for anyone's claiming evidence for a society of social equals, let alone one in which women dominate. It is true that there are societies in which women contribute more than men do to economic subsistence. There are also societies in which the descent of the family is *matrilinear,* that is, names and property descend through the mother's line. But not even in these cases are we observing a society "in which women have publicly recognized power and authority surpassing that of men."[10] All known societies, past and present, are male-dominated.

The archeological case is less certain, for here the evidence consists of interpretations of such physical remains as female burials, sculptures, and the like. A female burial, for example, might be evidence of a *matriarchy* (a female-dominated group), but it might also only be evidence of privileged women—the wives, mistresses, and concubines of male rulers. Sketchy as our knowledge of the prehistoric past is, there seems to be no convincing evidence that any societies were female-dominated.

✳ Variations in Female Power

If males have always dominated, it does not follow that women lack power altogether or have not exercised any influence. The record, to the contrary, reveals considerable variation, from little if any voice to a great deal.

Women's power and status are greater in those societies in which they have a role outside the family—particularly an economic role.[11] When they control money and goods and dominate the market, as female traders in many societies do, they have real if not dominant power. While most women in preindustrial societies contributed to the production of food, their having power depended on whether or not they *controlled* what they produced.[12] That is why women who were traders exercised more power than women who were tillers of the soil.

They can also have power if they are able to build a public sphere of their own. This can happen, for example, when men's activities take them away from the community. Among the Iroquois, according to anthropologist Judith Brown, the men engaged in hunting and warring and were gone from home for long periods. The women who were left behind worked together to produce and distribute food, decided on marriages, and basically controlled the affairs of the community.[13]

Such observations then bring us to industrial society. As industrialism developed in the Western world, it produced a society in which economy and family were separated into the household, the family sphere of women and children, and factory and office, the work sphere of men. Women lost power under such a development. Many scholars have noted, for example, that in the transition from a traditional agricultural society to an industrial one in the Third World, women lose in power and status.[14]

But Men Still Rule

Even where women have considerable power, men still have *authority* over women, that is, they have the *right* to decide a woman's actions and she must comply. Furthermore, it is always men's activities which are esteemed and valued, no matter what they are. Women have always been subject to male authority and have been culturally devalued.

In all societies there are some activities that are exclusively men's, and these are judged by both men and women as more important. That men can hunt wild game and fight wars, for which purpose women lack the needed strength, is one basis on which the claim of men to more important activity has been based. In those cases, women's work of gathering food, or cooking it, is defined as work that anyone can do and is given little esteem. Women's work seems to be least valued when women are largely confined to domestic work: preparing food and caring for children.

Yet the greater value placed on men's activities covers a wide range, well beyond the economic or that exhibiting men's superior strength. In those cases, for example, where women are the economic providers, men's leisure activities will be more esteemed. That was the case with the Tchambuli, one of Margaret Mead's three New Guinea tribes. The women were the economic providers, the men artists and specialists in ritual. Yet the women had to engage in rituals which signified they were morally and intellectually inferior to the men.

Margaret Mead said it well:

Men may cook, or weave, or dress dolls or hunt hummingbirds, but if such activities are appropriate occupations of men, then the whole society, men and women alike, votes them as important. When the same occupations are performed by women, they are regarded as less important.[15]

Explaining Male Domination

The domination of women by men is an apparent universal experience of human existence. Yet it remains unexplained. Only recently, under the stimulus of feminist scholars, has there been any attempt to provide an explanation that is essentially social, not biological, and while recognizing the fact of male domination, denies it is necessary for all time.

Let us look at three directions which such an effort at explanation has taken.

Domestic/Public That only women bear and nurse children has been used many times as a "natural" reason for women's being restricted in their activities and so made unequal to men. But anthropologist Michelle Rosaldo, while denying that this is either necessary or desirable, nonetheless theorizes that childbearing is the key to women being the "second sex."[16]

She does this by postulating an opposition of two spheres of human life, the *domestic* and the *public*. The differentiation of these two, she says, lies in the fact that "in most traditional societies, a good part of a woman's adult life is spent giving birth to and raising children . . . ."[17] Women, of necessity, become heavily absorbed in domestic activities; their economic and political activities are thereby constrained.

Men, in turn, "have no single commitment as enduring, time-consuming, and emotionally compelling —as close to seeming necessary and natural—as the relation of a woman to an infant child . . . ."[18] They are free, therefore, to form other, broader associations, to create a "public" sphere of laws, rules, and social linkages among kin groups and communities, and to engage in extra-domestic political and military activities, as well as artistic and recreational ones.

This "universal structural opposition" between domestic and public spheres means that women are most oppressed when they are confined solely to the domestic scene. They gain power when they enter the public sphere. Yet, Rosaldo says, women will never escape domination until the domestic/public opposition is minimized and each is no longer identified with only one sex. It is not enough for women to enter the work world, for "men who in the past have committed their lives to public achievement will recognize women as true equals only when men themselves help to raise new generations by taking on the responsibilities of the home."[19]

Man: Hunter and Warrior Only men, anthropologists have long argued, had the physical strength to hunt large animals or to fight to defend against attacks. The issue is not men's contribution to providing food, but the fact that these are skills which only men can acquire, and from which they gain a basis for establishing a claim to male domination. Anyone, it is believed, can do what women do, but only men can develop the special skills to perform these demanding tasks.

Hunting was usually a group activity, not an individual one, so hunting helped to create a community. Women as gatherers and gardeners usually worked individually, producing food for their own family. But hunters produced food for the whole community and developed the authority to decide on how the food was to be shared in the community.

In the same way, men as warriors developed skills in fighting which emphasized what came to be prized qualities: not only strength and stamina, but bravery and daring, the ability to lead and command, thus to be authoritative, and the assuming of responsibility for the safety of others, especially women and children.

The basic point of this thesis about the origins of male domination is that, besides physical strength, no other natural talent or ability distinguished male from female. Women were not naturally inferior to men, but neither did they have any special talent to offset the advantage that superior physical strength gave to men and which they could elaborate into a logic and ideology of male domination.

Woman/Mother, Man/Hunter-Warrior Man as hunter and warrior is not a direct contradiction of Rosaldo's theory of the opposition of domestic and public spheres, though she does not emphasize men's physical attributes. Rosaldo's theory stresses the demand on women to bear and care for children as a domestic confinement; the other stresses, in complementary fashion, men's unique capacity to hunt and defend. Each stresses how a biological endowment was socially developed and culturally interpreted in order to bring about a human possibility, male domination, but which is no longer, if it ever was, a social necessity. A fuller theory will undoubtedly encompass both perspectives.

The Coercion of Women   Any theory to explain the origins of male domination must give attention to a harsher aspect: the capacity and willingness of men to physically coerce women. Greater physical strength is also a greater capacity for violence.

The feminist, Juliet Mitchell, argues that:

historically it is women's lesser capacity for violence as well as for work, that has determined her subordination . . . . *Social coercion* has interplayed with the straightforward division of labor, based on biological capacity, to a much greater extent than is generally admitted.[20]

If men used their superior strength to protect women, they did so because they regarded women as their *property*. Early men *exchanged* women as easily as they did other things. Claude Lévi-Strauss, following a long line of anthropologists studying kinship, insists that the exchange of women is the most elementary of all forms of exchange, preceding the exchange of goods, and that kinship and society began with the social relations established among men by the first coercive exchange of women between those men.[21]

In most past human societies, women have not been free to choose their husbands. Instead, they have been exchanged or "given" by father or brother in arrangements which were primarily political or economic. When primitive men exchanged sisters, they created alliances among tribes; when peasant families arranged marriages, they protected and enhanced the family's economic status. Not even the daughters of kings have been exempt from this process.

The evidence that marriages were always exchanges of property is expressed in such ancient practices as the *bride-price* and in the *dowry,* the worldly goods the bride brought to the marriage.

A theoretical account of male domination, then, surely must take account of the exchange of women. The anthropologist, Gayle Rubin, insists that it would have to be a central issue:

Traditional concerns of anthropology and social science —such as the evolution of social stratification and the origin of the state—must be reworked to include the implications of matrilateral cross-cousin marriage, surplus extracted in the form of daughters, the conversion of female labor into male wealth, the conversion of female lives into marriage alliances, the contribution of marriage to political power, and the transformation which all of these varied aspects of society have undergone in the course of time.[22]

WOMEN IN AMERICAN SOCIETY

A cigarette marketed for women has in its advertising long popularized a slogan: "You've come a long way, Baby." Women in the United States have come a long way from the world of their mothers and grandmothers. But they are far short of reaching equality with men. And for women who are also black, there is a double disadvantage (see "Black and Female: The Double Negative").

Their advancement can be measured in gains in education, in greater participation in the labor force, in getting into occupations once restricted to men, and in the legal measures (both laws and court decisions) which have given women the legal basis for equal status with men in a wide range of educational and work situations.

Persistence of Sexual Inequality

Yet the historic inequalities between the sexes persist strongly into the present. If women have gained considerably in jobs, they have had but little success in reaching the income levels of men. If women have moved into employment in greater numbers, they still lack equality at work: they get paid less, are promoted less, and must often endure sexual harassment from male workers.

It is, however, not only in fairly objective evidence from women's experiences in the economy that the persistence of inequality is evident. It is evident also in whether men and women—especially women—continue to accept the sexual stereotype that has been so basic in the socialization of both sexes.

These stereotypes, to be sure, have come under challenge, but they have not been abandoned, not even by women. Many men and women continue to believe that men excel in ways which women can never match: in aggressiveness and independence; in ambition and ability to lead or command.

Are Women Less Ambitious?   The stereotype of women as less ambitious, less committed to success,

BLACK AND FEMALE: THE DOUBLE NEGATIVE

To be female instead of male is to be disadvantaged in American society; but so is it to be black instead of white. To be both, *to be a black woman,* is to carry the burden of a double negative.

There is ample evidence that black women pay a price for their disadvantaged status. They earn, on the average, less than either black men or white women do. They earn less than black men even when they are as well educated, do comparable work, are as experienced, and work as many hours. Poorly educated black women are the most economically disadvantaged of all.

Yet the earnings gap between males and females is less for blacks than for whites, and black women still exceed black men in education, even at the college level (in contrast to whites). Furthermore, black women constitute a larger proportion of the black professional community than do white women of white professionals.

Because of what racism has done to prevent so many black men from gaining steady employment and an adequate income, black women have long been used to holding jobs as well as to being mothers. The sex-role stereotype so prevalent among whites—strong, assertive men who are family providers and passive, nurturing women who are homemakers—has never applied to the same extent in the black community. There women are socialized to make a strong role in the family, to be resourceful, to be strong and independent persons, to be *doers.* The survival of their families often required it.

Perhaps that is why middle-class black women have been so much more successful than white women in utilizing higher education to gain status in an economic realm still dominated by white men.

For the majority of black women, though, the double negative remains their lot; as blacks and as women they are doubly disadvantaged in earning a living; far more of them end up as the sole parent working to support their children.

Notes

Sources: Joyce Ladner, *Tomorrow's Tomorrow: The Black Women* (New York: Doubleday, 1971); Carol B. Stack, *All Our Kin: Strategies for Survival in a Black Community* (New York: Harper & Row, 1974); Cynthia Fuchs Epstein, "Positive Effects of the Multiple Negative: Explaining the Success of Black Professional Women," *American Journal of Sociology* 78 (January 1973): 912–935; Donald Tremain and Kermit Terrell, "Sex and the Process of Status Attainment: A Comparison of Working Men and Women," *American Sociological Review* 40 (April 1975); 174–200.

persists even as women in large numbers turn to education and careers. Perhaps, because of that very fact, the idea gets greater currency.

An example of that is the wide dissemination of one psychological study of college women which claimed to find that women possessed "a stable, enduring personality characteristic" identified as "a mo-

tive to avoid success."[23] In the three or four years after its publication it became widely cited—and often by women—in the psychological and sociological literature, as well as in more popular literature, such as *Ms., Psychology Today,* and *The New York Times Magazine.*

Yet several efforts to replicate the study by others

Women are more and more to be found in occupations once restricted to men.

failed; comparable female populations seemed not to respond in the manner reported in the original study. The authors of one attempt identified what they regarded as technical flaws in the design of the original study and criticized the readiness of so many scholars to accept the research as authoritative.[24]

It is not at all unlikely that women conditioned to believe in their own inferiority may have doubts and anxieties about their capacity to succeed in a man's world. But that is not the same as possessing a "stable, enduring personality characteristic" which programs them to fail.

Women's Changing Perspective

Most women no longer fully accept the traditional stereotype of what women should be and do, but neither have all of them abandoned it entirely for a feminist ideology. They are caught between their roles in the family and those in the labor force.

A national sample of women in late 1970 found that three-fourths of all women still accepted the conventional sexual division as legitimate—men at work, women at home with children.[25] They agreed with the statement:

It is much better for everyone involved if the man is the achiever outside the home and the woman takes care of the home and the family.

However, a substantially smaller number—40 percent of the white women and 51 percent of the black women—agreed with the statement:

Women are much happier if they stay at home and take care of their children.

In addition, half of the white women and slightly more than half of the black women agreed that:

A woman should not let bearing and rearing children stand in the way of a career if she wants it.

Furthermore, 95 percent of the women believed in equal pay for equal work and two-thirds of them supported equal job opportunities for women.

What such a survey gives us is a picture of women's changing perspectives, not yet wholly consistent, and their contradictory feelings about old, familiar roles and new opportunities. During the 1970s, furthermore, changes in women's attitudes continued, and at a faster pace, toward an egalitarian position.

A comparison and analysis of several different studies revealed an especially strong increase from 1970 to 1974 in these attitudes:[26]

1. The obligations of husbands to share housework with wives (from 56 percent to 79 percent).
2. The right of women to keep their jobs while bearing children (from 50 percent to 83 percent).
3. The rights of women to be considered for a top job on an equal footing with men (from 67 percent to 84 percent).

There has also been a sharp decline (from about 70 percent down to 50 percent) among women who believe that a working mother is harmful for children.

While college-educated women are more egalitarian than others, these changes in the attitudes of women proceeded at about the same pace for all women, college and noncollege, since 1960.

By the middle 1970s there had already emerged in the United States a remarkably strong egalitarian, feminist perspective. More importantly, there is evidence that:

women's attitudes toward their roles in the home have become increasingly related to their attitudes toward their rights in the labor market since the rise of the women's movement . . . . However, whether caused by the movement or not, this change suggests that U.S. women's outlooks are converging with those of the movement's leaders.[27]

Women in the Labor Force   Women have entered the job market in ever larger numbers in the United States. To do so, they have had to break down barriers to their employment and to overcome the idea that married women should stay at home and raise children. But they have found that inequality between the sexes still persists. They have gained entry to the world of work, but not on equal terms.

The Earnings Gap   Women do not earn as much for their work as men do. As Table 12.1 shows, the gap between men's and women's incomes has remained remarkably stable for over two decades. Women get about 60 percent of what men do.

		TABLE 12.1 Differentials in Male and Female Income, 1955–1977		
Year	Women	Men	Earnings Gap	Women's Earnings as a Percent of Men's
1955	$2,719	$ 4,252	$1,533	63.9
1960	3,292	5,417	2,124	50.8
1965	3,823	6,375	2,552	60.0
1970	5,323	8,966	3,543	59.4
1975	7,504	12,758	5,254	58.8
1976	8,099	13,455	5,356	60.2
1977	8,618	14,626	6,008	58.9

Source: U.S. Department of Labor, *The Earnings Gap Between Women and Men,* 1979, Table 1, p. 6.

TABLE 12.2 Cumulative Earnings Distribution, by Sex, 1977		
Income	Women (percentage)	Men (percentage)
Less than $7,000	32.2	11.3
Less than $10,000	63.0	23.9
Less than $15,000	90.3	51.6
Less than $25,000	99.1	87.0
More than $25,000	00.9	13.0

Source: U.S. Department of Labor, *The Earnings Gap Between Women and Men*, 1979, Table 2, p. 7.

More compelling evidence comes from the data in Table 12.2. Almost one-third of all employed women in 1977 earned less than $7,000, and almost two-thirds of them earned less than $10,000. While 90 percent of women earned under $15,000, only slightly more than half the men did so. At the upper end, less than one percent of the women earned over $25,000, compared to 13 percent of the men.

The earnings gap may average about 60 percent, but there are notable deviations from that average. In some professional fields the gap is much smaller. Female health professionals in 1977, for example, earned 90.5 percent of what men did; computer specialists, 80.3 percent; engineering and science technicians, 76.4 percent; and teachers, 75.8 percent.[28]

The larger gap is between the self-employed, where women earn only 34.3 percent of what men earn, and between sales workers, where women are paid only 42.5 percent of what men are paid.

Why Do Women Earn Less? There are some logical reasons why women earn less than men do, but these are not sufficient to account for the earnings gap. Because so many women have entered the labor force so recently, they have less work experience and com-

mand fewer skills. Nor are they yet the equivalent of men in educational credentials, at least at the level where education counts the most. As recently as 1977 there were substantially fewer female college graduates—for persons 25 years and older, 12.4 percent of the white women, 20.2 percent of the white men.[29] (This sex differential did not apply to blacks, but they were a much smaller percentage of college graduates.)

But earnings are also affected by the occupation into which women go. While 64 percent of women in 1979 were in white-collar jobs, as Table 12.3 shows, more than half of them were in clerical jobs. Many fewer of them, furthermore, were managers and administrators. Similarly, more women than men were in service jobs (where pay is traditionally low), while far more men are in blue-collar jobs, where pay standards are better than in service jobs and often equal to or even better than many white-collar ones.

If these are some good reasons for women not to earn as much as men, there is not, however, reason for the gap in earnings to be as great as it is. In a recent study, sociologists David Feathermen and Robert Hauser concluded that, even accounting for those factors that would make income differences logical, there remains a large difference which represents inequality of opportunity, or "discrimination." "Discrimination accounts for 85% of the earnings gap in 1962 and 84% in 1973."[30]

Women, Children, and Work

At one time in the United States most women worked for a few years after leaving school, then left the labor force when they married and had children. As recently as the mid-1970s, we saw above, fully half the American women believed that a working woman could not properly care for young children. Even that figure, however, is a sharp drop from only 1970, suggesting that a major shift in attitudes is under way.

Such changes in attitudes accompany a rapid increase in the participation of women in the labor force. Half (51 percent) of women 16 and over were in the labor force in 1979 (see "Women in the Labor Force") and almost two-thirds of women between ages 20 and 54.

But what is significant is the increase in the number of married women with children who are not employed: 39 percent with children under six, 56 percent

While many more women have entered the labor force, large numbers of them still earn much less than men do. This is particularly true for women in traditional female jobs, such as sewing machine operator.

TABLE 12.3 Occupational Distribution, by Sex, November, 1979		
Occupational Categories	Men (percentage)	Women (percentage)
White-collar	41.4	64.1
Professional and Technical	15.1	16.0
Managerial and Administrative	14.1	06.4
Sales	05.9	06.9
Clerical	06.2	34.7
Blue-collar	46.1	14.9
Service Workers	08.5	19.7
Farm Workers	04.1	01.3

Source: U.S. Department of Labor, Bureau of Labor Statistics, *Employment and Earnings* 26, no. 11 (November, 1979), Table A-22, p. 35.

WOMEN IN THE LABOR FORCE

Over the past 40 years there has been a steady increase in women's labor-force participation.

1. *More and more women are now employed.* Women age 16 and over in the labor force numbered:

- 27 percent in 1940
- 35 percent in 1960
- 51 percent in 1979

In 1979, 69 percent of women aged 20–24 were in the labor force and 64 percent of women aged 25–54,

2. *Working women are no longer primarily young and/or single.* In 1940 slightly under 15 percent of married women (husbands present) were employed. In 1977, 47 percent of such women were; the figure was 54 percent for women aged 25–44.

3. *More married women with children are employed.* In 1950 only 12 percent of married women (husband present) with children under age 6 had jobs; only 28 percent with children aged 6 to 17. By 1977 employed women with children numbered as follows:

married (husband present):	
with children under 6	39 percent
with children aged 6 to 17	56 percent
divorced:	
with children under 6	66 percent
with children aged 6 to 17	82 percent

Notes

Source: *Statistical Abstract of the United States, 1978,* p. 404; U.S. Department of Labor, Bureau of Labor Statistics, *Employment and Earnings* 26, no. 11 (November 1979): Table A-4, p. 23.

with children aged 6 to 17. When we notice that a large majority of divorced women with children are also employed—over 80 percent, for example, of those with children aged 6 to 17—then we come to recognize that in the future women in the United States will continue to hold a job even as they choose to be mothers. The breach between childbearing and employment has now been broken, even as it already has in most other industrial societies.

Women in a Man's World

For college-educated women, seeking not so much a job as a career, the business world and the profes-

sions are still male-dominated. The discrimination exercised is usually more subtle but no less real in its consequences. We now take a brief look at three different situations women face in seeking to overcome sexual inequality.

Women and Authority   In a bureaucratized society, to succeed and win a high position means to have power over others and to possess authority. Though women have now become an integral part of the labor force, they are still underrepresented in positions of supervisory authority. In 1979, for example, men still outnumbered women in managerial and administrative positions better than two to one—14.1 percent for men, only 6.4 percent for women (see Table 12.3). There are fewer women, furthermore, as one moves up the ladder of authority; very few women are to be found at the top levels of major corporations.

This imbalance holds even for those professions where women easily outnumber men (nurses, librarians, schoolteachers, social workers). Women are much less likely to occupy positions of authority even when they are the equal of men in education and occupational status.

Such a discrepancy might be explained in three ways: (1) women have fewer qualifications; (2) some women, not having been socialized to be leaders, lack confidence in themselves and avoid positions of authority; or (3) male employers believe that women are unsuitable for supervisory positions and act accordingly.

Little is known about this process, for it has been little studied. One preliminary study, based on a sample of individuals at about age 37, concluded that: (1) women are less qualified than men, though this is the least important of the three factors; (2) women's attitudes about themselves are of greater significance; but (3) "the behaviors and policies of employers are much more important in the restriction of females from positions of authority."[31]

Professional Women: The Double Bind   Women have now begun to move rapidly into such professions as medicine, where in only the recent past they were rare. But once into professional training, they find themselves in a predominantly male world, one which subtly creates a "discriminatory environment." It is discriminatory because it is a traditionally masculine profession and its role expectations are built up around sexual stereotypes; in medicine, for example, a good physician should be assertive, egoistic, and independent—these are assumed to be masculine traits. Women, if they are typically feminine, are presumed not to possess such characteristics.

A study of the response of a medical faculty to the presence of female students found that many male faculty doubted the "pay off" of training women; as one put it: "I just have a feeling that we get considerably less working years out of women."[32]

The male faculty, and male medical students, too, put the female student in a *double bind*. As a *professional,* she is expected to be committed to her work, but as a *woman* she is expected to give priority to the

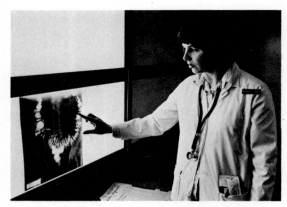

A woman in medicine is in a double bind; as a professional she is expected to be committed to her work, but as a woman she is expected to give priority to the needs of her husband and children.

needs of her husband and children. Men disapprove if women are hindered from a full professional commitment, but they also disapprove of their allowing work to interfere with family duties. One female student reported that during an admissions interview, she was asked: "Won't this interfere with your husband's career? You should be home with your child."[33]

Changes in the structure of medicine—the shift to group practice and the increased need for physicians in institutional settings (e.g., college clinics)—have created new roles which many males in medicine see as particularly appropriate for females. The work hours tend to be restricted to a regular schedule, thus allowing full attention to the family. That seems to make women acceptable to men in the profession. One female student described it thus:

> I've learned that you're supposed to say that you want to have children because that's normal. And you're supposed to have plans set up and assume that you'll work in group practice. And you're supposed to say that you'll wait until you're out (to have children) and you'll go into a field like pathology where you'll have good hours.[34]

Males also seem to think that women are better suited to certain kinds of patients, such as children (pediatrics) and women (obstetrics-gynecology).

The male-dominated environment of a medical school subtly pressures women to make choices in their career plans; it "channels" them to choose those "comfort zones" where they feel welcome, comfortable, and competent.

These subtle pressures have already created a distribution of physicians among medical specialities which differ considerably by sex. Women have chosen pediatrics, for example, three times as often as men have. They have chosen anesthesiology, pathology, and psychiatry twice as often, and public health two and a half times as often. Men, in turn, have chosen surgery, the specialty highest in prestige and income, three times as often as women; the margin of six to one in obstetrics-gynecology, which accounts for two-thirds of all female surgeons, is excepted.[35]

It is surgeons, both young as well as old, who express the greatest opposition to women in medicine, some venting outright hostility. A female student describes her experience:

. . . I had a bunch of residents who really did not appreciate women. They just plain don't think you belong. You're a foreigner. In a way you're not even there. That's very distressing. The residents I had, they were of the opinion that women couldn't do surgery, because they didn't have the stamina which is ridiculous. They kind of changed their minds by the time I was finished because obviously I could keep up with them.[36]

The Token Woman   The first woman accepted into a hitherto all-male work group becomes a *token,* identified primarily because she differs from the others, not in ability or in acceptance of work norms, but in some ascribed characteristic; in this case, gender. Sociologist Rosabeth Moss Kanter studied a group of such women who were the first to be hired and trained as saleswomen for a large industrial corporation.[37]

At the outset a token woman is highly visible, but what everyone notices is that she is a woman, not whether she is competent. As a consequence, she has to work twice as hard to prove her competence. Yet in doing that, she risks making the men look bad, which evokes retaliation.

One woman had trouble understanding this and complained of her treatment by managers. They had fired another woman for not being aggressive enough, she reported; yet she, who succeeded in doing all they asked and had brought in the largest amount of new business during the past year, was criticized for being too aggressive, too much of a hustler.[38]

In contrast to such overachievement, a more common response is to limit visibility by keeping a low profile. Such a woman downplays her sex, says little at meetings, and avoids too much exposure. But to her disadvantage, she also limits recognition for competence. What has so often been called "fear of success" in women may really be a fear of visibility.

When a token woman joins the group, men are suddenly aware of how much their male world is now threatened. They reassert their solidarity as men in several ways: by sexual teasing and innuendo, and by stories of their success with women; and by interrupting women with questions or apologies about whether such things as swearing, having a drink, or telling a joke are still permitted.

But men also exclude women from conversation when they confide they are looking for another job, talk office politics, or exchange ideas about getting around the rules. Yet the token woman is expected to demonstrate her loyalty. This she could do by allowing the men to make jokes about women without objecting, even when she feels insulted, and to accept kidding.

Then, too, the token woman has to run the risk of falling into four *role traps,* each of which would put her into a category convenient to men but would hurt her chances to perform well or to be given full credit for her competence. They are:

1. *Mother,* who gives comfort and to whom men bring their troubles.
2. *Seductress,* who becomes a sexual object but arouses resentment and jealousy.
3. *Pet,* who is treated as cute and amusing and complimented lavishly for displaying a competence typical for any man.
4. *Iron maiden,* the woman who successfully avoids the first three, but is trapped into appearing tougher and more militant than she is.

The Next Phase   For women who seek rewarding careers in business and the professions, there are now some difficult problems: that of gaining positions of authority, the double bind, and the role of token woman. These are problems that come *after* the legal provisions for equal opportunity have enabled woman to gain entry into what once were exclusively male domains.

When that occurs, the struggle for sexual equality simply moves to a second, more difficult phase. It is this that challenges what are often too simple ideas about achieving equality between the sexes and which force feminists to examine more closely the problems of sexual stereotypes and sex roles based on the division of labor between home and work. But that requires that we take a brief look at the feminist movement.

THE FEMINIST MOVEMENT: TOWARD SEXUAL EQUALITY

When women's struggle for equality took a more militant form and something called "women's liberation" came upon the scene, most men (and probably most women, too) thought that such a revolt of women against their traditional sex role was something new in American history. But it was not.

The struggle for women's rights, in fact, has deep roots. In Italy, for example, where women attended universities in the fourteenth and fifteenth centuries, they demanded equality of rights. As early as 1499 women in England petitioned for the right to vote. In London in 1790 Mary Wollstonecroft published her remarkable book, *Vindication of the Rights of Women.*

The American and French Revolutions, which advanced the cause of human rights and democratic government, only further added to women's claims to equality. During the American Revolution, for example, Abigail Adams wrote to her husband, John Adams, a member of the Continental Congress (and a future President of the United States):

> in the new code of laws . . . I desire you would remember the ladies and be more generous and favorable to them than were your ancestors. Do not put such unlimited power into the hands of husbands. Remember all men would be tyrants if they could. If particular care and attention are not paid to the ladies we are determined to foment a rebellion and will not hold ourselves bound to obey any laws in which we have no voice or representation.

But the women in that period were not in a position to foment rebellion. The feminist spirit was still largely restricted to a small group of women who were educated and middle or upper class. It was not until women's active involvement in social reforms in the early nineteenth century, and particularly in the movement to abolish slavery, that a firmer grounding for a

women's movement was established. And even then, it was still a movement of educated, middle-class women.[39]

Feminism and Abolition

The period of the 1830s and 1840s was one of ferment and change in a still young and developing United States. Utopian communities thrived, religious revivals swept the country, and a movement for the abolition of slavery began. A small but active number of middle-class women played a major role in these reform efforts.

They did so by using their acceptable involvement in church activities. Because so much of the reform efforts of that time drew inspiration from religious sentiments, women were able to get actively involved in various movements, especially the movement to abolish slavery.

But when female abolitionists were rebuked for being so outspoken (instead of "private and unobtrusive"), their consciousness of their lack of rights made them into feminists. The Grimke sisters of South Carolina were but two of the feminists who emerged from the abolition movement to act for women's rights. When some male abolitionists asked them to put off their struggle until slavery had been abolished, the sisters responded: ". . . what can woman do for slaves when she herself is under the feet of man and shamed into silence?"

The feminist consciousness aroused by women's participation in the antislavery struggle led to a national meeting in Seneca Falls, New York, in 1848, where 300 women and men issued a *Declaration of Sentiments,* a plea for ending the inequality of women in all aspects of life.

The Second Phase: Suffrage

After the Civil War women joined in forming an Equal Rights Association to promote the interests of both women and the new black "freedmen." They had hoped the Fourteenth Amendment (1868) would be extended to include women's rights, but soon they knew it would not. So, in 1869, the renowned Susan B. Anthony and other women's advocates formed the National Women's Suffrage Association. A second phase of the women's struggle in the United States was underway: the struggle to win the right to vote.

There was a point to focusing on a single issue. Since the Seneca Falls meeting in 1848, the idea of women's voting seemed a less radical concept and began to win wider support. It no longer seemed to be an assault upon the family and women's "place," but instead, a way to bring women's moral influence on government. To those concerned with social reform, the vote was a way to mobilize the female half of the population in support of child-labor laws and laws for better working conditions in factories. Then, too, women armored with the right to vote seemed to be a good starting place to assault the legally sanctioned discrimination against women.

In 1919, fifty years after the formation of the first suffragist group in 1869, a suffrage amendment finally passed the Congress. A year later, on August 26, 1920, having been ratified by 37 states, the Nineteenth Amendment became a part of the federal Constitution.

But passage of women's suffrage brought little of the changes hoped for by its advocates.[40] Though women were increasingly active in civic affairs, they also remained primarily in the home as wives and mothers.

The suffragists underestimated how much a victory in one area could lead to victory in others. They mistakenly anticipated that women would vote as a solid bloc, regardless of class and ethnic divisions. Also, they were simply wrong in thinking that suffrage would encourage women to fight for economic equality. Both the still-powerful traditional socialization of women and the reality of the existing distribution of sex roles were too much to be overcome simply by giving women the vote. The basic structure of the sexual division of labor remained unchanged.

The Third Phase: Women's Liberation

The sexual division of labor, which put women in the home, without an economic role, was only fully realized in the late nineteenth century, with the advance of industrialization. In all prior agrarian economies, women had essential economic tasks.

Leaving the Labor Force In the first days of industrialization, early capitalists did not hesitate to hire both women and children, for many of the new machine-tending jobs required no particular skill nor any great amount of strength. The horror of conditions under which children particularly, but women too, labored in mills and factories (and children in mines) brought on a powerful humanitarian movement to control or even eliminate their labor.[41]

Working men and their labor unions also joined in that struggle in order to eliminate women and children as lowly paid labor whose competition for jobs often undercut their own wage standards. They strongly supported protective labor legislation introduced to protect women's maternal status—restrictions on women's working hours, for example, or provisions to protect their health.

The political struggle over such legislation often pulled feminists in two directions and split them into opposing camps. In 1923, for example, the League of Women Voters opposed an early version of the Equal Rights Amendment, which would specifically have eliminated special legislation for women; the League contended that such legislation was needed to protect women. The National Women's Party, which proposed the amendment, argued that such legislation merely served to exclude women from better-paying jobs. (The argument that the present Equal Rights Amendment would deprive women of needed protective legislation has been one of the major arguments made by anti-ERA spokespersons.)

Coming Back In From 1920 to 1940, women's place in the economy changed but little, but the onset of World War II brought them into industry in large numbers to replace men conscripted for military service. There they soon demonstrated their capacity to learn quickly and carry out competently such skilled jobs as welding and riveting; "Rosie the Riveter" became the World War II symbol of women's economic contribution.

Though women had to give way to men after the war, they did not, in fact, fully return to domestic duties. Instead, women's share of the labor market increased steadily, and, as we saw, by 1970 even married women with children were more and more holding down jobs. The release of women from confinement to the home was a basic factor in creating the necessary conditions for a new, broad-based movement to arise.

There was also another factor—the steady decline in fertility rates in this as in all industrial societies. As a trend, it began over 200 years ago and is based on the recognition that in industrial societies children are not an economic asset. But the trend reached a critical level in this century. By the 1960s women were marrying later, delaying the birth of their first child, and planning to have fewer children. By the mid-1970s most young women planned to have no more than two children.

The Origins of a Movement If these were the necessary conditions for a new feminist movement, there still needed to be the more immediate circumstances that would crystallize women's diffuse, unorganized discontent into collective action. That came with the black civil rights protest that began in the 1960s and the antiwar actions that ended the decade. The question of basic human rights for blacks, for protesting youth, for the poor, indeed, for all minorities, created an egalitarian climate. In such a climate, according to sociologist Joan Huber, "women's awareness that the ideology of equal opportunity did not apply to them helped to precipitate the Women's Movement."[42]

Many young women in the 1960s joined fully in the radical activities of the New Left, only to discover that radical men were no more committed to sexual equality than were other men. Frustrated by the secondary roles handed them, and by the refusal of male leaders even to consider women's problems—while giving consideration to the problems of almost every other disadvantaged group—radical women moved off and soon were actively shaping a new radical feminism.[43]

Even before that, a more reformist branch of the movement began with the appointment by President Kennedy in 1961 of a President's Commission on the Status of Women. Its 1963 report, *American Women,* provided ample documentation of the denial of rights and opportunities for women.

When equal rights for women was included in Title VII of the Civil Rights Act of 1964, it seemed like a major step forward; but at first the Equal Employment Opportunity Commission (EEOC) ignored the provision altogether. The frustration in trying to get the law enforced led to the formation of the National Organization of Women (NOW) in 1966, a group that concentrated on extending women's rights, especially economic, and became a major force is support of the ERA.

Though today's feminist movement has no one dominant organization, and is marked by both radical and reformist emphases, it has, through its decentral-

ized, pluralist nature, enabled women to sustain a quite varied range of activities modifying the male-shaped environment around them. In a remarkably short period of time, women have redefined their sense of themselves as human beings and have committed themselves to equal rights and status in all spheres of society. Most women will now work for all of their adult lives. For college-educated women, the commitment to a professional or business career becomes central to their lives, not temporary or secondary.

Beyond Equal Opportunity

Even as women made good their claim to equal opportunity in jobs and schooling, they are nonetheless coming to recognize that sexual equality is still some distance away. They have not yet, for example, significantly narrowed the earnings gap. Furthermore, they have been denied positions of authority, channeled into "female" specialities in some professions, and suffered the dilemmas and pressures of being the "token" woman.

Each of these, presumably, are matters capable of being changed. But the effort to do so may mark a new and more difficult dimension of the process of changing sex roles; more difficult, because new demands here will encroach even further upon a diminishing turf long crucial to the male sense of masculinity.

But beyond those matters lies an even more basic one. Women have discovered that liberation from confinement to domestic roles has not, however, freed them from the burdens of housework and child care. Even as they work full-time, they remain almost full-time mothers and wives. Yet as far back as 1970 a majority of women had expressed the desire that men share their domestic duties. Sociologist Joan Huber made the point sharply:

> That women can bear children is, to date, a fact of nature, but that women are assigned the responsibility of rearing children is a man-made fact subject to change. Even though no man has a womb, it is now technologically possible for men to share equally in the important and delicate task of socializing the next generation.[44]

It is the responsibility for child care that will be ultimately decisive for woman's fate as the second sex or as the equal of man.

Part 5

INSTITUTIONS AND SOCIAL STRUCTURE

. . . [the family] simply cannot meet the pressure of being the only refuge in a brutal society.

Eli Zaretsky

Thirteen

THE FAMILY

Throughout the ages the family has been a fundamental social institution at the core of society. It has been called a cornerstone of society, credited with being a primary force for controlling behavior and civilizing the human animal, and viewed as a source of morality and decent conduct.

But when people talk loftily about the family, they really often mean the historic Western family, as it developed in Europe, and perhaps only the middle-class Western family, at that. Yet this is only one form of family among many. Anthropologists tell us that what may properly be called *family* is found worldwide in a varied set of forms.

THE UNIVERSALITY OF THE FAMILY

The family can be found in all known human societies, although not in the same form. According to anthropologist George P. Murdock, there is always a basic kinship group which provides for (1) permission of sexual access between adults, (2) legitimate reproduction, (3) responsibility for the care and upbringing of children, and (4) cooperation as an economic unit, at least in consumption.[1]

Apparently most social scientists agree that these four activities are of great importance in all human societies; they regulate and control in some stable manner the relationships of the sexes and provide for mating in order to reproduce. This is true even among so-called "primitives." But these same social scientists do not agree that it is always the same group which carries out these activities, or even in all cases that it is a kinship group.

The Family as a Group

Social scientists disagree also with Murdock's claim that the *nuclear* family of husband, wife, and children is *universally* the kinship unit by which these basic activities are carried out. There are well-known examples of societies in which at least some activities are carried out by other groups, some kinship-based, but some not.

In an Israeli *kibbutz* the mother-father unit does not raise and train the children alone; this is a communal responsibility. The *kibbutz,* according to anthropologist Melford Spiro, "can function without the family because it functions as if it, itself, were a family; and it can so function because its members perceive each other as kin, in the psychological implications of that term."[2] In China (at least prior to 1949) and in many traditional, preindustrial societies, cooperation as an economic unit and also the care of children have been carried on within an *extended* family group (one that includes more than the nuclear family).

Although the nuclear family is widespread, it is not, apparently, universal. Among the Nayar of India, for example, the resident family group consists of brother, sister, and sister's children. The father of the children resides elsewhere and is not part of the family as a group, though he is part of the institutional arrangement for mating and procreation.

Anthropological research shows us, in short, that no *one* form of human group must exist to carry out these activities, therefore, no *one* of them is universal.

The Family as Institution

To understand what is universal about the family we need to make a distinction between the family as an *institution* and the family as a *social group*. All societies work out ways to assure the reproduction, maintenance, socialization, and placement of the young.

1. *Reproduction.* Marriage sanctions a sexual union that leads to procreation and to a legitimate status for the new member of society.
2. *Maintenance.* In whatever way, there must be someone assigned to provide care for the human young, who is dependent for a longer period of time than any other animal.
3. *Socialization.* Also, someone (or several) must teach both the skills and norms essential for participation in society. Even though much learning does occur outside of any family group, particularly in modern society, socialization is still a primary family function.
4. *Placement.* Legitimacy of birth provides for a stable process of placement in society, by *inheritance* of property, *succession* of status, and *descent,* that is, placement at birth in ethnic, kinship, or even religious groups.

It is this *institutional* process that is *universal.* There is a range of group structures by which this can be done and to which the label, *family,* can be attached. As a social group, the family is a small, kinship-based, interacting unit (nuclear or extended), within which at least some of these familial functions are carried out.

Variations in the Family

An appreciation of just how varied in form the family can be is an essential element in a sociological perspective of the family, even if one's concern is only with the American nuclear family. What follows is a brief notation of some of the variations.

Mate-Selection   In any society mate-selection is never a chance procedure, but only in some societies is there a notion of romantic love as a basis for a *free* choice of mates by the individuals themselves. In a large number of traditional, agrarian societies, mate-selection has been a prerogative of the family. These are often crucial and complex decisions for families, involving many economic and status interests, since inheritance of position and property may be associated with marriage.

In addition, the selection process in most societies is also governed by rules of *endogamy* and *exogamy* (see "The Terminology of Kinship"). In traditional societies, such rules are formally prescribed. In modern societies there are few formal requirements, yet there are powerful informal expectations of endogamy and exogamy that often influence how young people make their choices. Race and religion are the most obvious examples of these, particularly race, for interracial marriages have long been forbidden by law in some states of the United States. (Recently, these laws were invalidated by the Supreme Court.) Yet the strength of these endogamous rules does not rely on law but on widely diffused cultural expectations.

Forms of Marriage   While the Western form of marriage is *monogamy,* many societies in the world have practiced *polygamy.* In polygamous societies for a man to marry several women means to be able to support them and their children and, consequently, can serve as an index of status and wealth. The lot of the common man is to be able to afford but one wife.

In the United States and some other Western societies, marriage, divorce, and remarriage (sometimes several times) is now so common that many observers have noted that this is a departure from traditional monogamy—"until death do us part"—and might be labeled *serial monogamy.*

Rules of Authority and Descent   Wherever the male is dominant and holds the authority of the family, the family is *patriarchal.* This is the Western tradition. Usually closely associated with this is a *patrilineal* tracing of descent through the male side of the family. Inheritance of name and property, for example, is frequently patrilineal.

But there are also rules of descent that are neither matrilineal or patrilineal. The tracing of descent may be *bilateral,* as it is, though imperfectly, in American society—imperfectly, because we are patrilineal in

THE TERMINOLOGY OF KINSHIP

Choice of Partners

Endogamy: marriage partners chosen from *within* a group: tribe, community, religious group, and so on.
Exogamy: marriage partner chosen from *without* a group—clan, tribe, kinship group, and so on.

Forms of Marriage

Monogamy: one man to one woman.
Polygamy: a plurality of mates.
  Polygyny: a man has several wives.
  Polyandry: a woman has several husbands.

Rules of Authority, Descent, and Residence

Patriarchal: authority held by the father.
  Patrilineal: descent (names, property) through father's line.
  Patrilocal: newly married couple reside with husband's parents.
Matriarchal: authority held by the mother.
  Matrilineal: descent through mother's line.
  Matrilocal: newly married couple reside with wife's parents.
Other
  Bilineal: descent follows both lines.
  Neolocal: newly married couple resides separately.

such things as transmitting names. But we do relate the child equally to each line of his descent; one set of grandparents is not favored over the other.

Authority in our system is still formally (and therefore legally) patriarchal, but in practice the trend has been steadily in the direction of an equal relationship, concomitant with gains in the status of women.

The Family as a Primary Group

When sociological analysis focuses upon the contemporary American family, there is an additional concern upon what has been called the "affectional function." The argument here is that the intense and close interaction of children and parents in a separate household creates a small, primary unit that is the major source of sustaining affection for both parents and children. The modern American family frequently lives away from other relatives, and this intensifies the interaction among mother, father, and children occupying a common household.

The frequent and intimate interaction of parents and children *universally* creates within some circumscribed circle of kin a basic *primary* group that can generate the deepest of human feelings of love and affection (and possibly also the opposite). But now, among most American families there is a very conscious *expectation* of happiness to be derived from the intimate and primary character of family relationships. In a study of 909 Detroit families, for instance, *companionship* was the aspect of marriage most valued.[3]

Apparently adults increasingly see in the family a fundamental source of primary response to a world more and more impersonal in its relationships. It is just when the individual is no longer so *economically* dependent upon the family that such expectations of happiness become so important to people.

CAPITALISM, INDUSTRIALISM, AND THE FAMILY

A generation ago many people, sociologists included, viewed with alarm the changes in the family that seemed to accompany the industrialization of society. The common theme in this bleak outlook was to predict the decline of the family as a consequence of a decline of its social functions. One influential formulation of this was that the family was passing "from institution to companionship."[4]

According to this interpretation, the agrarian family (even in the nineteenth century) was necessarily the center of life for the individual. It possessed major *economic* functions, for the agrarian family was a *productive* unit, organized by a division of labor to operate a farm. Except for a few who went into religious institutions or into the cities, individuals were tied into family status and their economic roles were found in the family as a work group.

In preindustrial societies the family performed many functions that have since become community or societal responsibilities. It not only socialized the young, it provided much other training of the child as well. Among European peasants and even later among American farmers, a boy learned his occupation by working with his father at a young age.

Furthermore, in an agrarian society the kinship group maintained the aged, nursed the sick, buried the dead, and provided for the mentally ill or physically crippled. It also ensured support for widows and orphans and made a place for the occasionally unmarried woman.

As a result one can understand how kinship became a most binding and obligatory relationship, regardless of personal feelings, requiring that family interests take precedence over individual ones. The individual was locked into a demanding structure of kinship obligations and duties that extended beyond the nuclear family to a wider network of kin.

The Transformation of the Family

The transformation of society by industrialization and capitalism thoroughly altered this organization of family life. Some of the major changes were:

1. *Separation of work and home.* A developing machine technology and capitalist production took work out of the home and into a factory; as a consequence, the family ceased to be a productive unit. Work, located elsewhere, became in time the almost sole responsibility of the father.

2. *Decline in family size.* Children were no longer economically necessary, unlike agrarian society, where a family with too few children might be able to maintain itself. Now they were mouths to feed, and the reward for having them was no longer in economic values. Birthrates declined as society industrialized, as did family size, particularly in the middle class, where children were viewed as competitive with other values.

3. *Decline of extended family system.* There was the decline of the extended family system of kinship obligation and an increase in the small, nuclear family maintaining a separate and independent household.

4. *Separation of family and education.* The need for a literate population for new kinds of occupational training, as well as more advanced education led to the emergence of a mass educational structure separate from the family.

5. *Loss of occupational succession.* As society industrialized, parents could less and less transmit an occupational status to their children, except where there was a family business—and with the development of corporate capitalism family-owned businesses (including farms) have declined rapidly. Children may pursue careers not even known or available to their parents.

How much industrialism and capitalism can be assigned responsibility for the decline of extended kinship units and the increase of the more isolated nuclear family is a matter of considerable scholarly argument. Sociologist Morris Zelditch points out that when economic changes effectively separate economic and occupational structures from the kinship structure, the traditional family structure is altered:

. . . the power and patronage on which the corporate descent group and extended family depend for their authority erode; after when their authority, in turn, erodes; and what is left is a primarily expressive kindred in which relatives

of the wage-earning working class and the salaried clerks and professionals. It could no longer adequately educate its children within the family only, and needed to send them to school. Nor did it need children for economic reasons. And with loss of authority and loss of social function came a decline in an extended family network. Increasingly, "family" came to mean father, mother, and children in a separate household—the nuclear family.

But the revolution in family was more than a re-shaping by loss of functions. It also brought new dimensions to the family not prominent in its traditional form: intimacy and sentiment; courtship and romantic love; a maternal value for the child over all other interests; and a new privacy and domesticity.

According to a historian of the family, Edward Shorter, in the traditional family "members of the family felt they had more in common with their various peer groups than with one another. In other words, the traditional family was much more a productive and reproductive unit than an emotional unit."[6]

In the transformation of the family it became a more private unit shielded from the larger community outside. The members were tied emotionally to one another:

> And the modern nuclear family was born in the shelter of domesticity. Thus sentiment flowed into a number of familial relationships. Affection and inclination, love and sympathy, came to take the place of "instrumental" considerations in regulating the dealings of family members with one another. Spouses and children came to be prized for what they were, rather than for what they represented or could do.[7]

With the industrialization of society, sweeping social changes have penetrated even into the less industrialized sphere. This nuclear group is a rural family in Mexico.

continue to find personal reasons for liking each other and helping each other but without the same compelling subordination to a common goal and common authority.[5]

Making the Modern Family

When the workplace was removed from the household, and economy separated from family, a revolution in family life was underway. As in any revolution, an old way of life was destroyed, while a new way of life emerged. The old order of family, a productive and reproductive unit tied closely to the community and in turn binding the dependent individual to it, eroded. In its place, a new form of family life emerged—the modern nuclear family.

The new family lacked the dominant economic and social functions that gave stability and authority to the premodern family. It could not transmit occupational succession to its children, especially in the case

The Family and Personal Life

The revolutionary shaping of the modern nuclear family was accompanied by a revolution in sexual attitudes and practices. Young people began to give more attention to their own feelings, less to parental wishes and the needs of property, according to Shorter, and "began to court whom they liked rather than whom their parents thought best."[8] Premarital sex increased considerably, and from 1750 to 1850 there was an enormous rise in premarital pregnancies.[9]

A new freedom of personal choice, of freer opportunities for romantic love and also sexual intimacy, had now entered society. The individualism which capitalism had created permeated all spheres of social life, not just the economic; it shaped the intimate and private spheres of life, as well as the public.

Just as capitalism separated the economy from the family, it also brought about revolutionary changes in courtship and sexual conduct. Capitalism forcefully freed people from land and traditional modes of agricultural life. It gave them no choice but to seek work as employed labor, and it required they be aggressively individualistic in looking out for themselves. When the new working classes internalized the sentiments of individual interest, this new egoism learned in the marketplace soon undercut the obligations to community and the ties to family and lineage. As Edward Shorter noted, "for young people in late eighteenth-century Europe, the sexual and emotional wish to be free came from the capitalist marketplace."[10]

But it did not come first to the propertied classes; instead, it was working people who were the vanguard of the sexual revolution. For the developing capitalist class, property was still significantly tied to family and its rights of inheritance, so the family remained firmly in control of the individual. But the working class had no property to preserve, no family business to transmit, "and so they were free to pursue individual rather than family objectives once the idea of doing so had occurred to them—which is to say, once they were able to shake free of *community* controls upon their intimate lives."[11]

The realm of freedom available to the individual under capitalism, nonetheless, remained limited, particularly for those who did not own property. Yet the separation of family from economy and the loosening of community controls had given to common people the idea of a personal life free from economic and political domination. The realm of family life, separated from economic production, came to be identified with such a personal life, one in which love and personal happiness were possible.

During the nineteenth century, then, the nuclear family came to be the one possible location for a personal meaning in life, for sharing a life with others trusted and loved. This was accompanied by the gradual elimination of child and female labor; children went to school and the woman remained at home as wife and mother.

In such a way, and certainly unintended, the development of capitalism had created the basis for a new form of the family. It was a nuclear family separated from economic production, and so for the nonproper-

The modern nuclear family offers privacy and domesticity, intimacy and sentiment; and it prizes children for what they are, not for what they represent.

tied classes a sphere of life free from economic controls, one conceived as making possible a personal life. It was also a form of family life in which, for perhaps the first time in history, the female role was confined inside the household and the male outside to income-producing work. The housewife and the wage-earning employed laborer as the two basic roles of the new form of family emerged as the unique outcome of capitalist development.

Eli Zaretsky sums up this development:

The split in society between 'personal feelings' and 'economic production' was integrated with the sexual division of labor. Women were identified with emotional life, men with the struggle for existence. Under these conditions a new form of the family developed—one that understood itself to be operating in apparent freedom from production, and that placed a primary emphasis on the personal relations of its members.[12]

These processes, begun two centuries ago, have continued to develop. The family retains even fewer of the social functions it once had, as schools, hospitals, nursing and old-age homes take on tasks that were once exclusively the family's. The family, furthermore, has become the sphere of personal life at a time when people are increasingly looking to themselves, outside of productive work, for meaning and purpose. As fewer people create a personal identity through their work, this split between "work" and "life" places greater weight on the significance given to the personal relations of the family. That weight, Zaretsky tells us, may be more than the family can now carry:

> Under capitalism almost all of our personal needs are restricted to the family. This is what gives the family its resilience, in spite of the constant prediction of its demise; it simply cannot meet the pressure of being the only refuge in a brutal society. [13]

At the end of the chapter we shall return to this issue in considering the future of the family.

CLASS, ETHNICITY, AND FAMILY LIFE

By and large, even in mobile societies, the family acts as a stabilizing factor in the class structure, for it is through the family that most individuals are placed in the class structure. In part this is done because the family has the resources, the knowledge, the "contacts" and influence, to locate their children in class positions similar to their own. An upper-class family, and even a middle-class family, knows how to choose educational lines of greatest advantage or how to gain entry into the corporate structure through personal contacts. Even skilled workers sometimes manage to get their own sons preferential entry into an occupation, where access depends on getting into an apprenticeship program or a union.

These are the factors that have made family more important in small towns than in big cities, more important for those of higher social status, and more important in the past than it is now or is likely to be in the future.

Social Class and Socialization

By socialization of the child, the family naturally and unconsciously transmits the attitudes and values, modes of individual action, and life-styles typical of the parents' social class. The child, therefore, becomes a person whose very approach to life makes him or her an appropriate member of a given social class.

Because of this, sociologists have concentrated on variation by social class in the family's socialization of the young and particularly in its child-rearing practices. But classes are broad and inclusive categories, and the assumption, for example, that there is a middle-class family may fail to notice differences in family patterns within the middle class.

In Chapter 5 we cited a study that compared families of the "old" middle class of independent business men and free professionals with families of the "new" middle class of salaried executives and professionals employed in large organizations. [14] The new middle-class parents taught their children the importance of adjustment to society, security, and getting along with peers, an orientation fitting in with an "organization-man" perspective of the world. The old middle-class parents, in turn, instilled in their children a more active and manipulative approach to life in which they learn the necessity of strong aspirations and hard striving toward their goals.

We also cited in Chapter 5 the work of Melvin Kohn, who showed how the characteristics of middle- and working-class occupations—requiring initiative and independent judgment in the one case, and routine and closely supervised repetition in the other—strongly affected parental conceptions of what children should learn to be. [15] Parents, in short, seemed to socialize their children to the world of work on the basis of their own work experience.

Perhaps it would be useful to repeat what we said there: Different social classes face quite different life situations. Parents are likely to try to teach their children what they think it requires to cope with the situations common to their social class, for that is what they know best from experience. That being so, we can expect to find that different social classes socialize their children in different fashions.

It is for this reason that the family is such a powerful force in reproducing the skills, attitudes, and lifestyles of the prevailing social classes, and in doing so, helping to sustain the class structure.

Class and Ethnicity

Within the United States, the peasant origin of many ethnic families has meant a tradition of strong and cohesive family, with meaningful interaction along lines of extended kin. Where class and ethnic culture meet in the same families, they modify one another. Perhaps one of the best expositions of this has been Herbert Gans's study of working-class Italians in Boston. Gans described their family type as one between the modern, and particularly middle-class, *nuclear* family and the *extended* family typical of peasant societies.[16] The *households* are nuclear, in that a single nuclear family lives separately, but the family maintains a rich and meaningful set of relationships with kin, particularly among adult brothers and sisters and their spouses.

There is, however, less interaction across the generations, with the important exception of the mother-daughter relationship, which remains close even after the daughter's marriage. The daughter usually locates her new home close to that of her mother's. The extended family pattern provides much of the social interaction for the adults, and they also depend upon one another for advice and help. Thus, interaction outside the family is limited by the high degree of interaction within it.

The relationship (in Gans's study) between the sexes, however, contrasts sharply with that of the middle class. First of all there is no easy interaction between the sexes, and men much prefer to interact only with men. Even within the same house, or within the same room, the men will speak to the men and the women to the women. Communication across sex lines, therefore, is limited, and men particularly *feel* ill at ease in such a situation, feeling that women talk faster and are more skillful at it; women, in turn, depend upon their ability to talk their husbands into things they want.

In husband-wife relations there is what Gans called a *segregated* relationship, in that there is a clear differentiation between the tasks and duties of husband and wife. There is much less, if any, of the joint relationship that characterizes the middle-class marriage. Husbands rarely assist in household duties, and women did not even feel it would be right to ask them to do so. Women assume entirely the very large task of caring for children, leaving perhaps only the most severe punishment to the father.

This family pattern is both ethnic and working class. Gans feels that the class dimension is the more important, and he compares this family pattern with the working-class family elsewhere, such as in England, to emphasize how much of the type is a consequence of social class.

The Lower-Class Family

Of all the issues relating family to stratification, none has been more controversial than the issue of the lower-class family in the urban slum. That proportionately more of these families are black than white brings a racial note to an already complicated issue. That many of these families are on welfare and characterized by higher than average illegitimacy rates makes any effort at an objective understanding particularly difficult.

Actually, the issue is not the families of lower-class people, nor those of lower-class blacks—it is lower-class families headed by a female. While the female-headed family occurs at any class level, both political and sociological interest has focused upon the mother-headed family in the lower class, where it is most frequent.

One basic fact about this family pattern is generally agreed on: the severe difficulty in earning a regular and adequate family-sustaining income by the lower-class male destroys his capacity to function as bread-winner and head of the family. As a consequence, women by default come to head the family. By work and by welfare they provide income, but in both instances it is a low income.

By the late 1970s, for example, the chances were one in three that a family headed by a female was below the poverty level; the chances were one in two if the female were black, one in four if she were white.[17]

In the United States a woman can receive AFDC (Aid to the Families of Dependent Children) if she has no male support. This policy encourages unemployed males to "disappear" in order that their families can be supported. (When he is able to earn a living the black male readily supports his family; in 1976, 80 percent of black families headed by a male were above the poverty line.)[18]

The most familiar interpretation of this pattern by sociologists (and others) is that it produces a *disorganization* of family life, with a set of harmful consequences for all members: illegitimate children, low educational ambitions, criminal and delinquent behavior, and mental and emotional disturbances in greater proportion than in other classes.[19]

The Matriarchal Black Family: Disorganized or Adaptive?

Drawing upon a wide range of available data about black lower-class families, the social scientist Daniel P. Moynihan, then Assistant Secretary of Labor under President Lyndon Johnson, in 1965 issued a controversial report arguing, first, that the lower-class black family was a consequence of poverty and racism, but secondly—and here was what made it controversial—that the "tangle of pathology" so created had in itself become a factor inhibiting further progress for blacks.[20] In short, the black lower-class family, Moynihan argued, now produced people who were severely handicapped in their ability to succeed and to take advantage of economic opportunities when and where—and if—they were offered:

Three centuries of injustice have brought about deep-seated structural distortions in the life of the Negro American. At this point, the present tangle of pathology is capable of perpetuating itself without assistance from the white world. The cycle can be broken only if these distortions are set right.[21]

What was the controversy about? None of Moynihan's critics disputed the evidence he cited about economic disadvantage and racial discrimination. Nor did they in large part deny the apparent outcome of this disadvantage: the lowered performance and achievement of blacks, as measured by tests, by educational attainment, by income, and by jobs.

What was in serious dispute, however, was Moynihan's interpretation of such facts. He had extended the frequent argument about the harmful effects of disadvantage by arguing that the black family in the ghetto, itself a consequence of such factors as poverty and discrimination, had now become a further cause of the plight of black people. No improvement could occur, Moynihan asserted, unless government programs were created to restore stability to the black family.

Moynihan's argument was supported by statistics about the condition of life in the ghetto, but also by the assumption that family disorganization *always* occurred under circumstances of poverty and racial discrimination. Families without male heads are almost automatically defined as "broken" or "disorganized." Illegitimate births in such families were taken as further evidence of disorganization.

A number of social scientists and civil rights leaders focused criticism on one matter in particular: that Moynihan's arguments had the effect of drawing attention away from what they took to be the fundamental issue—providing black males with regular employment at decent wages. This, they argued, should be the concern of social policy. If this were done, the plight of the black family would remedy itself. No tinkering with the family would be either helpful or desirable as a policy of the federal government. As sociologist Herbert Gans stated:

. . . however difficult it may be to improve and desegregate the schools and to provide jobs, it is easier, more desirable and more likely to help Negro family life than attempts to alter the structure of the family or the personality of its members through programs of "cultural enrichment" or therapy, not to mention irresponsible demands for Negro self-improvement.[22]

Gans argued that, in contrast to data offered by Moynihan, other data showed "no relationship between school performance and broken families," and that a study of mental health in Manhattan "demonstated that among whites at least, growing up in a broken family did not increase the likelihood of mental illness as much as did poverty and being of low status."[23]

Nor was the matriarchal family in itself the cause of social pathology:

Likewise, the matriarchal family structure and the absence of a father has not yet been proven pathological, even for the boys who grow up in it. Sociological studies of the Negro family have demonstrated the existence of an extended kinship system of mothers, grandmothers, aunts and other female relatives that is surprisingly stable, at least on the female side. Moreover, many matriarchal families raise boys who do adapt successfully and themselves make stable marriages. The immediate cause of pathology may be the absence of a set of emotional strengths and cultural skills in the mothers, rather than the instability or departure of the fathers.[24]

The lesson to be learned here is this: The lower-class matriarchal family is to be understood as an alternate type of family structure developed under circumstances in which the preferred nuclear family with both a male and a female parent is difficult to achieve because of poverty and unemployment.

The female-headed family in the United States is increasing. In 1978, 17.4 percent of all American children lived with their mother only, a percentage that has more than doubled since 1960. One in three of these female-headed families, we saw above, lives below the poverty level: one in four is white; one in two is black. The issue, then, is as important as it was in the 1960s when Moynihan, Gans, and others argued so warmly over what was to be done for one such type of family.

Nor is this family pattern peculiar to the ghettoes of urban America. Similar matriarchal family patterns occur elsewhere in the world.

The female-headed family is increasing in the United States among both blacks and whites, and among both poor and those not poor.

Hyman Rodman studied such families in Trinidad and asked whether they were universal for the lower class. They were not, he asserted.[25] Rather, they occur only where the occupational role is separated from the family role—as in industrial society—and where the man is expected to be the sole family provider. This does not hold, for example, in a peasant society in which the whole family works the land as a group.

Accordingly, we can expect to find a lower-class family pattern that is matriarchal and possesses a relatively high rate of illegitimacy in such societies, as long as unemployment, irregular employment, and even employment at low wages in dead-end jobs is all that is offered the lower-class male.

THE CHANGING AMERICAN FAMILY

The once pessimistic forecast about the future of the family, so common a generation ago, has since given way to a perspective that acknowledges that the family remains a significant institution. But there are changes underway, and possibly more to come, that have produced a whole new discussion about the meaning of the family for the individual and for American society, now and in the future.

Marriage and Divorce

The increasing rate of divorce in American society is often viewed with alarm as an indication of a decline in the American commitment to marriage and family. But evidence suggests something else (see "The Facts of Marriage and Divorce").

The facts so often cited as reason for alarm are such as these:

1. About 40 percent of all marriages, at the present rate, will end in divorce.
2. For every two marriages in any one year, there is one divorce.
3. But it is also true that from 75 to 80 percent of those who divorce get married again. The high rate of divorce, then, is not a vote against marriage and family by the American people.

Though it is no longer so uncommon to hear of divorce between partners who have been married for twenty years or longer, it is still the case that divorces occur largely among younger people who have been married less than seven years, and divorces are still less frequent among those longer married and with several children.

Nonetheless, an increasing number of American children experience the disruption of family life caused by divorce. Not only do they lose the regular company of one parent, they may have to move away from friends and familiar surroundings.

There has been almost a tripling of children affected by divorce over a 20-year period. In 1956, for example, there were 361,000 children whose parents divorced that year; since 1972, however, there are over one million such children each year.[26]

Many children become the custody of a single divorced parent. By 1978, 7.1 percent of children under the age of 18 were living with their divorced mother only, and an additional 0.7 percent with their divorced father only.[27] On the basis of present divorce rates, it is estimated that two of every five children born during the 1970s will spend at least part of their childhood in single-parent homes.

But if parents divorce, they also remarry. As a result of the present high divorce rate, 13 percent of all children in 1977 were living with two parents, only one of whom was a natural parent.[28] It is not uncom-

THE FACTS OF MARRIAGE AND DIVORCE

There were 2.2 million marriages in 1978, but there were also 1.1 million divorces. The *divorce rate* was 22.0 per 1,000 married women. This rate was 14.9 in 1970, 9.2 in 1960.

There were no children under age 18 in 43 percent of divorces in 1976; this compares to 40 percent in 1970.

Divorce affected 1,123,000 children in 1975, a high point in American family life; but in 1976 the figure fell to 1,117,000 and has leveled off since then. The figure has been over one million each year since 1972.

In 1960, 9.4 percent of children under age 18 were living with only one parent; by 1970, it was 12.2 percent; and by 1978, 19.2 percent—17.6 percent with mother, 1.6 percent with father.

In 1975, of all women whose first marriage ended in divorce: 64.5 percent were under age 30 at the time of divorce, and 76.3 percent of these women had remarried after an average 3.1 years of being divorced.

Of these, one-third had no children and one-third had one child. Another 24.3 percent were 30—39 years of age at time of divorce, and 56.2 of these women had remarried after an average of 4.5 years of being divorced. The remaining 11.3 percent were from 40 to 75 years of age at time of divorce, and 28.1 percent of these women had remarried after an average of 5.5 years of being divorced.

In 1976 the median age at first marriage was 22.9 for men, 21.0 for women. The median age of first divorce was 30.3 for men, 28.2 for women. The median age of remarriage was 35.1 for men, 31.7 for women. The median duration of a first marriage was 6.5 years.

At the current level of divorce, if continued over a lifetime, the proportion of marriages ending in divorce may be close to 40 percent.

Notes

SOURCES: U.S. Bureau of the Census, "Divorce, Child Custody and Child Support." (Current Population Reports: Special Studies: Series P-23: no. 84). U.S. Bureau of the Census, *Statistical Abstract of the United States: 1978* (99th Edition), Washington, D.C., 1979.

mon, furthermore, for two divorced parents both to bring children to the new family arrangement.

Whether it is the single parent going it alone, or the remarrying parent creating a new household, such new living arrangements require new forms of parental relations to children, as well as new problems with which both parents and children must cope. And there are no certain answers to be gained from counselors, classes, textbooks, clinics—or even Ann Landers.

Explaining Divorce

To measure the rate of divorce is simple compared to the task of explaining that rate. Why is there such an increase in the divorce rate in recent years?

There are several reasons that sociologists and psychologists have long given for divorce, but it is not obvious that these are also the reasons for the recent increase. For example, it seems that when people from quite different backgrounds marry, the necessary adjustments in role-expectations are more difficult and a divorce more likely. But the conflicting expectations which today intrude upon marriage may be more the consequence of *changing* expectations among men and women from basically the same kind of background, such as not having children; both partners working; and greater equality in family decision making.

In the past the rate of divorce was higher among the less educated and those of lower social status, sug-

Given the present rate of divorce, it seems that two of every five children born in the 1970s will spend at least part of their growing years in a single-parent home.

gesting that higher social status, with its greater economic security and material ease, helped to avoid some of the stresses which produced divorce.[29] But by 1975 the rate of divorce among men who had completed four years of college was the same as for all men. Women with four years of college, however, still have a divorce rate 10 percent lower than the total population.[30]

Some have argued that the ease with which divorce can be obtained, particularly with no-fault divorce laws, is the cause, but this is likely to be as much the effect of other changes as is divorce itself. Nonetheless, the ease of divorce reflects a greater acceptance of divorce in the population, and thus being divorced ceases to be a stigma, especially for women. This would encourage divorce among those dissatisfied with their marriage.

At the present time, certainly, changes in the relations between men and women are going on and these are, more than anything else, an outcome of changes in the traditional structure of sex roles that

have made marriage and childbearing so necessary for women. Women now have more options and are less dependent on men. Men, too, change under these circumstances. What both women and men want from marriage has been changing. An increased rate of divorce is surely to be expected under such circumstances.

Women: Family Role and Social Status

Throughout history the basic organization of the Western family has rested upon a sexual division of labor and a differential of power, justified by an ideology overtly claiming the superiority of males.

In modern times the status of women has been established by the capitalist development of industrial society, which, as we have seen, had notable effect upon the structure of the family and marital relations. That development isolated most women from employment outside the home, and defined for them a status built upon the female capacity for childbearing and assigned to them the exclusive task of keeping the home —in short, the role of *wife* and *mother*.

Rationalizations about the inferiority of women no longer have the same credence they once did. A long struggle going back over a century has brought women the vote, property rights, and an equality in civil status before the courts of the United States. Yet women are still far from equal to men in every phase of social life—and that is particularly true in the economic sphere.

Equal Within the Home? Yes and No

But what is true within the economy may not be true within the home. Here the received wisdom is that man's role as father and husband has declined radically in influence over both his wife and his children. His absence from the home, presumably, has given his wife, even if by default, more responsibility and consequently more authority. One sociologist argues that, "Based on the data on hand one has to conclude that the dominant-father model is neither practical nor functional in contemporary society and is tending to disappear."[31]

So, too, it is widely claimed, wives have become the equal of their husbands. Thus, in their Detroit study, Blood and Wolfe argued that power relations in marriage are an individual matter, an interpersonal relation testing the competency of two persons; therefore, the partner with more education, more organizational experience, and a higher status background is the one who makes the decisions.[32]

But this is strongly challenged by sociologist Dair Gillespie's argument that the "distribution of power is not an interpersonal affair but a class affair."[33] Women are in an inferior class position to men, therefore differences in individual competency will not offset the class advantages of men. Gillespie points out that Blood and Wolfe's own data show that, since higher status men are usually better educated than their wives, middle-class, white-collar suburban-residing males have more power over their wives—contrary to common myth—than do blue-collar, less-educated, city-dwelling males. To this, Gillespie adds the argument that women acquire their status from their husbands, that they are socialized to think of themselves as inferior, and they are psychologically conditioned—*programmed* is today's term—to be wives and mothers, noncompetitive with men because less able to compete. (Academic achievement suggests that little girls do not realize this until high school; before that they do as well or better than boys. An increasingly larger number, of course, now get a different message.)

Furthermore, women earn less than men, have less access to the more prestigeful, better-paying occupations, even when equally prepared. In addition, the laws still favor men; a wife has a legal claim to support, but not to her husband's salary—but he is entitled to her services; can legally decide where they will reside, and need not pay her any income.[34]

Having children increases the husband's power, for the wife becomes more dependent. In summary:

Thus, it is clear that for a wife to gain even a modicum of power in the marital relationship, she must gain it from external sources, i.e., she must participate in the work force, her education must be superior to her husband's, and her participation in organizations must excel his. Equality of resources leaves the power in the hands of the husband. However, access to these resources of power are structurally blocked for women.[35]

These disputes over the changing status of men and women tend to counter most claims about the gains in status made by women in recent decades, while not denying that change has occurred, change that also affects the family.

Working Wives

While the employment of women is nothing new, what is new is the rapid increase in recent years of working married women, particularly those with children. Sociologist Valerie Oppenheimer points out "that continued economic development in our society has increased the demand for female labor."[36] But there are other reasons, too, such as (1) the higher standard of living possible when both husband and wife work, (2) the increasing proportion of women who work to support children, and (3) the demand for greater economic opportunity for women as one dimension of the struggle for sexual equality.

In 1950 less than one-fourth (23.8 percent) of all married women were employed in some capacity, but by 1975 this figure had almost doubled to 44.4 percent.[37] Furthermore, having children no longer keeps women out of the labor force. In 1974, 50 percent of women with children aged 6 to 17 worked at some time during the year; one-third of those with children under 6 did so.[38]

While women in most cases do not earn as much as their husbands do, their employment nonetheless adds substantially to family income and gives the family an economic advantage over the family with only one breadwinner. In 1976 Howard Hayghe reported the following median family income: $14,885, when both husband and wife work; $12,360, when only the husband works; and $8,225, when only the wife works.

These facts about working wives suggest a basic change in the American family. The traditional nuclear household, in which the husband works and the wife remains home to care for the children, is no longer the most frequent pattern of family life. It holds true for only 34 percent of husband-wife families.[40]

The changing facts about the family are also supported, to a degree, by changing attitudes. In a New York Times/CBS News Poll in 1977, 48 percent of a national sample supported a marriage in which both partners worked and shared equally in housework and child care, while 43 percent supported the more traditional marriage. That suggests a serious national division, but when age is taken into account, the working wife finds strong support. Among 18- to 29-year olds, only 27 percent supported the traditional marriage, while among those over 45 years old, 59 percent preferred the traditional marriage.[41]

Effects on the Family

The new pattern of the working wife and mother cannot help but affect the family, but just how, and whether for good or bad, is not yet clear. Only a few things are now apparent.

As far back as 1965, sociologist Robert Blood pointed out how working wives changed the status of wife and daughter, and so of father and son. "Employment emancipates women from domination by their husbands and, secondarily, raises their daughters from inferiority to their brothers (echoing the rising status of their mothers)."[42] He cited other studies which found that sons become more dependent and more obedient, reflecting their observations of their father's lessened status, while daughters became more independent, more self-reliant, more aggressive, more dominant, even more disobedient.

In such ways, the shape of the American family is being altered by the exodus of women into the labor market. The roles of men and women are converging for both adults and children. As a result, the family will be far less segregated internally, far less stratified into different age generations and different sexes. This will enable family members to share more of the activities of life together, both work activities and play activities.[43]

From the vantage point of women seeking equality, Blood's interpretation of the changes in the American family signify positive gains for women. But the reality is also filled with problems and tensions.

While large numbers of men, as The New York Times/CBS News Poll indicated, agree on the preferability of a marriage of equal sharing, most of them seem in fact not to act that way. Working wives find that housework and care of children is still largely their task, quite unequally shared with husband.

Working wives and mothers find themselves compelled to work an average of 70 hours a week between both job and home. The weekend may be less a time for rest, more a time to catch-up on household tasks. Thus, as Giele notes, "more women have entered employment without having secured the needed adjustments in family life."[44]

The Unmarried Couple

A man and woman living together though unmarried—what was once called "common-law marriage" and found almost entirely in the lower class—has at-tracted much attention recently as a middle-class alternative to legal marriage. While unmarried couples were still only 3 percent of persons living together in 1979, there was nevertheless a strong trend toward such an arrangement during the 1970s—from 530,000 couples in 1970 to 1,346,000 couples in 1979. Furthermore, the trend was stronger among the young; 58 percent were couples without children in which the male was 34 years or younger. Fully 50 percent of all couples had never been married.[45]

In place of a legal marriage contract, some unmarried couples have entered into a private conjugal contract, in which they seek to spell out the extent and limit of their obligations to one another, as well as their individuals rights.[46] Many such contracts apparently seek to establish an equality between the partners. But if such a contract contradicts law in any of its provisions—if the man tries to avoid responsibility for any children born to his partner—these provisions would be held invalid or unenforceable.

The private conjugal contract is only binding, in any legal sense, then, if it can be upheld in a court of law. But then such contracts are no longer "private," and these couples are only the smallest step from being legally married.

The introduction of such private conjugal contracts is but one effort in a new time to find new ways—and usually more equal ones—to recreate the conjugal relationship. Americans may be redefining the meaning of marriage, but they are not abandoning it.

The Changing Family From the 1960s to the present these changes have come rapidly to bear upon the American family: an increasing divorce rate; a sharp increase in single-parent (usually female-headed) families; the working wife; and the difficult change toward equality between married partners.

Such changes in family life are not easy to interpret. Nor do the sociologists and psychologists who study the family necessarily agree on what they mean.

THE FUTURE OF THE FAMILY

On a worldwide basis the family is changing from old patterns and adapting to the kind of society that is coming into being everywhere. The industrialization of the world is accompanied by the emergence of the nuclear family on a world basis, with a decline of the extended kinship so predominant in more traditional family forms. William J. Goode emphasizes that this nuclear family pattern is in itself a world revolution, but that it is also one factor in a larger, more encompassing world revolution—the transition to the modern industrial society.[47]

As a part of the revolution the nuclear family emphasizes the freedom of the individual to choose his own life and control his own destiny, released in good part from the once rigid controls of extended kinship structures. At the same time, there is an obvious price: the shrinking of ties among kin reduces the sense of responsibility that family members have for one another.

Do We Need the Family?

Goode's argument proceeds on the generally accepted premise that the family in some modified pattern has survived the major social changes into industrialization, and has a future in modern society. Once the only significant contrary voice had been that of sociologist Barrington Moore, who has suggested that the family may not survive as an institution.[48] He raises the possibility that the family may be an obsolete institution or become one before long. Moore argues that there are conditions that "make it possible for the advanced industrial societies of the world to do away with the family and substitute other social arrangements that impose fewer unnecessary and painful restrictions on humanity."[49]

His basic argument is that there is no need for the family today, and that many of its basic features are outmoded if not useless. The obligation of affection among kin, for example, is characterized as a relic of barbarism. Moore regards the contemporary role of the wife and mother as one which makes demands that are impossible to meet, children as often a burden to parents, the troubles of adolescence as evidence of the family's inadequacy in stabilizing the human personality, and motherhood as frequently a degrading experience. He does not even believe that the necessity of affection and love for the infant requires family, though he acknowledges that the present bureaucratized hospital nursery now lacks the necessary warm and affectionate structure.

When Moore wrote in the 1950s, he was a lonely critic in a society that mostly accepted the nuclear family as an enduring and viable institution. No longer is this so. Since the 1960s marriage as a desired and idealized relationship has been challenged by those whose argument is basically quite simple: Wedlock "until death do us part" made sense in earlier times in which the family was necessarily a basic institution of society and dependence on the kinship structure was unavoidable for the individual. People change in interests and values, in aspirations and life-styles through life—changing careers in mid-life is now more frequent, for example—and therefore, it is claimed, a close, intimate relationship with the same person cannot reasonably be expected to persist over an adult life-time. The pattern of divorce in middle-class life is cited as testimony to that fact.

If this is so, assert the new critics of marriage, then new marital relations should be developed, relations that persist only so long as a mutually satisfying shared life is possible. No undue sacrifice by either partner for the other, it is felt, makes any sense, for both men and women are entitled to equal consideration from each other. Each is equally an individual, with equal rights and his and her own life to live.

The Attack on the Nuclear Family

These critics, in effect, would save the family by reducing it to marriage, detaching it from parenthood as well as from what they conceive to be unrealistic expectations of romantic love and a life-long commitment. In the popular writings of Nena and George O'Neill, adultery is held up as not necessarily a breach of faith—the couple can choose to be or not to be faithful to one another—for, they argue, "man is not naturally monogamous."[50] According to the O'Neills, the marital relation should be an undemanding interpersonal relation, what they (without any sense of contradiction) call "nonbinding commitments."

The conception that child-raising is an unrewarding burden, and a task too difficult to be left to mere amateurs, follows from the emphasis on marriage as an undemanding relationship. Margaret Mead once suggested that child-raising be left to couples specially trained and certified for parenthood. Others have suggested special clinics, or communes, or other extended families.

The unwillingness to make binding commitments into the future, or to assume the responsibilities of parenthood for a new generation, suggest a basic perspective that distrusts the future and instead seeks only to live in the present. What claims to be a newer, more optimistic view of human relationships, is, in fact, pessimistic. Christopher Lasch sums it up this way:

> The fear and rejection of parenthood, the tendency to view the family as nothing more than marriage, and the perception of marriage as merely one in a series of nonbinding commitments, reflect a growing distrust of the future and a reluctance to make provisions for it—to lay up goods and experience for the use of the next generation. The cult of interpersonal relations represents the final dissolution of bourgeois optimism and self-confidence.[51]

The Isolated Family

Another criticism of the nuclear family starts from the observation that the family is isolated from the larger social world, maintaining a "privatized" haven from the harsher demands of society. According to Kenneth Kenniston: "Each family is an island, insulated from public scrutiny, control, and interference, and because of its protected isolation able to function as a haven against the demands of the rest of society."[52]

Yet this isolation of the nuclear family, according to Kenniston, leads to unavoidable strains, for people come to expect too much of the family. Both parents and children suffer as a consequence. The isolation of family is an isolation of the mother, who may live vicariously through her children and so put unbearable burdens on them. The father, in contrast, is split between work and home; too often the demands of work take him away from family for the sake of a career. A careerist father and an overly mothering mother are not going to produce an emotionally balanced and secure young person. But a father who seeks all his satisfaction in the home seeks more in family life than it can produce, or, perhaps, asks more of his children than he has a right to.

Yet this critique of the "privatization" of the family somehow misses the point, for it assumes that in fact the family is truly isolated from the harsh reality of modern society. Such, however, is not the fact, as Christopher Lasch points out:

> Most of the writing on the modern family takes for granted the "isolation" of the nuclear family not only from the kinship system but from the world of work. It assumes that this isolation makes the family impervious to outside influences. In reality, the modern world intrudes at every point and obliterates its privacy. The sanctity of the home is a sham in a world dominated by giant corporations and by the apparatus of mass promotion.[53]

The family, then, is not by itself able to shelter its members from society and alone protect cherished values. Instead, as Lasch notes, the family but mirrors the conditions of society. Furthermore, "Americans can preserve what is valuable in their culture only by changing the conditions of public life itself."[54]

The future of the family in American society, and also in much else of the Western world, would seem to depend on what responses can be developed to the threat that modern society presents to the historic family.

The Loss of Function   That the family is no longer the encompassing social group it once was has long been offered by sociologists as reason for the decline of the extended family and the emergence of the nuclear form. But even with the coming of the nuclear family, the loss of function continued. Once only school and possibly church put children under the supervision of other adults. But now nursery school and organized recreation extends that control and lessens the family's. Earlier than ever children move into the sphere of the peer group, which now brings the young into the consumer-oriented culture of modern advertising. Much more learning, in short, is in neither the family nor the school.

Such loss of function continues to reduce dependency on the family, at an earlier age. The loss of function was the basis of defining the nuclear family as the source of emotion and sentiment not found in an impersonal, competitive world, for making it a haven in a heartless world. But the family, we have seen, has not been able to be any such privatized haven.

Love and Discipline   The world intrudes on the family in many ways, not least of which is the development of an industry of family experts: child psychologists, pediatricians, educators, family sociologists, all of whom purport to tell parents how to be parents. The authority of competency in child-raising is no longer conferred on mere parenthood. The precarious self-confidence of parents is undermined.

What the family should be like, how parents should raise their children, increasingly becomes a matter of "expert" knowledge and community judg-

Many of today's young couples, even when married, choose not to have children.

ment. The family loses authority, yet is presumed to be a source of love. When love and discipline are so separated, the family is further endangered and its future becomes more uncertain.

The Family in the Future

We have already seen some of the consequences of the weakening of the nuclear family: divorce rates rise to new levels; more adults live alone with one or more children after divorce. But there is the now basic hesitancy of young people to enter into marriage and institute a new family. According to the Bureau of the Census, since 1960 there has been an increase in the proportion of adults up to the age of 34 who have remained single. In 1977 the Bureau reported that the number of adults under 35 years of age who live alone had doubled since 1970. One pattern seems fairly clear: the young leave home earlier and now marry later.

Many young people today do not marry but also do not live alone; living together without benefit of marriage is no longer an uncommon situation. Such people are wary of marriage and its legal and emotional commitments.

Even when many young people do marry, they do not always have children. In 1957 the average number of children per family was almost four (3.8 was the statistical norm). By 1977 that figure had dropped to two.

Not all of these developments will necessarily continue. Even now a moderate increase in the birthrate is predicted. But the larger pattern remains clear: marriage as a binding commitment and the raising of the future generation no longer holds the central place that it once did in the value structure of many Americans.

The State and the Family If "experts" on marriage and family have intruded into the intimacy of family life, so, sometimes, has the state. In the United States,

CHILDREN AND FAMILY:
THE NEED FOR A SOCIAL POLICY

When the Carnegie Council on Children began its study of American children, it found that it necessarily had to examine the larger context of economic and social forces affecting parents and children. A social policy adequate to the needs of children and their families would, the Council said, have to provide the following:

1. A full employment strategy combined with a system of income supports so as to assure all families with children a minimum of at least half the current median income in any year.

But conventional economics and corporate capitalism oppose full employment as a social policy, and neither political party has ever worked for a family income policy. The opposition can be expected to be powerful.

2. A new program for flexible scheduling of work, part-time work, and time off for child-rearing.

But corporations will not readily accept a policy that reduces capitalism's historic separation of work and family, in which family needs have always been secondary to the demands of work.

3. A range of comprehensible and universally accessible public services to support and strengthen—not replace—families in the rearing of children.

But the opposition to this will come from those who oppose more government expenditures; from those who oppose any enlargement of government's role in social life; and from those who are indifferent to the poorer and racially minority children who most need such services.

4. A broad health policy for children and families that would include attention to non-medical influences on health; assure adequate health care for all children, regardless of income, race, or ethnicity; emphasize preventive care, primary care, and humane care; make health agencies publicly accountable for the quality of health care provided all children; and increase and strengthen parents and children's own capacity, as well as the local community's, to act as health advocates and caretakers.

But, these policies are such an indictment of the present organization of health services, and would require such a reorganization, that the defensive opposition of the present health-care establishment on most specific proposals to realize such policies is assured.

5. Those changes in law that would support the family's authority and maintain the family's integrity, while offering help and service during crisis.

But, while such a policy may get wider agreement than the others, any effort to change the law in the area of rights—family rights, and children's rights—opens up another dimension in a complex struggle over the rights and authority of individual, family, and state.

The Council's efforts to formulate social policy for the family makes one clear point: strengthening the family requires a significant alteration of economic practices, as well as the institution of new political programs. That, in turn, forces on us one sobering inference: accomplishing such policy requires an extended political struggle against established economic interests, which probably cannot be achieved independently of other struggles: for equal rights for women; against racial and class discrimination; against poverty; for economic security and full employment.

the federal government has not, up to now, developed any systematic family policy.

In some Western nations, governments have been committed to a policy of assuring the adequate financial support of all children with family allowances; Canada, for example, does that. More often, governments have also encouraged or discouraged higher birthrates, and so encouraged families to have more or fewer children. In Europe, where birthrates have fallen, it has been the former. In countries like India, where birthrates are high, the effort has been to develop policies to discourage birth by various means of birth control.

As one consequence of the rapid increase in working mothers, there has been a concerted effort to get government support for a national program of adequate day care for children. In other ways, too, the state finds reasons to intervene in the family: in the laws governing adoption procedures; in court authority to remove children from "incompetent" parents; and in rescuing abused children. Beyond that, however, there is little in the way of a national policy for children and family comparable to what has been done in other industrial societies.

Perhaps, however, a national debate over family policy is beginning. During the 1970s the Carnegie Corporation, a national foundation, created the Carnegie Council on Children and undertook a five-year study on the way children grow up in America. In their first volume they made an effort to make the case for a broad family policy in the interest of all children and families.[55] The fate of children, they clearly recognized, is bound up in the fate of the family. But they also discovered that to strengthen the family requires policies about jobs and health care, which implies a broad range of significant social reforms in the economic organization of society. (See "Children and Family: The Need for a Social Policy.")

Any society that cares for its children cannot avoid having a policy on family life and the care of children. The issue for the future is not whether to have a social policy, but rather what that policy is to be and what measure of national resources are to be used to support families in bringing a new generation into being. This implies a national discussion about conscious choices of acceptable forms of family life. At the least, it would seem, it would require debate and discussion over the following issues:

1. Whether the conventional nuclear form of the family should be continued.

2. Whether all adults should expect to share in the task of having and raising children.

3. How and in what way men and women should define the roles of husband-father and wife-mother.

4. How the needs of family and the rights of children should be recognized in the everyday workings of the world and economic activities.

5. What the proper and supportive, but not controlling, place of government should be in sustaining family life.

In a time that emphasizes personal rights and individual development, and rejects traditional roles and claims of moral obligation, the task may be more difficult than is first evident.

SUMMARY

The *universality* of family means the existence of a basic unit responsible for legitimate procreation, for the care and maintenance of children, and for their socialization and placement in society. However, the form of the group by which these functions are carried out is not always that of the *nuclear* family of father, mother, and children. To these universal functions can be added for modern society a renewed emphasis on an *affectional* function, which then emphasizes the family as a primary group.

Variation in family structure includes variations in accepted modes of mate selection (endogamy and exogamy); in forms of marriage (monogamy and polygamy); in rules of authority (patriarchal or matriarchal); in rules of descent and inheritance (patrilineal or matrilineal and sometimes bilateral); in rules of residence (patrilocal and matrilocal, and neolocal usually in modern society).

Industrialization and *capitalism* brought about these changes in the family: separation of work and home; decline in family size; decline of extended family system; separation of family and education; loss of occupational succession. ·

The family in modern society varies considerably by class and status in the way it socializes children. Working class and ethnic status merge in shaping a family structure: in child-rearing, in marital functions and relations between the sexes, and in sustaining kinship patterns over the generations.

The lower-class family headed by a female instead of a male has long been defined as family disorganization by social scientists. But a better sociological conception of it is as a family type developed in response to the fact that poverty, discrimination, and unemployment make unattainable the preferred, male-headed nuclear family.

A number of changes has come over the family since the 1960s. There has been a *sharp increase in divorce,* though almost 80 percent of divorced people remarry. The rising divorce rate has contributed to an *increase in single-parent (usually female-headed) families.* There has also been *an increase in working wives,* which is a gain for women in terms of achieving equality with men, but working wives find they are still left with most of the care of the children and the housework.

The future of the family is unclear. Attacks on the nuclear family by those seeking greater personal freedom from binding commitments, and on what its isolation presumably does to children, are not frequent. There is continued loss of family function and a challenge to family authority. Fewer people marry or have children.

The United States has no systematic family policy, as do other societies, but there is now discussion about what such a policy might be.

NOTES

[1] George P. Murdock, *Social Structures* (New York: Macmillan, 1949).

[2] Melford Spiro, "Is the Family Universal?" *American Anthropologist* 56 (5:1954): 844.

[3] Robert O. Blood, Jr., and Donald M. Wolfe, *Husbands and Wives: The Dynamics of Married Living* (New York: The Free Press, 1960), p. 172.

[4] Ernest Burgess and Harvey J. Locke, *The Family: From Institution to Companionship* (New York: American Book, 1953).

[5] Morris Zelditch, Jr., "Marriage, Family, and Kinship," in Robert E. L. Faris, ed., *Handbook of Modern Sociology* (Chicago: Rand McNally, 1964), p. 725.

[6] Edward Shorter, *The Making of the Modern Family* (New York: Basic Books, 1975), p. 5.

[7] *Ibid.,* pp. 5–6.

[8] *Ibid.,* p. 79.

[9] *Ibid.,* pp. 82–83.

[10] *Ibid.,* p. 259.

[11] *Ibid.,* p. 261.

[12] Eli Zaretsky, *Capitalism, the Family, and Personal Life* (New York: Harper & Row, 1976), pp. 64–65.

[13] *Ibid.,* pp. 140–141.

[14] Daniel R. Miller and Guy E. Swanson, *The Changing American Parent* (New York: Wiley, 1958).

[15] Melvin Kohn, *Class and Conformity* (Homewood, Ill.: Dorsey Press, 1969).

[16] Herbert Gans, *The Urban Villagers: Group and Class in the Life of Italian-Americans* (New York: The Free Press, 1962).

[17] U.S. Bureau of the Census, *Current Population Reports,* P-60, no. 119, "Characteristics of the Population Below the Poverty Level: 1977" (Washington, D.C., 1979).

[18] U.S. Bureau of the Census, *Statistical Abstracts of the United States: 1978* (99th edition), Washington, D.C., 1979, p. 468.

[19] For a review of the research on disorganization among blacks, see Thomas F. Pettigrew, *A Profile on the Negro American* (Princeton, N.J.: D. Van Nostrand, 1964), pp. 15–24.

[20] See Office of Policy Planning and Research, United States Department of Labor, *The Negro Family: The Case for National Action* (Washington, D.C.: U.S. Government Printing Office, 1965).

[21] *Ibid.,* p. 47.

[22] Herbert Gans, "The Negro Family: Reflections on the Moynihan Report," in Lee Rainwater and William L. Yancey, eds., *The Moynihan Report and the Politics of Controversy* (Cambridge, Mass.: The M.I.T. Press, 1967), p. 450.

[23] *Ibid.,* p. 451.

[24] *Ibid.,* p. 451.

[25] Hyman Rodman, *Lower-Class Families: The Culture of Poverty in Negro Trinidad* (New York: Oxford University Press, 1971).

[26] U.S. Bureau of the Census, "Divorce, Child Custody and Child Support" (*Current Population Reports:* Special Studies: Series P- 23; no. 84) 1979, Table 2, p. 8.

[27] *Ibid.,* Table 6, p. 11.

[28] Population Reference Bureau, as reported in *The New York Times,* November 27, 1977.

[29] William J. Goode, *After Divorce* (New York: The Free Press, 1965).

[30] Paul C. Glick and Arthur J. Norton, "Marrying, Divorcing, and Living Together," *Population Bulletin* 32 (5) Washington, D.C., Population Reference Bureau, Inc., p. 5.

[31] See Ersel E. LeMasters, "The Passing of the Dominant Husband-Father," in Hans Peter Drietzel, ed., *Family, Marriage, and the Struggle of the Sexes* (New York: Macmillan, 1972), pp. 110–111.

[32] See Blood and Wolfe, *op. cit.,* p. 37.

[33] Dair L. Gillespie, "Who Has the Power? The Marital Struggle," *Journal of Marriage and the Family* 33 (August 1971): 445–458.

[34] See Gail Putney Fullerton, 2d ed., *Survival in Marriage* (Hinsdale, Ill.: The Dryden Press, 1977), pp. 348–352.

[35] See Gillespie, *op. cit.,* p. 457.

[36] Valerie Kincaide Oppenheimer, "Demographic Influence on Female Employment and the Status of Women," *American Journal of Sociology* 78 (January 1973): p. 948.

[37] Janet Zollinger Giele, "Changing Sex Roles and Family Structure, *Social Policy,* January/February 1979, p. 33.

[38] *Ibid.,* p. 33.

[39] Howard Hayghe, "Families and the Rise of Working Wives—An Overview," *Monthly Labor Review* 99 (May 1976): 12–19.

[40] *Ibid.,* p. 16.

[41] *The New York Times,* November 27, 1977.

[42] Robert O. Blood, Jr., "Long-Range Causes and Consequences of the Employment of Married Women," *Journal of Marriage and Family Living* 27 (February 1965): 43–47.

[43] *Ibid.,* p. 47.

[44] Giele, *op. cit.,* p. 33.

[45] U.S. Bureau of the Census, Current Population Reports, Series P-20, No. 349, "Marital Status and Living Arrangements: March 1979," (Washington, D.C.: U.S. Government Printing Office, 1980), Tables E and F and pp. 3–5.

[46] For an interesting discussion of this arrangement, see Fullerton, *op. cit.,* pp. 616–634.

[47] William J. Goode, *World Revolution and Family Patterns* (New York: The Free Press, 1963).

[48] Barrington Moore, "Thoughts on the Future of the Family," in his *Political Power and Social Theory* (Cambridge, Mass.: Harvard University Press, 1958), pp. 160–178.

[49] *Ibid.,* p. 162.

[50] Nena O'Neill and George O'Neill, *Open Marriage: A New Life Style for Couples* (New York: Avon Books, 1973), p. 147.

[51] Christopher Lasch, *Haven in a Heartless World* (New York: Basic Books, 1977), p. 139.

[52] Kenneth Kenniston, *The Uncommitted: Alienated Youth in American Society* (New York: Harcourt, Brace and World, 1965), p. 277.

[53] Lasch, *op. cit.,* p. xxiii.

[54] *Ibid.,* p. xxiv.

[55] Kenneth Kenniston and the Carnegie Council on Children, *All Our Children: The American Family Under Pressure* (Harcourt Brace Jovanovich, 1977).

SUGGESTED READINGS

Jesse Bernard, *The Future of Marriage* (Cleveland, Ohio: World, 1972). A long-experienced sociologist writes knowingly—and sympathetically—of challenges to the institution of marriage.

Richard deLone, *Small Futures: Children, Inequality, and the Limits of Liberal Reform* (Harcourt Brace Jovanovich, 1979). A forceful critique of the failure to eliminate poverty

and provide an equal chance at a decent life for all American children.

William J. Goode, *World Revolution and Family Patterns* (New York: The Free Press, 1963). A world revolution toward the conjugal family is mapped out.

Herbert G. Gutman, *The Black Family in Slavery and Freedom, 1750–1925* (New York: Pantheon, 1976). A historian's brilliant depiction of the long black struggle to maintain family life in an often hostile environment.

Christopher Lasch, *Haven in a Heartless World: The Family Besieged* (New York: Basic Books, 1977). A leading historian and social critic offers a penetrating and controversial analysis and defense of the besieged modern family.

Kenneth Kenniston and the Carnegie Council on Children. *All Our Children: The American Family Under Pressure* (New York: Harcourt Brace Jovanovich, 1977). An analysis of the pressures which bear on the American family, with particular attention to the unmet needs of America's children.

Hyman Rodman, *Lower-Class Families: The Culture of Poverty in Negro Trinidad* (New York: Oxford University Press, 1971). A study of an alternate family type, with discussion of its meaning and significance.

Edward Shorter, *The Making of the Modern Family* (New York: Basic Books, 1975). A historian's analysis of how capitalism and industrialism affect the family.

Eli Zaretsky, *Capitalism, The Family, and Personal Life* (New York: Harper & Row, 1976). A probing, radical analysis of the relation between capitalism and the family.

Only the educated are free.

Epictetus

Fourteen

EDUCATION

Prominent among the dominant trends of this century is the growth of a complex and bewildering web of institutional arrangements called education. It commands an ever larger share of the resources of society and affects in varied ways more and more persons for longer and longer periods of their lives. It interlocks with economic and technological structures, with political structures and elites, and with economic development and world affairs in a manner never dreamed of a few decades ago. Education, apparently, is one of the central activities of modern society.

It has to be. The process of educating and training people is one of the major tasks in modern society. Now it has become a rapidly changing and profoundly complicating one. It becomes necessary, therefore, to examine education as one of society's institutions.

THE FUNCTIONS OF EDUCATION

The *universal* functions of education are to help socialize the young and to transmit the culture to the next generation. Transmitting the culture means to teach norms and values, to teach knowledge, and to train the young in useful skills. Any society does this, but preindustrial societies did so without schools and teachers, at least for the majority of people.

In these preindustrial societies, most learning took place within the interaction between adults and children in the routine of daily activities, but particularly within kinship structures. If some conscious training took place—as it necessarily did—still no full-time teachers were needed. Teaching was a task adults assumed as a regular part of their rearing of the young.

Even when reading and writing became a necessary skill for some in these societies, the peasant majority of the population remained illiterate; there seemed to be no need for them to be able to read. Education became a prerogative of particular groups: (1) priests and others who were the learned men of society; (2) the aristocratic and ruling stratum; and later, (3) merchants and others involved in commercial transactions.

But a modern, industrial society simply cannot function with widespread illiteracy. Increasingly, it requires people to have higher levels of literacy and professional or technical training. Thus, education as a mass process becomes essential for the functioning of modern society.

The Transmission of Culture

Education indoctrinates the young in the established beliefs of the culture and in that way becomes a conservative force in society. Even when education is not deliberately teaching prevailing values, it still does so. Values, for example, may play a large part in selecting both the kind of knowledge to be taught and the perspective from which it is taught. For instance, teaching history often becomes a process of inculcating a national self-image, and of indoctrinating the young into nationalistic and patriotic perspectives.

Pledging allegiance to the flag is part of the school's function of indoctrination of children into nationalistic and patriotic perspectives.

The School as Moral Authority

The task of moral training for the young was a highly pronounced emphasis in American education from elementary school through college in the nineteenth century, and continued well into the twentieth. But no longer can the school serve as moral authority.

For one thing, in a society where more people are educated, teachers are no longer the unique symbols of moral authority and intellectual competence they once were. No longer, therefore, can they speak authoritatively about moral and cultural standards.

For another thing, there is no longer any easy agreement as to what morality should be taught the young in American schools. Some parents, holding to more traditional values, want a moral training drawn from Christian teachings. Some others want newer teachings from modern psychology, which emphasize personal development and interpersonal relations, and a world of only relative rather than absolute values.

There has been throughout this century a continuing, sometimes bitter struggle in local communities over the moral atmosphere created by the school, as well as over its explicit moral teaching. The recurrent efforts in some communitites to return to prayers and reading of the Bible usually end up in courts, where the issue is most likely to be decided on the principle of separation of church and state.

An even more bitter struggle in a community can be brought about by the efforts of some parents to criticize what they believe are the wrong moral lessons learned by the reading of some textbooks or library books. Their efforts to remove such books from the curriculum, or from the school library, are then usually opposed as being an act of "censorship."

Nonetheless, many adults still look to the schools to carry out a moral function. In a Gallup Poll conducted in 1972, for example, "lack of discipline" emerged as the top issue, ahead of problems of school finance or racial integration.[1] On the question of specific educational goals for secondary schools the public gave first choice to "teaching students to respect law and order."

But teachers cannot be effective in teaching respect for law and order simply because an older generation wants them to do so. More to the point, teaching the young to respect the law and order is a weak substitute for teaching moral values. It comes about only in a society in which no agreement on and conformity to moral standards exists. Then only some reasonable conformity to law and order as the acceptable rules of the game prevents society from breaking down.

Such respect, however, is hard to gain when law no longer has the weight of moral authority behind it, and when it is often seen as a set of rules that benefit some in society more than others. Education cannot be expected to inculcate moral training in a society which no longer knows what its moral standards are.

What schools do teach, however, is conformity to rules in a bureaucratic society. They do this, in the first place, by organizing their internal structure in a bureaucratic manner and by being authoritarian. Schools reward conformity and obedience and have difficulty dealing with creativity, originality, and independence in their students.

The effect of this is to socialize each child into the acceptance of bureaucratic authority, and to become internally regimented and disciplined. In this way children learn that becoming an adult and advancing in the world requires conformity to the rules and role-expectations of bureaucratized organizations.

Education and the Economy

If the school becomes less significant for moral training, it becomes even more important in providing technical skills that certify an individual for the job market. As work shifts from skills traditionally acquired within the family or on the job to new types of work that require nonfamily training, new and demanding educational requirements emerge. Education and occupation become closely tied together, for educational achievement is the major route to preferred occupational roles. What people can do is increasingly defined by what education they have, and educational certification becomes necessary for improving one's life-chances. (For the increasing level of education in the United States, see Table 14.1.)

	Not High School Graduate (percentage)	4 Years of High School or More (percentage)	4 Years of College or More (percentage)
TABLE 14.1			
Level of School Completed by Persons 25 Years Old and Over, 1940–1977			
1940	75.5	24.5	4.6
1952	61.2	38.8	7.0
1959	56.3	43.7	8.1
1965	51.0	49.0	9.4
1970	44.8	55.2	11.0
1977	35.1	64.9	15.4

Source: U.S. Bureau of the Census, *Current Population Reports,* Series P-20, no. 243, "Educational Attainment: March 1972" (Washington, D.C., Government Printing Office, 1972); 1977 data from *Current Population Reports,* Series P-20, no. 314, March 1977.

If lack of education severely limits anyone's life-chances, and if getting an education is necessary for social mobility, then the *level* of education attained is a crucial matter to everyone—education is no longer the concern or the privilege of the few.

The economic value of education has a profound effect upon the structure of education. Changes in curriculum, efforts to upgrade academic and technical performance, the effort to provide a basic education for the most educationally disadvantaged, responses to the demand for more scientifically trained people—all these and other changes indicate education's effort to respond to changes in the "manpower" requirements of a modern economy.

SOCIAL CLASS AND EDUCATION

Those who constantly urge young people to continue their education are fond of quoting statistics to prove the economic value of education. Certainly, preparing people for an occupation is one of the significant functions of education, and one indication of the relationship between education and social class.

Sociologists have examined this relationship by testing the hypothesis that social class serves to distribute educational opportunity unequally—the children of the poor and uneducated get a poorer education; the children of the affluent and educated get a better education.

In an increasingly technological society, however, education cannot continue to be distributed to new generations in the same unequal proportions as it was to the previous ones. Constant changes in the occupational structure puts education to the task of developing the mass training of middle- and high-status persons. Thus, consciously or not, education becomes an instrument for selecting, training, and placing persons in occupations higher than those of their parents. This suggests a different hypothesis: that the educational process is the major mechanism for social mobility.

The Opportunity to Be Educated

When sociologist August Hollingshead described the pervasive influence of a community class structure on the educational process of the local high school in 1949, it came as a shock to many.[2] Hollingshead showed how the school's teachers and administrators acted toward students in ways determined more by the students' social-class position than by their qualities or abilities, even to the point of the distribution of grades and scholarships.

In such a community the school was subservient to the community's dominant classes. For the adolescent the school experience differed in no significant way from experience outside of school: the children of the lowest class were as disadvantaged in school as they were in the community.

Is inequality of educational opportunity to be explained, as Hollingshead did, by the advantages of higher class, including preferential experiences in school? Or do lower-class children fail to take advantage of educational opportunities available to them because they lack aspiration or possess little ability, or perhaps both?

A number of studies have shown—what is hardly surprising—that the higher the social class, the more likely one is to go to college. Several studies have also demonstrated that family position considerably influences even the desire to go to college, though none of these studies agreed on how much relative weight to give to family position and how much to the ability of the student.[3]

But family is not the only relevant dimension. Robert Havighurst and his associates found that children reflect the educational values of the neighborhood.[4] These different neighborhoods constitute what sociologist Alan B. Wilson called "climate of aspiration";[5] they are a result of the educational segregation created by locating schools in neighborhoods of different social classes.

The aspiration climate is lower in low-status neighborhoods and higher in high-status ones. Although most neighborhoods are homogeneous in terms of class, there is sometimes variation, too. Therefore working-class boys in a predominantly middle-class school are likely to raise their aspirations, but these same aspirations will usually be depressed in a slum-located school.

Can All Children Be Taught?

The confidence of teachers in the ability of their students to learn is an important factor in how well they learn. Many teachers seem to believe that lower-class and black children are less able to learn than are middle-class and white children, either because they believe there are genetic differences or because they believe "cultural deprivation" cannot be overcome in their classrooms (see "Jensen and the IQ Problem"). When that happens, there are nonlearning classrooms where teachers do not teach, students do not learn, and the educational process does not educate anyone.

What teachers expect of their students, then, matters very much on how well they learn. The "Pygmalion" experiment of psychologists Rosenthal and Jacobson documented just how much it can make a difference.[6] They gave IQ tests to 650 students in an elementary school in a working-class neighborhood, then told the teachers they would use the results to predict which students were about to take off intellectually. But the names they gave the teachers were drawn randomly from the class. So the teachers were led to expect more from a group of children no different by IQ test from the others.

Did it make any difference? It did, according to retests up to two years after the first one. For children in the first and second grades, their IQ scores improved beyond the level of change, though their "expectancy advantage" faded away after another year. But for older children, it increased still more in the second year.

Perhaps the most basic act of prejudice against the children of the poor and the minorities is to believe that they cannot learn. The 1972 Gallup Poll cited before said that 57 percent of the total sample and 67 percent of educators blamed the child's home life for educational failure. Only 6 percent blamed the school. The disadvantage of home background that poor children bring to school is now being used to excuse the school and to cover up the pervasive and compelling fact of unequal education.[7]

"Cooling Them Out"

In higher education this claim to equal opportunity is achieved by the *open door* policy of community colleges.[8] In addition, some state universities grant admission to almost any graduate of a high school within the state. But they use the freshman year as a screening process, eliminating large numbers by academic failure. These students do not recognize the class basis of their academic failure, for they have been led to believe that they were indeed "given a chance." Their academic failure is seen by them, by their families, and

Sorting students into different tracks means that some are prepared for college while others try to learn something vocationally useful.

JENSEN AND THE IQ PROBLEM

In the United States, no idea has been more tenaciously defended by many whites than that which asserts that blacks (and other nonwhites) are naturally inferior in intelligence, and so white children are more educable than black children.

But what was taken for granted by white Americans for a very long time has been seriously challenged and rejected by the vast majority of scientists concerned with the issue—sociologists, psychologists, geneticists, and anthropologists—for close to half a century now.

Nonetheless, the issue has remained stubbornly alive, and the results of thousands of IQ tests, used almost every day on schoolchildren, provide the evidence continually pointed to by those who insist on the superiority of whites over blacks.

What *do* IQ tests show? They show that:

1. In the United States, the average IQ score of black children is 10 to 15 points below that of white children.

2. Both black and white children achieve high and low IQ scores, though disproportionately more white children achieve higher scores, disproportionately more black children achieve lower scores.

Scientists do not dispute these differences of scores: they are demonstrated facts. What is in dispute is how to interpret them.

Most scientists believe that these test results would prove that blacks are innately inferior only *if* the IQ test adequately measures an inherited intelligence independent of other, environmental factors, that is, if they are culturally unbiased tests, and if their application in test situations takes adequate account of environmental differences in the test population. Few scientists believe this to be the case. Most IQ tests, according to the weight of scientific judgment, favor the socially and educationally advantaged.

In short, as long as *black* and *white* are social categories with significantly different life-chances and life experiences, there will be differences in average IQ scores.

Jensen's Thesis

The IQ controversy received new stimulus when a respected educational psychologist, Arthur Jensen, wrote a long article arguing the probability of different kinds of intelligence being unequally distributed among racial groups.* While acknowledging that environment does influence IQ, Jensen argued that 80 percent of IQ is inherited, and that discrimination and inequalities in education cannot account for the differences in achievement and in IQ scores of black and white children. (More recently, however, after studying some very poor black children in the South, Jensen has recognized environment to be more important than he first thought. Now he says that 50 percent of IQ is inherited.†

On that basis, Jensen argued for "differential educational treatment" based on these measured IQ differences, even though, as a result, there would not be an equal distribution of races and classes in each grouping.

Jensen's critics have argued in response that he has not proved his case,‡ that (1) he too uncritically accepts IQ tests as valid measurements of intelligence, (2) he does not adequately account for the great overlap in the genetic pools of blacks and whites in the United States—90 percent of blacks have some degree of white ancestry, (3) he draws together different test results and studies with different and often uneven controls and checks, many inadequate, (4) he does not adequately account for the problem of controlling for the effects of socioeconomic environment, and (5) he does not specify how much expectable differences in IQ scores are caused by different environmental opportunities. This last point views inherited ability as a potential developed differently in different environments.

Judging by Jensen's responses to his critics, he in turn is not moved by their criticism.

Some of Jensen's critics are less disturbed by his scientific arguments than by his suggestions for educational policy. Namely, from a young age to treat children differently who first measure differently. His advice emphasizes developing such cognitive abilities as abstract reasoning in children who first score higher; but developing different abilities in children who first score lower. Many feel that this would wrongly label many young children as incapable of learning, and result in unequal educational opportunities for different classes and races. Though ostensibly, Jensen himself does not want this outcome, but only the chance for each child to develop his or her inherent capacities, the consequences of such a policy, when widely used, would probably have such a result.

Notes

* Arthur R. Jensen, "How Much Can We Boost IQ and Scholastic Achievement?" *Harvard Educational Review* 39 (Winter 1969): 1—123.

† See the *Harvard Educational Review* 29 (Spring 1969) and 29 (Fall 1969), for a number of telling critiques of Jensen's work.

For further discussion of this issue of IQ, see Ronald J. Samuda, *Psychological Testing of American Minorities: Issues and Consequences* (New York: Dodd, Mead, 1975); and Jeffrey M. Blum, *Pseudoscience and Mental Ability: The Origins and Fallacies of the IQ Controversy* (New York: Monthly Review Press, 1978).

‡ Arthur R. Jensen, "Cumulative Deficit in IQ of Blacks in the Rural South," *Developmental Psychology* 13 (May 1977): 184—191.

by educators as evidence of the students' inadequacies. It looks as if they were *individually* eliminated by low grades and by counseling them out.

This is what Burton Clark calls *cooling them out.* He means public educational institutions confer legitimacy on social inequality by making academic failure seem to be an individual responsibility, an inadequacy of the person, not of the educational process.

The same thing can be accomplished by high school tracking. In about half the high schools in the United States today, students are sorted into different tracks, one being college preparatory; the others vocational, technical, industrial, business, general, and the like.

Though sorting into tracks is presumably done on the basis of ability, one study found that class and racial background strongly influenced which track a student took, quite apart from IQ score or achievement in

junior high.[9] Furthermore, track position had an effect on academic achievement greater than social class background, IQ, or past performance. The effect was to lower the academic performance of noncollege prep students and to raise that of the college prep ones. Not being in the college prep program hurt students' self-esteem; led to a deterioration of academic performance and to less participation in school activities; meant a greater likelihood of dropping out, and more frequent involvement in misbehavior problems in school and out.

Schooling and Inequality: The Jencks Report

A careful and detailed review of all American studies on the relation of class and race to educational and occupational achievement—known as the Jencks Report after its principal author—achieved a more wide-spread public recognition and discussion than scholarly research usually does.[10] Some of that discussion in the press distorted the findings and their policy implications.

The basic findings of the Jencks Report can be summarized as follows:

1. Though educational inequality has been reduced in the United States, educational opportunity is still very unequally distributed.

2. The distribution of cognitive skills, as measured by test scores, is unequal among the social classes and between black and white children. This inequality is largely a function of both genetic and environmental inequality, and could be reduced but not eliminated if educational inequality were eliminated and every one's economic status were equalized. Also, eliminating racial and class segregation would reduce inequality further.

3. Family background has more influence than any other factor on educational achievement. This means that a school's "output" depends largely on a single "input"—the background characteristics the children bring with them.

4. Individuals' occupational statuses are closely tied to their educational attainment.

5. But family background, cognitive skill, educational attainment, and occupational status does not explain much of the variation in *income*. Either there are other factors that do explain it—Jencks speculatively suggested "luck" and personality—or there has not been adequate measurement as yet. (For data on the relation of income and education, see Table 14.2)

From this analysis, Jencks came to the conclusion that schools can do little to make adults more equal. This particular finding has been widely disseminated, and one consequence was to use Jencks's work to argue for a lessening of efforts to improve education, thus relieving the schools of much responsibilty for the academic failure of children.

But Jencks did not intend to give aid and comfort either to complacent educators or to antireform political groups. He argues for a diversity of reforms in education, even though their outcome would not make us all equal. But making us all equal is exactly what Christopher Jencks does believe in, and for this he advocates a program of *income equality*. He ends his book with this statement:

TABLE 14.2
Income of Family Heads, 25 Years Old and Over, by Years of Schooling, by Race, 1977

	Under $10,000 (percent)	$10,000 to $14,999 (percent)	$15,000 to $24,999 (percent)	$25,000 and over (percent)	Median Income
White					
8 yrs. of School	45.0	20.7	23.7	10.6	$11,040
12 yrs. of School	19.1	19.4	38.1	23.4	$17,592
4 or more yrs. of College	6.6	10.2	33.0	50.3	$25,071
Black					
8 yrs. of School	58.1	19.9	17.3	5.3	$ 8,617
12 yrs. of School	41.2	21.8	27.6	9.4	$12,109
4 or more yrs. of College	8.2	16.9	38.9	36.1	$21,107

Source: U.S. Bureau of the Census, *Statistical Abstracts of the United States: 1978* (99th ed.) Washington, D.C., 1978.

As long as egalitarians assume that public policy cannot contribute to economic equality directly but must proceed by ingenious manipulations of marginal institutions like the schools, progress will remain glacial. If we want to move beyond this tradition, we will have to establish political control over the economic institutions that shape our society. This is what other countries usually call socialism. Anything else will end in the same disappointment as the reforms of the 1960s.[11]

Education and Social Mobility

In a changing and mobile society, education cannot continue to define the educational chances of children solely by reference to the status of their parents. Large numbers of people must be educated to fill the social positions created by the expansion of the salaried middle class. Determining who moves up from the lower ranks rests largely with the educational system, which then has two tasks: (1) it must locate and educate more people from lower-class levels for higher-class positions, and (2) it must increase the general level of education at all class levels in the society.

But this is a task for which schools and universities were not historically designed, and as yet they do not do it well.

Going to College At the turn of the century only 4 percent of those aged 18 to 21 were in college; this figure doubled about every 20 years, so that it was 16 percent in 1940. In October 1978, 35 percent of males aged 18–19 were in college, and 36 percent of females. Of the age group 20 and 21 years, 31 percent of males and 26 percent of females were in college.[12] (College attendance for men was highest in 1969, when it was up over 44 percent, but declined with the ending of the Vietnam war.)

This expansion does not necessarily do away with unequal chances, though it does reduce it. However, in 1976, 58.2 percent of young people from families earning $15,000 and over entered college, compared to only 20.4 percent of the poorest families earning under $3,000.[13]

Education for a Meritocracy

It has become a matter of faith of the modern, bureaucratic middle class that they hold their positions by virtue of personal achievement, and that they have risen by their own merit, not by the advantages of races or class. Furthermore, it is now a prevailing belief that this is exactly how the high and responsible positions in a modern society are to be filled, for then merit demonstrated by education and occupational success will give the best leadership.

The concept of *meritocracy* suggests a society in which people earn their social positions on merit and in which advancement through a hierarchy of social positions is based upon "objective" criteria, such as test scores, grades, degrees, and other forms of earned credentials. Presumably, the elite of such a society will be its most qualified people. And there will be elites, for meritocracy is a way of stratifying society from top to bottom. It is not a program for equality.

There is no actual meritocratic society today anywhere in the world, but there are powerful pressures in this direction in most modern and modernizing societies, regardless of ideological orientation. The idea is most attractive within the new middle class—that professionalized class which has succeeded in the process of becoming educationally qualified.

It is within bureaucratic structures that meritocracy is largely proclaimed as the basis for selecting the qualified. But the selection of people for advancement is never wholly a matter of their educationally certified merit. Political and ideological criteria are always important, however much they may be formally denied. Technical merit alone will not bring promotion if the individual's relations with colleagues and fellow workers are difficult—one must "relate" well to others—or if his social and political attitudes are too deviant.

But a more basic issue is that the opportunity to qualify is still very unequally distributed. Discrimination by social class, as well as by race and sex, begins so early in life that inevitably the successful meritocrats are drawn disproportionately from the middle and upper classes of society.

Furthermore, we have no scientific capacity to provide a genuinely equal process for determining merit. None of the objective criteria escape being culturally biased, particularly those of class. The qualified in present-day meritocracy win out mostly because of a head start in life, one that enables them to succeed in earlier grades in order to qualify for later education and the winning of the best credentials.

What is important, however, is that the meritocratic viewpoint may come to dominate more and more. Various testing processes from earliest childhood not only rank people but they label many of them as average or mediocre. Once such tags are firmly fixed, even the children labeled believe it, and in time they do in fact become academically mediocre. The children of the educated meritocrats will escape this fate more often than not, while the children of the less educated will most often be its victims.

RACE AND EDUCATION

In both quantity and quality of education, black people lag behind white people, as Table 14.3 shows. It has never been otherwise in the United States, but in the last two decades, since the Supreme Court decision of 1954, the differences in educational opportunities and educational achievement between the races has been a major concern of legislative policy and court decision.

Segregated Schooling

Segregation of the races in public facilities, including schooling, has been held to be constitutional since the Supreme Court ruled that separate facilities did not violate the 14th Amendment to the Constitution guaranteeing equal protection under the laws, *if* those facilities were otherwise equal. This was the famous *Plessy* v. *Ferguson* decision of 1896, the "separate but equal" ruling that remained basic federal policy until 1954, when in *Brown* v. *Board of Education* the Supreme Court overturned the earlier decision (see "Excerpts from Supreme Court Decisions on Racial Segregation"). The Court ruled that children, when required on the basis of race to attend separate schools, were deprived of the equal protection assured by the 14th Amendment.

Racially separate schools, the Court said in its written opinion, have "a tendency to retard the educational and mental development of Negro children and to deprive them of some of the benefits they would receive in a racially integrated school."

Desegregating Schools Though this decision became the law of the land, it did not lead to any rapid change in the segregation of the races in public schools in either the North or the South. Only slowly and grudgingly did change come. Indeed, as late as 1965, 80 percent of all white children were attending schools that were from 90 to 100 percent white and 65 per-

---

TABLE 14.3
Level of School Completed by Persons
20 Years Old and Over, by Age and Race, 1977

Age and Race	Median Years of School (percentage)	High School Graduate (percentage)	One or More Years of College (percentage)	Four or More Years of College (percentage)
White				
20–24 years	12.8	85.1	41.1	10.5
25 and over	12.5	67.0	30.0	16.1
Black				
20–24 years	12.6	75.3	31.7	6.0
25 and over	11.4	45.5	17.0	7.2
Spanish Origin				
20–24 years	12.3	61.5	25.3	4.3
25 and over	10.1	39.6	15.2	6.2

Source: U.S. Bureau of the Census, *Current Population Reports,* Series P-20, no. 134, "Educational Attainment in the United States: March 1977 and 1976," Washington, D.C., 1977, Table 2, pp. 19–28.

EXCERPTS FROM SUPREME COURT DECISIONS ON RACIAL SEGREGATION

Plessy v. Ferguson (1896)

. . . A statute which implies merely a legal distinction between the white and colored races—a distinction which is founded in the color of the two races, and which must always exist so long as white men are distinguished from the other race by color—has no tendency to destroy the legal equality of the two races. . . .

. . . Gauged by this standard, we cannot say that a law which authorizes or even requires the separation of the two races in public conveyances is unreasonable or more obnoxious to the 14th Amendment than the acts of Congress requiring separate schools for colored children in the District of Columbia, the constitutionality of which does not seem to have been questioned in the corresponding acts of state legislatures.

We consider the underlying fallacy of the plaintiff's argument to consist in the assumption that the enforced separation of the two races stamps the colored race with a badge of inferiority. If this be so, it is not by reason of anything found in the act, but solely because the colored race chooses to put that construction upon it. . . . The argument also assumes that social prejudices may be overcome by legislation, and that equal rights cannot be secured to the Negro except by an enforced commingling of the two races. We cannot accept this proposition. If the two races are to meet on terms of social equality, it must be the result of natural affinities, a mutual appreciation of each other's merits and a voluntary consent of individuals.

. . . If one race be inferior to the other socially, the Constitution of the U.S. cannot put them on the same plane.

Brown v. Board of Education (1954)

We come then to the question presented: Does segregation of children in public schools solely on the basis of race, even though the physical facilities and other "tangible" factors may be equal, deprive the children of the minority group of equal educational opportunities? We believe that it does.

. . . To separate them from others of similar age and qualifications solely because of their race generates a feeling of inferiority as to their status in the community that may affect their hearts and minds in a way unlikely ever to be undone.

We conclude that in the field of public education the doctrine of "separate but equal" has no place. Separate educational facilities are inherently unequal.

cent of black children were in schools that were at least 90 percent black.

Furthermore, what is most significant is that during the 1960s a trend for *increased racial separation* became evident. This is a consequence of increasing white concentration in the suburbs and conversely increasing black concentration in the central cities. In 15 large metropolitan areas in 1960, 79 percent of the nonwhite enrollment was in central city schools and 68 percent of white students attended suburban schools;

the trend through the 1960s and into the 1970s did nothing to alter that situation but instead intensified it.[14]

This trend holds in cities both North and South. In Atlanta, for example, only 30 percent of the schoolchildren were black in 1958, but fifteen years later, in 1973, black schoolchildren composed 80 percent of the total.[15] In Detroit, black schoolchildren were already 45.8 percent of the total by 1961, and had become 84 percent by 1979.[16]

An additional contributing factor in central cities is the increasing enrollment of white students in private schools. The trend is hardly new. By 1965, 40 percent of the total white elementary school population in St. Louis attended nonpublic schools; in Boston, 41 percent, and in Philadelphia, more than 60 percent.[17]

These patterns continued throughout the 1970s, increasing the racial separation of black and white children in schools. Thus, 66 percent of all black children in public schools in 1974 were still in schools where blacks were a majority. In fact, 35 percent of them were in schools that were 95 percent or more black, and 12 percent of them were in all-black schools.[18]

This further separation of the races occurs despite the fact that all public-opinion surverys reveal increasingly more positive attitudes about blacks by whites. Though prejudice seems to be declining, that fact has not made whites more ready to send their children to school with large numbers of black children.

Whites share two basic convictions about central city schools in which blacks are a majority: first, that the achievement level of the students is lower; and, secondly, that the schools are physically unsafe for students as well as teachers. It is these beliefs that account for the continued white movement to suburban and private schools.

The Coleman Report: Equal Educational Opportunity

There are, in fact, differences in the quality of education attained by white and black (and other minority) students in the United States—and the differences are substantial. A massive national study by sociologist James Coleman found that black students in the twelfth grade in the urban Northeast, for example, were reading at a ninth-grade level and doing math at a seventh-grade level. Eighty-five percent of black students were below the white average.[19]

In a massive collection of tables and statistical analyses, the Coleman Report found that such things as the physical quality of the school and its resources seemed to have little to do with the academic achievement of black students. Schools, the report found, have no "independent effect" on children. This means that schools do not make up for the considerable inequalities of home and neighborhood that children bring to school. The school does more educationally for children from affluent, educated homes and less for children from poorer, less educated ones.

What the Coleman Report did find, consistent with its overall result, was that when children from a disadvantaged background were in a class with less disadvantaged children, they did better than if their fellow students were all like themselves. Even when black disadvantaged students are in classes with similarly disadvantaged white students, they did better—this is a finding made much of by the supporters of school integration.

In a separate analysis of the Coleman Report data, it was reported that:

> The combined effects of social class integration and racial desegregation are substantial. When disadvantaged Negro students are in class with similarly situated whites, their average performance is improved by more than a full grade. When they are in a class with more advantaged white students, their performance is improved by more than two grade levels.[20]

Implications for Social Policy

The single most important conclusion to be drawn from the Coleman Report is this: that disadvantaged black students do better when placed in classes with more advantaged students. That conclusion led many (including Coleman himself) to argue that educational integration is the appropriate social policy for the problem of educating the disadvantaged minority.

Other social scientists and black intellectuals, however, while not necessarily disagreeing with the aim of integration, have offered a wide range of alternate ways to increase educational achievement by the disadvantaged child.[21] These include:

1. Reorganizing the public schools away from the neighborhood school to more inclusive systems, such as magnet schools, educational parks or clusters, which would bring together a larger mix of children.

2. A program of compensatory education, including, among others, remedial instruction, special tutors and counselors, the use of special teaching materials, cultural enrichment, and preschool (headstart) education.

3. Neighborhood or community control of schools, so that local people, particularly parents, could ensure that the school will meet the particular needs of their children.

Going Beyond Integration

A more basic critique of the Coleman Report has been made by Samuel Bowles, a political economist who contends, first of all, that Coleman's claim that the physical and economic resources going into education have no effect on outcome (achievement) is open to serious challenge.[22] Bowles argues that educational equality in outcome can only be achieved if the expenditure for black students and for poor white students is *greater* than that for more affluent students.

But Bowles makes two other basic arguments. One is that the school system alone cannot bear the burden of achieving equality of educational opportunity. As long as racial discriminatin and poverty exist, education alone will not equalize life-chances as these are measured by jobs and incomes. (This is the same point made in the Jencks Report.) Racial discrimination in the job market must be attacked directly, Bowles feels. Blacks earn less than whites even when their education is the same, and the greater the education, the greater the difference in earning power.

Bowles's third point is a basic challenge, namely, that whites gain competitively by the undereducation of blacks, so that achieving equality of educational op-

The federal courts' mandating of busing in order to desegregate schools has been a controversial strategy, often resisted, the gains from which remain in dispute among researchers.

portunity puts whites and blacks into a real conflict of interests. Therefore, according to Bowles, blacks must attain greater political power before education can be changed enough to provide equal opportunity for all.

Disagreement about Desegregation

In the 1960s and 1970s the Coleman Report was cited as justification for programs for school desegregation, including mandatory busing plans. Then in 1975 Coleman announced that he had changed his assessment of the issues and had decided that court-ordered desegregation (often by means of busing) did more harm than good.

Since then there has been heated debate among social scientists in interpreting the results of over 100 studies. Two matters are in disagreement: (1) whether court-ordered busing and similar desegregation measures only encourage "white flight" to the suburbs; and (2) whether school desegregation has any substantial positive effect on the achievement of minority students, or whether (as some argue) it has a negative effect.

As of now, competent researchers draw different, even contradictory readings from the same research. Even as they do so, others committed to improve education for disadvantaged school children are recognizing that, more and more, most disadvantaged children are to be found in large central cities, where there are fewer and fewer advantaged children with whom they can integrate. Other means, it would seem, must be found.

HIGHER EDUCATION

The changes in American higher education throughout this century have paralleled the changes going on throughout the whole of society. The small, private liberal arts colleges and the local normal schools for preparing local teachers have been overshadowed by the rise of the large universities. These have come to dominate higher education by their standards and criteria of what is academically excellent. As a result,

higher education has ceased to be a marginal, backward-looking enterprise shunned by the bulk of the citizenry. Today it is a major growth industry, consuming about 2 percent of GNP, directly touching the lives of per-

haps 4 percent of the population, and exercising an indirect effect on the whole of society.[23]

The Origins of the Modern University

The university is an ancient and prestigious structure, which has survived over centuries of radical transformation of society, from medieval to industrial. Yet rarely has it led in that transformation; instead, it typically has followed changes originating elsewhere in the society, and often only after considerable resistance.

Universities in the Middle Ages were closely tied to the religious structure. But even after they had freed themselves from close religious control, they were slow to adapt to the emerging industrial society. Most of all, they were resistant to democratizing higher education and making access to it more available to non-elites.

But when Wilhelm von Humboldt established a new university at Berlin in 1810, a new type of institution emerged. Others soon followed and within a decade or so they became centers of *scientific* learning in which the laboratory turned out to be as important as the lecture hall. This German model of the university, with its emphasis upon scientific training, in time influenced universities in the United States. The graduate school, for example, developed as a parallel to the German institute. According to Jencks and Riesman, "it was not until the 1880s that anything like a modern university took shape in America," and by World War I, "two dozen major universities had emerged."[24] Thus, within a space of forty years, a major transition in higher education had taken place.

Higher education is not what it was even two decades ago, and colleges and universities have undergone enormous changes. What are those changes? Two recent incisive analyses have argued that the *university* has been replaced by the *multiversity*, and that this in turn is but one component of an *academic revolution*.

The Multiversity

When Clark Kerr, a social scientist and former president of the University of California, coined the term *multiversity*, he meant that the university was now made up of several units that bore little relation to one another.[25] These units performed different services for different groups and clients, making the university a highly diversified organization. It no longer had a center that defined its mission in the world, as its liberal arts core of disciplines once did.

Among other changes, the large public universities have expanded to accommodate increased enrollments in their undergraduate divisions. But they have also grown as the major centers for training graduate students and thus for producing technicians, professionals, scientists, and scholars in greater numbers than before. And the university is the major site of scientific research.

This has meant a vast increase in students at American universities; campuses that contain 25,000 or more are no longer uncommon. Maintaining a single, cohesive sense of student life then becomes difficult — and perhaps no desire among many of the students that there even be one. But thousands of students on any large campus feel that they are a nameless face in a huge student body, unknown but to a few friends, and seemingly unable to find means for more personalized interaction with faculty. It is this alienated condition that most observers credit for so much of the student rebellion that first broke out at the University of California at Berkeley in the early 1960s.

However, it is not merely numbers that render the relationship of the student to the faculty so impersonal and frequently bureaucratized. In the large American university the student is by no means the only concern of the faculty and sometimes not the primary one. The vast research enterprise that large universities carry on now creates a different type of role for the professor that competes with his teaching role.

For most professors, the rewards of his occupation —recognition in his profession, publication of his work, offices in professional societies, and awards and honors—come, not from teaching, but from research and the publication of research. A good teacher is recognized only on his campus, but an outstanding researcher can have a national—even an international—reputation. He may travel to conferences on expense account, and his well-funded research may provide him with assistants, a second office, secretarial help, and a light teaching load, or even no teaching at all. None of this may be available to the teacher-professor.

The Academic Revolution

The basic changes in American higher education —which Jencks and Riesman have called an aca-

demic revolution—besides the transition to a multiversity, also include something more fundamental: the rise to unprecedented power of professional scholars and scientists within the university and in time with the society.

The Professionalization of Faculty   The *professionalization* of university professors and their assumption of greater power within the university are two related processes. Over the years professors in modern universities have been able to establish their right to choose their own colleagues, to control the curriculum, and even to determine criteria for choosing students. They have successfully imposed a professional claim to competency to make these decisions—a professional expertise that others as *laymen* presumably do not have.

Furthermore, the professors, organized in departments, control graduate instruction. "They turn out Ph.D.s who, despite conspicuous exceptions, mostly have quite similar ideas about what their discipline covers, how it should be taught, and how its frontiers should be advanced."[26] In addition, "they have established machinery for remaining like-minded," including national and regional meetings, national journals for publishing their research, and an informal network for job placement.[27]

The powerful graduate schools, expanding rapidly since World War II, have become pacesetters in the promotion of meritocratic values. They claim to choose their candidates by their demonstrated ability to do good academic work, ignoring other "particularistic" claims, such as class background. (Despite this claim, universities have not proved to be easily accessible to women and blacks.)

Beyond that, the graduate schools have led the way in extending meritocratic values to the professions themselves. The leading law firms and the most prestigious hospitals try to hire the best graduates of the leading professional schools, and colleges and universities seek after the most recommended graduates of the best graduate departments in their discipline. Since graduate education and professional training within universities increasingly finds an outlet in the best job opportunities, the training in values and outlook provided by graduate-school professors has increasing effect upon how the professions function. And professors are the reform-minded intellectuals of any profession, even in the business school.

This makes of higher education an instrument for

"meritocratic sorting and grading" of the future middle-class work force of modern society.

Training versus Educating This *training* of individuals for professional and technical labor markets, as well
as providing various forms of service to state and society, does not fit easily with higher education's historic
claim of *educating* people to a capacity for critical, objective thought. Training produces technically qualified
individuals who fit readily into corporate and governmental bureaucracies, while education equips people
to think independently, to pose critical questions, and
to challenge comfortable assumptions.

The meritocratic emphasis on training has an unintended but nevertheless real stultifying effect on educating the independent mind.[28] Furthermore, the emphasis on obtaining credentials to get a good job
creates in universities an atmosphere in which education of the mind loses out to a competitive scramble for
grades, credits, and degrees.

Change and Dissent in Higher Education

There have been other changes besides the ones
we have been describing, including some which were
a backlash against them.

During the late 1960s and early 1970s student dissent and protest erupted on American college campuses. Students protested the neglect of teaching, the
irrelevance to their lives of much that was taught, and
the dominance of research and graduate teaching over
undergraduate education. They also criticized the
close tie of some universities to the Department of Defense, the heavy dependency on the federal government for research funds, and the close association between universities and corporations. They argued for a
new consideration for the needs of blacks and other
minorities.

Behind the shouting and demonstrating students
were asking: What kind of university is it to be in what
kind of a society? They were asking that the university
rethink its conception of its public responsibility, and
that it become a force for social change, even radical
change. They argued that the university should be independent from other power centers and established
institutions of the society.

But the student rebellion, so closely tied to the
struggle against the Vietnam war, proved not to have
sustaining power, and its force receded as the war

Student protest and dissent in the late sixties and
early seventies centered on the Vietnam War, but
that activism dissipated as the war wound down
and ended in the middle seventies.

ended. By the late 1970s most of its criticism of the
university had receded, some even forgotten.

There have been some other lasting changes: increased admissions of minorities and programs geared
particularly to their needs, for one, and the participation of students with faculty in academic governance.

Other changes soon affected the relation of students to the university. Fewer jobs in a tighter economy produced a new concern for acquiring marketable skills. That, coupled with a corporate demand
that students have "practical" skills, and a refusal to
employ the liberal arts graduate once readily hired,
produced a student shift to more vocational fields of
study, away from the liberal arts.

Entering students in fall 1979, for example, expressed an *increased* interest (compared to such students in 1969) in majoring in the physical and biological sciences, in engineering, business, and in preprofessional programs. They expressed a corresponding *decline* in their intent to major in arts and humanities, in education, and in the social sciences.[29]

Student attitudes have changed, too, but not in any one direction. On some issues, the entering freshmen in 1979 were more conventional than they were in 1969, but in other areas they were at least as liberal,

suggesting that some changes in attitudes will be more enduring. (See Table 14.4 for a detailed comparison of entering college students in 1969 and 1979.)

Modern universities, and especially public ones, are now such integral parts of modern society and perform such critical functions for it that they cannot simply cease to perform the many teaching and research functions that make "multiversities" of them. Their relation to government and the corporate economy are close, and the changes of recent years make clear how responsive they always are to the needs of these larger clients.

TABLE 14.4
Percentages of Social Attitudes of Entering College Students: 1969 and 1979

	Women		Men	
	1969	1979	1969	1979
Students agree that:				
Marijuana should be legalized	22.4	43.6	28.1	48.6
The disadvantaged should receive preferential treatment	39.0	37.5	43.3	39.0
Capital punishment should be abolished	59.0	40.7	50.0	28.0
Criminals have too many rights	46.8	57.0	60.0	68.1
Abortion should be legal	74.1	53.6	77.9	53.0
Divorce laws should be liberalized	35.2	46.0	46.5	51.6
Objectives considered to be important:				
Achieve in a performing art	13.7	13.6	9.5	10.9
Be an authority in my field	54.3	70.5	62.9	75.3
Obtain recognition from peers	35.3	49.8	45.3	54.7
Influence political structure	12.0	12.0	19.6	19.1
Influence social values	37.1	33.9	31.5	29.8
Raise a family	77.8	64.8	66.5	65.0
Have administrative responsibility	16.4	34.5	29.8	39.5
Be very well-off financially	32.1	56.7	54.1	69.1
Help others in difficulty	75.0	71.4	58.2	55.4
Make theoretical contributions to science	5.5	11.2	14.0	17.6
Write original works	16.2	13.8	11.8	10.9
Create works of art	21.2	16.7	11.3	11.3
Keep up with political affairs	49.8	33.4	52.5	43.2
Succeed in my own business	33.1	42.5	55.5	55.9
Develop a philosophy of life	85.8	54.7	78.5	51.0

Source: *Chronical of Higher Education,* January 28, 1980. Data are from *The American Freshman: National Norms for Fall, 1979* (Los Angeles: Graduate School of Education, University of California at Los Angeles, 1980).

Blacks in Higher Education

Despite the handicap of financial and educational disadvantage, blacks have been attending college in ever increasing numbers since the early 1960s. Other minorities, too, have gained more admission to college.

College enrollment of blacks has increased substantially since 1964, when they were only 5 percent of all college students. But they were 7 percent in 1970 and by 1977 they were 11 percent.

However, while blacks in 1977 were 13 percent of all freshmen, they were only 9 percent of seniors and 6 percent of graduate students. This suggests that while blacks now enroll at a rate that equals their proportion in the population—blacks are 13 percent of all persons aged 18–21—they were not as successful as whites in completing four years of schooling. Further support for this observation is offered by evidence that, in 1977, only 41 percent of all blacks aged 25–29 who had started college had finished, compared to 54 percent for whites.[30]

It would seem that by now blacks have caught up with whites in their capacity to enter college, though they are overrepresented in two-year colleges and underrepresented in four-year ones. They will not catch up with whites in education, however, until they earn degrees at the same rate.

THE CONTROL OF EDUCATION

Whether public or private, the school system (or systems) of a society are subject to controls exerted from outside the educational process itself. To a considerable extent education has been a process of preparing young people to meet the requirements set down by other institutions of the society, and the changes in educational standards are a response to changing demands within the society.

But the educational structure is not equally responsive to the demands and interests of all the various sta-

Blacks now enter college at a rate equal to their proportion in the population, but they still lag behind whites in completing four years of schooling.

tus groups and classes. The established elites and privileged groups have always exerted control over education in two ways. First, they have usually established for their own offspring separate schools, such as the English public schools (which are really private schools), the German law faculties, the Ivy League universities, and the elite prep schools. Secondly, they have exerted a strong ideological control over the content and subject matter of the education of other social classes, once these other social classes gained voting rights and so had some political power.

Public education for most people began only in the nineteenth century, partly in response to the demands of working-class people for an education for their children. Labor unions and workingmen's parties, and the voting power of a newly enfranchised working class, put power behind such a demand.

But business classes and propertied elites, once the working class got the vote, pressed for universal education to accompany universal suffrage. They wanted working-class children in school in order to indoctrinate them with such values as respect for property and for law and order, hard work, frugality and savings, competition and achievement, belief in the capitalist system, and in America as the unequaled land of opportunity and freedom.[31]

What began at the outset as a democratic movement for *free* education became in time *compulsory* schooling for all social classes in schools controlled by the economic elite.

Since then, schools have always taught a political and economic perspective acceptable to dominant classes, and they are in trouble when they try to do otherwise. Though there is frequent lip service to the ideal of teaching the young to think critically, schools in fact are organized too authoritatively and teach too uncritically to accomplish that. A distinguished American political scientist put it:

In modern societies the school system, in particular, functions as a formidable instrument of political power in its role as a transmitter of the goals, values, and attitudes of the polity. In the selection of values and attitudes to be inculcated, it chooses those cherished by the dominant elements in the political order. By and large the impact of widely accepted goals, mores, and social values fixes the programs of American schools. When schools diverge from this vaguely defined directive and collide with potent groups in the political system, they feel a pressure to conform.[32]

What Is Not Taught

As important as what is taught is what is *not* taught in the schools. American public schools have taught American children very little about the American racial experience, particularly about the enslavement of blacks and the expulsion of Indians from their land holdings.

They have not taught black children anything about their own history, and as sociologist-historian George Rawick points out, they have failed to teach that black history is part and parcel of American history, not something apart.[33] Nor have they allowed Indian children to learn of the Indian heritage in their schools.

In both cases, schooling has been a means of *not* teaching their own heritage, history, and collective experience to subordinate groups. They have not even taught them enough of the dominant culture to allow them to succeed within it.

This is also true of working people and European immigrants. Their children have learned nothing about the life and struggles of immigrants, or of the history of labor violence that occurred so frequently until the 1930s.

In both these instances, the schools have treated American society as if there were no unequal groups and classes, when in fact such class and racial inequality is a fundamental key to the inequality that besets education.

From Local to National Control

In the United States education has been primarily a local enterprise, in contrast to Europe, where education has been under national control. This localistic pattern developed when the United States was primarily locally focused or at best regional in its economic structure.

But now, local markets are superseded by a national (and even international) market. Occupational opportunities are viewed increasingly in terms of national trends. Accordingly, the demands upon the local schools are to prepare young people to enter college and to enter job markets, neither of which is any longer a strictly local enterprise.

Education has become a matter of national policy and is receiving a steadily increasing share of national resources. The rapid growth of the U.S. Department of Education into a position of leadership in education, with resources for the support of varied types of programs for the development of education, is less than two decades old. The National Science Foundation has undertaken a national program for upgrading science training, as well as an extensive support of scientific research in universities.

There are other forces working against localism. Private foundations, for example, throughout this century have undertaken various projects intended to improve quality or to innovate in the area of curriculum. Increasingly, state governments have acted to minimize local differences through state certification of teachers, some common course requirements, and also through allocation of tax funds for education. Thus, state departments of education have long been a major force for removing local differences in education.

Professionalization   A highly significant development, consistent with the emergence of a more professionalized middle class, has been the *professionalization* of education on a national level, introducing national standards that put pressure on local school boards and shield both teachers and administrators from local pressures. More and more local systems must conform to nationally accepted standards in order to compete successfully for available good teachers, to remain accredited, and to place their graduates in decent colleges and universities.

This also means the growth of significant control agencies, including accrediting agencies. This leads to control over substantive curriculum matters by agencies outside the local school system or university. Frequently, a board of education or a board of trustees has no choice but to meet such requirements or have its programs disaccredited and its degrees devalued.

There has also been the growth of professional power by teachers and administrators, the professionals of education, over the day-to-day educational process. This increased professional power has developed "teacher power" and has been accompanied by economic action, including strikes, a behavior once defined as unprofessional. Now college professors, too, are organizing into faculty collective-bargaining organizations.

All of this movement away from local control has occurred without a great national debate over the issue of local versus national control. Yet local control takes on renewed meaning for citizens when they see its significance for controlling processes and decisions vital to their interests. School busing and community control of schools are two such recent issues.

Busing: Local versus Centralized Control   Busing children for integration touches upon racial attitudes, but on other issues, too. Proposals to bus children around and across a large metropolitan area (such as in and around Detroit, Michigan, and Richmond, Virginia) had other implications, if upheld by courts; they were not. One would be to reduce the power of the local school district and local citizen control. Citizen involvement in schools seems threatened if school attendance is assigned across community boundaries. Local boards will lose real power if the citizens who elect them and pay the taxes do not send their children to those schools. Parental participation will decline if children are to attend schools in distant districts. School busing is a complicated issue, but its effect on local control of education would be to reduce that control.

Community Control of Schools   That fact is not lost upon those blacks who have advocated that black people gain control of their own communities, particularly of the local schools that seem unable to educate their children well.[34]

Decentralizing large urban school districts (as has been done in New York City and Detroit) into several local boards became a political goal in the 1960s and early 1970s. Making it a political reality, however, proved more difficult.

To restore real power, not merely a pretence of power, to local districts within a large city—and thus to blacks and white ethnics and working-class people in their own neighborhoods—is an idea strongly resisted by established political leaders and by professional educators. Nor does it appeal to many middle-class people whose professional experience and training lead them to put their confidence in trained professional "expertise," and in the dominance of the more educated over the less educated. The professional organizations of teachers also have generally opposed community control in big cities.

The drift toward national control, centered in professional and governmental structures far beyond the influence of local people is a trend so far along that any reversal meets enormous resistance and opposition. But these two issues, busing and community control of schools, call attention to how much centralized control has already occurred in American education without any clear national decision to do so.

REFORMING EDUCATION

Education is under constant criticism. There are a number of difficult and pressing issues which bring about efforts at the reform of education as it now is.

Basically, education has the task of fitting children into a modern society—a technological, complex, and stratified society. It is not an instrument for reforming society. Instead, it has always been shaped and reformed by other forces and groups within society. This produces demands upon education not always consistent, sometimes contradictory.

Here are a few of the more difficult and pressing issues.

Preparing People for Jobs The belief that the school has the task of preparing people for jobs and for getting ahead is widespread, held as tenaciously among the poor and disadvantaged as among the affluent. Here is where much intended reform fails to meet the issue. Schools have no independent power to transform themselves into educational processes that do other than fit people into the existing society. Variations in ways of educating children compete for attention and support, but all must finally meet the same tests—and these are the credential-winning tests imposed on the schools. Schools cannot retain credibility if they fail to teach children to take exams and achievement tests and do well on them.

The schools, in short, will carry out the tasks of preparing the young for society, but the schools do not on their own decide what that preparation is to be. Increasingly, schooling is a process of teaching and testing for the skills and values that make for success in the world of jobs and careers, on terms set down by those who are the gatekeepers to jobs and careers. (Note, though, that professional educators usually come to believe thoroughly in these same skills and values as the essential curriculum.) Schools provide instruction and then sort and sift to stamp best grade on some,

only good to average on others, and mark some as rejects.

Educating Equally If even the poorest people expect the schools to prepare their children for jobs and getting ahead, they want them to do so in some reasonably *equal* manner. The public schools have always claimed to provide equal opportunity for all to learn, though in fact they have never done so. Even now millions of ordinary people believe this is what schools should do.

Yet the Gallup-conducted poll on the problems of education quoted before found that 57 percent of the total sample and 67 percent of the educators blamed the home life of the children for their doing poorly; only 6 percent blamed the school.

When one adds to this that as many as 52 percent of educators would allow children to leave school at age 16, you see developing among educators a new perspective, one which reduces their obligation to educate equally, and instead to legitimate what has happened anyway, the providing of lesser education for those below the comfortable middle-class level.

In a society organized unequally, schools have neither the ability nor the mandate to educate all—rich and poor, black and white—equally. They do not expect to do so; dominant classes do not want them to do so; nor do they have the will or desire to do so. Equality in education cannot be realized, so the *Jencks Report* told us, if we do not achieve equality in the economy.

Equal Opportunity But most reformers are not asking that each child be equally educated, only that each one be given an equal opportunity. The disabilities of class and the discriminations of race are to be removed, so that all children will learn according to their natural ability. Some will learn more than others, for, many believe, abilities are different. This, of course, is the meritocratic goal, where the better-educated elite outstrips the average-educated mass, not because of class advantage or racial privilege, but because of natural talent given equal opportunity to learn.

But providing an equal opportunity to learn is not a workable goal in industrial society as long as its class structure perpetuates inequality in life-chances. A society organized into social classes, as all industrial societies are, could not achieve equality of opportunity with upsetting its structure of class advantages and privileges. Achieving equal opportunity, therefore, requires a radical restructuring of basic institutions; that takes a political revolution, not educational reform.

Big-City Schools Perhaps nowhere is the inequality of education more painfully evident than in many big-city school systems. Many are debt-ridden and on the verge of bankruptcy. They are often poorly and inefficiently managed, with cumbersome, unresponsive bureaucracies.

In all but six of the nation's big-city school systems, white students are now a minority. According to Diane Ravitch, a historian of education, between 1968 and 1977 Atlanta lost 78.3 percent of its white enrollment, Detroit lost 61.6 percent, San Francisco lost 56.4 percent, and San Antonio 53.3 percent.[35]

This loss of white students also means the loss of working- and middle-class families, so that, not only big-city schools have largely nonwhite students, they also have very poor ones.

It is in these schools that the quality of education has declined seriously. It seems that teachers cannot, will not, or do not believe they can teach these children effectively. As a result, their levels of achievement are usually three to five years below the national average, and even worse in some cases.

The school buildings are not environments conducive to learning. Violence in the halls and classrooms, against both students and teachers; vandalism; high rates of truancy; the selling and using of drugs in hallways and bathrooms; the lack of effective authority and discipline—all of these prevent serious learning.

Some five million school children attend these big-city schools, 10 percent of the public population. They come from the most disadvantaged backgrounds, and they are likely to remain there unless there is effective reform. That probably requires two things: a conviction that all children, even the most disadvantaged ones, can learn; and a significant influx of funds to pay for the teachers and resources necessary to enable them to catch up and in that way have an equal chance to be educated.

Deschooling Society

Perhaps the most radical idea for reforming education has been advanced by Ivan Illich, a Latin-American intellectual whose book, *Deschooling Society,* has

been widely read in the United States. Illich argues that *schooling* and *learning* are not the same thing. Yet schools seek to monopolize all learning experiences, with a consequent enforced dependency of individuals on the schools.

> Rich and poor alike depend upon schools and hospitals which guide their lives, form their world view, and define for them what is legitimate and what is not. Both view doctoring oneself as irresponsible, learning on one's own as unreliable, and community organization, when not paid for by those in authority, as a form of aggression or subversion. For both groups the reliance on institutional treatment renders independent accomplishment suspect. The progressive underdevelopment of self- and community-reliance is even more typical in Westchester than it is in the northeast of Brazil. Everywhere not only education but society as a whole needs "deschooling."[36]

What Illich advocates is creating alternate ways to promote learning on an equal basis. He emphasizes the wide range of human possibilities, including self-learning and learning from one's peers. He also advocates giving people access to learning centers on an equal basis, without regard to previous certification. His concerns are with the failure of obligatory schooling to do its assigned task adequately, with its failure to provide equal educational opportunity, and with its making people dependent on elites and elite-controlled institutions. Therefore, if we deschool society, he argues, "our reliance on specialized, full-time instruction through school will now decrease and we must find more ways to learn and teach; the educational quality of all institutions must increase again."[37]

Illich's notion of deschooling society is probably too impractical to be a serious basis for educational reform in this society now, and probably in most societies in the world. He imagines it would be easier to revolt against school than against government and corporations, but in fact schools are so important to reproducing the values and skills of any society that they are going to be defended as zealously as any other institution. Society cannot be deschooled short of a political attack on all its institutions.

Yet, despite his political impracticality, Illich's contribution is significant. He provides us with a highly penetrating critique of the place of school in contemporary society the world over, while emphasizing what he regards as its negative outcomes: supporting inequality; making people too dependent and docile;

making the less educated feel inferior to the more educated; institutionalizing and legitimizing the values of elites. These make more difficult the construction of a world in which we can discover how to use technology "to create institutions which serve personal, creative, and autonomous interaction and the emergence of values which cannot be substantially controlled by technocrats."[38]

Illich's critique reminds us of a basic principle: Education is not an independent institution but is responsive to the demands of other institutions for training and certifying people for a class structure and for socializing them to the established values. If education is to do anything more humane and liberating, it requires a basic reform of education that is part of a basic reform of society.

SUMMARY

The *function* of education is to *socialize* the young and to *transmit the culture*—functions which necessarily support the established order.

Education relates to *social class* in two ways. First, educational opportunity is distributed unequally, reflecting existing differences in class and status. *Family* and *neighborhood* reinforce quite different educational aspirations for youth of different social classes. Teachers often assume that children are not equally educable, with the result that less effort is made in teaching the children of the poor and minorities. But this is never acknowledged. Rather, *cooling them out* leads such youth to believe that their lower achievement is their own fault. The *Jencks Report* emphasized that family background has a greater effect than anything else on educational achievement.

Secondly, since salaried, middle-class positions are expanding and these positions require more skill, education must provide a new generation with more education, so that some people from lower-class levels can move up to higher-class positions.

Meritocracy is a process in which educationally established merit will determine how individuals are placed in the class structure. It appeals most to the professionally educated, but merit is hard to measure, and other factors, political and ideological, always intrude to affect how people are selected.

Despite legal efforts, racial segregation in schools has increased. The *Coleman Report* found children's achievement depends more on their home background than on their school, but that disadvantaged black children improved in classrooms shared with more advantaged students. But Coleman and other researchers now disagree sharply over whether busing helps or hinders school integration.

Modern universities have become *multiversities,* organizations to train scientists and professionals, do research, and educate undergraduates. These several goals create tensions; for example, teaching suffers if research is maximized.

But this is only one aspect of an *academic revolution;* the emergence of a relatively autonomous and professionalized body of scholars and scientists, who reproduce themselves in graduate training, promote meritocratic values, and altogether dominate and reshape higher education in its central feature.

Controlling education is important to dominant elites, for they see it as a way of indoctrinating the young of all social classes with the values necessary to maintain the institutional structure.

Education in the United States has gone from a locally controlled system to a nationally coordinated one, influenced by national needs and concerns. Recent efforts to restore community control encounter a powerful drift to centralized and professional control.

Today many people advocate reforming education. Some issues of reform are: preparing people for jobs; educating equally; equal opportunity; and big-city schools. Ivan Illich advocates deschooling society, because established school systems monopolize all learning, make people dependent on schools, yet they support inequality, make people too dependent and docile, and legitimize the values of elites.

If education is to do more than socialize children to established values and train and certify them for the class structure, society must be basically reformed.

NOTES

[1] *The New York Times,* September 3, 1972.

[2] August H. Hollingshead, *Elmtown's Youth* (New York: Wiley, 1949).

[3] See, for example, Natalie Rogoff, "Local Social Structure and Educational Selection," in A. H. Halsey, Jean Floud, and C. A. Anderson, eds., *Education, Economy, and Society* (New York: The Free Press, 1961), pp. 241–251.

[4] R. J. Havighurst, P. H. Bowman, G. P. Liddle, C. V. Matthews, and J. V. Pierce, *Growing Up in River City* (New York: Wiley, 1962).

[5] Alan B. Wilson, "Residential Segregation of Social Classes and Aspirations of High School Boys," *American Sociological Review* 24 (December 1959): 836–845.

[6] Robert Rosenthal and Lenore Jacobson, *Pygmalion in the Classroom* (New York: Holt, Rinehart and Winston, 1968).

[7] Ray C. Rist, *The Urban School: A Factory for Failure* (New York: Doubleday, 1973).

[8] Burton Clark, *The Open Door College* (New York: McGraw-Hill, 1960).

[9] Walter E. Schafer, Carol Olexa, and Kenneth Polk, "Programmed for Social Class: Tracking in High School," *Trans-action* 7 (October 1970): 39–46. Reprinted in William Feigelman, ed., *Sociology Full Circle: Contemporary Readings on Society* (Praeger Publishers, 1972), pp. 145–158.

[10] Christopher Jencks et al., *Inequality: A Reassessment of the Effect of Family and Schooling in America* (New York: Basic Books, 1972).

[11] Jencks, *op. cit.,* p. 265.

[12] U.S. Bureau of the Census, *Current Population Reports,* Series P-20, no. 335, "School Enrollment—Social and Economic Characteristics of Students: October 1978" (Advance Report), Government Printing Office, 1979.

[13] U.S. Bureau of the Census, *Current Population Reports,* Series P-20, no. 319, "School Enrollment—Social and Economic Characteristics of Students: October 1977," Washington, D.C., 1977, Table A-5, p. 68.

[14] U.S. Commission on Civil Rights, *Racial Isolation in the Public Schools,* Vol. I (Washington, D.C.: Government Printing Office, 1967), p. 3.

[15] James E. Blackwell, *The Black Community: Unity and Diversity* (New York: Dodd, Mead, 1975), p. 107.

[16] *The Detroit News,* March 22, 1979.

[17] *Racial Isolation in the Public Schools,* Vol. I, pp. 38–39.

[18] U.S. Bureau of the Census, *Statistical Abstracts of the United States: 1978* (99th ed.), Washington, D.C., 1979.

[19] James S. Coleman, et al., *Equality of Educational Opportunity* (Washington, D.C.: Government Printing Office, 1966).

[20] *Racial Isolation in the Public Schools,* Vol. I, p. 91.

[21] See Harvard Educational Review, *Equal Educational Opportunity* (Cambridge, Mass.: Harvard University Press, 1969).

[22] Samuel Bowles, "Toward Equality of Educational Opportunity?" in *ibid.,* pp. 115–125.

[23] Christopher Jencks and David Riesman, *The Academic Revolution* (Garden City, N.Y.: Doubleday, 1968), p. 13.

[24] *Ibid.,* p. 13.

[25] Clark Kerr, *The Uses of the University* (Cambridge, Mass.: Harvard University Press, 1963).

[26] Jencks and Riesman, *op. cit.,* p. 14.

[27] *Ibid.,* p. 14.

[28] See Ted Vaughn, "The Educational Institution: The Indoctrinating Appendage," in Larry T. Reynolds and James T. Henslin, eds., *American Society: A Critical Analysis* (New York: McKay, 1973), pp. 225–247.

[29] *The Chronicle of Higher Education,* January 28, 1980. (See "Social Attitudes of Entering College Students: 1969 and 1979" for source of the data.)

[30] U.S. Bureau of the Census, *Current Population Reports,* Series P-20, no. 333, "School Enrollment—Social and Economic Characteristics of Students: October 1977" Washington, D.C., 1978, p. 1.

[31] See Samuel Bowles and Herbert Gintis, *Schooling in Capitalist America: Educational Reforms and the Contradictions of Economic Life* (New York: Basic Books, 1976), Chaps. 3 and 4; and Bernard Bailyn, *Education in the*

Forming of American Society (Chapel Hill: University of North Carolina Press, 1960).

[32] V. O. Key, Jr., Politics, Parties, and Pressure Groups (New York: T. Y. Crowell, 1964), pp. 12–13.

[33] George Rawick, From Sundown to Sunup (Westport, Conn.: Greenwood Press, 1972).

[34] See Alan A. Altschuler, Community Control: The Black Demand for Participation in Large American Cities (New York: Pegasus, 1970).

[35] Time, September 12, 1977.

[36] Ivan Illich, Deschooling Society (New York: Harper & Row, 1970; paperback edition, 1972), pp. 3–4.

[37] Ibid., p. 33.

[38] Ibid., p. 2.

SUGGESTED READINGS

Alan A. Altschuler, Community Control: The Black Demand for Participation in Large American Cities. New York: Pegasus, 1970.

Samuel Bowles and Herbert Gintis, Schooling in Capitalist America: Educational Reform and the Contradiction of Economic Life. Basic Books, 1976.

Martin Carnoy, ed., Schooling in a Corporate Society. New York: McKay, 1972.

Burton Clark, The Open Door College. New York: McGraw-Hill, 1960.

James Coleman et al., Equality of Educational Opportunity. Washington, D.C.: Government Printing Office, 1966.

Harvard Educational Review, Equal Educational Opportunity. Cambridge, Mass.: Harvard University Press, 1969.

Ivan Illich, Deschooling Society. New York: Harper & Row, 1970.

Christopher Jencks and David Riesman, The Academic Revolution. New York: Doubleday, 1968.

Clark Kerr, The Uses of the University. Harvard University Press, 1963.

Robert Rosenthal and Lenore Jacobsen, Pygmalion in the Classroom. New York: Holt, Rinehart and Winston, 1968.

Fifteen

RELIGION AND SCIENCE

Religion and science can be viewed as different ways—sometimes competing and even in conflict, sometimes complementary—to interpret the natural order of things and to explain and come to terms with the events of our lives. Since both are viewed as major institutional structures in modern society, and since they provide important ways to look at life (worldviews), both must be examined by the student of society.

RELIGION AND SCIENCE AS WORLDVIEW

Up until now the long-term historical view suggests that science is more likely to be dominant in the future than is religion. Secularization has put much of social life under the domination of the rational processes of science—and under the control of bureaucratic and technological structures whose logic and legitimation is derived from science.

At one time it seemed that science has emerged triumphant in a "war" with religion, and religion would eventually fade away as scientific thinking was inculcated into modern populations. Then there seemed to be a new accommodation in which religion acknowledged the domain of science in explaining all *natural* things and occupied a more restricted sphere of its own, primarily concerned with finding a larger set of meanings for human existence, meanings that an empirical science did not even claim to supply.

Yet this never became a fully dominant position. Many people still felt that religion was unnecessary and archaic. In turn, fundamentalists—those who make a literal interpretation of the Bible—never conceded the validity of scientific explanations over Biblical ones, as evidenced by the renewal of the debate over evolution (based on Darwin's theory) and creation (based on the Book of Genesis in the Bible) in the education of children.

The issue has never been closed. Much that has occurred in the last few years can be seen as a radical and remarkably strong counterassault on the domination of science and its rational view of the world, and the restoration of some sense of the sacred to human life. This is so even though many of those involved had no conception of being religious in doing so.

(Many in fact were conventionally antireligious, or at least antiestablished religion.)

It would be incorrect, however, to think that the resistance to rational science began only recently. Instead, it has deep roots in modern history, as the controversy over the "two cultures" makes evident.

The Two Cultures: Science and Humanism

The scientific worldview seems to be one that few other intellectuals have ever shared or for that matter, even understood. This is the theme pursued by C. P. Snow in *The Two Cultures and the Scientific Revolution.*[1] By *two cultures* Snow meant the one of science and the other of humanist intellectuals. He saw these two cultures as complete opposites: "the intellectual life of the whole of Western society is increasingly being split into two polar groups."[2]

Scientists, Snow argues, know too little of the world of literary culture, and literary intellectuals do not have even a glimmer of understanding of the world of science. From his own experience as both scientist and novelist, he documents this mutual ignorance. Snow sides with the scientists; he believes an ignorance of science is the more deplorable, because it is dangerous for the future of the human race.

Snow opts for industrialization and technology and the science that makes this possible. He sees in the scientific revolution of modern, electronic technology a potential force for eliminating the great gap between rich and poor that now plagues the world.

The Pessimism of the Humanists

Humanists over the past century have been pessimistic to the point of despair. They saw the world becoming increasingly rationalized—more and more calculable, planned, and unspontaneous, and in that sense less free.

Humanists were repelled, not so much by the ugliness of industrialism as by its relentless intent toward uniformity, manipulation, and rationalized bureaucratic control. Science, from this perspective, is the servant of the bureaucrat and the modern politician. The scientist is not only partner to the crime, he is its intellectual godfather.[3]

Generations of talented humanists (including religious thinkers) for over a century now have built an established rage against this ever more scientific and rational society. It has bred in them a deepened sense of disenchantment with the world. They share with Max Weber a despair about the future of humanity in a thoroughly rationalized world, yet see no reason to believe that the course of history could be altered.

Here are two radically opposed ways of viewing the world. The viewpoint of science is abstract, analytical, and piecemeal, and it approaches all phenomena with the single intention of viewing them objectively and with no value-preference about them. Its worldview is congruent with much of a technologically and bureaucratically organized world, which looks to science, not literature, for its standards and norms. The humanistic mind rejects that same world and rebels against it.

This rebellion is the source for the development of a new religious consciousness among many youth. It is also the source of a renewed effort to restore the sacred to spheres of human life from which the powerful processes of secularization once removed it. For that reason, religion, though in forms possibly strange and never before experienced, moves back to the center of human experience.

In this chapter, accordingly, we will look at religion first, for there was religion before there was science.

RELIGION AND SOCIETY

How to explain or even define religion has probably yielded less scholarly agreement than almost any other matter studied. Religion is so diverse in historical development, so culturally varied, that definitions developed from our own Western experience often fail to encompass it adequately.

What comes out of these scholarly efforts, however, is the recognition that religion emerges from common experience in society and offers explanations that transcend whatever mundane, factual knowledge is available. These are explanations expressed in symbolic forms and acts which relate a people to the ultimate conditions of their existence.

As human societies have evolved over long periods of time, so also have religions. Each of the world's religions, in its own distinctive way, has conferred a sacred meaning upon the circumstances of a people's existence.

Some religions, such as Christianity and Islam, have grown far beyond their social origins, now counting their believers in the hundreds of millions. If Christianity can now claim the largest number of adherents, Christians nonetheless are less than 40 percent of all religious believers in the world (see Table 15.1).

We have no historical or archeological reason to believe that religion began full-blown. Instead, it developed slowly with the evolution of human society, and in its more primitive forms—itself an evolutionary development beyond the earliest prereligious people—possessed no organization or special roles (no church or clergy), only a communal sharing in rituals that gave expression to religious symbols.[4]

As religion and society evolve, a sense of *sacredness* takes concrete form in objects and images that become sacred, whether these are persons, animals, or natural objects, human artifacts or symbolic expressions. The sacred also becomes conveyed and expressed for the living in *ritual,* where behavior gives objective form to mood and feeling. A division among the sacred and the *profane* eventually marks off religious from nonreligious activity.[5]

TABLE 15.1
Religious Populations of the World

Religion	Members
Christian	983,620,900
Roman Catholic	566,686,800
Eastern Orthodox	72,815,000
Protestant	344,119,100
Jewish	15,032,378
Islam (Muslim)	576,160,200
Zoroastrian	233,550
Shinto	55,156,000
Taoist	31,116,100
Confucian	174,189,200
Bhuddist	260,685,550
Hindu	517,897,450
Total	2,614,091,328

Source: *The World Almanac and Book of Facts, 1979 and 1978 Yearbook of American and Canadian Churches.*

The Functions of Religion

Of all possible ways to understand the connection between religion and society, the *functional* interpretation has been the dominant one. It asserts that every society has a number of necessary conditions that it must successfully meet in order to survive, and one of these is the cohesion or solidarity of its members. Religion, it is asserted, provides this function for society. But it provides two other functions as well: a mechanism for social control; and a source of psychic and emotional support for individuals.

Religion as Social Cohesion According to the functionalist perspective, sharing the same religious interpretation of the meaning of life unites a people in a cohesive and binding moral order. This was what Émile Durkheim meant when he defined religion as:

. . . a unified system of beliefs and practices relative to sacred things, that is to say, things set apart and forbidden—beliefs and practices which unite into one single moral community called a Church, all those who adhere to them.[6]

But these members of the moral community also share a common social life. The religious community and the society have the same members. When that occurs, religion, by providing a moral unity, then provides a society with a powerful social "cement" to hold it together.

When the *moral* community of believers is identical with the *social* community, as is common in more traditional societies, then the symbolism of the sacred supports the more ordinary aspects of social life. Religion then *legitimizes* society; it provides sacred sanction for the social order and for its basic values and meanings.

Furthermore, the commitment of individuals to these shared beliefs is renewed and refreshed each time the members come together to worship, when, that is, they become a *congregation.* Such a sense of renewal is even stronger when they come together on ceremonial occasions of great sacred meaning, such as, for example, on Easter and Christmas for Christians. But the unifying rituals of faith are also called upon by individuals on the most significant occasions for family and for the individual: at birth, at marriage, and at death.

In traditional societies the religious and the nonreligious spheres of life are not sharply differentiated. But in modern, industrial societies, religion and society are not the same. The emergence of different modes of life-experience leads to different meanings about life, producing a religious differentiation. The all-encompassing church gives way to competing religious groups. Religion may still provide cohesion, but now only for subgroups of society.

Civil Religion If religion can no longer serve to morally unify the people of a modern society, it may, however, serve to provide a legitimation of society and its major social institutions. At least, says sociologist Robert Bellah, that is what happens in the United States with the emergence of what he calls a *civil* religion.[7]

Civil religion means a use of religion to sanctify American society and celebrate its secular ways of life. In recent years, for example, Congress voted to place "under God" in the pledge of allegiance. "In God we trust" is on all coins. Presidents of the United States take the oath of office with one hand on the Bible and most formal public meetings are opened with a prayer. The Boy Scouts have a "God and country" award. American orators proclaim our opposition to "atheistic communism," thus linking religion to our political system.

This civil religion requires no specific creed, only the confidence that God is in his heaven and blesses this society. Nor is it a new development. Will Herberg had earlier observed that each of the three major religious groups—Protestant, Catholic, and Jewish—had been "Americanized," that is, each had reinterpreted its beliefs to fit the American experience.[8] American churches, he felt, really worshiped "the American way of life."

Religion as Social Control

Whether it is fear of fire and brimstone, as prevailed for so long among Christians, or the injunction to do good works, religious belief can influence the conduct of those who believe. The recognition that religion can control human action and keep people "in line" makes it a useful instrument for a ruling class, and throughout history these classes have consciously recognized such an instrumental value. Frank E. Manuel said that in the eighteenth century even skeptics and atheists recognized that "religion was a mecha-

nism which inspired terror, but terror useful for the preservation of society . . . ."[9]

This recognition carried on into the twentieth century. Such prominent Protestants as industrialist Mark Hanna, railroad baron James Hill, and President William Howard Taft all found in the Catholicism of millions of immigrant workers a strong bulwark against socialism and "anarchy."[10] Hill explained his donating a million dollars for the establishment of a Catholic seminary on the grounds that, with "millions of foreigners pouring into this country," the Catholic Church is "the only authority they fear or respect."[11]

While conservatives have valued religion for this protective function, radicals have also often recognized that religion can be a support of the established order, and have, consequently, been critical of religion. Marx's life-long associate, Friedrich Engels, for example, once noted that the bourgeoisie in England discovered that religion could make the masses "submissive to the behests of the masters it had pleased God to place over them."[12]

Marx, in turn, recognized that religion was more than simply an instrument for class control, though it could be so used; it was solace and comfort for those who suffer the injustices of this world:

> *Religous* suffering is at the same time an *expression* of real suffering and a *protest* against real suffering. Religion is the sigh of the oppressed creature, the sentiment of a heartless world, and the soul of soulless conditions. It is the *opium* of the people.[13]

Religion as Emotional Support

If religion can be a form of social control, that is because it also performs another basic function: it is a source of comfort and solace for the suffering, a faith to which people turn when they are most troubled. It gives them emotional support and provides a moral strength they would not otherwise have to sustain themselves in the face of trials and defeats, personal losses and unjust treatments.

Religions as Psychotherapy

In twentieth-century America there is another way in which religion sustains people; it becomes a supporting psychology, a form of psychotherapy. Religion is viewed in upbeat terms, and God is conceived of as a humane and considerate God; such a hopeful perspective turns away from the older Christian conception of a stern and demanding God.

Psychologizing Religion   This "psychologizing" of religion has created an "Americanized religion" (as sociologists Louis Schneider and Sanford M. Dornbusch have called it) for which someone like Norman Vincent Peale, a prominent Protestant clergyman, with his "power of positive thinking" serves as a typical example.[14] It provides peace of mind, promises prosperity and success in life, as well as effective and happy human relations. It is thus a source of security and confidence, of happiness and success *in this world*.

But it does not stop there. Pastoral counseling—for which clergymen get psychological training—is apparently a more significant function of American clergy than it is of European clergy. According to one careful observer:

> The more routine but flourishing engagement of religion in the affairs of a very large proportion of Americans consists in their submitting hurts and hopes to the care and help of pastors. Gauged by both consumer demand and by clergymen's self-evaluation, the chief business of religion in the United States is now—as it has probably long been—the cure of souls.[15]

The religious practitioner has now moved into a relevant place in the mental health field as a helping professional. Consequently, pastoral counseling has become so much a specialty that a national organization—the American Association of Pastoral Counselors—has been formed, to set professional standards, regulate practice, and certify practitioners.

The Organization of Religion

While religion is basically a matter of faith and creed, most religions develop an organizational form. These religious structures vary considerably in size, in form, and in their relation to society. To say they are all *churches* is to lump together a wide range of social forms; they need to be distinguished from one another. To do this, sociologists usually identify four basic forms; ecclesia, denomination, sect, and cult.

The *ecclesia* is defined, fundamentally, by its acceptance of society in all its imperfections. It does not fight society, nor does it withdraw. It is both *in* and *of* the world and seeks to be a power within the world.

This leads it to engage in a close set of relationships with the secular institutions of the society, particularly the governmental.

As a universal church, the ecclesia defines as members all those born within a given territory from all social classes. This inclusiveness—of a large and diverse religious community—requires large-scale organization, a formal and hierarchical organization, a religious bureaucracy, with a chain of command from top to bottom.

By definition the ecclesia is a universal world church. But this is an ideal type which is only approximated by historical cases. The Roman Catholic Church in the Middle Ages is perhaps the nearest historical approximation to the type, at least in the Western world. The Anglican Church in England and the Lutheran Church in Germany, in turn, are examples of national ecclesia, in contrast to the international scope of the Roman Catholic Church.

The *denomination* is also a stable church that does not fight or withdraw from the world, but, unlike the ecclesia, does not seek a close tie with government and does not monopolize a territory. The larger Protestant churches, which originated in a break with the Roman Catholic ecclesia, are examples of denominations.

Some denominations began as sects, but in time have made peace with the world, frequently when their members are no longer disadvantaged in society. They have become well established and accepted in status, and now possess a bureaucratic structure with trained clergy and other officials.

The *sect* is typically a small and exclusive religious group whose members are not born into it but voluntarily join it. Those who choose to belong to a sect must be accepted on its rigorous terms. (To be sure, the children of sect members are often thoroughly socialized to a commitment early in life, particularly when the sect's way of life isolates them from other contacts.) Its discipline extends into their personal lives. What it lacks in controlling organization (and sects develop only a rudimentary formal structure), it more than makes up for in fervent commitment to a belief.

Typically, sects are *in* but not *of* society, for they reject the worldly society. Some sects take a radical stance toward secular government by refusing to pay taxes, to serve in any civil or political capacity, or even to take oaths (Jehovah's Witnesses is a contemporary

The Roman Catholic Church is an ecclesia with a worldwide membership exceeding half a billion persons. In a break with tradition, a non-Italian, the Polish Cardinal Karol Wojtyla, the Archbishop of Cracow, is inaugurated in 1978 as Pope John Paul II.

sect often in difficulty with government for such reasons).

While some sects have taken a militant posture toward the world, seeking to change it, others have been passive and withdrawing, seeking to remain as removed from society as possible. The Old Order Amish in Pennsylvania and the Hutterites in the midwestern states and Canada, for example, reject and withdraw from the world.

The *cult,* in turn, is a small and almost formless religious group, formed around a charismatic leader. It is often short-lived. Unlike the sect, it lacks a coherent doctrine and does not impose any such set of beliefs as a condition for membership. Instead, it attracts members through the spellbinding quality of a leader.

The cult appears most frequently in urban centers, where its appeal is often to those who feel lost and without a sense of belonging in an impersonal and anonymous city life. Cults flourish in slums and among minorities and can be found, for example, among the "store-front" churches in ghetto areas. The Black Muslims began in this way in Detroit in the 1930s. But cults also appeal to middle-class people, who no less experience loneliness and frustration.

Religion in Society These distinctions in the forms of religious organization are intended to draw attention to the inherent tension between the sacred concerns of religion and the secular interests of society. Religion constantly draws closer to society and then draws away. It accepts it, ignores it, or rejects it.

Sects, for example, draw their members mostly from the less attached and more disadvantaged in society; in this way, religion gives expression to the social experiences of groups and classes within society. As sects become denominations, dissident religious groups come to terms with society, and tensions lessen as the worldly status of its members improves.

But new sects and cults constantly appear among those who are materially and socially disadvantaged, or among those who find no rewarding sense or meaning in life. There is thus constant religious *movement,* an increasing or lessening of tension between the sacred and the secular, between religion and society. Religion never completely embraces society, nor does it completely reject it.

Religion and Stratification

Churches cannot avoid the simple fact that stratification separates the population into higher and lower classes; and religious organization undeniably mirrors the class structure of society. Whatever may be their doctrinal position, churches usually develop a membership drawn disproportionately from one social class or another. Furthermore, membership in church, like membership in a voluntary association, varies directly with social class: higher class, higher membership; lower class, lower membership.[16]

For reasons that have less to do with doctrine and more to do with historical origins, such denominations as the Episcopalians have been high-status churches, the Presbyterians have been middle-class churches, and such large denominations as the Baptists have been lower-middle and working-class churches. But this must be qualified. Though the Episcopal Church is a high-status church, it enrolls many middle- and working-class members. A report of the National Council of Churches, for example, showed that about 42 percent of the Episcopal membership was in the working class, despite its strong appeal to high-status people.[17] The major, large denominations always draw membership from all social classes; they only differ from one another in the proportions from each class.

The Suburban Church   When the middle-class moves to the suburbs, the churches follow their most consistent parishioners. In many instances, congregations move—lock, stock, and barrel—from the city to the suburb, selling their former church building to those left behind, which often means to black people.

This movement to the suburb often removes the middle class from the harsher problems that beset those who remain within the city—those of race and poverty, for example. The church that follows them also turns from such problems, organizing itself instead around the central interests of the middle-class congregation: family and teen-agers, leisure, and the concerns of morality and values typical of the affluent. The church is captive to the suburban interests and perspectives of its memberships.[18]

The Church and the Working Class   The greatest failure of the Christian mission has been its inability to hold the industrial working classes within the church. The estrangement of the working class from the Christian churches has been greater in Europe than in the United States, but religious data from Great Britain, France, Italy, Germany, Belgium, *and* Latin America provide detailed support of the idea that the working class has largely abandoned any significant attachment to or involvement in the church, Catholic or Protestant.

There have been two basic reasons given for the inability of organized religion to attract the working classes in industrial society. The first of these—stressed by American sociologists—sees a cultural affinity between church atmosphere and middle-class life-style, an atmosphere in which people of lower social status feel strange and out of place, even unwanted.[19] Their studies have stressed how much liturgy, the sermon, the pattern of Sunday school, women's guilds, youth groups, and the like, reflect the tastes and standards as well as the interests and concerns of the middle class.

Religion and Radical Politics   European sociologists give a second reason, based on the observation that where radical politics flourish among workers church membership declines. French sociologists E. Pin and A. Dansette, for example, assert that the French worker is not integrated into modern society, that he suffers from a sense of an unjust world, and his political orientation is anticapitalist. French workers vote communist in large numbers, and in equally large numbers stay away from the Catholic Church. Pin argues that French workers are estranged from the Church precisely because it gives no promise of pursuing justice *in this world.*[20]

A similar pattern comes from other European societies. Surveys from Britain and the Netherlands, for example, reveal that the working class is less likely to attend church or even hold religious views than are members of other social classes, and that those who are supporters of socialist and communist parties are less religious than supporters of conservative parties.[21] Sociologist Rodney Stark has examined British data and asserts that "the strength of lower-class radicalism in Britain partly accounts for lower-class religious apathy."[22]

In some other countries, the United States in particular, the estrangement of workers from religion is not so pronounced. Indeed, the Catholic Church in the United States has managed to hold its immigrant, working-class members very well. This may be because, for the European immigrant, the church was a haven and source of both spiritual and material assistance when so little else was available. Also, these immigrants were very largely from rural, peasant backgrounds, among whom religion has always been strong. Nonetheless, though there is considerable variation from one society to another, the general pattern remains clear and is supported consistently by data: those of lower social status are least attracted to the Christian churches.

Working-Class Sects

In the United States, Great Britain, and some few other countries where Protestantism has been dominant, there is another response of the working class and others of low social status — they break off and regroup in newly created small churches of their own. Each time this is done, another sect is born.

Such sects are often hostile to the dominant churches and reject the world as essentially corrupt. Yet their energies go into apolitical activities, and they find their hope, not in justice in this world, but in a just heaven or in a millennium to be brought about by the second coming of Christ. As a consequence, they drain off potential radical commitment by alienated workers, and such sects are therefore viewed by radical parties as competitive.

An influential English historian, E. P. Thompson, has suggested that one important reason for much less revolutionary action in England, compared with other European nations, was the attraction to nonconformist religion, especially Methodism, among English workers.[23] Sociologist Robert Blauner similarly accounts for the failure of labor unions and labor-oriented politics among Southern white workers to the growth of evangelical sects in that region.[24]

Religion Among the Oppressed

Sects and cults have often appeared first among social groups subject to conditions of oppression and cultural destruction. Frequently these are racial and cultural minorities, colonized people overrun by powerful industrial and military powers, unable to continue their traditional way of life, yet not able or even permitted to share fully in the life of their conquerors.

Their responses to such conditions often took the form of *nativistic* movements which proclaimed the restoration of the traditional ways and that the invaders were to be driven from the land. The "Cargo" cults among the natives of Melanesia in the South Pacific, which began in the later nineteenth century as a mode of resistance to white, European control, is a notable example of such a movement.[25]

As the natives saw it, the white people did not manufacture any of the goods they needed, but instead received abundant supplies by ship; in return they merely sent back scraps of paper. According to the legend which grew up, these cargoes were made by the natives' own ancestors and were stolen from them by the whites according to some secret. Prophets of the new cult appeared and propounded a system of belief and ritual by which the secret could be learned, the cargoes secured, native independence reestablished, and the white man defeated.

In the 1870s and again in the 1890s a Ghost Dance spread among such Indian tribes as the Cheyenne, the Arapaho, the Pawnee, and the Sioux, promising to restore the buffalo and the old ways of life. The movement ended once and for all at the Battle of Wounded Knee. Among the Utes and Shoshones of the Rocky Mountain area a Sun Dance cult emerged, with a ceremony from which these Indians obtained a sense of power and redemption despite their oppression by whites.[26]

While such religious sects of protest among the powerless do not succeed in overthrowing their conquerors, and are usually impermanent, they nevertheless have an impact. At the outset they provide a sense of dignity and personal integrity for people oppressed and often treated without respect. They enable them better to survive as persons, escaping the personal despair that invites personal disorganization, so often evident in alcoholism, suicide, and the like.[27]

Religion and Race in the United States

When revolt and protest by native peoples took religious form, as we saw above, religion could be radical in its implications, rather than conservative. In the American case, the overall effect has to be seen as largely conservative, even though both aspects are present.

When slavery began in the American South, slaveholders came to view religion as an effective means of social control, and so slaves were Christianized. According to a noted historian, slaves were taught that slavery had divine sanction, that the Bible commanded servants to obey their masters, and that there were "punishments awaiting the disobedient slave in the hereafter."[28] Despite such instruction by slavemasters, the slaves created a Christianity that kept alive their resistance to accepting slavehood as their natural condition.[29]

When slavery ended, the black church became central to black life, the one unique organization usually safe from white invasion, the nearest thing to an untouchable sanctity.[30] Consequently, and since few opportunities for leadership existed, capable blacks were disproportionately attracted to the ministry. Black clergy were leaders to an extent never attained by their white counterparts. The historic record of black churches for a century now has been one of being largely accommodative, yet also invariably being central to black protest and militancy.

The black church sought to turn its parishioners into black puritans, rigorous upholders of the puritanic virtues of abstention from sex, liquor, and gambling. It has been a basic institution in the construction of lifestyles of sobriety and respectable behavior, particularly for middle-class blacks. Thus, one significant effect of the Christian religion on blacks has been to promote traditional Protestant morality and so to render a disprivileged group more amenable and conforming to the dominant culture.

At the same time, such religious faith made it possible for black people to sustain a sense of personal dignity and worth. It provided a capacity to endure indignities and hardships by taking seriously the Christian belief that "the meek shall inherit the earth." Reward in an afterlife sustained a people that otherwise could not have made sense of the conditions of their existence, for there was certainly no reward in this life.

Yet such Christian dignity could also produce political passivity. Sociologist Gary Marx found that many black Christians avoided demonstrations, even though they wanted integration to take place.[31] They believed that, since God was on their side, they did not need to do anything on their own. Marx found that the more religious blacks were less militant, and conversely, the more militant ones were less religious.

Nonetheless, many religious blacks have been militant. The black church was central to the civil rights action during the 1960s. It was the meeting place for protest; and black ministers were major figures among the civil rights leadership, particularly in the South. Many of the protest songs, such as "We Shall Overcome," are secularized versions of hymns, and their mood and style is that of the spiritual. It is no accident that such a major leader of protest as Martin Luther King was a minister.

Religion: Radical and Conservative Religion, now and in the past, obeys the biblical injunction: "Render unto Caesar the things that are Caesar's." Even when a religious sect rejects the world, it may yet endure hardships patiently, believing that "the meek shall inherit the earth."

Yet there is always a basic tension between religion and the secular world, and a reforming and even revolutionary impulse in religion seems never to be extinguished. However buried under conformity to secular order, it manages to break out and seek again to redo the world.

Religion as Culture

Max Weber always understood religion to be a set of meanings by which people interpreted their social life and their society and sought to alter it or adjust to it or even reject it. Religion not only interpreted the world, it provided an orientation of ethical conduct; it helped shape the world, even as it, too, was fashioned by its encounter with the world. Whatever may be its organizational features, religion is primarily belief and perspective and value.[32]

Weber undertook a monumental effort to demonstrate that ideas were not merely a reflection of human behavior and organization, but that ideas *interacted* with what Marx called the "material forces" to be a (but never the only) determinative force in shaping human society. For the realm of ideas Weber chose religion; for the realm of action he chose the economic.

The Protestant Ethic and the Spirit of Capitalism is but one of several works that Weber wrote around a specific problem, the emergence of rational capitalism.[33] His study of religion in Europe, in China, and in India explored the reasons why capitalism emerged or was blocked from development. In each case he found reasons in the character of religion as a set of fundamental meanings that led people to favor or disfavor certain modes of action, such as the type of economic conduct that produced capitalism.

In each society the religious outlook on life produced an economic ethic, a religiously sanctioned standard of economic conduct. The emergence of Protestantism in Christian Europe led to an ethic that encouraged the kind of economic behavior that supported the emergence of rational capitalism. But in China and India religion discouraged the economic behavior necessary for the emergence of capitalism.

The Protestant Ethic The religious revolt generally known as Protestantism ushered in a period of significant breaks from the hitherto secure unity of Christendom. Some of the new sects that broke away were both socially and religiously radical.

To these people revolutionary preachings by such men as John Calvin and John Knox provided a new religious perspective. Calvin's teachings were religiously radical in their central challenge to a basic tenet of Catholic teaching: that the church, as the valid Christian ecclesiastical system, was the duly authorized administrator of sacraments.

Calvin argued that the granting of sacraments could not influence the assignment of the person to an eternal life in heaven. The Catholic faithfuls' reliance on Mary and on saints was not only disputed, it was criticized. Only God, said Calvin, knew who was saved and who was eternally damned, and the intervention of no others, mortal or immortal—priests and bishops, Mary, Jesus, or saints—would change it. This God of Calvinism was a stern and terrible God who had predestined humans to either heaven or hell, and neither their individual good works nor sacramental grace would save them.

Belief in predestination created for Calvinists an anxious concern about their own unchangeable eternal fate. They possessed a terrible fear of hell and eternal damnation, and they were saddled with the frightening necessity of facing God alone, without the intervention of the church. In the face of this fear they understandably sought some evidence of their predestined fate. Instead of being frozen with fear, Calvinists engaged in an active campaign against the external world, warning the powerful that they were in danger of eternal doom.

Although Calvinists believed that people were predestined to an eternal fate, and could not change it, yet it mattered how one lived one's life. They insisted that each person should act as if he or she were one of the elect and live life for the greater glory of God.

Central to this was the Protestant conception of a religious theory of signs. The Calvinists came to argue that one's earthly fate was a sign of one's eternal fate. Accordingly, prosperity in worldly efforts signified election or salvation, whereas poverty and worldly failure signified an eternal damnation.

The consequences of such a belief were revolutionary. Calvinists practiced industry, self-denial, and thrift. They considered it sinful to indulge themselves in worldly goods or to lust after worldly pleasures. They became what Weber called "inner-worldly ascetics" by exercising their virtues in their occupation as a calling. Their hard work led to savings and surplus, and so to investment that made an expanding capitalism possible.

Over time the belief in predestination diminished and ceased to be significant in religious belief, but the economic ethic that developed out of Calvinism stood independent, detached from any particular religious faith. What Weber had called the Protestant Ethic came to be the dominant ethical orientation to work for the middle classes of Western industrial societies. It culminated in secular versions that placed a central value on work and made of economic success a this-worldly goal that needed no relation to anything beyond this life.

Secularization

This decline in the religious permeation of other social institutions is *secularization*. For a long time secular has meant "worldly" contrasted to "religious" or "sacred." Fundamentally, secularization means "the process by which sectors of society are removed from the domination of religious institutions and symbols."[34] Secularization, then, is a *desacralization* of the world, one in which there is no overarching religious symbolism for the integration of society, and in which an understanding of human beings and their society is no longer stated primarily in religious terms.

The Sources of Secularization   Secularization is hardly a new or even a modern process. Its origins in the Western world lie in the Christian religion, even though the process is interpreted as a loss of the power and effectiveness of religion. The religion of ancient Israel, for instance, divorced God from the "natural" processes of the world, and there were significant consequences from this: God was not manipulable by magic; He did not confer divinity upon humans, even kings; and His divinity was not expressed in nature worship.

Max Weber credited Calvinism and the emergence of the Protestant Ethic as being a major development in the rationalization of the world—and secularization is part and parcel of that rationalization. Protestantism divested the world of much of the magic and the miracles of medieval Catholicism. It reduced the sacraments in number and eliminated all the intermediaries between God and man: saints, the Virgin, angels, miracles, and the sacraments through which grace could be dispensed. "At the risk of some simplification, it can be said that Protestantism divested itself as much as possible from the three most ancient and most powerful concomitants of the sacred—mystery, miracle, and magic."[35]

Yet no one would claim that secularization has driven religiosity entirely from modern life. Rather, religion has remained more closely associated with the institution of the family, and is not yet entirely divorced from education. It has been most thoroughly removed from the economy and the state, probably most of all from the economy, for industrial capitalism has long been a dynamic force for secularization.

In those societies not fully industrialized, in turn, and not historically Christian, such as the Islamic nations, a deliberate resistance to further secularization is now a major aspect of social and political developments (see "Islam and the Secular World").

Furthermore, secularization has not affected modern societies uniformly. Its impact has been stronger on men than on women, on the middle-aged than on the young or the old, in the cities than in the country, on Protestants and Jews than on Catholics, and on those social classes directly linked to modern industrial production than on such more traditional occupations as artisans and small shopkeepers. Political and economic institutions have developed their own independent symbolic systems, and thus secular ideologies have emerged.

The loss of religion's capacity to be the integrating symbol-system for society means that religion has lost that basic function that once defined it sociologically as an institution. Secularization, therefore, has been *deinstitutionalizing* for religion. In such a world, the rational perspective of science becomes a major organizing belief for a secular and increasingly rationalized world.

Modernizing the Christian churches in recent years has meant that some women in some churches were able to become practicing clergy.

ISLAM AND THE SECULAR WORLD

The world of Islam (its members are called Muslims) is a wide band that reaches from western Africa, across that continent to the Middle East, including all Arabic states and Iran, into Asia, including southern parts of the Soviet Union, and India, Malaysia, Indonesia, and the Philippines. It includes 576 million people in that vast geographic stretch.

The Islamic faith does not distinguish between church and state, though such a secular separation is now characteristic of some Islamic nations. Yet there is an annual meeting of Islamic foreign ministers; it is difficult to imagine a meeting of Christian foreign ministers.

The Soviet Union has encroached upon these historic Islamic lands. Some of that power's South Asian population is Muslim, as is neighboring Afghanistan, which the Soviet Union had been seeking to control for several years and which it invaded in the winter of 1979–80. But it has also been encroached upon by the Western nations, and some of its lands have at different times been European colonies.

In recent years a renewed Islam has been reinvigorated by a sense of its own valued identity and religious faith. Islamic leaders, particularly in the Middle East, have been seeking to meet the threat to Islam they see in Communism, which they regard as atheistic, but also in the threat they see in the Western world's secular mode of life.

These threats have served to reinforce a conservative movement among the Muslims, a return to a more traditional way in order to preserve Islam. Many Muslims believe that Westernization is secularization and that it produces an eventual disrespect for Islamic ideas and principles. The revolution in Iran, which brought into political power a religious leader and created an Islamic republic, provides a vivid illustration of this. The intent of the religious revolutionaries in Iran is to purge Iran of the Western "corruption" of Islam's historic faith and way of life.

A new tide of Islamic faith becomes a powerful force in the world, for the Muslims are one of the world's larger religious populations. Furthermore, they are interested in spreading that faith, and they have been successful in recent years in converting many people in Africa to Islam. Not the least of the complexities it adds to the world's scene is its rejection of the secular trend that inevitably accompanies modernization, and its effort to create an Islamic world independent of both the superpowers.

Secularization as Modernizing and Being Relevant

Secularization induces a response in modern churches that encourages greater acceptance of the modern, secular world by the church, and presses for new ways to get religion back into social life to make it relevant again. In the Catholic Church Pope John XXIII coined the term *aggiornamento* ("bringing up to date" in Italian), which became a powerful symbol of the reform and modernizing movement within the church itself.

Changes in liturgy have been accompanied by other developments, such as the shedding of the traditional, distinctive garments by nuns and priests—one symbol of moving from cloister to street and of redefining their relation to the congregation and even to the larger body of the nonreligious. A strong plea for release from celibacy comes from young priests, and many young nuns seek new ways to express their vocation, ways that bring them into closer contact with a secular world and protect them less from its more everyday aspects.

In other ways, too, various churches have tried to

come to terms with newer social developments. In 1978, for example, the Episcopal Church decided to ordain women, to revise the Book of Common Prayer, and to modify its traditional stands on such matters as abortion and homosexuality. The resulting disagreement, however, produced a split among Church members and a sizable minority withdrew to form the Anglican Church of North America.

In that same year the Church of Jesus Christ of Latter-Day Saints (Mormons) revoked its policy of excluding blacks from its priesthood. This was probably the most significant change in Mormon policy since its renunciation of polygamy in 1890.

Not all churches accepted change however, at least not in all areas of life. The United Presbyterian Church, for example, at its 1978 convocation, voted not to ordain homosexuals to the ministry, though at the time the delegates went on record in support of the civil rights of homosexuals.

Religion and Political Action   Another way of being modern and relevant is through political action. Both Catholics and Protestants, black and white, plunged into the civil rights movement in the 1960s. Perhaps the former Father Groppi and the Rev. Martin Luther King were the best known of dedicated civil rights leaders among clergy—and the most controversial. The activism that led such clergy as the two brothers and former Catholic priests, Daniel and Phillip Berrigan, to oppose the Vietnam war by destroying draft records and consequently being imprisoned is testimony to the power of religious vision to sustain a radical stand against the secular state.

Beyond the borders of the United States, too, a more radical political stance comes from a once conservative Catholic Church. In Spain the Church, which once backed Franco's holy crusade to restore Christendom, has become a powerful force in restoring democracy. Even more dramatically, Catholic priests in a number of Latin American countries have joined the radical political struggle against dictatorial regimes and for democracy and even socialism, in some instances with the backing of their bishops. Some of them have been jailed and, like other political prisoners in such regimes, tortured.

In all these efforts the religious have gone forth into the secular world and joined movements and developments stemming from the needs of the poor and dispossessed. Such political action is in the secular world,

but it seeks always to be more than secular, to find a deeper religious significance and legitimation for taking sides in political disputes between the dispossessed and powerless and the powerful elites and established institutions. That religion can be and has from time to time been a radically moral critique of worldly institutions and secular practices should be evident from such contemporary examples.

The *liberation theology* developed by Catholic clergy in Latin America is a powerful example of this. It stresses religious support for the struggle *against* economic and political oppression and *for* social reforms like democratic participation, redistribution of land, and the more adequate feeding, clothing, and educating of millions of impoverished children.

Religious Change: From Social Activism to Personal Salvation

During the 1960s the major Protestant denominations and the Catholic Church in the United States were actively involved in the controversial social issues of that decade: civil rights and racial protest; the peace movement, the antidraft movement and the anti-Vietnam war movement. But as the 1960s receded, a change began to appear in the religious concerns of many Americans.

First, there was an overall modest decline in church membership, but most of that loss was concentrated in the larger Protestant denominations, those which had participated in and had supported various social movements. While these churches lost members, other churches gained members; those which gained were mostly smaller churches, and more likely to be evangelical and fundamentalist. A more conservative theology was also actively asserted and liberal theology criticized. In 1975 eighteen Protestant, Catholic, and Eastern Orthodox theologians met and reaffirmed traditional Christian beliefs and condemned thirteen "heresies" of modern religious thought.

Second, there was a renewed interest in personal salvation offered by evangelical Christianity, but again, outside the larger, mainline churches. Evangelicalism presents a form of Christianity that emphasizes individual response to the fullness of salvation in Jesus Christ. According to a Gallup Poll in 1976, 34 percent of Americans have had a "born-again" experience and four in ten Americans believed the Bible to be the literal word of God.

The New Religious Consciousness

Since the 1960s in the United States, a renewed interest in religion has emerged among American youth. The roots of this renewed concern came out of the countercultural movement of the 1960s and has survived the demise of that movement.

The forms the new religious interest has taken are diverse and follow no single pattern. Some youth have returned to religion in the Western tradition, though not to the conventional practices of the established churches but outside of them in the Jesus movement and the Catholic Charismatic Revival. Others turned to the Asian tradition—to the Hari Krishna and Zen Bhuddism—to seek a radically new approach to spiritual meaning.

To understand this development, we need to recognize that a biblical tradition has rooted itself deep in the American experience since the seventeenth cen-tury. But so did a highly secular mode of thought, utilitarian individualism, which came from the effort to apply science to understanding humanity and was both atheistic and deterministic.[36] Robert Bellah contrasts them this way:

> Whereas the central term for understanding individual motivation in the biblical tradition was "conscience," the central term in the utilitarian tradition was "interest." The biblical understanding of national life was based on the notion of community with charity for all the members, a community supported by public and private virtue. The utilitarian tradition believed in a neutral state in which individuals would be allowed to pursue the maximization of their self-interest, and the product would be public and private prosperity.[37]

The utilitarian tradition was never wholly compatible with the biblical tradition, Bellah tells us, although adding:

One of the first expressions of a new religious consciousness among American youth was participation in Hare Krishna.

But the most pervasive mechanism for the harmonization of the two traditions was the corruption of the biblical tradition by utilitarian individualism, so that religion itself finally became for many a means for the maximization of self-interest with no effective link to virtue, charity, or community. A purely private pietism emphasizing only individual rewards that grew up in the nineteenth century and took many forms in the twentieth, from Norman Vincent Peale to Reverend Ike, was the expression of that corruption.[38]

The new religious consciousness is a repudiation of the dominance of utilitarian individualism, a dominance associated with the related dominance of science, technology, and bureaucratic organization. To call into question the central place these have in our lives is to suggest a crisis in the legitimacy of the American way of life; a crisis, says Bellah, that is a crisis of meaning, a religious crisis. It was brought on by "the inability of utilitarian individualism to provide a meaningful pattern of personal and social existence, especially when its alliance with biblical religion began to sag because biblical religion itself had been gutted in the process."[39]

Whether Christian or oriental in form, the new religious consciousness expresses an image of established society so lost to materialism as to be unsavable. The result of such conviction is a withdrawal from a society seen as corrupt and illegitimate.

Different as they are, the new religious expressions have one common theme: They emphasize immediate experience instead of doctrinal belief. They give higher value to firsthand encounter over abstract logic.

What the new religious consciousness gets from the oriental religions is *nondualism,* the unity instead of the duality of all being. We are not separate selves, according to this perspective; there is no difference between one person and another, for we are all one. If that is so, then there is no basis for the exploitation of any one person by another: rich by poor; black by white; woman by man.

Oriental religions have also been influential in deemphasizing the importance of literal, dogmatic belief. Many beliefs and symbols, instead, are taken to be appropriate for different groups in their unique, historical experiences. Each is a unique expression of the fundamental truths of nondualism.

Belief in certain doctrinal or historical statements (Jesus is the Son of God, Christ rose from the tomb on the third day) has been so central in Western religion that it has

been hard for Westerners to imagine religions for whom literal belief in such statements is unimportant. But the impact of oriental religion coincides with a long history of the criticism of religion in the West in which particular beliefs have been rendered questionable, but the significance of religion and myth in human action has been reaffirmed.[40]

How widespread the new religious consciousness is, and how appealing it may be in the future, cannot now be known. But one social aspect of the new religiousness deserves note: the new converts are a younger and better-educated group. Some argue that the better educated have more influence on social life, suggesting that these new movements will grow and have more lasting effects on society over time. They also argue that, because these people are younger, the movement will spread and increase as they grow older. But neither of these possibilities is certain. Others argue that the commitment of young people to a renewed religious consciousness may be a stage of their development, rather than a lasting commitment, and that as they mature, marry, and have families, they will move into more conventional and more institutionalized forms of religion.[41]

Religion and the Secular World

The increasing secularity of modern society leaves many people feeling empty of personal and social meaning for their existence, and the several recent religious developments are expressions of that.

One development was to be more relevant to the problems of the secular world and to enter directly into its social conflicts, taking the side of the poor and dispossessed, in an effort to challenge social injustice in religious and moral terms. The greater moral concern for all persons to be accomplished by often radical social reform would make society less secular.

In the United States this effort to offset the meaningless secular life produced in the 1960s the counterculture, which, in the 1970s became a new religious consciousness among the young. This youth movement had a parallel and overlapping development in the decline in the membership of mainline churches and a growth of evangelical churches which offer a personal salvation through Jesus Christ—the born-again Christian. But the more fundamental and conservative theology also weakened the social gospel. Social reform through religion lost support, personal salvation gained.

Whether these developments will continue and grow is not obvious at the present time. Religious movements have too often gone in cycles of growth and decline to be sure about what the future now holds for the present ones.

Yet, in attempting to assess the consequences of secularization for contemporary religion, several sociologists have attempted to see into the religious future. Both sociologists Peter Berger and Robert Bellah, for example, suggest that as religion becomes more subjective and personal, it becomes, as Bellah notes, less orthodox, and established belief gives way to personal interpretation.[42] He observes that "for many churchgoers, the obligation of doctrinal orthodoxy sits lightly indeed, and the idea that all creedal statements must receive a personal reinterpretation is widely accepted."[43]

Sociologist Thomas Luckmann, too, suggests that in the modern world different social institutions are each autonomous within their own sphere; this then leaves a private sphere for the individual in which he may develop a private worldview that may or may not be congruent with an official model of religion. Thus, there emerges the basis for a noninstitutionalized, *privatized* model of religion.[44] When this happens, religion recedes from the public stage and becomes socially and politically innocuous. "The gods of traditional religions live on as private fetishes or the patrons of congenial groups, but they play no significant role in the public life of the secular metropolis."[45]

SCIENCE IN SOCIETY

It would be unimaginable today to try to understand society without accounting for the influence upon it and the place within it of modern science. Science is a highly rational activity with immense practical consequences for almost every phase of social life.

When the natural scientist talks about science, he does so primarily in terms of theory and method, though he sometimes acknowledges that science is committed to certain values. He is less likely to recognize that modern science is socially organized, and, indeed, is now an institutionalized sector of modern society.

Yet it is this fact that makes science important to the student of society. Science is more than theory and method; it is a complex and extraordinarily influential process in modern society, and the role of the scientist is now one of the more important roles in the organization of that society.

The Growth of Science

Science as we know it in our time is the historic outcome of several centuries of significant social development in the Western world and is inextricably interwoven with Western culture and history. In a rudimentary manner, science is found in all cultures, even "primitive" ones. All people have made empirical observations about nature, generally related to practical considerations, and have developed arts and skills from these.

Yet science has taken major developmental steps forward only at particular times and in particular cultures. Over a thousand-year span, for example, the Greeks developed an impressive science with a large number of significant achievements to their credit.[46]

But knowledge of this science was lost in Europe after the fall of Rome. Not until well into the Middle Ages did renewed trade and commerce bring Greek and Islamic science back into a Europe in which technology was already well developed.

During the sixteenth and seventeenth centuries, usually defined as the period of the rise of modern science, a major breakthrough occurred in scientific discovery and achievement. A complex set of processes produced an atmosphere that was congenial to scientific creativity, and thus developed one of the truly great periods in the history of science.[47]

Perhaps most significantly, René Descartes provided a new rational philosophy for science that stressed the need to make precise observations and rigorous logical and mathematical calculations in order to establish necessary relations among events. There was also a refinement of experimental techniques, aided by the invention of new instruments of observation and measurement: the telescope, the microscope, the thermometer, the barometer, the pendulum clock, and the air pump. A new mathematical rationality combined with a new emphasis on empirical observation to create a powerful modern science.

The concern for practical inventions useful in mining and other industries led to technological innovations that in turn made possible new scientific tools of observation and experimentation. At this point in his-

Although men like Galileo Galilei (1564–1642) were highly controversial, even persecuted, in their own time, they subsequently received recognition and praise for their brilliant experimental and theoretical studies.

century, science has grown to enormous proportions. According to a historian of science, Derek de Sola Price, "Whereas in the mid-seventeenth century there were a few scientific men—a denumerable few who were countable and nameable—there is now in the United States alone a population on the order of a million with scientific and technical degrees.[48]

The growth of scientific manpower over the past 250 years, according to Price, has been at an exponential rate whereby it doubles about every fifteen years. But we have reached the point where such growth cannot continue. If we did, says Price, ". . . we should have two scientists for every man, woman, child, and dog in the population, and we should spend on them twice as much money as we had."[49]

There is, however, another development that may be even of more social significance: The enormous lead in scientific development once held by such scientifically developed nations as Great Britain, the United States, and Germany, is now lost in the face of rapid gains from other nations, such as Japan and the Soviet Union, and even the less-well-developed societies—the Chinese scientific population, for example, is doubling every three years.[50] Science is diffusing rapidly throughout the world, and the scientifically underdeveloped nations are rapidly catching up.

Developing Science in Underdeveloped Nations
Max Weber said that Protestantism encouraged the development of capitalism and science in the Western world, and the lack of such a rational worldview was a barrier to developing science in other parts of the world. This argument has often been liberally applied today in explaining the lesser development of science in Asia and Africa. But what may have been significant in explaining a historical development two or three centuries ago may be less relevant today.

Indian scientists, for example, in examining the very real problems of developing science in their own society, point out that inadequate technological development, a scarcity of resources for science, and a weak educational base in the population, are now the basic factors inhibiting the development of science.[51]

tory, technology was better developed than science and did not depend on science; actually, science gained from technology.

This period also saw religious changes and developments; and the emergence of Calvinism provided a new, strong impetus to science. Max Weber claimed Western society was more congenial to the development of science than any other, in particular because its religious view presumed a rational God revealed in nature and discoverable by the rationality of man. At this early period science and religion were not yet seen as opposed forms of truth. Science, instead, was conceived to be the rational process for understanding the order of things God had created.

These several factors, coming together at a particular time in history, brought into existence a social climate in which science flourished and grew, and a great panorama of giants of science came upon the scene in a relatively short period—men such as Newton, Leibnitz, Copernicus, Kepler, Galileo, and Boyle, among others.

Nonetheless, the number of persons who were scientists remained but a tiny fraction of the human community, literally, a handful of people. In the twentieth

The Scientific Community: Ethos and Autonomy

Though science has more than its share of creative talent, it has always been more than a collection of bright, scientific minds; it is also a communal effort. Every separate science has one or more scientific organizations, but more than that, there is a scientific community, a widely shared sense of a common enterprise that is different in a basic way from the other enterprises found in modern society—or at least, so scientists confidently think.

Scientists, for example, have always proclaimed the free dissemination of knowledge as a basic principle, so that all scientific claims can be publicly scrutinized by other scientists. Also, science does not recognize national, racial, or religious boundaries. Nothing was more offensive to scientists than the Nazis' effort to discredit Albert Einstein's scientific work because he was a Jew.

Another principle that scientists claim is the free-

dom to choose their own problems, so that they can follow new leads and hypotheses on the frontiers of knowledge, unrestrained by the practical interests of others. From these values, scientists have long stressed independence from political and economic interests— an autonomy seen as essential for science.

Basic and Applied Science   Within the scientific community there is a fundamental distinction between basic and applied scientific research. Logically and historically, the distinction is one between ''pure'' research—concerned with advancing fundamental, theoretical knowledge—and ''practical'' research— applying already existing scientific knowledge to the solution of practical problems.

Among scientists, basic research is more prestigeful

This nuclear reactor—itself a complex technological process—is an application of principles developed by basic science.

than applied, and some basic scientists are quite disdainful of applied scientists and engineers. Their assumption is that applied scientists depend completely upon basic science, and thus that technology rests exclusively upon science, so that advances in technology are only possible after advances in scientific theory.

But this is an incomplete and inaccurate reading of the historical and contemporary record. Technology and science mutually interact and influence one another, rather than one being wholly dependent on the other. Although technology does in fact advance by applying scientific principles to practical problems, its own successes often contribute in unanticipated ways to the advance of basic science.

The Autonomy of Science   Historically, the scientific community has enjoyed a relatively high degree of autonomy from the economic and political power structures of society. There have been a number of reasons for this.

First of all, until perhaps World War II, science was small science, not influential in the society, marginal but respected. This autonomy also benefited by the fact that science was primarily housed within the university with which it shared many values. If the university has, at least in part, been an "ivory tower," somewhat detached from the rest of society, this has served the scientific and scholarly communities well. It enabled them to pursue rational inquiry and intellectual life somewhat away from the impassioned scrutiny of partisan interests and from ideological (and sometimes anti-intellectual) perspectives. (To be sure, government and business did not subsidize and use the university then as they do now.)

In the last half century, however, science has been useful; and modern industrial society has had a major payoff for its investment in modern science. Science has become indispensable to the modern world, so that even totalitarian societies have had to concede some autonomy to science. To be sure, they have done this more for physical science than for biological science, and least of all for social science.

There have been, nonetheless, some noted instances in which government—particularly dictatorial government—has interfered severely with scientific autonomy. Hitler's Germany and Stalin's Russia are the two most noted examples. In these two cases scientists were subjected to political controls and direction, and forced to make scientific theory compatible with the ruling ideology.[52]

In democratic societies such as the United States there has been no such crude political subjection of science to party and ideology, but no less persistently, as we shall see, the autonomy of science has been seriously breached.

Science has also benefited by its own success. The enormous fruits of natural science have given to it an unchallenged prestige, superior to that of any other kind of scholarship. This has worked to keep science well supported and, more importantly, relatively free from interference by others. The scientist has become a major authority figure in the modern world, and scientific method has become the major standard for determining what to believe.

Yet two related developments now suggest that the relation of the scientific community to modern society is undergoing—if it has not already completed—a significant transformation. There is, first of all, the emergence of what a number of observers have come to call "Big Science," and secondly, the closer involvement with and control by national government of science, which threatens its prized autonomy.

Big Science

Since 1940 there has been an enormous change within the scientific community. We have noted the growth in the number of scientists, but there is also a vastly increased flow of funds for the support of scientific research, and in the importance that government and military now attach to scientific activity. Science has become Big Science.

As a consequence of its enormous growth, science is no longer housed entirely within the university, though this still remains its primary home. Private research institutes, industrial laboratories for applied work, and governmental laboratories now employ a large part of the scientific population of the United States. Many basic researchers—not to mention applied researchers—are neither students nor teachers in universities. Yet, as recently as 1940, "perhaps 90 percent of all basic scientific research in the United States was done by professors, or by students working under their direction."[53]

There have been a number of other important changes in science as a consequence of its changed size and status:

1. A newly found affluence has created a scientific elite who enjoy high status and rewards; who com-

mute among visiting appointments, conferences, and the like; and by such "commuting" are able personally to exchange ideas, as well as to constitute a select list for mailing preprints and otherwise unpublished material. These scientists make up an *invisible college* of creative and productive elites, whose significance cannot be observed only by consulting published journals.[54]

2. The way in which research is carried on has changed from the single, creative scientist, working alone or with a few students, to team work and organization reminiscent of large-scale organization.

> Just as the modern corporation has supplanted free partnership and apprenticeship in industry, so a more complex form of organization may be supplanting free collaboration and the professor-student association in science. Both changes involve the development of a more complex division of labor, the separation of the worker from the tools of production, and the greater centralization of authority.[55]

Team work occurs within large research organizations, which have sources of support usually far superior to those that scientists can get elsewhere—this being one of their attractions. The scientific community seems divided as yet on whether or not the team work of Big Science is superior to the individual project typical of "little science." Proponents of both are still to be found in the scientific community.[56]

3. Applied research has grown far more rapidly than has basic research, both in large government laboratories and in the industrial laboratories of corporations. Some of this research is still basic—at least from the scientist's perspective—but from the organization's viewpoint it is supported because it is likely to have useful (and for corporations, profitable) application.[57]

Scientists in Politics

Two significant developments alter the older pattern of a highly autonomous and politically remote science. One is that scientific knowledge and technology are so closely involved in military and political decisions that scientists now assume new roles of administrators and advisors in which they must make judgments that are not only technical but also political and moral. The other is that modern society now sees in science a major instrumentality for solving problems of military power, food production, physical disease, and the like; and thus has attempted to harness science more closely than ever before to national policy.

The new place of science in modern society has imposed upon many scientists, and particularly the leadership of science, advisory roles that are essentially political. The creation of numerous advisory boards and committees to governmental agencies and offices is an official acknowledgment of the need for scientific consultation. During the 1950s a Special Assistant to the President for Science and Technology was appointed, and this was followed by the President's Science Advisory Committee.

Ideally, scientists are presumed to advise on matters that are within their technical competence, but experience with the hydrogen bomb, atomic power, and the radiation fallout and testing controversy in the 1950s suggests that these technical matters are often inseparable from political and moral issues. In addition, some scientists have not hesitated to speak out in moral terms, with the result that they have often been in the position of publicizing quite contradictory advice. The near-disaster of a nuclear power plant in Pennsylvania in the spring of 1979 similarly found the scientific community split. Many scientists defended the feasibility and safety of such plants, but scientists associated with the Association of Concerned Scientists severely criticized the federal government and the power industry for inadequate safety standards and for failing to assure public safety.

There is another kind of role that may very well have as much influence on science as the political one: the role of the scientific advisor on those decisions about how government can advance science. A modern government that wants to use science extensively knows that it also has to support science. It is here that the scientific advisor becomes a political emissary from the scientific community to the government, bringing the position of scientists about what should be done and what is needed in strengthening science: science education, recruitment of scientists, participation in international conferences, and investment in various new areas of scientific exploration.[58]

Increasing involvement in the political process has rarely turned scientists into social and political critics of the government. Their ideological outlook seems to be little different from that of the military and political leaders whom they advise. Donald N. Michael characterizes a "new breed" of scientist, a science entrepreneur, deeply involved in the politics and power of Washington:

The science entrepreneurs are supported by and in turn support big business, big publicity, big military, sometimes big academic and parts of big government. They are both the captives and the kings of these powerful coalitions—kings for obvious reasons, captives because in reaping the benefits of affiliation they capitulate in some degree to the operating principles of these institutions. They have climbed to power through conservative hierarchies and tend to hold conservative values.[59]

Politics in Science

No modern society can now do without a national policy on science. Congress, for example, established the National Science Foundation (NSF) as an agency to support scientific education and also to provide funds for scientific research. Governmental support of research, however, comes from a whole variety of governmental agencies, including the military establishment.

But the support that government so generously gives science is not without its costs. What is lost is some of the autonomy and independence scientists have long prized and judged so necessary for science. Here are some of the consequences:

1. Others besides scientists have an impact upon the direction of scientific research. When a government amply funds one kind of scientific research and not another, it affects the disposition of scientific talent and thus the development of science. Sociologist Normal Kaplan puts it this way ". . . the 'market place of ideas' determining the choice of scientific problems is rapidly being replaced by a deliberate attempt to link the goals of society with the research goals of science."[60]

The feasibility and safety of nuclear power plants like this one in Oregon has deeply divided the scientific community.

Scientists are not compelled to study what political leaders think important, but they find it easier to fund a project—and remember that research in physical science is highly expensive—if they choose to work in those areas of scientific endeavor that are consonant with national policy. From the scientific point of view, nonscientists frequently fail to appreciate the importance of basic research designed only to advance scientific theory without regard for any immediate application.

2. Scientists have always opposed *secrecy:* instead, all scientific research should be publicly available for scrutiny. But scientist Barry Commoner notes, "now even *basic* scientific work is often controlled by military and profit incentives that impose secrecy on the dissemination of fundamental results."[61]

3. The technology that scientific advance makes possible often puts these military or other use before scientists have had a chance fully to measure the consequences, particularly the hazardous impact on life itself. Scientists have been unable to stop this—and some have aided and abetted it—with the results that the integrity of science has been seriously eroded, according to a report of a major scientific organization.[62]

But this report and the critical comments by Barry Commoner are evidence of another, significant development: that in recent years the scientific elite, and through them, the whole scientific community, have been subject to widespread and often severe criticism for their uncritical participation in governmental policy-making. Such an organization as the Federation of Atomic Scientists illustrated the possibilities of an independent and critical function carried on by qualified scientists. The federation originated in the moral concerns of atomic scientists engaged in research at atomic energy research laboratories during World War II. The terribly destructive potential of atomic energy, when harnessed to war uses, disturbed these scientists; more so when the first atom bomb fell on Hiroshima.

More recently, new groups of scientists have come forth to widen the range of those qualified to express positions on policy matters independent of—and often in opposition to—the government and the scientific advisory bodies attached to it. They have addressed themselves to issues of ecology and population, chemical hazards and toxic pollution, nuclear dangers, and industrial and commercial threats to the environment.

There is, then, a growing struggle within the scientific community to restore some of the independence it lost in becoming Big Science and so to free it from the control of government and the corporate economy.

THE FUTURE OF SCIENCE AND RELIGION

All those who have long hailed a world without religion are likely to prove to be poor prophets. But those who have raged against soul-less science are no more likely to be predicting with any accuracy what the future will be like.

It would seem there are two issues for the future of *science:*

1. Science has suffered enormously in prestige from being a too-willing partner of worldly power, and for letting go so much of its once prized autonomy. Critics both outside and inside science are engaged in a struggle over the responsible uses of science, so that science will no longer be a tool of governments and corporations but will put into practice some larger sense of purpose.

2. More basically, science has suffered for its basic contribution to bureaucratic, technological domination in an overrationalized world. To recognize that science is a powerful instrument for dealing with nature but is not, as Max Weber well knew, a source of ultimate wisdom, is the beginning of understanding both the power and limits of science. Weber's point was that science cannot tell us how to live our lives; at best, it may be one of the means to achieve a desired world. But it is never enough. What is *desirable* in the world today is a political and moral matter, not a scientific one.

For *religion* there are also two important developments:

1. The long humanistic resistance to stripping life of sacredness has resurged powerfully in our time, but in new unforeseen ways. The vitality of religion probably cannot be measured by the bank accounts and membership lists of the established churches. A renewed sense of the sacred in life challenges the domination of science and rationality, while raising new and as yet unanswered questions about life in postindustrial society.

2. Religious groups, even established churches,

are caught in renewed tension with society, as on a worldwide scale religious groups break partnership with secular powers and seek social change to provide justice in this world. This puts religion in opposition to governments and ruling classes, and makes of them a movement to withhold legitimacy from societies as they now are.

The consequences of these new developments are not fully apparent. But it is unlikely that science or religion can long remain unchanged.

SUMMARY

The rational and secular worldview of science has seemed to be assured of dominance, but religion has also seemed to make a strong counterattack on the domination of science and has tried to restore some sense of the sacred to human life.

Religion gives expression to this sense of sacredness in human life; a division between the *sacred* and the *profane* marks off religious from nonreligious activity.

A *functional* interpretation of religion stresses how sharing in religious beliefs creates moral cohesion and thus makes society morally legitimate. But religion also provides a mechanism for *social control* and a source of *psychic and emotional support* for individuals.

The *ecclesia* is an inclusive religious organization that accepts the world as it is. The *denomination* is a stable church that has made peace with the world. The *sect* is a small religious group that is *in* society but not *of* it, for it rejects the worldly society. The *cult* is a small, almost formless religious group formed around a charismatic leader that attracts the alienated in society.

Religious organization reflects the *class structure* of society, usually in the proportion of members it draws from different social classes. In industrial societies, the established churches have had least success in holding onto the working classes. But when working-class people form sects, these often compete with radical politics.

Among the oppressed, religion may produce *nativistic* and *revivalistic* movements in criticism of those who rule them. In the United States, religion has been a powerful force in the black community in providing dignity and self-respect. While this has often meant accepting the social order, it has also been an important source of support for civil rights.

Weber described the *Protestant Ethic* as a powerful set of religious ideas that contributed enormously to the development of both capitalism and rational science.

Secularization, the process of removing sectors of society from sacred domination, has been a pervasive process in the modern world.

Since the 1960s there has been a new religious consciousness among American youth. It takes various forms, including the Jesus movement and the Charismatic Catholic Revival, as well as an interest in Asian forms, such as Zen Bhuddism. It is a rejection of the materialism of modern society and of the domination of that society by utilitarian individualism.

There is a scientific *community* sharing an ethos of scientific values, including the *autonomy* of science.

Big science has developed since 1940, based on vastly increased funds for scientific research provided by government, and in a new involvement of scientists in making decisions about scientific development as well as about the uses of science by government, including the military.

This has put science into *politics,* reduced its autonomy, and opened it to criticism about the role of scientists in making decisions that include military *secrecy* and that direct funds to purposes other than the development of basic science.

For the *future* of science there are two issues: the struggle over the responsible uses of science, so it will no longer be a tool of government and corporations; *and* the recognition that science has contributed to an overrationalized world by being a powerful instrument for dealing with nature yet cannot tell us how to live our lives or what is morally desirable.

The *future* of religion is affected by two important developments: the resurgent sense of the sacred in life offers new ways to renew religion, but often outside established churches; and religious groups are caught in renewed tension with society, which puts them into opposition to governments and ruling classes.

NOTES

[1] C. P. Snow, *The Two Cultures and the Scientific Revolution* (New York: Cambridge University Press, 1961).

[2] *Ibid.,* p. 4.

[3] Cesar Grana has provided a brilliant analysis of the development of this humanist perspective. See his *Bohemian versus Bourgeois: French Society and the French Man of Letters in the Nineteenth Century* (New York: Basic Books, 1964).

[4] See Robert Bellah, "Religious Evolution," *American Sociological Review* 29 (June 1964): 358–374.

[5] Peter Berger, *The Sacred Canopy: Elements of a Sociological Theory of Religion* (Garden City, N.Y.: Doubleday, 1967), p. 26.

[6] Émile Durkheim, *The Elementary Forms of Religious Life,* trans. Joseph Ward Swaine (New York: The Free Press, 1948), p. 47.

[7] Robert Bellah, *Beyond Belief* (New York: Harper & Row, 1970).

[8] Will Herberg, *Protestant, Catholic, Jew* (New York: Doubleday, 1960).

[9] Frank E. Manuel, *The Eighteenth Century Confronts the Gods* (Cambridge, Mass.: Harvard University Press, 1959), p. 240.

[10] Louis Schneider, "Problems in the Sociology of Religion," in Robert E. L. Faris, ed., *Handbook of Modern Sociology* (Chicago: Rand McNally, 1964), p. 784.

[11] E. Digby Baltzell, *Philadelphia Gentlemen* (New York: The Free Press, 1958), p. 224.

[12] Karl Marx and Friedrich Engels, *On Religion* (Moscow: Foreign Language Publishing House, 1955), p. 303.

[13] T. B. Bottomore, *Karl Marx: Early Writings* (New York: McGraw-Hill, 1964), pp. 43–44.

[14] Louis Schneider and Sanford M. Dornbusch, *Popular Religion* (Chicago: University of Chicago Press, 1958).

[15] William A. Clebsch, "American Religion and the Cure of Souls," in Donald R. Cutler, ed., *The Religious Situation: 1969* (Boston: Beacon Press, 1969), p. 993.

[16] See Nicholas J. Demerath III, *Social Class in American Protestantism* (Chicago: Rand McNally, 1965), p. 4.

[17] *Ibid.,* p. 2.

[18] Such is the theme of G. Winter's study, *The Suburban Captivity of the Churches* (Garden City, N.Y.: Doubleday, 1961).

[19] See James West, *Plainville, U.S.A.* (New York: Columbia University Press, 1945); W. Lloyd Warner et al., *Democracy in Jonesville* (New York: Harper & Row, 1949); and Robert J. Havighurst and H. Gerton Morgan, *The Social History of a War-Boom Community* (New York: Longman's, 1951).

[20] For a review of the work of these French sociologists, see Schneider, *op. cit.,* pp. 796–799.

[21] See Charles Glock and Rodney Stark, *Religion and Society in Tension* (Chicago: Rand McNally, 1965), Chaps. 10 and 11.

[22] Rodney Stark, "Class, Radicalism, and Religious Involvement in Great Britain," *American Sociological Review* 29 (October 1964): 706.

[23] E. P. Thompson, *The Making of the English Working Class* (New York: Vintage Books, 1966).

[24] Robert Blauner, "Industrialization and Labor Response: The Case of the American South," *Berkeley Publications in Society and Institutions* (Summer 1958). Also, Liston Pope's *Millhands and Preachers* (New Haven, Conn.: Yale University Press, 1942) remains a useful study examining the formation of sects by working-class people in the South.

[25] The foremost study of the "Cargo" cults is Peter Worsley, *The Trumpet Shall Sound: A Study of the "Cargo" Cults in Melanesia* (London: MacGibbon and Kee, 1957).

[26] See James Mooney, *The Ghost-Dance Religion and the Sioux Outbreak of 1890* (Chicago: University of Chicago Press, 1965), and Joseph G. Jorgensen, *The Sun Dance Religion: Power for the Powerless* (Chicago: University of Chicago Press, 1972). See also Vittorio Lanternari, *The Religions of the Oppressed: A Study of Modern Messianic Cults,* trans. Lisa Sergio, (New York: Knopf, 1963).

[27] See Milton Yinger, *Sociology Looks at Religion* (New York: Macmillan, 1961), Chap. 2.

[28] Kenneth Stamp, *The Peculiar Institution* (New York: Knopf, 1956), p. 158.

[29] See Eugene D. Genovese, *Roll, Jordan, Roll: The World the Slaves Made* (New York: Pantheon, 1974), pp. 208–284.

[30] See E. Franklin Frazier, *The Negro Church in America* (New York: Schocken, 1964).

[31] Gary T. Marx, *Protest and Prejudice: A Study of Belief in the Black Community* (New York: Harper & Row, 1967).

[32] See Max Weber, *The Sociology of Religion* (Boston: Beacon Press, 1963).

[33] Max Weber, *The Protestant Ethic and the Spirit of Capitalism* (New York: Scribner's, 1958). Other works are *The Religion of China* (New York: The Free Press, 1951); *Ancient Judaism* (New York: The Free Press, 1952); and *The Religion of India* (New York: The Free Press, 1958).

[34] Berger, *op. cit.,* p. 107.

[35] *Ibid.,* p. 111.

[36] For an analysis of the relations between biblical religion and utilitarianism, see Robert Bellah, *The Broken Covenant: American Civil Religion in Time of Trial* (New York: Seabury Press, 1975).

[37] Robert Bellah, "The New Consciousness and the Crisis in Modernity," in Charles Y. Glock and Robert N. Bellah, eds., *The New Religious Consciousness* (Berkeley: University of California Press, 1976), p. 335.

[38] *Ibid.,* p. 336.

[39] *Ibid.,* p. 339.

[40] *Ibid.,* p. 348.

[41] See Robert Wuthnow, "The New Religions in Social Context," in Glock and Bellah, *op. cit.,* pp. 285–293.

[42] Peter L. Berger, "A Sociological View of the Secularization of Theology," *Journal for the Scientific Study of Religion* 5 (Fall 1966): 3–16; and Robert Bellah, "Religious Evolution," *American Sociological Review* 29 (June 1964): 364.

[43] Bellah, *op. cit.,* p. 372.

[44] Thomas Luckmann, *The Invisible Religion* (New York: Macmillan, 1967).

[45] Harvey Cox, *The Secular City,* rev. ed. (New York: Macmillan, 1966), p. 2.

[46] Brian Tierney et al., *Ancient Science* (New York: Random House, 1968).

[47] The following discussion is drawn from Bernard Barber, *Science and the Social Order,* Chap. 2 (New York: The Free Press, 1952; Collier Books edition, 1962).

[48] Derek J. de Solla Price, *Little Science, Big Science* (New York: Columbia University Press, 1963; paperback edition, 1965), p. 8.

[49] *Ibid.,* p. 19. Price's Chap. 1 is a good discussion of the exponential growth of science and its implications.

[50] *Ibid.,* p. 101.

[51] See Surajit Sinha, "Indian Scientists: The Socio-Cultural and Organizational Context of Their Professional Environment," pp. 105–153, and Purnima Sinha, "Social Constraints on Science in India," pp. 154–160, in Surajit Sinha, ed., *Science, Technology and Culture* (New Delhi: India International Center, 1970).

[52] On Germany, see Joseph Needham, *The Nazi Attack on International Science* (London: Watts and Cox, 1941), and Sir Richard Gregory, *Science in Chains* (London: Macmillan, 1941). See also Joseph Haberer, *Politics and the Community of Science* (New York: Van Nostrand Reinhold, 1969).

On Russia, see Julian Huxley, *Heredity East and West: Lysenko and World Science* (New York: Henry Schuman, 1949), and Conway Zirkle, ed., *Death of a Science in Russia* (Philadelphia: University of Pennsylvania Press, 1949).

For a brief review of both cases, see Barber, *op. cit.,* Chap. 3.

[53] Spencer Klaw, *The New Brahmins: Scientific Life in America* (New York: Morrow, 1968), p. 155. See especially Chap. 6, "Scientists Without Students," pp. 155–167.

[54] See Price, *op. cit.,* Chap. 3, "Invisible Colleges and the Affluent Scientific Computer," and Diane Crane, *Invisible Colleges: Diffusion of Knowledge in Scientific Communities* (Chicago: University of Chicago Press, 1972).

[55] Warren Hagstrom, "Traditional and Modern Forms of Scientific Teamwork," *Administrative Science Quarterly* 9 (December 1964): 251.

[56] For the flavor of some of this, see Klaw, *op. cit.,* Chap. 5, "The Styles of Big Science," pp. 134–154.

[57] See *ibid.,* Chap. 7, "The Vineyards of Utility," and Chapter 8, "The Industrial Labyrinth."

[58] See *ibid.,* Chap. 9, "Movers and Shakers," for a discussion of scientific advisors in Washington. See also, Daniel A. Greenberg, *The Politics of Pure Science* (New York: New American Library, 1966), and Don K. Price, *The Scientific Estate* (New York: Oxford University Press, 1968).

[59] Donald N. Michael, "Science, Scientists, and Politics," in John G. Burke, ed., *The New Technology and Human Values* (Belmont, Cal.: Wadsworth, 1966), p. 359.

[60] Norman Kaplan, "Sociology of Science," in *Handbook of Modern Sociology* (Chicago: Rand McNally, 1964), p. 871.

[61] Barry Commoner, *Science and Survival* (New York: Viking Press, paperback edition, 1967), p. 48.

[62] Committee on Science in the Promotion of Human Welfare, American Association for the Advancement of Science, "The Integrity of Science," *American Scientist,* June 1965.

SUGGESTED READINGS

Robert Bellah, *The Broken Covenant: American Civil Religion in Time of Trial.* New York: Seabury Press, 1975. A historical analysis of the relation between biblical religion and utilitarianism in American society.

Peter Berger, *The Sacred Canopy: Elements of a Sociological Theory of Religion*. Garden City, N.Y.: Doubleday, 1967. A foremost sociologist of religion maps out the range and concerns of sociology in examining religion.

J. D. Bernal, *The Social Function of Science*. Cambridge, Mass.: M.I.T. Press, 1967. An American reprinting of an influential English scientist's analysis of the place of science in society, first published in 1939.

Barry Commoner, *Science and Survival*. New York: Viking Press, 1966; paperback edition, 1967. A highly articulate plea for a humanely responsible science, by a scientist actively involved in criticizing the inadequate structure of science.

Nicholas J. Demerath III, *Social Class in American Protestantism*. Chicago: Rand McNally, 1965. A sociological analysis of the relations between status and religiosity among American Protestants.

Émile Durkheim, *The Elementary Forms of Religious Life*. New York: The Free Press, 1948. Durkheim's classic study that established religion as a social phenomenon and developed a functional theory of religion.

Joseph Haberer, *Politics and the Community of Science*. New York: Van Nostrand Reinhold, 1969. A penetrating examination of the relation of science to politics, including the politics of science under the Nazis, and a good review of the Oppenheimer episode of the 1950s.

H. H. Gerth and C. Wright Mills, *From Max Weber: Essays in Sociology*. New York: Oxford University Press, 1946. Weber's superb essay, "Science as a Vocation," remains as fresh today as it was in 1918.

Charles Y. Glock and Robert N. Bellah, eds., *The New Religious Consciousness*. Berkeley: University of California Press, 1976. A fascinating discussion of the diverse forms of the new religious consciousness among American youth.

Spencer Klaw, *The New Brahmins: Scientific Life in America*. New York: William Morrow, 1968. A very readable account of how science and scientists have changed from little to big science, with particular emphasis on the lives and careers of scientists.

Thomas Luckmann, *The Invisible Religion*. New York: Macmillan, 1967. The persistence of religion but without the organized church is predicted by a sociologist of religion.

Derek de Solla Price, *Big Science, Little Science*. New York: Columbia University Press, 1963. a distinguished historian of science weighs the significance of the emergence of big science.

Louis Schneider and Sanford M. Dornbusch, *Popular Religions*. Chicago: University of Chicago Press, 1958. A study of the "Americanizing" of religion from the middle of the nineteenth century to now.

Max Weber, *The Protestant Ethic and the Spirit of Capitalism*. New York: Scribner's, 1958. This is perhaps the greatest classic, certainly the most influential, in the sociology of religion.

Bryan Wilson, *Religion in Secular Society*. Baltimore: Penguin Books, 1969. Britain's foremost sociologist of religion explores the modern process of secularization and what it means for religion and for modern society.

Sixteen

ECONOMY AND SOCIETY

Without sustenance and shelter no other human activity is possible. It is only a step beyond that truism to recognizing that this necessary economic activity has an enormously shaping impact on all other aspects of social life.

It has long been assumed that economics and politics are separate activities, but in fact they are not and never have been. Instead, they are closely integrated with one another, producing in all modern societies a *political economy.*

In this chapter and the next we will deal separately with economic and political institutions, but our analysis will give full recognition to the close involvement of each with the other.

THE ORGANIZATION OF AN ECONOMY

Every society must provide some organized way for satisfying those material wants—food, shelter, and clothing—without which life could not be sustained. In a cooperative and interdependent process, many different persons contribute in some manner to a total task of producing and distributing goods.

Production

The productive factors—land, capital, labor, and organization—are combined in cooperative efforts at producing goods, and these efforts in turn bring about a division of labor and a system of occupations, however simple. Work is always done in social groups, whether that is the family, the small household unit, or the large, modern factory.

Distribution

Distributive processes are organized around the claims of each person to a share of the goods produced by the collective efforts of the group. Goods have always been relatively *scarce;* that is, demand exceeds supply, and distribution has always been unequal once there exist enough goods beyond the minimum necessary to sustain life in the group. Distribution then becomes a problem focused on *surplus,* that is, on any supply beyond that minimum.

At this point economy intersects with both the political structure and class structure. Differences of power permit some to gain a larger share of the economic surplus, and these more powerful classes, in turn, always control the political process. By such control unequal distribution is both enforced and justified. In all known societies such political control has been one factor in the allocation of economic surplus.

In the most primitive of economies—the hunting and gathering societies—there probably was never any regular surplus, so there was no established mechanism for distributing surplus in such societies. Life was necessarily on a day-to-day basis. Even a modest surplus of production—food, housing, tools and weapons, and ceremonial goods, for example—probably did not appear until the emergence of horticultural societies. That surplus then made possible an elite, which benefited from the surplus by getting a larger share for itself.[1]

Surplus and Economic Growth   There is another important aspect of the distribution of goods: Only when there is a surplus beyond a subsistence minimum can there be economic growth and development. Such a surplus is then not consumed; instead it is invested in further development of economic production. To invest surplus rather than consume can only be done if there exists the organized power to make such decisions. As sociologist Leon Mayhew observes:

> Surplus alone is not enough to insure development; it is necessary that there be some form of social organization for concentrating surplus and committing it to the tools of production and the equipment of civilization. Hence the intimate connection between systems of economic distribution and social stratification. The distribution and concentration of surplus defines the social strata that can control wealth and power and make the crucial allocative decisions.[2]

The controlling social strata that make such decisions has always had to enforce them upon an unwilling people. Extracting a surplus is always a politically coercive process. Payments of tribute and systems of taxation have been the major mechanisms for doing this, and these mechanisms required power to make them effective.

Marx's View of Surplus   These conceptions of surplus treat it as a problem in distribution and of political power, but Karl Marx among others treated it as a problem in production and of economic power. Marx developed his conception of capitalist production around the idea that the capitalist extracted surplus production from the worker by getting from each worker more production than was paid for in wages.

For Marx the value (not price) of anything is measured by the labor-power necessary to produce it. Workers must be paid for their labor and they must be paid sufficient to buy their "daily necessaries," as Marx called it; that is, enough to maintain their established standard of living. Suppose, said Marx, the worker was a cotton spinner who needed three shillings a day to sustain himself and his family; and suppose he could do that by six hours of work. But the capitalist, who pays him his three shillings, can make him work more than six hours, indeed ten to twelve hours. By working twelve hours, Marx said, the spinner produces six shillings of value, but gets paid for three. The capitalist takes the other three. In this fashion, says Marx, he extracts a *surplus labor* from the worker, "which surplus labor will realize itself in a *surplus value* and a *surplus produce*."[3]

Property

Property, too, rests on the conception of scarce resources, for if resources were unlimited and inexhaustible, no one would need to claim ownership of anything. The most common confusion about property is to think of it as a material object—land or tools—when property is *ownership* of an object, not the object itself. Ownership means the right to use, consume, or have access to and control of an object.

A further distinction is necessary. Private ownership of *personal* goods—from clothes and household goods to automobiles and television sets—does not distinguish one social system from another; all economic systems permit private ownership of these goods. But *ownership of the means of production*—of land and natural resources, of tools, machinery, and factories—is what defines a society as one of private or socialized property.

Whatever their form, property rights are sustained by collective agreement within the society and legally enforced by political authority. This is no less true of private property than any other kind. A person has private property rights only because laws and courts will protect and enforce such rights.

If property rights are socially defined and enforced, it follows that such rights are always limited. Laws regulate the use of property, and in any modern society there is a whole set of restrictions on private owners: fire and health regulations; zoning ordinances; and safety regulations, are examples. Furthermore, property may be confiscated for public use under specified circumstances, as when buildings are taken in order to build highways. Lastly, taxes are levied on property and if they are not paid, property rights are forfeited.

Types of Property   The emergence of private ownership of the means of production is a relatively late feature of societal development. In the earliest of societies, the land and its resources were defined as the *common* property of the community. Only when a resource was appropriated and used, as when an animal was killed for food, did it become private property. Even then, powerful customs ensured a sharing of food with others, so that little inequality actually existed.

When human society developed into more complex forms, as in the agrarian societies that preceded industrial society, property became a more complicated matter. Communal ownership often gave way to ownership by a family or kinship unit. The right of property was often divided between a ruling monarch and the individual peasant-farmer who actually worked the land and produced a crop.

With the advent of capitalism and the emergence of industrial production, however, land was no longer the basic means of production or source of wealth; industrial machinery was. Within such societies, (but not necessarily in their distant colonies), the rights of property were *formally* available to all, though not so in actual practice.

Private and Public Ownership   In capitalist society there is private ownership of the means of production, but there are also significant forms of public property. A factory is private property, but the street leading up to it and servicing it is public property. Besides streets, a capitalist economy requires a considerable infrastructure of public property: highways, sewerage systems, fire and police protection, schools for training people, and the like.

From Private to Public Ownership   In modern industrial, or at least industrializing society, public own-ership usually means state ownership. The national government is the public body which claims ownership in the name of all the people and for a social purpose rather than private profit.

Yet the state as the instrument of public ownership does not exhaust the possible social forms of property. Consumer and producer cooperatives, municipal ownership (as of public utilities), nonprofit corporations (e.g., hospitals, homes for the aged, and orphanages run by churches and civic groups) provide some examples of forms of ownership alternative to both private corporations and national governments already known and practiced in society. Each of these is an example of a form of social ownership in a more decentralized, local form.

CAPITALISM AS AN ECONOMIC SYSTEM

It would be a gross oversimplification to say that capitalism is defined only by private ownership of the *means of production*—land, tools and machines, and raw materials. It is much more than that. Private ownership, in fact, is not unique to capitalism; the artisans and merchants of the Middle Ages, for example, also owned their tools, their shops, and the goods they made or imported. Private ownership of land also came before the emergence of capitalism.

What Is Capitalism?

What distinguishes capitalism as an economic system—what Marx called a *mode of production*—are several closely interwoven features: private ownership of the means of production; wage-labor; the market; profit; capital accumulation; investment; and economic growth.

Since private ownership and the market for disposing of goods long existed, it is the addition of the others into a single economic system which makes an economy capitalist. We can understand that by distinguishing simple commodity production from capitalism.

Commodity Production   Under simple commodity production the individual producers own their own necessary means to produce—land, tools, and the

This cabinetmaker reminds us of the precapitalist system of commodity production, when skilled artisans crafted completed objects by themselves.

like—and they use them to produce goods that are then exchanged for money, which they then use to purchase goods they need and want. The "butcher, the baker, the candle-stick maker" were each producers—as were the shoemaker, the blacksmith, the tailor—who made things each other needed, and used the money they earned in order to buy each others' goods. Money served as a medium of exchange, not an end in itself. Commodities were the beginning and the end of the transaction.

Capitalist Production Capitalism changes simple commodity production in several ways:

1. Under capitalism ownership of the means of production belongs to one set of individuals, but the work is carried out by others. The labor expended to make useful products no longer belongs to a class of independent producers who make products, own them, and exchange them for other products. Now the artisan's skill becomes a quantity of *labor-power* bought by the capitalist. Labor-power, too, is then a commodity. The buying and selling of labor-power is one of the distinguishing features of capitalism.

2. Under commodity production the process of exchange is Commodity for Money for Commodity. But under capitalism it is Money for Commodity for Money. The capitalist begins with money (capital), which is used to buy the means of production and labor-power and to organize these into a process which produces a commodity, which is then sold on the market. Money is the beginning and the end of the process. But the money gained at the end of the process is intended to be more than the money originally invested. It is this gain that is *profit* and is the income of the capitalist.

The Elements of Capitalism

The process of capitalist production involves several basic elements, some of which we have already noted. The following are the necessary elements for an economic system to be capitalist:

1. *Private ownership of the means of production,* a process, we previously noted, which did not begin with capitalism.

2. *Wage-labor,* which is created by converting labor-power into a commodity, which the capitalist purchases. It is this process which produces the working class and that basic and inherently hostile relation in capitalist society: worker versus capitalist, employee versus employer. The worker under capitalism is *free* labor, meaning that the workers are not slaves or serfs, but are free to sell their labor-power to any employer who will pay for it. In fact, of course, in order to live workers have no choice but to sell labor-power.

3. The *market* in any economy is a system of exchange. Under capitalism it was originally intended to be (and is still often described as) a competitive arena in which producers buy and sell goods freely, with prices being determined by the balance of supply and demand. It is up to capitalists to produce that which is in greatest demand and will be most profitable to sell at any one time.

4. *Profit* is the income derived by the capitalist from selling on the market. It is the difference realized between the capital first invested and that gained in re-

turn after commodities are produced and sold. Under capitalism, then, commodities are produced for profit and what is not profitable will not be produced.

5. *Capital accumulation* is a necessary activity for capitalists, for unless there is capital to invest, the system will fail. Profits produce capital when they are reinvested. Accumulating capital is so basic a process that its encouragement is a matter of national tax and fiscal policy.

6. *Investment* and *growth* are accomplished by using accumulated capital to expand an enterprise or create a new one. Capitalism is more than a system of accumulating personal wealth, though it is that, too.

Since, in realizing a profit, the capitalists extract more money from the system than was first invested, in time wealth would accumulate in their hands, gradually stultifying the system. This can only be offset by an expansion of the system of production, which means by constantly reinvesting; capital must constantly circulate. Capitalism, then, as an economic system, requires constant investment and constant economic growth.

From Competitive to Corporate Capitalism

Capitalism, perhaps once in fact and for longer in myth and ideology, was an economic system of small, competitive, individual producers, each one taking his chances in a free market, where there was no political or other interference with the competitive market's ability to set prices for goods and for labor solely on the basis of demand and supply. This was laissez-faire capitalism.

Laissez-faire capitalism has been succeeded by *corporate* capitalism. The modern corporation has been an effective means of concentrating ever larger investments and gaining control over larger concentrations of technology and highly skilled manpower. This gives to fewer but larger corporations greater power over economic processes. Competition declines when a few firms dominate a large industry.

While many small businesses remain in such an economy, small business no longer sets the economic pattern. It does not control the direction of investment or affect the level of prices. Indeed, much small business is in fact controlled by large business, as small retail outlets are dependent upon the large firms that produce the goods they sell. An increasing number are local, franchised outlets for national brands or services

—automobile dealers, service stations, fast-food outlets, and the like.

The Corporate Concentration Most efforts to analyze the concentration of business size in American capitalism concentrates on the top 500 corporations, which are listed each year in *Fortune* magazine. But this obscures as much as it reveals, as economist Robert Heilbroner points out, for the top 50 industrials have an aggregate of sales as large as the bottom 450, and the profits of the top 10 companies are equal to almost half the profits of the rest.[4] A more useful measure, Heilbroner says, would be the top 150 supercorporations, each of which owns a billion dollars' worth of assets or sells a billion dollars' worth of goods and services. This "tiny group of immense corporations constitutes a bastion of formidable economic strength within the sprawling expanse of the American economy . . . ."[5]

Managers and Capitalists

The invention of the legal corporation was a significant step in the development of capitalism. It made it possible for many people to invest in a single enterprise, instead of relying on the capitalizing abilities of the few rich, while still protecting these many investors by limiting the liability of ownership they incurred.

The Separation of Ownership and Control But this development of the corporation had an unanticipated consequence: dispersing ownership among a large body of stock-holders apparently separated ownership from the actual, operating control of the enterprise. Increasingly, actual decision-making rested with *management,* which not only directed and supervised the employees in the internal daily operations, but also made fundamental policy decisions for the firm. It seemed that a *managerial class* had emerged to take control of the corporation away from a *capitalist class*.

The argument that this separation meant a basic change in capitalism was first made in the early 1930s by two economists, and soon came to be widely accepted among social scientists.[6] It was believed to refute Marx's claim that a capitalist class, which owned the means of production, through that ownership dominated society. The capitalist class, it was claimed, had lost its dominant place. The ownership of industry was not widely dispersed among millions of stockholders.

Not all economists and social scientists agree fully with this analysis; some, not at all. However, none disagree that there is a split between ownership and management in most large corporations. But many reject any implication that this has led to the emergence of a managerial class taking over from a capitalist class.[7]

What turns out to be a rather complex issue, as Maurice Zeitlin notes, needs to be separated into two issues:[8]

1. Whether owners continue to control the large corporations, despite their being managed by a professional group of nonowners.

2. Whether the emergence of managerial functions, carried out by salaried professionals, means the rise of a new social class to power, different in origin and interest from the ownership class.

The Concentration of Ownership Some social scientists believe that a class of large property owners still retains control of many large corporations. While over 30 million Americans own stock, according to the New York Stock Exchange, there is nonetheless a high concentration of ownership in the hands of a relatively small group. Economist Robert Lampman, for example, found that some 75,000 adults, each with total assets of $500,000 or more, owned at least 40 percent of all the corporate stock in the United States, and that this stock represented over 55 percent of their personal wealth.[9] The top 1 percent of wealth holders, about 1.5 million people, owned at least 80 percent of all stock. A social class marked by substantial ownership of the means of production still exists.

Large stock owners, furthermore, do not need to own anything like a majority of the stock of a large corporation to exert control. Most analysts today have accepted a mere 10 percent ownership as sufficient to have control, because stock is so widely dispersed. (In fact, a recent government study "concluded that effective control could be assured with even *less* than a 5% holding, 'especially in very large corporations whose stock is widely held.' "[10]

Management and Control But does such a capitalist class in fact control large corporations, or does management? Answering that exactly, Zeitlin tells us, is not now possible on the basis of what is known, and on the basis of the limited information which corporations have been forced to make public. There are very few events which put the proposition to the test.

One event which did, came when the socialist government of Chile nationalized American-owned copper companies in 1971.[11] The Kennicott Copper Corporation had prepared for such a possibility, and as a result emerged from nationalization with no loss. But the management of Anaconda Company, the other big copper corporation, had not, and it lost a considerable investment. Within two months, the president of the company and at least 50 percent of the managerial staff were fired, and its chairman took early retirement. A vice-chairman of Chase Manhattan Bank took over as chief executive officer. Zeitlin noted that: "The decimation of Anaconda's allegedly controlling management illustrates the general proposition that those who really have control can decide when, where, and with respect to what issues and corporate policies they will intervene to exercise their power."[12]

If this example tells us anything, it suggests that "management" and "control" are not necessarily identical. If the managerial functions are no longer carried out by the owners, this does not mean owners have lost control, but instead they have delegated a managerial *function* to others.

The Crises of Capitalism

Capitalism is a complex system; its development over the last 200 years has been of enormous growth, but not slowly and evenly. Instead, development has been irregular, at times rapid, characterized by disturbances and disruptions, producing crises of economic collapse and depression that have social consequences for all of society.

Capitalism is vulnerable to any action which would disrupt the necessary circulation of capital. When goods are produced, they must be consumed; the profits earned must then be reinvested, in an endless cycle. At any number of points, the process can be disrupted and often has; capitalism has never been a smoothly working economic system. Its dynamic, developing character always produces recurrent inflation, recession, and sometimes depression.

The crisis of *overproduction* and *underconsumption*, which produces recession are the two sides of one basic problem: the productive capacity produces more than can be consumed at one time within one market and profits fall. When that occurs, capitalists withhold investment while seeking new commodities to produce for new markets.

Severe recessions are not merely economic crises of capitalism; they are also *social crises* of society. They cause great human suffering; governments are then forced to take some actions both to rescue people from unemployment and bankruptcy and to restore production. Thus, the recurrent economic recessions of capitalist production necessarily stimulate social changes, including the emergence of a strong government to regulate and even control the economy.

These collapses also give rise to working-class demands for action on its own behalf. Working-class interest in greater economic security brings about a set of reforms, such as unemployment compensation and pensions, as well as the growth of labor unions and collective bargaining. The rise of the *welfare state* can be attributed, at least in part, to an effort by government to respond to working-class discontent by providing social programs which alleviate the distress and suffering brought on by these social crises.

Yet, if capitalism is beset with recurrent crises, no total collapse of capitalism has yet occurred. It has always managed to recover, though it has been changed in the process. Each recession and recovery eliminates some marginal producers, and so the concentration of capital in corporate form has accompanied the passage of capitalism through these periodic crises. Each crisis always involves the national government further in economic matters.

Counteracting Collapse   If economic recession is an inherent feature of capitalism, there is also counteraction which either offsets a possible collapse or which stimulates a recovery from one. Here are some examples:

New Industry   Once an economy has been industrialized the possibilities of offsetting recession through the introduction of new industry is possible. Technological developments provide new opportunities for investment and production which stimulate the economy. The growth of an electronics industry, of computers, and new advances in medical knowledge and technology, for example, have had such a stimulating effect.

State Expenditures[13]   The government is a major employer and a major consumer, and its activities always have an economic impact. Expenditures which are intended to stimulate production or consumption help to offset possible crises: for example, buying up grain or other surplus agricultural commodities; and funding public works, such as parks, schools, and other public buildings. (The construction industry depends heavily upon public expenditures.)

There is also a *transfer* process in which the state accumulates revenue through taxes and then pays it out to others: to subsidized industries; to the unemployed and poor people; to retired people; to schools, nursing homes, hospitals, and the like. Such transfer policies increase the capacity for consumption by providing payments and income where private means would be unsufficient.

Another important source of public expenditures is for military purposes. The purchase of armaments — planes, ships, vehicles, guns, and various forms of sophisticated technology — is an expenditure which encourages production and consumption and ensures employment. The result is a powerful military-industrial complex with a vested interest in continuing and expanding such expenditures.[14]

Within any capitalist society, there is a growing reliance on state expenditures. That dependence gradually transforms both the government and the economy by the penetration of each other. Not only is there a *political economy,* instead of separate political and economic processes, there is now a *capitalist state.*

State Capitalism

The term laissez-faire once suggested that a free society was best promoted by the separation of the economic and political institutions from one another. Specifically, it admonished the government to let the economic order alone, except for the enforcement of laws against criminal and fraudulent behavior.[15]

Perhaps only in the United States is there still a widespread public belief that government involvement is an unnatural and unnecessarily interfering process, and that government and the "free" market ought to be kept apart. But in fact a complex capitalist economy, organized largely through very large corporations, cannot function without a strong government.

In the United States the development of a political economy makes it impossible to pretend any longer that politics and economics are distinct enterprises unrelated to one another. Government regulation of various forms of economic activity is now well established. There is a complex *welfare state* that includes some effort to reduce the impact of the market on those subject to low income and unemployment, and an equivalent welfare for business in the form of *tax breaks* and *subsidies*.

The federal government now tries to protect the dollar, improve the balance of trade, and both protect and promote private investments abroad. At home, it tries to reduce inflation, control interest rates, increase sources of energy, reduce unemployment, protect natural resources and the environment, reduce pollution, encourage capital accumulation and investment in new businesses, and regulate a wide sphere of economic activities in the interest of public health and welfare. Economic policy is a central concern of government, perhaps its most important activity.

A capitalism that is closely integrated with the national government is then *state capitalism*. That does not mean that the state has taken over the capitalist system, nor does it mean that capitalists control the government. Instead, it means that the nation-state's economic policies are intended to protect and promote a capitalistic economy.

INDUSTRIALISM AND TECHNOLOGY

In the Western world industrialism and capitalism developed together, yet they are not the same thing. A society can be both industrial and capitalist, as the United States is, but it need not. The Soviet Union is industrial without being capitalist, and many of the industrializing nations in Asia and Africa are not capitalist. Socialism has always shared with capitalism a positive value on technology and industrial production.

If industrialism is not to be confused with capitalism, then what is it? *Industrialism* is a system of machine technology, and the organization of work to fit the social uses of that technology for production.

Technological Determinism

The idea of *technological determinism*—that technology produces changes in social organization—has been a widely accepted concept in social science. Modern technology is viewed as having a logic of its own and as producing most social changes in society. Thus, technology determines social order; industrial machinery produces industrial society.

The invention of the automobile is often given as a powerful case in point. It created a whole new industry and many new occupations, while eliminating others, such as buggy makers and blacksmiths. It stimulated mass production and the modern assembly line. In time it promoted the invention of paved highways. It also made possible suburban neighborhoods, shopping centers, and motels. In these and so many other ways the invention of the automobile changed American life.

Yet in doing that, the technology was not the only factor. The decision to mass-produce automobiles, rather than have them be a privilege of the rich, was an economic decision, not a technological one, and was possible only because capitalism had available sufficient raw materials, labor, and investment capital, as well as cheap energy. That made possible a new, profitable industry.

Changes in technology will always have some effect on social life, but the extent and significance of that change depends on other factors. Such changes can be limited or can be far-reaching.

In a recent work David Noble has shown how, between 1880 and 1930, corporate capitalism combined with an advanced scientific technology to revolutionize production and reshape American society.[16] It did so by fostering the development of a technical specialty—modern engineering.

It was in the creation of the professional engineer, university-educated but corporate-employed, that the industrial corporation got control of scientific technology and was able to control technical innovation for corporate purposes. In such a situation technology is not an independent force and it does not alone determine the shape of society.

Technology and the Division of Labor

Industrialization brought about a reorganization of work impelled by the introduction of new and complex machinery, before which all other historically known technologies seem primitive and crude. Vast social consequences flow from this change from the simple to highly productive technology.

Perhaps the most significant consequence is the development of a historically new form of the division of labor. Human beings have divided labor since the earliest organization of society. But until the onset of industrial capitalism, such a division was what Marx called the *social* division of labor: one person was a farmer, another made shoes, another spun cloth, still another baked or butchered. While society's labor was divided, each person performed a whole task, and each of these tasks usually involved a number of developed skills.

The days of the old craftsman who made a total object with a few tools and his remarkable skills are gone. Now the human-made object is the end-product of a vast system of production that involves many special tasks. Each person contributes but one small part to the finished product.

As against this social division of labor, there stands the division of labor in detail, the manufacturing division of labor. This is the breakdown of the processes involved in the making of the product into manifold operations performed by different workers.[17]

Two things, it should be noted, are involved here: (1) the replacement of the human hand by the machine, which is a *technological* change; and (2) the subdividing of the whole task into many small, detailed tasks, which is a *social* change.

There are two significant consequences to be derived from these changes. The first is the greater production of goods at cheaper cost. The second is the routinizing and deskilling of work.

Unlike the craftsmen of an earlier era, these workers perform only one step in the assembly of the automobile, a striking example of the division of labor in detail.

When capitalists first were able to replace skilled hands with machines, they found it profitable to break the work up into small, detailed parts, each one of which was likely not to be a skill. Thus labor was deskilled and so was cheaper for the manufacturer.

These technological and social changes have not merely replaced the craftsman with the machine-tending worker. Gradually but irrevocably the worker lost control over tools, quality of work, hours of work, the pace and rhythm of work, and the like. The alienation of the worker, as Karl Marx fully recognized, is rooted in this process of the "degradation of work."

Automation   The social consequences of technology have been made vividly apparent in recent years by the development of automation. Automation is not merely more advanced mechanization. It involves two principles: a continuous process of production, whereby machine-controlled parts move from one point to another without being touched by human hands; and, self-control by means of a feedback process, in which machines provide information on which decisions can be made, such as the decisions ordinarily made by inspectors or maintenance men.

Automation eliminates many of the machine-operative positions that once provided most of the jobs on an assembly line. Its long-run consequences on the need for labor are not yet quite clear and are still subject to contradictory interpretations. But it is quite evident that automation reduces the need for lesser skills and increases the need for more technically skilled people. Within the factory, a few technicians replace unskilled and semiskilled positions.

The Mechanization of Clerical Work   As the large corporation replaced the small family business, a large white-collar office staff came into being to undertake clerical. But this work, too, has been subject to the same processes of mechanization, detailed division of labor, and now automation, as has factory work.

In a small office one clerk or secretary might answer the phone, sort the mail, make out bills, type letters, record orders, make payments, and file. In a large office the work will be divided into separate jobs: mail clerk, billing clerk, order clerk, bookkeeper, filing clerk, typist, and the like. In the office, too, work becomes routinized and deskilled.

Many of the traditional skilled occupations associated with office work have been declining or have even been replaced by machines. Braverman reports on the decline of the bookkeeper:

> The decline of the bookkeeper . . . was helped along by the bookkeeping or posting machine, which converted a certain amount of skilled ledger work into a mechanical operation. The decline was continued, especially in banking, by the development of electronic bookkeeping machines, which complete the conversion of bookkeepers into machine operators and at the same time reduce the demand for them sharply. Thus one multibranch bank reported that within eighteen months after installing electronic bookkeeping machines, the bookkeeping staff of 600 had been reduced to 150, and the data-processing staff had grown to 122. This is in line with the experience of most banks, which achieve a reduction in overall labor requirements of 40 to 50 percent for the same volume of work, and in the process cut down the bookkeeping people sharply and replace them with machine operators.[18]

The Effect on Occupations   As should now be evident, there is a constant process of a detailed division of labor, accompanied by mechanization, which tends to reduce skills and eliminate jobs, while reducing labor costs and increasing productivity. In a capitalist economy, the maximization of profits provides a constant impulse in this direction.

But that is hardly the whole story. Two other developments need to be noted. One is that an advanced industrial society also develops many highly skilled occupations: scientists, engineers, and technicians, and various other professions, as well as a huge army of managers and administrators to run the large bureaucratized corporations and public agencies.

This development (as we saw in Chapter 9) has provided the expansion of what social scientists call the *new* middle class. The combined professional and managerial categories, which accounted for 10 percent of the occupations in 1900 made up about 25 percent of all occupations in 1975.[19]

A second development is an enormous shift from, first, agriculture, and second, from manufacturing to a rapidly increasing sector of service occupations. Agriculture now absorbs barely over 3 percent of the work force, and manufacturing employed only 25 percent of the work force in 1968, and it is in a steady decline.[20]

The industrialization of society has so mechanized the production of food and manufactured goods that an even smaller part of the work force can easily produce enough for the entire population.

CONFLICT AND CONTROL IN THE ECONOMY

One does not have to be a Marxist to recognize an economic basis for social conflict. Many scholars, both Marxist and not, have observed peasants struggling against rich landowners, workers against employers, the poor against the rich, and even nations fighting over (1) access to markets and raw materials; (2) land; (3) trade routes; and (4) sources of food for their populations.

From a Marxian perspective, the basic struggle in life is always a *class struggle,* in which the *interests* of a subordinate class (peasants or workers) are pitted against a dominant class (landowners or employers) in an irreconcilable conflict. These class struggles shape quite different kinds of societies, and through these struggles societies are changed. "The history of all hitherto existing societies is the history of the class struggle."[21] Thus, for Marx, conflict is the significant source for historical change; to deplore conflict is to accept the dominance of established patterns and to fail to understand how society changes.

Ideology in Conflict and Control

Early capitalists and modern management have not hesitated to claim authority over the worker.[22] At one time in the United States, and until the 1930s, most American industry espoused an "open shop" position, rejecting the right of workers to organize unions and bitterly opposing every such effort. Extensive labor violence was often the result.

This class position of dominance was maintained by force, including the police power of the state, which invariably intervened on behalf of the employers. In response, socialist parties and militant unions put forth counterideologies. Unions challenged the authority of management, at least in those aspects affecting workers, and claimed the right of workers to act collectively on their own behalf.

Labor Unions

Labor unions are organizations that represent the class interests of workers, but this function does not necessarily make them revolutionary. Historically, in fact, unions have tended to be pragmatic and reformist. Even in periods of violent conflict and forceful repression, when they are usually militant, unions' ultimate goals are not usually revolutionary.

In the United States, labor unions won legitimate status as collective-bargaining agents through the Wagner Act of 1935. Before 1935 they were a struggling, class-based social movement fighting to be recognized as the legitimate voice of the workers. After that, they became stable social organizations with a legitimate function in society defined and protected by legislation.

Long and difficult as was the struggle by labor unions and some allied middle-class reformers, the victory was not simply a conquest of a stubborn capitalist class forced to come to terms despite itself, even though this could accurately be said of many individual corporate leaders. But from the turn of the century on, a more sophisticated group of business leaders saw the need to accept many reforms which would stabilize the continued expansion of the economy, en-sure continued influence over government, and yet undercut the growing threat of socialism.

This was done by accepting, indeed promoting, many liberal reforms, including, first, workmen's compensation for work-related injuries and finally, the recognition of unions as the legitimate representative of workers in collective bargaining.[23]

Today both management and labor operate within a legal order that insists both parties bargain in good faith and enter into contractual relations. Social mechanisms—such as bargaining elections, federal mediation of prolonged disputes, and union-management contracts as the legal basis for worker-management relations—have become institutionalized.

As a consequence, American labor unions have accepted capitalism and in turn have been accepted as the legitimate representatives of workers' interests. Through collective bargaining they seek to get "more and more" for workers while not altering the basic pattern of property relations under capitalism.

But if unions now represent workers *within the*

Workers in the United States possess the legal right to bargain collectively and to be represented by a union. These white-collar workers at a university are demonstrating against the university administration's resistance to entering into bargaining relations.

capitalist system, rather than organize them to oppose capitalism, then they become agencies for *integrating* workers into capitalist society. (A more critical perspective would say that unions have been used to coopt the workers.)

But if American labor unions have come to accept capitalism and reject socialism, they have, at the same time, never accepted laissez-faire capitalism. Instead, they have been an active and decisive element in a political coalition of liberal reformist groups—including representatives of corporate capitalism—steadily building a welfare state. They have put political force behind legislation for social security, unemployment compensation, civil rights, housing, welfare, education, medical care, and care of the aged.

Work and Alienation

From the earliest days of industrial society, work was supposed to be the central life-interest of an industrial people, their dominant and rewarding role. But do workers actually find their work to be so central to their lives? Do they find it more rewarding than other activities? There is much evidence to suggest they do not. For the working classes, work has always been a necessity, not a joy.

Robert Dubin, an industrial sociologist, for example, attempted to determine the "central life-interests" of industrial workers.[24] He discovered that these interests were not in work but in human associations outside of the job. Less than 10 percent of workers preferred the informal relationships on the job to other possibilities.

The Alienated Worker   Ever since Karl Marx spoke of the *alienation* of the worker, critics of modern industry under capitalism have maintained that the worker typically feels that his work is only for the purpose of earning a living, and that he is not in any way fulfilled by work itself, that it is not a rewarding activity. Marx was concerned with a *social process* of alienation occurring under certain conditions, which affected workers more than any other social class (see "Marx on Alienation").

Sociologist Robert Blauner undertook an ambitious sociological effort to study alienation in work.[25] His major innovation was to compare *type of work:* craft work with machine-tending and then with assembly work and lastly with a continuous process industry,

such as the chemical industry, where work is highly automated.

Blauner discovered a regular progression of feelings of greater alienation, particularly powerlessness and meaninglessness, from craft work, where it was low, to automobile assembly work, where it was highest, with a reversal under the newer circumstances of automated continuous production. Both craft workers and those operating automated processes felt they had control over their jobs, were freer from close supervision, and were not merely appendages to the technological processes.

What Blauner's research optimistically suggests is that the greatest sense of alienation from work may have been reached in the mass, assembly-line production process, and that its eventual replacement by automated processes may produce work environments less conducive to feelings of powerlessness and meaninglessness in work, less isolating and estranging. But this may actually hold true only for a technical elite of highly skilled workers and not for others.

But another sociologist, after reviewing the available studies on automated work, comes to a different conclusion. Though automated work is an improvement over previous conditions, he says:

> . . . there are, in addition, other features and tendencies of automated work which are strongly alienating. In the factory these include: destruction of the work group and ensuing social isolation; fewer promotional opportunities; continuous stress, anxiety, and tension arising out of fear of damaging expensive equipment; the need for constant alertness; increased production rates; increased levels of supervision; and so on.[26]

Blue-Collar Blues   It has been fashionable to say that intellectuals have made too much of alienation because they think factory jobs are dull and boring, but that workers do not necessarily find them so, and that they are really fairly content. But now greater worker absenteeism and turnover, especially among younger workers, have provided separate evidence that most factory workers do not like the jobs or the conditions under which they work, find them demeaning, yet do not (at least as yet) put much blame on anyone or anything besides themselves.[27]

As a consequence, there is now much talk about how to make the routinized factory job more interesting—*job enrichment,* it is called. Both management and union leadership have been reluctant to change established ways, or to think differently about workers.

MARX ON ALIENATION

Under the conditions imposed by capitalism, according to Marx, the worker is required to sell his labor for a wage in order to live; work becomes a commodity, for sale like any object; work is divided up to suit technological efficiency; and since property is private, neither the machines nor the product belong to the worker. The result is alienation.

Marx's own words:

What, then, constitutes the alienation of labor? First, the fact that labor is *external* to the worker, i.e., it does not belong to his essential being; that in his work, therefore, he does not affirm himself but denies himself, does not feel content but unhappy, does not develop freely his physical and mental energy but mortifies his body and ruins his mind. The worker therefore only feels himself outside his work, and in his work feels outside himself. He is at home when he is not working, and when he is working he is not at home. His labor is therefore not voluntary, but coerced; it is *forced labor*. It is therefore the satisfaction of a need; it is merely a *means* to satisfy needs external to it. Its alien character emerges clearly in the fact that as soon as no physical or other compulsion exists, labor is shunned like the plague. External labor, labor in which man alienates himself, is a labor of self-sacrifice. Lastly, the external character of labor for the worker appears in the fact that it is not his own, but someone else's, that it does not belong to him, that in it he belongs, not to himself, but to another.

Notes

From *Economic and Philosophic Manuscripts of 1844,* trans. Martin Milligan, with an introduction by Dirk J. Struik, ed., (New York: International Publishers Company, 1964), pp. 110–111.

Despite such coolness of management and union leadership, ideas for new work arrangements have begun to gain attention in the United States; they have long been talked about and tried out in Europe.

The proposals range from ones which permit workers to trade jobs back and forth, as well as make more flexible time arrangements (both of which still leave management in control) to *group assembly*, which assigns a group of workers the task of assembly and allows them to carry it out as a group project. This is an innovation borrowed from Europe, particularly from Sweden and Yugoslavia.[28] How extensively it will be adopted in the United States, and whether it will alter in any significant way the deep estrangement of many blue-collar workers from the conditions of their work-life, are not now evident.

Is Work Valued? Discussions of alienated workers imply that people in other occupations do like their work and find reward in it. There is as yet little systematic evidence, but sensitive observers of American life, such as sociologist David Riesman, have sensed a perceptible shift from the older, religiously sanctified values on work to leisure pursuits as the sphere of life which provides a significant meaning for living.[29]

Two recent trends lend support to Riesman's idea that work is no longer as valued an activity for all workers, not merely blue-collar ones.

1. *Early retirement.* Fewer people are now working to age 65, and many are now retiring before age 60 if they can do so. In 1954, for example, the average wage worker at General Motors retired at age 67, the average salaried worker at age 63. By 1977 both were retiring at age 58 or 59.

While some argue that early retirement is most favored by autoworkers, steelworkers in foundries, and others doing routinized or physically hard work, the evidence suggests otherwise. At General Motors salaried workers quit as early as do these on the assembly line.

According to the Bureau of Labor Statistics, the proportion of men in the labor force—that is, working or seeking work—in the 55—64 age bracket fell from 89.6 percent in 1947 to 74.5 percent in 1976.[30]

2. *Job satisfaction.* Self-employed people and the more educated workers in well-paid jobs have always found more satisfaction in work than have blue-collar workers and those with little skill or education. This is still true.

But a 1977 study by the Institute for Social Research at the University of Michigan for the U.S. Department of Labor showed a marked decline in job satisfaction among the college-educated and among those under 30 years of age.[31]

For all respondents in the national sample, only 27.2 percent were satisfied with their pay, and only 31.9 percent were satisfied with the opportunity to develop their abilities. In each case there was a decline of over 10 percent since 1973.

The trend to early retirement and the decline in levels of job satisfaction are evidence that work in capitalist society no longer offers an ethical value. It is a source of necessary income and a basis for sharing in the material goods capitalism provides in such abundance. But the search for meaning in life is now largely pursued in other kinds of human activities and in social relations other than those found in the corporation.

Socialism and the Alienated Worker

Some sociologists have argued that routinized industrial work is inherently alienating and that this is true whether the system is capitalist or socialist. This is part of the conception that what gives modern society its basic form is industrialization.

Industrialization, however, as we have already asserted, is not an independent force; historically, it developed under the control of capitalism. Does that mean that under socialism there are no alienated workers?

If what is meant by socialism is *state socialist* systems of the Soviet Union and Eastern Europe, where an authoritarian state owns and controls the means of production, the answer is clear: There are alienated workers in such societies.

After the Russian Revolution in 1917, under the leadership of Lenin, the new Soviet Union began to industrialize and at a rapid rate. To industrialize rapidly it had no choice but to borrow industrial technology and the social system of industrial organization which had been created in the capitalist nations of Europe and the United States. That meant: the factory system; the production line; the detailed division of labor; wage-labor; close supervision of workers; piece-work and incentive systems; a hierarchy of positions differentiated by pay, privilege, and authority; and the bureaucratic organization of the entire system of production.

The consequence of this was that the Soviet Union's rapid industrialization *reproduced* the capitalist relations of production inside any Soviet factory. In addition, the development of engineers who controlled the work process by impersonal criteria of output and production quotas denied to workers any possibility of self-management. Furthermore, the concentration of economic control at the top, in the hands of the state, without independent unionism and democratic practices, only reinforced the system of authoritarian control.

When work is a system of domination and control, it is alienated work. When the worker's relation to work remains that of selling labor for wages, with no control over any aspect of the work or no claim upon what is produced, there are alienated workers. There is, then, alienated work and alienated workers in those societies, capitalist and socialist, in which these conditions prevail.

THE WORLD AS AN ECONOMIC SYSTEM

Most people think of an economy as being part of a society—thus, the American economy or the Soviet economy—though always engaging in some trade beyond the society's borders. But the economic systems of modern nation-states have always extended well beyond their borders. Now those modern economies are but units of a worldwide complex economic system.

The idea that from the sixteenth century on there has been a long historical development leading to a world capitalist economy was only recently described and analyzed by sociologist Immanuel Wallerstein.[32] Capitalism became a world system because capitalist development never stopped at national boundaries or at the development of only a national economy.

Empires and Colonies

When capitalism developed in European societies, so did colonialism. By the seventeenth century major European nations were interested in a secure supply of raw materials from sources outside Europe, usually Asia and Africa. This led Western nations to take political control over large areas of Asia and Africa and convert them into colonies. Furthermore, profits from trade with colonies provided much of the capital accumulation for expansion of the European economy.

The classic pattern of colonialism was an international division of labor in which the colony provided raw materials and was a market for finished goods, while the European nation used the raw materials to manufacture goods for both domestic and foreign markets. It was a political and economic structure of domination and control, evident in political subordination of a non-Western people to a Western people, and in the enormous differences in the standards of living between the two societies.

But the old pattern of colonies and empires is gone. There are very few outright colonies in the world any longer. New economic and political arrangements have emerged in this century, providing new forms of domination and control, to fit the emergence of an economic system that now involves the entire world.

The New World Economy

Now, the growth and change of any national economy seems to depend less on national concerns and objectives, more on how that economy fits into a world system. The markets for most goods are worldwide; rich economies penetrate poor ones; and every nation is caught up in a worldwide market structure.

In speaking of the fate of traditional peasant economies and their market, Mayhew noted that "remote events in the larger world alter the fate of peasants in the village."[33] What is true for Asian peasants is no less true for American farmers and workers. The income of many farmers may depend less on selling wheat for American loaves of bread, more on the price of wheat on the world market and on political deals to sell grain to China and the Soviet Union. So, too, the job of an American worker may be eliminated as production is shifted by a multinational corporation from factories in the United States to a nation with a cheaper wage-scale.

Rich and Poor in the World Economy

In the new world economy, there is great inequality. There are rich nations and poor nations, and the gap between the rich and poor is widening. But there is also a three-way division that reflects both historical differences in development and differences in social organization and ideology:

The *First World* is made up of the capitalist nations of North America and Europe, plus Japan, among which the United States has been the most powerful and influential.

The *Second World* is the communist bloc of nations in Europe, dominated by the Soviet Union.

The *Third World* is a complex of mostly new nations, former European colonies, located primarily in Asia, Africa, and Latin America. They have achieved political independence but are economically poor and industrially underdeveloped.

Among the Third World nations there is a group of them so impoverished and with such poor prospects for economic development that some scholars claim they constitute a *Fourth World*.

The political elites who lead Third World nations borrow ideas of economic and political organization from the major nations, but they are intent on building new societies that are *not* simply imitative of either the Soviet Union or the United States. The future they wish to shape for themselves is rooted in their own distinctive history and culture. Nonetheless, more of them are moving toward some form of socialism, rather than capitalism.

A number of major nations of the world are First World powers. They wield enormous economic and political control over poor nations, maintain a flow of raw materials from these former colonies, and compete with one another for control over sources of raw materials and markets for finished goods. These are rich nations producing 60 percent of the world's wealth with only 20 percent of its people.[34] The United States is the first of these nations. Japan and the larger nations of Western Europe are the others.

This small number of powerful, technologically developed societies are the *core* —the dominant, organ-

In many places in the Third World the evidence of a preindustrial economy is quite visible yet; this is the market in Old Delhi in India, operating just as it has for centuries.

izing center—of the world system. Each has a strong state apparatus, a strong economy diversified between agriculture and industry, and its industrial production is composed of highly processed goods produced by skilled, relatively highly paid labor.

The *periphery* of the world system is a large set of societies with a weak state and an economy specializing in the production of one or two unprocessed goods (raw materials) by unskilled, low-wage labor. These are the underdeveloped societies of the Third World.

There is also a *semiperiphery*, the economies of which are between the others—more diversified than the peripheral ones, but much less so than the core

economies. Mexico and Brazil are examples of such economies.

The three zones do not receive equal shares from the workings of the world system. The core gets a disproportionately larger share of the surplus generated by worldwide economic activity, for the exchange of goods on the world market is always an unequal exchange. Though no one nation controls the entire system, the strong ones can make sure that the unequal flow of surplus to the core zone is maintained.

What happens to underdeveloped societies, then, is primarily a matter of how they fit into the worldwide division of labor. If the system allows for core economies, it also requires ones on the periphery. If there must be developed societies, there also must be undeveloped ones.

Though it is not impossible for a peripheral society to develop and reach a level of semiperipheral or even core status—the place of particular societies in the system is not fixed forever—the odds against any one underdeveloped society doing so are tremendous. For that reason, most of them are likely to remain in a state of *dependency:* dependent on world markets for disposing of their raw materials at prices beyond their control; dependent on core states for loans and technical assistance; and dependent on the world system's investment decisions for a chance to develop even limited aspects of their own resources.

What About Socialism?   The political elites of some of these dependent societies, we noted earlier, are attracted to socialism because it provides a more effective system for controlling and planning the factors of development. It also symbolized their ideological rejection of capitalism.

Yet, when an underdeveloped society becomes socialist, it must still participate in the world system's division of labor; being socialist does not give it another choice. As a peripheral society it will still be forced to contribute to the profit-making of the core's multinational corporations. Viewed that way, socialism in one or a few peripheral (or even semiperipheral) societies does not threaten capitalist domination.

The United States in the World Economy

The dominant place of the United States in the new world economy is itself a recent development. Only after World War II did the United States establish itself as the dominant military power of the "free world" and acquire military bases around the world. Accompanying this military and political development, American corporations increased their investments abroad, seeking new outlets for American capital. Foreign investment of American firms increased more than seven times from 1946 to 1966.

In the decade and a half after 1950, sales of American goods in foreign markets tripled. By 1965 the size of the foreign markets of American firms equaled approximately 40 percent of the domestic production of farms, factories and mines. In the process a number of the larger corporations became multinationals.

The Multinational Corporation

The largest of America's large corporations have become even larger in recent years, but mere growth is not the only change. They now operate in many countries at once, investing in European, Asian, and Latin American markets, buying up local firms or creating their own subsidiaries. They are *multinational* corporations.

Such a development is still a recent one, but there are a few aspects that are evident, even now:[35]

1. There are 187 giant American firms that are multinationals (according to economist Raymond Vernon[36]), and these are as yet most of the multinational corporations of the world so far. They are "supergiants" and in a class by themselves when measured against *Fortune*'s list of America's 500 largest firms. They account for about a third of all sales in the United States, and they perform a dominant role in U.S. exports, so that their activities are important for the balance of trade, the value of the dollar, and, in general, America's national trade policy.

2. The new multinational corporate leadership regards the nation as a political constraint, only hindering its global activities. Even more, it views a primary attachment to the nation as sentimental and irrational, merely an impediment to an effective global pursuit of profits.

3. Multinational firms do not, contrary to their claims, benefit developing nations. Often, as in places like Brazil and Mexico, they make possible an economic growth which raises the living standard of a minority, even enriches a few, while increasing the poverty and misery of the majority.

4. As a consequence, American multinational

This branch of the Chase Manhatten Bank in Hong Kong is one example of the multinational reach of American corporations and banks.

firms are often resented and feared abroad, where they are sometimes seen an an extension of American power and control, thus, as evidence of the growth of an American empire. Their sheer size and power easily matches if not exceeds that of small nations, nations which control fewer resources than do many American corporations. ("General Motors' $25 billion in sales is . . . larger than the Gross National Product of about 130 countries."[37]) One threat to the multinational firms, then, is nationalization by a Third World nation seeking to control its own economic development.

5. Multinational firms are increasingly viewed as a threat by American labor unions.[38] First, they are larger and management has more options, so that pinning them down to a contractual agreement in an American high-wage industry is harder than with other corporations. As labor unions see it, multinational firms *export jobs* as well as capital investments.

6. The power of the multinational corporations is based on its effective control of knowledge in three areas: technology, marketing, and finance capital.

Through its superior, sometimes monopolized knowledge, they are able to develop efficient, centralized plans for a worldwide operation.

7. Democratic governments can no longer effectively control the multinationals in the public interest. The corporations have too many means to escape regulation; they can, for example, neutralize a nation's antiflationary policy by tie-ins with global banks and by manipulation of money markets. The regulatory capacity of any national government is both restricted to its national boundaries, while the corporations operate worldwide, and is too far behind the corporations in knowledge adequate to cope with them.

The economic changes induced by the emergence of the giant multinationals, then, suggests several sources of tension and conflict for the future. One lies in the fact that most multinationals are American, so that resistance to their dominations also becomes a worldwide anti-Americanism. Such resistance, furthermore, sparks both nationalism and socialism as ways of creating alternatives to domination by this new pattern of world capitalism.

But perhaps an equally severe strain lies within the United States. Exporting jobs threatens much of the American working class and also a sizable section of its technically skilled personnel. While vast amounts of money might flow back to the United States as profits

of multinationals, that fact does not promise to offset lost jobs. Since the top one percent of shareholders own about 75 percent of personally held corporate stocks and about 85 percent of corporate bonds, such wealth is not shared sufficiently to ensure the welfare of the nation as a whole.

But even more basic is a potential clash between the logic of multinational corporate growth and operation on a global scale and the interests and values of particular nations, even (perhaps especially) the United States. Raymond Vernon symbolizes this issue by calling his book *Sovereignty at Bay*. He opens his study with these words:

> Suddenly, it seems, the sovereign states are feeling naked. Concepts such as national sovereignty and national economic strength appear curiously drained of meaning . . . [multinational corporations] sit uncomfortably in the structure of long-established political and social institutions. They sprawl across national boundaries, linking the assets and activities of different national jurisdictions with an intimacy that seems to threaten the concept of the nation as an integral unit.[39]

What this suggests is a significant new tension between capitalism and nationalism, and so, between corporate interest and national interest. What is good for General Motors may no longer be good for the United States.

SUMMARY

From a sociological perspective the economy is a system of *productive* and *distributive* processes for meeting material wants. It requires cooperative organization for production, but distribution is a problem focused on *surplus*. A surplus makes possible an elite of power; it also makes possible economic *growth* and *development*. For Marx, the surplus extracted from the worker by the capitalist is the source of profits.

Property consists of the *rights in objects*, not the objects themselves. It is ownership of the means of production that distinguishes private property systems from socialized ones. Property can be *communal*; it can be in family and kinship groups; it can take shared forms; and it can be *private* or *public*.

Capitalism is an economic system in which ownership and productive work are separated, and labor becomes a commodity bought by the capitalist. Capitalism invests money to produce goods in return for money, but the intention is that the money earned be more than the money invested. That is profit and the capitalist's income.

The *elements* of capitalism are private ownership of the means of production; wage-labor; the market; profit; capital accumulation; and investment and growth. Capitalism requires constant circulation of capital.

Capitalism has changed from a competitive, laissez-faire form to a *corporate* form, with a small set of very large corporations dominating the economy.

The rise of *management* in the corporation is said to have brought about the *separation of ownership and control.* But the evidence does not prove that a capitalist class has been superseded by a new managerial class.

Capitalism has always been an unstable system and has always had *crises* of depression and inflation, though there has never been a total collapse. Each recession advances the concentration of capital.

New industry, new markets, and state expenditures are means to counteract crises.

State capitalism means the state's economic policies are intended to protect and promote the capitalist economy, but also to control and regulate the economy.

Industrialism and capitalism are not identical; industrialism is a system of machine technology, and the organization of work to fit the social uses of that technology for production.

Industrial technology does not *determine* the shape of society and is not an independent force for change. Industrial technology and capitalism developed together and capitalism has been able to control technology for corporate purposes.

There has long been a *social* division of labor, where one person does a whole, though specialized task, as does a shoemaker. Capitalism has created a *detailed* division of labor, wherein each task is further subdivided so that work is de-skilled and is cheaper for the manufacturer, who also increases his control over the work process. Even clerical work is subject to this deskilling process.

It is also subject to processes of *automation,* which reduce the amount of labor while requiring some more skilled functions.

Two other changes are involved: the increase in a new middle class of scientists, engineers, technicians, and professionals; and a rapid shift from agriculture to industry and now to a service economy.

The economy always produces problems of conflict and integration. *Labor unions* under capitalism have become representative of workers' interests, accepting capitalism but seeking social reforms. Industry, in turn, has used *human relations* to try to integrate workers at the place of work.

Alienation of workers occurs when work becomes a thing apart from the worker, an alien force beyond his control. Modern workers do not make work their central life interest, and their degree of alienation varies with the type of work—craft less so, assembly work more so. Ideas about job enrichment have been introduced from Europe.

Work is alienating in socialist societies when the worker is subject to the same conditions of wage-labor and also deprived of any control over work as under capitalism.

The world is now a single economic system. The empires and colonies of the nineteenth century have been replaced by a system of politically independent but economically dependent nations.

There is a system of international stratification made up of a First World of the capitalist nations of Europe and North America; a Second World of the communist bloc of nations; and a Third World of poor nations, former colonies, primarily in Asia, Africa, and Latin America.

According to this position, the world capitalist system is divided into a core of powerful, dominating economies; a periphery of weak, poor ones producing largely raw materials; and a semiperiphery of economies between these two. The dominant core economies get a larger share of the surplus in a system in which exchange is always unequal.

The multinational corporations, mostly American, dominate the world economy, and cannot be controlled by national governments, putting capitalist and national interests in tension.

NOTES

[1] See Gerhard Lenski, *Power and Privilege* (New York: McGraw-Hill, 1966), esp. Chaps. 5 and 6.

[2] Leon Mayhew, *Society: Institutions and Activity* (Glenview, Ill.: Scott, Foresman, 1971), p. 106.

[3] Karl Marx and Friedrich Engels, *Selected Works* (Moscow: Progress Publishers, 1968), p. 212.

[4] Robert L. Heilbroner, *The Limits of American Capitalism* (New York: Harper & Row, 1966), p. 10.

[5] *Ibid.,* p. 14.

[6] See A. A. Berle and Gardner Means, *The Modern Corporation and Private Property* (New York: Macmillan, 1933).

[7] For a full discussion of the issues involved, see Maurice Zeitlin, "Corporate Ownership and Control: The Large Corporation and the Capitalist Class," *American Journal of Sociology* 79 (March 1974): 1073–1119.

[8] *Ibid.,* p. 1078.

[9] Robert Lampmann, *The Share of Top Wealth-Holders in Personal Wealth, 1922–1956* (Princeton, N.J.: Princeton University Press, 1962), Tables 75–80.

[10] Zeitlin, *op. cit.,* p. 1087.

[11] *Ibid.,* pp. 1092–1094.

[12] *Ibid.,* p. 1094.

[13] James O'Connor provides the best discussion of state expenditures in relation to capitalism; see his *The Fiscal Crisis of the State* (New York: St. Martin's Press, 1973).

[14] See Seymour Melman, *Pentagon Capitalism* (New York: McGraw-Hill, 1970).

[15] See Sidney Fine, *Laissez-Faire and the General Welfare State* (Ann Arbor: University of Michigan Press, 1966).

[16] David Noble, *America by Design: Science, Technology, and the Rise of Corporate Capitalism* (New York: Oxford University Press, 1977).

[17] Harry Braverman, *Labor and Monopoly Capital: The Degradation of Work in the Twentieth Century* (New York: Monthly Review Press, 1974), p. 72.

[18] *Ibid.,* pp. 338–339. See his Chapter 15, "Clerical Workers," for a detailed analysis of the effect of mechanization on clerical occupations.

[19] Data for 1900 are from *Historical Statistics of the United States,* 1960, p. 74; for 1974, U.S. Department of Labor, *Employment and Earnings,* vol. 21, no. 8 (February 1975), p. 41.

[20] See Daniel Bell, *The Coming of Post-Industrial Society* (New York: Basic Books, 1973), pp. 129–137.

[21] A famous quote from *The Communist Manifesto* of Karl Marx and Friedrich Engels.

[22] See Reinhard Bendix, *Work and Authority in Industry* (New York: Wiley, 1956).

[23] For studies on these historical changes by dominant groups within American captialism's leadership, see Gabriel Kolko, *The Triumph of Conservatism; A Reinterpretation of American History, 1900–1916* (New York: The Free Press, 1963), and James Weinstein, *The Corporate Ideal in the Liberal State: 1900–1918* (Boston: Beacon Press, 1968).

[24] Robert Dubin, "Industrial Workers' World: A Study of the 'Central Life-Interests' of Industrial Workers," *Social Problems* 3 (Winter 1956): 131–142.

[25] Robert Blauner, *Alienation and Freedom* (Chicago: University of Chicago Press, 1964).

[26] Paul Blumberg, *Industrial Democracy: The Sociology of Participation* (New York: Schocken, 1973), p. 60.

[27] See Harold L. Sheppard and Neal Q. Herrick, *Where Have All the Robots Gone? Worker Dissatisfaction in the 70s* (New York: The Free Press, 1973), and Richard Sennett and Jonathan Cobb, *The Hidden Injuries of Class* (New York: Knopf, 1972).

[28] See Benot Abrahamsson, *Bureaucracy or Participation: The Logic of Organization* (Beverly Hills, Cal.: Sage Publications, 1977).

[29] See David Riesman, *Abundance for What: And Other Essays* (Garden City, N.Y.: Doubleday, 1964).

[30] *The New York Times,* July 10, 1977.

[31] *The New York Times,* December 17, 1978.

[32] Immanuel Wallerstein, *The Modern World-System: Capitalist Agriculture and the Origins of the European World-Economy in the Sixteenth Century* (New York: Academic Press, 1974).

[33] Mayhew, *op. cit.,* p. 108.

[34] Gustav Lagos, *International Stratification and Underdeveloped Countries* (Chapel Hill: The University of North Carolina Press, 1963), p. 41.

[35] The following summary is drawn from two studies: Raymond Vernon, *Sovereignty at Bay: The Multinational Spread of U.S. Enterprises* (New York: Basic Books, 1971), and Richard J. Barnett and Ronald E. Muller, *Global Reach: The Power of the Multinational Corporations* (New York: Simon and Schuster, 1974).

[36] Vernon, *op. cit.,* p. 11.

[37] *Ibid.,* p. 7. Gross National Product (GNP) is the total goods and services produced by a nation within any one year.

[38] Gus Tyler, "Multinational Corporations vs. Nations," *Current,* September 1972, pp. 52–63. Originally published as "Multinationals: A Global Menace," *The American Federationist,* July 1972.

[39] Vernon, *op. cit.,* pp. 3 and 5.

SUGGESTED READINGS

Richard J. Barnett and Ronald E. Muller, *Global Reach: The Power of the Multinationals* (New York: Simon and Schuster, 1974). A probing, critical assessment of the effect of multinationals on both the United States and Third World nations.

Robert Blauner, *Alienation and Freedom: The Factory Worker and His Industry* (Chicago: University of Chicago Press, 1964). A comparison of alienation as a consequence of types of work.

Harry Braverman, *Labor and Monopoly Capital: The Degradation of Work in the Twentieth Century* (New York: Monthly Review Press, 1974). A brilliant, award-winning study of how capitalism accomplishes the deskilling of work.

Robert Heilbroner, *The Limits of American Capitalism* (New York: Harper & Row, 1966). A provocative examination of the future prospects of the corporate sector of the American economy.

Clark Kerr, John T. Dunlop, Frederick Harbison, and Charles A. Myers, *Industrialism and Industrial Man* (Cambridge, Mass.: Harvard University Press, 1964). A major effort to explore the consequences of industrialism.

Karl Marx, *Selected Writings in Sociology and Social Philosophy,* trans. T. B. Bottomore (New York: McGraw-Hill, 1956). A good set of briefer selections from Marx's discussion of capitalist and precapitalist society.

Seymour Melman, *Pentagon Capitalism* (New York: McGraw-Hill, 1970). An analysis of a "second" political economy combining the Pentagon and defense industry.

David F. Noble, *American by Design: Science, Technology, and the Rise of Corporate Capitalism* (New York: Oxford University Press, 1977). A remarkable historical analysis of the interrelated rise of a scientific technology and corporate capitalism.

Harold Sheppard and Neal Q. Herrick, *Where Have All the Robots Gone? Worker Dissatisfaction in the 70s* (New York: The Free Press, 1973). A detailed exploration of the blue-collar "blues."

Raymond Vernon, *Sovereignty at Bay: The Multinational Spread of U.S. Enterprises* (New York: Basic Books, 1971). A look at one aspect of the new world economy, the multinational corporation.

Immanuel Wallerstein, *The Modern World-System: Capitalist Agriculture and the Origins of the European World-Economy in the Sixteenth Century* (New York: Academic Press, 1974). A path-breaking analysis of the conception of capitalism as culminating in a world economy.

James Weinstein, *The Corporate Ideal in the Liberal State: 1900—1918* (Boston: Beacon Press, 1968). A fine historical analysis of the capitalist cooptation of liberal reform.

*Governments derive their just power from the consent of
the governed.*

The Declaration of Independence

Seventeen

POLITICS AND SOCIETY

Political parties, Max Weber once said, live in a house of power. Whatever else politics is about, it is about power.

To speak of power often evokes in us unpleasant images: of the few who rule and the many who are ruled; of special interests and privileged classes; of bosses and dictators; and of the struggles of class against class. But the political process also includes the actions of democratic citizens, where the majority decide and the authority of law commands respect and obedience.

In traditional, preindustrial societies, the political process often is only partially differentiated from the religious and economic processes, and political authority is embedded in customs and traditions of ancient origin. But in modern society the political process has developed specialized structures and roles, and authority is legally specified in charters, constitutions, and by-laws.

POWER AND AUTHORITY

What is power? Among social scientists there is an increasing tendency to define power in terms of group or societal decision-making. From that perspective, power is a social process, not an object or "thing" divided among power-holders. To have power is to participate in a decision-making process. To be powerful is to control decision-making in a group or at least have a very strong influence on what decisions are made. To be powerless, in turn, is to be excluded from decision-making.

Authority

Power cannot be understood apart from authority. When a President of the United States vetoes a bill, he exercises the authority of his office, as does the legislature when it votes on a bill. City councilmen and mayors, governors and senators are all political roles in which some authority is vested. Authority is *legitimate* power, the right to make a decision that is based on an

The exercise of legitimate decision-making in modern society is a legal-rational process, according to Weber. These state legislators are studying an issue with the intent of writing legislation.

acceptance of the claims of decision-makers that their decisions are binding on all members of the social organization involved.

The sources of legitimation are diverse. Max Weber has indicated that in stable social orders the legitimacy of authority may be *traditional,* as in the authority of the village elders or a tribal chief, rooted in custom and cultural tradition, or it may be *legal-rational,* as in modern societies, derived from documents (laws, charters, and constitutions). In situations of instability and change, authority is often *charismatic;* that is, based upon the personal devotion of the followers of a leader, who attribute to him the great qualities.[1] When this happens, masses of people, no longer accept the traditional or legal-rational system of authority as legitimate.

Yet others besides those with authority do exercise power. In a complex process of reaching decisions others participate when they have *access* to those who have authority. Those who have such access are *influentials.*

Influence and Authority   Some influentials, such as party bosses, lobbyists, and businessmen, are often credited with having more to say about decisions than those who possess authority. "Real" power, it is often claimed, rests with dominant influentials, behind-the-scenes actors not even known to the larger public. Officials are then regarded as mere puppets who respond to the order of party bosses, the pressures of lobbyists or large party contributors, or the demands of economic influentials.

However weak the system of authority may be and however dominant a structure of influence, nonetheless, the exercise of power still cannot dispense with legitimate authority. For without it, decision-making by powerful people can only be regarded as a system of naked coercion, as well as one of corruption and fraud. Authoritarian systems in the past always claimed legitimacy, as by divine right of kings. Modern totalitarian systems also develop and propagate an ideology to justify the monopoly of power by the party. Decisions must always seem to be the acts of those who hold the symbols of authority.

This suggests that power can be defined as the distribution of influence, pressure, and authority within a social system for the making, legitimizing, and executing of decisions.

This last point is basic: A decision is not a decision until it has been carried out. Perhaps only in the literature of bureaucracies has there been recognition of the problems involved in the execution of decisions. In the middle level of bureaucracies officials can significantly modify or even subvert a decision taken at higher echelons, so that the outcome is not what was intended when the decision was made. Presidents of the United States at least since Harry Truman have admitted being frustrated in trying to carry out decisions against subtle but effective sabotage by the permanent civil service bureaucrats.

Inclusion and Exclusion

If all members of the society had equal access to authority, influence and pressure would be no issue. But in fact this is not so. Even in democratic societies, some sizable segment of people are excluded from decision-making. In general, the higher the social status, the more are people included and able to influence decisions; the lower the status, the more are they excluded, despite formal rights of inclusion.

Sometimes people are legally excluded: slaves in a slave society, and aliens without the rights of citizenship, for example. Convicted criminals may lose the right to vote or hold office. Once women had no legal rights, but in time most modern societies (as the United States in 1920) extended the franchise to women. Earlier in history the working class could not vote, but property restrictions on voting were abolished to bring workers into political society.

Even when legal exclusion has been eliminated, an effective, informal exclusion may still be practiced. Though the Fifteenth Amendment to the Constitution was adopted in 1870, ensuring political rights for black people, such rights were still denied in practice in much of the South for almost a hundred years after. It took federal marshals in 1962 under direct orders from President John Kennedy intervening in some southern counties, to get county registrars to register blacks.

Inclusion in the political process through voting is the formal right most widely extended, yet it provides a very limited way to participate in decision-making. It may come down to merely endorsing decisions made elsewhere. In 1972 the Democratic Party made procedural changes in order to include representative numbers of women, racial minorities, and youth. Even this, however, did not change the domination of the Party's convention by people of middle- and upper-class position, whether measured by occupation, education, or income. (This is even more true of the Republican Party.)

One projected solution to the student unrest on campuses in the late 1960s was to give students some representation in academic government, which presumably made sit-ins and the taking over of buildings unnecessary. In an earlier time, accepting labor unions as legitimate gave workers participation through collective bargaining in decisions about wages and working conditions.

What this tells us is that, historically, there has been a gradual extension of the legal right to participate, as in voting and holding office, to ever larger numbers of people, but beyond that, a closer participation in decision-making, or even influential access to such, has continued to be restricted to those who control economic resources and possess higher status: men over women, whites over blacks, middle-aged over youth, affluent over poor, employers over employees, the propertied over the nonpropertied, middle class over working class, the educated over the less educated.

In any society power is distributed unequally, reflecting the class structure and the unequal control of economic resources. That is what is meant by the concept of *power structure*.

NATION AND STATE

In the modern world almost everyone is a citizen of a nation, and so everyone has a nationality. Yet the process of creating nations is still recent history in Europe and America—note that Germany and Italy only became nations within the last century. Nation-building, furthermore, is a central component of the process of economic development throughout the non-Western world.[2]

That is the significance of nation for the modern world: It unites populations larger than the tribal village structures of the past, breaks down local barriers to trade and commercial development (industrialism and capitalism encouraged nation-building), and integrates a population under a central government.

In the process, it turns that population into a *people,* sharing a common language and a common heritage. (To be sure, there often remain old cultural groupings, loyalties, and languages within nations; for example, the cultural and linguistic divisions in Belgium, in Yugoslavia, and in India.) National identity and loyalty come in time to supersede the former limited and localized identities that were once so central to people's lives: village, tribe, kinship, and church.

Nations unavoidably bring into being a more powerful government, one controlling a larger population and governing a wider territory than did earlier forms of government. This is the *state,* which governs the nation.

Max Weber defined the state as a political organization that claims binding authority and a legitimate monopoly of force within a territory.[3] In the modern nation the state is an inclusive group from which there is no escape. A stateless person belongs nowhere and is, in terms of rights and status, a nonperson. All other social groups are subordinate to the authority and power of the state.

The State and Society

Social scientists and historians have long tried to explain the state in relation to society, to define it as the *institutionalization* of social power. But their efforts to do so have led to some differing conceptions. Following the work of Theda Skocpol, we shall put these diverse efforts into three broad approaches:[4]

1. *The state is an arena in which conflicts over economic and social interests are fought out.* The *liberal* version of this conception of the state is that it is an arena of legitimate authority operating within established rules of the game accepted by the majority of citizens. This majority consensus then permits the state to resolve conflicts, usually without violence or coercion, and so to maintain internal peace. One side can

win out in an election, but there is also much emphasis on compromise.

The *conflict* version, in contrast, is that the state is an arena of conflict marked by organized coercion. Charles Tilly, for example, defines the state as "an organization which controls the principal concentrated means of coercion within the population."[5] The state, according to this view, resolves conflict by domination and coercion, rather than by democratic consensus. Its basic function is to support the dominant classes over subordinate ones. This fits the often expressed Marxian view that the state is simply an instrument of the ruling class.

2. *The state is a capitalist state.* Most contemporary Marxian theorists do not claim that the state is simply an instrument of the ruling class. Instead, they see the state as possessing a limited degree of autonomy, and capable, when the occasion arises, of opposing specific demands of the dominant class, or a segment of it, in order to develop policies that preserve the class structure and the economic system as a whole. From this perspective, the state is often in a better position to understand and act effectively on the needs and interests of the economic system than is the often shortsighted dominant class. While the state in capitalist nations is not a tool of the capitalist class, it is, nonetheless, a *capitalist state.*[6]

A somewhat different approach has been taken by those Marxists who argue that, while the state is not controlled by a dominant class, it is shaped by the struggles that go on between the social classes. The effort to resolve and control class conflict in the interests of the whole economic system nevertheless puts the state into making policy that is not always what the dominant class wants.[7]

3. *The state is an autonomous organization.* This perspective sees the state as an organization with a logic and interest of its own. While it will operate within the context of the social relations of the economic system and the divisions between dominant and subordinate classes, the state is not simply an expression of these class relations or of their conflicts:

The state properly conceived is no mere arena in which socioeconomic struggles are fought out. It is, rather, a set of administrative, policing, and military organizations headed, and more or less well coordinated by, an executive authority. Any state first and fundamentally extracts resources from society and deploys these to create and support coercive and administrative organizations . . . the administrative and coercive organizations are the basis of state power as such.[8]

States, therefore, are actual organizations attempting to control territories and people. For that reason, the state has a basic interest in maintaining order, and to that end, it usually maintains the existing class structure. Its interest in doing that and the interest of a dominant class may then be the same, but not necessarily and not always. In a period of crisis it may force the dominant class to make concessions to subordinate classes. "These concessions may be at the expense of the interests of the dominant class, but not contrary to the state's own interests in controlling the population and collecting taxes and military recruits."[9]

But the state is not only concerned with keeping the peace inside the nation, it also operates externally in a geopolitical environments of other states. Within such an environment it develops a network of international relations. The interest of state rulers in maintaining an international position, and its response, for example, to foreign military competition, may lead to policies that drain resources from dominant classes or undermine their class interest.[10]

Internal pressures and conditions, on the one hand, and internal class-structured economies and politically organized interest groups, on the other, are not independent of one another in their effect on state organization. "The state, in short, is Janus-faced [two-faced] with an intrinsically dual anchorage in class-divided socioeconomic structures and an international system of states."[11]

These three positions on defining the state focus around the issue of *power*—how political power is related to economic and class power. The first two positions—the state as arena and the state as capitalist state—do not recognize the state as an organization of power in its own right, while the third position does. In all cases, however, the effort is to understand the state as a concentration of power for the control of society.

This fits Max Weber's often quoted definition of the state as the one form of social organization that "claims the *monopoly of the legitimate use of physical force* within a given territory."[12]

The Function of the State If the state is a concentration of power for the control of society, and if it legitimately monopolizes violence within a given territory,

then it would seem that its relation to society can be stated in terms of these basic functions:[13]

1. Limiting internal power-struggles to maintain internal peace.
2. Bringing power to bear on other societies in defense of national interest or in expanding and building empire.
3. Controlling the members of society so as to bind them to the pursuit of collective goals.
4. Recognizing and implementing the interests and demands of various groups, thus, by combination and compromise, aligning interests in the making of public policy (see "Governing by Subsidy").

The Bureaucratic State

The need to develop an efficient administrative structure leads modern nation-states to become increasingly bureaucratic. Max Weber's observation fits:

> It is obvious that technically the great modern state is absolutely dependent upon a bureaucratic basis. The larger the state, and the more it is or the more it becomes a great state power, the more unconditionally is this the case.[14]

Yet few sociological studies have sought to determine the significance of bureaucratization for the nature and functioning of the state.

One can argue, as does sociologist Seymour M. Lipset, that governmental bureaucracy provides a neutral function that reduces political conflict, for the bureaucrat is an impartial expert, not a political partisan.[15] Impartial experts in government can perform two integrative functions for democratic society. First, they can provide a stable and routine administration of established political functions, rendering less disruptive the change of power from one party to another. Secondly, they can turn issues of conflict into administrative decisions and expert judgments, thus making sources of conflict more manageable and less disturbing within the social order.

Perhaps the outstanding American example of this is the complex social mechanism of federal mediation for resolving labor-management conflicts and insisting upon establishing a workable agreement in a binding contract. This requires a body of experts—both within

The state always claims the right to use violence if necessary to maintain internal order.

and without government—that can be called upon to provide a technical skill for resolving a dispute and finding the grounds for agreement.

By this process issues of class conflict are removed from the political arena and cease to be the basis for conflicting ideological positions taken by corporations, unions, and political parties. A possibly disruptive issue within the political process is then minimized.

But this stabilizing effect of bureaucracy can also be viewed as conservative in its significance, for it serves to keep the peace and preserve established interests. Lipset, for example, described how a socialist party in Canada, after having won office, was then blocked in carrying out its program by the resistance of the permanent bureaucracy of civil servants.[16]

Max Weber recognized that control over administrative implementation of decision making was decisive for political power, and he doubted the chances of democratic politicians to keep such control from the permanent bureaucrats. Although bureaucracy may be stabilizing and a mechanism for reducing conflict, this, in Weber's view, did not make it supportive of democracy. His ultimate view about the impact of bureaucracy upon democracy was pessimistic, and he thought it essential to prevent a bureaucratic domination of all social life.

THE POLITICAL PARTY

Since the state is the politically dominant and controlling force within a society, with binding authority, political struggles in a nation are struggle to influence

GOVERNING BY SUBSIDY

One way in which the American government recognizes and implements the interests and demands of various groups is by providing them with a *subsidy*. Subsidies offer a form of economic support to meet a need or a problem, as, for example, school lunches for poor children, or, to induce people to carry out economic policies, as, for example, tax deductions to encourage business to invest in order to create jobs.

The extensive use of subsidies not only makes government a powerful force in directing and regulating the economy, it also blurs the line between the private and public sectors. Well over $100 billion of tax funds are spent each year for various subsidies.

Here are the important forms of subsidy:

Cash Payments. These include payments to sugar beet and cane growers to protect the domestic industry; to sheep raisers to improve the quality of wool; to medical schools to train doctors; to employers to move workers off welfare; and to the shipping industry to compete with foreign shippers.

Tax Subsidies. Tax deductions permit some to pay a smaller tax than would normally apply. There are tax incentives to encourage capital investment; states and cities grant tax abatements to get business to invest in plant expansion or in new plants within their boundaries. *Capital gains* allows those who make a profit on investment to get a lesser tax rate. Deducting from taxes the interest paid on home mortgages is intended to encourage home ownership.

Credit Subsidies. These involve a government-guaranteed loan to provide a lower rate of interest than the market alone would be able to provide: loans to finance a student through college is one example, as is the financing of public works projects.

Benefits-in-kind Subsidies. These involve providing a product or service paid for by the Government. Food stamps and Medicare are familiar examples.

Besides subsidies, there are other forms of governmental action for the same purpose. High tariffs to protect domestic producers from foreign competition, for example, is one major form. So are those regulations, such as in the trucking industry, which reduce competition and keep up the rates charged customers.

---

the policies and decisions of the state; they may even be struggles for control of the state. Of the kinds of groups that organize for this struggle, the *political party* is the most significant. As Weber said, parties "live in a house of 'power,'" and "are always structures struggling for domination."[17]

The political party originated in England from political clubs that organized to support candidates who, once in office, could reflect the interests and concerns of some citizens more than others. The existence of parties, then, testifies to differences in class and group interests, the propertied and nonpropertied classes, the richer and the poorer, who want different kinds of political action and different kinds of social policies from the state.

The relation of the party to the state is varied, ranging from one-party states to multiple-party states. In one-party states, one powerful political group, committed to a dominant ideology and program, completely controls the state and allows no alternative choice of program and policy. The forms of party and electoral process are retained but are not used to make political choices. Instead, they are used to provide symbolic expressions of support by loyal citizens.

Democratic states are, theoretically and constitutionally, multiple-party states, for its citizens have the right to form any party they choose. But among democratic nations there are in fact some varied patterns. In France and Italy there is a governing coalition of procapitalist parties of the right and a strong opposing coalition of anticapitalist parties of the left. Since no single party even has a majority, a coalition of parties to form a government is always necessary.

A second pattern is found in the nations of the British Commonwealth—Britain, Canada, New Zealand, and Australia—and those of northwestern Europe.[18] Here two parties usually dominate, but for the most part they offer sharper ideological alternatives to the voter, based as they are on social classes. One of them is either called the Labor Party (as in the British Commonwealth nations, except Canada), or the Social Democratic Party. These working-class-based parties have in some cases introduced elements of socialism into the national life.

In the United States, a still different situation prevails. While, constitutionally, multiple parties are always possible, and many small parties always exist, there is nonetheless a powerful two-party ideology that severely restricts the chances of other parties becoming seriously contending forces.

The two American parties are not primarily *ideological* parties but, instead, both have liberal and conservative wings and so overlap. American politicians are rarely spokesmen for clearly defined ideologies, or for the specific groups and classes such ideologies speak for. Instead, they are primarily political brokers who seek to create winning coalitions of groups and classes within the parties before the election instead of among several parties after an election.

The American Party System

What is distinctive about the politics of the United States is the failure to develop a party of the left, based

In Italy the Italian Communist Party, mobilizing an anticapitalist sentiment, has become the nation's second largest political party.

In democratic societies, political parties meet in conventions to choose their top slate of candidates and construct their platform. Here delegates to the 1980 Democratic convention apparently respond differently to a convention speaker.

solidly on the working class and espousing socialist programs. In that way the American party structure differs from practically all other industrial capitalist nations. According to sociologist Richard Hamilton, this accounts for the inadequacy of social welfare and for the relatively unlimited growth of the military complex in the United States.[19]

Given the American two-party system, what are the consequences for control and direction of the state? When both parties strive to be political canopies that stretch widely over a diverse range of social groups and classes, they come into competition for at least some of the same ones, thus tending to push the parties nearer to an ideological center. They become more alike in program and purpose. Indeed, for purposes of winning elections, the parties must exaggerate their differences, relying increasingly on the political personality of candidates, rather than issues and programs, to bring victory. They constantly risk being seen as Tweedle-dum and Tweedle-dee.

Despite that, some perception of ideological differences between the parties persists in the American population. A majority of adults perceive the Democratic Party as the party of the poor and the working man and the Republican Party as the party of the rich and of business.[20] Furthermore, if all American workers do not vote Democratic, most do, and that fact is significant in determining the character of both the Democratic and Republican parties. So is the fact that most Jews and Catholics, most blacks, and most poor people also vote Democratic (see Table 17.1).

The American two-party system operates within a pervasive political culture that demands that the parties and their major candidates stray not too far from some presumed ideological center, and then defines any fairly sizable deviation as unacceptably "radical" or "extremist" and calls for a "landslide" defeat of a candidate. The defeat of Republican candidate Barry Goldwater in 1964 and Democratic candidate George McGovern in 1972 occurred at least in part out of such circumstances.

Perhaps the basic point is not apparent: In the United States party politics operates within a political culture that works to restrict issues and programs for elective choice.[21] This is possible only because both parties accept as given and beyond political discussion the main structural features of the society, particularly the economic: the distribution of property and wealth, the class structure, corporate control and organization of the economy. Furthermore, both parties draw their leadership from upper-middle-class levels of American society.

Money and Votes Political parties in democratic societies are the organizations by which an electorate is mobilized. To do that, parties must appeal to masses of people, promising programs that will solve problems, ease burdens, or protect their interests. But elections cost money and since little money comes from the voters, the parties turn elsewhere. In the United States, at least, various groups then provide financial support to make campaigns possible.

Thus the political party links two separate and sometimes incompatible forces: masses of ordinary citizens, who supply votes, and powerful economic and

TABLE   17.1
Party Affiliation by Social Characteristics, 1976, by Percentages

	Republican	Democratic	Independent
National	22	46	32
Race			
White	24	43	33
Nonwhite	7	69	24
Education			
College	27	36	37
High School	20	48	32
Grade School	19	59	22
Age			
Under 30 years	15	41	44
30–49 years	20	49	31
50 years and over	29	48	23
Income			
$20,000 and over	31	35	34
$15,000–19,999	22	44	34
$10,000–14,999	19	47	34
$7,000–9,999	21	49	30
$5,000–6,999	18	51	31
$3,000–4,999	20	53	27
Under $3,000	16	61	23
Religion			
Protestant	28	43	29
Catholic	15	54	31
Jewish	9	57	34
Occupation			
Professional and Business	28	37	35
Clerical and Sales	24	40	36
Manual	15	52	33
Farmers	35	42	23
Union Membership			
Labor Union Families	15	54	31
Non-union Families	24	44	32

Source: *Gallup Report Index*, no. 131, June 1976.

social interests, who supply money. There is corruption inherent in such a process. To make it work, interest-serving activity is concealed from votes. While such concealing can be successful in specific cases, over the long run it is not. The result is a widespread contempt by citizens for politics and politicians, a situation that discourages political participation and weakens confidence in the democratic process.

Recently, there have been several reforms intended to restore public confidence in the integrity of elections. These have included limitations on the amount of campaign funds from a single source; public disclosure of all contributors; and public funding in order to reduce the need for private funds. There is yet no substantial evidence that such measures have restored public faith in the electoral process or encouraged any greater participation.

The Future of the American Parties

The American two-party system has been so long and so well established that most Americans assume its indefinite continuity. Yet no system lasts forever and changes may be coming.

Richard Hamilton's assessment of political poll data suggests to him that the United States may develop a party-and-a-half, because much of the Republican base in the population (older people, rural and small-town people) is shrinking and that of the Democratic Party is increasing.[22] If the Democratic Party were to be the dominant one, he predicts, then the dominant groups will join it in order not to be left out of the permanent ruling party. If this were to happen, however, it is possible that the Democratic Party might break into the two parties, or more, and the result would be an end of the two-party system as we have known it.

Another development of importance is that more and more voters are detaching themselves from the parties. According to political analyst David Broder, this is true of the electorate as a whole throughout the United States, and as a consequence many more voters now split their tickets.[23] A Gallup Poll in 1968 reported that 84 percent of the voters said they voted for the person, not the party. Increasingly, neither of the parties has a loyal constituency on whom it can count to vote the party's straight ticket.

Nonetheless, the parties suffer less from this than does the disenchanted voter. Even when the independent voters vote for the person, not the party, they are still voting for the candidates of one party over another, and one party always then wins and becomes the majority.

Still another development is the steady decline in the number of people who even bother to vote, a fact which serves as a measure of the alienation of voters from the parties and their programs. The function of political parties is to mobilize the citizenry and get them to participate in an election. Any failure to do so, over the longer run, would compel radical changes in the nature of a party system.

Still other possible changes come to mind, such as a "capture" of the Republican party by self-avowed conservatives, or the emergence of a populist, or even democratic socialist party, on the left of the Democratic Party.

It may be that none of these possibilities will occur in the near future, and that instead, the parties will realign voters and revitalize themselves. Whatever it is, some kind of change in the two-party system in the United States is likely.

Parapolitical Groups

Political parties are not the only political groups that operate in the house of power. In the United States, as in most democratic societies, the right of assembly makes legitimate the organization of private citizens into groups that can seek ways to influence government and change social policy. (Political parties exist under this same right.)

This makes political many private and voluntary associations that are not ordinarily so defined: chambers of commerce; labor unions; manufacturers' associations; civic groups; taxpayers' associations; veterans' associations; and almost any other organized interest in the society. These are parapolitical groups.[24]

These groups can and do operate in different ways, aiming their efforts at different targets. Some groups concentrate primarily on the legislative and executive branches of government. They lobby; that is, they try to influence policy and legislation to suit their own interests. Powerful groups, especially economic ones (including corporations) lobby on a permanent basis, with a consequent advantage in affecting policy. Other groups emerge temporarily around new and controversial issues, and their lobbying is limited and sporadic.

Some groups concentrate on *issues,* formulating programs and policies for change and seeking to "educate" people to their desirability. These groups publicize problems and projected solutions outside of party structure, and in time mobilize sufficient support to command serious attention from governmental agencies and political parties. (To be sure, they may also do some limited lobbying and they may testify before legislative committees.) The case for ecological reform, antipollution measures, conservation of natural resources, as well as the case for and against birth control and abortion, and for constraints on population growth, are all issues that were first developed through the activities of voluntary, parapolitical groups.

ELITES AND POWER

In the long record of known human societies, so it has seemed, the select few, however chosen, seem always to rule over the many. Not even the emergence of political democracy has seriously weakened the idea that political power always rests in the hands of an *elite.*

Though by no means new, this somewhat dispiriting idea was systematically developed in the late nineteenth and early twentieth centuries in the face of rising power by mass-based socialist parties in Europe. For a while it seemed that masses of ordinary people, through such working-class parties, would take power by democratic means in a number of European nations. To show this was not at all humanly possible was the intent of three influential sociologists: Gaetano Mosca, Vilfredo Pareto, and Robert Michels.

The Rulers and the Ruled

In his *The Ruling Class,* Gaetano Mosca (1858–1941) asserted that all human societies were always and everywhere ruled by a controlling social class and thus human society always divided between the rulers and the ruled.[25] Every ruling class, furthermore, to *legitimate* its power, uses the dominant values prevailing in the culture, as when kings presume to rule by the will of God and elected presidents by the mandate of the people.

Mosca is hardly original in arguing that there is always a ruling class; this has been taken for granted by many scholars for centuries. However, the timing of his study coincided with serious intellectual concerns about new forms of political power and the possibilities of democratic rather than elite rule.

Vilfredo Pareto (1848–1923), in turn, took the existence of ruling class for granted, and concentrated, instead, on "the circulation of elites."[26] He was basically concerned with the consequence of "open" and "closed" elites; they were open when access to elite position is possible for persons of nonelite origin, and closed when an elite class monopolizes its position for those born into it, as a hereditary aristocracy. Since no elite has an inherited monopoly of brains and skills, a stable political process required that the ruling elite co-opt into its own ranks the best talent from the ranks of the nonelite.

Yet elites always tend to close their ranks to those from below, says Pareto, for a ruling class imputes superiority to itself and inferiority to subordinate classes. A closed aristocracy inevitably decays, producing cleavage and dissension within its own ranks. When that happens, new elites emerge from other classes to give leadership to revolutionary change. Then, a new ruling class will take over from a deposed one.

The Iron Law of Oligarchy

"Who says organization, says oligarchy." With these famous words, Robert Michels expressed in modern language an ancient pessimism about the human capacity to achieve freedom and democratic order within social organization.[27] Oligarchy means the rule of the few over the many. Michels considered it to be an *inevitable* outcome of social organization, and his "iron law of oligarchy" was a sociological formulation of this idea.

Michel's argument has two aspects. First, he argues for the necessity of leadership, and secondly, he tries to show how such leadership always becomes an oligarchy. Leadership, Michels argues, is necessary in any group that organizes for collective action, for this requires a division of labor and an assignment of specialized and skilled functions on behalf of the group to some of its membership. Leadership *roles* necessarily emerge from this problem.

But why does this necessarily result in oligarchy? First of all, because the delegation of tasks and authority to a leadership places in its hands a concentration of skills and prerogatives that the members do not have. Leaders become specialized in carrying out tasks that others know little about, and the experience of being a leader sets these members apart from the others.

Leadership also makes possible an internal power. It affords the opportunity to build a staff of people who are loyal; it gives control over the channels of communication; and it can practically monopolize access to the members. Only the leaders control the membership files, the official records, and the treasury, and without in a way being dishonest or illegal, they can use these to their own advantage.

But what about the followers? According to Michels, the members of any large social organization contribute to the emergence of oligarchy because of their indifference to running the organization and their unwillingness to become greatly involved. Furthermore, Michels argued, the members appreciated the greater skills and ability of leaders and they feel beholden to them. Thus they have no inclination to prevent their leaders' growing power.

But does all of this make any difference in how the organization pursues its goals? It does. An oligarchic leadership becomes conservative and cautious, and it develops interests of its own that may be quite different from what the organization publicly claims its goals to be. The more these organizations grow and prosper, the more do they become stable and bureaucratic organizations. Michels had studied the great socialist parties of Western Europe, and he observed that their original goals of effecting radical change in society diminished as they became more oligarchic.

Social organization, then, creates a set of conditions that makes oligarchy possible. Michels's theory did not require any psychological explanations, such as a lust for power or a desire to dominate. Instead, his perspective is basically sociological, for he interprets oligarchy as an inevitable outcome of a set of structural conditions that begins with the division of labor. Nor does this theory require any moral charge against leadership. Oligarchy is not the intent of leaders, nor did Michels doubt their personal integrity.

But Is It Inevitable?   Michels's thesis of the inevitability of oligarchy is an impressive if dismaying argument. And it takes only a little astute observation of political parties, labor unions, and civic organizations to see how often presumably democratic leadership can ef-

fectively perpetuate itself, seemingly indefinitely. But does it have to be that way?

One important sociological study sought to test that out by studying a union that seemed to be the exception to the usual oligarchic process—the International Typographers Union (ITU).[28] The major finding of the study was that the ITU had remained democratic by institutionalizing a two-party system within the union, creating *effective* opposition to any incumbent leadership—effective because they had access to necessary information, resources, and to the membership. There could be, then, structural conditions of opposition and contest that would reduce the likelihood of oligarchy.

Community Power Elites

In studying power in the community, some sociologists have claimed the existence of an elite, but other social scientists have projected instead a more pluralistic model of the community, one in which varied groups compete to influence the outcome of social issues.

In *Community Power Structure,* sociologist Floyd Hunter described in detail an economic elite—mostly corporate executives and bankers—who by informal communication and because of a similar social point of view agree on the major decisions affecting the lives of all the citizens of the community.[29] This is an elite not known to the community, for its members do not usually hold official positions, and its decision-making activities are not publicly visible.

Power, then, seems to be centered at the very top of the social structure in the hands of the community's "economic dominants." They exercise social power because they control the community's economic resources: the banks and credit, the corporations and jobs. The elite decides, but others, whom the community identifies as leaders, then go about the task of carrying out the decisions, including mobilizing community support.

These community leaders, including elected public officials and the heads of the well-known large organizations of the community, are not, according to Hunter, decision-makers in their own right. They are, rather, individuals of second and third rank in the a power structure, whose function is to carry out decisions, not make them. So are the organizations they run: the Chamber of Commerce, for example, and the numerous civic organizations. This leads to the inference that these organizations are not controlled by their membership but are used, instead, to control that membership; their support is mobilized for decisions made by the elite.

Robert Dahl, a political scientist, has insisted that Hunter's study does not apply to all American communities.[30] He criticized Hunter for centering on *who* the decision-makers are but not on *how* decisions are made. In turn he has insisted on the importance of observing the *issues* in the community over which decisions are made and of observing the actual decision-making process that goes on. The same people, he notes, are not necessarily involved in the different areas of decision-making—education, city government, and community welfare, for example. Dahl's perspective gives a different image of community power structure, with less concentration in an elite and a wider citizen participation in decision-making.

It occurred to more than one critic of Hunter's work that the concentration of community power in an economic elite was not necessarily true of all communities, and that differences in the attributes of communities could account for a concentration of power in one community, a dispersion of power in another.

With that in mind, sociologist Michael Aiken reviewed fifty-seven studies of community decision-making undertaken by sociologists and political scientists.[31] He found a number of important community characteristics related to variations in the diffusion of power. Perhaps the most interesting of these findings was that decentralized community power was more characteristic of communities that *economically* were dominated by absentee-owned firms rather than locally owned ones, were more industrialized, and were more industrially diverse.

In *political* terms reform municipal government, marked by city managers and small city council's elected at large, are likely to be more concentrated in power, while old-fashioned, unreformed political structures—mayor-council form of government, direct election of mayors, and large councils elected by ward or district—are associated with a decentralized power structure. Given the familiar imagery of machines and bosses, this may be a surprising finding.

Reform governments that promised to clean up corrupt politics put more control in the hands of the city manager and often, by reducing city councils in size and eliminating local districts, made it easier for the economic elite to succeed in citywide elections. In contrast, the representation of many other groups, particularly ethnic and working-class ones, is increased by large councils elected by districts. In short, the "reform" of civic government earlier in this century restored community power to the economically dominant elements and reduced participation in decision-making by those with less status.

There were other related political characteristics. Cities with concentrated power, for example, have strong executives and have more bureaucratized city governments, though they are likely to be more efficient. Cities with decentralized power are more likely to have a liberal electorate.

When Aiken compared communities, he found that decentralized power and nonreformed government was more likely to be found in cities with a large working class population, many Catholics, and a high degree of ethnicity. (Interestingly, Aiken could find no relation between the proportion of the population nonwhite and the degree of diffusion of power.) In turn, cities with a higher proportion of white-collar workers, and a higher proportion of high school graduates, as well as a higher than average medium income are more likely to have concentrated power structures. In short, the more heterogeneous a city, the more diffused in power, while homogeneous, middle-class communities are more concentrated in power.

All of the relations that Aiken found, as summarized above, were measured statistically, and the measurements were all moderate, some even weak. Therefore there were many exceptions to what has been said, and the findings are not to be taken as hard and fast generalizations that apply in all cases.

One thing can be noted. Cities with concentrated power are more likely to be those whose political structure has been reshaped by the business community to be more efficient, which they are, and to be run like a business, which requires a strong executive. This does not encourage a wider sharing in community decision-making.

National Power Elites

Until recently most studies of power in the United States have been community studies. However, the late C. Wright Mills undertook a sociologically bold and imaginative effort to delineate the national power structure of American society, describing an elite of the very rich and of the top leaders in industry, labor, government, and the military united by a common ideological outlook.[32]

In contrast, other social scientists view social power as more pluralistic. They perceive a wide and diversified array of interest groups, each with access to authority and each managing to bring pressure upon official decision-makers. The complexity of the decision-making process and the fact of social change, it is felt, makes it unlikely that a single elite can control all decisions.

This was the argument of sociologist Arnold Rose, who deliberately challenged Mills's argument and offered instead a pluralistic model of power.[33] Rose did not deny there were elites. He simply saw many instead of a single one, and furthermore claimed that "the top business elite are far from having an all-powerful position; that power is so complicated in the United States that the top businessmen scarcely understand it, much less control it; and that since 1933 the power position of businessmen has been declining rather than growing."[34] The political elite, Rose believed, in the political arena, at least, is not subordinate to the economic elite.

A social scientist, G. William Domhoff, took basic issue with Rose and sought to detail how a national power elite protecting and advancing the interests of an upper class was able to shape social legislation by working through universities and their scholarly experts, through foundations funding research, and through nonpartisan civic groups.[35] Such an elite, said Domhoff, controlled, not by resisting change but by developing a moderate program of social reform. In turn, this elite more clearly controlled foreign policy—even Rose conceded that a power elite did in fact control foreign policy. Both Domhoff and Rose point out the power of secret groups, such as the CIA, and the influence of organizations such as the Foreign Policy Association and the Council on Foreign Relations, in making foreign policy. Domhoff described the upper-class control of these influential organizations.[36]

Who Rules—and How? Subsequent literature arguing the issue of an American capitalist elite controlling the major decisions of the society has revealed, more than anything else, how little such a basic issue has been studied by American social scientists—a revealing point in itself. But there would seem to be two questions that need to be answered:[37]

1. Has an ideological domination been obtained, ruling out serious alternatives to the economic and political structures now prevailing?

Corporate capitalism destroyed its small-scale business and farmer opposition in the "critical" election of 1896, according to political scientist Walter Dean Burnham. The election was critical because "this brought to a close the 'Civil War' Party system and inaugurated a political alignment congenial to the dominance of industrial capitalism over the American political economy."[38]

By World War I, according to historian James Weinstein, significant liberal social reforms led by a segment of the corporate leadership had won out over what had been a serious conflict between capital and labor, wherein an anticapitalist perspective had made inroads into organized labor and the working class.[39] In more recent decades, a strong anticommunism among almost all social classes has associated socialism with totalitarianism and "free enterprise" with liberty and democracy.

Corporate capitalism seems to have achieved an ideological legitimacy among the nonelite classes; one that restricts public discussion and competitive party platforms to choice among alternatives which do not threaten capitalism's dominant position.[40]

2. Is there class-consciousness and a cohesive sense of purpose and unity in the economic elite?

Arnold Rose says no, that business has not effectively expressed its own interests. As a consequence, he argues that the economic elite has given way to the political elite in the making of decisions.[41]

But Domhoff, Weinstein, and Gabriel Kilko[42] argue that the disunity of the business class is more apparent than real, and that there has been a highly articulate segment of the business elite who have been able to shape government policy through a structure of influence that backs reforms and changes in such a way as to protect basic class interests. Sometimes this put them in to outright opposition to such "unenlightened" members of their own class as the Chamber of Commerce and the National Association of Manufacturers (NAM).

This argument does not claim any complete unity in an economic elite in either political action or ideological outlook. Indeed, Domhoff insists there is both a more liberal and a more conservative segment of this class; they differ, not on fundamental interests, but on means by which their interests can best be advanced in American society.

There is a host of other questions to ask and answer before a ruling class can be clearly identified: how it manages to control important decisions, for example, and what decisions are important and acted upon, what are unimportant and left to others. And very little is known about upper-class consciousness, except inferentially, for the economic elite does not usually submit to interviews or make frank comments on their worldviews.

CENTRALIZING AND DECENTRALIZING POWER

The dominant trends of modern society—industrialization, bureaucratization, and nationalism—are powerful organizing forces that tend to concentrate power. Even without any plans or schemes by antidemocratic groups, democracy is threatened by the possibility of total power concentrated in central organs of the state.

De Tocqueville and Pluralist Society

One of the great classics of political sociology is *Democracy in America* by Alexis de Tocqueville, a Frenchman of aristocratic origin who visited the United States in the 1830s, intent on observing the democratic process as it functioned in this new nation.[43] While accepting the democratization of society accomplished by the French Revolution, De Tocqueville was yet concerned about the potentiality for amassing total power in the governments of the new, industrial nations.

De Tocqueville's solution to the danger of concentrated power was the *pluralist society*—one in which there are several sources of power other than the state, and in which there is a potentiality for engaging in conflict and struggling for goals against other groups. Thus, political (but peaceful) conflict is an insurance against the domination of society by a single center of power.

In the United States, De Tocqueville thought, the *local, self-governing community* and the *voluntary association* could be the significant sources for a pluralism of power. As active sources of political engagement, experience, and training for citizens, they would be an independent source of politically capable leadership. They would also generate new centers of power

to compete both among each other and with the state for a basis for a democratic consensus.

What concerned De Tocqueville was the existence of centers of power located between the individual citizen and the nation-state. As an unorganized mass, aggregates of individual citizens could not oppose the centralized power of the state. Political organizations that had free access to masses of citizens and the opportunity to organize them to engage in political contest, whether in competition for office or in conflict over policy, was a guarantee of a democratic society.

However, a local self-government has by now become less significant as a source of independent social power. It has clearly declined as an autonomous unit in society (as we saw in Chapter 8).

Furthermore, local government is often controlled by local dominant majorities and the local elites based upon them, which often choose *not* to act upon major issues, such as race, housing for the poor, and the like. Also, in the metropolitan areas of the United States, the shared powers of a pluralistic society produce a proliferation of local governments that are too small to act effectively upon metropolitan problems (see this discussion in Chapter 8).

Perhaps more so than Europeans, Americans have made a virtue of the voluntary association. These have been the parapolitical groups that have organized citizens to seek and demand rights and services, to advance causes, and to enlarge the political choices available to a democratic electorate.[44]

But the theorists of pluralism also make an assumption about voluntary associations—that they are reasonably equal to one another in the capacity to influence decisions; but this is unlikely to be so. Some represent the interests of those with wealth, power, and privilege; others speak for those who lack any such advantages. All voluntary associations, therefore, are not equal in their ability to influence decisions that affect their interests.

Decentralizing Power

The undeniable trend toward the concentration of power at the top of hierarchies of decision-making is a common theme that runs through discussions about the future prospects of democracy and individual liberty from quite varied perspectives: liberal, conservative, and radical. A cynical acceptance of power located beyond the reach of ordinary citizens has been a component of American political culture for generations now. Our grandfathers were likely to say: "You can't fight city hall." Today people are just as likely to say that, as well as "You can't fight the corporation."

"Power to the People" Radical critics of American society have called for more power to the people to reverse the trend toward centralizing power. By this they meant to include people not previously included in decision-making: students, racial minorities, women, and the poor. Extension of voting rights once denied—enfranchising the disenfranchised is an example of this—but so is an extension of representation for groups once not considered legitimately due any representation—such as students in academic government.

Beyond this is the organization of those who had not previously been organized. A notable early example is Saul Alinsky's organization of a working-class area of Chicago near the stockyards—the now renowned "Back-of-the-Yards" movement.[45] By such organization otherwise powerless people were in a position to act together to press for consideration of their interests at city hall. The organization of tenants and renters is another example, as is the organization of welfare mothers, and the organization of migrant workers under Cesar Chavez.[46]

Such groups as these then move into the political arena, taking their place alongside already established groups and competing with them to affect decision-making. Organizing the unorganized, thus integrates into the political system people once left out or at best only marginally involved. It extends further the right of democratic participation, and as a social reform strengthens the existing political structure.

But radical critics want more than integrating people into the existing system. Sociologist Richard Flacks advocates *participatory* democracy to provide more direct participation in and control of decisions by the people affected by such decisions. Self-management in work organizations, decentralization of political structures, and local community organizations with real control are among the changes advocated.

For that purpose he calls for the development of community-based, self-determining organizations. He sees them as carrying out the following functions:

1. Achieving community control over previously centralized functions, through local election of school and police administrators; by forming community-run cooperatives in housing, social services, retail distribu-

tion and the like; by establishing community-run foundations and corporations.

2. Maintaining close control over elected representatives; running and electing poor people to public office; ensuring direct participation of the community in framing political platforms and in shaping the behavior of representatives.

3. Acting like a trade union in protecting the poor against exploitative and callous practices of public and private bureaucracies, landlords, businessmen, etc.[47]

Much of this is an effort to restore local control and so to make community once again a viable location of decision-making. (Relevant here is our earlier reference in Chapter 8 to Milton Kotler's thesis about neighborhood government and in Chapter 10 to the effort to develop community control of schools and other functions in large cities.[48]) But there are problems with such efforts.

Local, grass-roots decision-making, for one thing, is meaningless unless there is also local control over resources. Thus local power implies local economies. But the economy has long since been integrated into national and international markets. Control of economic resources—of property, jobs, and capital—now lies in corporate structures that are neither controlled by nor dependent upon local communities or groups.

Restoring power to the people may require more than decentralizing political structures. It requires coping with the fact that economic resources are concentrated in great corporate organizations which, by virtue of the right of private property, are difficult to hold *accountable* for decisions that can so drastically affect people's lives.

That such a possibility is at least technologically feasible, given the development of a cybernated technology, one operated by self-regulating control mechanisms rather than human labor (which does not require either the huge factory or the large corporation to be economical) is an argument carefully reasoned out by anarchist Murray Bookchin. He says:

I do not profess to claim that all of man's economic activities can be completely decentralized, but the majority surely can be scaled to human and communitarian dimensions. *It is enough to say that we can shift the overwhelming weight of the economy from national to communitarian bodies, from centralized bureaucratic forms to local, popular assemblies in order to secure the sovereignty of the free community on solid industrial foundations.* This shift would

The New England town meeting, where local citizens gather to make all community decisions, is America's historic example of decentralized, participative democracy.

comprise a historic change of qualitative proportions, a revolutionary social change of vast proportions, unprecedented in man's technological and social development.[49]

(Anarchism is an antipolitical philosophy that opposes the state and all centralized political authority and seeks to replace them with new, local forms of human association.) Anarchists share with liberals a high valuation on individualism and with socialists an opposition to private ownership of the means of production, yet it stands in basic opposition to both. "In a sense too socialist for the liberals and too liberal for the socialists, the anarchists found capitalism and Marxism equally distasteful."[50]

Accountability

Decentralizing power into the hands of ordinary citizens, including the poorer and lesser educated, encounters another source of opposition, too: The claimed authority and autonomy of professionals and experts, a claim that implicitly asserts the incompetency of ordinary citizens. Technical and professional competence does exist, but many times these experts have been "servants of power," using their very real technical expertise for the benefit of the corporate or governmental organization that employs them, and so for the specific class and group interests these organizations serve, rather than for some larger public interest.

Decentralizing power may require holding accountable both corporations and government agencies, and the professionally qualified experts employed by them. This is one of the most difficult problems of a highly complex and differentiated society: How to prevent private and public groups from serving their own or other special interests rather than the interests of citizens, customers, clients, or some version of a public interest.

THE NADER NETWORK

Ralph Nader is:

President of *Public Citizen*, which is supported by contributions and provides funds for these groups: Congress Watch (lobbying); Litigation Group (lawsuits); Critical Mass (energy); Health Research Group; Aviation Consumer Research Group; Retired Professional Action Group; and Public Citizens Visitor Center, as well as Public Interest Research Groups and Citizen Action Groups in various states.

Managing Trustee of *Center for Study of Responsive Law*, which provides funds for Consumer Complaint Research Center; Clean Water Action Project; and Freedom of Action Clearinghouse.

Ralph Nader uses income from speaking and writing to support the Corporate Accountability Research Group and the Public Interest Research Group.

Nader also has close working ties to several independent groups: Center for Auto Safety; Center for Concerned Engineering; Washington Office of Consumers Union; Professional Drivers Council for Safety and Health; Disability Rights Group; and Pensions Rights Center.

Notes

Source: *The New York Times*, January 29, 1978.

Who Watches the Watchman? But there is a further aspect. Public agencies are supposed to protect and advance public interests, while private groups are expected to pursue their own interests, though within limits. But when private interests and public agencies are in collusion, public interests are unguarded. Thus the United States Department of Agriculture (USDA) presumably looks after the interests of farmers, as well as the larger public interest concerning the production and distribution of agricultural products. But for some time now, USDA has been charged with being part and parcel of an *agribusiness complex,* composed of land-grant universities and their agricultural extension services and experiment stations, the Farm Bureau, the large food-processing firms, the farm machinery and chemical companies, and the major food-distributing chains. USDA has been accused of fostering corporate farming at the expense of family farming, of benefiting big farmers over small farmers, of helping the processors at the expense of consumers, of hindering ecological efforts to protect the environment, and of doing research to displace farm laborers by ma-

chinery but doing nothing to help such displaced farm labor get back into the labor force.[51]

But if public agencies fail to look out for public interests, who does? *Who watches the watchman?* Public-interest research groups, modeled after Ralph Nader's efforts, have partially filled the gap. Small resources, limited access to records, and no legitimate public status of their own hinder them, though the credibility of Ralph Nader has given enormous impetus to this effort to cope with power by holding it accountable.

More to the point, Nader has created a now widely copied model of independent research and investigative organizations that probe into any situation where private power and public authority combine to thwart public interest. Since then he has challenged a wide range of industries and governmental agencies with revealing investigations (see ''The Nader Network''). By probing and publicizing, he has made facts public that often force governmental action.

Beyond that, he has tried to encourage—perhaps revive would be a better term—a pattern of independent citizen action in behalf of consumer, citizen, and taxpayer interests without depending on political of-fice-holders. Indeed, these office-holders are often part of the problem, rather than part of the solution. Nader-inspired Citizen Action Groups and John Gardner's Common Cause, as well as a wide range of independent local groups in many urban communi-ties, have sparked a renewed spirit of independent citi-zen investigation that has increased moderately the prospects of holding government and business ac-countable for the consequences of their actions on the interests of others.

POLITICAL PARTICIPATION

All politicians in democratic societies know that there are differences among the social classes in both interests in and participation in politics. It is a truism, for example, that in the United States a heavy vote favors the Democrats, since it is the workers and the poor who vote less consistently, and they are more likely to vote for the Democrats.

A large quantity of research on political participa-tion seems to confirm what politicians instinctively know: that people higher in class position are more likely to participate in politics than are people in lower class position.[52] Whether status is measured by in-come, education, or occupation, the result is the same: those of higher status participate more than to those of lower status. Furthermore, in the United States, blacks participate in politics to a much lesser extent than do whites.[53]

Apathy and Alienation

In American elections, two parties compete for votes within the same groups and classes, and only in national elections does even more than half of the electorate bother to vote. This fact is often both noted and lamented; there is perhaps no more frequently ex-pressed value in American society than that everyone should vote.

But there are also those social scientists who argue that a low turnout of voters aids the democratic pro-cess. It indicates, they say, that there is a general agreement on social matters and that people are confi-dent that the outcome of an election will not disturb

things. A high turnout, in contrast, is viewed as indicat-ing a high level of conflict that threatens social stability and a possible breakdown of the democratic process.[54]

The Powerless Apathetics But other social scientists define the issue differently. They see the apathetic as alienated voters who cannot find in elections a solution to the problems that most concern them. For them the two-party system offers too little choice, too little change from the status quo. Thus the politically alien-ated are likely to be the socially and economically dis-advantaged.

Electoral data support this argument in that partici-pation in elections is lowest by the poorest and least-educated. They do not see their interests, however they conceive them, as served by existing political par-ties and groups and by elections as contests for power and resolution of issues. They feel they are without power.[55]

Complaining about apathetic voters does not do justice to the problem of political participation. Full participation and high voter turnout may mean that the issue at stake strains the existing consensus in the community, producing high levels of opposition vot-ing, but, at the same time, such an election serves as a rough measure of the extent of the uncommitted and alienated, who normally find no reason for electoral participation.

This suggests an important question: Can a demo-cratic order survive the alienation from politics of a large segment of its citizens? Although nonvoting by the alienated may, in the short run, conveniently con-tribute to the stability of the democratic process, this apathy is indicative to the sources of dissension that the political process may be failing to resolve. As ten-sions grow and the number of alienated voters in-crease, there may occur a serious conflict, fought out in other, possibly violent ways until a new basis for so-cial order is achieved.

The New Alienated

Recent examination of both electoral and survey data suggests that an increasing number of citizens are detaching themselves from the parties, are splitting their tickets, or are not bothering to vote. A Gallup Poll in 1976, for example, reported that these percentages of Americans responded in this manner when asked their party affiliation: Democratic, 46 percent; Republican, 22 percent; and Independents, 32 percent. As Table 17.2 shows, since 1937 this is a decline of almost one-third of people identifying as Republican and a doubling of the Independents. The Democrats, in turn, have changed only a little.

An increasingly larger number of voters split their tickets. More than 50 percent of the ballots cast are now split. In 1968 a Gallup Poll reported that 84 percent of the voters said they voted for the person not the party.

Nor are these independents the same as those formerly identified as the alienated: those low in social status and less educated or politically involved. Instead, they are the more educated, an increasingly larger segment of the middle class.

In recent years it has been common to designate certain social categories as alienated: the young, the blacks, the blue-collar workers, the "middle Americans," white ethnics, and so on. But a study of increasing political alienation among the American electorate during the 1950s and 1960s discovered there was no strong relationship between alienation and such demographic factors as age, race, income, education, and the like.[56] Alienation, in short, is distributed uniformly across various classes and groups in American society.

The Alienated Voter Splitting tickets when voting and ceasing to make an identification with either of the two major parties are both ways in which the American electorate expresses its alienation from a process which it seems increasingly to feel does not serve them well, if at all. Not taking the trouble to vote would be another.

Voting as one form of political participation never has been a major activity of American adults, except for presidential elections once every four years. In the postwar years, the turnout has been less than two out of three adults:

- 1952   62.7 percent
- 1956   60.4 percent
- 1960   63.5 percent
- 1964   62.0 percent
- 1968   60.8 percent
- 1972   53.7 percent
- 1976   56.5 percent

The 1972 election shows a striking decline in voter participation, and only a small improvement in 1976. When you figure that the winning candidate in 1976 got about 50.5 percent of the votes cast by the 56.5 percent who voted, then only a little more than one adult in four chose the president of the United States.

In the 1978 congressional elections, according to Tables 17.3 and 17.4 (when no president was being elected), less than half of all voters claimed to have voted (and the claims are inflated). Also, less than one-fourth of the new voter groups, ages 18–20, claimed to have voted. Furthermore, the less-educated, the lower-income people, and the blue-collar workers voted in considerably fewer numbers than did the better-educated, those of higher income, and white-collar workers.

This difference in voting has some very real consequences for democratic politics in the United States. For one thing, it gives greater political weight to those who *do* vote; these are often people more thoroughly committed to one or the other of the parties; people who may not be representative of all potential voters.

Such a decline, in the second place, tends to separate a public opinion, as expressed in polls, from political action. Not the majority opinion, but the actively mobilized opinion of a minority can then win out when large numbers fail to vote.

TABLE   17.2
Party Affiliation of American Voters, 1937–1976

	Repub- lican	Demo- cratic	Inde- pendent
1937	34	50	16
1940	38	42	20
1950	33	45	22
1954	34	46	20
1960	30	47	23
1966	27	48	25
1970	29	45	26
1974	26	43	31
1976	22	46	32

Source: *Gallup Report Index*, no. 131, June 1976.

TABLE 17.3
Reported Voting by Age, Education, and Income, November 1978

Years of Schooling	18 Years	18–24 Years	25–34 Years	35–64 Years	65 Years and over
Elementary					
8 years	41.4	6.5	15.0	40.2	50.4
High School					
1–3 years	35.1	11.0	18.5	43.1	56.5
4 years	45.3	21.4	33.1	58.9	66.1
College					
1–3 years	51.5	33.2	45.0	66.6	71.8
4 years or more	63.9	40.2	54.5	73.1	77.0
Income					
Under $5,000	30.6	14.4	21.0	34.0	43.9
$5,000–9,999	39.2	18.4	26.0	43.7	59.8
$10,000–14,999	44.0	23.4	36.3	52.1	67.1
$15,000–19,999	49.8	27.5	44.0	59.2	64.3
$20,000–24,999	53.1	27.9	46.3	63.3	65.4
$25,000 and over	60.1	32.5	52.2	70.9	66.1

Note: These are inflated figures, for they represent what people said about their voting. What is important about these figures are the differences by age, income, and education.

Source: U.S. Bureau of the Census, *Current Population Reports,* Series P-20, no. 344 "Voting and Registration in the Election of November, 1978" U.S. Government Printing Office, Washington, D.C., 1979, Tables F and H, pp. 4–5.

These consequences only serve to further increase alienation, for they heighten rather than decrease the widespread conception that the political process is not responsive to the needs and concerns of the majority of citizens. That, in turn, may further increase apathy, or it may lead many people to take more direct action than voting: to demonstrate and picket, to disrupt and interfere, even to defy the law. Sit-ins, sit-downs, and new forms of organizing and bargaining develop as preferred ways to participate in politics. The politics of conflict and confrontation replace electoral competition.

The shift of even a minority of people from electoral politics to the politics of confrontation threatens the very integrity of political parties and elections. If they are to be restored as central institutions of a democratic society, then nothing less than a radical reform of political parties as forms of political participation is required.

ON POLITICAL ECONOMY: A FINAL NOTE

To study society the sociologist must study politics, for a society, as Max Weber told us, is a delicate balance among conflicting forces, an arena of groups contending for dominance in status power. Conflict, therefore, is always present in society.

Social scientists once studied politics as a process separate to a large extent from other processes, especially the economic. The liberal ideal of capitalism and democracy, the economic and the political, as two structures that touched each other but very little was always more an ideal than a reality. But this no longer applies in any modern society. The economy and the polity are thoroughly interwoven with one another. We made this point at the outset of examining the eco-

TABLE 17.4
Reported Voting by
Occupational Groups, November 1978

Occupational Groups	Male	Female	Both
Total Employed	45.8	46.1	45.8
White-Collar	58.6	51.9	55.1
Blue-Collar	35.4	31.2	34.6
Service	43.6	36.7	39.1
Farm	49.6	40.9	48.1

Note: These are inflated figures, for they represent what people said about their voting. What is important about these figures are the differences by sex and occupational group.

Source: U.S. Bureau of the Census, *Current Population Reports,* Series P-20, no. 344 "Voting and Registration in the Election of November 1978" U.S. Government Printing Office, Washington, D.C., 1979.

nomic structure in Chapter 16. It is useful to stress it again in ending this brief examination of the political.

The dominance of the economic and political in human life surely needs no emphasizing here. But the lesson for students of society should be clear: no understanding of modern society can be carried out without its starting point being in the structures of power and domination that originate in the economic and political processes, as well as in the class structure.

SUMMARY

Power is *decision-making* and *authority* is the right to make decisions, that is, *legitimate* power. However, other actors, by influence and pressure, participate in decisions, but still others, mostly of low status, are excluded.

The *nation-state* organizes a large population into a modern society; it claims binding authority and a legitimate monopoly of force within a territory. Social scientists offer three different conceptions of the state: (1) it is a political *arena* in which conflicts over economic and social interests are fought out; (2) it is a *capitalist state* which possesses some autonomy in deciding policies to preserve the class structure and the economic system as a whole; and (3) the state has *autonomy* in possessing a logic and interest of its own, and is an administrative organization to control territories and people. The state carries out four *functions:* (1) maintaining internal peace; (2) promoting the national interest among other nations; (3) controlling its members in pursuit of collective goals; and (4) compromising among various interests in making public policy.

Political parties are organizations to mobilize citizens to get control of the state. There are one-party states and multiple-party states. The American two-party system manages to restrict ideological competition; it is the only party system in Western nations not to develop a party of the left.

Parapolitical groups are citizen groups that lobby in behalf of interests and promote various issues.

Rule by *elites,* even in democratic societies, is the claim of an influential body of literature that insists *oligarchy* is inevitable—an "iron law"—in all organizations. Recent sociological literature has presented both elite and nonelite (*pluralist*) versions of power in American communities, and more recently, in American society.

Alexis de Tocqueville thought that in the United States *decentralized* power was possible in a *pluralist* society, one in which such organizations as the *local, self-governing community* and the *voluntary association* could mediate between the unorganized citizen and the powerful state. But local government is no longer a source of much power and voluntary associations are not equally influential. Consequently, new ideas for decentralization include *participatory democracy,* a *decentralized* economy, and citizen action groups to hold *accountable* those in authority.

Political participation in democratic society varies with class: those higher in class generally participate more. *Voting* is, according to one version, a means to settle issues and achieve consensus. There is, however, an issue over whether *apathy* promotes or hinders democracy. Some social scientists argue for only moderate participation, on the ground that high participation by the lower class and the alienated threatens democracy. Others have disputed the evidence behind this claim, insisting that low participation is evidence of alienation induced by failure of the political system to respond to their needs.

New trends show less commitment to the parties and the increase of independent voters, more ticket-splitting among voters, and decreased participation even in national elections.

The combination of closely related political and economic processes—the political economy—and the associated class structure are basic to an understanding of modern society.

(NOTES

[1] Max Weber, *The Theory of Social and Economic Organization,* trans. A. M. Henderson and Talcott Parsons (New York: Oxford University Press, 1947), p. 328.

[2] See Clifford Geertz, ed., *Old Societies and New Nations* (New York: The Free Press, 1963), and Reinhard Bendix, *Nation Building and Citizenship* (New York: Wiley, 1964).

[3] Hans Gerth and C. Wright Mills, *From Max Weber: Essays in Sociology* (New York: Oxford University Press, 1946), p. 78.

[4] Theda Skocpol, *States and Social Revolutions* (New York: Cambridge University Press, 1979), pp. 24–33.

[5] Charles Tilly, *From Mobilization to Revolutions* (Reading, Mass.: Addison-Wesley, 1978), p. 52.

[6] See Ralph Miliband, *The State in Capitalist Society* (New York: Basic Books, 1969; Nicolas Poulantzas, *Political Power and Social Class,* trans. Timothy O'Hagan, (London: New Left Books, 1973); Perry Anderson, *Lineages of the Absolutist State* (London: New Left Books, 1974); Goran Therborn, *What Does the Ruling Class Do When It Rules?* (London: New Left Books, 1978); and Claus Offe, "The Theory of the Capitalist State and the Problems of Policy Formation," in Leon N. Lindberg et al., eds., *Stress and Contradiction in Modern Capitalism* (Lexington, Mass.: D.C. Health, 1975), pp. 125–144.

[7] See Gösta Esping-Anderson, Roger Friedland, and Erik Olin Wright, "Modes of Class Struggle and the Capitalist State," *Kapitalistate,* no. 4–5 (Summer 1976): 186–220.

[8] Skocpol, *op. cit.,* p. 29.

[9] *Ibid.,* p. 30.

[10] *Ibid.,* pp. 30–31.

[11] *Ibid.,* p. 32.

[12] Gerth and Mills, *op. cit.,* p. 78 (italics in original).

[13] Leon Mayhew, *Society: Institutions and Activity* (Glenview, Ill.: Scott, Foresman, 1971), p. 127.

[14] Gerth and Mills, *op. cit.,* p. 211.

[15] Seymour Martin Lipset, "Political Sociology," in Robert K. Merton, Leonard Broom, and Leonard S. Cottrell, Jr., eds., *Sociology Today* (New York: Basic Books, 1959), p. 102.

[16] Seymour Martin Lipset, *Agrarian Socialism* (Berkeley: University of California Press, 1950).

[17] Gerth and Mills, *op. cit.,* pp. 194–195.

[18] For a comparison of political parties in Great Britain, Australia, Canada, and the United States, see Robert Alford, *Party and Society* (Chicago: Rand McNally, 1963).

[19] Richard Hamilton, *Class and Politics in the United States* (New York: Wiley, 1972), p. 541.

[20] Alford, *op. cit.,* p. 100.

[21] For an analysis of how the two-party system can thwart and block majority desires., see Hamilton, *op. cit.,* pp. 3–15.

[22] *Ibid.,* pp. 534–537.

[23] David Broder, *The Party's Over* (New York: Harper & Row, 1972).

[24] See Scott Greer and Peter Orleans, "The Mass Society and the Parapolitical Structure," *American Sociological Review* 27 (October 1962): 634–646.

[25] Gaetano Mosca, *The Ruling Class* (New York: McGraw-Hill, 1939).

[26] Vilfredo Pareto, *Mind and Society* (New York: Harcourt Brace 1935).

[27] Robert Michels, *Political Parties* (New York: The Free Press, 1949). This book was first published in German in 1911; in English in 1915.

[28] Seymour M. Lipset, Martin A. Trow, and James S. Coleman, *Union Democracy: The Internal Politics of the International Typographical Union* (New York: The Free Press, 1956).

[29] Floyd Hunter, *Community Power Structure* (Chapel Hill: University of North Carolina Press, 1953).

[30] Robert A. Dahl, *Who Governs? Democracy and Power in an American City* (New Haven, Conn.: Yale University Press, 1961).

[31] Michael Aiken, "The Distribution of Community Power: Structural Bases and Social Consequences," in Michael Aiken and Paul Mott, eds., *The Structure of Community Power* (New York: Random House, 1970), pp. 487–525.

[32] C. Wright Mills, *The Power Elite* (New York: Oxford University Press, 1956).

[33] Arnold M. Rose, *The Power Structure: Political Processes in American Society* (New York: Oxford University Press, 1967).

[34] *Ibid.,* p. 490.

[35] G. William Domhoff, *The Higher Circles: Governing Class in America* (New York: Random House, 1970).

[36] *Ibid.,* Chap. 5, pp. 111–155.

[37] A good review of these issues, arguing that there is such a ruling elite, is Milton Mankoff, "Power in Advanced Capitalist Society: A Review Essay on Recent Elitist and Marxist Criticism of Pluralist Theory," *Social Problems* 17 (Winter 1970): 418–430.

[38] Walter Dean Burnham, "The End of American Party Politics," *Trans-action* (December 1969), p. 13.

[39] James Weinstein, *The Corporate Ideal in the Liberal State: 1900–1918* (Boston: Beacon Press, 1969).

[40] For sophisticated discussion of the legitimacy of capitalism in Western industrial societies, see Norman Birnbaum, *The Crisis of Industrial Society* (New York: Oxford University Press, 1969), and Ralph Miliband, *The State in Capitalist Society: An Analysis of the Western System of Power* (New York: Basic Books, 1969).

[41] See Rose, *op. cit.,* pp. 89–92. Richard Hamilton also supports this position; see his *Class and Politics in the United States,* p. 516.

[42] See Gabriel Kolko, *The Roots of American Foreign Policy: An Analysis of Power and Purpose* (Boston: Beacon Press, 1969).

[43] Alexis de Tocqueville, *Democracy in America,* Vols. I and II (New York: Vintage Books, 1954).

[44] For studies of voluntary associations in contemporary urban life, see John N. Edwards and Alan Booth, *Social Participation in Urban Society* (Cambridge, Mass.: Schenkman, 1973).

[45] See Saul D. Alinsky, *Reveille for Radicals* (Chicago: University of Chicago Press, 1946).

[46] See Robert K. Binstock and Katherine Ely, *The Politics of the Powerless* (Cambridge, Mass.: Winthrop Publishers, 1971).

[47] Richard Flacks, "On the Uses of Participatory Democracy," in Matthew F. Stolz, ed., *Politics of the New Left* (Berkeley, Cal.: Glencoe Press, 1971), p. 30.

[48] Two useful works cited in those chapters and relevant here are Milton Kotler, *Neighborhood Government: The Local Foundations of Political Life* (Indianapolis: Bobbs-Merrill, 1969), and Alvin A. Altschuler, *Community Control: The Black Demand for Participation in Large American Cities* (New York: Pegasus, 1970).

[49] Murray Bookchin, *Post-Scarcity Anarchism* (Berkeley, Cal.: Ramparts Press, 1971), p. 112. Italics in original.

[50] Marshall S. Shatz, ed., *The Essential Works of Anarchism* (New York: Bantam Books, 1971), p. xvi. See also David Apter and James Joll, eds., *Anarchism Today* (Garden City: Anchor Books, 1972).

[51] See Jim Hightower, *Hard Tomatoes, Hard Times: The Failure of the Land Grant College Complex* (Washington, D.C.: Agribusiness Accountability Project, 1972). On the role of the Farm Bureau in the agribusiness complex, see Samuel R. Berger, *Dollar Harvest* (Lexington, Mass.: Health Lexington Books, 1971).

[52] Lester W. Milbrath, *Political Participation: How and Why Do People Get Involved in Politics* (Chicago: Rand McNally, 1965), Chap. 5, pp. 110–141.

[53] *Ibid.,* p. 138. For a detailed analysis of black participation in southern politics, see Donald R. Matthews and James W. Prothro, *Negroes and the New Southern Politics* (New York: Harcourt Brace Jovanovich, 1966).

[54] Seymour M. Lipset, "Political Sociology," in Merton et al., *op. cit.,* p. 95.

[55] For an empirical study of the sense of powerlessness among municipal voters, see Murray Levin, *The Alienated Voter: Politics in Boston* (New York: Holt, Rinehart and Winston, 1960).

[56] James S. House and William M. Mason, "Political Alienation in America, 1952–1968," *American Sociological Review* 40 (April 1975): 123–147.

SUGGESTED READINGS

Murray Bookchin, *Post-Scarcity Anarchism*. Berkeley, Cal.: Ramparts Press, 1971. A radical, but anarchist and libertarian (not Marxist) approach to reorganizing society.

G. William Domhoff, *The Higher Circles: Governing Class in America*. New York: Random House, 1970. The most recent sociological work to provide empirical evidence for the existence of a national ruling class.

Richard Hamilton, *Class and Politics in the United States*. New York: Wiley, 1972. A thorough analysis of survey data on political attitudes which challenge some sociological received wisdom.

Floyd Hunter, *Community Power Structure*. Chapel Hill: University of North Carolina Press, 1953. The first and most influential of the studies of community power asserting there is a community power elite.

Charles E. Lindblom, *Politics and Markets: The World's Political-Economic Systems*. New York: Basic Books, 1977. A renowned moderate social scientist writes a sharp critique of the ill fit between democracy and corporate business.

Seymour M. Lipset, Martin A. Trow, and James S. Coleman, *Union Democracy: The Internal Politics of the International Typographical Union*. New York: The Free Press, 1956. An influential effort to test empirically the thesis of the "iron law of oligarchy" on modern organization.

Donald R. Matthews and James W. Prothro, *The Negro and the New Southern Politics*. New York: Harcourt Brace Jovanovich, 1966. A thorough analysis of how blacks have begun to participate in politics in the South.

Robert Michels, *Political Parties*. New York: The Free Press, 1949. The work that advanced the famous thesis of the "iron law of oligarchy."

Ralph Miliband, *The State in Capitalist Society: An Analysis of the Western System of Power*. New York: Basic Books, 1969. A penetrating analysis of the relationship between capitalism and the democratic state.

C. Wright Mills, *The Power Elite*. New York: Oxford University Press, 1956. The first work to describe the outlines of a national power elite in America.

Gaetano Mosca, *The Ruling Class*. New York: Harcourt, Brace, 1935. A classic study proclaiming the inevitability of a ruling class in human society.

Arnold Rose, *The Power Structure: Political Processes in American Society*. New York: Oxford University Press, 1967. The most influential work from the pluralist perspective, challenging Mills's thesis of a power elite.

Theda Skocpol, *States and Social Revolutions*. New York: Cambridge University Press, 1979. A brilliant case is made for the state as an autonomous, coercive organization.

Alexis de Tocqueville, *Democracy in America*, Vols. I and II. New York: Vintage Books, 1954. The great, unsurpassed classic on the problems and prospects for democracy in the United States.

James Weinstein, *The Corporate Ideal in the Liberal State: 1900—1918*. Boston: Beacon Press, 1969. A historical documentation of the relation between the liberal, reforming state and a dominant capitalist class.

Alan Wolfe, *The Seamy Side of Democracy: Repression in America*. New York: McKay, 1973. A probing analysis of how repressive the state can be even in a democracy.

Part 6

CONFLICT AND CHANGE IN MODERN SOCIETY

> *. . . all of us, except those who live alone in caves, run necessary risks of being publicly denounced as deviants.*
>
> **Jack D. Douglas**

Eighteen
SOCIAL DEVIANCE AND SOCIAL PROBLEMS

Too often people feel that the troubles that affect their lives are crosses they bear alone, and for which they and no one or nothing else is responsible. The goals they did not reach, the dreams which never became real, they believe, are due to their own personal deficiencies and failures. When a society like the United States emphasizes personal action—"stand on your own feet"; "do for yourself"; "take care of number one"—the effect is to ask people to see their troubles as only their own personal fault.

People bearing troubles or suffering disappointments do not easily see—as we noted back in Chapter 1—how structural changes and social conflicts lie behind the personal traps from which they cannot manage to escape. They lack the sociological imagination that would enable them to place their troubles in a wider context of social issues.

Take the matter of the city—decaying, getting poorer and uglier, losing its middle class, its streets becoming less safe. The personal solution for this has been, for those with the means, to move to the suburbs. Those without the means—the older, the mi-

norities, the poor—stay behind, the quality of their lives declining along with their neighborhoods. For others—realtors, builders, merchants—the suburban drift has been an opportunity to make money by constructing sprawling housing developments and large shopping centers.

The spread of suburbia steadily engulfs farms and green space, while behind it urban blight moves relentlessly outward from the black ghetto and innercity slums to lap threateningly at the edges of older suburbs. Insofar as dying cities and urban sprawl are the outcomes of leaving urban growth to the process of profit-making and unregulated markets, the troubles and problems of urban life cannot be altered by personal actions.

If this is so, it is the task of the sociologist to make clear to troubled people how and why their troubles are located in the arrangements of social structure, rather than in personal failure. The use of the sociological imagination—as C. Wright Mills told us—lets us understand that our *private* troubles are rooted in *public* issues.

Social Problems

Sociologists have always paid serious attention to social problems, the term they use more commonly than public issues. The concept of a social problem was first developed in two pioneering essays by sociologists Richard Fuller and Richard Myers some forty years ago as a way of resolving a difficulty for sociologists who wanted to deal with public issues while yet remaining scientifically objective.[1]

Defining a Social Problem Those conditions or situations which members of the society regard as a threat to their values were defined by Fuller and Myers as social problems. Social problems are what people say they are. Two things must be present: (1) an *objective condition* (crime, poverty, racial tensions, and so forth) the presence and magnitude of which can be observed, verified, and measured by impartial social observers; and (2) a *subjective definition* by some members of the society that the objective condition is a "problem" and must be acted upon. Here is where values come into play, for when values are perceived as threatened by the existence of the objective condition a social problem is defined.

Recognizing an undesirable condition and defining it as a social problem, however, are two different things. There can be disagreement if some people believe the situation, though undesirable, is unavoidable —part of the human condition or the price we pay for "progress." For most of human history, for example, poverty was the common lot of the mass of people. With only a primitive technology, the existing economies were incapable of producing enough to raise the level of living above some minimum level of survival. Poverty was the unavoidable fate of the masses, not a social problem.

Even now there are those who do not believe that poverty is a social problem. They believe, instead, that poor people are to blame for their own condition of poverty; they "blame the victim," as we saw in Chapter 16. They define it as the personal failure of those who are poor, not a consequence of the arrangement of social structure.

The steadily rising rate of accidental deaths involving automobiles in the United States—to take another example—was long considered to be unavoidable, the regrettable price we paid for all the obvious advantages the mobility of the automobile gave us. But with the invention of seat belts and shoulder straps, and the effective criticism of Ralph Nader, among others, automobile safety became a social problem. Something could be done about it. Whether automobile manufacturers sacrificed safety for speed and salability finally became a public debate and a matter of congressional investigation.

But some people may not define a condition as a problem because it is to them desirable and natural, and not a threat to their values. Racial discrimination, for example, is not a problem for those who believe the races to be naturally unequal. They would deny that differential treatment is "discrimination." (For them, integration is a threat to their values, and thus a social problem.) It requires a belief in equality in order to define discrimination as a social problem.

There are significant cultural differences in the readiness of people to accept objective conditions as inevitable. Some people in the world are more ready to bow to the inevitable, to be philosophically resigned to the hardships imposed by nature and society. Western people, however, have generally been more activist in their orientation. The outlook that characterized the Protestant Ethic, the emergence of science, and the development of numerous technical inventions, is one of activist mastery of the environment. Such an outlook is more likely to demand that objective conditions be changed and to believe they can be. In American life, this leads to the frequent demand that somebody (usually government) "do something."

Two Types of Social Problems

Sociologists distinguish between two types of social problems: first, problems of *deviance* having to do with the adjustment of people to conventional ways of behaving; and, second, problems of *social organization* which are created by the way the community or the society is organized.

Deviance When some people do not conform to established ways of behaving and violate social expectations and social rules which others uphold, their behavior is deviant. Delinquency and drug-addiction among adolescents is defined as deviant behavior; so is alcoholism, mental illness, various forms of sexual behavior (rape, incest, sodomy), bigamy, vandalism, and a host of other behaviors, most of which are forbidden by law.

Social Organization In modern society, many social problems are created by the way the organization of community or society produces situations that some members of the society refuse to accept as right or necessary or even inevitable. That 10 percent of the population is below the poverty level becomes a social problem for those who do not think such an amount of poverty needs to be tolerated in an affluent society. So, too, the existence of slum housing, the lack of equal opportunity for nonwhites and women in education and employment, the abuse and neglect of children and the elderly, and the cost and distribution of health care among all social classes and racial groups.

DEVIANT BEHAVIOR

The study of deviant behavior by sociologists—and by psychologists—has deep roots in persistent social concerns about problems of conformity and social control. In an effort to understand deviant behavior the major effort of past social research for at least half a century has concentrated on the *deviant person.* Criminals, juvenile delinquents, prostitutes, and the like have been studied in detail, with an emphasis upon both their biological and psychological characteristics and their environment.

Criminals, for example, were first defined as a *biological* type; their criminal behavior was interpreted as being *inborn,* a consequence of some genetic makeup. In 1876 Cesare Lombroso, an Italian criminologist, advanced the idea that the criminal was a genetic throwback to a more savage and primitive person. He reached this conclusion by examining the skulls of convicts and claiming he found them to be characterized by enormous jaws, cheekbones, and prominent superciliary arches (eyebrows); these and other features, he said, were found only in savages and apes.

Lombroso's theory was widely accepted until 1913. Then Charles Goring, an English physician, published the results of his study, which measured the physical characteristics of both convicts and nonconvicts, and found there was no significant difference.[2]

That shifted concern to the *psychological* makeup of criminals. They were thought to have a weak ego structure and a poorly developed moral sense; in short, an inability to meet the demands and expecta-

tions of society, or to possess the same moral values as other people, or to be capable of self-control.

Many social scientists thought that the psychological factors producing such behavior were the outcome of a type of environment: a broken home, a brutalized or neglected childhood, poverty and lack of social opportunity, a slum neighborhood, and the like.

This focus on a psychological explanation sought to find the cause of deviancy in some attribute or characteristic of the person. Such an approach concentrated on the deviant individual and asked: Who is this person? How did such a person become deviant?

But social research failed to provide any clear explanation. The studies only partly supported one another, and many provided contradictory findings.

A British scholar, Barbara Wooten, for example, undertook a careful, systematic critique of research on juvenile delinquency.[3] She selected twelve factors most commonly reported in both the popular and professional literature as being causes of delinquency and then looked to see what twenty-one major empirical studies in three countries over a period of four decades had discovered. Her results produced a bewildering array of findings, frequently noncomparable, and usually subject to overgeneralization. She then joined others in declaring that the psychological study of the individual offender as a bundle of traits or deviant-producing factors had about exhausted its value. A new perspective was emerging.

A New Perspective on Deviancy The new effort to define deviancy insisted that a sociological analysis had to focus upon deviant *behavior,* rather than some conceptions of deviant *personalities.* One of the leading students of delinquency, Albert Cohen, insists that "much—probably most—deviant behavior is produced by clinically normal people."[4]

If deviancy is not in the attributes of persons, then it must be rooted in the structure of society. An earlier, influential essay by Robert Merton had pointed out one way for deviancy to occur as a consequence of structural conditions: in the gap between goals and means in society.[5]

Anomie and Deviancy

Merton took Émile Durkheim's classic concept of *anomie* and adapted it to the explanation of deviance. As we saw in Chapter 3, Durkheim developed the concept of anomie to identify those situations in which the power of social norms to regulate social interaction among the members of society no longer held.

Merton's starting point was a significant insight: his recognition that, if a set of socially approved *goals* were to be effectively upheld by the members of a society, then those members had to have available to them effective, socially approved *means* to attain those goals. Becoming a "success," for example, is supposed to be gained by hard work and educational achievement. Yet, for one thing, a good education is not equally available to all social classes and races. Some people, furthermore, despite hard work and educational achievement, will be held back by racial, class, or sexual discrimination.

In effect, then, there is unequal, not equal opportunity for educational and occupational achievement in American society (a point that should come as no surprise after our analysis of social inequality). In the gap between goals approved *for all* and means *limited to some* lies a source of deviant behavior. Merton made the point clearly: deviant behavior, he noted, will occur on a large scale when a society holds out, above everything else, "certain *common* success goals for the *population at large,* while the social structure rigorously restricts or completely closes access to approved modes of reaching these goals *for a considerable part of the same population* . . . ."[6]

Merton was interested in how the members of society *adapted* to this discrepancy between goals and means. Some people accept both the goals and the socially approved means as legitimate and *conform* to them, even sometimes when they do not personally succeed. Many others, however, adapt in a deviant fashion, which, Merton said, takes any one of four possible forms: ritualism, innovation, retreatism, and rebellion.

Ritualism is a giving up on the goals while still going through the motion of the means, conforming to the prescribed patterns of behavior even though no longer expecting to be successful. The lower middle-class citizen who no longer aspires for high office and is content with his small gains and limited mobility, who "plays it safe" and asks nothing, is an example of ritualism.

Innovation is the opposite of this, where the goal of personal success is strongly adhered to, but new, illegitimate means are employed to get there. This generates a wide range of illegal activities by which people

seek money and recognition. Note that deviants do not want anything different from what other people do. They are conformists in terms of the major value of success; they are deviants only in how they go about attaining success. The lower-class boy who wants to "make it big" but lacks the acceptable credentials for a rewarding career in business or a profession may turn to drug-dealing as a way to wealth and power.

The emphasis upon success and winning is so strong in the United States that it has produced the highest rate of property crime among the richer industrial nations of the world. Deviancy, therefore, occurs at all class levels in American society, not merely among those who are the poorest and most disadvantaged.

Among the poorest, criminal behavior is largely conventional property offenses: mugging, holdups, car thefts, breaking-and-entering. At an earlier time it was various immigrant groups who were highest in such crimes: the Southern and Eastern Europeans in the late nineteenth and early twentieth century. But their rate of offenses declined rapidly as they won access to legitimate opportunities in society. At the present time it is blacks and Hispanics.

But there is also an extensive pattern of white-collar deviance, crime, and political corruption. Some examples are the college student who cheats on an important examination because of the intense competition to get into medical school; the college coach who recruits athletes by doctoring transcripts, or offering money and jobs; the doctors who cheat on Medicare, operate a kickback scheme with laboratories, and do not report all their income to the Internal Revenue Service; or the Watergate offenders who arranged a break-in to Democratic headquarters and then covered it up.

Retreatism, in turn, produces the "true aliens," those who give up on both goals and means. They are *in* society but not *of* it. These are the individuals who had first strongly internalized both goals and means but were unable to use the means effectively to achieve the goals. This may be for lack of opportunity due to discrimination, or because they found themselves revolted by the need to engage in intense personal competition with others. But they also cannot bring themselves to use illegal means. They resolve their intense personal dilemma by withdrawing from the process altogether. They escape the system by "dropping-out." They are the vagrants and tramps,

In every large city we can see society's dropouts: the homeless men and women who have given up on both legitimate goals and means.

the homeless men of skid row, chronic alcoholics and drug addicts, and some psychotics.

Rebellion takes the form of renouncing the established goals and the social structure that support them and seeking, instead, to create a social structure in which new goals and means are possible. A revolutionary movement is an example of this type. The countercultural intention to reject highly individualistic and competitive behavior, as well as personal success and wealth as an individual goal, and to replace these with a conception of a cooperative, communal existence is another.

Perhaps the major value of Merton's essay was his clear demonstration of the idea that deviancy is rooted in the structure of society, not in the attributes of persons. Yet even here Merton emphasized the *motivations* of individuals to deviate from the accepted patterns of behavior. He defined a deviant as one whom most people *called* a deviant, making a social-scientific

concept out of the labeling conventional people apply to unconventional people. In reaction to this, a new generation of sociologists undertook to redefine deviant behavior.

The Outsiders

Perhaps the most provocative of this new work has been that of sociologist Howard S. Becker, who refuses to accept society's definition that people *are* deviant, but recognizes that in fact society does *label* people as deviants.[7] And the majority do so when the others violate the rules that the majority have made and insist on. Becker says:

. . . *social groups create deviance by making the rules whose infraction constitutes deviance,* and by applying those rules to particular people and labeling them as outsiders. From this point of view, deviance is *not* a quality of the act the person commits, but rather the consequence of the application by others of rules and sanctions to an 'offender.'[8]

What this new approach does is shift the analysis from the supposedly deviant person to the interaction between the rule-applier and the rule-breaker. People are labeled deviants by others and thus become "outsiders," even though they may have violated a rule but once, while others have done so several times with impunity.

The Deviant Career   A permanent involvement in deviant behavior does not come quickly, once the deviant act has been committed. There can be much experiment and withdrawal before there is that progressive involvement that defines a "deviant career," as Becker calls it.

The first nonconforming act may be accidental and unintended, undertaken in a spirit of fun, an act of shoplifting, for example, but without any clear intention to deviate. It may be a response to taking a "dare" or while out for fun and feeling less responsible and conventional than usual. Put this way, it is evident that deviant behavior is not peculiar merely to some people, but in fact is experienced by all people. Most people, probably, do in fact commit one or more deviant acts in their lifetime, particularly when young. But most of them do not follow a deviant career. Instead, they become "committed" to conventional rules and behavioral patterns of their own groups in society. Some others, however, become progressively drawn into some kind of deviant behavior.

To be pulled into a deviant career is to be drawn into closer association with others who deviate in the same manner, say, in taking drugs, and to associate less and less with those who clearly disapprove of such behavior. An association with other deviants provides support for the deviant behavior and protection from the enforcers of the rules.

Becker, for example, studied drug-taking among jazz musicians, where continued involvement by the individual over a period of time was strongly encouraged by close association with other jazz musicians, who defined themselves as different from "squares" in every way.

For many others, becoming a career deviant may be simply the brutal fact of being caught in a deviant act and then publicly labeled a deviant—a delinquent,

a criminal, a dope addict, or as insane. The label may then stick to them, regardless of anything else they may do. Thus, defined by others as deviant, the person so labeled may find it hardly possible to be anything else but a deviant. Perhaps their only viable role is to move toward a deviant career and close association with other deviants.

The Deviant Group

The labeling conception of deviancy is particularly concerned with how individuals become deviant in a society in which the line between deviance and conformity is not a sharp one. But another approach has been concerned with social groups which are marginal or disadvantaged in society and because of that develop a perspective on social life that is deviant. Such a group rejects at least some of the rules and norms of the larger society and develops norms of its own. It creates a *subculture* that is deviant and that provides a strong group basis for deviant behavior.

As far back as the 1920s and 1930s sociologists were strongly impressed by the fact that certain social areas of the city were characterized by high rates of delinquent acts committed by youths in association with others, rather than alone. From such research in Chicago came Edwin Thrasher's *The Gang,* a study of a large number of gangs in the immigrant, lower-class neighborhoods of Chicago.[9]

Thrasher pointed out that boys *learned* to be delinquent by their participation in the gangs that were the normal part of life in their urban neighborhoods. They were not deviating from the conventional behavior of others; rather, they were conforming by being gang members and acting as gang members did. Delinquency was the "natural history" of a juvenile under such circumstances. It involved no psychological problems of frustration or deprivation.

The key idea here is that individuals *learn* to be deviant through their association with others who are already so. They are *socialized* to deviant norms. The late distinguished criminologist, Edwin Sutherland, developed a theory of *differential association* as an explanation of delinquent behavior, asserting that youth become delinquent

to the extent that they participate in settings where delinquent ideas or techniques are viewed favorably, and that the earlier, the more frequently, the more intensely, and the longer the durations of the associations in such settings, the greater the probability of their becoming delinquent.[10]

Deviant Subcultures

In time sociologists shifted from the socialization process by which a boy learned delinquency to the conditions from which delinquent gangs emerged. The key concept became *delinquent subculture,* which points to the existence of norms and values that place positive value on delinquent behavior and that confer status on gang members for delinquent acts. Such a subculture also defines the attitudes to and behavior toward those outside the group.

The source of the subculture lies in the experiences of boys low in social status, who suffer when judged by "middle-class measuring rods," as Albert Cohen called them.[11] Middle-class success seems out of reach and they find themselves facing low status in adult life. In reaction, they form groups which exhibit the *opposite* of middle-class values—malicious destruction and vandalism, nonutilitarian thefts (stealing cars for joyrides, not profit), as well as fighting and aggressive behavior directed against others.

But the kind of activity that will be exhibited by delinquents, according to one study, will depend on the opportunities available in their neighborhood.[12] They will engage in criminal activities like theft only if adult theft, including fences, already exist as a process from which they can learn and which they can join. Otherwise, their delinquent activity may consist largely of fights with rival gangs or they may engage in such escapist activity as drug-taking.

How extensive such quite distinctive subcultures are in any large urban area is not obvious. Some sociologists have argued that perhaps only in very large cities like New York and Chicago can such specialization of youthful gangs be found. One investigation found that the delinquent groups tended not to be so specialized but to shift their activities from one form of delinquency to another.[13]

The lack of opportunity for achieving conventional social goals creates problems of status in society for which delinquent subcultures are one solution. Those who share common problems develop collective solutions in the form of organized group activities oriented around norms and values peculiar to the disadvantaged group, as we have said, and provide rewards of esteem and status from within their own ranks.

If the subculture of delinquent youths is a prominent case of a *deviant* subculture there are nonetheless others. Some examples:

Professional Thieves. Those who make a living from stealing property develop a subcultural world around their illegal activity. They need considerable secrecy and subterfuge, for one thing; of necessity they operate in an underworld of concealed actions. They rely on a network of others who provide assistance, including, especially, "fences," those illegal dealers who market stolen goods.

Pimps and Prostitutes. The peddling of sex for a price violates both moral norms and laws, yet it also depends on the patronage of large numbers of straight "johns." Pimps acquire a number of prostitutes, organize and manage their work, and collect a portion of their pay. They are also crucial in locating young women who can be lured into a life of prostitution.

Thieves and fences, and pimps and prostitutes live in a criminal subworld—an underworld—where their occupation is, by definition, illegal, and they live by their ability successfully to violate moral standards and law. They are part of an even larger criminal world of pick-pockets, drug peddlers, gamblers, professional arsonists, street muggers, swindlers, and the like. It is here that a deviant subculture rationalizes and justifies the life-style of those who live outside the law and, in most cases, without stable patterns of association with those whose lives are not deviant, or at least not so by occupation or cultural outlook.

Homosexuality   A different kind of deviant subculture is that of *homosexuality.* Homosexuality is not a criminal occupation but homosexual acts were illegal in all the states of the United States until recently. Even now, in most states, they are subject to severe penalty. As a consequence, homosexuals have had to conceal their activities both to avoid prosecution and also to avoid harassment and punitive treatment by "straights." Homosexuals are, therefore, forced to live in two worlds, the heterosexual world wherein they work and even, in some cases, maintain heterosexual lives, and a homosexual world wherein a sexual life is practiced that is often both repugnant to heterosexuals and difficult for them to understand.

In the 1970s homosexuals, both male and female, began to claim the right to be homosexual without fear of punishment from others. In effect, they have been denying that they are deviant, only that their homo-

Homosexuals have been demanding that their homosexuality be defined, not as deviant, but as an alternate life-style.

sexuality is an *alternative* sexual preference. If they succeed in this campaign, then what has long been a deviant subculture will be an alternative one; a once deviant life-style will become simply one alternative among others. Deviant subcultures like all other aspects of social life, are not frozen into place forever but are subject to redefinition and change.

Explaining Deviant Subcultures   Social deviancy only exists because any organized society develops rules to guide behavior (social norms) and because some people are unable or unwilling to follow those rules. When detected by others, their norm-violating behavior brings punishment and rejection. In some cases, deviants (particularly young ones) gradually discard their deviant ways and eventually become relatively conforming adults.

But in other cases deviants are the victims of a *labeling* process: defined as deviant and then treated as deviant by others, they move from conventional associates to deviant ones, finding in fellow deviants support for their deviant life-style, as well as rationalizations and justifications for their rule-breaking conduct.

Deviants become *outsiders* whose actions and lifestyles are labeled as morally offensive, or as criminal, and they live on the margins of conventional society. But very few can do so alone; deviants can practice a deviant life-style when they find a compatible group with a supporting set of cultural outlooks and norms. If they are to be outside the main groups of society, they must become *insiders* in a subworld of fellow deviants. Within that world is a subculture providing a set of beliefs and attitudes that justify deviant conduct. It also defines its own world and conventional society and how the interaction between them is to occur. Its norms govern conduct so as not to endanger friends or associate too much with foes.

But most of all the deviant subworld and its subculture provides the place where the deviant can be deviant. Without it, the lone person has little opportunity to escape surveillance and punishment. Deviancy requires established social relations, as well as the sustaining norms and values which a subculture provides.

Deviancy and Dominant Values   From this emphasis on deviants as outsiders, it would seem that we are speaking of people whose own values are opposed to those of the dominant society; that they possess a subculture because they do not share in the values expressed in the dominant culture. Yet such is not the case.

In many ways the carriers of deviant subcultures adhere to many dominant values. They share in the importance of making money, even though they may use illegal means to get it. They participate in the same consumption styles and seek esteem and high status, even though, again, they may use somewhat different standards. They are not, in short, indifferent to, and certainly not opposed to, much of the dominant culture. They are more likely to be *norm-violating* persons, rather than *value-rejecting*. Often what distinguishes deviants from others is the use of deviant means to attain conventional goals: money, success, and high status (homosexuals are an exception to this; their deviancy hinders their attainment of conventional goals).

Nor are deviant subcultures the source of political radicalism. Instead, their political values are more likely conservative. Inmates of prisons, for example, are often quite nationalistic and patriotic. (The emergence of a radical political consciousness among black prisoners is a development of only the 1960s.)

Mental Illness as Deviant Behavior

Some forms of deviant behavior, it should be noted, do not easily provide a basis for a deviant group or a deviant subculture. Mental illness is one. Becoming mentally ill isolates the individual from his or her usual groups, but does not provide in their place deviant groups to which he or she might turn for support or protection.

Mental illness is by now a widely recognized social problem in American society, and also one of the more costly. Providing mental health services and staffing mental hospitals and clinics requires an enormous expenditure of public funds.

The harsh and fearful treatment of the mentally ill in the past is now a well-told story. By now, the long struggle for humane treatment of such people has reached a fairly wide level of acceptance in modern society. At the core of such a struggle has been the effort to win public acceptance of mental illness as just that, *an illness,* to be treated as any illness, not punished but cured. In addition, there has been the long effort to convince the population that most mental illness is not genetically based, and so is not inherited, and therefore does not reflect upon a family's genetic quality. And much progress has been made.

The Myth of Mental Illness   It took several generations to convince the American population to think of the mentally suffering as *ill* in the same fashion that the physically suffering are ill. Just about the time the concept of mental illness was finally winning public acceptance, the psychiatrist Thomas Szasz undertook a fundamental attack upon it. He asserted that there is no such thing as mental illness, it is a myth.[14] What is regarded as mental illness, he said, are *problems of living.*

Szasz's principal point is that *mental illness* is a label placed upon certain deviant behavior. Such behavior, he claimed, is taken as evidence of mental illness, and then mental illness is offered as the cause of the behavior. This is logically fallacious, but, according to Szasz, is only one of the fallacies inherent in the concept of mental illness.

The idea of *being ill,* Szasz says, is derived from medicine, where a malfunctioning of the organism presents itself in various symptoms that are then regarded as amenable to medical treatment (see "From Sin to Sickness: The Medicalization of Deviance"). In mental problems, he says, what happens is that behavior, much of which may be the person's verbal communications about his problems, is then measured by the psychiatrist's reference to norms of what one expects from "normal" people. These are not medical standards being applied; they are *psychosocial, ethical,* and *legal* ones. The judgment that a chronic hostility is evidence of mental illness, for example, is because it is seen as a deviation from the ethical norm of love and kindness. Yet medical remedies are undertaken. The disorder is defined by one set of terms and its remedy defined by another.

Note that Szasz is not arguing that there are not emotionally troubled people. Instead, he insists that

FROM SIN TO SICKNESS: THE MEDICALIZATION OF DEVIANCE

Back in the Middle Ages, a theological definition of deviance prevailed; deviance was *sin*. After the advent of the Industrial Revolution and the emergence of nation-states, most deviance was defined as *crime*. Now, in the twentieth century, when science more often guides our conceptions of reality, deviance is increasingly designated as a medical problem; deviance is *illness*, physical and mental. Medicine has achieved the authority to define many deviant individuals as "ill" rather than as immoral or criminal.

While not all forms of deviance have been medicalized, the following have come increasingly to be treated within medical jurisdiction: alcoholism, drug abuse, obesity, hyperactive children, mental retardation, violent behavior, suicide, child abuse, wife-beating, sexual offenses, including rape, incest, and child molestation, as well as crime and delinquency.

Medicine's growing authority to define the meaning of much social behavior then becomes a basis for social control. However much medicine may be committed to treating individuals rather than punishing them, medicine is mandated to provide treatment for the behavior defined as deviant. Medicine *intervenes* in order to limit, modify, regulate, isolate, or eliminate such behavior by medical practices. Medicine, then, is becoming society's major agent for the control of deviant behavior.

Medical control begins with medicine's power to define some behavior in medical terms and thus bring that behavior within its domain of treatment. In doing so it makes use of new medical technologies, such as:

Psychoactive medications: tranquilizers and stimulants; amphetamines for overeating and obesity; disulfiram for alcoholism; methadone for heroin; and many others. These medications are easily administered, quite potent in their effects, and less expensive than other treatments.

Psychosurgery: Surgical procedures, such as prefrontal lobotomy, fell into disrepute in the 1950s because of such "side effects" as general passivity and difficulty with abstract thinking. Now a new form of psychosurgery, including laser technology and brain transplants, has emerged. Despite continued opposition, in 1976 a national commission reporting to the Department of Health, Education, and Welfare endorsed the use of psychosurgery and judged its risks to be "not excessive."

Human genetics: Genetic screening and genetic counseling, particularly in decisions to have children, are becoming commonplace. While genetic causes for such deviant behaviors as alcoholism, hyperactivity, schizophrenia, manic-depressive psychosis, homosexuality, and mental retardation are often claimed, there is little as yet developed to a level permitting medical intervention. However, the enormous interest in this expanding area of medical and scientific knowledge strongly suggests much future effort to develop modes of genetic control.

When medicalization of a deviant behavior, such as alcoholism or drug addiction, occurs, it may then be *decriminalized,* that is, no longer defined in law as a crime. Control of the problem is then shifted from the judicial system to the medical system. On the other hand, some deviant behavior, such as homosexuality, demonstrates a movement toward both *decriminalization* and *demedicalization* and being defined, instead, as an alternate life-style.

If the medicalization of deviant behavior is the dominant trend, what are the *conse-*

quences? Sociologists Peter Conrad and Joseph W. Schneider suggests that it is part of a long-time *humanitarian* trend; it allows the deviant to assume the *sick role,* rather than be a sinner or a criminal; it is *optimistic* about the individual's future (sick people are usually curable); it lends the *prestige of the medical profession* to designating and treating deviance; and it is more *flexible* and *efficient* than the legal and judicial systems.

But, Conrad and Schneider point out, there is also a darker side of much less desirable consequences:

1. Individuals in the sick role are not held responsible for their own behavior, but they are then placed in a position of dependence on experts and the responsible nonsick; they are no longer responsible, self-controlling adults.

2. Defining deviance as disease allows society's moral and social definitions of behavior to be hidden behind a facade of scientific objectivity and neutrality.

3. Defining a problem as medical removes it from the public realm of discussion and debate to where only medical experts can presumably speak competently about it.

4. Defining deviant behavior as a medical problem allows experts to do things to the person that could not otherwise be done: cutting into the body, for example, or requiring a person to take certain medications.

5. Defining a problem as deviance and medically treatable produces a widespread tendency to look for causes and solutions in individuals rather than in social structure.

6. This individualizing of deviant behavior as sickness, furthermore, detracts from developing any political issues. This opiate addict in the ghetto, for example, is treated as sick, deflecting attention from the structure of the ghetto life that produces such behavior.

7. Finally, defining destructive, pain-producing or oppressive action as sick keeps us from seeing evil intent or even evil consequences in human behavior. Claiming that evil consequences are the product of a "sick mind" makes them seem like accidents. In this way medicalization contributes to the exclusion of a conception of evil in modern society.

Notes

Source: Peter Conrad and Joseph W. Schneider, *Deviance and Medicalization: From Badness to Sickness* (St. Louis, Mo.: C. V. Mosby, 1980), Chaps 1, 2, 9, and 10.

the problems of living in modern society prove to be troublesome and disturbing for many people. But they are not "ill" in some medically objective sense.

What Szasz says about mental illness as a myth is close to what Howard Becker said about deviancy. When people deviate in certain disturbing ways in their interactions with others, then, being mentally ill is the label that others place on them. And like other cases of deviancy, the people so labeled may sometimes come to accept the label and to believe themselves to be mentally ill.

The problem of mental illness, therefore, is only partly a problem of those so labeled. It is also a problem of definition; that is, a problem of how definitions of normality and reality are made in society and used as judgments of what is conventional and what is deviant behavior.

Labeling Deviants: A Caution

The concept of deviancy has developed from that of a deviant person to deviant behavior to deviant groups and cultures. A deviant person or deviant behavior was thought of as a problem in conformity and control. Since deviance is a violation of group norms, labeling some person's actions as deviant serves to define what is acceptable behavior. After being labeled deviants, such persons are pressured to conform, or to hide their deviant behavior from others, or to leave the group—and they can be made to leave by being ostracized or expelled.

But when deviants come together to form groups and create a subculture, is there still deviancy? There are now groups with contrasting, even contradictory norms. A majority of the population, or at least larger and more influential groups, may label smaller and less influential groups as deviants. Are homosexuals, for example, deviants or are they now an alternate lifestyle? What may be defined as deviancy, like homosexuality, depends upon majority views. But these change over time, are sometimes vague, and are always inconsistently applied.

Deviancy is a normative term, and it is easy to forget that sociologists call deviants those who are labeled deviant from the perspective of the more dominant (but by no means universal) norms of the society. Exaggerations of normative consensus lead some sociologists to label all rule-breaking behavior as deviancy, forgetting that rules reflect power as much as consensus, and that it is the more influential people in society who make the rules. It is doubtful, also, if there is any gain, sociologically, in applying the label of deviancy to organized crime or the evasions of moral standards by corporations. The concept of deviancy needs to be used with care if its scientific value is to be maintained.

PROBLEMS OF SOCIAL ORGANIZATION

Although there has been a predominant interest in problems of deviant behavior in recent years, problems of social organization, such as race relations, poverty, and urban renewal, persist as compelling issues. Most such problems prove to be significantly interrelated; and this interrelatedness makes it hard for the sociologist to study a single problem as if it existed without reference to others. Housing as a problem, for example, involves the problem of poverty (low-income housing) and the problem of race (segregated housing).

It may be useful to sort out three ways in which sociologists pursue the study of social problems. The distinctions are not precise; they simply suggest different ways to focus on complex issues:

1. Some sociologists follow a basic issue such as race across institutional areas like the economy and education, and across levels: from interpersonal interaction to community processes to national policy-making.

2. Others focus on a single institution, such as education, which is one locus for a problem like race and a source of problems of its own.

3. Still others analyze the often grievous inadequacies of structures and programs built to handle social problems, such as welfare or mental hospitals.

Basic Issues

Some complex issues pervade the entire social structure, having no single institutional locus, for they are not exclusively economic, political, or educational problems; they are all of these. *Racism,* for example, ramifies throughout the social structure, creating problems of job discrimination, educational disadvantage, community tensions, and many others. It complicates other social problems: housing, poverty, the schools, urban renewal, law enforcement, and the like. Few aspects of social life escape its contamination.

Another such problem is *poverty.* It too affects education, housing, and employment. It is a problem of the changing labor force, of upgraded job requirements, of unneeded workers with few skills, of school dropouts, of poor housing and poor health, of malnourished children and impoverished elders, of inadequate welfare programs, and basically of the social neglect by all societal institutions of the lower economic fifth of the nation.

The *status of women* is another encompassing issue, one that shows up in the practices and policies of almost all social institutions and groups. All three of these—race, poverty, and women's status—are basic issues because they are rooted in one of society's most fundamental and difficult matters: the problem of inequality.

Ecology is a different, though similarly pervasive, issue. It concerns the practices of community, government, and industry about waste disposal, pollution of air and water, preservation of wildlife, protection of natural resources, development of land for profit, and provision of recreational facilities. It cuts across the *vested* interests of a wide range of social groups and classes while demanding attention to a more compelling *public* interest.

Institutional Problems Other social problems have an institutional locus.

Education becomes a social problem—more accurately a set of social problems—when performance in education fails to meet people's expectations and needs. The value placed on equal educational opportunity, for example, may be threatened by obvious differences in educational chances provided for different social classes and racial groups. There is seemingly no end to educational problems: teacher strikes, school dropouts, innercity schools, segregated schools, schools and delinquency, teaching deprived children, updating curricula, and community control of schools.

Government is a social problem when it responds too slowly to changing needs and demands, or when its democratic character is violated by special interest control, or when its growing bureaucracies impinge increasingly on those very civil liberties government is supposed to protect.

The *law* is a social problem when its dispensation of justice fails to treat people equally, so that being poor or a member of a minority means less chance for justice than being rich or dominant. It is also a problem when courts take so long to bring criminal and civil cases to trial that witnesses are unavailable, making impossible the retribution or restitution the law is supposed to provide.

Even the *family* does not escape this. To many who claim the family is a basic institution, it seems to have been weakened; others see it as unable to socialize children adequately. The fate of children with divorced or working parents, the problems of adoption, the difficulties of marital relations in a changing moral climate, the feminist challenge to male domination—all these suggest the family as a set of social problems.

The *economy* is a set of social problems, too: un-employment and underemployment, racial and sex discrimination in hiring and promoting, inflation, the working poor, the changing needs of the labor market, and the inability to provide without subsidy adequate housing for low-income people. There is also the concentration of economic control in huge corporations, and the as yet uncharted functions and powers of multinational firms.

When Solutions are Problems Agencies of society are created to carry out social policy, remedy ills and solve problems; but each in time also becomes a social problem. The mental hospital is one example. In the past mental hospitals have not been organized primarily for purposes of *therapy* but for *custody* of mentally disturbed people who are socially disruptive in their normal surroundings. Such hospitals, in this case, take the mental patient out of and away from society.

Erving Goffman characterizes mental hospitals as one among the "total" social institutions of modern society that are organized to move whole blocks of people through routines of activity according to schedules, to keep close surveillance on them, and to enforce close association with others, so unlike ordinary life.[15]

Sociological work has shown how the internal social organization of hospitals affected patients, particularly the chance of recovery.[16] Many features of the ordinary routines of the mental hospital, it seemed, detracted from recovery, particularly the rather insensitive and impersonal "handling" of patients by nonprofessional attendants, by which dignity and respect were effectively denied. The need for radical alteration of hospitals if they were to be genuinely therapeutic was shown. Alternatives have been proposed; an outpatient program, a community health clinic, and a "half-way house" for those who are not quite ready to cope with society. But that only creates another problem: local residents always resist placing a half-way house in their neighborhood.

Some other examples follow:

Prisons are intended to reform criminals, but the "reformatories" badly need reform. They are inefficient and fail to reform most of those assigned to them. In many cases they are breeders of criminal careers and attitudes; inmates become brutalized as a condition of survival. Most ex-convicts return to crime and are usually again convicted. Prisons contribute, in short, to the problem they were once designed to solve.

A prison is one kind of "total" institution, wherein whole blocks of people are closely supervised, kept under constant surveillance, and moved through disciplined routines of activity.

Welfare rolls grow, yet inefficiency and redtape deprive many of what is legally their due. Welfare agencies can be degrading to many poor, yet they do little if anything to assist the poor in getting out of poverty. The welfare system was designed in the 1930s for temporary but widespread Depression-induced unemployment and economic insecurity. The set of problems today is entirely different.

Housing programs were undertaken to help low and moderate income people to get decent shelter, but doing so has produced some horrendous results. Public housing agencies built enormous high-rise apartments inhabited by many welfare poor and fatherless families, often racially segregated (though no longer by official policy). Frequently their corridors became unsafe from attack, haunts of criminals and drug peddlers; in a short time they were badly vandalized, falling into disrepair. As environments, they are in

some cases socially if not physically worse than the slums they were to replace.

More recently the effort to subsidize single-family homes for the poor in presumably sound, older sections in the innercity turned into a fraudulent game perpetrated by property owners, realtors, and even some housing officials; a scandal that robbed poor people of money and a housing opportunity, the government of public funds, and seriously discredited the Department of Housing and Urban Development (HUD).

Each of these institutions reflect in specific ways the carrying out of social policies that encompass older solutions to social problems. Sometimes their programs never were adequate for the task; sometimes circumstances have changed too much. These institutions have taken on a life of their own with a vested interest in their own continuity and perpetuation. Once they

Prisons are ineffective institutions, and their living conditions occasionally produce riots. This shakedown is a search for weapons in the aftermath of one such riot.

both; a federal agency with vast regulatory powers over railroads, or airlines, or public utilities, or public lands comes into the control of those who are to be regulated when these groups provide most of the experienced experts who serve as professional staff or even as commissioners. Public interest gives way to self-interest.

What should be apparent is not only that there are many social problems but that *very little is not a social problem.* Our social institutions are each a set of social problems; so are all large social groups and organizations; and so are all social agencies claiming to act on social problems. Every aspect of American society is a social problem from the perspective of some group's values.

The Problem of Social Problems   But if everything is a social problem, can the concept of social problems be any longer useful to us? To answer that, we must examine critically what is assumed in labeling some things as social problems.

Sociologists, it seems, make three assumptions:

1. that society's social problems require a program of *social reform;*
2. that agreement can be reached by the public on what is or is not a social problem; and
3. that resolving social problems requires a *welfare* approach.

Let us look at each of those in turn.

Social Problems as Social Reform

The existence of social problems supposedly indicates some unsatisfactory and value-threatening aspects of an otherwise satisfactory society. Society is not a problem, it is assumed, but it does contain a number of social problems. This assumption, then, leads to a *reformist* approach to society. There is no quarrel with basic values and institutional structure, only a concern with some specific features. Social reforms are called for, not revolution.

Given this assumption, the source of social problems is seen in terms of three not wholly separate ideas:

1. Social problems occur because modern society is so complex, so intricate in its internal organization that an inconsistent and loosely meshed social struc-

were an effort to solve problems; now they are part of the problem, complicating the social troubles that brought them into being. By emphasizing the failures of official agencies and programs, sociologists raise questions about the official (and sometimes also popular) definition of the problem, pressing for a new understanding of causes and sources as a basis for new efforts at resolution.

Perhaps one could also put in this category the numerous regulatory agencies of the community, the state, and the federal government. A municipal agency intended to regulate construction or protect public health becomes corrupt or bureaucratically slow or

The failure of public housing to solve the problem of housing the poor is dramatically illustrated in this photo of the demolition of an eleven-story building, one of 35 such buildings of the massive Pruitt-Igoe project in St. Louis. The entire project became a haven of criminals and was so vandalized that it became unlivable and was finally demolished this way.

ture cannot help but generate strains and social tensions.

2. Even if modern society is highly productive and highly rewarding in status and material goods for so many, it still has a dark side to it. There are costs and casualties to any social system; progress has its price.

3. Social change continually alters social structure and therefore disrupts established relations among social groups, redefines social roles, renders outmoded or dysfunctional once respected and productive beliefs and behavior patterns. From this come social problems.

Each of these conceptions of the source of social problems then suggests a social perspective that is cautiously reforming. Society cannot be perfect, it is claimed, so utopian expectations are unwarranted. What is clearly being said is that the kind of social problems we have are the price we pay for the kind of society we have. We can expect always to have them,

though specific social problems will change as the society changes.

However, there is some difficulty with this way of reasoning about social problems. As we have noted, most problems are intricately interwoven with other problems, so that one social problem, like racism, cannot be examined in isolation from others, like slums and poverty. Increasingly, we see social problems to be the undesirable consequences of the normal and routine practices of existing social institutions.

More and more, these undesirable outcomes grow and increase the social costs necessary to cope with them. Now, in some cases, the price we pay for progress outweighs the progress. The growing debate in the United States over the extensive use of toxic chemicals in industry and in the production of food, with consequent harm to natural resources, to the food chain, and eventually to the long-run health interests of human beings, is just such an issue.

It may no longer be radical to say that American society does not have social problems, American society *is* a social problem.

The Politics of Social Problems

When a social problem is defined as an objective condition that threatens established social values, and when society is thought to be organized around a consensus of values, then it leads easily to the assumption that a society readily achieves agreement on what its social problems are. But successfully defining a social condition as a social problem is a complex political process that involves struggle among unequally competing groups, some more powerful, some with little capacity to get recognition. It is, says Herbert Blumer, "a highly selective process," and the most "harmful" conditions are not necessarily the ones to receive attention and be defined as problems.[17]

There are, Blumer points out, conflicting interests and differences of power in getting public attention to social problems. The feminist movement, for example, has in recent years acted vigorously to have rape defined as a serious social problem.[18] Rape has long been a crime, but enforcement has been limited and ineffective; neither public officials, the criminal justice system, nor the general public seemed to have been greatly concerned.

Now, through feminist pressure and action, rape has received the attention that befits a serious problem. That is so even though there has also been considerable resistance to defining rape as a social problem; males in law enforcement have been reluctant to change long-established attitudes and practices. As in any such situation there are conflicts over whether the social condition (the frequent occurrence of rape) deserves to be defined as a social problem for which some reform should be developed.

Prior to the feminist movement women lacked the power to have rape defined as a social problem deserving of social reform. That power was realized in the political force of the feminist movement, even against resistance.

Political power, then, and conflict, bargaining, pressuring, and propagandizing are the elements by which a condition becomes defined as a social problem. In that process differences of social power are decisive.

The Welfare Model of Social Problems

Social scientists and practicing professionals have together defined and promoted a welfare model for dealing with social problems.[19] They seek useful reforms to assist troubled people, but the programs they develop still assume that professionals will be in charge and will exercise control, however benevolent, over deviants and over the victims of problems, such as the poor. These problem people are to be taken care of and helped within a program designed and operated by professional "experts."

This is the process we have identified before — turning political conflict into manageable issues that can be legally and administratively controlled. (Turning class conflict into collective bargaining between unions and management is, as we have already observed, perhaps the outstanding historical example of this.)

When this is done, these professionals are the dominant actors in the administration of a social program intended to control, change, or reform a social problem. These are social workers, psychologists, urban planners, and professionals in medical care, criminal justice, housing, education, community services, among others. They plan and design the social programs and exercise authority and make decisions about and for others: deviants, the poor, minorities, the elderly, and all those confined to "total" institutions, such as prisons and hospitals.

Furthermore, it is these professionals' definition of the problem that is likely to become the official one, for they are supposed to be the "experts." Because deviants and the victims of social problems have not been politically organized, their conception of the problem is not heard or given consideration.

But it is just that situation, claim Horowitz and Liebowitz, that is changing. Social problems become political in a new way when the deviants, the poor, or the minorities offer *their* definition of the problem and organize to act upon it. The problem of rape, we saw above, got consideration as a serious social problem when women, the victims and potential victims, not the "experts" in medicine, psychology, and criminal justice, exerted strong political pressure to bring reform into the handling of rape.

Recent political history offers a number of other examples. Youth have exerted political pressure on drug laws and on the draft; welfare mothers have organized to obtain more adequate expenditures for welfare; and elderly people have organized into such groups as the Grey Panthers to fight the abuse of elderly patients in nursing homes. Homosexuals have fought openly to end being labeled deviant.

These actions are political actions, and when they occur, social problems are no longer the monopoly of "experts." Instead, the victims of the problems become a political factor in whatever social reforms are adopted.

SOLVING SOCIAL PROBLEMS

Most Americans seem to believe that something can be done about almost any undesirable situation, that social problems can always be solved. They expect, therefore, that some mode of action can be devised that will make a difference and reduce if not eliminate a social problem.

For that reason the pressure to bring about desired changes, to reform the practices and institutions of American life, is very strong. Yet if most Americans have confidence that something useful can always be done, they very often do not appreciate or even understand the complexities of reform as a social process and the fact that there are considerable differences among ways of bringing about social reform.

Reform and Social Change

To reform means to change, and changes in social life threaten those who benefit by things as they are. Any reform, therefore, is likely to be opposed by those who believe they have something to lose if the reform is adopted. The political struggle is then between *reformers* and *antireformers*.

While it is difficult to deny that social problems exist, or that they are better left alone to work themselves out naturally, that is just what antireformers do. The basic antireformer argument is that the intervention of "do-gooders" does more harm than good. Changes that do improve social life, it is argued, come gradually and naturally, without any planned intervention, when able, productive people are allowed to work and produce without the restrictions and regulations imposed by reformers. Such an argument

emerges from the ideology of capitalism and the image of a free, competitive market.

Yet very often antireformers end up being reformers anyway. They do so when they advocate that various controls and plans be abandoned and there be a return to market processes. This can be illustrated by examining the efforts of two competing interest groups to reform health care in New York City.

The Problem of Health Care

Health care has long been a focus of social reform, for its problems affect the interests of everyone. One problem is the *maldistribution* of health services (both physicians and hospitals or clinics), which are often in short supply in innercities and rural areas but plentiful in suburbia. Another one, which has received major public attention, is the rapidly increasing *cost* of medical services, especially hospital care, which has run ahead of inflation.

The problem of maldistribution then produces another problem: the *lack of quality* medical care for many people but especially for the poor and elderly in nursing homes. These three problems come together as one: the inadequate and unequal *delivery of health services* by the health-care organizations and professions.

Any attempt to understand why this is so must look at the organization of health-care services and of the medical profession. Health care in the United States is organized around the professional monopoly of physicians over the dispensing of medical services. As sociologist Robert Alford notes, "The physicians in private practice and the voluntary hospitals still constitute the core of the health system."[20] Despite many investigations and reports on the problems of health care, and many varied recommendations for reform, none has ever dared to challenge this professional monopoly.

The medical profession has maintained a continuous control over the provision of medical services and no other changes or innovations have altered that. For one thing, physicians have been able to define their skills legally as their property to be sold for a price, and have managed to create social beliefs that such a process is in the best interest of all. Secondly, physicians have dominated the organization and operation of hospitals, hospital accreditation, and in this way have exerted a powerful influence over health-resource allocation.

Physicians also maintain a control over the training and licensing of physicians, and, among other things, there are too few physicians and too many specialists, especially surgeons. According to sociologist David Mechanic, it would be reasonable for one-fifth of all physicians to be specialists, but approximately four-fifths of American physicians practice as specialists. Surgeons are the most numerous, resulting in a rate of surgical operation double that of England and Wales.[21] Unnecessary surgery is one of the recognized abuses of American medicine.

The monopoly of health services by private practitioners, according to medical sociologist Eliot Freidson, makes of medicine a consumer-oriented industry dependent upon sales and volume. "The major pressures of the system are directed toward increasing the number of services and decreasing the professional quality of those services."[22]

Reforming Health Care

In examining the problems of health care in New York City, Alford discovered that one powerful group within health care—"market reformers"—blames "bureaucratic interference and cumbersomeness for the defects of the system and calls for the restoration of market competition and pluralism in health-care institutions."[23] Alford labels this approach the *pluralist perspective,* since its advocates call for a competitive market among several different sources of health care. Pluralists accept health insurance and government subsidy for the poor and elderly in order to ensure that no one is left out, but otherwise want no governmental subsidy, control, or planning for health care. This is basically a conservative approach, since, from this perspective, no reorganization of health care is required, only a program for those individuals and families who are unable to procure adequate care.

The market reformers are the *professionals* of health care: the biomedical researchers, physicians in private and group practice, as well as salaried ones, and other health-care professionals, who share a common interest in maintaining professional autonomy and a control over the conditions of their work. Their reforms are intended to preserve their interest in a *professional monopoly,* which, according to Alford, is the dominant structural interest within the organization of health care.

The other major reform group—the "bureaucratic reformers"—puts the blame for the problems of health care on market competition "and calls for increased administrative regulation and government financing and control of health care."[24] Bureaucratic reformers emphasize

need for integration of all the basic elements of health care in order to overcome duplication (which the pluralists hail as diversity), lack of coordination (which the pluralists welcome as competition), and lack of planning (which the pluralists condemn as both unnecessary and impossible).[25]

This is essentially a liberal solution, in contrast to the conservative view of the market reformers.

Bureaucratic reform, in turn, is advocated by the *organizations* of health care: the medical schools, hospitals, insurance companies, and health planning agencies. They are intent on maintaining and extending the control of their organizations over the work of the professionals. Their goal of an efficient and systematically planned health system is one of *corporate rationalization.*

There are at least two things to note about these reform efforts. One is that both the market and bureaucratic reformers are groups which dominate and operate the health care system and so have an enormous stake in how it operates. And each is the basic opposition to the other. Neither group wants to change things radically; they both would stand to lose from that.

Secondly, there is no organization of comparable influence advocating a more basic reform. There are "the 'equal-health advocates,' who seek free, accessible, high-quality health care which equalizes the treatment available to the well-to-do and to the poor."[26] They are as yet, however, relatively weak in the politics of health care.

The Limits of Social Reform

What can be learned about the reform of social problems in American society from the example of health care reform?

First of all, note that the dominant reform groups are a part of the structure which needs reform. Two implications flow from this:

1. The dominant reformers for many social problems are "insiders," people who provide the actual services and operate the social programs which have been legally established and publicly funded to pro-

vide needed services. Sometimes, as in health care, the service itself is the problem. In other cases, the service was developed to handle a social problem—as prisons for rehabilitating convicted criminals—and has in time compounded the problem by becoming a part of it, rather than a solution.

2. By virtue of their professional training and experiences, these insiders are more knowledgeable than ordinary citizens and can speak as "experts" on the problem. But their expertise is partisan, not impartial. As Alford showed about health care, both professionals and bureaucrats, as experts, offer solutions that are limited because they protect their own stake in the system as it is.

What this means is fairly clear, but it is basic: The social reforms developed by insiders fall short of solving the problem, for the practices and procedures of the would-be reformers; for example, those of the bureaucrats and professionals in health care, are part of the problem. The professional monopoly of the physician and the organizational authority of the bureaucrats are so deeply imbedded in law and in long-established practice and custom, and so uncritically accepted even by outside critics, that, as aspects of the problem, they remain untouched by any suggested reform. In such instances, most reforms fail to live up to their promise, and some even make the problem worse.

Furthermore, what sometimes passes for reform is in fact something else. Alford makes the point, for example, that the bureaucratic effort to bring coordination and integration into health care, and the opposition to this by professionals seeking to protect their own professional autonomy, "are part of a battle—sometimes manifest, sometimes latent—of deeply embedded structural interests for control of key health care resources and institutions."[27] Such a struggle uses the facade of reform but does not constitute reform.

The Difficulty of Reform Another lesson is evident: Reforms which really reform are difficult to achieve. Sometimes social reforms not controlled by dominant interests achieve a political success. Then the "repressed" interests of others (as Alford calls them)— the people who do not get adequate medical care, for example—becomes a political factor in the struggle for reform. Because no institution or political structure serves these interests, it requires great political and or-

ganizational energies to offset the structural domination of those in control, such as bureaucrats and professionals.

Even when a concrete reform has been won and politically forced upon the dominant interests, it can be lost over time if the dominant interests get control of the reformed process. They will gradually change a law or program—often by controlling its day-to-day operation—from what was originally intended and promised into something that at least does not threaten their interests. Here again is a familiar case: those who are supposed to be regulated in the public interest, as we saw before, get control of the regulating process and operate it for their own interest.

Structural Reforms Not all reforms really do reform. Some reforms are too limited and superficial, and some are designed to protect the vested interests of the "insiders" who already benefit by the existing system. Such limited reforms are adopted because they promise to improve the system while not altering the basic structure of privilege and power, such as the professional monopoly in medicine, which, we saw above, controls the distribution of health resources.

This means, therefore, that if there are to be reforms which really reform, they must go beyond such limited reforms to make some changes in the basic structure of the system. There must be *structural* reforms.

A structural reform is more than a new program or a change of policy; unlike limited reform, it changes the established structure of power, privilege, and authority of the system being reformed. Structural reform, according to the French social critic André Gorz,

> is conceived not in terms of what is possible within the framework of a given system and administration, but in view of what should be made possible in terms of human needs and demands.
>
> And finally, it bases the possibility of attaining its objective on the implementation of fundamental political and economic changes.[28]

Structural reform does not ignore the value of specific, limited reforms; instead, it incorporates them into a political program that seeks to go further and make some fundamental structural changes.

While bureaucrats and professionals in all areas, not just health care, are capable of generating useful reforms, they are not capable of structural reforms, that is, of larger structural changes. They view their area of interest and expertise in isolation from other areas (in which they admit not to be experts), while structural reformers recognize that health care, education, family life, and more are interdependent, so that reforms in only one and not in the others are of limited value.

This, in fact, was the conclusion to which Alford came in his analysis of the competing claims of the market and bureaucratic reformers in health care. While both groups offered useful specific proposals, according to Alford, no specific one of them "can cure the symptoms of illness in the health-care system." That requires "a must more fundamental struggle to change American social institutions."[29]

Reforms and Reformers The history of social reform is a history of efforts that have promised much but done little to remove social problems. Few social prob-lems are really new, though more and more of the structures and institutions of society seem to be so problem-filled that very little, as we noted earlier, is not a social problem. If that is so, then not all reforms really reform, and not all reformers are really re-formers.

Social problems are more than the deficiencies of otherwise healthy social structures, to be easily re-moved. Instead, they persist and stubbornly resist re-form because, as Alford points out, from this perspec-tive, they are "a disease of the entire social organism which must be diagnosed and treated as a whole."[30] That cannot be done by bureaucrats or professionals, who have a vested interest in making some reforms but protecting their own privileged position. It can only be done by a social movement with a broad program of social change. (Social movements are our concern in the next chapter.)

SUMMARY

For sociologists, a social problem is defined as an *objective* condition defined as posing a *threat* to *values*.

There are two types of social problems: problems of *deviance* and of *social organization*.

Behavior is deviant when individuals do not conform to established ways of behaving and violate social expectations and social rules which others uphold.

Deviants were first defined as deviant *persons;* they were once thought to be *biological* types, their behavior inborn. Later their deviant behavior was defined as *psychological,* the product of a weak ego structure and a poorly developed moral sense.

Robert Merton developed a theory of deviancy which related it to *social structure.* He saw deviancy as a consequence of socially approved *means* not being available to some persons to pursue socially approved *goals.* In the gap between goals approved *for all* and means *limited to some* is a source of deviant behavior. The results are: *ritualism:* giving up on goals but still acting out accepted means; *innovation:* employing illegitimate means to achieve goals; *retreatism:* giv-ing up on both goals and means; and *rebellion:* renouncing established goals and the social structure that supports them and seeking to create a social structure in which new goals and means are possible.

More recently, deviants are defined as those *labeled* deviant by the majority or by powerful groups. Such labeling often forces people into deviant careers.

Another approach sees disadvantaged and marginal groups in society developing a deviant perspective on social life; they create a deviant *subculture.* Members are socialized into deviant behavior. Deviant subcultures develop among delinquent youth, among those in the criminal world, and among homosexuals.

Problems of social organization include these *basic* issues: race, poverty, women's status, and ecology, as well as *institutional* issues: education, government, law, family, and the economy, within which are many specific problems.

In addition, many past solutions—welfare, housing, and mental hospitals, for example— have themselves become problems. Not only are there many problems but there is very little not a problem.

Sociologists assume a *reformist* conception of social problems, *consensus* on the definition of problems and a *welfare model* of how problems are taken care of.

On this basis, the source of social problems is seen in terms of (1) the *complexity* of modern society; (2) the *costs* and *casualties* of progress; and (3) social *change*. This is a cautiously reforming approach to social problems.

But Blumer stresses how conflict, bargaining, pressuring, and propagandizing affects what problems get public attention. While sociologists generally assume that problems are *apolitical*, they become political when the poor, the deviants, or the minorities offer and press for their definition of the problem.

Solving social problems leads to efforts at social reform, which means to make changes. Reform is opposed by those who have something to lose, but these antireformers often advocate changes in their interest and become reformers, anyway.

Robert Alford's description of social reform in health care points up the limits of social reform:

1. Dominant reform groups are often part of the structure which needs reform, and so offer reforms which protect their interests.

2. Reforms which really reform are difficult to achieve, for dominant interests usually change reforms into something not threatening to them.

3. Only those reforms which seek to make basic structural changes can really reform. These structural reforms include basic structural changes and short-run substantive changes into a program of change carried out by a social movement.

NOTES

1 Richard C. Fuller and Richard R. Myers, "Some Aspects of a Theory of Social Problems," *American Sociological Review* 6 (February 1941): 24–32, and "The Natural History of a Social Problem," *American Sociological Review* 6 (June 1941: 320–329.

2 For a discussion of the development of criminal explanation, see Richard Quinney *The Problem of Crime* (New York: Dodd, Mead, 1970), Chap. 3.

3 Barbara Wooten, *Social Science and Social Pathology* (New York: Macmillan, 1959).

4 Albert K. Cohen, "The Study of Social Disorganization and Deviant Behavior," in Robert K. Merton, Leonard Broom, and Leonard S. Cottrell, Jr., *Sociology Today* (New York: Basic Books, 1959), p. 463.

5 Robert K. Merton, "Social Structure and Anomie," *American Sociological Review* 3 (October 1938): 677–682. Reprinted in Robert K. Merton, *Social Theory and Social Structure,* 2d ed. (New York: The Free Press, 1968).

6 Robert K. Merton, *Social Theory and Social Structure,* rev. ed. (New York: The Free Press, 1957), p. 146.

7 Howard S. Becker, *Outsiders: Studies in the Sociology of Deviance,* 2nd ed. (New York: The Free Press, 1973).

8 *Ibid.,* p. 9.

9 Edwin Thrasher, *The Gang* (Chicago: University of Chicago Press, 1936).

10 Quoted in Howard Becker, *Social Problems: A Modern Approach* (New York: Wiley, 1966), p. 229.

11 See Albert Cohen, *Delinquent Boys: The Culture of the Gang* (New York: The Free Press, 1954).

12 Richard Cloward and Lloyd E. Ohlin, *Delinquency and Opportunity: A Theory of Delinquent Gangs* (New York: The Free Press, 1960).

13 James F. Short, Jr., and Fred L. Strodtbeck, *Group Process and Gang Delinquency* (Chicago: University of Chicago Press, 1965).

14 Thomas Szasz, *The Myth of Mental Illness* (New York: Harper & Row, 1961).

15 See Erving Goffman, *Asylums: Essays on the Social*

Situations of Mental Patients and Other Inmates (New York: Doubleday, 1961).

[16] See, for example, Alfred Stanton and Morris Schwartz, *The Mental Hospital* (New York: Basic Books, 1954); and William A. Caudill, *The Psychiatric Hospital as a Small Society* (Cambridge, Mass.: Harvard University Press, 1958).

[17] Herbert Blumer, "Social Problems as Collective Behavior," *Social Problems* 18 (Winter 1971): 302.

[18] Vicki McNickle Rose, "Rape as a Social Problem: A Byproduct of the Feminist Movement," *Social Problems* 25 (October 1977): 75–89.

[19] See Irving Louis Horowitz and Martin Liebowitz, "Social Deviance and Political Marginality: Toward a Redefinition of the Relation Between Sociology and Politics," *Social Problems* 15 (Winter 1968): 280–296.

[20] Robert R. Alford, *Health Care Politics: Ideological*

and Interest Group Barriers to Reform (Chicago: University of Chicago Press, 1975), p. 195.

[21] David Mechanic, *Politics, Medicine, and Social Science* (New York: Wiley, 1974), p. 38.

[22] Eliot Freidson, *Professional Dominance: The Social Structure of Medical Care* (New York: Atherton Press, 1970), p. 73.

[23] Alford, *op. cit.,* p. 1.

[24] *Ibid.,* p. 1.

[25] *Ibid.,* p. 265.

[26] *Ibid.,* p. 191.

[27] *Ibid.,* p. xiv.

[28] André Gorz, *Strategy for Labor* (Boston: Beacon Press, 1967), pp. 7–8.

[29] Alford, *op. cit.,* pp. 265, 266.

[30] *Ibid.,* p. 265.

SUGGESTED READINGS

Robert R. Alford, *Health Care Politics: Ideological and Interest Group Barriers to Reform* (Chicago: University of Chicago Press, 1975). A detailed study of how dominant interests control the processes of social reform in health care.

Howard S. Becker, *The Outsiders: Studies in the Sociology of Deviance,* 2d ed. (New York: The Free Press, 1973). A provocative presentation of the idea of labeling as basic to understanding deviance.

Richard Cloward and Lloyd E. Ohlin, *Delinquency and Opportunity: A Theory of Delinquent Gangs* (New York: The Free Press, 1960). The subcultural variation in big-city gangs is explored.

Albert Cohen, *Delinquent Boys: The Culture of the Gang* (New York: The Free Press, 1954). An influential study defining lower-class delinquency as a subcultural process.

Robert Ash Garner, *Social Change* (Chicago: Rand McNally,

1977). This radical analysis of social change includes a discussion of reform.

David Matza, *Delinquency and Drift* (New York: Wiley, 1964). That delinquency does not in most cases lead to a delinquent career is the theme of this thoughtful study.

C. Wright Mills, *The Sociological Imagination* (New York: Oxford University Press, 1961). Our private troubles must be seen as public issues, else we cannot understand what happens to us.

James F. Short, Jr., and Fred L. Strodtbeck, *Group Process and Gang Delinquency* (Chicago: University of Chicago Press, 1965). A review and analysis of the group basis of delinquency.

Thomas Szasz, *The Myth of Mental Illness* (New York: Harper & Row, 1961); also *The Manufacture of Madness* (New York: Harper & Row, 1970). In these two works Szasz develops his famous thesis about mental illness.

The most general function of collective behavior, then, is to maintain an element of flexibility in the workings of society.

Ralph Turner

Nineteen

COLLECTIVE BEHAVIOR
Crowds, publics, and social movements

For the most part people interact within the patterns set by social structure, within the routines that give form and stability to social life—but never completely. The clash of whites and blacks in a race riot or the violence between striking workers and police that destroys property and injures people, are both instances of action that is neither routinized nor governed by the social norms that control more institutionalized action.

Some social interaction exhibits a specific set of norms that define and limit people's conduct but other situations do not. There are population aggregates with no clear definition of group membership, little division of labor, no clear role expectancies, no established authority, and an absence of stable leadership. Compared to bureaucracy or the highly integrated folk society, these are "loosely" structured.

Social scientists label such phenomena *collective behavior.* It encompasses three major areas:

- *Crowds:* the fighting, violent mobs, the great masses of spectators, the ceremonial crowds either gay or solemn as occasion requires.
- *Publics:* the physically dispersed aggregates of people who share an interest in some event or issue, political or cultural.
- *Social movements:* the collective action of social groups or classes seeking to bring about or to resist social change—a matter of social protest, of reform or revolution.

THE CROWD

In everyday language the presence of large numbers of people at a shopping center or of people pouring out of office buildings at the end of the workday is usually called a crowd. A mob bent on violent attack on others is also called a crowd; so, too, is a political demonstration.

These different situations have in common only the fact of the physical presence of many people. But these people may have no common concern, no particular awareness of one another. "Crowds" of busy shoppers and people hurrying home from work are involved in their own private objectives—making a purchase or catching the next bus. In the sociological sense, this is not a crowd.

A crowd emerges when an aggregate of people share a common focus. They are no longer merely individuals; there is a common interest or concern, as well as interaction and communication among members of the crowd.

Casual Crowds People on the street watching the police handle an accident, or watching a building going up, or listening to a pitchman trying to sell his wares, are *casual* crowds. People's interest is moderate and their emotional involvement is low. The individual has little difficulty leaving the crowd. Nor do the norms of conventional behavior lose their force.

Conventional Crowds In every society there are crowd situations which are well established and in which the culture provides a model of acceptable crowd behavior. These are *conventional* crowds. A crowd at a political convention and a crowd at church on Sunday morning are different in behavior and mood, yet each has a conventional way of acting.

An *audience* is also a conventional crowd. It is usually quite restrained in its behavior. A lecture audience, or one at a concert or play, may be relatively passive, for each individual is intent on the speaker or performer and is less conscious of the others in the audience.

There are, nonetheless, opportunities for emotional expression in the audience situation, particularly at the end of a performance, when applause expresses approval, and a standing ovation may express appreciation for a particularly good performance.

Expressive Crowds Conventional crowds sometimes provide an opportunity for release of emotions in ways that are not socially threatening, as, for example, at a football game or a rock concert. These are *expressive* crowds. They give people an opportunity to express themselves freely and to release emotions and ten-

sions. People can scream, yell, cheer, boo, wave their arms, stamp their feet, and shout at the tops of their lungs. When the game or concert is over, they may be both physically and emotionally exhausted.

The Acting Crowd

The fears aroused by the thought of a crowd are not from casual or conventional crowds, not even expressive ones, but fear of the crowd in action, violent and destructive, bent on riot. In situations of conflict and tension, whether these are political struggles, labor disputes, or race conflicts, the possibility of such crowd action emerges.

There have always been such crowds throughout history, and they have often been a significant political force, even a revolutionary one.[1] A strong fear of politically acting crowds emerged among the propertied classes in Europe, and particularly in France, in the nineteenth century. The rise of mass-based socialist parties only added to this great fear of masses of ordinary people taking their political demands to the streets.

A French scholar, Gustave LeBon, incorporated these conservative sentiments into a theory of the crowd which was to have enormous influence on sociological ideas of crowd behavior until quite recently.[2]

LeBon perceived the crowd as an organized aggregation with a collective mind, in which the person loses any individual mentality. The crowd mind gives freer play to the subconscious, and highly emotional qualities and instincts became dominant. The crowd, therefore, is defined as being incapable of highly rational or intellectual effort but reflects the common mediocrity of its members.

American social scientists stripped LeBon's theory of its more obvious antidemocratic bias, but otherwise built upon his work to develop a conception of crowd behavior built upon two assumptions:

1. That collective behavior was radically different from the "normal" actions of the individual, controlled as these usually are by social norms.

2. That the basic explanation for such "abnormal" action of the individual lies in *contagion* induced by a crowd situation. The usual predispositions of the individual are overcome by unanimous, intense feelings that permit action otherwise blocked by normative controls.

Why the individual loses control of himself in a

The end of a college graduation ceremony is a fit occasion for a happy, expressive crowd.

crowd situation has been explained by such psychological mechanisms as *emotional contagion, imitation,* and *suggestion,* as well as the *anonymity* of the crowd and its restricted attention. Perhaps *suggestibility* due to contagious excitement and a sense of power in the crowd has been the most frequent explanation. The result, presumably, is an irrational and deviant individual, stripped of his civilized veneer.

Such contagion, according to the theory, produces an acting crowd characterized as suggestible, destructive, irrational, emotional, paranoid, spontaneous and uncontrolled, and made up largely of the lower classes.

Sociologist Carl Couch calls these terms *stereotypes* of the acting crowd.[3] He makes the point that irrationality, for example, is a component of many aspects of social life, not just crowd behavior, and that what is called rational and what is irrational is often an official definition that makes rational whatever supports the established system while opposition to current institutions is considered irrational.

The Emergent Norm Theory

An effort to move beyond an inadequate psychologizing about collective behavior has been developed most by sociologist Ralph Turner. His central thesis is that, even in the most violent and dangerous crowds, there is also social interaction, in which a situation is defined, norms for sanctioning behavior emerge, and lines of action are justified and agreed upon. Turner calls this an *emergent norm* theory.[4]

The emergent norm perspective has particularly challenged the empirical description of crowd situations so often produced in the past, descriptions that seem to overemphasize the unanimity of the crowd and the contagion which captures the emotions of all. Rather, careful observers of crowds note that many people stand around, not involved actively or even emotionally, and some are even opposed to the dominant orientation of the crowd. A crowd is rarely unanimous or undifferentiated.

The theory of crowd behavior has moved away

from the older perspective that viewed the individual as coming under the sway of the crowd and losing his capacity for rational judgment before the onsweep of an overpowering emotional contagion. Instead, sociologists now explain crowd behavior by the same sociological concepts that explain social groups. Crowds are best understood as a *developing collectivity*, in which interaction leads to defining what its members feel to be justifiable action, even when this violates established ways or proceeds in the face of official opposition.

Yet even then there must be the proper combination of elements before a crowd becomes an acting crowd. A crowd must be able to direct hostility against a definitely focused object: there has to be something to act *against*. The interaction must build up an unambiguous imagery of friend and foe, *we* and *they*.

When this is done, the prevailing culture comes into play. It provides symbols, whether of nation, class, or race, which clearly and sharply define the object of hostility, simplify the character of the threat or problem, and create the situation in which it becomes possible to define as legitimate a course of action that would usually be defined as extreme.

In the confusing situation in which a crowd gathers, *rumor* plays an important part in defining the situation for the crowd in such a way as to encourage direct action. In race riots, for example, rumors have swept through crowds, presenting some actual event in such a way as to arouse either whites or blacks to violent action. Rumor is the act of dealing with ambiguous situations when institutionalized forms of communication (the newspapers or radio) do not provide sufficient information. The resulting improvised definitions of what is happening is then a form of news, not necessarily false.[5]

Even when a crowd acts violently, not every one present in the crowd does so. Sometimes only a small active core commits any action, while the larger part of the crowd watches. But they do give moral support and serve both to encourage and protect the active core. Usually young males will make up the active core, with females, older people, and even children constituting the larger supporting crowd. (Perhaps it is evidence of cultural change that young women have recently been in the forefront of political demonstrations.)

Many potential situations do not produce an acting crowd, which is evidence that one or more of the necessary elements is not present. Perhaps the crowd cannot focus upon a common object of hostility, or the symbols are too ambiguous to provide a clear definition of the situation encouraging action. The gathering of crowds in tense situations always presents the *possibility* of crowd action, of mobs and riots, but it does not guarantee it.

Crowds and Violence

Although mob behavior may seem spontaneous and the least predictable of human action, it is possible to find some rough relationship between crowd violence and social structure. Violent crowds are most likely to occur around issues and situations that mark the deepest cleavages of values and interests within the society, where there is the least consensus to provide controlling norms, and where conflict between social groups and classes is the most bitter.

The struggles of blacks, of Chicanos, Indians, immigrants, farmers, and of workers in the United States is a long, unrelieved record of periodic violence during most of American history.[6] Action by college students in the 1960s against the draft pales by comparison with the extensive destructiveness of the draft riots in 1864 in New York City by improverished Irish immigrants.

Violent action in revolt against economic loss and destitution has been characteristic of American farmers for over two centuries. In the 1930s, bankrupted by mounting debts and little income, farmers burned crops, obstructed sheriffs' foreclosure sales of farm property, and even bought back foreclosed properties for mere pennies at "shotgun sales": they threatened to shoot any outsider who would bid on a property.

Nor is the use of violence only a weapon of the disadvantaged. In the South until recent years, the Ku Klux Klan demonstrated the white capacity for deliberate force and terror to keep blacks "in their place." The usually spontaneous lynch mob, in turn, was a white weapon to punish alleged black offenders against white women and by that means to terrorize the entire black community.

Labor and Violence From the Civil War until the 1930s, labor strife periodically broke out in the United States. In fact, according to two noted students of labor relations, "The United States has had the bloodiest and most violent labor history of any industrial nation in the world."[7]

Labor unions during this period were much smaller and weaker organizations than at present, and there was as yet no legal right to organize and to be represented in collective bargaining. Furthermore, law enforcement in the form of police and courts was usually on the side of the employer.

A strike, therefore, pitted the superior number of the workers against the superior armed force and legal power of the employer. Such a combination of numbers against arms led often to violent action, usually resulting in bloodshed, injuries, and death, largely of the strikers, and to jail and imprisonment for the strike leaders. The presence of almost any size crowd was usually sufficient excuse for the authorities to direct organized violence against the strikers.

Racial Violence

Racial violence, both before and after slavery, has been persistent in American life, though the 1960s brought a sustained pattern of urban violence throughout much of a decade probably unmatched in our history.[8]

An outbreak of violence which rent Harlem in the summer of 1964 was soon followed by similar violence in seven other cities, including Brooklyn and Chicago. In the summer of 1965 there was extensive rioting in Watts, the black area of Los Angeles, among five cities where violence erupted. Violence flared in twenty cities in 1966, and then in 1967 there were well over twenty outbreaks of violence, including the major burnings and destruction in Newark and Detroit.

Unlike the great race riots of the past (Chicago,

Racial violence has been a continuing pattern in the United States. When people come together to form an angry crowd demanding some redress of grievance, as these blacks in Brooklyn, New York, are doing, the potential for violence is considerable.

1919; Detroit, 1943) these were not a direct confrontation between white and black crowds. Instead, these were riots by blacks directed primarily against white-owned property in the ghetto, accompanied frequently by looting.

The results were devastating. Between 1964 and 1967, about 130 civilians, mostly black, and twelve civil personnel, mostly white, were killed.[9] 4,700 people, again mostly black, were injured, and over 20,000 persons were arrested during the riots. Property damage was in the hundreds of millions of dollars. Whole areas of Newark and Detroit looked like cities destroyed in war.

In describing the pattern of disorder the Report of the National Advisory Commission on Civil Disorders notes that there was no "typical" riot.[10] Riots did not always spring from a single precipitation incident, and the rioters were not "hoodlums," criminals, or the least educated. Instead, they were more knowledgeable than the average, even though they were also largely young high school dropouts. But they were race-conscious, race-prideful young men, hostile to both whites and middle-class blacks.[11] Furthermore, a large segment of the community supported them, though passively, and took satisfaction in the results, viewing the riot as a useful and legitimate form of protest.[12]

Violence and Politics

Most of the significant violence in American history, then — and there has been a lot — is the violence of rebellion and protest. It can only be understood by putting it into a political context. It is political because it is an act of violence against a prevailing situation of power, after efforts to use more conventional political means have failed, either because political authority was unresponsive to appeals, or because disadvantaged people were also disenfranchised and otherwise lacked legal rights.

It is for this reason, Jerome Skolnick argues, it is inadequate to analyze riots in terms of "tensions" and "frustration":

It is not that this perspective is wrong, but that it tells at once too little and too much. Too little, because the idea of "tension" or "strain" does not encompass the subjective meaning or objective impact of subordinate caste position or political domination. Too much, because it may mean almost anything; it is a catchall phrase that can easily obscure the specificity of political grievances. It is too broad to explain the specific injustices against which civil disorders may be directed; nor does it help to illuminate the historical patterns of domination and subordination to which the riot is one of many possible responses.[13]

Violence and Order   Riots are destructive events, and when they occur there is usually a call for law enforcement accompanied by pious assertions by civic leaders that there are better ways to accomplish worthwhile goals. But if more legitimate forms of social action — the courts and legislative action — cannot seem to accomplish significant change, if a group continues in its powerlessness and its felt oppression, a resort to violence may seem morally defensible. At least to many young blacks it did during the urban riots of the 1960s.[14] And so it has throughout history with other peoples.

The moral case against violence is a preference for more rational and humane action. But any moral case must rest upon the assurance that democratic society offers alternatives for effecting significant social change. When such alternatives do not prove effective for those who feel oppressed, the moral argument against violence becomes less and less convincing. It is then that situations of collective behavior produce redefinitions of norms to make legitimate action that would earlier have been illegitimate.

Authority and Violence   Violence is always a threat to the established order and so always brings a response from those in authority, sometimes more violent than the violent action they would put down. When authorities make official explanations of riots, they insist that they are senseless and irrational outbursts, even though they may be the product of pent-up frustration. As Skolnick notes, "The essential problem with this perspective is that it neglects the intrinsically political and rational aspects of collective protests and fails to take seriously the grievances that motivate riots."[15]

In addition, the official position is always that violence can accomplish no good purpose: "Violence cannot build a better society," or "violence will not solve problems," and the like. But to claim that "violence doesn't pay" is to make a moralizing judgment, not a historical or sociological one. Rioting, in fact, by different social groups and classes in the past has produced social reforms intended to get at the very source of the grievances that produced the riots. Not to make such concessions in the face of deeply felt grievances is often to invite escalation of such conflict. The only alternative is a ruthless repression, itself notably violent, and possibly the extermination of the group that is in revolt.

To say this is not to celebrate violent riots:

> This is not to maintain that violence always works or is always necessary. We do not wish to create a new myth— a myth of violent progress—which could be disposed of easily by citing examples of violence without much progress (like the American Indian revolts) and progress with little violence (as among Scandinavian Americans). The point is that political and economic power is not as easily shared or turned over to powerless outsiders as one had thought.[16]

And just because power is not shared, or a more sensitive responsiveness in authority developed, acting crowds will seek to achieve by violence what people have been unable to achieve more peaceably. Racial violence in Miami and several other southern cities in 1980 is evidence that this is a persistent feature of American society.

PUBLICS AND PUBLIC OPINION

Publics and public opinion are creations of the revolutionary changes that created democratic society. Democratic elections and freedoms of speech and press made possible free discussion of issues on which public decisions had to be made. The growth of newspapers, too, providing both information and partisan opinion, contributed to the place of public opinion in democratic societies.[17]

The Public

The public lacks the structure that one associates with well-organized groups; it has no officials, though there may be opinion leaders; there is interaction and communication, though there is no definition of membership. The public furthermore has no process of physically coming together—its interaction is not face-to-face.

The concept of the public includes several elements:

1. Some (but not all) members of a society who have some concern or interest in a public matter.
2. An issue that requires resolution or decision within that society.
3. A process of discussion among these interested individuals, carried on through available means of communication.

From these elements it would seem that the concept of public denotes not so much a group of people as a social process—a process of public discussion leading to the formation of one or more widely shared opinions as to the advisability or desirability of a public policy or a mode of action by government.

In everyday discussion the concept of public is commonly used to refer to the fans of movie and TV stars and the more devoted followers of public figures. It is also used to refer to the idea of everyone without restriction, as "the public is invited." Another use is to denote the customers and clientele of the mass producers of entertainment and material goods: the movie public, the auto-buying public, and so on. In these cases what might be called public opinion is usually *mass customer reaction* to products offered to consumption. Although this mass reaction may certainly influence production policies, it is not public opinion in a sociological sense.

There are other common misconceptions about the nature of public. One is to speak of *the* public as if it included everyone in the society. Potentially it does, but in practice it is more restricted. If the public includes those who are interested in an issue and participate in public discussions of the merits of that issue, this excludes those who are not interested and have not participated.

Furthermore, there is not *the* public—there are *publics*. Different issues are of concern to different segments of the population: school busing, abortion, energy, taxes, inflation, and national defense are issues that do not interest the same or the same number of people. The public concerned with school busing will be smaller than that concerned with taxes. The public concerned with national defense has been in the past larger than that concerned with energy, but this probably is no longer the case.

The Public: A Political Process If *public* refers to the discussion of public issues, then the public is a *political* process. According to sociologist Hans Speier, public opinion is

opinion on matters of concern to the nation freely and publicly expressed by men outside the government who claim a right that their opinions should infuence or help determine the actions, personnel, or structure of their government. . . .[18]

Ideally, then, the public is a process of political citizens—rational, intelligent, informed—discussing fully and seriously the important social issues facing the society, with free access to all relevant facts through the media of communication. Rational people in a free society—this is the image of the public. Only a democratic society could fill the requirements set forth from this perspective.

The State of Public Opinion

The actual state of public opinion in modern democratic society falls far short of the ideal process. For over forty years now, beginning with an influential work by Walter Lippman,[19] social scientists, marketing researchers, journalists, and professional pollsters have been measuring public opinion in the United States, and more recently throughout the literate world (see "Publics and Polls"). We now know a vast amount about public opinion on a vast array of issues.

What comes through from even a modest sampling of expressions of public opinion is this: Often the public seems neither well informed nor deeply concerned with many issues. Nor does public opinion seem to be the outcome of informed and serious public discussion. The image of the public that emerges from analyses by many social scientists, then, is a sorry one, damaging to the hope for an elightened public.

Dismay at the seemingly low state of public opinion is based upon the expectation that (1) all issues are within the intellectual grasp of the public, and (2) all citizens ought to be rational participants in public discussion. But many social scientists have come to the conclusion that what we know about public opinion warrants no such confident position.

Yet such a judgment may be unduly pessimistic in assessing the possibilities of intelligent public opinion while expecting too much from things as they now are. The late V. O. Key, a distinguished political scientist, wrote a sober defense of the rational capacity of the voting public, challenging seriously the unflattering image now so widespread.[20]

It does not follow, for example, that people are not rational when they take opinion cues from leaders and group representatives whom, they believe, are closer to an issue and understand all its implications better. Nor could we expect that people would approach public issues with a blank mind, innocent of any predispositions. Before they belong to publics, people belong to social groups and classes, and they think about the world in ways shaped by these group memberships. Through these they are made conscious of their interests, so their participation in public discussion is shaped by these prior experiences in social groups. We say "rationally" because it is not irrational for people to be aware of their values and interests and to assess issues against these in developing an opinion.

The Problem of Public Opinion

The shaping of public opinion does not occur in a social vacuum. It occurs within the framework of political parties and their contests for public office. One cannot understand public opinion except as one also understands something about parties, their leadership, and the structure of power in American society. And none of these encourages the development and expression of a rational public opinion.

The connection between the public and the political leader, for example, does not translate every serious concern into an issue, or turn every issue into legislative action. The political system is not that responsive. Why not? Why should it be that, according to sociologist Richard Hamilton, "there are some rather solid reasons for parties to refuse the mobilization of potential support."[21]

To understand why the political parties are only partly and incompletely responsive to the opinions of the citizens who elected them, the following need be noted.

1. Party organization is controlled by professionals, who link two basic groups: the mass of citizens, who supply votes, and the organized interest groups, who supply money. What the party does is, at a minimum, a compromise between those two interests.

2. The mass of voters, therefore, are not in direct control of the parties. They can translate their opinion

PUBLICS AND POLLS

For over forty years now, public opinion polls have been carefully developed and refined; by now *Gallup* is a household word in the United States. After literally hundreds of polls a vast amount of information has been gathered. Can we now make an assessment of the place of polls in American society? The following are some useful points in attempting any assessment:

1. *Techniques.* After much experience, and some embarrassing failures (such as *Liberty* magazine's prediction of Franklin Roosevelt's defeat in 1936, and Gallup and other polls' prediction of Dewey's election over Truman in 1948), careful probability-sampling now permits a surprisingly small number of respondents to provide an accurate sample of the population as a whole. A sample of 3,000 is sufficient to predict the outcome of a national election within a very small and measurable range of error.

Sampling is not everything; the questions asked must be clear and unambiguous in their meaning to respondents. But even here much experience has sharpened and refined the techniques of asking questions.

2. *Predicting elections.* The polls are most successful in predicting elections; now they rarely miss by more than 2 percentage points. This is because they ask people their *intention* shortly before people actually have an opportunity to act on that intention. Perhaps their greatest technical problem lies in the number who express an opinion but fail to vote.

But is this technical success of any social value? Are elections any better because pollsters can tell us the weekend before how it will come out? And is the result itself affected by the publishing of polling results?

3. *Testing political support.* Polling is now a standard tool used by politicians and parties to sound out in advance how voters might respond to a candidacy, and how they are responding during a campaign. It is of practical use, therefore, in deciding on candidates and on shaping campaigns to make the greatest appeal.

But only some of these polls are public. Those done for candidates and parties are often kept secret. If politicians then know what others do not know, particularly what the public does not know, are such polls then contributing to public understanding or to public manipulation?

4. *Public opinion.* Polls have provided much information on attitudes and opinions of the adult population on a wide range of important issues; on how opinion has changed over time; and on how such opinion varies in the population by age, race, occupation, income, region, religion, sex, and other pertinent variables. Through persistent polling we know a great deal about the state of public opinion in the United States.

5. *But is it public opinion?* What is measured by opinion polls, however, is not public opinion—a crystallized and widely shared opinion developed after much public discussion —but the aggregated mass opinions of the population. It is individual opinion counted and added up, including in this mass aggregate many individuals who really have no opinion, are not concerned with an issue, and may even know little if anything about it. Often polling occurs before any public discussion has occurred, or at least before it has advanced very far.

6. *Is the opinion poll useful?* What value do we derive from its information? Social scientists, and eventually historians, have much to learn from it, particularly in terms of trends measured over time. Carefully assessed within its limits it has a scholarly usefulness.

But is the opinion poll useful to society, not just to scholars? No ready answer can be given. It depends on what *uses* are made of the poll, and here we know much less than we know about the polling process itself.

7. *Polls and policy-making.* We do know that a favorable opinion poll does not guarantee that an issue will become policy. Gun control, for example, wins in the polls but loses in the Congress. Polls may have some role in policy-making but other factors do also—the successful pressure of various groups, the power of dominant classes in the society.

However, no one claims that polls should be translated directly into legislation. Decision-making by polls, given their character as expressing aggregate mass opinion rather than public opinion, would not be better democracy than what we now have. Judiciously used, the opinion poll can be the one important communication between citizens and their government. We need to know more about this and other possible functions of the poll before we can arrive at any adequate assessment of its place in democratic society.

into political action only by choosing the limited and often unclear options offered by the parties. They can choose one or the other of the two parties, or they can choose not to vote at all. With only rare exceptions, the general population has not been able to intervene in the "political process in order to make clear the direction of majority sentiment."[22]

3. The parties and the candidates do not deliberately make "unmistakably clear" what they stand for or will do. Instead, they often deliberately obscure the issues. Elections are interpretable in a number of ways as to what if any "mandates" were given by the voters. Indeed, the intention of the majority can be so obscured, says Hamilton, that it becomes "a relatively simple matter to 'misdefine the majority.'"[23]

The discrepancy between what the people want and what the parties deliver is considerable,and most Americans know that. Neither the parties nor politicians are held in high esteem. More to the point, a sizable number of Americans have constantly recorded their suspicion and distrust of the parties, the political leaders, and of government. The apathy of which the voting public is so often accused can be traced to a widespread feeling that government and party act in ways determined by other than the interests or wishes of the majority. Public opinion cannot help but be affected by such a feeling.

Public Opinion and Expertise

Even for many educated and concerned people, some public issues are so complex that an informed public is hard to obtain. Furthermore, leaders who must make decisions, such as legislators, governors, and presidents, cannot be expertly informed on so many matters. As a consequence, they are guided by the advice of experts as well as by the positions taken by the spokesmen for groups with definite interests in the issue. Interest groups, in turn, employ experts to advance their cause—teaching us that experts are not always objective and disinterested. Moreover, it is often to the advantage of administrators, experts, and elites to let the public assume its own incompetence to judge technical matters.

Few citizens expect that major decisions over national defense, such as the problem of choosing among alternate weapons system, are matters to be decided by public opinion, and not because so much relevant information is a military secret. Even if the information were not, the technical complexity of the matter can exceed the capacity of all but the specially trained. Even where issues are not as technical as military weapons systems, the issues are still complex—involving economic, political, administrative, financial, and tax factors understood only by those trained in these specialties. As a consequence, any concern for the function of public opinion in a democracy must recognize that the average citizen does not expect—and is encouraged not to expect—to have an informed opinion on such matters. He or she does expect the nation's political leadership to be able to make informed judgments, with the assistance of disinterested experts, and to be held accountable for the decisions it makes. How to be sure that the experts are objective, however, and how to hold political leadership accountable, become serious issues for the public as electorate.

Furthermore, interest groups often deliberately obscure and becloud issues, rather than clarify them. While lobbying and pressuring within the legislative and administrative structure, they intervene in the opinion-making process with deliberately constructed appeals. They resort to propaganda.

Propaganda: The Manipulation of Public Opinion

The formation of public opinion is rarely left to chance. Interest groups always seek to shape it to suit their own ends. As a consequence, it is rarely the spontaneous outcome of public discussion; rather, *manipulation by propaganda* is a major process.

Propaganda is the deliberate distribution of partisan (one-sided) communication in order to influence the formation of public opinion. It may be, but it does not have to be, untruthful. What distinguishes propaganda is its intent: to focus attention on an issue in such a way as deliberately to create a choice in public opinion and reduce the probability of alternative choices of opinion being made.

Unlike academic scholarship and science, its concern is not the pursuit of truth, but to convince people of a point of view. This does not mean that propagandists are intentionally dishonest, only that they are highly partisan about an issue.

In modern society propaganda is a major factor in public life, diffused extensively through the mass media. Systematic, professional work in propaganda comes from those professionally skilled in mass communication and from the communication professions.[24] Advertising and public relations provide a professional source of skilled propagandists. Public relations firms in the United States have become major businesses manufacturing propaganda for clients.

Corporations, trade associations, government agencies, and the military now regularly employ the professional skills of propagandists, who work skillfully to "fool all of the people all of the time," though they do not succeed all of the time. The basic task of these professionals is to provide the mass media with information, just as much information as they want made public—no more—selected and organized so as to put the best possible light on the organization and its interests.

The Hidden Persuaders In contemporary America, terms like "hidden persuaders" and "Madison Avenue" symbolize public awareness of these efforts to manipulate opinions about products, personalities, politicians, issues, and ideas. Vance Packard's *The Hidden Persuaders,* became a national best seller by exposing the techniques by which advertisers and public relations practitioners sought to influence opinion.[25] Its very title implies a sinister process; its major theme was that people did not know that so much of the material in mass communications to which they were exposed was deliberately contrived, without their knowledge, to shape their opinion.

How Do Mass Persuaders Persuade?

A propaganda message is built by appealing to *values* and *attitudes* in order to influence opinions. The propagandist invokes *symbols* of these underlying values and attitudes to link his particular objective to these values and, as a consequence, mold opinion in the desired direction. *Freedom, equality, socialism, private enterprise, individualism, big government, bureaucracy:* these are some of the major symbols, both negative and positive, that signify underlying values and attitudes. For example, when the public relations firm of Whittaker and Baxter undertook to direct the American Medical Association's campaign against President Truman's program for national medical insurance, they labeled it "socialized medicine" so effectively that the label remained attached to the program until long after.

Tricks of the Trade The label of "socialized medicine" is an example of *name-calling,* one of seven major "tricks of the trade" employed by propagandists. These are enumerated in an enlightening little book, *The Fine Art of Propaganda.*[26]

1. *Name-calling* means to place a bad label on something: *bureaucratic,* for example, or *communistic,* or *totalitarian.*

2. *Glittering generality* means to place a good label on it, using such "virtue words" as *American, democratic, fair-minded,* and the like.

3. *Transfer* means to identify something with something else which is highly valued. Opponents of legalized abortion practices, for

example, identify their political position as upholding the sacredness of life (*prolife*), while proponents of such practices identify legalized abortion as *freedom of individual choice* ("the right to choose").

4. *Testimonial* is the process of obtaining statements (endorsements, testimonials, etc.) from famous or respected persons to support or oppose an issue. Athletes and movie and TV stars are favorite candidates for testimonials.

5. *Plain folks* is a process of identifying the propagandist's ideas with ordinary people, making them seem down-to-earth and commonsensical.

6. *Card stacking* refers to the development of an argument that so arranges facts and falsehoods as to lead people almost inevitably to a particular conclusion.

7. *Band wagon* seeks to build support by leading people to believe that everyone is for an idea or candidate, and therefore they would do well to join the others.

The Influence of Propagandists

What accounts for the influential role of propagandists in shaping public opinion to suit special interests? The unstable character of public opinion in a changing society is bound to bring efforts at influencing it. Powerful groups of one kind or another develop vast stakes in programs and activities, and are not going to allow public opinion to develop spontaneously if that opinion has some bearing on their interests. Furthermore, the complexity of many public issues allows the propagandist to present simplified answers in acceptable symbolic terms.

In America the fears and anxieties of masses of people about world trends; about the prospects for world peace; their insecurities about a changing, uncertain future, individual and collective; their unspoken concerns about shifts and transitions in power—all these concerns give the propagandist an opportunity to influence the shaping of public opinion. Such a situation not only sets the stage for the manipulation of mass opinions, it damages belief in an informed and intelligent public opinion as a function of democracy.

Social science has contributed considerably to this damaged image of democracy by its emphasis on the low state of public opinion and the manipulation of it by propagandists. But students of social science need to keep clear the distinction between the present state of affairs—*what is*—as objectively described by social science, and an image of a future, more ideal state of affairs—*what might be*. The present state of public opinion is not in itself sufficient reason for abandoning a belief in the possibilty of a more rational process of forming public opinion. But it is a basis for understanding the present gap between the reality and the ideal, and also for understanding what characteristics of modern society prevent the ideal from being more nearly approximated.

The state of public opinion is not low because people are stupid or irrational—and is probably not as low as social scientists have been saying—but because too many interests are served by confusing, not clarifying public issues. In the face of technical complexity,

These workers are attaching such "glittering generalities" as "American" to their demands by waving the flag and putting up a patriotic sign.

ordinary citizens are encouraged to assume their own incompetency and so to rely on experts to shape public opinion. But experts are only sometimes on the public's side; often they are partisan actors in struggles for advantage and gain.

SOCIAL MOVEMENTS

People rarely accept change without making some effort to give it direction, to reshape things according to some human design—an old order to be restored or a new one to be created. *Social movements* are the conscious attempts of masses of people to bring about change in the social structure.

Social movements have arisen throughout history, from all social classes and groups: peasants and farmers, workers and shopkeepers, oppressed minorities and declining classes. Some of them are limited in their objectives: *reform* movements accept the basic values and institutions of society but seek to change what they define as abuses, defects, or inadequacies. *Revolutionary* movements, in turn, try to bring about a fundamental change in social structure, as in replacing capitalism with socialism.

Identifying Social Movements

Like crowds, social movements have been hard to study, for they are large and complex processes. Rarely can they be observed at one time or at one place. They differ from crowds and publics, however, in that they develop some structure—a core of organization, however weak and inconsistently integrated, even fragmented—and they develop a leadership.

A definition of social movement that fits our conception is: "A collectivity acting with some continuity to promote or resist a change in the society or group of which it is a part."[27]

That people act collectively, not individually, to promote or resist change is Killian's basis for claiming there are four basic features of a social movement:[28]

1. The existence of *shared values*—a goal or an objective, sustained by an ideology.

2. A sense of *membership* or participation—a "we-ness," a distinction between those who are for and those against.

3. *Norms*—shared understandings as to how the followers should act, definitions of outgroups, and how to behave toward them.

4. A *structure*—a division of labor between leaders and followers and between different classes of each. This is not a comprehensive structure, however.

Although it would be correct to say that social movements arise because people want to change the order of things, this is hardly an adequate statement of why social movements come to be. To some extent people always and everywhere would like to change things. In fact, one long and persistently puzzling question about human life is why more people do not rebel against the circumstances of their lives, why they so patiently endure oppressive and burdensome conditions.

The emergence of a social movement is not an automatic process. For one thing, individuals must communicate their dissatisfactions and share with others a *collective* sense of a common lot in life. They must identify with others who share their same fate. Spontaneous acts of rebellion and protest, silent acts of sabotage and vandalism—these may signify an underlying sense of grievance. So may voting "Communist" (or whatever is most heretical), or a withdrawal and refusal to be involved in society.

The emergence of a social movement from the appropriate underlying conditions requires the development, not only of a sense of collective fate, but of a belief in the chance to act collectively toward new goals that will bring a new life. In the absence of any *hope,* there will be no social movement.

Many social scientists believe that a social movement is most likely to occur when by an objective measurement the life of an oppressed people has improved. A mood of *rising expectations* makes people impatient with the actual pact of social change, and a movement develops to bring about change more quickly.

Yet this explanation fits some movements, not others. It does not fit movements that emerge among once dominant classes and groups, who try to resist change that benefits others to their disadvantage. The radical right movement is a fairly recent example of this;[29] another is the Southern white movement against blacks;[30] and the Know-Nothing movement against immigrants in the 1840s and 1850s is an older one. Nor does it fit nativistic movements among colonized peoples, who reject their rulers' culture but do little to change the relations of power and control. (See the discussion of nativistic movements in Chapter 15.)

Many social scientists agree that objective conditions alone will not create a social movement. There needs to be a social consciousness that finds a basis for hope. For this to happen, says Louis Killian, there must be leadership, an active nucleus sharing a "vision, a belief in the possibility of a different state of affairs, and there must be enduring organization devoted to the attainment of this vision."[31]

This is the crux of a social movement: Not merely that people are in situations which lead to a strong sense of grievance, dissatisfaction, and resentment but that they develop a perspective which makes concerted, collective action possible. Working out such an interpretation of things is the function of ideology.

The Ideology of a Social Movement

For any class or group generating a social movement, their ideology expresses a sense of grievance and injustice about society, provides a specific criticism of the existing social structure, and projects goals which are to be sought by collective action. (In turn, dominant groups and classes develop defensive ideologies to oppose such changes.) An ideology interprets an historical situation from the perspective of a group or class in order to legitimate its social movement:

Ideology performs *four* functions for a social movement:

1. It links *action* and *belief*. Ideology gives politically oriented expression to basic beliefs about justice, rights, human nature, freedom, and property, among others; thus, it interprets these basic values in concrete human situations to justify action. As political scientist David Apter points out, "ideology helps to make more explicit the moral basis of action."[32] In that way ideology provides the deepest of moral sanction—and often passionate support—for political action.

2. Ideology is *unifying*. It concentrates the energies of people onto specific projects and unites them around symbols and slogans that give specific content to their hitherto vague feelings of discontent. Thus, it provides *solidarity* to what might otherwise be a diffuse and weakly organized collectivity.

3. It provides a *collective sense of identity*. Ideology defines *we* against *them,* and *we* may be the people, the working class, la raza (the race), the chosen ones, the nation, or whatever is the collective basis of the solidarity. (It also helps shape personal identity, particularly for the young: see "Erik Erikson: Ideology and Identity".)

4. It makes a utopian future seem both *believable* and *attainable*. A movement's ideology generates a *utopian* mentality that fastens firmly on a belief in a future state of affairs. The utopian myth may seem to reach for impossible goals, but the effort to reach utopia may radically change society, even though it is not utopia which is eventually constructed.[33]

Organization and Leadership

A social movement is not the same thing as an organization, yet it needs some degree of organization if it is to mobilize people for collective action. A political party, for example, usually provides the organized core for political movements, but so can civic organizations and labor unions.

It requires an organization in order to carry out basic activities: plan rallies, publish newspapers and pamphlets, hold meetings, and work out a strategy for the campaign. Without organization, leaders lack the resources with which to function.

There are almost always competing organizations in a social movement. The civil rights movement in the South, for example, never focused around one organization. There was Martin Luther King's Southern Christian Leadership Conference, but there was also the National Association for the Advancement of Colored People (NAACP), the Student Non-Violent Coordinating Committee (SNCC, called "Snick"), the Congress of Racial Equality (CORE), and other, more local groups, as well.

In this case, as in others, new organizations came into being as the movement developed, usually over differences of ideology and tactics. When some degree of success makes an organization more moderate, a more radically uncompromising organization may be created. In other cases, a failure of strategy may lead to new groups that adopt new strategies. In the radical youth movement of the 1960s, the original Students for a Democratic Society (SDS) splintered into fractions, such as the Maoist-oriented Progressive-Labor Party and the Weathermen.

ERIK ERIKSON: IDEOLOGY AND IDENTITY

While most students of ideology have emphasized its functions of creating solidarity and legitimizing action and program, Erik Erikson has in complementary fashion pointed to the place of ideology in the formation of personal *identity.* Maturation in the person comes when personality is shaped by the search for identity and role. Because youth are the ones who have not yet found themselves, who are searching for an identity, they become particularly responsive to ideologies, for ideology helps to provide identity. That is why youth are so much more easily mobilizable for social movements than are adults, and why they are particularly responsive to dramatic action.

In explaining the appeal and the significance of ideologies for youth, Erikson says:

Ideologies offer to the members of this age-group overly simplified and yet determined answers to exactly those vague inner states and those urgent questions which arise in consequence of identity conflict. Ideologies serve to channel youth's forceful earnestness and sincere asceticism as well as its search for excitement and its eager indignation toward that social frontier where the struggle between conservatism and radicalism is most alive. On that frontier, fanatic ideologists do their busy work and psychopathic leaders their dirty work; but there, also, true leaders create significant solidarities.*

Notes

* Erik Erikson, *Young Man Luther: A Study in Psychoanalysis and History* (New York: W. W. Norton, 1958), pp. 38–39.

Leadership Many leaders of movements of the oppressed classes are themselves from more advantaged status. But whatever their social origins, leaders of emerging social movements are *charismatic;* they can rally masses of people in opposition to the established order and require no institutionalized positions in bureaucracies or traditional social structure to legitimize their leadership.

A social movement also needs more pragmatic leaders who are skilled organizers, as well as those who can devise strategy and tactics. Emphasis on charismatic leaders and intellectuals, in fact, has neglected the crucial role of the organizer, particularly in the early days of the movement.

When Movements Succeed

A movement may succeed in achieving some or all of its goals or it may fail. If a revolutionary movement succeeds, the changes in society its reforms bring

Through his demonstrated ability to rally masses of people for revolutionary action and in support of a socialist transformation of Cuba, Fidel Castro has proven himself to be a charismatic leader.

about transforms it from a protest movement into a legitimate participant in the established order. This is what happened to the labor movement of the 1930s. Its unions won legal status as the representative of workers entitled to engage in collective bargaining.

Becoming legitimate meant a significant new status for unions. They were no longer illegitimate organizations in American society; they were no longer underdogs; and they were no longer carrying on something resembling a class struggle.

Unions were transformed by this very process. The labor movement became organized labor—less a social movement, more integrated into society, less alienated from it. This transformation brought a change in leadership as well. Old leaders who had excelled at organizing workers and leading strikes now had to excel at negotiations around the bargaining table. Those who could not make the change lost out to newer leaders who could.

Labor's gradual loss of the verve and orientation of a movement was evident in the 1960s, when the new consciousness about race, peace, and poverty found organized labor either taking no significant part or even opposing protesting movements. Labor was no longer the representative of the poor; its position on race was compromised by practices of discrimination in some unions; and many of its top leadership (with some notable exceptions) were unsympathetic to the various peace groups and their demonstrations, particularly over the Vietnam conflict.

Labor found itself no longer thought of as an underdog, and no longer the spokesman for underdogs in this new period. In fact, labor was defined by the new social movements as part of the "establishment." The New Left's effort to create a movement turned away from labor and to students, poor people, black people, to strongly antiwar segments of the middle class, and to women, for its social base.

When Movements Fail

When a social movement fails to attain power, and when it fails to convert any significant number of people to its cause, frustration and bitterness and sometimes more desperate action may result. More importantly, the inability to achieve any significant goal deprives the movement of that morale-sustaining idea that the future lies with it. It loses adherents, retaining perhaps only a core of the most dedicated true believers. Even some of them may seek answers in more promising movements (see "The True Believer").

But whether a movement fails or succeeds is not an obvious matter. Socialism, by all normal accounts, failed in the United States. Yet Normal Thomas, the Socialist Party's candidate for president for six elections, has quite correctly pointed out that one of the factors in the "failure" of socialism was that its pragmatic program of social reform was "stolen" by the major parties, though not, of course, its more radical measures.

The reforms the Socialists introduced and promoted on behalf of various disadvantaged groups gradually won acceptance and were politically adopted. Legislation on behalf of working women and children, the eight-hour day, unemployment compensation and social security, union representation— these once "radical" measures have in time become social policy.

Social Movements Today

During the 1960s and the 1970s, the issue of race, peace, equality for women, and the environment have produced new social movements in the United States.

The Civil Rights Movement   A civil rights movement has been going on in American society almost throughout this century. It has been largely a middle-class movement, joining whites and blacks in common action. In that form, with Martin Luther King providing inspired leadership, it enlarged the scope of protest in the South in the early 1960s. Its most active members were recruited from black colleges, where there was a disciplined commitment to follow King in nonviolent action and passive resistance.

Integrating schools, eliminating de facto segregation, and expanding educational and job opportunities for blacks were basic objectives of the movement. If state and local government in the South was the enemy and needed to be changed, federal government was seen as an ally. This was particularly apparent in the effort to strike down Jim Crow restrictions on the use of public facilities: bus terminals, restaurants, parks, swimming pools, and the like. (Remember: it all began by sitting on a lunch counter.) No less important was the effort to get blacks registered to vote.

THE TRUE BELIEVER

Mass movements attract large numbers of alienated and disaffected persons who find a meaning for their life in a complete dedication to the movement. In doing so, they may find a solution to their personal problems or at least some therapy for them. Eric Hoffer—a brilliant, self-educated intellectual who worked most of his life as a longshoreman—called such people *true believers*. The *frustrated,* the *rejected,* and the *disaffected* who flock to a social movement give to it some of their unreasoned zeal and enthusiasm, according to Hoffer, regardless of what that movement is all about.*

But care must be taken not to confuse the true believers with others who are strong and devoted adherents of a movement, but not in any way disoriented or incapable of rational judgments. It would be a poor and very biased analysis to claim that a social movement emerged because people are irrationally disoriented by the problems of their own life. The bias, obviously, is in making it seem that those attracted to a movement demanding social change are people with psychological problems, while more rational people are therefore not attracted to any movement. This kind of conservative psychologizing is inadequate sociological analysis. When great mass movements arise, it is because established institutions are not meeting the interests and demands of large numbers of people, and they turn to a movement as a way of remedying their lot in life.

Notes

* Eric Hoffer, *The True Believer* (New York: New American Library, 1951).

But as the movement spread and involved more people, and as its young black leadership, in particular, learned from hard (and sometimes brutally violent) experiences, a rethinking took place. Even before Martin Luther King was assassinated, the first Southern phase of the movement was over.

As new and competing leaders and organizations emerged, there was no single thrust to the developing movement and no single strategy. More moderate developments competed with more militant ones, strategies of confrontation contrasted with strategies of legal petition and conventional political action. Peaceful marches led to peaceful demonstrations, but sometimes also to violence. And there were urban riots.

Two threads ran through the varied activities of the movement. One was *cultural,* a growing sense of independence and collective identity as a black people and a black community, strongest among youth. This was a rejection of assimilation into the culture and institutions of a white society.

The second was *political,* concerned with finding ways to change the economic and social inequality of blacks. These included (1) building black political power, based upon black population concentrations in central cities and in rural southern towns and counties; and (2) pressing for federal programs for affirmative action in employment and education, and for job training, housing, and urban assistance for cities.

It is evident that the equality between the races the movement has struggled for so long and so hard has not been attained. White and black, as we have seen in Chapters 10 and 11, are still two separate and very unequal social worlds.

Yet the long struggle for civil rights has changed the United States. Perhaps most importantly, the federal government is not officially and constitutionally committed to a national policy of equal opportunity and affirmative action. Furthermore, most of the old patterns of segregation, once legally sustained, are gone.

What is at issue for this movement is a basic question: Can the interests and needs of the black poor be best met by sharing in a struggle with middle-class blacks, *or* by joining forces with other poor people, white and Hispanic? The answer to that will be decisive for the future direction of the civil rights movement.

The Antiwar Movement The Vietnam war brought into being a large if amorphous base of opposition that was never one organization and never united around a single ideology. From the outset the movement was overwhelmingly a middle-class movement, and also predominantly white.[34]

Opposition to the war had a variety of bases. Some people were opposed to any war; they were truly pacifists. Others maintained a historic "isolationist" position, opposing American involvement in foreign controversies. But most opposed, not war in general, but the Vietnam war in particular, from a political perspective that opposed American intervention in the social and political struggles in southeast Asia.

From the start the antiwar movement had to fight for its legitimacy. It suffered the stigma of not being thought patriotic by many Americans. Support for military symbols and activities—respect for the uniform, for undertaking military service voluntarily, for flag-saluting and pledging allegiance—were all natural sources of support for the war, even among many Americans who thought involvement in Vietnam was a mistake. When opposition to the war produced draft resistance among college youth—including in some cases flight to Canada—"draft dodging" was seen by many as further sign of disloyalty.

For millions of Americans there was a deep, conflicting response to the war: on the one hand, their natural inclination to support their country in time of military and political crisis abroad; on the other, their growing doubts as to the wisdom of having ever become involved in Vietnam.

What the antiwar movement succeeded in doing was shifting the bulk of public opinion from approval to opposition. The vigorous debate over the legitimacy of the war undermined confidence in the validity of its objectives and in the purported reason for being there, as well as making painfull apparent the cost of the war in lives, in national unity, and in international respect.

For young Americans who became involved in the protests against the war, the experience often had fur-

ther implications. It led them into a critical position on the military, its place in American society and its ties with corporate power—the military-industrial complex. It made them conscious of the natural affinity between business; patriotic, civic, and veterans organizations; and the military, uniting politically around conservative programs. It brought them into contact with ideas about American imperialism, the cold war, and a Third World struggling to be liberated from the controls of great, dominating powers, of which the United States was perhaps the most powerful. In short, it was a radicalizing experience. From then on, for many youth the United States could never be "my country, right or wrong."

The end of the Vietnam war ended the movement as it had functioned from 1965 to 1973, but some of the changes it brought about will have permanent consequences.

The Feminist Movement Movements protesting the lot of women and seeking to change it have been prominent in the United States for over a century.[35] The suffrage movement—to make women voting members of society—brought militant action by women into the political arena until it succeeded in getting a constitutional amendment in 1920. The cause of equality for women moved slowly on, but in recent years has taken on new spirit and direction, activating a large number of women in a revival of feminism.[36]

Like other social movements, the feminist movement has no single organizational core, no one set of objectives, no single ideological orientation. Feminists can and do vary considerably on what changes they seek in the lives and status of women.

Though feminism addresses itself to the conditions of all women, its active involvement has come largely from white, middle-class, college-educated women. It is they who have forthrightly taken up arms against *sexism.* The movement is more evident at universities and in the professions than elsewhere, and its greatest successes to date have been in advancing equal employment and education for professional women.

Since we have examined the feminist struggle in Chapter 12, we shall not pursue it here. It has already changed the status of women in the society and significantly altered the relations of women to men. From now until the end of this century, the feminist struggle

Large numbers of women have now renewed the feminist struggle. This demonstration for ERA in Washington, D.C., brought together women of different backgrounds, including these members of a labor union.

for equality will be the source of a potentially radical transformation of modern society.

The Environmental Movement

A concern with the natural environment, and the harm which so many social practices do to it, is hardly new in the United States. A *conservation* movement began in the early years of this century with the objectives of conserving natural resources, protecting unspoiled wilderness, and saving endangered species of birds and animals. An impressive system of national parks and wilderness areas is an achievement of that movement.

More recently, however, the movement has undergone a significant change. While the earlier concerns remain important, a new set of issues has moved to the fore: pollution of air and water, the depletion of natural resources, alternative sources of energy, and—a central issue—the problem of nuclear power.

What is now basic to the newer phase of the environmental movement is a simple but fundamental consideration: that there is a contradiction between the established practices of the industrial economies and the preservation and maintenance of a livable, healthy environment. Necessarily, then, the environmental movement has become far more than an effort to preserve vanishing wildfowl, but a basic struggle to change long-entrenched economic practices and political policies.

In the concluding chapter (Chapter 20), we provide a more detailed examination of the issues around which this is new, significant social movement is developing in the United States.

The Significance of Social Movements

Many social scientists have been skeptical about the importance of social movements in effecting social change. They have often viewed them as so much shoving and shouting by people who feel more keenly than others the effects of changes in cultural or in social structure. Perhaps movements are interesting, they say, even exciting, because of their drama and conflict, but they are of little importance in changing society.

But sociologist Lewis Killian points out that "The

study of social movements reminds us of the irrepressible conviction of sentient men that they can collectively, if not individually, change their culture by their own endeavors."[37] When people commit themselves to social movements, that is, they assume their actions can make a difference. But can they?

The outcome of a great social transformation, such as the Industrial Revolution, may be inevitable and perhaps would have occurred without the shouting and shoving of social movements. Some social scientists, in fact, imply that all that people can do is adjust rationally to inevitable social change. This is the underlying assumption of the famous *culture-lag* theory advanced by sociologist William Ogburn.[38]

For Ogburn, the adequate use of technological and scientific innovations was usually incompatible with older cultural ways, producing the "lag" of cultural and social processes behind technological change. Human beings had to adapt to technology, rather than the other way around.

But such a thesis leaves the issue unresolved. Social change may be necessary and inevitable, but *what* social change? Are there some choices, some options for the historical actors? Industrialization and technology makes social change unavoidable, but do such changes demand any one new form of social organization to replace the old one? It would seem not. Both capitalist and communist structures, and an infinite variation within these, are institutional arrangements compatible with advanced technology.

Only a true believer in free will would assert that people can change society in any manner they choose. Probably all social scientists agree that people are bound within the framework of social institutions by which they are socialized and from which they get a perspective on the world. Karl Marx once said:

> Men make their own history, but they do not make it just as they please; they do not make it under circumstances chosen by themselves, but under circumstances directly encountered, given and transmitted from the past. The tradition of all the dead generations weighs like a nightmare on the brain of the living.[39]

Somewhere between a position that sees people as unconscious puppets of historic processes and an opposing position that sees people freely able to choose what history will be, lies a defensible ground. When people want to change their world, they rethink and re-assess and judge; and they act. What they do makes a difference, though what comes about may not be what they intended.

That is why studying social movements is useful. It tells us something important about the conscious efforts of people to determine *within limits* their destiny and to direct the processes of change in terms of their values and goals.

COLLECTIVE BEHAVIOR: A CONCLUDING NOTE

Collective behavior is not an occasional irrational outburst in an otherwise stable social order. It is, instead, a frequent and significant aspect of modern society. The frequency of its occurrence points up a major historical development: the emergence of masses of people—as crowds, publics, and social movements—to direct involvement in the great decisions of modern times.

If the evidence of collective behavior is to be taken seriously, we must learn not to overemphasize sociological ideas about stability and order. The "shouting and shoving" of crowds and movements tells us that modern people are not wholly governed by unchangeable social relations nor uncritically committed to some fixed set of cultural traditions. There is too much fluidity and change in modern culture and social relations to assume that.

Nor can we dismiss collective behavior as the irrational acts of ignorant common people blindly responding to social tensions and threatening social change. LeBon's antidemocratic bias distorts any sociological analysis of collective behavior and reduces our capacity to understand how social change occurs.

All of this reminds us once again of Karl Marx's brilliant aphorism: "Men make their own history, but they do not make it just as they please; they do not make it under circumstances chosen by themselves. . . ."

SUMMARY

Collective behavior includes all those loosely structured collectivities for which there is little division of labor, no established authority, no clear definition of membership; these include *crowds, publics,* and *social movements.*

A *crowd* is more than an aggregate of people at one place, but emerges when interaction among such individuals gives them a common focus, and concern.

It is the *acting crowd* that is the major concern of crowd theory, beginning with LeBon's, which emphasizes the loss of individuality in an emotional *contagion.* But the *emergent norm* theory argues that a crowd is a developing *collectively,* in which a situation is defined, norms emerge, and lines of action are agreed upon.

Crowd *violence* occurs around issues that mark deep cleavages of values in a society, such as race and labor in the United States. Such violence then is a form of *political protest,* which may or may not produce social reform.

The *public* came into being in democratic society, and is a *political* process of free discussion of important social issues. There are publics of varying size, depending upon issues. They are presumably *rational* processes of discussion and opinion-formation, but the reality is less than the ideal.

The public is not as irrational or uninformed or apathetic as many have said. Political leaders and parties often confuse rather than clarify issues for publics, and are often unresponsive to many concerns.

Interest groups intervene in the opinion-forming process to *propagandize,* and skilled experts in mass communication are professionals at this task.

A *social movement* is a collectivity with some continuity to promote or resist change. Its basic features are shared *values,* a sense of *"we-ness",* shared *norms,* and a *structure.*

While movements arise out of social conditions breeding grievances, they do not occur unless people have reasons to be *hopeful.*

Ideology performs four functions for a movement: it links action and belief; it provides a collective sense of identity; it unifies; and it makes a future seem both believable and attainable.

A movement must have some *organization* and *leadership.* Most movements are characterized by competing organizations.

When a movement succeeds, it brings about change, but it, too, is changed, especially by being integrated into society. A failure, however, is not obvious, since other groups often take over those of a movement's programs with greatest appeal.

In the 1960s and 1970s the issues of *race, peace, equality for women,* and the *environment* generated new social movements in the United States. The feminist movement and the environmental movement have developed into major social movements by the end of the 1970s.

NOTES

[1] See George Rude, *The Crowd in the French Revolution, 1730–1848* (New York: Wiley, 1964).

[2] Gustave LeBon, *The Crowd: A Study of the Popular Mind* (London: Benn, 1896); paperback edition New York: Viking, 1960).

[3] See Carl Couch, "Collective Behavior: An Examination of Some Stereotypes," *Social Problems* 15 (Winter 1968): 310–322.

[4] See Ralph Turner, "Collective Behavior," in Robert E. L. Faris, ed., *Handbook of Modern Sociology* (Chicago: Rand McNally, 1964), pp. 382–425, esp. pp. 384–392.

[5] Tamotsu Shibutani, *Improvised News: A Sociological Study of Rumor* (Indianapolis: Bobbs-Merrill, 1967).

[6] For a historical review, see Richard E. Rubenstein, *Rebels in Eden: Mass Political Violence in the United States* (Boston: Little, Brown, 1970).

[7] Philip Taft and Philip Ross, "American Labor Violence: Its Causes, Character, and Outcome," in Hugh Davies Graham and Ted Robert Gurr, eds., *The History of Violence in America,* A Report to the Commission on the Causes and Prevention of Violence (New York: Bantam Books, 1969), pp. 281–395.

[8] See Allen D. Grimshaw, ed., *Racial Violence in the United States* (Chicago: Aldine, 1969).

[9] Joseph Boskin, "The Revolt of the Urban Ghettoes, 1964–1967," *The Annals* 381 (March 1969): 7.

[10] The National Advisory Commission on Civil Disorders, *Report* (New York: Bantam Books, 1968). The official *Report* has also been published by the Government Printing Office.

[11] See *Report,* p. 111.

[12] See Jerome Skolnick, *The Politics of Protest, A Report of the Task Force on Violent Aspects of Protest and Confrontation of the National Commission on the Causes and Prevention of Violence* (New York: Simon and Schuster, 1969), pp. 147–148.

[13] *Ibid.,* pp. 337–338.

[14] See Boskin, *op. cit.,* pp. 12–13.

[15] See Skolnick, *op. cit.,* p. 340.

[16] See Rubenstein, *op. cit.,* p. 111.

[17] See Hans Speir, "Historical Development of Public Opinion," *American Journal of Sociology* 55 (January 1950): 376–388.

[18] *Ibid.,* p. 376.

[19] Walter Lippman, *Public Opinion* (New York: Harcourt, Brace, 1922).

[20] V. O. Key, Jr., *The Responsible Electorate: Rationality in Presidential Voting, 1936–60* (Cambridge, Mass.: Harvard University Press, 1966).

[21] Richard Hamilton, *Class and Politics in the United States* (New York: Wiley, 1972), p. 84.

[22] *Ibid.,* p. 138.

[23] *Ibid.,* p. 135.

[24] For several case studies of the techniques employed by such professionals, see Stanley Kelly, *Professional Public Relations and Political Power* (Baltimore: Johns Hopkins University Press, 1956).

[25] Vance Packard, *The Hidden Persuaders* (New York: McKay, 1957).

[26] See Alfred McClung Lee and Elizabeth Brant Lee, *The Fine Art of Propaganda* (New York: Harcourt, Brace, 1939; reprint, Octagon Books, 1972).

[27] Ralph H. Turner and Lewis M. Killian, *Collective Behavior* (Englewood Cliffs, N.J.: Prentice-Hall, 1957), p. 308.

[28] Lewis Killian, "Social Movements," in Robert E. L. Faris, *op. cit.,* p. 430.

[29] Daniel Bell, ed., *The Radical Right* (New York: Anchor Books, 1963).

[30] See David Chalmers, *Hooded Americanism* (New York: Doubleday, 1965).

[31] See Killian, *op. cit.,* p. 435.

[32] David Apter, "Introduction: Ideology and Discontent," in David Apter, ed., *Ideology and Discontent* (New York: The Free Press, 1964), p. 17.

[33] For a brilliant exposition of the political meaning of utopian myths for the modern world, see Karl Mannheim, *Ideology and Utopia,* trans. Louis Wirth and Edward A. Shils (New York: Harcourt, Brace, 1936).

[34] See Skolnick, *op. cit.,* Chap. 2, "Anti-War Protest;" and Irving Louis Horowitz, *The Struggle Is the Message: The Organization and Ideology of the Anti-War Movement* (Berkeley, Cal.: Glendessary Press, 1970).

[35] See William L. O'Neill, *The Woman Movement: Feminism in England and the United States* (Chicago: Quadrangle Books, 1971), and also his *Everyone Was Brave: The Rise and Fall of Feminism in America* (Chicago: Quadrangle Books, 1969).

[36] A useful source on its development is Judith Hole and Ellen Levine, *Rebirth of Feminism* (Chicago: Quadrangle Books, 1971).

[37] See Killian, *op. cit.,* p. 454.

[38] William F. Ogburn, *Social Change* (New York: Viking, 1922).

[39] Karl Marx, "The Eighteenth Brumaire of Louis Bonaparte," in Karl Marx and Friederich Engels, *Selected Works* (Moscow: Progress Publishers, 1968), p. 97.

SUGGESTED READINGS

David Apter, ed., *Ideology and Discontent* (New York: The Free Press, 1964). A collection of essays on the place of ideology in the modern world. See in particular essays by Apter and by Clifford Geertz.

Allen D. Grimshaw, ed., *Racial Violence in the United States* (Chicago: Aldine-Atherton, 1969). A collection of papers that covers the long historical record of violence in race relations in the United States.

Richard Hamilton, *Class and Politics in the United States* (New York: Wiley, 1964). This is a very thorough, detailed study of what survey research tells us about class and political opinion. Hamilton's Chap. 3 in particular bears directly on this chapter.

Irving Louis Horowitz, *The Struggle Is the Message: The Organization and the Ideology of the Anti-War Movement* (Berkeley, Cal.: Glendessary Press, 1970). A review of organization, idealogy, and mobilization of the movement against the Vietnam War.

Lewis M. Killian, *The Impossible Dream?* (New York: Random House, 1968). A fine study of the origins and dilemmas of the black movement in the United States in the 1960s.

Alfred McClung Lee and Elizabeth Briant Lee, *The Fine Art of Propaganda* (New York: Harcourt, Brace, 1939; reprint, Octagon Books, 1972). After more than thirty years, this remains a little gem that never loses its informative value.

Karl Mannheim, *Ideology and Utopia,* Louis Wirth and Edward A. Shils, trans. (New York: Harcourt, Brace, 1936). A twentieth-century classic on the political meaning of utopian myths for the modern world.

The National Advisory Commission on Civil Disorders, *Report* (New York: Bantam Books, 1968). Known as the Kerner Report, this is the most influential of the government-inspired reports that seek to make sense of racial violence in the late 1960s.

William L. O'Neill, *Everyone Was Brave: The Rise and Fall of Feminism in America* (Chicago: Quadrangle Books, 1969). A fine history of the feminist movement that brought the vote to women, among other things.

Richard Rubenstein, *Rebels in Eden: Mass Political Violence in the United States* (Boston: Little, Brown, 1971). A study that emphasizes the political meaning of violence in American history.

Jerome Skolnick, *The Politics of Protest, A Report of the Task Force on Violent Aspects of Protest and Confrontation of the National Commission on the Cause and Prevention of Violence* (New York: Simon and Schuster, 1969). A major sociological analysis that places violence in a political framework.

We are indeed travellers bound to the earth's crust . . . Yet we collectively behave as if we were not aware of the problems inherent in the limitations of the Spaceship Earth.

René Dubos

Twenty

ENVIRONMENT AND SOCIAL CHANGE

To focus on society, as sociologists do—on groups and classes, social structure and social change—is to risk losing sight of the fact that human society is embedded in an environment. It is also to risk losing sight of the fact that the human being is first and foremost an animal, sharing living space with other animal species in an environment on which they are mutually dependent. We forget that only at our peril.

It may be useful, then, as we approach the end of our introduction to the study of society, to restate some fundamental points we have made from time to time:

1. A human population needs to be organized in some way in order to collectively adapt to a natural environment. The cooperative activity necessary to provide the material basis for life is fundamental in the formation of society. While technology can radically alter the terms of human adaptation to the environment, modern populations are not released from the need to adapt.

2. The growth of technology enables people to extract more sustenance from nature, and so to support a large population. The *evolution* of human society from wandering bands of food-gatherers to vast urban-industrial societies has its source in this development of technology. The domestication of animals, the cultivation of crops, and successive technological improvements and innovations made possible larger, settled populations and more expanded societies. The Industrial Revolution was a recent, radical change in the adaptation of society to environment, expanding human society to undreamed of scope and permitting population growth to unprecedented size.

Such evolutionary change is accompanied by *ecological expansion,* a process of absorbing once unrelated populations into a single society extending over a wide territory. This is also accompanied by ever greater internal complexity of such enlarged societies, especially in its division of labor and its class structure.

3. The era of empires and colonies developed an international division of labor in which the colony provided raw materials and a market for finished goods, while the colonizing Western nations used the raw materials to manufacture goods for both domestic and foreign markets. Though nineteenth-century colonialism is gone, a group of modern nations, including the United States preeminently, are twentieth-century *neocolonial* powers, wielding enormous political con-

trol over supposedly independent nations, maintaining a flow of raw materials from underdeveloped nations (former colonies) and competing with one another for sources of raw materials and markets for finished goods.

These economic processes, always including trade and exchange, have rarely been contained within the boundaries of a single society. Now there is a world economy. Markets are worldwide, rich economies penetrate poor ones; and Third-World peasants and American farmers alike find their economic fate far beyond their individual control but dependent upon remote political events and distant markets.

It then becomes necessary to think of the world as a single *ecosystem*—a complicated, intricately interrelated process of interaction of environment with population on a global scale. However sophisticated technology may be, that population still must derive its sustenance from that planetary environment. Whatever are the powers of science and technology, and however removed urban people feel they are from raw nature, the link that ties human beings to nature can never be broken—not, at least, if they are to survive. Humankind cannot escape its dependence upon planet earth.

THE ECOLOGICAL PERSPECTIVE

A human ecology does not let us forget that society is but one component of human life. A society is the *organization* of a *population,* but the size and characteristics of any population depend also upon the sustaining *environment.* Organization is a collective capacity for interacting with environment; cooperative effort will be more productive than will single individuals working alone. *Technology* is a crucial factor in the interaction of people with environment. It changes the terms and conditions of that interaction; it provides more sustenance, and permits population to grow. But in turn it has resulted in more complex organization of society, more specialization and differentiation.

There is a complex interactive process among population, organization, technology, and environment. The student of society legitimately concentrates on the study of social organization while yet maintaining a perspective in which these other factors are duly noted.

Technology and Ecology

The relation of human population to nature has always involved technology. As sociologist Otis Dudley Duncan notes:

> . . . apart from language, the most distinctive feature of eco-systems that is due to the inclusion of man is the modification, or even the creation, of flows of materials, energy, and information occasioned by technology. . . . From this point of view, technology is an *extension* of the species capacity—often a very great extension indeed. . . ."[1]

Of these extensions, the greatest one has been the Industrial Revolution. Yet the ground for it was set by a long history of technological development in Europe, from perhaps as early as the eighth century. The use of fossil fuels, beginning with coal, thoroughly altered the relation of humankind to environment. From 1850 to 1950, according to Duncan, population increased at a ratio of 6.5:1 but work output grew by 65:1.[2]

Population expanded enormously, as new and unprecedented ecological expansion linked Western and non-Western peoples in systems of production and exchange, while standards of living in the Western world grew to undreamed of levels for larger numbers of people.

Such a revolutionary development apparently encourages the naive and illusory notion that technology has freed humanity from any dependence upon the environment. What can and sometimes does happen is that technology frees people from a complete dependence on the environment of a limited region, but only because technology enables a dominant people to successfully exploit the environment of another people. Thus, imperial control of other people's regions only extends human dependence on the environment to a wider area. Human populations cannot escape dependence upon environment any more than animal populations can, even if the artificial urban environment fosters such an illusion among many people.

The power of modern technology is immense, and its often indiscriminate use has altered the environment in ways unimagined only a few decades ago. As Duncan notes, "Taking more from the environment and reacting back upon the environment in more drastic and varied ways, industrial man has carried the process of 'living into' the environment beyond any precedent."[3]

The cumulative consequences of this have produced a crisis in the relation of society to environment, the full implications of which seem yet to be "unthinkable" to complacent Western people unable to imagine that high and wasteful consumption cannot be carried on indefinitely, if not extended. All the assumptions of growth and development so basic to Western ideology and social science are challenged by the somber messages coming from the ecological scientists. If we interpret these messages correctly, they tell us that some change in social organization—and probably quite radical—has to occur.

THE ECOLOGICAL CRISIS

Throughout most of human existence, the earth seemed large and limitless, and what human beings could do to it was little enough compared to what nature, in turn, could sometimes do to them. It required back-breaking toil for most people to wrest a living from nature, and their actions, however temporarily or locally harmful, had no long-run or widespread malconsequences for the environment.

That point in human history is now behind us. The immense power of technology, the spreading poison of industrial chemicals, the insatiable demand of huge populations for food and water, the vast polluting processes of modern industry—all these threaten the environment more severely than most people realize. There is an ecological crisis on the human population.

This crisis appears in a number of different forms, each one of which is technically complicated and each one of which is related to the others. We can summarize this crisis in terms of four issues:

1. *Population.* The rapid growth of population in recent centuries, and its continued growth throughout the world, presses hard on the adequate supply of food and water, even in a technically sophisticated world. All experts acknowledge that some limit on the human population is essential, though just what limit achieved how soon by what means remains a source of much disagreement.

There is some popular tendency to define the ecological crisis almost exclusively on the threat posed by the population "explosion." But population growth is intricately related to the organization of society, as well as to the distribution of resources among the societies of the earth. Even if population were to level off now, the accelerating use of energy, for example, would not, for per capita consumption of natural resources is on the increase. (We will pursue the issue of population in a little more detail later on in this chapter.)

2. *The depletion of natural resources.* If the environment is conceived of as a complex of natural resources, some of these are finite and irreplaceable—the fossil fuels (coal, gas, and oil), and minerals—supplies of which cannot last but a limited time into the future, particularly given the present rate of consumption, and increasing technological development increases this rate of consumption.

Land used for food production is increasingly lost to urban development, to soil depletion by erosion and overuse. In the same manner, *usable* water diminishes.

Furthermore, raising the standard of living throughout the world threatens to exhaust the environment even faster. To bring everyone in the world up to present American standards would require 75 times as much iron, 100 times as much copper, 200 times as much lead, 75 times as much zinc, and 250 times as much tin as is now extracted annually from the earth.[4]

Plants, too, interact in complex food chains with animals. But land clearance, deforestation, the paving over of good land, the destruction of many wild plant species, the overuse of grazing land, the building of dams, and the liberal application of defoliants destroy organisms, deprive others of food supply, and simplify the ecosystem. Cutting trees, for example, leads to erosion of the soil, which diminishes the water-retaining capacity of the area, reduces the supply of fresh water, and causes silting of dams.

Human activity, it seems, has already produced a great increase throughout the world in desert and wasteland. "In 1882 land classified as either desert or wasteland amounted to 9.4 percent of the total land on earth. In 1952 it had risen to 23.3 percent."[5] Such great deserts as the Sahara desert in Africa and the Thar desert in India are largely human-made, due to deforestation and overgrazing, and the potentiality for more such deserts in the world is considerable. Both deserts are spreading at the rate of several miles per year.

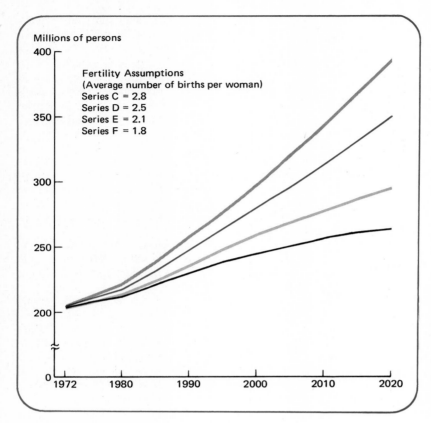

FIGURE 20.1
Projections of total population, 1972–2020. *Source:* U.S. Bureau of the Census, *Current Population Reports,* Series P-25, #493, "Projection of the Population of the United States, by Age and Sex: 1972 to 2020" (Washington, D.C.: U.S. Government Printing Office, 1972), cover.

3. *Depletion of living organisms.* People often act as if they were the only living organisms with a right to live. The destruction of other animals, from insects to elephants, even other human beings, occurs deliberately and also unintentionally but no less effectively. Animals are deprived of a living environment as human beings take over more space, or they are slaughtered to make room or to be used. Many species have vanished in the last two hundred years or so, and many more are on the endangered list.

Living organisms interact in complex ecosystems, but when some are wiped out, the ecosystem that connects one organism with another is simpler, and in that lies danger. A disruption in a simple system is more threatening to its very existence and all the organisms dependent on it, including the human one. (See "Food Chains and Ecosystems.")

4. *Pollution and poison.* Not only does human activity use up natural resources, it also pollutes and poisons. Pollution of water and air is probably the best known to publics, for drinking water and recreational use is at stake, and air fit to breathe is an issue everyone can grasp, even without knowing the technical facts. Still, there is too little understanding of the pollution potential in modern industrial processes. As Ehrlich and Ehrlich note, "Nowhere is man's ecological naivete more evident than in his assumptions about the capacity of the atmosphere, soils, rivers, and oceans to absorb pollution."[6]

Industrial waste, spilled oil, and insecticides also creep into ecosystems and food chains to poison living organisms, deplete available food, and simplify ecosystems dangerously. Poisons seeping into water enter into organisms which feed in the water, and the poison

Except for the drilling of oil wells, Alaska remains one of the last wilderness areas untouched by the resource-depleting actions of industrial capitalism.

concentrates in their system in a higher concentration than found in the water itself. (Again, see "Food Chains and Ecosystems.") An outbreak of cholera in Naples, Italy, in September 1973, for example, was traced to the eating of mussels, which came from the highly polluted Bay of Naples. A desperate government tore up the mussel beds in the bay, destroying the livelihood of many small fishermen.

Air pollution has spread from industrial cities out over oceans even to the North Pole. It kills people and destroys crops and forests. "A 1968 UNESCO conference concluded that man had only about 20 more years before the planet started to become uninhabitable because of air pollution alone."[7]

The destruction of the environment is proceeding rapidly and efforts to halt it and reverse direction are as yet small and feeble. In part this is because too many people have a naive notion that the magic of science will ultimately solve all problems. More significantly, powerful and dominant societies, such as the United States, contribute disproportionately to the ecological crisis as a consequence of enjoying a disproportionate share of the world's goods. Its political-economic structure cannot stop destroying the environment without being radically modified. But neither can there be remedy until there is a change in long-accepted beliefs and values. The roots of the ecological crisis go deep into Western history, and are not simply the consequence of industrial profit and the thoughtlessness of complacently affluent people.

The Roots of the Crisis

There is a message of some import in recognizing that the people most successful in ecological expansion—the people of Europe and America, builders of

FOOD CHAINS AND ECOSYSTEMS

Human beings and other animals survive only by obtaining energy and nutrients for growth, development, and sustenance by eating plants, or by eating animals which have eaten plants, or even by eating animals which have eaten animals which have eaten plants. Whatever may be the length of the *food chain,* it begins with plants.

Through the process of photosynthesis green plants capture energy in the form of radiation from the sun and use it to bond together small molecules into the large (organic) molecules characteristic of living organisms. When animals eat plants, they break down these organic molecules and use some of the energy in daily activity and some of it to build up large molecules of animal substance. Animals that eat other animals repeat this process of breaking down the large molecules, putting its energy to use.

In this way energy flows through a food chain. Food chains can be several steps long, as when insects eat from plants, small fish eat insects, large fish eat small fish, and birds and humans eat the fish. Humans may kill and eat the birds, too.

Sometimes there are several interlinked food chains within an ecosystem. Then organisms feed on several other organisms, and prey organisms are attacked by more than one predator.

These interlinked food chains make up a more complex ecosystem, which is then also more stable; it can the more easily compensate for changes imposed upon it.

Complex communities such as an oak-hickory forest are stable and persist unless interfered with by human beings. A cornfield, in contrast, is a very simple community, consisting of a human-made stand of a single kind of grass. It is unstable and easily subject to ruin unless constantly managed.

When toxic substances enter the food chain through, for example, a river, poison is not dissipated but instead is concentrated in organisms at each trophic (feeding) level. In predatory birds, for example, the concentration of DDT may be a *million* times as high as that in estuarine waters. Oysters constantly filter the water in which they live, and they live in shallow water in which pollution is concentrated. As a consequence their bodies contain much higher concentrations of radioactive substances of lethal chemicals than does the water from which they got them.*

Notes

* For these and other examples, see Paul R. Ehrlich and Anne H. Ehrlich, *Population, Resources, Environment: Issues in Human Ecology* (San Francisco: W. H. Freeman, 1970), pp. 159–161.

a complex industrial society—are the people of the earth who seem least of any to respect nature or see themselves as part of it.

The Religious Root According to historian Lynn White, Jr., Christianity must bear much responsibility for this perspective, for it has long taught that man has dominion over the world and all its creatures. White called Western Christianity the most anthropocentric (human-centered) religion the world has seen. "Christianity, in absolute contrast to ancient paganism and Asia's religions (except, perhaps, Zoroastrianism), not

Many large cities throughout the world suffer from constant air pollution.

But the basic perspective about the mastery of nature remained. Ecology critic Barry Weissberg reminds us of such statements as Descartes's in exclaiming the benefits of his new method for a more rigorous science: "To render ourselves the masters and possessors of nature;" and of Francis Bacon's: "Our main object is to make nature serve the business and conveniences of man."[10]

Science, too, then, reflects values that promote destruction rather than protection of nature. This is particularly the case when science is linked to technology and practical goals. The natural world becomes a thing apart and hostile, and humans feel they must conquer it.

> Unfortunately, to bastions of applied science such as the Army Corps of Engineers, conquering nature means paving it over with dams, highways, and airports, poisoning all the bothersome insects, killing off the wild animals that could frighten or attack people, filling in the swamps, chopping down the trees, and installing several chlorinated swimming pools where there was once a lake . . . there has to be a radical rethinking of the initial premise that the universe is something "out there" apart from us and hostile to us.[11]

The Technological Root   For many centuries now Western people have been superb technicians. They advanced technology well before they developed science. According to historian White, between A.D. 800 and 1000 Europe moved well ahead in technological development, not merely in craftsmanship, far outstripping the more sophisticated cultures of Byzantium and Islam. By the end of the fifteenth century the technological superiority of Europe enabled its small nations to conquer, loot, and colonize much of the rest of the world.[12]

Ecology and Capitalism

Western capitalists have shared this same orientation to nature that had its origin in Christianity—nature is to be mastered. From this perspective, land, water, minerals and fossil fuels, forests and animals, all the components of the environment, are but commodities in a market system—*valuable* if they can be used for producing goods or sold for some human use, *worthless* if that is not the case.

Competitive capitalists were long unrestrained in their exploitation of natural resources—and of human beings, too—dumping waste material into streams

only established a dualism of man and nature but also insisted that it is God's will that man exploit nature for his proper ends."[8]

By destroying the pagan religions which paid respect to the spirits residing in natural objects, Christianity bred in people an indifference to feeling in nature:

> The whole concept of the sacred grove is alien to Christianity and to the ethos of the West. For nearly 2 millennia Christian missionaries have been chopping down sacred groves, which are idolatrous because they assume spirit in nature.[9]

The Scientific Root   The early roots of modern science lie in religious motivations, for generations of early scientists studied nature for the better understanding of God. It was not until the late eighteenth century that scientists outgrew this religious underpinning of their scientific work.

and cutting down forests without regard to the needs of future generations. In the early decades of this century a new generation of corporate capitalists recognized that their own self-interests were better served by stopping such wanton destruction of natural resources; as a consequence, they made conservation their own cause.

Though American corporate capitalism may have adopted conservation as a useful cause, other practices destructive of the environment have multiplied —the pollution of rivers, for example. Even now land and natural resources are not yet defined as a natural resource. Instead the logic of private property still applies; land and oil and minerals, even water, are defined as the property of individuals (including corporations), to be used in the market as they see fit in making profit. Whether the private entrepreneur is the sole individual or the large corporation, the conception of environment as property for profit largely prevails. The very fact that economic growth depends on increased consumption of energy, and that such consumption is a major source of corporate profits, suggests a fundamental conflict between American capitalism's basic practices and attaining ecological balance.

Capitalism and Social Costs   One reason that capitalism has apparently been so successful in providing us with a mass of consumer goods and thereby increasing the standard of living is that all the costs of production are not added in under present systems of cost-accounting or of economic analysis. Many of the social costs of production are shifted onto individuals or on the community or even onto future generations.

According to economist K. William Kapp, social costs are "all direct and indirect losses suffered by third persons or the general public as a result of private economic activities."[13] It includes those consequences of production which do damage and cost someone something to repair—air and water pollution, depletion of animal and energy resources, soil erosion and depletion, or deforestation, for example. But many social costs are the impairment of human beings through injury, disease, and loss of livelihood. The long and as yet not fully successful struggle to assign medical and other costs arising from "black lung" disease among coal miners to the coal industry as a necessary cost of production is a striking example.

Given the ideology of free enterprise, it has always been difficult to measure and assess these costs (which economists call "externalities"). Given the power of corporate capitalism, it is even more difficult politically to fix the responsibility for such costs on private enterprise. Forcing industry to take steps to reduce pollution leads many businessmen to complain that their individual competitive position will be reduced by additional costs, or to seek to enlist consumer support on the grounds that such costs will have to be passed on to the purchasing public. More recently, given the poor view the public has of governmental bureaucracy, it has been fashionable to complain of the costly burden of federal regulations.

The production of automobiles that no longer create physically harmful smog will raise the price of such products to the consumer. Apply that to a large range of products, from residential construction to transpor-

Strip mining for coal is but one of the many profitable practices so destructive of the environment.

tation to food and clothing, and it becomes clear that the high material standard of living produced by American capitalism has been facilitated by transferring social costs to individuals and publics or to future generations, or sometimes leaving the cost unpaid, as when polluted Lake Michigan and Lake Erie beaches are simply closed and withdrawn from public use.

Kapp's thesis that private enterprise escapes paying the social costs of doing business, and that this is a major factor in the ecological crisis, is not intended to place sole responsibility for ecological damage on capitalism alone. When a municipality dumps raw sewage into a river and pollutes someone else's water supply, or when a socialist government builds up industrial production with little thought to water pollution, as the Soviet Union has done,

. . . they sacrifice the quality of the environment for revenues by choice; that is, their action is similar to that of a private firm operating in accordance with the principle of investment for profit. Both try to maintain an artificial, purely formal short-run financial solvency by ignoring social costs.[14]

It would seem sufficiently apparent that the ecological crisis of our time is deeply rooted in the religious, scientific, and technological values of Western culture, as well as the structure and practices of economic production. But no discussion of this crisis is possible without also examining the growth of human population and its relation to the natural environment and to the organization of social life.

POPULATION

In recent years a popular emphasis upon the "population explosion" has pointed to high birthrates throughout the world, attributing to them an alarming growth of the world's population. But this only obscures the complex process of population growth or stability that must be understood if population is to be examined as one component of the ecological complex.

There is a subtle but profound relationship among population, organization, technology, and environment. Significant changes in the structure of society usually produce changes in the composition or characteristics of population, and these interact with the environment—usually altering it in some fashion—which then has further impact on society and on population. Population, therefore, is but one factor in a dynamic process of ever changing relationships.

Demography

The specialized activity that studies the characteristics and composition of human populations is *demography*. Its most basic and reliable information is obtained by census. (See "Counting People: The Census.") As yet, there is no fully reliable census data for much of the world so that demographers must still estimate some population factors from various indices and indirect information.

The demographer studies three basic phenomena: *births, deaths,* and *migration*. Taken together, these describe the growth and decline of a human population in a given region or geographical area. On a world basis, migration cannot add or subtract from the total, but the shift of population from rural to urban, or from one continent to another, is still an important factor in understanding population growth.

Environmental factors begin with the fertility of the soil, the abundance of game, the character and distribution of plants and other vegetation, and the availability of water, and the climate. But these components do not remain virginal. Human practices may, for example, hunt out game or reduce the fertility of the soil, either reduce the water supply or pollute some of it, or destroy useful vegetation. Thus the environment is always modified in interaction with a food-producing population, and that modification has implications—sometimes severe—for the level of population that can be sustained by the environment.

Cultural factors include knowledge and skills of a practical kind for producing food, warding off disease, and promoting nutrition. But customs about mate selection, religious and moral beliefs about conception and birth, values about marriage, family, and children, dietary habits, sanitation and health practices—these and other cultural factors also influence the population structure of a society.

Social factors must also be taken into account: the degree of urbanization, the efficiency of social organization to exploit technology and environment, the formation of a labor force, the class structure, migration patterns, the organization of the economy, and the level of technology.

COUNTING PEOPLE: THE CENSUS

The effort to make an accurate count of the people in a region or a country is very old; in Babylon and China there were population censuses as far back as 3000 B.C.

Yet these censuses were never popular with ordinary people, and for good reason. Too often it meant conscription, confiscation, or higher taxes. It was an instrument of political and economic control, and for that reason, rulers tried to keep results secret, even as the people tried to escape being counted.

Modern censuses began in the French and British colonies in what is now Canada in 1665, then in Iceland in 1703. A census was introduced in Sweden in 1748, in Denmark in 1769, and in the United States in 1790, followed by Great Britain in 1801. Russia did not undertake a full enumeration of its population until 1897, and Turkey not until 1927.

The United States census was provided for in the Constitution (Article I, Section 2) as the basis for determining apportionment of representatives in Congress among the states. Thus, Congressional seats are always reapportioned after every census.

By now the census does not merely count the number of people in the country. It enumerates them by age, sex, race, national origin; it records their education, occupation, income, and place of residence. It counts their houses, with and without plumbing or electricity. It records their migration from rural place to city, from city to suburb, from one state and region to another. It also undertakes censuses of manufacturing, farming, and business every five years.

Nor does the Bureau of the Census, first established in 1902, content itself with the decennial counting. In between it undertakes samples of changes in population characteristics, so that fairly accurate projections can be made each year.

In tracing the movement of population from rural to urban places, the Bureau of the Census invented such things as the small *census tract,* and defined for us what we have come to mean by *urban,* by *metropolitan area,* the *urban fringe* and the *central city.* (See "Measuring the Urban Population" and "Defining the Metropolitan Area" in Chap. 8.)

Fertility and Mortality

Demographers measure the growth of a population by the relationship between birthrates and death rates, between fertility and mortality. (For explanation of demographic terms, see "The Language of Demography.") Migration can add to or subtract from this.

If we start with the idea that the birthrate can be high or low, and the death rate can also, this allows for four logically possible combinations: (1) high birthrates and high death rates; (2) low birthrates and low death rates; (3) high birthrates and low death rates; and (4) low birthrates and high death rates.

High Birthrates, High Death Rates   The first of these—the combination of high birthrates and high death rates—has been most common throughout human history. It is the pattern even now in many agrarian, nonindustrialized sections of the world, even as it was found in the Western world prior to the Industrial Revolution.

In tribal and peasant societies the large extended family is the basic organizing unit of social life, the work group of an agrarian economy. Such societies put a high value on fertility for high fertility has been necessary for survival in societies in which life expectancy was short and in which the infant mortality rate

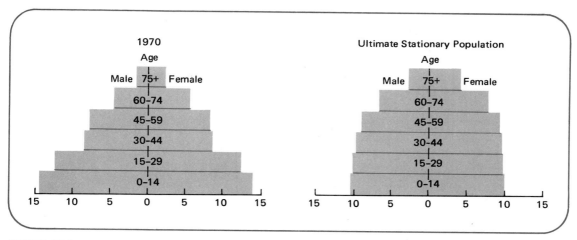

FIGURE 20-2
Percent distribution of the population by age and sex, 1970, and ultimate stationary population. *Source:* U.S. Bureau of the Census, *Current Population Reports,* Series P-25, no. 480, "Illustrative Population Projections for the United States: The Demographic Effects of Alternate Paths to Zero Growth" (Washington, D.C.: U.S. Government Printing Office, 1972), p. 5.

was high. In some past societies perhaps most infants failed to live to a reproducing adulthood.

In these societies, then, a high birthrate is balanced off by a high death rate. A low standard of living, hard physical toil, exposure to disease, poor diet, a lack of sanitation, even periodic famine in some cases, and a limited technology all promote a high death rate and a short life expectancy. According to demographer Irene B. Taueber, life expectancy typically fluctuates around 25 years, and the death rate averages around 40 per 1,000 total population.[15]

This often means that such societies have a higher proportion of their population below the age of 14 than any modern society does and also a much smaller proportion over 65 years of age—even a smaller proportion over 40. The birthrate fluctuates with circumstances but averages 40 per 1,000 population. Although population changes both upward and downward in the short run, there is no persistent trend in either direction.

The Western Demographic Transition

Over the last 300 years or so, the Western world has gone through a major change in the relation of births to deaths—a process usually called the "demographic transition"—that has led to an enormous gain in population. Economic, technological, and social development in the seventeenth and eighteenth centuries, followed by increased industrialization in the nineteenth, reduced the death rate dramatically, while the birthrate changed only moderately. It gave Europe a tremendous growth in population, from 103 million in 1650 to 274 million in 1850, while millions more migrated to the Western Hemisphere.

In the United States the surplus of births over deaths produced a doubling of population once every 23.5 years between 1790 and 1860. But this was only a transitional phase; in due time birthrates fell. The gap between births and deaths that produced such leaps in population growth occurred in a demographic transition from a high birthrate-high death rate society to a low birthrate-low death rate society.

Mortality

Unlike fertility, death is not a major positive value in any society. That people are mortal is accepted from one or another religious orientation, but any society will reduce the death toll by whatever means is avail-

THE LANGUAGE OF DEMOGRAPHY

There is a number of terms that demographers use, each of which is given a statistical expression. Some of the more basic ones are the following:

The *birthrate* is computed on the basis of every 1,000 persons in a specified population in a given year. Thus, a birthrate of 18 means an average of 18 births for every 1,000 persons in the population.

This is a *crude* birthrate, in contrast to *specific* birthrates, computed on the number of births per 1,000 living persons of designated age, sex, or of family status in a specified population in a calendar year.

Like the birthrate, the *death rate* is computed on the basis of every 1,000 persons in a specific population in a given year.

The *fertilty rate* is the number of births in a particular population for every 1,000 women of childbearing age, generally defined as from fifteen to forty-five.

The *population growth rate* measures the growth of a population as a percent annual increase. A growth rate of 2 percent, for example, means that 20 persons per thousand (2 per every 100) are added to the population each year. The rate of *natural increase* (or *decrease*) is obtained by subtracting deaths from births. In addition, gains or losses by migration need to be measured to measure population growth.

able to it, except where such means would violate sacred values. Until recently, few societies had any effective means for warding off an early death, and life for the vast majority of people was short. Poorly fed populations were ravaged by diseases that they little understood and over which they had no control.

The first year of life has always brought the greatest danger of death; death in this first year—infant mortality—is always high in impoverished, agrarian populations. In the United States, infant mortality has only dropped significantly since 1900 when the infant death rate was 162.4 per 1,000 live births. By 1930 it was 64.6, and by 1977 it was 14.0.[16]

This reduction in the death rate has increased life expectancy in the United States and in other societies in which the same changes have taken place. By 1977 in the United States life expectancy was almost 73 years—fairly typical for a modern society.

When the decline in mortality increases life expectancy, significant changes occur in the population. Since people live longer, a higher proportion of them are in the older age brackets. In the United States those over 65 have increased, not only in absolute numbers but as a proportion of the population. They have in fact increased from 4.1 percent of the population in 1900 to 11 percent in 1978.[17]

Because more people live longer, but not necessarily better, either physically or psychologically, there has been an accelerated interest in the field of gerontology (the study of the aging process) in the last two decades. The physical, mental, and social needs of people who have mostly retired, voluntarily or not, from regular employment, and who are allowed no useful, respected role in society, has made aging a social issue of growing importance. Despite much sentimental rhetoric about "senior citizens" and "golden years," the lack of any useful function for most people over 65 years of age robs increased life expectancy of the kind of cultural and moral value it could have.

Fertility

In the United States, as in most Western countries, a long-run decline in the rate of fertility has occurred. In the United States the low was reached in the mid-1930s, but then it increased again, and the birthrate increased (see Table 20.1), contrary to what demographers had expected.

The increased birthrate peaked at 26.6 in 1947, but remained around 25 through the 1950s. After that it steadily declined to an historic low of 14.8 in 1975 and 1976; then it again showed an increase.

TABLE 20.1
Crude Birthrates in the United States, 1920–1977

Years	Number of Births per 1,000 population
1920	27.7
1930	21.3
1935	18.7
1940	19.4
1945	20.4
1950	24.1
1955	25.0
1960	23.7
1965	19.4
1970	18.4
1971	17.2
1972	15.6
1973	14.9
1974	14.9
1975	14.8
1976	14.8
1977	15.3

Source: U.S. Bureau of the Census, *Statistical Abstract of the United States: 1978* (99th ed.) Washington, D.C., 1978.

The Future American Population

Since 1970 there has been a sharp decline in fertility and during the 1970s an equally sharp decline in the birth expectations of young wives. This has led the U.S. Bureau of the Census to develop new projections for the future of the population, including the possibility of achieving zero population growth.

A new set of assumptions of completed cohort fertility (average number of births per woman upon completion of childbearing) range from a high of 2.8 to 2.5 to 2.1 to 1.8. The difference, then, is 1.0 child per woman. Between 1970 and 2000 such a seemingly small difference of one birth per woman for future childbearing cohorts means a difference of about 50 million in the population by the year 2000. There would be 300 million Americans in the year 2000 if the higher assumption prevailed, 250 million if the lower assumption prevailed (See Figure 20.1). A very small change in the birthrate can have large conse-

quences for the rate of population growth, given the already large population and the relatively high proportion of females in the childbearing years.

Zero Growth When? Under certain assumptions, zero population growth in the United States could come by the year 2028, which is 56 years from projections based on 1972 data. Under other assumptions, it could be as late as 2062. The first assumption is that the total fertility rate moves down to 1,500 (equivalent to 1.5 birth per woman) in 1980 and then gradually moves up to 2,110 (2.11 per woman, which is the level of fertility required for a population to replace itself exactly under projected mortality rates and in the absence of immigration). Table 20.2 provides some examples of projecting the year of zero growth and the size of the American population when that is achieved. Figure 20.2 contrasts the distribution of the American population by age and sex in 1970 with an ultimate stationary population brought about by zero growth.

World Population Growth

Whatever may be the prospects for limiting population growth in the United States, such prospects for the world's population are quite another matter. The present trends in Europe and the United States differ considerably from those in other parts of the world, particularly in the underdeveloped countries.

Measuring the world's population is at best a hazardous process, and even now large areas of the world possess no accurate census. Careful estimates of population and of rate of growth are necessary.

The following is a demographic assessment from the best available evidence of world population since 1650.[18]

YEAR	POPULATION (IN MILLIONS)
1650	545
1750	728
1800	906
1850	1,171
1900	1,608
1950	2,406
1977	4,257

What the above figures say is that world population is increasing rapidly, and that it has increased almost sevenfold since 1650. Prior to that, demographers believe, it increased only slowly, with high birthrates offset by high death rates.

TABLE 20.2
First Year of Zero Growth and Population Attained
Under Selected Projection Series Assuming No Immigration.

	Series T	Series V	Series W
First Year of Zero Growth			
Early Timing Pattern[1]	2,062	2,028	2,038
Late Timing Pattern[1]	2,058	2,028	2,034
Total Population in First Year of Zero			
Growth (in millions)			
Early Timing Pattern[1]	310,187	255,426	294,522
Late Timing Pattern[1]	297,933	249,433	276,224

[1] Mean age of childbearing: early timing pattern, 25.0; late timing pattern, 27.8.

Series T: Total fertility rate remains at 1970 level until 1980 and then declines to 2,110 (replacement level)

Series V: Total fertility rate drops to 1,500 by 1980, then gradually increases to 2,110.

Series W: Total fertility rate drops immediately to 2,110.

Source: U.S. Bureau of the Census, Current Population Reports, Series B-25, No. 480, *Illustrative Population Projections for the United States: The Demographic Effects of Alternate Paths to Zero Growth.* Washington, D.C., 1972.

The growth rate of the world population, according to the estimates of demographers, is 1.9, meaning 19 people are added to each one thousand in the world population each year. At such a rate world population will double again in 37 years. Demographer Irene Taueber points out that with the world's present population "increasing at rates of growth four or five times those of recent centuries, simple forward projections for a few more centuries yield numbers that are not possible on a finite earth."[19]

Comparing Developed and Underdeveloped Worlds Even a simple contrast built upon a few statistics makes it plain that the developed world stands in sharp contrast to the underdeveloped world in its demographic structure. Table 20.3 compares a selected set of countries in both the developed and underdeveloped world on some basic demographic phenomena: birthrates and death rates, infant mortality rates, life expectancy, and population under 15 years of age.

Within the developed countries, the range of any one of the rates if fairly small. The birthrate ranges from 10.0 (West Germany) to 18 (Hungary and USSR), while the death rate ranges from 6 (Japan) to 12 (West Germany, Great Britain, and Hungary). There is a somewhat greater range in infant mortality,

from Sweden's 8 to Hungary's and the USSR's 30. The life expectancy range is narrow, from 70 to 74. The percentage of people under 15 years of age ranges from 21 percent (Hungary, Sweden, and West Germany) to the United States 28 percent.

The underdeveloped countries, in contrast, offer a strikingly different profile. Birthrates run from 37 to 49, death rates from 12 to 20, and infant mortality from 71 to 130. Life expectancy is much lower, and the percent of their population under 15 years of age is in every case over 40 percent—from 41 to 48—suggesting what an enormous potential they have for sustaining a high birthrate in the near future, and consequently for rapidly increasing population, even if fertility should decline.

An inspection of Table 20.3 reveals that the underdeveloped nations have a greater gap than do the developed ones between their birthrates and their death rates. Mexico, indeed, has a death rate lower than some developed nations. In part, this is because such countries have so large a part of their population in the younger age categories; the age structure in a country affects the death rate.

But since 1940 underdeveloped countries have experienced a greater decline in their death rates than in their birthrates, and have done so without signifi-

TABLE 20.3
Demographic Aspects of Selected Developed and Undeveloped Countries

	Birth Rate	Death Rate	Infant Mortality	Live Expectancy	Population Under 15 years (percent)
Developed Countries					
United States	15	9	15	72	28
Great Britain	12	12	14	72	23
Sweden	12	11	8	75	21
West Germany	10	12	17	71	21
USSR	18	9	30	70	26
Hungary	18	12	30	70	21
Japan	16	6	10	74	24
Undeveloped Countries					
Egypt	39	13	108	53	NA
Ghana	48	17	115	49	46
Tanzania	45–49	16–18	120–130	45–59	44
India	37	17	134	47	41
Philippines	40	12	80	58	46
Indonesia	42	20	126	42	43
Mexico	44	10	71	61	48

Source: U.S. Bureau of the Census, *World Population: 1977 —Recent Demographic Estimates for the Countries and Regions of the World,* Washington, D.C., 1978.

cantly altering their social structure. Rather, deliberate intervention by developed countries helped to control infectious diseases and to introduce measures of public health. The Ehrlichs call this "exported death control." Control of malaria, yellow fever, smallpox, cholera, and other infectious diseases have been responsible for sharp reductions in the death rates of most of the underdeveloped countries.

In the decade 1940–1950 the death rate declined 46 percent in Puerto Rico, 43 percent in Formosa, and 23 percent in Jamaica. In a sample of 18 undeveloped areas the average decline in death rate between 1945 and 1950 was 26 percent.[20]

Implications of Population Growth   Whatever may have been the intention and justification for controlling diseases and reducing the death rate in these underdeveloped countries, humanitarian or otherwise, the

consequences for the future are sobering. Ehrlich and Ehrlich assert that by lowering the death rates in these societies, "the world growth rate moved from 0.9 (doubling time 77 years) in the decade 1940–1950 to a rate of 1.8 percent (doubling time 39 years) in the decade 1950–1960."[21] By the 1970s the growth rate was 1.9 (doubling time 37 years).

The rapid growth of population in poor countries will not only contribute to world population growth but will also mean that population in underdeveloped countries will grow faster than in developed countries, and thus become a larger proportion of the world population. Table 20.4 provides evidence for this. The underdeveloped countries, which by 1975 already had over 70 percent of the world's people, by the year 2000 will have about 80 percent.

Further evidence comes from Table 20.5, where the moderate growth rates of the United States, as well as the Soviet Union and Japan, contrast sharply with

A high birthrate in India and other Third World countries is one factor contributing to the rapid increase in world population.

the high growth rates of some of the world's poorest countries.

If the evidence from these two tables is a fair estimate of population growth in the world—and assuming no great catastrophe: nuclear war or a worldwide famine—in the quarter century from 1975 to 2000 the world's population will grow from 4.10 billion to 6.35 billion.

Population Growth in Perspective

From the time of Malthus to now, this sobering prospect of more people than the earth can feed, with consequent human misery, has been a spectre of fear and concern (see "Malthus: The Problem of Human Survival"). Yet to make population growth alone the central factor in the present ecological crisis may—conveniently, for the people of the developed nations—put the blame on birthrates in underdeveloped countries and in effect define them as responsible for the world crisis. That would be a distortion of a complex problem.

To put the problem in perspective, the basic issue is that to sustain population requires an adequate supply of food and water. But the largest and fastest growing populations do not necessarily consume the most. Living standards vary considerably, and the Asiatic nations with the most people still do not consume most of the world's natural resources. The *richest* nations, of which the United States is first, do that.

The domination of underdeveloped countries by developed ones becomes even more politically strained than it is now when population growth increases the poor countries' share of the world's people but not of the world's wealth.

TABLE 20.4
Population Estimates of Growth of World Population: 1975–2000 (Medium Series)*
(population in millions)

	1975	1980	1990	2000
World	4,090	4,470	5,340	6,350
More Developed Regions	1,131	1,170	1,252	1,323
Less Developed Regions	2,959	3,300	4,088	5,027

* Based on assumptions, this is a medium estimate of population growth. See the source cited for high and low series.
Source: U.S. Bureau of the Census, *Illustrative Populations of World Populations to the 21st Century* (Current Populations Reports: Special Studies: Series P-23; no. 79), 1979, pp. 17–18.

THE CRISIS OF GROWTH

The concept of growth—of steadily increasing material production, growing national and personal wealth, and rising standards of living—has been an explicit fundamental value in the development of Western industrial-capitalist societies for over two centuries. And most socialist societies have retained those same values.

But if "more" and "bigger" have been prized, the various social consequences of growth until now have

TABLE 20.5
Total Population and Net Growth, 1975 to 2000, and Average Growth Rate,
for Selected Countries (Medium Series)

	Total Population (millions)		Net Growth, 1975 to 2000		Average Annual Growth Rate	Percent of World Population	
	1975	2000	Millions	Percent	Percent	1975	2000
China	935	1,329	394	42	1.4	22.9	20.9
India	618	1,021	403	65	2.0	15.1	16.1
Indonesia	135	226	91	68	2.1	3.3	3.6
Pakistan	71	149	78	111	3.0	1.7	2.4
Nigeria	63	135	72	114	3.0	1.5	2.1
Brazil	109	226	117	108	2.9	2.7	3.6
Mexico	60	131	71	119	3.1	1.5	2.1
United States	214	248	34	16	0.6	5.2	3.9
USSR	254	309	55	21	0.8	6.2	4.9
Japan	112	133	21	19	0.7	2.7	2.1

Source: U.S. Bureau of the Census, *Illustrative Projections of World Populations to the 21st Century* (Current Population Reports: Special Studies: Series P-23; No. 79), Washington, D.C., 1979, p. 8.

MALTHUS: THE PROBLEM OF HUMAN SURVIVAL

In 1798, in his "Essay on the Principle of Population," Thomas Malthus (1766–1834) advanced the proposition that population growth tends to exceed the food supply. Specifically, Malthus postulated that population grows at a geometric ratio of $1:2:4:8:16$, whereas the food supply grows only at an arithmetic ratio of $1:2:3:4:5$. When this happens, human misery in the form of war, famine, plagues, and infanticide increases until population is checked.

These *positive* checks occur if people do nothing to prevent population exceeding food supply. *Preventive* checks, in turn, which Malthus advocated, are basically a moral restraint: abstention from sexual relations outside of marriage, postponement of marriage for the individual male until he can support a family, even celibacy for some. But Malthus was pessimistic about very many people being capable of practicing such restraints; accordingly, he foresaw misery in the human future.

Demographers have long since abandoned the details of Malthus's theory, but his basic thesis—that population tends to grow in excess of food supply—has come alive again as one of the significant issues of our time. In the shorter run of time, for a century beyond Malthus, his dire predictions seemed not to fit the Western situation. Even though population grew, the rapid spread of industrialization and the opening up of the grassy plains of North America to cultivation seemed to negate Malthus's warnings. Even Malthus acknowledged he did not anticipate the great increase in cultivable land, nor the improvement in agricultural techniques that increased food production several times over.

But the growth of the world population in the last half century or less, and its projected growth if unchecked in the next 30 years, coupled with an insatiable consumption of natural resources particularly in the rich societies, all become aspects of an ecological crisis that makes Malthus's concerns, if not his specific theory, relevant again.

been largely ignored. One of these consequences has been population growth in the world as a whole. From the perspective of the present social organization of human populations and supporting technology and resources, there may already be too many people:

Taking into account present population densities and the other factors involved in carrying capacity, we arrive at the inescapable conclusion that, in the context of man's present patterns of behavior and level of technology, *the planet Earth, as a whole, is overpopulated.*[22]

The Ehrlichs' sober comment is one of a growing school of scientists who have warned that we are soon to exceed, if we have not already, the earth's carry capacity.

The threat of world population growth, however, is not merely a threat of an impending Malthusian disaster at some further time, or of famine and starvation among the least fortunate. It also implies increasing political struggle and a revolt against the now quite unequal distribution of the planet's sustenance among the *have* and the *have-not* peoples of the world.

But the troublesome growth of population is only one of the threatening consequences of economic growth; so also is the increase in pollution to a point endangering human survival. At the same time, the earth's natural resources, the exploitation of which made growth possible, are being rapidly depleted. Furthermore, the inequality in the shares accorded different peoples of the earth in the benefits of economic growth threatens a worldwide struggle over sharing.

The Limits of the Earth   The earth is a limited ecosystem, capable of sustaining only a limited though perhaps quite large population. The sources of food and water are not infinitely expansionable. The world's population, however, is increasing so rapidly that it cannot go on indefinitely growing at its present rate without ensuring disaster.

The problem, however, is not simply one of population and environment. In the underdeveloped societies population is growing most rapidly, but in the developed societies the much higher standards of living consume greater quantities of the earth's finite resources. If the underdeveloped societies change into developed ones, they will also develop a different population structure, one of lower birthrates and lower death rates. But the rising standard of living that accompanies modernization may threaten even more the finite limits of the earth.

The Limits of Growth

The sense of an impending crisis was sharpened during the 1970s by the publication of a report from the Club of Rome, a group of American and European scientists, industrialists, economists, and others, who organized a research project at the Massachusetts Institute of Technology on the environmental crisis facing all of mankind. The report offered little comfort: the industrial societies, it said, face an inevitable catastrophe, a total collapse, unless radical measures to limit both population growth and industrial growth are instituted soon.[23]

The present pattern of growth, if it continues, threatens to deplete the nonrenewable natural resources on which industrialism depends. Such depletion would result in the breakdown of industrialism and this, in turn, would bring death by famine to millions. However, if new sources of these depleting resources were discovered, the impetus given to further industrial growth would bring about a new, destructive level of the pollution of water, air, and soil. If pollution is successfully controlled, the unchecked growth of population would soon surpass the earth's capacity to feed that population.

The only way to avoid disaster, according to the study, is by putting a severe limit on growth. World population has to be stabilized, so that birthrates do not exceed death rates. Industrial growth must be severely limited; pollution reduced; the demand for consumer goods also reduced; eroded soil restored and agriculture improved and extended so that food production is increased; and natural resources used at a sharply reduced level.

But this radical solution of no-growth is as unwelcome to industrial societies as are predictions of impending disaster. A program of no-growth would seriously disrupt the world's industrial systems, for they are committed to steady growth. Furthermore, a program of no-growth would seem to deny to the many impoverished and dependent societies of the Third World the opportunity to industrialize and so to raise their standards of living. In both cases, then, there are strong reasons to refuse to accept the message, no matter how convincing the evidence may be.

This combination of dire predictions of disaster and a drastic and unwelcome solution has prompted challenges and criticisms from scientists, engineers, and economists, who see other possibilities of solution than are offered by these "models of doom."[24] The Club of Rome argument for impending disaster, they point out, is built upon certain assumptions; their conclusions, therefore, depend upon the correctness of these assumptions. It assumes *geometric growth* of population (as did Malthus) and economic production and it also assumes *absolute limits* upon natural resources and technological development. Sooner or later, if these assumptions are valid, growth will overtake the limits and a collapse is inevitable.

But to the opponents of no-growth, these assumptions are highly dubious. Accordingly, the advocates of growth have answered the Club of Rome by arguing that modern technology gives us good reason to look optimistically to the future. Their reasoning can be summarized as follows:

1. Already existing and usable technology could, if more efficiently and widely applied, adequately take care of many problems, such as food. Only 3 percent of the earth's surface is not farmed and much of that inefficiently by outmoded methods and techniques.

2. The supply of natural resources has never remained fixed but instead has expanded as technology has improved our ability to extract resources. Now it is possible to drill oil wells as deep as 30,000 feet and also to drill beneath the oceans. Each technological advance increases the supply of usable resources.

3. Technology also provides new resources and materials to substitute for old ones. No one even knew of plastics, now so widely used, until a short time ago. Once wood was the basic source of energy, then coal, petroleum, and natural gas. Now, new technologies offer us nuclear, solar, and geothermal power.

These arguments reflect great confidence in modern science and in science's ability to use and further develop technology to solve ecological problems. Certainly, the past record of science and technology is an impressive one; technology has provided enormous advances in material comfort and human health. There is every reason to believe that technological capability can continue to offer humankind new means to support a large population at even greater levels of material comfort, health, and leisure.

Technological Fix   Yet there is a danger that an understandable enthusiasm for technological achievement could lead us to believe that all crises can be met by technological solutions—a technological fix. But technology, as we saw in Chapter 16, is not an independent force to solve problems or make social changes; its effects depend on the economic and political structure in which it is developed and used. The crisis to which the Club of Rome was referring is also a crisis of social and political practices, of vested interests and established inequalities.

The Faustian Bargain   Americans in particular have faith in technological fixes. They believe that technology can readily cleanse the environment, produce abundant food, and find new sources of inexhaustible energy at little cost and requiring no sacrifice. Few scientists today maintain such an optimistic view.

Many technological solutions, such as those to reduce air pollution, require more time for scientific development than the ecological crisis may allow, and may also be so costly as effectively to reduce the standard of living. Others pose further ecological threats. In any case, there is no basis for complacently assuming that scientists and engineers can solve all problems.

To assume that a technological fix is possible is to mistakenly define the problem as a technological one. But the ecological crisis is social, political, and cultural first, and only secondarily technological. To press ahead with proclaimed technological solutions—such as building a vast network of nuclear power plants—may very well be to risk the future of humankind in what the authors of the second report to the Club of Rome called a "Faustian bargain." (Faust, according to legend, sold his soul to the devil for power and knowledge.):

We need hardly belabor the point. A technological fix might very well become a Faustian bargain—and worse,

for we would be selling not merely *our* souls to satisfy our immediate comfort needs, but the well-being and perhaps the very existence of *generations still unborn*. [25]

Making Social Changes   The opponents of no-growth do recognize that social changes have to be made and that there cannot be complete reliance only on technology. They argue that social practices can also change and offer as evidence the decline in the birthrate in human societies which have attained higher standards of living. The dangers of population growth do not exist in these advanced industrial societies, they argue, so therefore let other societies use economic growth to reach a higher standard of living and the resulting decline in the birthrate will take care of population growth.

But the decline in the birthrate is an example of changed behavior which is individual and voluntary, action taken by couples who decide that it serves their personal self-interest not to have more children. But how many ecological problems can be solved that way? Giving up smoking, perhaps; but not the problems of toxic waste disposal, water and air pollution, the threat to the food chain, spreading deserts, and the widespread risks of radiation and nuclear disaster. Those require collective action by authorized agencies.

The issues at stake are obviously complex and offer no easy solution. The advocates of no-growth point to the social costs which current practices entail, and to the possible destructive consequences of heedless, unchecked consumption of resources. Their critics keep us from being doomsayers and show us the technological possibilities that science can offer, though, again, the ecological crisis is always more than a technological problem.

RESHAPING SOCIETY: FINDING AN ECOLOGICAL BALANCE

We started this chapter by making a basic point: that human society is necessarily linked to the environment and that human beings, organized into human societies, are not and can never be independent of that environment. Now, in the twentieth century the relationship of society to environment has become critical. No society has ever survived by remaining persistently out of balance with the environment. It is the arrogance of an advanced technological society that it could forget that basic point, or ignore it.

The critical problem of society and environment—the ecological crisis—is a complex matter. The difficulty of providing enough food for the needs of the world, while unchecked population growth continues; the exhaustion of finite resources by the consumption practices of affluent societies; and their destruction of the environment by pollution and poison constitute much of what is basic to the ecological crisis.

But no statement of the problem would be complete without recognizing that the relation of developed to underdeveloped society is also basic to the world's unbalanced ecology. America, the most advanced technological society, with the highest standard of living, and the greatest capacity to waste and pollute, has often served as a model of what an advanced society could become. Perhaps the most difficult lesson to learn is that the whole world cannot imitate the United States if ecological balance is to be achieved.

America: The Impossible Model

The United States is a society with a voracious appetite for natural resources. Though it has less than 6 percent of the world's population, it consumed (in 1966) over a third of the world's tin; over a fourth of its phosphate, potash, and nitrogenous fertilizer; half of its newsprint and synthetic rubber; more than a fourth of its steel; and about a fifth of its cotton.[26]

To do that, and to be the world's most industrially productive society, the United States is highly dependent on foreign sources for most of its basic industrial raw materials, except coal. Since 1961, for example, we have been importing 90 percent of our nickel and 30 percent of our copper.[27] Though the United States possesses vast quantities of oil, it nonetheless imports about half of what it consumes.

To raise other countries to the standards of the United States—to repeat some information we cited early in the chapter—would require 75 times as much iron as is now mined annually, 100 times as much copper, 200 times as much lead, 75 times as much zinc, and 250 times as much tin. With the exception of iron, this would exceed all known or inferred reserves.[28] Biochemist H. R. Hulett, for example, asserts that ". . . [about] a billion people is the maximum population supportable by the present agricultural and industrial system of the world at U.S. levels of affluence."[29] The population of the earth is already four and a half times that maximum.

Not only is the United States not a viable model for other nations, but efforts to develop to the same level of affluence and consumption threaten to add an already overpolluted global system, and to use up even faster already depleting natural resources. The sheer competition for oil and for minerals necessary for industrial production threatens to produce conflicts of worldwide and possibly globally destructive proportions.

The United States (and other industrial societies) can only retain their own levels of production and consumption and maintain their cherished process of growth if they manage to maintain relations of domination and control over other parts of the globe; in short, to maintain a pattern of imperial relations. The present position of the United States depends on this. If the United States is to overconsume, other countries must remain largely underdeveloped and must underconsume.

This basis for American domination in the world is not likely to be publicly acknowledged. It is, however, the source of a powerful ideological appeal to continue economic growth and expand energy sources to maintain a high standard of living.

Against that there is a spreading concern for ecological values, and an unfocused and sporadic (but growing) environmental movement, but as yet with little political power. Nonetheless, the effort to act upon the many diverse aspects of the problem-ridden ecosystem suggests that struggles over conflicting interests and goals will be central to American political life for decades to come.

The Environmental Movement

Since the early 1970s, there has been a steady growth in the environmental and ecological movement in the United States. Such a movement is a resurgence of an interest which Americans have taken before in their natural environment. In the early decades of this century, a conservation movement grew up to conserve such rapidly depleting natural resources as forests; the great national parks are an outcome of that early effort. More recently, efforts to protect various birds and animals in danger of extinction by human predators led to legislation to protect all endangered species.

This concern for trees and forests, birds and animals is still an aspect of the movement, but now it has made a crucial next step: to seek the protection of human beings from dangers to health and safety in the environment around them. Americans are now beginning to realize the true extent of environmental hazards. The threat to air and water on which all life depends; the toxic hazards found in prepared foods, on many jobs, and in manufactured goods; the nuclear threat; the numerous carcinogens present in our human-made environment—all these and more testify to the ever-growing risk for all in industrial society.

The opposition to nuclear power has probably been the major issue around which the movement has mobilized a mass of citizens, mostly middle class and largely young. It is on this issue that the movement has been most militant, its tactics including nonviolent tres-

passing on nuclear sites, as at the large Seabrook nuclear plant in New Hampshire. The incident at Three Mile Island in Pennsylvania in 1979 only served to dramatize the dangers about which the movement has warned.

The environmental movement did not originate out of any ideological opposition to the status quo; it was not anticapitalist nor advocating any radical structural changes. But its actions have put it into opposition to the large public utility and energy corporations and to the federal government. Its struggles have, therefore, served to develop within the movement a growing sense that the ecological crisis and the threat to the environment is not an accidental consequence of our technological ignorance or our affluent life-style, but is imbedded in economic practices and interests which are at present basic to the existing structure of all advanced industrial societies.

What is at stake in the struggle between the move-

Opposition to nuclear power has become the major organizing issue for the environmental movement.

ment and the nuclear industry is not merely a problem of nuclear safety, but a question of basic policies in all industrial societies about their relation to the natural environment, the use of natural resources, the value of economic growth, and the kind of human future desired and found possible.

SUMMARY

Society is but one component of human life and is never independent of an environment; instead there is a complex, interactive process among *organization (society)*, *population*, *technology, and environment.*

Technology extends the human capacity to modify environment but indiscriminate use is the root of an *ecological crisis.* This crisis takes these forms: (1) a rapid growth of world population; (2) the depletion of natural resources; (3) the depletion of living organisms; and (4) the pollution and poisoning of the environment.

Its roots can be traced to (1) a *religious* perspective (Western Christianity) that viewed man as apart from and destined to be master of the natural world—*man-conquers-nature;* (2) a *scientific* perspective that absorbed this attitude to nature from the religious one; and (3) a superb *technology* which enabled the small nations of Europe to conquer, loot, and colonize much of the rest of the world.

Western *capitalism* also absorbed this perspective, defining natural resources as commodities in a market system—valuable or worthless only in terms of exchange value. Corporate capitalism, however, puts some restraints and rational controls on previously unrestrained competitive capitalism, as in conservation practices. Capitalism has also pushed many *social costs* of production onto individuals, publics, and future generations.

The study of population—*demography*—examines three basic phenomena: *births, deaths, and migration.* A change from high birthrates and high death rates to low birthrates and low death rates is the *demographic transition*, which Western nations have gone through and which largely differentiates their populations from those of underdeveloped societies.

A recent sharp decline in fertility in the United States makes *zero population growth* possible anywhere from 2028 to 2062.

The population of the world has grown 7 times since 1650 and its present rate of growth of 1.9 will double it again in 37 years, a rate of growth that cannot go on indefinitely.

Developed and *underdeveloped* countries contrast sharply on such major demographic factors as birthrates, death rates, infant mortality, life expectancy, and percent of population below age 15. For underdeveloped countries, birthrates and death rates are higher (with some exceptions on death rates), as is infant mortality, and the percent of population under age 15; life expectancy is lower. Death rates have been lowered in underdeveloped countries by public health measures introduced by developed countries. This has further increased population growth in these societies.

The implications of this are: *a rapid world population growth* that threatens the carrying capacity of a finite planet and renews Malthusian fears of disaster in the future; and *increased political strains* between developed and underdeveloped nations, particularly since developed nations will be perhaps only 20 percent of the world's population. In addition, further development increases the rate of consumption of natural resources; the developed societies and particularly the United States, now consume far more than do underdeveloped societies despite their greater populations.

If ecological balance is to be achieved, America is an *impossible model* for the world, for its consumption of resources is at a rate that could not sustain more than a billion people, and there are now about 4.5 billion people on the earth (Table 20.4).

There is now a growing environmental movement in the United States; it is a response to the extent of environmental hazards all face in industrial society.

NOTES

[1] Otis Dudley Duncan, "Social Organization and the Ecosystem," in Robert E. L. Faris, ed., *Handbook of Modern Sociology* (Chicago: Rand McNally, 1964), p. 42.

[2] *Ibid.,* p. 62.

[3] *Ibid.,* p. 69. For an effort to assess just how the environment has been altered, see the scientific symposium, edited by W. I. Thomas, Jr., *Man's Role in Changing the Face of the Earth* (Chicago: University of Chicago Press, 1956).

[4] Paul R. Ehrlich and Anne H. Ehrlich, *Population, Resources, Environment: Issues in Human Ecology* (San Francisco: W. H. Freeman, 1970). pp. 61−62.

[5] *Ibid.,* p. 166.

[6] *Ibid.,* p. 159.

[7] *Ibid.,* p. 118.

[8] Lynn White, Jr., "The Historic Roots of our Ecologic Crisis," in Fred Carvell and Max Tadlock, eds., *It's Not Too Late* (Beverly Hills, Cal.: Glencoe Press, 1971), p. 22. This article originally appeared in *Science* 155 (March 10, 1967): 1203−1207.

[9] *Ibid.,* p. 24.

[10] Barry Weissberg, *Beyond Repair: The Ecology of Capitalism* (Boston: Beacon Press, 1971), p. 17.

[11] Anthony D'Amato, "The Politics of Ecosuicide," in Leslie L. Roos, ed., *The Politics of Ecosuicide* (New York: Holt, Rinehart and Winston, 1971), p. 25.

[12] White, *op. cit.,* p. 19.

[13] K. William Kapp, *The Social Costs of Private Enterprise* (New York: Schocken Books, 1971), p. 13.

[14] *Ibid.,* p. xvi.

[15] Irene B. Taueber, "Population and Society," in Faris, *op. cit.,* pp. 87−88.

[16] U.S. Bureau of the Census, *Statistical Abstract of the United States: 1978* (99th ed.), Washington, D.C., 1978, p. 59.

[17] U.S. Bureau of the Census, *Social and Economic Characteristics of the Older Population: 1978* (Current Population Reports: Special Studies: Series P-23, no. 85), 1978, p. 2.

[18] United Nations Department of Social Affairs, Population Division, *The Determinants and Consequences of Population Trends* (New York, 1953), Table 2, p. 11. Figure for 1977 from U.S. Bureau of the Census, *World Population: 1977—Recent Demographic Estimates for the Countries and Regions of the World,* Washington, D.C., 1978.

[19] Taueber, *op. cit.,* pp. 85−86.

[20] Ehrlich and Ehrlich, *op. cit.,* p. 22.

[21] *Ibid.,* p. 23.

[22] *Ibid.,* p. 22.

[23] Donnella H. Meadows and Dennis L. Meadows et al., *The Limits to Growth* (New York: Universe Books, 1972).

[24] See, for example, H. S. D. Cole et al., eds., *Models of Doom: A Critique of the Limits to Growth* (New York: Universe Books, 1973), and John Maddox, *The Doomsday Syndrome* (New York: McGraw-Hill, 1973).

[25] Mihajlo Mesarovic and Eduard Pestel, *Mankind at the Turning Point* (New York: Dutton, 1974; paperback edition New York: New American Library, 1976), p. 135 in paperback edition.

[26] See Ehrlich and Ehrlich, *op. cit.,* p. 61.

[27] *Ibid.,* p. 61.

[28] *Ibid.,* pp. 61−62.

[29] *Ibid.,* p. 202.

SUGGESTED READINGS

Harrison Brown, *The Challenge of Man's Future.* New York: Viking, 1954. A renowned study of population and resources.

Rachel Carson, *Silent Spring.* Boston: Houghton Mifflin, 1962. The classic work that did more than any other to awaken people to the dangers of destroying the environment.

Barry Commoner, *The Closing Circle* (New York: Knopf,

1971); and *The Politics of Energy* (New York: Knopf, 1979). A renowned ecologist offers thoroughly critical analyses of the ecological and energy crises of our day.

Paul R. Ehrlich and Anne H. Ehrlich, *Population, Resources, and Environment: Issues in Human Ecology*. San Francisco: W. H. Freeman, 1970. A wide-ranging, informative review of all aspects of the ecological crisis.

K. William Kapp, *The Social Costs of Private Enterprise*. New York: Schocken Books, 1971. An economist's examination of the failure to include social costs in economic analysis of private enterprise.

John Maddox, *The Doomsday Syndrome*. New York: McGraw-Hill, 1973. A British scientist finds reason for more hope than does the Club of Rome.

Donnella H. Meadows and Dennis L. Meadows et al., *The Limits to Growth*. New York: Universe Books, 1972. A Club of Rome analysis of the perils of population and ecology on spaceship earth.

Mihajlo Mesarovic and Eduard Pestel, *Mankind at the Turning Point* (New York: Dutton, 1974; paperback edition, New York: New American Library, 1976). A more updated grim warning from the Club of Rome.

Leslie L. Roos, Jr., *The Politics of Ecosuicide*. New York: Holt, Rinehart and Winston, 1971. A collection of essays that stresses possibilities and problems in instituting change.

William Thomas, Jr., ed., *Man's Role in Changing the Face of the Earth*. Chicago: University of Chicago Press, 1956. A scientific symposium on what has been done by humans to the one planet they inhabit.

Barry Weissberg, *Beyond Repair: The Ecology of Capitalism*. Boston: Beacon Press, 1971. A highly readable introduction to the radical perspective on ecology: problems and solution.

Dennis Wrong, *Population and Society* (New York: Random House, 1976). A brief, clear summary of what demographers know about population and its growth.

GLOSSARY

Accountability. The means of holding private and public groups to the service of public interest rather than their own or other special interests.

Acculturation. Absorption of ethnics into the dominant culture.

Adaptation. An adjustment to a natural environment in such a way as to extract sufficient resources to sustain life.

Affirmative action. A conscious, deliberate effort to seek out and find minorities for equal opportunities in such basic areas as jobs, housing, and education.

Alienation. A condition in which the social world, or aspects of it, is beyond the reach of people's power and understanding and society seems to be controlling them. Also, individual feelings of powerlessness, meaninglessness, normlessness, isolation, and self-estrangement.

Anarchism. An antipolitical doctrine opposed to centralized political authority, strongly valuing individualism, and seeking new and freer forms of human association.

Anomie. According to Durkheim, a condition in which social relations have disintegrated until moral rules no longer effectively regulate social action.

Ascribed identity. A personal identity assigned at birth, as sex and race.

Authority. Legitimate power; the right to make decisions or exercise control over others in social organization.

Automation. A continuous process of production whereby machines control movement from one part to another without human aid and where a feedback system by machines allows for machine control of this process.

Birthrate; see **Crude birthrate.**

Bureaucracy. Rational administration for the control and coordination of a formally established organization. (see **Formalization**)

Capitalism. An economic system characterized by these closely interwoven features: private ownership of the means of production; wage-labor; the market; profit; capital accumulation; investment; and economic growth.

Caste. A permanent, very rigid form of social stratification sanctified by religion.

Census. The effort to make an accurate count of the people in a region or country.

Charismatic authority. Authority based upon the personal devotion of followers, who attribute great qualities to a leader.

Class system. An open system of stratification (in contrast to caste and estate) in which mobility from lower to higher strata is not forbidden by religion or law.

Collective behavior. Social interaction so loosely structured that prior normative controls, role expectancies, and authority are lacking.

Colonialism. An international division of labor in which the colony provides raw materials and a market for finished goods and the dominant nation manufactures goods for its own and foreign markets.

Community. The organization of social life with a geographical locality, characterized by shared social identity.

Contranormative. Norm-violating.

Control group. The group in experimental research which is deliberately not exposed to the experimental stimulus or action.

Core. A small number of powerful, technologically developed societies that are the organizing center of the world economy. (see **Periphery**)

Correlation. A consistent relationship between two variables, usually measured statistically.

Corporate Capitalism. An economic system which effectively concentrates large investments, technology, and labor power in a relatively few dominant corporations.

Counterculture. A confrontation and contradiction of the dominant culture, especially concerning the rebellion among American youth in the 1960s.

Crowd. A large, physical aggregate of people who share a common focus and who interact and communicate.

Crude birthrate. Computed on the basis of every 1,000 persons in a specified population in a given year.

Crude death rate. Computed on the basis of every 1,000 persons in a specified population in a given year.

Cult. A small and almost formless religious organization grouped around a charismatic leader.

Cultural pluralism. The maintenance of separate ethnic identity in a society.

Cultural relativism. The assertion that all human cultures are equally legitimate.

Culture. An ordered system of meanings and understandings.

Death rate, see **Crude death rate.**

De facto segregation. Segregation in schools not legally required but produced by other restrictive practices such as residential segregation.

Deferred gratification. The ability to save, to postpone pleasure for future rewards.

Definition of the situation. People act in a situation consistent with what they define that situation to be.

Delinquent subculture. The existence of norms and values among delinquent actors that place a positive outlook on delinquent behavior and confer status on those who commit delinquent acts.

Demography. The study of the characteristics and composition of human populations.

Denomination. A stable church that does not withdraw from the world but does not seek to control it either, and does not monopolize a territory.

Dependent variable. The variable that varies or changes by the effect of another variable on it.

Deviant behavior. The conduct of those who act contrary to established norms and the rules of society.

Differentiation. Specialization of roles, classes, and occupations which creates a more complex social structure. (see **Division of labor**)

Discrimination. Differential (therefore unequal) treatment of persons because of race or ethnic status.

Division of labor. A process whereby specialization in social roles leads to a more complex social structure.

Dysfunctional. Disruptive of established social relations and interfering with ongoing social processes.

Ecclesia. A basic type of religious organization that is both in and of the world and seeks to be a power in society.

Ecological expansion. The process of absorbing once unrelated populations into a single society extending over a wide territory.

Economy. The organization within a society to produce and distribute material goods so as to promote the basic sustenance of life.

Ecosystem. A complicated, intricately interrelated process of interaction of environment with oppulation.

Education. The process by which the young are inducted into the culture and trained in necessary skills and values.

Elite. Those at the top of a hierarchical social system who control decision-making in the system.

Emergent-norm theory. The idea that even in a violent crowd social interaction defines the situation and establishes norms for sanctioning behavior.

Empirical. Based on observation or experiment, thus factual.

Endogamy. Where marriage partners are chosen from within a group.

Estate. A series of social strata in medieval Europe rigidly set off from one another and supported by custom and law.

Ethnic group. People who are visibly different from others by such cultural dimensions as language, place of origin, and heritage.

Ethnocentrism. Using one's culture as the standard by which all other cultures are judged.

Exogamy. Where marriage partners are chosen outside of the group.

Family. A social arrangement to legitimize mating and the care and socialization of the young.

Family group. A kinship group that regulates and controls the relationship of the sexes in an institutionalized manner and provides mating in order to reproduce.

Feral children. Those who grow up in virtual isolation from human contact and are thus denied the humanizing influence of the socializing process.

Fertility rate. The number of births in a particular population for every 1,000 women of childbearing age.

Folk society. Small groups of people who are organized on a kinship basis, with little specialization of occupation or economic function but with a shared culture.

Folkways. Customary ways of doing things that are usually accepted as the right way.

Food chain. The interlinked system by which animals and human beings survive by obtaining energy and nutrients from plants and other animals.

Formal structure. The official and explicit designation of the positions and relations of an organization, independent of the characteristics of the position-holders.

Formalization. A process of making organization increasingly formal in structure.

Function. The contribution each interrelated part makes to the maintenance of the whole entity (group or society).

Gender. The cultural aspects of being feminine and masculine, in contrast to the biological aspects of being male and female.

Ghetto. A section of the city where members of a minority people are forced to live.

Goal specificity. Clearly and precisely defined aims of a formal organization.

Group. A plurality of persons sharing in a common pattern of social interaction.

Hierarchy. The ranking of social positions from top to bottom in a social structure.

Hypothesis. A testable proposition; it predicts a specific relationship expected to be found in the data.

Identity. An image obtained from membership and a role in a group that is particularly valued.

Identity crisis. A difficulty in knowing what socially recognized identities would allow one to become the person one wants to be and to be able to live in accordance with one's values.

Ideology. The interpretation of a situation from the perspective of a group or class in order to legitimate modes of social action.

Independent variable. The variable that produces change by its effect on another variable, called the *dependent variable.*

Indicators. Particular observations from which sociological inferences about invisible phenomena (such as morale) are made for research purposes.

Individuality. The uniquely individual character of each person.

Industrialism. A system of machine technology and the organization of work to fit the social uses of that technology for production.

Industrialization. The transformation of society from predominantly agricultural to predominantly industrial forms of production, which then radically alters other institutions of the society.

Informal controls. Nonofficial mechanisms invoked for social control.

Informal structure. The network of spontaneous, unplanned social relations in a bureaucracy that are not formally prescribed.

Inner city. The area beyond the central business district that includes transient residential areas, slums, and racial ghettoes.

Institution. A normative order of social action deemed morally and socially crucial for a society.

Integration. The internal logic by which a culture becomes a harmonious entity.

Interaction. The process by which two or more persons are interacting toward and responding to one another at the same time.

Internalization. Through interaction with others, learning to feel and think as they do.

Labor force. The segment of the population in employed work, plus those unemployed but available for work.

Laissez-faire capitalism. An economic system of small, competitive, individual producers in a free market based solely on demand and supply.

Language. A complex system of verbal, written, and gestural symbols created to convey meaning.

Latent function. An unrecognized and unintended but no less objectively real function. (see **Function**)

Laws. Mores put into a written code with specific punishments for violations enforced by designated authority.

Manifest function. A recognized and intended function. (see **Function**)

Mass culture. A culture manufactured and marketed by a culture industry; it is a consumer culture.

Mass society. The tendency in modern society to break down communal relations and to isolate local groups from centers of power, ending in totalitarianism.

Matriarchal. Where authority is held by the mother.

Meritocracy. A society based on assignment of position and greater social reward for those presumed to be more qualified.

Metropolitan. A concentration of urban population distributed among a central city and a complex of the smaller satellite cities and villages surrounding the central core.

Minority. Members of society who are blocked from full and equal participation in all phases of social life because of their racial, ethnic, or other identifiable status.

Monogamy. One man married to one woman.

Mores. Those standards people regard as crucial for the welfare of the group.

Multinational corporation. A process of expansion achieved by large organizations, who also seek to influence government and change social policy in their own interests.

Participant-observation. Taking part in the social life of a group or community to observe what happens from an insider's viewpoint.

Party. A political structure organized to acquire power and achieve domination.

Patriarchal. Where authority is held by the father.

Peer group. A form of primary group whose members are equal in social status.

People. A population that shares a common language and heritage.

Periphery. The large number of underdeveloped societies with a weak state and an economy specializing in the production of one or two raw materials by unskilled, low-wage labor.

Political economy. The close involvement of the economic and political institutions with one another.

Politics. The process whereby humans utilize power and authority to make decisions.

Polity. A governing system of power and authority.

Polyandry. A woman married to several husbands.

Polygamy. A plurality of mates.

Polygyny. A man married to several wives.

Population growth rate. A measure of the growth of a population as a percent of the annual increase.

Power. The distribution of influence and authority for the purposes of making, executing, and legitimizing decisions.

Prejudice. Negative attitudes and feelings toward people because of race or ethnic status.

Primary group. A small, intimate group with face-to-face interaction, of reasonably long duration, sustaining close personal relations.

Primary relation. Direct, face-to-face interaction; a relation valued as an end in itself.

Production. Land, capital, labor, and organization combined in a cooperative effort to produce goods.

Propaganda. The deliberate dissemination of partisan communication in order to influence the formation of public opinion.

Property. The ownership of an object, not the object itself, which means the right to use, consume, or have access to and control of the object.

Protestant ethic. A religious orientation to the world which encouraged self-discipline, hard work, initiative, material acquisition, and competitive individualism.

Public. Some members of a society who are interested in a public matter that may require discussion or resolution by the society. A process of free discussion by which such decisions can be made, and the emergence of public opinion from such discussion.

Racism. Beliefs about the inherent superiority of one race over another, and practices based on such beliefs. Also, **institutional racism,** which is control of social institutions by one racial group to the disadvantage of another.

Reform movement. A social movement that accepts the basic values and institutions of society but seeks to change what are defined as abuses, defects, or inadequacies.

Religion. Explanations that transcend mundane, factual knowledge, expressed in symbolics forms and acts, which relate a people to the ultimate conditions of their existence.

Resocialization. Socialization later in life that makes a sharp break with an individual's past identity.

Revolutionary movement. A social movement that tries to bring about a fundamental change in the structure of society.

Role. The patterned way in which people in various social positions interact with others based on mutual expectations.

Role set. A differentiated set of role expectations that orient an occupant of a role toward other actors who are in different relations and situations.

Role conflict. When an actor in a role cannot seem to meet expectations for one role fully without violating another role.

Sample. A small proportion of the total population drawn so that the variation in the characteristics of the population will be present in the sample in the same proportion as they appear in the universe of study.

Scientific method. The logical, rational processes that provide reliable and objective means for acquiring systematic and accurate knowledge.

Sect. A basic type of religious organization that is small and exclusive and whose members voluntarily join it.

Secularization. The decline of religious influence on other institutions.

Segregation, racial. Separate residential areas and schools based solely on race.

Sex role. The social role and behavior culturally defined as appropriate for male and female.

Sign. A physical thing or event that stands for another thing or event.

Social change. Any alteration in roles, relations, or in the structure of a group or society.

Social class. Economic strata distinguished by unequal rewards from participation in the production processes of the society.

Social conflict. A struggle over values or over scarce resources in which two contesting groups each seek to impose their values or their claim on resources over those of the other.

Social control. The use of negative and positive sanctions (punishment and reward) to get people to act in conformity with group norms and expectations.

Social evolution. The growth and development of human society by greater spans of integration and control of population, accompanies by greater internal differentiation and complexity.

Social mobility. When property and position are open to all persons and are not transmitted through a system of inheritance.

Social movement. A collective action to promote or resist change that includes shared values, a sense of membership, shared understandings, and a structural system between leaders and followers.

Social position. A socially identified place in a system of interaction, such as chair of a committee.

Social problem. A condition or situation which some persons in a society regard as a threat to their values.

Social relation. Interaction between people in a somewhat stable and persistent pattern.

Social structure. The integration of social roles into a systematic pattern of social interaction.

Socialization. The basic process by which the human being becomes a person and a functioning member of social groups.

Society. All the systems of social interaction carried on by a population within a specified territory.

State. A political organization that claims binding authority and a legitimate monopoly of force within a territory. The state governs the nations.

State capitalism. A form of capitalism that is closely integrated with the national government.

Status. A position in society; often used to classify someone as high in rank.

Status group. A number of individuals who occupy a similar position in the prestige ranking of their community and who regularly interact with one another and recognize each others as equals.

Stereotype. Culturally based images of a category of people, attributing to them uniformly a common set of characteristics.

Stratification. The division of society into a series of levels, ranking one above the other by virtue of the unequal distribution of social assets such as power and privilege.

Structural assimilation. The movements of ethnics into social positions in a group or community controlled by a dominant group.

Structural mobility. Social mobility created by changes in the occupational structure of the society; sometimes called *forced* mobility.

Structural reform. A reform that is more than a new program or a change of policy; it is a change in the established structure of power, privilege, and authority of the system being reformed.

Subculture. Distinctive versions of the dominant culture carried by particular segments and groups of the society.

Suffrage. The right to vote, particularly associated with making women voting members of the nation.

Symbol. Human-made signs— objects including words—for which human beings have a set of shared meanings and values.

Symbolic interaction. Interaction that proceeds through the communication of meanings by language and other symbol-using processes.

Technological determinism. The idea that the single factor of technology produces changes in social organization.

Technological fix. The belief that there is a technological solution to all societal problems.

Theory. A selection and organization of facts which provides the basis for a generalized explanation of empirical relationships among some phenomena.

Theoretical orientation. A perspective on social life which examines it from a particular angle, such as the functional.

Third World. The former European colonies that have achieved political independence but are economically poor and industrially underdeveloped.

True believer. Someone who sees dedication to a social movement as a way of giving meaning to his life.

Urban ecology. The distribution of people, functions, and services in a community, and the location of the community in its physical environment which influences its shape and form.

Urbanism. The values and lifestyles associated with urban life.

Urbanization. A shift of the population from predominantly rural to predominantly urban locations.

Values. End states that people would like to achieve; conceptions of what is good and desirable in society.

Variable. An observable attribute of persons or groups that can vary in degree, as by age or income, or in status, as single or married.

Zero growth. The level of fertility required for a population to replace itself exactly under projected mortality rates and in the absence of immigration.

NAME INDEX

Adams, Abigail, 280
Aiken, Michael, 396
Alford, Robert, 428, 429, 330, 431
Alinsky, Saul, 399
Anthony, Susan B., 280

Bales, Robert, 111, 112
Barnard, Chester, 151
Baron, Francis, 463
Becker, Howard S., 415, 416, 421
Bell, Daniel, 23, 133, 135, 136, 137, 138, 139, 142, 143, 207
Bell, Wendell, 179
Bellah, Robert, 339, 349, 350, 351
Bendix, Reinhardt, 209
Benedict, Ruth, 84, 245
Bensman, Joseph, 114
Berger, Bennett M., 180
Berger, Peter, 351
Berkley, George, 162
Berrigan, Daniel, 348
Berrigan, Philip, 348
Blau, Peter, 159, 209
Blauner, Robert, 252, 253, 343, 373
Blood, Robert O., Jr., 300, 301, 302
Blumer, Herbert, 427
Bookchin, Murray, 186, 399
Booth, Charles, 9
Boskoff, Alvin, 174
Bowles, Samuel, 323
Braverman, Harry, 202, 371
Broder, David, 393
Bronfenbrenner, Urie, 87
Brown, Judith, 269

Burgess, Ernest, 173, 175
Burham, Walter Dean, 397

Calvin, John, 345
Caplovitz, David, 225
Carmichael, Stokeley, 250, 252
Carnegie, Dale, 157
Carter, Jimmy, 47
Cassirer, Ernst, 34
Chavez, Cesar, 399
Chinoy, Eli, 210
Chomsky, Noam, 54
Clark, Burton, 317
Cloward, Richard, 230
Cobb, Jonathan, 96
Cohen, Albert, 413, 417
Commoner, Barry, 357
Conrad, Peter, 421
Cooley, Charles Horton, 83, 85, 86, 105, 109
Crozier, Michel, 160
Couch, Carl, 436

Dahl, Robert, 396
Dahrendorf, Ralf, 192
Dalton, Melville, 154
Dansette, A., 342
Davis, Kingsley, 78
Descartes, René, 351, 463
De Tocqueville, Alexis, 398
Deutscher, Irwin, 89
Dombusch, Sanford M., 340
Domhoff, G. William, 203, 397
Dubin, Robert, 373

Duncan, Otis Dudley, 209, 458
Durkheim, Emile, 7, 12, 84, 93, 107, 116, 338,
    413

Ehrlich, Anne H., 460, 471, 474
Ehrlich, Paul R., 460, 471, 474
Emerson, Ralph Waldo, 141
Engels, Friedrich, 339
Erikson, Erik, 96, 448
Erikson, Kai, 28
Ewen, Stuart, 72, 74

Featherman, David, 275
Filene, Edward, 72
Firey, Walter, 174
Flacks, Richard, 65, 399
Freeman, Jo, 89
Freidson, Eliot, 429
Freud, Sigmund, 85
Fromm, Erich, 132
Fuller, Richard, 412

Gans, Herbert, 73, 74, 95, 109, 176, 180, 183,
    206, 295, 296, 298
Garner, Robert Ash, 43
Geertz, Clifford, 53, 60
Gesell, Arnold, 87
Giele, Janet Zollinger, 302
Gillespie, Dair, 301
Glazer, Nathan, 242, 244
Goffman, Erving, 23, 423
Goldfarb, William, 79
Goldwater, Barry, 391
Goode, William J., 303
Gordon, Milton, 244
Goring, Charles, 413
Gouldner, Alvin W., 18
Greer, Scott, 27
Groppi, Father, 348

Haley, Alex, 62
Hall, Richard C., 185
Hamilton, Charles, 250, 252
Hamilton, Richard, 391, 393, 441, 443
Hanna, Mark, 339
Harrington, Michael, 206, 207, 218, 219, 220
Harris, Chauncey D., 173
Hauser, Robert, 275
Havighurst, Robert, 314

Hayghe, Howard, 301
Heilbroner, Robert, 366
Herberg, Will, 339
Hill, James, 339
Hoffer, Eric, 450
Hollingshead, August, 314
Horowitz, Irving Louis, 427
Hoyt, Homer, 173
Huber, Joan, 282
Hunter, Floyd, 396
Huxley, Aldous, 93

Illich, Ivan, 332, 333

Jacklin, Carol H., 268
Jacobson, Lenore, 315
Jacoby, Henry, 162
Jencks, Christopher, 318, 324, 325
Jensen, Arthur, 316, 317
John XXIII, Pope, 347

Kanter, Rosabeth Moss, 268, 279
Kaplan, Norman, 356
Kapp, K. William, 464, 465
Kennedy, John F., 385
Kenniston, Kenneth, 304
Kerr, Clark, 324
Key, V.O., 441
Killian, Lewis, 446, 447, 452
King, Martin Luther, 348, 449, 450
Knowles, Louis L., 250
Knox, John, 345
Kohn, Melvin, 87, 157, 295
Kolko, Gabriel, 397
Kornhauser, William, 132, 133
Kotler, Milton, 399

Lampman, Robert, 216, 367
Lash, Christopher, 304
LeBon, Gustave, 435, 453
Lee, Alfred McClung, 93
Lee, Dorothy, 54
Leeds, Ruth, 154
Lenski, Gerhard, 210, 243
Lever, Janet, 266, 267
Lévi-Strauss, Claude, 271
Lewis, Hylan, 227
Lewis, Oscar, 131, 227
Liebow, Elliot, 23

Liebowitz, Martin, 427
Lind, Robert, 114
Lippman, Walter, 55, 441
Lipset, Seymour M., 209, 387, 388
Locke, John, 192
Lombroso, Cesare, 413
Long, Norton, 184
Luckmann, Thomas, 351
Lynd, Helen, 114
Lynd, Robert, 17, 114

Maccoby, Eleanor, 268
Maccoby, Michael, 157
MacDonald, Dwight, 73
McGovern, George, 391
Malthus, Thomas, 472, 474
Manuel, Frank E., 339
Marx, Gary, 22, 344
Marx, Karl, 13, 17, 43, 46, 97, 143, 192, 195,
    196, 208, 211, 339, 363, 364, 366, 370,
    371, 373, 374, 386, 453
Mayhew, Leon, 123, 363, 376
Mayo, Elton, 106
Mead, George Herbert, 15, 34, 55, 79, 80, 85,
    86, 266
Mead, Margaret, 265, 269, 303
Mechanic, David, 429
Merton, Robert, 84, 155, 413, 414, 415
Meyer, Marshall, 159
Michael, Donald N., 355
Michels, Robert, 394, 395
Milgram, Stanley, 22
Mills, C. Wright, 11, 16, 17, 156, 157, 192, 396,
    397, 411
Moore, Barrington, 303
Mosca, Gaetano, 394
Moskos, Charles C., Jr., 108, 109
Moynihan, Daniel P., 242, 244, 296, 297
Muller, Max, 56, 80
Murdock, George P., 289
Myers, Richard, 412

Nader, Ralph, 401–402, 412
Neumann, Franz, 158, 159
Noble, David, 369

Ogburn, William, 453
O'Neill, George, 303
O'Neill, Nena, 303
Oppenheimer, Valerie, 301
Orwell, George, 140

Packard, Vance, 444
Parenti, Michael, 244
Pareto, Vilfredo, 394
Park, Robert, 114
Parkin, Frank, 198, 204, 205, 210, 211, 212,
    217, 218
Pateman, Carole, 162
Peale, Norman Vincent, 340
Perrow, Charles, 154
Pin, E., 342
Plato, 140
Pliven, Frances Fox, 230
Prewitt, Kenneth, 250
Price, Derek de Sola, 351
Pryor, Frederick, 230

Rainwater, Lee, 228
Ravitch, Diane, 332
Redfield, Robert, 130, 131
Riesman, David, 94, 155, 324, 325, 374
Rinehart, James, 206
Rodman, Hyman, 227, 228, 298
Rogers, Harrell R., Jr., 246
Rosaldo, Michelle, 270
Rose, Arnold, 397
Rosenthal, Robert, 315
Ross, H. Lawrence, 180
Roszak, Theodore, 65, 66
Rousseau, Jean-Jacques, 192
Rubin, Gayle, 271
Ryan, William, 226, 227

Samuelson, Paul, 138
Sapir, Edward, 54
Schneider, Joseph W., 421
Schneider, Louis, 340
Schrank, Jeffrey, 73
Seeman, Melvin, 97
Selznick, Philip, 158
Sennett, Richard, 96, 179
Shils, Edward, 107
Shorter, Edward, 293, 294
Simmel, Georg, 46, 111, 115
Skinner, B. F., 93
Skocpol, Theda, 25, 386
Skolnick, Jerome, 24, 439
Slater, Philip, 65, 66, 69
Snow, C. P., 337
Speier, Hans, 441
Spiro, Melford, 289
Spitz, René, 79

Spock, Benjamin, 87
Stalin, J., 158, 204
Stark, Rodney, 343
Stein, Maurice, 114
Sumner, William Graham, 57, 128
Sutherland, Edwin, 416
Suttles, Gerald, 176
Szasz, Thomas, 419, 421

Taft, William Howard, 339
Taueber, Irene B., 467
Thomas, Norman, 449
Thomas, W. I., 35
Thompson, E. P., 343
Thrasher, Edwin, 416
Tilly, Charles, 386
Toennies, Ferdinand, 130
Touraine, Alain, 135
Turner, Ralph, 37, 436

Ullman, Edward I., 173

van den Berghe, Pierre L., 250–251
Vernon, Raymond, 378, 379
Vidich, Arthur J., 124
von Humboldt, Wilhelm, 324

Wallerstein, Immanuel, 375
Warner, William Lloyd, 114, 199

Weber, Max, 15, 147, 148, 150, 152, 160, 163,
    196, 197, 337, 344, 345, 346, 352, 357,
    383, 384, 386, 387, 388, 389, 404
Weinstein, James, 397
Weiss, Robert S., 82, 83
Weissberg, Barry, 463
White, Leslie, 34
White, Lynn, Jr., 462
Whorf, Benjamin L., 54
Whyte, William, 23, 94, 155
Wilensky, Harold, 230, 231, 232
William, Robin, Jr., 58
Wilson, Alan B., 314
Wilson, James Q., 176
Wilson, William J., 254
Wirth, Louis, 175, 176, 236, 238
Wolfe, Donald M., 300, 301
Wollstonecraft, Mary, 280
Wood, Robert, 181
Wooten, Barbara, 413
Wrong, Dennis, 84

Young, Michael, 191

Zaretsky, Eli, 294, 295
Zeitlin, Maurice, 367
Zijdervald, Anton C., 116, 117

SUBJECT INDEX

abolition, and feminism, 280
accountability, 399, 400–402
acculturation, 244
achieved identity, 95
acting crowd, 435–436
adaptation, 6, 56–57
adolescence, peer groups in, 86, 89, 110, and sex
    roles, 89
adult socialization, 89
adultery, 303
advertising, and consumption, 72
affirmative action, 253–257
African tribes, 124
age, and poverty, 224
aggiomamento, 347
aggregate, 102
agrarian family, 292
agrarian societies, 125–126
agribusiness, 401
Aid to Families with Dependent Children (AFDC),
    229, 296
alienation, 97–98, 402–404
alternate life style, 64–69
American Association of Pastoral Counselors, 340
American culture, 65, 69
American Indians
    as minority group, 237, 239, 241
    group, 237, 239, 241
    and religion, 343
    women among, 269
Amish, 62, 341
anarchism, 400
Anglican Church, 340, 348
anomie, 116
    and deviance, 413–415
anthropology, 4

anthropology (cont.)
    and culture, 52, 60
    fieldwork in, 23
    origins of, 8
    and the primitive, 131
anticipatory socialization, 89
antiwar movement, 451
apathy, and political process, 402
Appalachian people, 62
Arapesh, 265
armies, and rise of cities, 167
artifacts of culture, 53
ascribed identity, 94–95
Asian-Americans, 241–242
assembly-line production, 373
assimilation, 244
assimilationist model, 251–252, 253
Association of Concerned Scientists, 355
Athens, ancient, 142
athletics, and social mobility, 210, 211
attitudes
    and family socialization, 295
    and social class, 295
audience, as conventional crowd, 435
authority
    in bureaucracies, 149, 150–151, 153–154,
        158, 162, 163
    charismatic, 384, 448
    and complex structure, 41
    and influence, 384–385
    legal-rational, 384
    and power, 383–385
    rules of, 290, 291
    and violence, 439–440
    and women, 277–278
automation, 370, 373

automobile industry, 369, 412
autonomy, local, decline of, 114–115, 171–172
averages, 26

Bakke case, 256
Baptists, and social class, 342
beats, 65
behavioral controls, 93
belongingness, to social groups, 103–104, 109
best-liked person, in small group, 111, 112
bilateral descent, 290
biology
    and culture, 77–78
    and human nature, 77
    and inequality, 191
    and sex differences, 262–263
birthrates, 465, 466, 467, 468, 469, 470, 471
black(s)
    in higher education, 328
    in inner city, 183
    life-style of, 62, 64
    matriarchal family of, 296–298
    as minority group, 241
    and negative identity, 95
    subculture of, 62, 64
    and voting, 249
    women, 272, 273
Black Muslims, 341
blaming the victim, 226–227, 412
blue-collar blues, 373–374
blue collar occupations, 205–207
    in communist societies, 205
    and family power relations, 301
    and sex, 275, 276
bohemian life-style, 64–65
Bolshevism, 158
bonds, tax-free, 219
born-again Christians, 348, 350
boundaries, of social groups, 103–104
brainwashing, 89, 91
bride-price, 271
Brown v. Board of Education, 320, 321
bureaucracy
    components of, 149
    formal structure of, 149–152, 385
    functional meaning of, 148–149
    and individuality, 94
    informal structure of, 152–153
    origins of, 147–149
    in postmodern society, 137, 160–163
    as rationalizing force, 150
    and rise of cities, 167

bureaucracy (cont.)
    and social power, 158–160, 161, 162
    as trend, 130
bureaucratic personality, 155–158
bureaucratic state, 387–388
bureaucratization, 115, 117, 118, 147
bureaucrats, 153–154, 155–158
Bushmen, 6
busing, 250, 324, 330

Calvinism, 345, 346, 352
capital accumulation, 366
capital gains, 219
capitalism
    competitive, 366, 368, 463–464
    corporate, 366, 397, 464
    crises of, 367–368
    cultural contradiction of, 137
    and ecology, 463–465
    as economic system, 364–369
    and the family, 292–295
    and ownership of means of production, 364
    and Protestantism, 345, 351
    state, 139, 368–369, 386
    and surplus, 363
    as trend in modern society, 129
    as world system, 375–377
cargo cults, 343
Carnegie Council on Children, 306, 307
case study method, 23
caste, 193–194
casual crowds, 435
cataclysmic events, 42
Catholic Charismatic Revival, 349
census, 23, 466
central cities, 183–185, 220
Central Intelligence Agency (CIA), 397
central tendencies, 26
change (see culture change; social change)
charismatic leaders, 384, 448
Chicanos (see Mexican Americans)
child care
    men's role in, 265
    women's role in, 263, 265, 270, 282
child custody, 298
child labor, 281
child-rearing, 303, 304–305
    practices, 87, 295
childbearing, 262, 270, 282
childhood dependence, 78
children
    feral, 78–79

children *(cont.)*
    and poverty, 224
    and social policy, 306, 307
    socially deprived, 79
    and transformation of family, 292
Chile, 367
China, extended family in, 289
Chinese-Americans, 241–242
Christianity, 337
    as root of ecological crisis, 462–463
chronic illness and poverty, 226
Church of Jesus Christ of the Latter-Day Saints, 348
city (cities)
    crisis of, 182–185, 258, 411
    and density, 175
    growth of, 173–175
    and heterogeneity, 175–176, 177
    impersonalization of social interaction in, 115
    and insolvency, 172
    and market, 173–175
    medieval, 167, 173
    negative view of, 175–176
    power in, 396
    rise of, 126, 167
    schools in, 332
    and size, 175
civil politics, 48–49
civil religion, 339
Civil Rights Act, Title VII, 282
civil rights movement, 447, 449–451
class, social *(see* social class)
clerical work, mechanization of, 370–371
closed systems, 193–194, 208
Club of Rome, 475, 476
coercion, organized, 386
cognition, 56–57
Coleman Report, 322–323, 324
collective behavior, 434, 453
    see also crowds; public; social movements
colonial model, 252–253
colonialism, 376, 457
commodity production, 364–365
communal dimension, of good society, 140–141
communes, 67, 140–141
communication channels, in bureaucracy, 151–152
communist societies and communism
    income in, 217
    inequality in, 211–212
    Marx's view of, 143
    social mobility in, 210
    social services in, 230–231

communist societies and communism *(cont.)*
community
    and city, 166, 176–177, 181
    and counterculture, 67
    future of, 185–186
    local self-governing, 398
    and social class, 199
    as social group, 40
    and status, 199
community control, 399
community decision making, 395–396
community power elites, 395–396
companionship, as valued aspect of marriage, 291
competitive capitalism, 366, 368, 463–464
complex structures, 41
computer, in postindustrial society, 137
concentric zone model, 173, 174
conflict, 41, 45–50, 404
    and class struggle, 45–46, 192
    and control of economy, 371
    and cultural differences, 123–124
    forms of, 47–49
    functions of, 46
    roots of, 45, 47
    and social structure, 50
    state as arena of, 386
conflict resolution, 49
conflict theory, 13
conformity, 93
congregation, 338
conscience, 81, 83
consumer culture, 70, 71–72, 73
consumer purchasing, and poverty, 225
contractual relation, 105, 116
contranormative actor, 84
control
    centralization of, 137
    of education, local, 329, 330
    and good society, 141
conventional crowds, 435
"cooling them out," 315, 317
cooperation, 6
corporate capitalism, 366, 397, 464
corporate domination, 74
corporations, and local community finance, 172
corporations, multinational, 124, 137–138, 377, 378–379
correlation coefficient, 27
cosmopolites, 183
Council on Foreign Relations, 397
counterculture, 64–69, 117, 349
    contradictions in, 66–67
    end of, 67, 69

counterculture *(cont.)*
  lasting effects of, 69
  origins of, 64–65, 66
  versus culture, 65–66
creation, and religion, 336
criminals
  conviction of, and social class, 197
  immigrants as, 414
  theories about, 413
  white-collar, 414
  see also deviant behavior
crime, as normative, 84
crowd, 434–440
  acting, 435–436
  and emergent norm theory, 436–437
  types of, 435
  and violence, 436, 437–438
cults, 341, 342, 343
cultural differences, 123–124, 127, 131
cultural pluralism, 243
cultural relativism, 60–61
culture, 52–75
  artifacts of, 53
  and biology, 77–78
  conflict of, with social structure, 137
  definition of, 52
  elements of, 56–60
  in folk-modern comparison, 131
  and human nature, 77
  integration of, 60
  and language, 54–56
  religion as, 344–345
  and sex differences, 263–265
  and social structure, 53
  transmission of, 311
  versus counterculture, 65–66
culture change, 53
culture lag theory, 453
culture of poverty, 227–228

data collection, 20–21
day care, 307
decentralization, 398–402
  of bureaucracy, 162, 163
  of city, 183–184, 396
  and good society, 142
decision making
  in bureaucracy, 149, 162, 163
  community, 395–396
  and expertise, 443
  and group size, 117
  local, 399

decision-making *(cont.)*
  in postindustrial society, 137
  process of, 383
  of task groups, 110–111, 112
  see also power
definition of the situation, 35
deinstitutionalization, 346
delinquent subculture, 417
democracy
  and bureaucracy, 159–160, 161, 162
  participatory, 399
  as value, 59
Democratic Party, 391, 393, 402, 403
  social characteristics of members of, 391, 392
democratic state, 389–390
demographic transition, 467
demography, 43, 465–468
denomination, 340, 342
dependency, of underdeveloped nations, 377
dependent variables, 20
depression (economic), and social change, 42, 43
deschooling society, 332–333
descent, rules of, 290–291
desegregation, and education, 320–322, 324
deviant behavior, 413–422
  and anomie, 413–415
  and labeling, 415–416, 418, 419, 421, 422
  medicalization of, 419, 420–421
  and values, 417, 419
deviant career, 416
deviant groups, 416–417
deviant subcultures, 416, 417–419
differential association theory, 416–417
diffusion, 43, 45
discrimination, 297
  definition of, 244
  function of, 246
  and prejudice, 244–245
  and pursuit of success, 84
  as social problem, 412
  structure of, 246–250
  and women's earnings, 274–275
diseases, infectious, control of, 471
distribution, 362–363
division of labor, 6, 41, 93
  in family, 292, 300
  in folk-modern comparison, 130–131
  international, 376
  and oligarchy, 395
  sexual, 262, 263, 269, 273, 281
  in social groups, 102
  and technology, 369–371
divorce, 298–300

documentary research, 23
domination, sexual, 268–271
double bind, 278
dowry, 271
dysfunctional, 13
dystopian images, 140

Eastern Europe
   inequality in, 204–205
   social mobility in, 210
   women's role in Jewish ghettos of, 264
   see also specific country
ecclesia, 340
ecological balance, achieving, 476–479
ecological crisis, 6, 459–465
   and capitalism, 463–465
   roots of, 461–463
ecological expansion, 457, 458
ecological perspective, 458–459
ecology, as social problem, 423
   and technology, 458–459
   urban, 172–175
economic class model, 252, 253, 254
economic discrimination, 246–247
economy
   control of, and conflict, 371–375
   as institution, 128
   organization of, 362–364
   as social problem, 423
   world, 375–379
education
   control of, 328–331
   and discrimination, 247, 248, 250, 258
   financial support of, differential basis of,
      250
   functions of, 311–314
   and income, 25, 318
   and inequality, 314–320, 331–332
   as institution, 128
   level of, increasing, 313
   mass, as trend in modern society, 131
   and poverty, 225–226
   and race, 25, 320–324
   reforming, 331–333
   separation of, from family, 292
   and social class, 197, 314–324, 329
   and social mobility, 209
   as social problem, 423
   see also higher education
efficiency, as value, 59
egalitarian socialism, 212, 218
ego, 85

elderly
   as minority group, 238
   and poverty, 224
   and social services, 232
elites, and power, 394–398
Elizabethan Poor Laws, 226
emergent norm theory, 436–437
emotional contagion, 435, 436
emotional support, and religion, 339
empirical, 11–12, 21
endogamy, 194, 290, 291
entertainers, and social mobility, 210, 211
entrepreneur, 199
environment, adaptation to, 6, 56–57
   destruction of (see ecological crisis)
environmental movement, 452, 477–479
Episcopal Church, 342, 348
Equal Rights Amendment, 281
equality before the law, 211, 233
estate, 194
ethics, of social control, 93
ethnic minorities, 236–244
   rediscovering, 243–244
   see also specific minority group
ethnic neighborhood, 176, 183, 186
   and identity, 95, 96
   peer groups in, 109
ethnic status, and stratification, 196, 198
ethnic subcultures, 62
ethnicity, and the family, 295–296
   meaning of, 239
   persistence of, 244
   and social class, 295–296
ethnocentrism, 61
Europe
   and growth of cities, 175
   income in, 217, 218
   rise of cities in, 167
   social mobility in, 209–210
   social services in, 231, 232, 233
   socialism in, and inequality,
      211–212
   see also Eastern Europe; specific country
evangelicalism, 348, 350
evolutionary process, in development of complex
      society, 124, 143
evolutionary theory
   and religion, 336
   and social change, 43
exclusion, from political process, 385
exogamy, 290, 291
experimental research, 22–23
expertise, and public opinion, 443–444

expressive crowds, 435
extended family, 289, 292

family, and capitalism, 292–295
    changing American, 298–302
    division of labor in, 102
    and ethnicity, 295–296
    extended, 289, 292
    future of, 302–307
    as a group, 289–290
    and industrialism, 292–295
    as an institution, 128, 290, 303
    isolation of, 304–305
    nuclear, 289, 292, 293, 294, 301, 302–305
    and personal life, 293–295
    as a primary group, 85–86, 291–292
    sex role learning in, 265–266
    and social class, 294, 298
    and social mobility, 208–209
    as social problem, 423
    as socializing agent, 85–86, 87
    and the state, 305–307
    and suburbs, 179
    transformation of, 292–293
    universality of, 289–292
    variations in, 290–291
family allowances, 232, 307
federal income tax, 216–217, 219
    "loopholes" in, 219
federal revenue sharing, 172
Federation of Atomic Scientists, 357
female-headed households, 224, 258, 296–298
feminist movement, 280–282, 427, 451–457
feral children, 78–79
fertility, 466, 467, 468, 469, 470
fieldwork, 23, 24, 28
First World, 376
fiscal crisis, 138
folk community, 166
folk culture, 69, 70
folk society
    individuality in, 93
    modern society contrasted with, 130–132
    social group in, 101
folkways, 57
food chains, 460, 462
food supply, and population, 474
forced mobility (see structural mobility)
Foreign Policy Association, 397
formal group, 40
formal organization, 147, 149
Fourth World, 376

France, workers in, 342
freedom, and social control, 92–93
functionalism, 12–13
    and inequality, 192
    and religion, 338–339
fund of sociability, 82–83
fundamentalists, 336
future societies, 138–140

Gallup polls, 442
gamesman, 157
gemeinschaft, 130
gender, 263–265
generalized other, 80, 86
genetic control, 93
genetics, and view of poor, 226
Germany, science in, 354
gerontology, 468
gessellschaft, 130
gestures, 34, 80
ghetto, Jewish, 243
Ghost Dance, 343
global structure, emerging, 118
goal-specificity, in large organizations,
    146–147
goals
    of bureaucratic organization, 146–147,
    154
    and means, discrepancies between,
    414–415
    professional, 154
good society, the, 140–142, 143
gossip, 91
government
    local, 172, 181–182
    of metropolis, 181, 185
    and scientific research, 356–357
    as social problem, 423
graduate schools, 325
gratification deferred, 227
Great Britain
    National Health Service in, 232
    social class and religion in, 343
Greece, ancient, slavery in, 191
Greenwich Village, 64–65
Gross National Product, percentage of, spent for
    social services, 230–231, 232, 233
growth
    concept of, 473
    crisis of, 473–476
    economic, 363, 366
    limits of, 475–476

Haiti, women's role in, 264
Hari Krishna, 91, 349
haves and have-nots, struggle between, 138, 139
Hawthorne studies, 106
health, and social class, 197
health care, 428–429
hidden agenda
    of schools, 86
    in small groups, 112
hidden injuries of class, 96, 97
hierarchy, in bureaucracy, 149, 150–151
    in complex structures, 41
high culture, 69–70, 73
higher education, 315, 317, 319, 324–328
Hinduism, 194
hippies, 65
historical research, 23, 25
homosexuality, 238, 417–418
Hopi language, 54
Horatio Alger myth, 92
horticultural societies, 125
housing
    and discrimination, 249–250
    and poverty, 225
housing programs, 424
human nautre, 77–78, 85
humanism, 337, 357
Hungary, social mobility in, 210
hunting and gathering societies, 125, 166
    division of labor in, 263, 270
    economy of, 363
Hutterites, 62, 341
hypothesis, 20

"I," 85
id, 85
idea person, in small group, 111–112
identity, personal, 448
identity crisis, 96–97
ideology
    in conflict and control of economy, 371
    of social movements, 447, 448
    and societal boundaries, 124
impersonal relations
    in bureaucracy, 149
    in mass society, 132, 133
immigrants, 242–243, 251, 253
    Catholicism of, 339, 343
    and crime, 414
    as ethnic status group, 197, 198
    illegal, 43
    view of, as unfit, 226

imprisonment, 197, 423
inclusion, in political process, 385
income
    distribution of, 216, 217, 218
    and education, 25, 318
    and race, 25, 247
    and sexual inequality, 274–275
    source of, and social class, 194
    and Spanish origin, 247
independent variables, 20
India, caste in, 193–194
    Nayar of, family among, 289
individual
    and mass culture, 73
    in mass society, 132
    and society, 6–7, 8
individualism, 93–94
    and bureaucracy, 94, 155, 157
    and counterculture, 67
    and family, 293–294
    and group size, 117
Industrial Revolution, 129, 457
industrial societies, 126–127, 129
    social class in, 199–204
    women's loss of power in, 269
    see also modern society
industrial technology, 127, 129
industrialism, 369–371
    and family, 292–295, 302–303
industrialization
    and basic trend from small to large social
        groups, 113, 114
    and caste system, 194
    and child labor, 281
    and humanism, 337
    and science, 337
    and social change, 70
    and structural mobility, 208
    and urbanization, 166, 167
    and working women, 281
industry
    and deterioration of cities, 181
    suburban relocation of, 178, 182–183
inequality
    and conflict, 13, 192
    equalitarian view of, 192
    functional view of, 192
    future of, 233
    justifying, 191–192
    persistence of, 211–212
    sexual, 262–282
    and schools, 13
infant mortality, 466–467, 468

influence, and authority, 384–385
information storage, 92–93
inheritance, 208–209, 294
inner city, 183, 220
inner-directed individual, 155
innovation, 43, 45, 414
instincts, 77, 85
institution, total, 423
institutional norms, 128
institutional problems, 423
institutional racism, 250
institutional roles, 128
institutional spheres, 128
integration, 104, 107
intellectual technology, 136–137
interaction, 60
interactionist perspective, 13, 15
interest groups, 393–394
internal colonialism, 252
internalization, 81, 83, 84, 85, 86, 88, 91
International Typographers Union, 395
interracial marriage, 290
invasion, 173
investment, 366
IQ, 316–317
Iroquois, 269
Islam, 338, 346, 347
isolated groups, 62, 64
Israeli kibbutz, 289
Italian-Americans, and family, 295–296

Japanese-Americans, as minority group,
    241–242
Jehovah's Witnesses, 340–341
Jencks Report, 317–319, 323, 331
Jesus movement, 349
Jewish ghettos, women's role in, 264
Jews, as minority group, 242–243
job enrichment, 373
job satisfaction, 375
juvenile delinquency, 413, 416–417

Kerner Report, 250
kibbutz, 289
kinship, in folk-modern comparison, 131

labeling, of deviants, 415–416, 418, 419, 421,
    422
labor, wage, 365
labor leaders, and social mobility, 210, 211
labor movement, 202, 206, 449

labor movement (cont.)
    and violence, 437–438
labor-power, 365
labor unions, 371–375, 378
laissez-faire capitalism, 366, 368
language, 78
    and culture, 54–56
    in socialization process, 79–80
large groups, small groups within, 110–112
large organizations, nature of, 146–147
    see also bureaucracy
latent functions, 13
Latin America
    church and political action in, 348
    growth of cities in, 175
law(s), and property, 364
    as social problem, 423
leadership
    charismatic, 383, 448
    labor, 210, 211
    and oligarchy, 394–395
    of social movements, 448
learning, and culture, 53
    process of, 6
legal-rational authority, 384
liberation theology, 348
life chances, and social class, 196, 197, 198
life expectancy, 197, 468, 470, 471
line organization, 154
literature review, 19–20
living organisms, depletion of, 460, 462
lobbying, 393, 394
looking-glass shelf, 83
lower class, and black family, 296–298
Lutheran church, in Germany, 340

male domination, 268–271
management, and control, 366, 367
manifest functions, 13
manufacturing, in postindustrial society,
    137–138
market
    under capitalism, 365
    and city, 173–175, 182
    world, 118
marriage, 298–299, 303
    companionship as valued aspect of, 291
    and exchange of women, 271
    forms of, 290, 291
    interracial, 290
Marxism, 139, 192, 195–196, 204, 206
mass culture
    commercialization of, 73

mass culture *(cont.)*
  differentiated from popular culture, 71, 74
  and the individual, 73
  and mass media, 70
  and mass society, 74
  and societal boundaries, 124
mass education, as trend in modern society,
  130
mass media
  and mass culture, 70
  and sex role socialization, 266
mass society, 132–133
mate selection, 290, 291
material interests, social conflicts of, 45
matriarchal family, 269, 291, 296–298
matrilineal descent, 291
matrilinear family, 269
matrilocal residence, 291
"Me," 85
mean, 26
means of production
  communal, 364
  ownership of, 363
  private, 364, 365
  public, 364
median, 26
medical profession, control of health services by,
  428–429
Medicare, 232
medicine, control of deviant behavior by,
  420–421
medieval cities, 167, 173
medieval Europe, estate in, 194
megalopolis, 170–171
"melting pot," 242, 243, 244
membership, in social groups, 103–104
mental health
  and religion, 339–340
  and social class, 197, 226
mental hospital, as social problem, 423
mental illness
  as deviant behavior, 419–422
  myth of, 419, 421–422
meritocracy, 142, 191–192, 211, 233
  definition of, 191
  education for, 319–320
meritocratic socialism, 212, 218
Methodism, 343
metropolis, 180–182
metropolitan area, 168–171
Mexican-Americans
  as minority group, 239–240, 241, 252,
  253
  and voting, 249

Mexican-Americans *(cont.)*
  see also Spanish origin
Middle ages, cities in, 167, 173
  estate in, 194
  Roman Catholic Church in, 340
middle class, 199, 201–202
  and deferred gratification, 227
  and family power relations, 301
  lower, 201–202, 204
  new, 201–202, 295, 319
  and occupation, 202
  old, 201, 202, 295
  and religion, 342
  and socialization, 295
  values of, and delinquency, 417
military, and socialization, 89–91
military-industrial complex, 368
ministry, blacks in, 344
minority groups
  definition of, 198, 236
  types of, 236–242
minority status, 244–250
  definition of, 198
  and discrimination, 244–245, 246–250
  and prejudice, 244, 245–246
  and social power, 245
mobility, social (*see* social mobility)
mode, 26
modern society, 129–133
  abstract nature of, 116–117
  bureaucracy in, 146–163
  folk society contrasted with, 130–132
  as mass society, 132–133
  master trends in, 129–130
money economy, 147, 365
monogamy, 290, 291
Moonies, 91
moral community, 338
moral obligations, 116, 137
moral training, 312–313
morals, and view of poor, 226
mores, 57, 128
mortality rates, 466, 467–468, 470, 471
mothers, working, 79, 275, 277, 282
multinational corporations, 124, 137–138,
  378–379
multiple nuclei model, 173, 174
multivariate technique, 27
multiversity, 324–325
Mundugumor, 265

name-calling, by propagandists, 444
nation-building, 385–386

nation-state, 113, 130
National Council of Churches, 342
national power elites, 396–398
National Science Foundation (NSF), 356
National Socialism, 158–159
nativistic movements, 343
natural resources, depletion of, 459
nature, and society, 6
Nayar, family among, 289
Nazi Party, 158–159
near-poor, 224, 225
negative identities, 95–96
neighborhood
    and educational values, 314
    ethnic (*see* ethnic neighborhood)
    urban, 176, 177
neocolonialism, 457–458
neolocal residence, 291
New Guinea
    sex and personality in, 265
    sexual division of labor in, 269
nondualism, 350
norms
    changes in, 57
    definition of, 57
    and interaction, 60
    internalization of, 83, 84, 85
    in social groups, 102
    violation of (*see* contranormative actor)
nouveau riches, 198
nuclear family, 289, 292, 293, 294, 301,
    302–305

objectivity, 26–27
occupation
    and discrimination, 246–247
    and division of labor, 371
    and identity, 95
    inheriting, 209
    and social class, 87–88, 201, 202, 205–208
occupational distribution by sex, 257, 276
    and voting, 405
occupational personality, 89
occupational succession, 292
offices, in bureaucracy, 147, 149
Old Order Amish, 341
oligarchy, 394–395
open door policy, 315
open systems, 192, 194, 208
oppressed, and religion, 343
organization man, 94, 155–156, 157, 160, 295
Oriental religions, 349, 350

other-directed individual, 94, 155
overproduction, 367–368
oversocialized image, 84, 85

parapolitical groups, 393–394
participant-observers, 23, 24, 28
participatory democracy, 399
particular other, 80, 86
passing, 95
pastoral counseling, 340
patriarchal family, 290, 291
patrilineal descent, 290, 291
patrilocal residence, 291
peasant societies, 60, 61, 131
peasants, urban migration of, 166–167
peer groups, 40, 105–110
    in adolescence, 110
    in bureaucracy, 153
    importance of, 110
    and integration, 107
    power of, and social control, 106–107
    and resistance, 110
    role allocation in, 102
    and sex role learning, 266, 268
    as socializing agent, 86, 106, 110
    and subcultures, 107, 109
    in war, 107
personal development, 4
personal failure, 411
personal identity, 448
personal salvation, 348
personality, bureaucratic, 155–158
    occupational, 89
    and sex, 265
    and success, 92
personality market, 156–158
physically handicapped, as minority group, 238
physician, female, 278–279
pimps, 417
planned changes, 43, 45
play, and sex roles, 267
Plessy v. *Ferguson,* 320, 321
pluralism, 133, 398
pluralism perspective, on health care, 429
pogrom, 243
poisons, 460–461
political action, and religion, 348
political economy, 404–405
political participation, 393, 402–404
political party, 388–394, 402
    financial support of, 391, 393
    and public opinion, 441, 443

political party *(cont.)*
    and stratification, 198–199
political process, public as, 441
politics, and counterculture, 66–67
    and discrimination, 247, 249
    and new professional class, 207–208
    and science, 355–357
    and social mobility, 210, 211, 242
    and violence, 439–440
polity, as institution, 128
polls, public opinion, 442–443
pollution, 460–461
polygyny, 291
polygamy, 290, 291
polyandry, 291
poor, internal shifts in, 224
    location of, 220
    profile of, 220–234
    stereotype of, 215
    and welfare, 226, 228–230
    see also poverty
popular culture, 70, 71, 74
population growth, 458, 459, 465, 466
    implications of, 471–472
    in perspective, 472
    suburban, 169–170
    United States, 467, 468, 469
    urban, 168
    world, 469–472, 473, 474
postindustrial society, 135–139, 143
poverty, 218–230
    and age, 224
    and blaming the victim, 226–227, 412
    culture of, 227–228
    and race, 220, 224
    rate of, 218, 219
    as social problem, 422
    trap of, 225–226
    see also near-poor; poor
poverty area, 220
poverty index, 221
power, and authority, 383–385
    and bureaucracy, 158–160
    concentration of, 114, 117, 118, 398
    decentralizing, 396, 398–402
    definition of, 383, 385
    and economic surplus, 363
    and elites, 394–398
    in family, 300–301
    and peer groups, 106–107
    in postindustrial society, 137
    and the state, 386, 387
predestination, 345

preindustrial societies
    family in, 292
    learning in, 311
    political process in, 383
    women's power in, 269
prejudice
    definition of, 244
    and discrimination, 244–245
    function of, 245–246
preliterate societies, 57, 60, 61
Presbyterians, 342, 348
President's Commission on the Status of Women, 282
President's Science Advisory Committee, 355
priesthood, as administrative elite, 167
primary group, 40, 105–110
    definition of, 86
    family as, 85–86, 291–292
primary relations, 105
    in bureaucracy, 152–153
    and city, 176
prisons, 423
privacy, right of, 92–93
private conjugal contract, 302
private troubles and public issues, 11, 411
production, 362
    capitalist, 365, 367–368
    commodity, 364–365
    social costs of, 464–465
profane, 337
professional authority, 153–154
professional autonomy, 160, 161
professional monopoly, in health care, 428, 429
professional class, new, 207–208
professional occupations, in postindustrial society, 136, 137
professional thieves, 417
professionalism versus populism, 137, 142
professionalization
    of education, 330
    of university faculty, 325–326
professionals
    in bureaucracy, 153–154
    goals of, 154
    self-employed, and social class, 201
profit, 365–366
progressive tax system, 219
propaganda, 444–446
property, 294, 363–364
property crime, 414
prostitutes, 417
Protestant churches, 340
    see also specific denominations

Protestant ethic, 137, 345, 346, 352
psychotherapy, religion as, 339–340
public, 440–441
    as political process, 441
    and polls, 442–443
public agencies, and public interests, 401
public-interest research groups, 401
public opinion
    and expertise, 443–444
    manipulation of, 444–446
    problem of, 441, 443
    state of, 441, 445
public opinion polls, 442–443
Puerto Ricans
    as minority group, 240
    see also Spanish Origin
punishment, in social groups, 103

quantitative methods, 26, 27

race, 95, 198
    and education, 25, 320–324
    and income, 25
    and IQ, 316–317
    meaning of, 238–239
    and poverty, 220, 224
    and religion, 344
race relations, future of, 257–259
racial minorities, 236–244
racial violence, 438–439
racism, 250–253, 422
    see also discrimination
radical politics, and religion, 342–343
rape, 427
reality, and symbols, 56
rebellion, 49, 415
recession, 367–368
reform, social (see social reform)
reform governments, 396
reform movements, 446
regressive tax system, 216, 219, 232
regulatory agencies, 425
relationships, categories of, 82–83
religion, and change, 348
    civil, 339
    as culture, 344–345
    functions of, 338–340, 344
    future of, 357–358
    as institution, 128–129
    organization of, 340–342
    and the secular world, 350–351

religion, and change (cont.)
    and secularization, 336, 345–348, 351
    and stratification, 196, 198, 342–343
    and race, 344
    renewed interest in, 349–350
    and resocialization, 89–90, 91
    as root of ecological crisis, 462–463
    as worldwide, 336, 337
religious movements, 117
remarriage, 298, 299
Report of the National Advisory Commission on
    Civil Disorders, 250
Republic of South Africa, 236, 247
Republic of Zimbabwe, 236
Republican Party, 391, 393, 403
    social characteristics of members of, 391, 392
Research, social
    major methods of, 21–25
    and objectivity, 26–28
    steps in, 18–21
    and theory, 21, 25–26
reservation, city as, 185
residence rules, 291
residential segregation, 249–250
resistance, subculture of, 110
resocialization, 89–91
restricted covenants, 249
retirement, early, 374–375
retreatism, 414–415
revolution, 49, 139, 446
rewards
    in bureaucracy, 151
    as social control, 91, 92
    in social groups, 103
    see also social rewards
rich, stereotype of, 215
ridicule, 91
ritual, 337
ritualism, 414
role(s), social, 36–38
    acquisition of, 88–89
    in groups, 102
role-allocation, 41
role-change, 38
role-conflict, 38
role expectations, 36–38, 102
role models, 89, 95
role-playing, 117
role-set, 38
role-taking, 102
role traps, 279
Roman Catholic Church
    and immigrant workers, 339, 343

Roman Catholic Church *(cont.)*
  international scope of, 340
  in Middle Ages, 340
  and political action, 348
romantic love, 293, 303
rules, in bureaucracy, 149
ruling class, 394
rumor, 437
rural areas, poor in, 220

sacred, 131, 337
sampling, 21
sanctions, 91, 103
scarce resources, conflict over, 47
scarcity, belief in, 65
school, hidden agenda of, 86
  sex role learning in, 266
  as socializing agent, 86
  see also education
science, 56, 65
  applied, 353–354, 355
  autonomy of, 353, 354, 356
  basic, 353–354, 355, 357
  big, 354–355
  in folk-modern comparison, 131
  future of, 357
  growth of, 351–352
  as institution, 128–129
  and new religious consciousness, 350
  and politics, 355–357
  in postindustrial society, 136
  as rationalizing force, 150
  as root of ecological crisis, 463
  as trend in modern society, 130
  as world view, 336–337
science-fiction, 93, 140
scientific community, 352–354
scientific method, 18–21
Second World, 376
secondary relations, 115, 117, 175, 176
sector theory, 173, 174
sects, 340–342, 344
secularization, 336, 345–348, 351
segregation
  in housing, 249–250
  in schools, 320–322
self, emergence of, 81, 83
  and society, 83–85
self-control, 83, 91
self-employed professionals, and social class, 201
self-fulfillment, in good society, 142
self-government, 142, 162–163

serial monogamy, 290
service economy, in postindustrial society, 135–136, 137, 138
sex, biology of, 262–263
  and earnings, 274–275
  and occupational distribution, 275, 276
  and temperament, 265
sex, premarital, 293
sex differences, 263, 268
sex ratio, 263
sex role(s), acquisition of, 88–89, 95
  and identity, 95, 96, 97
  and socialization, 263, 265–268
sexes, relationship between, 296
sexual domination, 268–271
sexual revolution, 293, 294
sick role, 421
significant symbols, 34
signs, 34
single-parents, 298, 299
  see also female-headed households
slavery, 191, 344
small groups
  in laboratory, 111–112
  within larger groups, 110–112
  research on, 111–112
  significance of, 112
  types of roles in, 112
small towns, 114
social category, 102
social change, 7, 41–45
  and advertising, 72
  and conflict, 50
  and environment, 457–480
  and growth, 476
  and industrialization, 70
  reform as, 428
  and role conflict, 38
  and social awareness, 8–9
  and social research, 19
  and social structure, 50
  ways of coming about, 42–45, 50
social class(es), 194–196
  and conflict, 371
  in communist societies, 204–205
  and community, 199
  control of, 339
  and distribution, 263
  and education, 314–320, 329
  and ethnicity, 295–296
  and family, 294, 295–298
  hidden injuries, 96, 97
  and income, source of, 194

social class(es) *(cont.)*
  in industrial society, 199–204
  and life chances, 196, 197, 198
  Marx on, 19
  and occupation, 87–88, 201, 202, 205–208
  as open system, 194
  and political force, 207–208
  and political participation, 402
  and political party affiliation, 391, 392
  and race, 252, 254
  and religion, 339, 342–343
  and self-identification, 200
  in socialist societies, 204–205
  and socialization, 86–87, 295
  and status, 198, 199
  struggle among, 45–46
  and suburban residents, 178, 180, 181
  Weber on, 196, 197
social cohesion, as function of religion, 338–339
social community, 338
social control, 83, 91–93
  and group power, 106–107
  and religion, 339, 344
  in social groups, 103, 117
social costs of production, 464–465
social deprivation, 79
social facts, 7
social group(s), 40, 102–119
  and basic trend from small to large, 101–102,
    112–118
  components of, 102–104
  definition of, 40, 102
  family as, 289–290
  in mass society, 132–133
  see also large groups; small groups; *specific type*
social heritage, 53
  see also culture
social identity, 94–97
  achieved, 95
  and alienation, 97–98
  ascribed, 94–95
  and crisis, 96–97
  negative, 95–96
  occupation as, 95
  racial, 95
social institutions, 128–129
social interaction, 33–50, 115
social life, nationalization of, 150
social mobility, 95–96, 208–211
  and education, 313, 314, 319
  of European immigrants, 242
social movements, 47–48, 446–453
  examples of, 449–452
  failure of, 449

social movements *(cont.)*
  identifying, 446–447
  ideology of, 447, 448
  leadership of, 448
  organization of, 447
  significance of, 452–453
  success of, 448–449
social norms *(see* norms)
social organization, problems of, 413, 422–428
  see also social structure
social policy, and children, 306, 307
  and social change, 45
social problems, defining, 412
  politics of, 427
  as social reform, 425–427
  solving, 423–425, 428–431
  types of, 412–413
  welfare model of, 427–428
  see also deviant behavior; social organization,
    problems of; *specific problem*
social ranking, 102–103
social reform
  and distribution of wealth, 216
  and health care, 429
  limits of, 429–432
  and religion, 348, 350
  and social change, 428
  social problems as, 425–427
  sociology used for, 16–17
social relations, 35–36
  in city, 176
  in folk community, 166
  in mass society, 132, 133
  see also specific type
social reward, 191, 192, 196, 197, 204, 205
social self, 83
social services, 230–232
social status, 36
  and community, 199
  and decision making, 385
  roles not linked to, 38–39
  and social class, 198
social structure, 40–41
  and change, 41, 50, 56
  complex, 41
  and conflict, 50, 137
  and culture, 53
  of social groups, 102
  and stability, 41
socialism
  and alienated worker, 375
  failure of, 449
  and income, 217–218
  and inequality, 211–212, 217–218

socialism *(cont.)*
  state, 139
  and underdeveloped societies, 377
socialization, 78–91
  adult, 89
  agents of, 85–87
  anticipatory, 89
  in bureaucratic family, 155
  childhood, of sect members, 340
  definition of, 78
  to deviant norms, 416
  in entrepreneurial family, 155
  and family, 155, 290, 295
  and sex roles, 263, 265–268
  and social class, 86–88, 295
  in social groups, 103
socially supportive role, 39
society
  basic elements of, 123
  boundaries of, 124
  complex, development of, 124–127, 129
  concept of, 123–124
  definition of, 123
  evolution of, 338, 457
  and individual, 6–7, 8
  legitimation of, and religion, 338, 339
  meaning of, 4–8
  measuring, 142–143
  modern, 129–133
  and nature, 6
  nature of, 123–124
  postindustrial, 135–139, 143
  as problematic, 8–9
  reality of, 7–8
  reasons for, 4, 6–8
  and self, 83–85
  as social group, 40
  and the state, 387, 389
  study of, 18–28
  types of, 125–127
socioemotional specialists, 263
sociological imagination, 11, 17, 411
sociology, 8–11
  origin of, 8, 9
  perspective of, 9, 10
  as a science, 15
  uses of, 15–18
Soviet Union
  income in, 217
  industrialization of, 375
  inequality in, 204, 211, 217
  science in, 354
  structural mobility in, 208
Spanish Origin, 240, 249

specialization, 116
  in agrarian societies, 126
  in bureaucracies, 149
  in horticultural societies, 125
  in industrial societies, 127, 129
staff organization, 154
Standard Metropolitan Statistical Area, 169
state
  bureaucratic, 387–388
  definition of, 386
  democratic, 389–390
  and the family, 305–307
  functions of, 387, 389
  and political party, 389
  and society, 386–387, 389
state capitalism, 139, 368–369, 386
State Capitalist City, 185
state socialism, 139
stereotypes
  definition of, 245
  and minority status, 245
  of poor, 215
  of rich, 215
  sex role, 265, 266, 268, 271–273
stock-holders, 366, 367
stratification
  definition of, 191, 192
  multidimensionality of, 196, 198, 199
  and religion, 342–343
strength, physical, of males, 263, 270
structural assimilation, 244
structural mobility, 208
student protest, 326
subcultures, 61–64
  definition of, 61
  deviant, 416, 417–419
  ethnic, 62
  and peer groups, 107, 109
  regional, 62
subsidies, governing by, 389
suburbs, 177–180
  church in, 342
  and family life, 179
  growth of, 169–170, 411
  life styles of, 179–180
  myth of, 179–180, 181
  residents of, characteristics of, 178–179, 180
  and social class, 178, 180, 181, 206
success, and personality, 92
  pursuit of, 84
succession, 173
suffrage, 280–281
suicide, 12, 107
Sun Dance cult, 343

success, and personality *(cont.)*
  sunbelt, population increase in, 170, 171
  superego, 85
  surplus, economic, 336, 362, 363
  survey research, 21–22
  survival, 4, 6, 52, 57
  Sweden, inequality in, 211–212
  symbolic interaction, 15, 34–35
  symbolic values, 175
  symbols, 34, 52, 55–56
    and reality, 56
    significant, 34
    of Western culture, 35

taboos, 57
task-centered role, 39
task specialists, 263
tax(es)
  federal, 216–217, 219
  progressive, 219
  property, 181–182
  regressive, 216, 219, 232
  subsidies, 389
Tchambuli, 265, 269
teachers, and expectation of students, 314–315
technical occupations, in postindustrial society,
    136, 137
technological determinism, 369
technological development, 368
technological domination, 65, 66
technological fix, 476
technology, 369–371
  and displaced workers, 220
  and division of, labor, 369–371
  and ecology, 458–459, 463
  new, 43, 45, 56
  and popular culture, 70–71
  in postmodern society, 160
  and science, 354, 357
technology assessment, in postindustrial society,
    136
theoretical knowledge, in postindustrial society,
    136
theory, 11–15, 25–26
  see also specific theory
Third World, 376, 377
total institutions, 423
totalitarian power, 158–159
tracking, in school, 13, 317
transfer policies, 368
tribute, 363
Trinidad, family in, 298

Trobriand Islanders, 54
true believers, 450

underclass, 252
underconsumption, 367–368
underdeveloped nations, and development of
    science, 352
unemployment, 11, 43, 258
United States
  as poor ecological model, 477
  women in, 271–280
United States Bureau of the Census, 168, 169,
    466, 468
United States Department of Agriculture, 401
United States Department of Education, 330
unmarried couples, 302, 305
unplanned changes, 43
upper class, 198, 203, 209, 342
urban ecology, 172–175
urbanism, 175–177
urbanization, 166–168
  and basic trend from small to large social
    groups, 113, 114
  and decline of local autonomy, 171–172
  as trend in modern society, 129–130
  in United States, 167, 168
  world, 168
utilitarian individualism, 350
utopias, 93, 140

value-neutrality, 15
values, 57, 58–60
  and advertising, 72
  in American society, 58–59
  conflict over, 46–47
  contradictions in, 58, 59–60
  and counterculture, 64, 65
  and delinquency, 417
  and deviance, 417, 419
  and education, 311, 327, 329
  and family socialization, 295
  and inequality, 233
  and interaction, 60
  and lower class, 227–228
  and middle class, 417
  and social class, 227–228, 295, 417
variables, 20
Vietnam War, 108–109, 451
violence, and crowds, 435, 437–438
  and politics, 439–440
  racial, 438–439

voluntary associations, 398
voting, and alienation, 393
  and apathy, 402–404
  and blacks, 249
  and political process, 385
  and social characteristics, 403, 404, 405
  and Spanish origin, 249

wage-labor, 365
Wagner Act, 372
war
  primary groups in, 107, 108–109
  and social change, 42
  Vietnam, 108–109, 451
wealth, 211, 216–218
Weber case, 257
welfare model, of social problems, 427–428
welfare
  myths, 229
  recipients, 226, 228–230
  as social problem, 424
welfare state, 230–233, 368, 369
white-collar occupations, 201, 205–208
  and sex, 275, 276
white-collar crime, 414
wives, working, 301–302, 307
women
  and authority, 277–278
  black, 272, 273
  domination of, 268–271
  and earnings gap, 279–280
  exchange of, 271
  family role and social status of, 294, 300–302, 307
  and identity, 95, 96, 97
  as minority group, 238

women (cont.)
  ordination of, 348
  power of, variations in, 269
  professional, 278
  status of, as social problem, 422–423
  in U.S., 271–280
  work of, 11, 13, 264–265, 269, 274–280, 281–282, 301–302, 307
women's liberation movement, 281–282
work, arrangements of, new, 374
  and Protestant ethic, 345
  school as preparation for, 313–314, 331
  value of, 374–375
  of women (see women, work of)
  work groups, 106–107, 110, 132–133
worker, alienation of, 370, 373–375
  participation of, 162–163
  and socialism, 375
working class(es), 202–203, 204
  decline in, 205–206, 207
  and economic reforms, 368
  and the family, 295–296
  new, 206–207
  and religion, 339, 342, 343
working poor, 203, 204
world economic system, 138, 375–379

Yankee City, 199
Yoruba, women's role among, 264
Yugosiavia, social class and occupation in, 205

Zen Buddhism, 349
zero population growth, 469, 470